WITHDRAWN

D1420448

The Collected Courses of the Academy of European Law
Series Editors: Professor Marise Cremona,
Professor Bruno de Witte, and
Professor Francesco Francioni,
European University Institute,
Florence
Assistant Editor: Anny Bremner, *European University*
Institute, Florence

VOLUME XIX/1
International Humanitarian Law and
International Human Rights Law

The Collected Courses of the Academy of European Law
Edited by Professor Marise Cremona,
Professor Bruno de Witte, and Professor Franceso Francioni
Assistant Editor: Anny Bremner

This series brings together the Collected Courses of the
Academy of European Law in Florence. The Academy's mission is to
produce scholarly analyses which are at the cutting edge of the two
fields in which it works: European Union law and human rights law.
A 'general course' is given each year in each field, by a
distinguished scholar and/or practitioner, who either examines the
field as a whole through a particular thematic, conceptual, or
philosophical lens, or who looks at a particular theme in the context
of the overall body of law in the field. The Academy also publishes
each year a volume of collected essays with a specific theme in each
of the two fields.

International Humanitarian Law and International Human Rights Law

Pas de Deux

Edited by
ORNA BEN-NAFTALI

OXFORD
UNIVERSITY PRESS

OXFORD
UNIVERSITY PRESS

Great Clarendon Street, Oxford OX2 6DP

Oxford University Press is a department of the University of Oxford.
It furthers the University's objective of excellence in research, scholarship,
and education by publishing worldwide in

Oxford New York

Auckland Cape Town Dar es Salaam Hong Kong Karachi
Kuala Lumpur Madrid Melbourne Mexico City Nairobi
New Delhi Shanghai Taipei Toronto

With offices in

Argentina Austria Brazil Chile Czech Republic France Greece
Guatemala Hungary Italy Japan Poland Portugal Singapore
South Korea Switzerland Thailand Turkey Ukraine Vietnam

Oxford is a registered trade mark of Oxford University Press
in the UK and in certain other countries

Published in the United States
by Oxford University Press Inc., New York

British Library Cataloguing in Publication Data
Data available

Library of Congress Cataloging in Publication Data
Data available

Typeset by Newgen Imaging Systems (P) Ltd., Chennai, India
Printed in Great Britain
on acid-free paper by
CPI Antony Rowe, Chippenham, Wiltshire

ISBN 978–0–19–100160–4

1 3 5 7 9 10 8 6 4 2

Acknowledgements

This collection was developed from a series of lectures given at the European University Institute in Florence as part of the Academy of European Law's annual summer course in the field of international human rights law. Some books, like some children, have been nourished by many parents. This book has been thus blessed. I am grateful to Francesco Francioni for having decided to devote the 2008 summer course to the interaction between international humanitarian law and international human rights law, for having given us the opportunity to explore this intricate issue with a group of amazing students, and for his warm hospitality (matched only by the temperature in Florence that summer), so crucial for the creation of a community of scholars. In addition to essays submitted by the lecturers in the course (Christine Bell, Paola Gaeta, Andrea Gioia, Marco Sassóli, Ana Filipa Vrdoljak, and myself), the book was further enriched by the contributions solicited from Yuval Shany and Marko Milanović, for which I am especially thankful.

For superb assistance in the editorial process, I am forever indebted to Jennifer Shkabatur, SJD candidate at Harvard Law School. Special thanks are due to the inimitable Anny Bremner, the assistant editor of this series.

This book is dedicated to Silvia and Antonio Cassese.

Orna Ben-Naftali
Tel-Aviv

Contents

Contents

IV. *CODA*

Notes on Contributors

Christine Bell is Professor of Public International Law and Associate Director of the Transitional Justice Institute at the University of Ulster. Professor Bell read law at Selwyn College, Cambridge (1988) and gained an LL M in Law from Harvard Law School (1990). In 1990 she qualified as a Barrister at law and she subsequently qualified as an Attorney-at-law in New York. From 1997–99 Professor Bell was Director of the Centre for International and Comparative Human Rights Law at Queen's University of Belfast. She has been active in non-governmental organizations, and was chairperson of the Belfast-based Human Rights organization, the Committee on the Administration of Justice from 1995–97, and a founder member of the Northern Ireland Human Rights Commission established under the terms of the Belfast Agreement. In 1999 she was a member of the European Commission's Committee of Experts on Fundamental Rights. Professor Bell authored the book *Peace Agreements and Human Rights* (Oxford University Press, 2000), and a report published by the International Council on Human Rights Policy entitled *Negotiating Justice? Human Rights and Peace Agreements* (2006). In 2007 she won the American Society of International Law Francis Deak Prize for an article on peace agreements. Her most recent book *On the Law of Peace: Peace Agreements and the Lex Pacificatoria* (Oxford University Press, 2008) won the (UK) Socio-Legal Studies Association Hart Book Prize.

Orna Ben-Naftali is Professor of International Law and Dean of the Law School at the College of Management Academic Studies in Israel. A graduate of the Law Faculty of Tel-Aviv University, the Fletcher School of Law and Diplomacy, Tufts University, and Harvard University (History), she taught at Brandeis University and at the Fletcher School of Law and Diplomacy, and worked in the Department of Peacekeeping Operations of the United Nations. Professor Ben-Naftali's publications focus on international humanitarian law, most particularly, the law of belligerent occupation; international criminal law; and on the cultural study of law. She is a member of the Editorial Board of the *European Journal of International Law*; founding member of the Executive Board of *Concord — the Research Center for the Interplay between International Norms and Israeli Law*, and a member of the Executive Board of *B'tselem — the Israeli Information Center for Human Rights in the Occupied Territories*.

Paola Gaeta is Professor of International Criminal Law at the Law Faculty of the University of Geneva and Director of the LL M Programme in International Humanitarian Law of the Geneva Academy of International Humanitarian Law and Human Rights. In February 2010, she joined the Graduate Institute of International and Developments Studies in Geneva as Adjunct Professor. Previously she was Full Professor of International Law at the University of Florence. Professor Gaeta graduated with a degree in Political Science from the University of Florence and obtained a PhD in Law from the European University Institute. She is a Member of the Editorial Boards of the *Journal of International Criminal Justice* and of the *European Journal of International Law*. Her publications include *The UN Genocide Convention: A Commentary* (ed) (Oxford University Press, 2009) and *The Statute of the International Criminal Court: A Commentary* (co-edited with A Cassese and J R W D Jones, Oxford University Press, 2001).

Andrea Gioia is Professor of International Law at the Faculty of Law of the University of Modena and Reggio Emilia, where he is also a member of the Doctoral School in Legal Sciences. From September 2010, he is on leave from the University of Modena and Reggio Emilia and is serving as Senior Legal Officer at the International Atomic Energy Agency (IAEA) in Vienna. A graduate of the Law Faculty of the University of Pisa, he obtained his PhD in international law at the University of Rome I ('La Sapienza'). Professor Gioia is a member of the Editorial Committee of *The Italian Yearbook of International Law* and is a member of the Italian Society of International Law, the American Society of International Law, and the International Law Association. He served on the Italian Delegation to the Standing Committee on Liability for Nuclear Damage of the IAEA, was the Scientific Advisor to the IAEA International Expert Group on Nuclear Liability, and served as IAEA Consultant.

Marko Milanović is a Lecturer in Law at the University of Nottingham School of Law. He obtained his first degree in law from the University of Belgrade, his LL M from the University of Michigan Law School, and is completing his PhD at the University of Cambridge Faculty of Law. He clerked for Judge Thomas Buergenthal at the International Court of Justice, and has worked for several years for a Serbian NGO, the Belgrade Centre for Human Rights, of which he remains an associate. He has acted as counsel or advisor in cases before the Constitutional Court of Serbia, the European Court of Human Rights, and the International Court of Justice, and has published in leading academic journals.

Marco Sassòli is Professor of International Law and Director of the Department of International Law and International Organization at the University of Geneva. He was Professor of International Law at the Université du Québec à Montreal, where he remains Associate Professor. He is also Associate Professor at the University Laval. He chairs the Board of Geneva Call, an NGO engaging non-state armed actors to respect humanitarian norms, and is Vice-Chair of the Board of the *International Council of Human Rights Policy*. Professor Sassòli graduated as doctor of laws from the University of Basel and was admitted to the Swiss bar. He worked from 1985–97 for the International Committee of the Red Cross (ICRC) at the headquarters, *inter alia*, as deputy head of its legal division, and in the field, *inter alia*, as legal adviser of the ICRC delegation in Israel and the Occupied Territories, as head of the ICRC delegations in Jordan and Syria, and as protection coordinator for the former Yugoslavia. His publications and research are dedicated to international humanitarian law, human rights law, international criminal law, the sources of international law and the responsibility of states and non-state actors.

Yuval Shany is the Hersch Lauterpacht Chair in International Law at the Law Faculty of the Hebrew University of Jerusalem. He serves as Director in the International Law Forum at the Hebrew University and the Project on International Courts and Tribunals (PICT). He is a member of the steering committee of the DOMAC project (assessing the impact of international courts on domestic criminal procedures in mass atrocity cases) and is a senior research fellow at the Israel Democracy Institute. Professor Shany has degrees in law from the Hebrew University, New York University, and the University of London. He has published numerous books and articles on international courts and arbitration tribunals, and other international law issues such as international human rights and international humanitarian law. Professor Shany has taught in a number of law schools in Israel, and has been in recent years a research fellow at Harvard and at Amsterdam University, and a visiting professor at the Georgetown University Law Center, Michigan University Law School, the Faculty of Law of the University of Sydney, and Columbia University Law School.

Ana Filipa Vrdoljak is Professor in the Faculty of Law, University of Western Australia and Visiting Professor in the Department of Legal Studies, Central European University, Budapest. She holds a Doctor of Philosophy (in Law) from the University of Sydney. Professor Vrdoljak is a member of the Cultural Heritage Committee and Rights of Indigenous Peoples Committee of the International Law Association. She was Marie Curie Fellow at the European University Institute, Florence (2006–08), where she worked on her forthcoming book entitled *Law and Cultural Heritage in Europe*. She has been Jean Monnet Fellow, Law Department European University Institute, Florence (2004–05); Visiting Fellow, Faculty of Law, University of New South Wales (2008); Visiting Scholar at the Lauterpacht Centre for International Law, University of Cambridge (1999); and Global Law School, New York University (2000). She is the author of *International Law, Museums and the Return of Cultural Objects* (Cambridge University Press, 2006) and numerous academic articles on international law and cultural heritage.

Table of Cases

INTERNATIONAL COURTS AND TRIBUNALS

EUROPEAN UNION

Court of First Instance

International Military Tribunal, Nuremberg

Supreme National Tribunal of Poland

United Nations Human Rights Committee

Permanent Court of International Justice

Special Court for Sierra Leone

NATIONAL COURTS

Table of Cases

Table of Legislation

I
ENTRÉE

1

Introduction: International Humanitarian Law and International Human Rights Law— Pas de Deux

Orna Ben-Naftali

This book begins *in medias res* and ends with no climactic, much less absolutist, conclusion. This is not to say that the collected essays in this volume do not hope to contribute to the development of international law or that they have lost sight of the 'lighthouse', of justice.[1] It is, however, to acknowledge that navigating forward is, as it has always been, a process wrought with interpretive twists and turns in the often turbulent waves of a multitude of competing narratives, shifting paradigms, polar doctrines, and a patchwork of governing norms, where we, the participants (both writers and readers), are engaged in the 'art of establishing the probable by arguing from our sense of the possible'.[2] Such indeed is the nature of our métier.

The book, thus, enters an ongoing, fluid conversation. The conversation explores the movements unfolding between international humanitarian law (IHL) and international human rights law (IHRL). Taking this conversation seriously is often an exercise at once humbling and exalting: it requires engaging in the sometimes weary rehashing of debates (such as between realism and idealism; states' sovereignty and human rights; universal values and bright-line rules; hard and soft law), while knowing that even our best efforts will at most advance towards, but invariably fail to reach, the 'lighthouse' and nevertheless retaining faith in the tenability of its promise and, *ergo*, in the necessity of the voyage.

---

[1] Woolf, *To the Lighthouse* (1994); Morgan, *The Aesthetics of International Law* (2007) offers an insightful analysis of the parallel between *To the Lighthouse* (where the Ramsey family strives towards, while simultaneously deferring to a later day, their ultimate goal) and international law: 'participatory interaction in the movement towards, as opposed to the substantive definition of, truth…In moving towards substantive rights…in providing the framework for the expression of conflicting viewpoints, process doctrine move towards substance, thus hinting at the ultimate form of the dispute's resolution' at 34.

[2] White, *Heracles' Bow: Essays on the Rhetoric and Poetics of Law* (1985) at 31.

Taking IHRL to armed conflicts of varying kinds is a humanistic project. Its promise is the humanization of IHL.[3] Premised on the idea of the universality of human rights,[4] and buttressed by the similarity of the core values underlying both normative regimes,[5] the project has set out to weave a net, thicker than hitherto available, for the protection of the rights to life, liberty, and dignity of all individuals under all circumstances.[6]

The idea that IHL and IHRL are complementary, rather than alternative regimes, has represented a paradigmatic shift in the international legal discourse, replacing the former convention which maintained that the two are mutually exclusive.[7] The coupling of the consciousness of the changing face of war from inter-state to intra-state or mixed conflicts, with the experience that 'the first line of defense against international humanitarian law is to deny that it applies at all',[8] generated a new paradigm according to which IHL is not an alternative to IHRL but an exception to the full application of the latter.[9] Normative developments originating in the 1968 International Conference in Teheran,[10] and including the 1977 Protocols Additional to the Geneva Conventions;[11] references made to humanitarian law in human rights conventions;[12] the 1990 Declaration of Minimum Humanitarian Standards;[13] and the Statute of the International Criminal Court,[14]

---

[3] Meron, 'The Humanization of Humanitarian Law', 94(2) *AJIL* (2000) 239–278.

[4] Universal Declaration of Human Rights, 10 Dec 1948, GA res 217A (III), UN Doc A/810 at 71 (1948) art 2.

[5] Judgment, *Furundžija* (IT-95-17/1), Trial Chamber, 10 December 1998, § 183.

[6] Droege, 'The Interplay between International Humanitarian Law and International Human Rights Law in Situations of Armed Conflict', 40 *Is. L.R.* (2007) 310–355, at 312.

[7] See eg Draper, 'Humanitarian Law and Human Rights', *Acta Juridica* (1979) 193–206.

[8] Baxter 'Some Existing Problems in Humanitarian Law' in Pilloud (ed), *The Concept of International Armed Conflict: Future Outlook* (1974) 1–2.

[9] Ben-Naftali and Shany, 'Living in Denial: The Co-application of Humanitarian Law and Human Rights Law to the Occupied Territories' 37 *Is. L.R.* (2004) 17–118.

[10] Resolution XXIII (Human Rights in Armed Conflicts), Final Act of the International Conference on Human Rights, 13 May 1968, UN Doc A/Conf.32/41, reprinted in 63 *AJIL* (1969) 680 (Resolution adopted on 12 May 1968).

[11] Protocol Additional to the Geneva Conventions of 12 August 1949, and relating to the Protection of Victims of International Armed Conflicts, 8 June 1977, 1125 UNTS 3 (hereinafter *AP I*); Protocol Additional to the Geneva Conventions of 12 August 1949, and relating to the Protection of Victims of Non-International Armed Conflicts (Protocol II), 8 June 1977, 1125 UNTS 609 (hereinafter *AP II*). The Protocols reflect, *inter alia*, the influence of IHR by either making explicit references to certain rights (see eg *AP I*, Art 72; *AP II*, preamble), or by taking human rights into consideration (see eg *AP I*, Art 1(4)—referring to the right of self-determination; *AP I*, Art 75(4)—borrowing some of the language of ICCPR, Art 14). See generally, Schindler, 'Human Rights and Humanitarian Law' 31 *Am. U.L. Rev.* (1982) 935–977.

[12] See Convention on the Rights of the Child, 20 November 1989, 1577 UNTS 3; UN General Assembly, Optional Protocol to the Convention on the Rights of the Child on the Involvement of Children in Armed Conflict, 25 May 2000, GA Res 54/263.

[13] Declaration of Minimum Humanitarian Standards, UN Doc E/CN.4/Sub.2/1991/55 (adopted by the Meeting of Experts at Human Rights Institute of Abo Akademi, Turku, Finland) (2 December 1990).

[14] Art 7 of the ICC Statute (hereinafter: ICCSt) defines crimes against humanity. The concepts underlying these crimes derive from IHRL (eg the right to life, not to be tortured, the right to liberty and to security of person), as distinct from war crimes in the ICCSt, deriving from IHL. Note that as crimes against humanity may be committed in times of peace as well as in times of armed conflict, it further stands to reason that they can be committed against both civilians and members

which proscribes crimes against humanity and genocide in both peace and war-time situations, confirmed the validity of the new paradigm. Taken together with jurisprudential pronouncements in both international and domestic fora as well as wide scholarly support,[15] it seems that the confluence of the regimes currently enjoys the status of the new orthodoxy. This indeed is the point of departure of all the contributors to this book.

In the DNA of new orthodoxies, however, erstwhile beliefs and nascent heresies are the twining strands of the helix. Thus, the taxonomy of the current scholarly discourse on the interaction between IHR and IHRL may be delineated as follows:

(a) Some scholars still maintain the position that the twain do not and indeed should not meet.[16] Some other writers, while sympathetic to the humanizing project, are concerned that it may fail to achieve its objective and may result in less, rather than more, protection to human rights.[17]

(b) Most scholars hold that there is a large measure of convergence between IHL and IHRL, which invites each to be enriched by insights from the other, and can thus be used for interpretative purposes to improve the law and advance its humanistic purpose.[18] Opinions diverge, however, on the scope and methods of dealing with norm conflicts: some hold that existing interpretive mechanisms—most specifically the *lex specialis* principle—

---

of the military. Judgment, *Tadić* (IT-94-1-T), Trial Chamber, 7 May 1997, § 643; Art 6 ICCSt, reproducing Art II of the Genocide Convention, defines the crime of genocide, which could be viewed as a distinct subcategory of crimes against humanity.

[15] See eg *Legality of the Threat or Use of Nuclear Weapons*, Advisory Opinion, ICJ Reports (1996) 226, paragraph 25; *Legal Consequences of the Construction of a Wall in the Occupied Palestinian Territory*, Advisory Opinion, ICJ Reports (2004) 136, paragraph 106; *Armed Activities on the Territory of the Congo (Democratic Republic of the Congo v Uganda)*, ICJ Reports (2005) 116 at 69–70, paragraphs 216–217. On the domestic level, the practice of the Israeli Supreme Court operating in its capacity as a High Court of Justice and exercising judicial review over actions of the military in the occupied Palestinian Territory is noteworthy. See eg HCJ 7957/04 *Mara'abe v The Prime Minister of Israel*, available online at <http://elyon1.court.gov.il/files_eng/04/570/079/a14/04079570.a14.pdf> [last accessed 24 March 2010]; HCJ 769/02 *The Public Committee against Torture in Israel v The Government of Israel (Targeted Killings)*, available online at <http://elyon1.court.gov.il/files_eng/02/690/007/a34/02007690.a34.pdf> [last accessed 24 March 2010].

[16] See eg Bowring, 'Fragmentation, *Lex Specialis* and the Tensions in the Jurisprudence of the European Court of Human Rights', *J.C. & S.L.* (2009) 1–14 maintains that IHL and IHRL are not even 'fragmented', as there is 'no unity there in the first place to be fragmented', and that 'chalk is being compared with, or even substituted by, cheese. Or still worse, the two are being mixed together: chalky cheese is horribly indigestible, while cheesy chalk is no good at all for writing on the blackboard', at 2–3.

[17] See eg Lubell, 'Challenges in Applying Human Rights Law to Armed Conflict', 860 *International Review of the Red Cross* (2005) 737–754; Schabas '*Lex specialis?* Belt and Suspenders? The Parallel Operation of Human Rights Law and the Law of Armed Conflict, and the Conundrum of *Jus ad Bellum*' 40 *Is. L.R.* (2007) 592–613; Shany, 'Human Rights and Humanitarian Law as Competing Legal Paradigms for Fighting Against Terror' in this volume; Ben-Naftali, 'PathoLAWgical Occupation: Normalizing the Exceptional Case of the Occupied Palestinian Territory (OPT) and other Legal Pathologies' in this volume.

[18] See eg Orakhelashvili, 'The Interaction between Human Rights and Humanitarian Law: Fragmentation, Conflict, Parallelism, or Convergence?' 19(1) *EJIL* (2008) 161–182.

adequately resolve the relatively narrow scope of norm conflicts;[19] others posit that, in some areas, legitimate methods of interpretation will fail to harmonize the two regimes, indicating a conflict that can be resolved only by the political process.[20]

(c) Some scholars believe that the convergence between the two paradigms is as substantive as it is substantial, indicating a 'movement towards a new merger' of both bodies of law into one.[21] Such 'fusion',[22] in reshaping both IHL and IHRL, invites the generation of new paradigms designed to redeem anew the promise of the humanistic project.[23]

This multiplicity of movements of the *Pas de Deux* of IHL and IHRL is reflected in the contributions to this volume.

Part I: *Adagio*, focuses on the paradigmatic and the normative complexities of the interaction between both regimes. In *Human Rights and Humanitarian Law as Competing Legal Paradigms for Fighting Terror*, Yuval Shany surveys the various developments and counter-developments of the first decade of the twenty-first century relating to identifying the governing legal paradigm of the 'war against terror'. Shany posits that the controversy over the proper legal framework, featuring an intense struggle between a human rights-centred 'law enforcement' paradigm and a security-centred, IHL-based 'armed conflict' paradigm, exposes the meta-differences between IHRL and IHL. 'The considerable political capital and legal efforts invested in jockeying between the two competing paradigms,' argues Shany, 'cast doubt on the increasingly common narrative' of the merger between IHRL and IHL. Indeed, ideological tensions between the two camps supporting the competing paradigms cannot be avoided even if a mixed paradigm were to be developed as such a development would likely simply channel the same ideological struggles to disagreements on the contents and direction of the new mixed paradigm. Apprehensive of a utopian tendency of some institutions (specifically the European Court of Human Rights and the Goldstone Committee[24]) to use IHRL to 'hijack' IHL, Shany concludes with a qualified endorsement of a mixed paradigm, namely one that does not fail to consider existing realities.

The enfolding movements of Marco Sassòli and Marko Milanović focus on the interaction of particular norms of IHL and IHRL that regulate specific situations

---

[19] Sassòli, 'The Role of Human Rights and International Humanitarian Law in New Types of Armed Conflicts', in this volume.

[20] Milanović, 'Norm Conflicts, International Humanitarian Law and Human Rights Law', in this volume.

[21] Arnold and Quenivet (eds) *International Humanitarian Law and Human Rights Law: Towards a New Merger in International Law* (2008).

[22] Judgment, *Kunarac, Kovac, and Vuković* (IT-96-23 and 96-23/1-A), Trial Chamber, 22 February 2001, § 467: 'With regard to certain of its aspects, international humanitarian law can be said to have fused with human rights law' (note that the Tribunal still specified that with respect to other aspects IHL remains the *lex specialis*, § 471).

[23] Bell, 'Post-conflict Accountability and the Reshaping of Human Rights and Humanitarian Law', in this volume.

[24] See *Report of the United Nations Fact Finding Mission on the Gaza Conflict*, A/HRC/12/48 (25 September 2009). Available online at <http://www2.ohchr.org/english/bodies/ hrcouncil/ docs/12session/A-HRC-12-48.pdf> [last accessed 24 March 2010].

and on the adequacy of existing mechanisms for resolving norm conflicts. In *The Role of Human Rights and International Humanitarian Law in New Types of Armed Conflicts*, Sassòli expands Shany's interest in the 'war on terror' to additional types of new conflicts (asymmetric conflicts, conflicts in failed states, and UN peace operations). Noting that from the perspective of the application of either IHL or IHRL, the novelty of the conflicts is overstated, the chapter compares them to the archetypes of conflicts for which IHL was originally designed; determines the threshold questions relative to the applicability of both regimes *ratione materiae, ratione personae*, and *ratione loci*; and proceeds to focus on their co-application. The latter is explored in the light of the *lex specialis* principle on both a general level and in relation to the pertinent questions of the targeting and preventive detention of members of an armed group. This discussion generates the conclusion that existing law, properly interpreted, contains realistic, albeit controversial and situation-dependent, solutions for the legal problems arising in these types of conflicts.

Norm Conflicts, International Humanitarian Law and Human Rights Law disagrees with this conclusion: the *lex specialis* maxim, posits Milanović, 'must be abandoned as a sort of magical, two-word explanation of the relationship between IHL and IHRL as it confuses far more than it clarifies'. Sharing Shany's concern that a shift towards the utopian edge of progress may slide the humanizing project into irrelevance, Milanović's discussion of the interaction of particular norms of IHL and IHRL that regulate specific situations advances the following argument: (a) such interaction will frequently result in a norm conflict, for which there are numerous tools for either conflict resolution or avoidance; (b) *lex specialis* is at best a fairly limited tool of norm conflict avoidance, which cannot be used to describe the relationship between human rights and humanitarian law as a whole; and (c) there are situations in which all legitimate interpretive tools will fail us, where a norm conflict will be both unavoidable and irresolvable due to a fundamental incompatibility in the text, object and purpose, and values protected by the interacting norms, and where the only possible solution to the conflict will be a political one. The chapter identifies three such possible situations of irresolvable antinomy—targeted killings, preventive security detention (offering a reading different from Sassòli's), and positive obligations during occupation—and discusses them in the light of recent cases.

Part II: *Variations* comprises three 'solo' chapters, each discussing the interplay between IHRL and IHL in the context of a specific international regime: indefinite belligerent occupation, the European Court of Human Rights, and the Protection of Cultural Heritage.

In *PathoLAWgical Occupation: Normalizing the Exceptional Case of the Occupied Palestinian Territory (OPT) and Other Legal Pathologies*, I focus on the legal discourse of the most legalized occupation in world history (in terms of the co-application of numerous legal regimes, including IHL and IHRL, the multitude of cases where judicial review over the actions of the occupying power was exercised, and vast scholarly interest) to posit that more laws may not only fail to generate more justice, but may actually facilitate, sustain, and legitimize this failure. The argument rests on two interrelated propositions: first, that the Israeli control of the OPT is an illegal occupation, the defining feature of which is the blurring of boundaries, both physical and legal, which has culminated in the reversal of the relationship between the rule and the exception.[25] The second proposition focuses on the normative implications of this regime. It suggests that once law is implicated in the shaping of such a regime, law itself becomes infected, and is likely to operate in a manner that will defy its normative purpose on both an individual and a systemic level: its application to individual cases (through judicial review) would typically entail a 'dynamic' interpretation designed to advance the interests of the occupying power at the expense of the occupied people and it will contribute to and facilitate the formation of an environment (indicative of a systemic state policy) of tolerance towards systematic violations of human rights. This tolerance, in turn, may transform grave such violations from war crimes into crimes against humanity. This 'pathoLAWgy', it is suggested, provides the proper context for understanding both the manner with which the most recent military operation in Gaza ('Operation Cast Lead', 27 December 2008–18 January 2009) was exercised and the consequential Report of the Goldstone Committee.

In *The Role of the European Court of Human Rights in Monitoring Compliance with Humanitarian Law in Armed Conflict,* Andrea Gioia focuses on the relationship between the European Convention on Human Rights (ECHR) and IHL. In the first part of this chapter, Gioia analyses the relationship between the ECHR and IHL from a general point of view: having determined that the ECHR continues to apply in times of armed conflict, both international and non-international, the discussion proceeds to examine the Convention's extraterritorial application, the relationship between the ECHR and IHL, and the competence of the European Court of Human Rights to take IHL into account when applying the Convention in situations amounting to armed conflict. The second part discusses the Court's case-law relating to situations of armed conflict in order to ascertain what role IHL has so far played in the Court's decisions: special reference is made to cases relating to the right to life, to the right to liberty, and to the protection of property. The possible explanations for the Court's marked reluctance to refer to IHL are discussed in this context (explanations which differ from those provided by Milanović), while pointing out that generally the Court has not so far adopted decisions squarely contradicting the applicable rules of IHL. Gioia concludes with an implicit plea for the Court to depart from its 'ivory tower' (or 'ivory dungeon') attitude towards IHL, so as to contribute to a convergence of the two legal regimes towards a more coherent as well as a more realistic regulation of conduct in armed conflicts in general and in non-international armed conflicts in particular.

In *Cultural Heritage in Human Rights and Humanitarian Law,* Ana Filipa Vrdoljak discusses the protection of cultural heritage by IHL, IHRL and international criminal law (ICL). The chapter points to change over time in the rationale

---

[25] This proposition rests on a co-authored article, Ben-Naftali, Gross, and Michaeli, 'Illegal Occupation: The Framing of the Occupied Palestinian Territory', 23(3) *Berkeley J. Int'l L.* (2005) 551–614; Reprinted in Kattan (ed), *The Palestine Question In International Law* (2008).

of this protection due to the interplay between these legal regimes: the exceptionalism originally afforded to cultural heritage in IHL arose from its perceived significance to humanity through its advancement of the arts and sciences, and knowledge. By the mid-twentieth century, and with the rise of human rights in international law, this rationale was recalibrated to emphasize its importance to the enjoyment of human rights and promotion of cultural diversity. This shift in rationale manifested itself most clearly in the articulation and prosecution of war crimes, crimes against humanity, and genocide. The protection of cultural heritage was thus no longer based on its exclusivity but on its intrinsic importance to people and individuals, to their identity and their enjoyment of their human rights. In examining the protection of cultural heritage in this chapter, Vrdoljak focuses on this shifting rationale to highlight the ever-present interplay and interdependence between IHL and IHRL in the following manner: (a) positing the exceptional treatment of cultural heritage in general IHL instruments, and its overlap with IHRL; (b) detailing how this protection has been built upon by the specialist regime for the protection of cultural heritage during armed conflict and belligerent occupation developed under the auspices of UNESCO; and (c) analysing ICL jurisprudence from the International Military Tribunal, Nuremberg (IMT) to the International Criminal Court for the former Yugoslavia (ICTY), to show how efforts to prosecute violations of the laws and customs of war relating to cultural heritage have been intrinsic to the articulation and prosecution of crimes against humanity and genocide. The chapter concludes with a consideration of the evolving and potential future normative trends in this field in the light of recent developments.

In concluding, Part III: *Coda*, Paola Gaeta and Christine Bell discuss some of the manifold possibilities introduced by the merging of IHL and IHRL.

Gaeta provides an affirmative answer to the question presented in the title of her chapter *Are Victims of War Crimes Entitled to Compensation?* Drawing on the transformation of IHL in the light of IHRL as well as on developments in the regime regulating State Responsibility and in case-law, Gaeta proposes that individuals possess primary rights towards states in the event of armed conflicts and are thus entitled to obtain reparation from the responsible state for their violations.

In her *Post-conflict Accountability and the Reshaping of Human Rights and Humanitarian Law*, Bell posits post-conflict accountability as a site for the merging of the IHL and IHRL regimes, generating an otherwise missing synthetic clarity. The aftermath of conflict often makes two distinct demands for post-conflict accountability: first, that those responsible for human rights or humanitarian law violations during the war are held accountable for violations; and second that third parties with post-settlement responsibility for 'implementing the peace' are held accountable where they themselves violate the rights of local populations. Both demands are variously made post-conflict by local populations and by international actors. This chapter considers the ways in which IHRL and IHL have been argued to impose post-conflict accountability in both these senses. It proposes that in both cases a lack of fit between each specific regime and the post-conflict political landscape to which it has applied, has involved an interpretative revision of what the regimes require, generating a fairly loose merged-regime and institutional innovation for the existing regimes of human rights and humanitarian law. The chapter examines and evaluates three suggested conceptualizations of the current legal landscape and its future direction. The first conceptualization ambitiously involves the attempt to articulate a new third-way combined regime—a *jus post bellum*—that is, a coherent attempt to develop a combined humanitarian law and human rights regime tailored to the political goals of internal constitutional revision. The second conceptualization is of a project of piece-meal reform aimed at producing new norms specifically targeted at filling in some of the 'gaps' between existing norms and post-conflict accountability demands. The third conceptualization of the way forward involves an attempt to narrate a form of transnational accountability which would build on, rather than attempt to rationalize, the legal pluralism and mess of current developments. The chapter concludes by advancing the possibility of drawing on all three conceptualizations as reflecting different underlying meta-level understandings of the current 'situating' of international law itself.

The *Pas de Deux* of IHL and IHRL, as the various contributions to this book reflect, consists of multiple narratives, paradigmatic shifts, doctrinal perplexities, and a hodgepodge of governing norms. This patchwork texture and lack of taxonomic elegance are not, however, reason for despair. Quite the contrary: they mirror the process through which international law—p(l)aying deference to political realities while simultaneously seeking to transcend them—charts new waterways leading to the lighthouse.

II
ADAGIO

2

Human Rights and Humanitarian Law as Competing Legal Paradigms for Fighting Terror

Yuval Shany

In a recent article on the interplay between international law and politics, Martti Koskenniemi wrote that 'much about the search for political direction today takes the form of jurisdictional conflict, struggle between competing expert vocabularies, each equipped with a specific bias'[1] and that '[p]olitical intervention is today often a politics of re-definition, that is to say, the strategic definition of a situation or a problem by reference to a technical idiom so as to open the door for applying the expertise related to that idiom, together with the attendant structural bias'.[2]

The 'war on terror' in the first decade of the twenty-first century exemplifies such political struggles over the governing legal paradigm. Not only is the meaning of the term 'terrorist' itself controversial; the legal framework governing the fight against terrorism is also highly contested, and features an intense struggle between a human rights-centred 'law enforcement' paradigm and a more aggressive humanitarian law-based 'armed conflict' paradigm. Describing the paradigm struggle in Koskenniemic terms not only reveals, once again, the potential for the strategic use of the law; it also exposes the meta-differences between human rights law and humanitarian law. The considerable political capital and legal efforts invested in jockeying between the two competing paradigms casts doubt on the increasingly common narrative of the growing merger between human rights law and humanitarian law and the irrelevance of distinguishing between the two. Moreover, it is now clearer than before that the ideological tensions between the two camps supporting the competing paradigms cannot be avoided even if a mixed paradigm were to be developed to govern the fight against terror (as is increasingly alleged). Such a development may simply lead to the channelling of the same ideological struggles that had been held over the choice of paradigm to disagreement on the contents and direction of the new mixed paradigm.

In Part 1 of this chapter, I describe the jurisdictional struggle between the two principal legal paradigms that purport to regulate the international fight

---

[1] Koskenniemi, 'The Politics of International Law—20 Years Later', 20 *EJIL* (2009) 7, at 9.
[2] Ibid, at 11.

against terror: the law enforcement and the armed conflict paradigms. Arguably, many disagreements concerning the lawfulness of specific counter-terrorism, such as targeted killings or detention without trial, are actually disagreements on the applicable legal framework and the stories on the nature of the threat of terrorism that is being offered. In Part 2, I consider the emergence of a mixed paradigm which borrows contents from both human rights law and humanitarian law. I argue that such normative crossover illustrates the difficulty of maintaining rigid paradigmatic distinctions in light of the complexities of the fight against terror; but also that some key differences in emphasis between the two paradigms nonetheless remain. Most significantly, I argue that the development of a new mixed paradigm merely recontextualizes pre-existing jurisdictional struggles over the proper legal framework to govern the fight against terror. Part 3 concludes.

1. The Development of Competing Paradigms

A. The 'law and order' paradigm

1. The classic 'law and order' paradigm

The traditional point of departure for discussing the international law response to terrorism, or the international fight against terror, used to be a belief that terror (understood hereby as serious violence directed by non-state actors against civilians or civilian targets in order to terrorize the population and/or facilitate a change in government policies)[3] essentially is a criminal phenomenon.[4] True, the very existence of international treaties that seek to suppress terrorism suggests that terrorism constitutes a particularly serious criminal phenomenon: it entails a common threat of global dimensions to vital state interests (national security, life of the citizenry, stability of political institutions); but the international aspect of the problem of terrorism has been understood to simply suggest that a greater degree of international coordination and cooperation may be needed in order to effectively address the threat of terror. In this respect, terror constitutes a phenomenon analogous to other cross-border criminal activities such as drug

---

[3] See eg, SC Res 1566 (2004), 8 October 2004, at 3 (alluding to terror as 'criminal acts, including against civilians, committed with the intent to cause death or serious bodily injury, or taking of hostages, with the purpose to provoke a state of terror in the general public or in a group of persons or particular persons, intimidate a population or compel a government or an international organization to do or to abstain from doing any act, which constitute offences within the scope of and as defined in the international conventions and protocols relating to terrorism); International Convention for the Suppression of the Financing of Terrorism, Art 2(b), 9 December 1999, 39 ILM (2000) 270 (referring to terror as any act 'intended to cause death or serious bodily injury to a civilian, or to any other person not taking an active part in the hostilities in a situation of armed conflict, when the purpose of such act, by its nature or context, is to intimidate a population, or to compel a government or an international organization to do or to abstain from doing any act').

[4] See eg Bassiouni, 'Methodological Options for International Legal Control of Terrorism', in *International Terrorism and Political Crimes* (Bassiouni ed, 1973) at 485; Blakesley, *Terrorism, Drugs, International Law and the Protection of Human Liberty* (1992) at 140–143.

trafficking, money laundering, and organized crime.[5] Indeed, the 13 global anti-terrorism treaties, concluded under UN auspices which are in force,[6] focus on criminalizing specific terrorist practices: plane hijacking, hostage taking, use of bombs etc, and on imposing on states an obligation to extradite or prosecute (*aut dedere aut judicare*). In addition, the treaties provide for a range of cooperative measures designed to prevent and punish terror offences. In short, the international terror treaties clearly embrace a 'law and order' paradigm as the dominant framework governing the fights against terror.

There is a growing body of opinion, in political, military, academic, and other circles, that the traditional approach embraced by the international community has not been successful in suppressing terrorism, and that, in any event, this approach cannot be expected to effectively address the greater threats posed by new terrorist groups or by new means and operational strategies at the disposal of 'old' terrorist groups. These perceptions are based on a number of inter-related factors:

1. The existing international treaties are not comprehensive in their scope of coverage, leaving the acts and omissions of some crucial states, and some manifestations of terrorism unregulated or under-regulated.[7] The lack of an accepted definition of terrorism is often cited as indicative of international law's ineffective approach to the problem.[8]

---

[5] See eg United Nations Convention against Illicit Traffic in Narcotic Drugs and Psychotropic Substances, 20 December 1988, 28 ILM (1989) 493; Convention on Transnational Organized Crime, 15 November 2000, UN Doc A/55/383 (2000).

[6] Convention on Offences and Certain Other Acts Committed on Board Aircraft, 14 September 14 1963, 704 UNTS 219; Convention for the Suppression of Unlawful Seizure of Aircraft (Hijacking), 16 December 1970, 860 UNTS 105; Convention for the Suppression of Unlawful Acts Against the Safety of Civil Aviation (Sabotage), 23 September 1971, 974 UNTS 177; Protocol for the Suppression of Unlawful Acts of Violence at Airports Serving International Civil Aviation, 23 September 1971, 1589 UNTS 473; Convention on the Prevention and Punishment of Crimes Against Internationally Protected Persons, 14 December 1973, 1035 UNTS 167; Convention on the Physical Protection of Nuclear Materials, 26 October 1979, 1456 UNTS 125; International Convention Against the Taking of Hostages, 17 December 1979, 1316 UNTS 205; Convention for the Suppression of Unlawful Acts Against the Safety of Maritime Navigation, 10 March 1988, 1678 UNTS 221; Protocol for the Suppression of Unlawful Acts Against the Safety of Fixed Platforms Located on the Continental Shelf, 10 March 1988, 1678 UNTS 303; Convention on the Marking of Plastic Explosives for the Purpose of Identification, 1 March 1991, UN Doc S/22393 (1991); International Convention for the Suppression of Terrorist Bombings, 15 December 1997, 37 ILM (1998) 249; Financing Convention, *supra* note 3; International Convention for the Suppression of Acts of Nuclear Terrorism, 13 April 2005, UN Doc A/59/766 (2005).

[7] Saul, *Defining Terrorism in International Law* (2006) at 135.

[8] Much ink has been spilled on the problem stemming from the lack of a definition for 'terror' in international law and the inconclusive state of negotiations over the text of a comprehensive terror convention. See eg Saul, *supra* note 7; Acharya, 'War on Terror or Terror Wars: The Problem in Defining Terrorism', 37 *Denv. J. Int'l L. & Pol'y* (2009) 653; Di Filippo, 'Terrorist Crimes and International Co-Operation: Critical Remarks on the Definition and Inclusion of Terrorism in the Category of International Crimes', 19 *EJIL* (2008) 533; Gaeta and Jessberger (eds), 'Symposium: Responding to Terrorism: The Quest for a Legal Definition', 4 *JICJ* (2996) 894. See also *United States v Yousef*, 327 F 3d 56, 98 (2003) ('[C]ustomary international law currently does not provide for the prosecution of "terrorist" acts under the universality principle, in part due to the failure of States to achieve anything like consensus on the definition of terrorism'). Although the lack of a clear definition is problematic, its implications should not be exaggerated. First, many international law concepts are not fully defined (aggression, self-determination, sustainable development, etc), and

2. The principle of universal jurisdiction reflected in the *aut dedere aut judicare* principle, which is situated at the heart of the 'law and order' paradigm that the treaties have instituted, has proven to be a relative failure.[9] Many states appear reluctant to try, or even extradite, suspected terrorists whose acts do not implicate them directly (a phenomenon explained in large part by the high material and political costs of universal jurisdiction trials and extradition procedures).

3. The threat of terror itself has undergone a major transformation in recent years which has led to its perception as a threat of a different magnitude altogether than other cross-border criminal activities. These transformations include *inter alia*: (a) a shift from acts of terror committed by groups seeking to promote specific political goals (and therefore guided, to some degree, by pragmatic calculations) to terror acts committed by fundamentalist groups featuring violence almost boundless and anarchical in nature that is carried out by extremely highly motivated operatives;[10] (b) the increased access of terrorists to sophisticated and devastating technology (including, perhaps, weapons of mass destruction);[11] and (c) the use of failed states as training bases and launching pads for terror operations.

One may question the prevalent view that the international legal regime on terror is seriously flawed due to the lack of a definition of terrorism and other design flaws in the existing legal infrastructure. Such a view may largely derive from manipulative rhetoric used both by those actors that want to use the lack of a definition as an indication of international law's irrelevance (justifying thereby extra-legal measures) and those who cite the lack of a definition as an excuse for inaction against terror groups. To be clear, there is also genuine concern about the fairness of the existing legal rules governing the fight against terrorism which criminalize some forms of violence (typically violence perpetrated by disempowered groups against more powerful states) and authorize other forms of violence (typically violence

---

international law has developed a number of methodologies to tackle such ambiguities (eg review of state practice, case law, literature, etc). See eg Koskenniemi, *From Apology to Utopia: The Structure of International Legal Argument* (2nd edn, 2005) at 590–592. Secondly, a consensus exists with regard to the prohibited nature of most manifestations of terrorism (which are covered in the 13 treaties). Finally, one can argue that Security Council Resolution 1566 (2004) has implicitly endorsed a comprehensive and binding definition of terrorism and rectified the legal situation. See *supra* note 3.

[9] See eg Kirsch, *Inclusion and Exclusion at the Global Arena* (2006) at 280–281; Hale, 'The "Roaming ICC": A Model International Criminal Court for a State-Centric World of International Law', 35 *Denv. J. Int'l L. & Pol'y* (2007) 429, at 441 ('sovereign States using universal jurisdiction have patently failed and will continue to fail at bringing justice to the commission of international crimes').

[10] See eg Ben-Dor and Pedahzur, 'The Uniqueness of Islamic Fundamentalism and the Fourth Wave of International Terrorism', in *Religious Fundamentalism and Political Extremism* (Weinberg and Pedahzur eds, 2004) 71; Thacjrah, *Dictionary of Terrorism* (2nd edn, 2004) 210–217.

[11] See eg Second Annual Report of the Advisory Panel to Assess Domestic Response Capabilities for Terrorism Involving Weapons of Mass Destruction, *Towards a National Strategy for Combating Terrorism* (2000) 20; Bellany, 'Material Dangers', in *Terrorism and Weapons of Mass Destruction: Responding to the Challenge* (Bellany ed, 2007) 13.

applied by states against non-state actors such as separatists of terrorists).[12] Such 'double standards' underscore the importance of legal framings for the attainment of political legitimacy. Thus, a look at the relevant interplay between law, politics, and morality, suggests it is the lack of will by states to address terror within the existing boundaries of the law, and not a problem of definitional nature, that seems to account for the exaggerated focus on the present law's shortcomings.[13]

Still, the forceful images of 9/11 have conferred great urgency on calls by states and other influential actors to re-evaluate the adequacy of the traditional 'law and order' paradigm for addressing the heightened terrorist threat posed by terror groups. This process of re-evaluation has led to two types of government reactions (applied jointly or severely): (a) the emergence of a revised 'law and order' with fewer human rights protections; (b) a paradigmatic shift from 'law and order' to an 'armed conflict' paradigm.

2. *The revised 'law and order' paradigm*

One dramatic response to the perceived inadequacy of the traditional 'law and order' paradigm in meeting the challenges of the enhanced terror threat has been the emergence of a revised legal framework which strikes a new balance between security interests and individual freedoms. This 'revised law and order' paradigm is characterized not only by a normative shift in the equilibrium between competing values and interests; it also features a new allocation of responsibilities among the branches of government: as a rule, the revised paradigm entails the transfer of decision-making power from courts and legislatures to the executive.

One example of the application of the 'revised law and order' paradigm at the international sphere, is the 'targeted sanctions' or 'smart sanctions' regime first introduced by the UN Security Council in Resolution 1267(1999) against members and supporters of the Taliban.[14] This regime entails the administrative freezing of assets and bank accounts of blacklisted individuals and organizations and the introduction of concomitant movement restrictions upon them. Such harsh measures have been implemented without judicial review; instead, listing and delisting decisions are subject to a mostly non-transparent inter-state process of deliberation.[15]

---

[12] See Žižek, *Welcome to the Desert of the Real!: Five Essays on September 11 and Related Dates* (2002) at 91–94.

[13] For support, see Bennoune, 'Terror/Torture' 26 *Berkeley J. Int'l L.* (2008) 1, at 23 ('[T]his perception of outstanding definitional lacunae leads to nervousness about even using the word "terrorism" with the definitional challenges in question sometime exaggerated').

[14] SC Res 1267 (1999), 15 October 1999, The regime has been extended in Resolution 1333 (2000) also to individuals associated with Al Qaeda. SC Res 1333 (2000), 19 December 2000.

[15] For a review of the Security Council process, see eg Andrés-Sáenz-de-Santa-María, 'Collective International Measures to Counter International Terrorism', in *International Legal Dimension of Terrorism* (2009) at 91; Feináugle, 'The UN Security Council Al Qaida and Taliban Sanctions Committee: Emerging Principles of International Institutional Law for the Protection of Individuals?', 9 *German Law Journal* (2008) 1513; Bothe, 'Security Council's Targeted Sanctions against Presumed Terrorists', 6 *JICJ* (2008) 541; Bianchi, 'Assessing the Effectiveness of the UN

An analogous normative shift has been taking place in the last decade in many national jurisdictions. Countries such as Australia, Canada, France, India, Israel, Russia, the United Kingdom, and the United States have passed legislation in recent years designed to facilitate more flexible standards of investigation, detention, and prosecution of terror suspects. Such legislation has provided, *inter alia*, for longer periods of initial detention periods for terror suspects,[16] introduced more liberal rules on evidence admissibility (including reliance on generous evidentiary presumptions and the use of secret evidence in terror-related proceedings),[17] and the establishment of special courts or chambers to hear terror-related cases.[18] In Israel, restrictions were also placed on the right of terror suspects to meet with their legal representatives.[19]

Some responses to terror threats by democratic states represent an even more radical departure from the classic 'law and order' paradigm and involve the application of executive means against terrorists outside the criminal law process. A number of countries have provided for prolonged detention without trial of terror suspects through administrative detention laws, citing the need for prevention of future attacks (as opposed to notions of individual guilt), as the dominant reason for depriving the liberty of terror suspects.[20] Other jurisdictions have reached similar results through an aggressive application of their immigrations laws;[21] and some jurisdictions have introduced a system of liberty restrictions in the form of 'control orders', as supplementary or alternative methods of supervision exercised over terror suspects.[22]

Other examples of attempts for radical reconfiguration of the 'law and order' paradigm can be found in the authorization and regulation of coercive interrogation

---

Security Council's Anti-Terrorism Measures: The Quest for Legitimacy and Cohesion', 17 *EJIL* (2006) 881.

[16] See eg Anti-Terrorism Act 2004 (Australia), Sch 1, ss 5, 7; Criminal Justice Act 2003 (UK) s 306; Terrorism Act 2006 (UK), s 23; Code of Criminal Procedure (France), Art.78-2-2 (as amended in 2001); Criminal Procedure Law (Detainee Suspect of a Security Offence)(Temporary Measure) 2006 (Israel), Art 35.

[17] See eg Terrorism Act 2000 (UK), s 109; Anti-Terrorism Act 2001 (Canada), Part 3; Criminal Procedure Code (Germany), Art 110a; Military Order of 13 November 2001: Detention, Treatment, and Trial of Certain Non-Citizens in the War Against Terrorism, Art 4(c)(4), 3 *CFR* 918 (2002).

[18] See eg Prevention of Terrorism Act 2002 (India), s 23; Military Order of 13 November 2001, *supra* note 17. See also Country of Origin Information Report; Turkey, State Security Courts (Devlet Güvenlik Mahkemesi), <http://www.ecoi.net/> (Turkey/Topics & Issues/Judiciary/State security courts and heavy penal courts) [last accessed 1 May 2010]

[19] Criminal Procedure Law (Enforcement Powers—Detention) 1996 (as amended in 2005) (Israel), Art 35.

[20] See eg Emergency Powers (Detention) Law 1979 (Israel); Code of Criminal Procedure 1973 (India), Arts 107, 151; Anti-Terrorism Act (No 2) 2005 (Australia), Sch 4, Div 105. For a discussion, see Hakimi, 'International Standards for Detaining Terrorism Suspects: Moving Beyond the Armed Conflict-Criminal Divide', 33 *Yale J. Int'l L.* (2008) 369.

[21] See eg Anti-Terrorism, Crime and Security Act 2002 (UK), Part 4; Uniting and Strengthening America by Providing Appropriate Tools Required to Intercept and Obstruct Terrorism Act of 2001 (US), Title 4; Immigration and Refugee Protection Act 2001(Canada), ss 77–85.

[22] See Anti-Terrorism Act (No 2) 2005 (Australia), Sch 4, Div 104; Prevention of Terrorism Act 2005 (UK).

of terror suspects by Israel and the United States,[23] and in Israel's policy of punitive house demolitions—a policy designed to disincentivize would-be terrorists
(who may be willing to sacrifice their own lives as suicide bombers) by adopting responsive measures that adversely affect their immediate family members.[24]
One may also briefly mention a host of other measures introduced by some states
in order to increase their long-term counter-terrorist preventive capabilities,
which have significant adverse effects on individual liberties. These measures
include wide-scale wire-tapping programmes[25] and other invasions of privacy,[26]
and limits on terrorist-sympathetic speech and political participation.[27]

The common denominator to all of these new counter-terrorism measures is
the erosion of the human rights of terror suspects that they entail, and the weakening of judicial controls that had been put in place to guarantee such rights.
The cumulative impact of such measures represents a major shift in the equilibrium between individual rights and the general security interests of the society in
question.[28] Such an outcome raises a number of concerns. First, states may over-
react and excessively erode human rights. What is more, governments interested
in accumulating more power (at the expense of other branches of government)
may inflate the actual threat of terror to justify their empowerment under the
revised paradigm.[29] In addition, there is a concern that a 'slippery slope' type of
dynamics would cause the spillover of restrictions applied vis-à-vis the human
rights of terror suspects to other members of society, thus leading to an erosion of
liberal values across-the-board, and to a fundamental change in the nature of the
right-restricting society.

---

[23] See *Report of the Commission of Inquiry Regarding the GSS' Interrogation Practices with Respect to Hostile Terrorist Activities 1987* in 1 *Landau Book* (Barak and Mazuz eds, 1995) (in Hebrew); Greenberg and Dratel, *The Torture Papers: The Road to Abu-Ghraib* (2005).

[24] For a discussion of this policy and its dubious effectiveness, see Kretzmer, *The Occupation of Justice: The Supreme Court of Israel and the Occupied Territories* (2002) 145; Farrell, 'Israeli Demolition of Palestinian Houses as a Punitive Measure: Application of International Law to Regulation 119', 28 *Brooklyn J. Int'l L.* (2003) 871; Zemach, 'The Limits Of International Criminal Law: House Demolitions in an Occupied Territory', 20 *Conn. J. Int'l L.* (2004) 65; Darcy, ' Punitive House Demolitions, the Prohibition of Collective Punishment, and the Supreme Court of Israel', 21 *Penn St. Int'l L. Rev.* (2003) 477.

[25] See Klosek, *The War on Privacy* (2007) at 36 *et seq.* For a legal analysis of the NSA wiretap-ping program, see eg Baldwin and Shaw, 'Down to the Wire: Assessing the Constitutionality of the National Security Agency's Warrantless Wiretapping Program: Exit the Rule of Law', 17 *U. Fla. J.L. & Pub. Pol'y* (2006) 429; Kitrosser, 'Macro-Transparency' as Structural Directive: A Look at the NSA Surveillance Controversy', 91 *Minn. L. Rev.* (2007) 1163.

[26] See eg BBC, 'The Most Spied Upon People in Europe', <http://news.bbc.co.uk/2/hi/europe/7265212.stm> [last accessed 1 May 2010]

[27] See eg SC Res 1373 (2001) 28 September 2001, UN Doc S/RES/1373 (2001) at 2; Organic Law 6/2002 on Political Party (Spain), Art. 9; Basic Law: The Knesset (as amended in 2008) (Israel), Art 7a.

[28] Although one may argue that enhancing general security also leads indirectly to improved individual protections for the population of the threatened society, the introduction of the 'revised law and order' paradigm changes the manner of burden allocation within society, facilitating a sacri-fice of the rights of a few suspects, in order to promote the rights and interests of the majority.

[29] See eg Žižek, *supra* note 12, at 107.

3. Resistance to the 'revised law and order' paradigm

Attempts by governments to strike a new balance between human rights and security concerns have attracted some legislative support, but have also encountered serious resistance from certain legislatures, and more typically from the judiciary. In particular, international and national judges have tended to view with suspicion some of the justifications put forward by executives for specific measures adopted under the 'revised law and order' paradigm and characterized some executive counter-terrorism actions as ineffective (perhaps even counter-productive), excessive, or contrary to core values.

For example, in *Kadi,* the European Court of Justice held that the EU regulation that implemented the Security Council's 'smart sanctions' violates fundamental principles of EU law and cannot therefore be given effect.[30] Similar outcomes have also been subsequently reached by the EU Court of First Instance[31] and the UN Human Rights Committee.[32]

No less strong resistance can be encountered in the domestic sphere. For example, in *Hamdan,* the US Supreme Court struck down the Military Commission procedures designed to try Al Qaeda members under standards that fell short of international due process guarantees;[33] in *Boumediene,* the US Supreme Court also struck down the parallel Combatant Status Review procedures (judicial procedures designed to review the prolonged detention of 'enemy combatants') for falling short of constitutional due process standards.[34]

In the same vein, the UK House of Lords has declared the incompatibility of an Act permitting the indefinite detention of some foreign terror suspects pending their deportation from the UK[35] with the European Convention on Human Rights. The Law Lords also prohibited the use of evidence procured through torture, restricted the use of secret evidence in terror-related judicial proceedings, and criticized the extreme implications of 'control orders' issued by the government (as a substitute for prolonged detention).[36] The House of Lords, acting in its legislative function, also rejected Parliament's attempt to extend to 42 days the maximum period of detention without indictment.[37]

The Israeli Supreme Court, in a series of decisions, has also repudiated some of the government's attempts to significantly deviate from established human rights norms. It struck down governmental decrees detaining without trial foreign

---

[30] See Joined Cases C-402/05 and C-415/05, P *Kadi and Al Barakaat International Foundation v Council and Commission,* Judgment of 3 September 2008.

[31] Case T-341/07, *Sison v Council,* Judgment of 30 September 2009.

[32] *Sayadi v Belgium,* Comm no 1472/2006, Views adopted by the Human Rights Committee on 22 October 2008, UN Doc CCPR/C/94/D/1472/2006 (2008).

[33] See *Hamdan v Rumsfeld,* 548 US 557 (2006).

[34] See *Boumediene v Bush,* 128 S Ct 2229 (2008).

[35] See *A v Secretary of State for the Home Dept* [2004] UKHL 56. The House of Lords judgment was essentially affirmed in *A v UK,* Judgment of 19 February 2009 (ECtHR). One may note that the Supreme Court of Canada has also struck down in *Charkaoui* an immigration law-based system of prolonged detentions without trial. *Charkaoui v Canada (Minister of Citizenship and Immigration),* 2007 SCC 9.   [36] *Secretary of State for the Home Department v JJ* [2007] UKHL 45.

[37] Coates, 'House of Lords Deals a Fatal Blow to 42-Day Terror Detention Plans', Times On-line 14 October 2008.

terror suspects as 'bargaining chips' for future prisoner exchange;[38] it revoked a military ordinance passed in the Occupied Territories permitting the detention without judicial review of terror suspects for a period of up to 18 days;[39] and nullified a military order seeking the deportation of family members of suspected terrorists (a measure which may have been intended to serve as a form of collective punishment).[40] It also outlawed the use of coercive interrogation techniques.[41]

Certainly, not all new counter-terrorism measures have been successfully challenged before courts, nor revisited by parliaments.[42] Moreover, some of the aforementioned decisions challenging governmental counter-terrorism policies have been late in coming;[43] others may not have been carried through fully by the executive.[44] Still, the cases mentioned above illustrate an aversion by some judiciaries and parliaments of attempts by the executive to stray too far off acceptable human rights concepts and standards. The commitment to core human rights values even in the face of a significant terrorist threat is impressive and laudable—as it ensures that liberal societies fighting terror would not surrender the same liberal values they are defending during the course of the fight.[45] Still, with the rise in perceived terrorist threats, the adequacy of the 'law and order' framework—understood as compelling states to fight terror with 'one hand tied behind the back'[46]—is being increasingly questioned. Furthermore, key features of the 'law and order' paradigm, even if somewhat revised, do not lend themselves easily to

---

[38] *Plonim [Anonymous parties] v Minister of Defence*, ILDC 12 (IL 2000).

[39] *Mar'ab v Commander of IDF Forces in Judea and Samaria*, HCJ 3239/02, PD 57 (2) 349.

[40] *Ajuri v IDF Commander in West Bank*, HCJ 7015/02, 56(6) PD 352.

[41] *Public Committee against Torture v State of Israel*, HCJ 5100/94, 53(4) PD 817.

[42] For example, the right of the executive to indefinitely detain 'enemy combatants' has survived constitutional challenges in the US and in Israel. *Hamdi v Rumsfeld*, 542 US 507 (2004); Cr A 6659/06, *A and B v Israel* Crim A 6659/06, ILDC 1069 (IL 2008). The Canadian Supreme Court did not rule out the possibility, in extreme cases, of 'deportation to torture'. *Suresh v Canada (Minister of Citizenship and Immigration)* [2002] 1 SCR 3. The Israeli Supreme Court also failed to meaningfully curb the practice of punitive house demolitions. See eg *Abu Dahim v IDF Home front Commander*, HCJ 9353, Judgment of 5 January 2009.

[43] For example, the 2000 *Anonymous* judgment (*supra* note 38) was issued more than a decade after the first Lebanese 'bargaining chips' were detained; *Hamdan* (*supra* note 33) was issued four years after the first terror suspects were interned in Guantánamo.

[44] For example, NGOs in Israel have alleged that the 1999 *Public Committee against Torture* (*supra* note 41) has not been fully implemented by the Israeli Security Agency. HCJ 5100/94 *Public Committee against Torture v State of Israel*, Judgment in Motion for Contempt of Court, 6 June 2009.

[45] See eg *Morcos v Minister of Defence*, HCJ 168/91 45(1) PD 467, 470 ('The power of society to stand against its enemies is based on its recognition that it is fighting for values that deserve protection. The rule of law is one of these values.'); *Beit Sourik Village Council v Israel and the Commander of the Israeli Defence Force in the West Bank*, HCJ 2056/04, ILDC 16, at 86 (IL 2004) ('Regarding the state's struggle against the terror that rises up against it, we are convinced that at the end of the day, a struggle according to the law will strengthen her power and her spirit. There is no security without law. Satisfying the provisions of the law is an aspect of national security.'). See also *Report of the High-level Panel on Threats, Challenges and Change, A More Secure World: Our Shared Responsibility*, UN Doc A/59/565 (2004) at 147.

[46] See *Public Committee against Torture*, *supra* note 41, at 39 ('A democracy must sometimes fight with one hand tied behind its back. Even so, a democracy has the upper hand. The rule of law and the liberty of an individual constitute important components in its understanding of security. At the end of the day, they strengthen its spirit and this strength allows it to overcome its difficulties.')

the fight against terror: the 'law and order' paradigm revolves around the concept of individual responsibility and the punishing of the guilty. It struggles, as a result, to address collective phenomena such as mass disturbances and widespread terror, where individual guilt is harder to identify or uphold. It also encounters difficulties in adopting preventive measures against individuals before establishing their guilt—a state of affairs compatible with the human rights framework's willingness to assume some degree of risk to society as an acceptable price to be paid for preserving liberty. But what if the risk associated with the operation of terror groups has become much more probable and extremely dangerous? In this case, there is a growing body of opinion that using the 'law and order' paradigm's standard 'tools' for fighting terror may prove to be 'too little too late'.

B. The 'armed conflict' paradigm

The perception—real or imagined—that the changing nature of the threat of terrorism has outgrown the capacities of the 'law and order' paradigm underlies the decision by the US after 9/11 to fight terrorism through a different paradigm—the 'armed conflict' paradigm. Key aspects of the US's decision to declare a 'war on terror' have received support from both the UN Security Council[47] and NATO.[48] Israel, another terror-stricken country, made a similar move in 2000 following the eruption a year earlier of a violent uprising in the Occupied Territories, which entailed a sharp rise in suicide bombing attacks within Israel (the second Palestinian *Intifada*).

According to this new legal paradigm, terror represents a threat equivalent in its magnitude to an inter-state war. True, terror groups are much smaller in size than regular armies, but they may compensate for this shortcoming with access to new technologies, a heightened motivation to cause harm and lack of meaningful restraints in the application of force. So, if the 'war on terror' really looks like war, in the sense that it involves the application of large-scale deadly force by organized groups, then the rules of war may provide a natural starting point for ascertaining the rights and obligations of the warring parties.

The attractiveness of this new paradigm to governments is clear. An 'armed conflict' paradigm provides governments with a new 'tool-kit' to handle terror threats, which may be more commensurate with the gravity of the perceived threat. The legitimacy it seems to confer upon the use of military force (including in the territory of foreign states) has dramatic consequences for the direction of counter-terror efforts. Whereas the civilian police and prosecutors operating under the 'law and order' paradigm focus on neutralizing concrete threats and establishing individual responsibility, the military is trained to physically weaken adversary groups and

---

[47] See SC Res 1368(2001), 12 September 2001; SC Res 1373(2001) 28 September 2001, UN Doc S/RES/1373 (2001).

[48] See Statement issued at the Ministerial Meeting of the North Atlantic Council held at NATO Headquarters, Brussels, on 6 December 2001, <http://www.nato.int/cps/en/natolive/official_texts_18848.htm> [last accessed 3 May 2010] 'Enduring Freedom', the NATO operation in Afghanistan initiated after the 9/11 terror attacks is still ongoing at present.

reduce their capacity to pose a future risk. The conceptual move from individual-based to collective-based counter-terrorism measures represents a radical shift of the balance between human rights and security interests. Such a shift is further reflected by some specific measures adopted pursuant to the 'armed conflict' paradigm that entail dramatic human rights-limiting implications (eg, targeted killings of suspected terrorists and the indefinite detention of 'enemy combatants'). Indeed, the invocation of the 'armed conflict' paradigm has sometimes been accompanied by derogations from human rights treaties (similarly conveying a shift in the equilibrium existing between security and liberty).[49] These moves also have serious institutional implications since they facilitate the removal of large parts of the fight against terror from the purview of domestic legal systems to an underdeveloped international legal framework, with fewer hard and fast rules in place, and even more limited supervisory mechanisms.

Surprisingly perhaps, the invocation of the 'armed conflict' paradigms may enjoy not only the support of 'security hawks', but also that of some 'rule of law' purists. This latter group may regard the extra-legal approach to the fight against terror that the 'armed conflict' approach entails as a useful way of insulating domestic legal systems from the 'contaminating' spillover effects that result from processing terror cases in the ordinary legal system.[50] Erecting a 'separation barrier' between terror and most other social threats also helps society maintain an illusion of normality even when the most abnormal measures are resorted to.[51]

Of course, the shift to an 'armed conflict' paradigm also raises many objections. Most obviously, the move from a framework that tolerates a limited set of counter-terrorism measures directed against a small group of individuals whose guilt can be legally established to a framework that permits the targeting with deadly violence of members of armed groups (even individual members that pose a marginal threat to the society in question), raises concerns of overreaction and unjustified right-deprivation. Moreover, the move from one legal environment, where judicial and political institutions closely supervise counter-terrorism efforts, to another legal environment, where such supervision is non-extant or ineffective,[52] invites lawlessness and massive abuse of power.

---

[49] See eg the derogations by United Kingdom (2001–05) and France (2005–06) to the International Covenant on Civil and Political Rights, Notifications under Art 4(3) of the Covenant (Derogations).

[50] See eg Sajo, 'From Militant Democracy to the Preventive State?', 27 *Cardozo L. Rev.* (2006) 2255, 2261 ('[I]t is increasingly likely that the legal policies of counter-terrorism will have inevitable spillover effects'); *Final Report Poelgeest Seminar on Counter-terrorism strategies, human rights and international law: meeting the challenges* (2007), <http://media.leidenuniv.nl/legacy/Final%20Report%20Counter%20Terrorism%20Expert%20Seminar.pdf> [Last accessed 3 May 2010] ('[S]tates might consider adopting special anti-terrorism legislation providing for administrative measures rather than incorporating changes in the regular criminal law system. For such changes may affect the system and "contaminate" it.').

[51] See eg Gross, 'Chaos and Rules: Should Responses to Violent Crises Always Be Constitutional?' 112 *Yale L.J.* (2003) 1011, at 1044–1045.

[52] For example, in Israel, courts may exercise judicial supervision over military operations and have done so on a number of occasions. See eg *Barake v The Minister of Defence*, HCJ 3114/02, 3115/02, 3116/02, ILDC 369 (IL 2002); *Physicians for Human Rights and ors v Commander of the Israeli Defence Force in the Gaza Strip*, HCJ 4764/04, ILDC 17 (IL 2004). Still, the effectiveness of

In addition, the very analogy between the 'war on terror' and inter-state wars can be challenged, as it is difficult to transfer notions relating to the definition of 'combatants', the 'battle ground', and the 'beginning and end of hostilities' from one context to the other. In the case of many terror groups, distinctions between 'combatants' or 'civilians taking a direct part in hostilities' and 'non-combatants' are hard to draw; there is often no identifiable 'battlefield' and the violence exercised is of an ongoing nature, without a clear ending-point in sight.[53] Hence, specific rules permitting the killing of 'combatants' or the deprivation of their liberty for the duration of the conflict may be ill-suited to govern the 'war on terror'—even from a 'laws of war' perspective. In other words, treating the 'war on terror' under the laws of war may be problematic in the sense that such a norm-application exercise may disrupt the internal balance between humanitarian and military interests that the laws of war seek to establish. Still, as a matter of legal doctrine, the application of the 'armed conflict' paradigm appears to be permissible in some circumstances under existing law.[54] The key doctrinal question that has emerged in recent years has not been whether the laws of war apply at all to the fight against terror; but rather, which sub-set of international humanitarian law rules (IHL) apply (ie, whether one should invoke IHL rules governing international or non-international armed conflicts).[55]

2. The Emergence of a Mixed Paradigm?

A. The co-application of international humanitarian law (IHL) and human rights law

There is growing evidence that the gulf between the 'law and order' and 'armed conflict' paradigms as competing international legal frameworks for conducting the fight against terror is not as deep and ascertainable as one may have imagined. At first glance, this detracts from the significance of the paradigmatic shift

---

such supervision is, generally speaking, very limited, and some human rights activists have argued that these proceedings only create a veneer of judicial review over the military, which ultimately serves more to legitimate power than to curtail it. See eg Sfard, 'The Price of Internal Legal Opposition to Human Rights Abuses', 1 *Journal of Human Rights Practice* (2009) 37.

[53] See eg Duffy, *The 'War on Terror' and the Framework of International Law* (2005) at 332 *et seq*; Bond, 'The Language of War: A Battle of Words at Guantanamo Bay', 10 *Appeal* (2005) 70; Balendra, 'Defining Armed Conflict', 29 *Cardozo L. Rev.* (2008) 2461; Rona, 'Interesting Times for International Humanitarian Law: Challenges from the "War on Terror"', 27 *Fletcher F. Wld. Aff.* (2003) 55.   [54] *Prosecutor v Boškoski*, Case No IT-04-82, Judgment of 10 July 2008 (ICTY) at 190.

[55] See *Hamdan v Rumsfeld*, 548 US at 630–631; *Public Committee against Torture in Israel v Israel*, HCJ 769/02, ILDC 597 (IL 2006) at 21. At least from one normative aspect, the *Hamdan* approach appears to me to be preferable: while all, or almost all, inter-state violence is governed by IHL (See Dinstein, *The Conduct of Hostilities under the Law of Armed Conflict* (2004) at 15–16) IHL applies in non-international contexts only when violence reaches a high threshold of intensity: long duration, extensive casualties, use of heavy weaponry, expanding battle ground etc. See eg *Prosecutor v Haradinaj*, Case No IT-04-84-T, Judgment of 3 April 2008 (ICTY) at 37–62. Thus, the move from the 'law and order' paradigm to the 'armed conflict' paradigm is justified only when the phenomenon is of such a magnitude that it escapes the scope of coverage of 'law and order' measures. This standard appears to limit the discretion of governments on when and how to invoke the exceptional powers conferred upon them by the armed conflict paradigm.

described above. But at a deeper level, the separate existence of the two paradigms notwithstanding their growing substantive convergence underscores the importance of providing particular framings for the narrative of the 'war on terror'. In other words, the choice of a paradigm may still control the manner in which the increasingly similar rules governing the war on terror under both paradigms are interpreted and applied.

The normative gaps between the 'law and order' and the 'armed conflict' paradigm are narrowed due to the cumulative impact of three legal developments. First, some specific rules of common contents have emerged under both legal frameworks that purport to govern the fight against terror—human rights law and IHL. The prohibition against torture under the 1949 Geneva Conventions (applicable in both international and non-international armed conflicts) and the 1984 Convention against Torture is a clear example of such a common rule.[56] Other examples may include the duty not to deliberately deprive non-combatants of their lives,[57] the prohibition against hostage taking,[58] and numerous obligations pertaining to the respect for the rights of individuals in occupied territories, which limit the counter-terrorism options available to the occupying forces.[59] With regard to such rules, the choice between paradigms appears to be irrelevant, and at least one national court has cited such normative similarities as a justification for refraining from offering a precise classification of the situation at hand.[60]

A second avenue for the increased convergence between the two paradigms has been the role of international human rights law norms as IHL gap-fillers, and thereby, as a source of law under the 'armed conflict' paradigm as well. The important assertion by the International Court of Justice in the *Nuclear Weapons* advisory proceedings, that human rights treaties continue to apply in time of war (although the laws of armed conflict constitute *lex specialis*),[61] has created a space for the invocation of human rights law in respect of those areas not regulated by IHL. This approach can be used to generate new obligations for states applying military force against terror groups that go beyond the requirements of IHL; it may also be used to fill concepts already existing under international humanitarian law with new and more specific normative contents. An example of a 'new'

[56] See eg Convention Relative to the Treatment of Prisoners of War, 12 August 1949, Arts 3, 14, 75 UNTS 135; Convention Relative to the Protection of Civilian Persons in Time of War, 12 August 1949, Arts 3, 32, 75 UNTS 287 (*GC IV*); Convention against Torture and Other Cruel, Inhuman or Degrading Treatment or Punishment, 10 December 1984, Art 1-2, 1465 UNTS 85. In fact, one may argue that some of the prohibitions against torture under the laws of war are more stringent than those existing under human rights law. For a discussion, see Shany, 'The Prohibition against Torture and Cruel, Inhuman and Degrading Treatment and Punishment: Can the Absolute be Relativized under Existing International Law?' 56 *Cath. U.L. Rev.* (2007) 837, 849.

[57] See eg Protocol Additional to the Geneva Conventions of 12 August 1949, and Relating to the Protection of Victims of International Armed Conflicts, Article 51(2), 8 January 1977, 1125 UNTS 3 (*AP I*)('The civilian population as such, as well as individual civilians, shall not be the object of attack. Acts or threats of violence the primary purpose of which is to spread terror among the civilian population are prohibited'); International Covenant on Civil and Political Rights, 16 December 1966, Art 6, 999 UNTS 171   [58] See eg *AP I*, Art 75(2)(c); ICCPR, Art 9.

[59] See eg *GC IV*, Art 27; ICCPR, Art 17, 23.

[60] See *Mara'abe v Prime Minister of Israel*, HCJ 7957/04, ILDC 157 (IL 2005) at 27.

[61] *Threat or Use of Nuclear Weapons*, ICJ Reports (1996) 226, 240.

human rights norm may be the emerging duty of states to pay individual reparations to individuals whose rights have been violated during counter-terrorism
military operations (such as 'targeted killings').[62] As an example of a 'content-
filling' human rights norm, one may note due process guarantees: although IHL,
including the laws governing non-international armed conflicts (which constitutes according to the US Supreme Court's *Hamdan* judgment a minimal normative benchmark), affirms the need to respect 'judicial guarantees which are
recognized as indispensable by civilized peoples',[63] human rights law may offer its
rich jurisprudence on what constitutes due process in order to inform the contents
of this parallel IHL notion.

But even more dramatically, some writers have identified the emergence of a
mixed legal framework to govern the 'war on terror', which borrows rules and
concepts from both human rights law and IHL.[64] This mixed legal framework
responds to the criticism directed against the sub-optimal 'fit' between the laws of
war and the 'war on terror' by introducing human rights norms and sensibilities
as an additional restraining factor, limiting military decision-makers' freedom of
action and mitigating some of the more problematic consequences caused by the
application of IHL to counter-terrorism operations. The mixed framework, implicitly endorsed by the International Court of Justice in the *Wall* Advisory Opinion
(a case dealing with the legality of one dramatic counter-terrorism measure—the
construction of a physical obstacle in an occupied territory),[65] uses human rights
law as a robust gap-filler by tending to construe the absence of individual rights
under IHL as a legal *lacuna*, and not a 'negative arrangement'. It also encourages a
reinterpretation of traditional IHL norms and concepts in ways that correspond to
human rights principles.

Several decisions of the Israeli Supreme Court may illustrate the emergence of
a mixed paradigm. In the *Targeted Killing* case, President Barak opined that the
principle of proportionality—a key IHL principle—should be reconceptualized
so as to incorporate *inter alia* the duty to opt for the least harmful measure even in
relation to enemy combatants.[66] Hence, militants should not be killed when they
can be arrested—an outcome that deviates from classic IHL that does not similarly

[62] See *Public Committee against Torture in Israel* (2006), *supra* note 55, at 40; *Report of the Special Rapporteur on Extrajudicial, Summary or Arbitrary Executions*, 25 January 2000, UN Doc E/CN.4/2000/3, at 34.   [63] See eg *GC IV*, Art 3.
[64] See eg Kretzmer, 'Targeted Killing of Suspected Terrorists: Extra-Judicial Executions or Legitimate Means of Defence?, 16 *EJIL* (2005) 171, at 201 *et seq*; Prud'homme, '*Lex Specialis*: Oversimplifying a More Complex and Multifaceted Relationship?', 40 *Is. L.R.* (2007) 356, 388; Watkin, 'Controlling the Use of Force: A Role for Human Rights Norms in Contemporary Armed Conflict', 98 *AJIL* (2004) 1, 34.
[65] *Legal Consequences of the Construction of a Wall in the Occupied Palestinian Territories*, ICJ Reports (2004) 136, 178 ('[S]ome rights may be exclusively matters of international humanitarian law; others may be exclusively matters of human rights law; yet others may be matters of both these branches of international law.').
[66] *Public Committee against Torture in Israel* (2006), *supra* note 55, at 40 ('among the military means, one must choose the means whose harm to the human rights of the harmed person is small-est. Thus, if a terrorist taking a direct part in hostilities can be arrested, interrogated, and tried, those are the means which should be employed.').

bar the killing of enemy combatants.[67] In the *Unlawful Combatant Incarceration* case, President Beinish forcefully made the point that enemy combatants not entitled to prisoner of war status cannot be detained merely on the basis of their group affiliation; consequently, the state must establish the individual risk attendant to each and every one of them.[68] This last position regards the absence of an international regulation governing the detention of combatants not entitled to prisoner of war status as a legal *lacuna* that has to be filled not by extension of the scope and logic of existing IHL rules on detention of enemy soldiers, but rather with what are essentially human rights norms. Finally, in the *Bassiouni* case (a case dealing with Israel's obligations vis-à-vis the population of Gaza after Israel's withdrawal therefrom), President Beinish held that although the occupation of Gaza may be over (and, hence, most IHL rules are inapplicable to the situation there), Israel continues to be responsible for maintaining a minimum level of humanitarian conditions in Gaza.[69] Arguably, the conclusion of the Court in *Bassiouni* is based upon human rights norms and principles, or at least, human rights sensibilities.[70]

B. The remaining paradigmatic choice

Although the emergence of a mixed paradigm appears to take the edge off the move from the 'law and order' to the 'armed conflict' paradigm, one has reason to believe that identifying the competing paradigms at play remains a useful and meaningful exercise. First, the 'armed conflict' paradigm has some important *jus ad bellum* implications, which human rights law, in its present form, does not adequately capture.[71] Hence, the very right to resort to military force as a counter-terrorism measure—ie, to engage in targeted killings or to invade a foreign country—may still depend in many circumstances on the existence of extremely violent conditions that would qualify under international law as an 'armed conflict of a non-international nature'[72] and/or 'armed attack'.[73] While a few human rights bodies

---

[67] See Cohen and Shany, 'A Development of Modest Proportions: The Application of the Principle of Proportionality in the *Targeted Killings* Case', 5 *JICJ* (2007) 310.

[68] *A and B v Israel*, CrimA 6659/06, ILDC 1069 (IL 2008). President Beinish also insinuated that a provision in the Unlawful Combatants Incarceration Law of 2002 that reverses the burden of proving individual risk to the detained individual may be unconstitutional and urged the state not to invoke this 'presumption of dangerousness'. Ibid, at 24.

[69] *Ahmad v The Prime Minister*, HCJ 9132/07, ILDC 883 (IL 2008).

[70] See Shany, 'The Law Applicable to Non-Occupied Gaza', 42 *Is. L.R.* (2009) 101. For a general theory about the role of human rights sensibilities across legal regimes, see Teitel, 'Humanity-Law: A New Interpretive Lens on the International Sphere', 77 *Fordham L. Rev.* (2008) 101.

[71] But see some interesting future directions proposed in Schabas, 'Lex Specialis? Belt and Suspenders? The Parallel Operation of Human Rights Law and the Law of Armed Conflict, and the Conundrum of Jus Ad Bellum', 40 *Is. L.R.* (2007) 59.

[72] See eg *GC IV*, Art 3. See Pictet (ed), *IV Geneva Convention Relative To The Protection Of Civilian Persons In Time Of War: Commentary* (1960) at 36 ('[I]t must be recognized that the conflicts referred to in Article 3 are armed conflicts, with armed forces on either side engaged in hostilities—conflicts, in short, which are in many respects similar to an international war, but take place within the confines of a single country. In many cases, each of the Parties is in possession of a portion of the national territory, and there is often some sort of front.').

[73] UN Charter, Art 51. See Dinstein, *War, Aggression and Self-Defense* (4th edn, 2005) 183–184; Simma (ed), I *The Charter of the United Nations: A Commentary* (2002) at 796.

have shown some willingness to adopt a flexible interpretation of what constitutes an 'absolute necessity' that could justify the use of force under a 'law and order' framework,[74] there still remain many less-than-immediate threats that would justify the application of lethal force under IHL, but not under human rights law. Consequently, as a legal matter, the choice of paradigms would have great significance with regard to violence-'triggering' situations.

Secondly, and perhaps more importantly, even if one accepts that most rules and principles applicable under both legal paradigms governing the fight against terror are relatively similar, a question arises as to the manner in which these rules and principles are implemented in specific fact patterns. Human rights law is founded upon a number of fundamental ethoi that profoundly affect the way in which it is interpreted and applied: individual fault or risk serve as the basis for sanction imposition, and the deep suspicion of the way governmental power is employed leads to a general preference for insisting that governments choose what are the least freedom-curbing measures and err, if necessary, on the side of restraint (the introduction of 'beyond reasonable doubt' as a standard of criminal conviction is illustrative of such ethoi).[75]

At the same time, the laws of war appear to be more receptive to notions of collective responsibility (eg, targeting and detaining combatants on the basis of their group affiliation; the imposition of collective movement restrictions, such as siege and curfew, on enemy populations),[76] and confer broad discretion upon military decision-makers. Hence, military commanders are not always required under IHL to select the least harmful measures (eg, they may adopt troop safety precautions at the expense of increased collateral damage, or kill enemy soldiers in circumstances where they can be captured).[77] Furthermore, IHL subjects military decision-makers to a relatively liberal 'reasonableness' standard and tolerates operational mistakes and a certain degree of collateral harm.[78]

Significantly, the different points of departure of human rights law and IHL derive not only from differences in the ideological inclinations of their forefathers, but also from structural reasons relating to the typical factual and institutional conditions that they are designed to govern. IHL governs situations of massive violence employed by collectives, often under conditions of considerable uncertainty

[74] See eg *McCann v UK*, Judgment of 27 September 1995, at 200 (ECtHR).

[75] See eg Malanczuk (ed), *Akehurst's Modern Introduction to International Law* (7th revised edn, 1997) 209; Raday, 'Privatising Human Rights and the Abuse of Power', 13 *CJLJ* (2000) 103, at 111–112; Meron, 'The Humanization of Humanitarian Law', 94 *AJIL* (2000) 239, at 250.

[76] See eg Abi-Saab, 'International Criminal Tribunals and the Development of International Humanitarian and Human Rights Law', in *Liber Amicorum Judge Mohammed Bedjaoui*, Yakpo and Boumedra (eds), (1999) 649, at 650; Meron, *supra* note 75, at 243; Fletcher and Ohlin, *Defending Humanity: When Force is Justified and Why?* (2008) at 208.

[77] See eg *Public Committee against Torture in Israel* (2006), *supra* note 55, at 46; Fletcher and Ohlin, *supra* note 76, at 24.

[78] See eg *Final Report to the Prosecutor by the Committee Established to Review the NATO Bombing Campaign Against the Federal Republic of Yugoslavia*, 39 ILM (2000) 1257, at 50. For criticism of this tolerant standard, see Ben-Naftali and Michaeli, '"We Must Not Make a Scarecrow of the Law": A Legal Analysis of the Israeli Policy of Targeted Killings', 36 *Cornell Int'l L.J.* (2003) 233, at 250 ('Bystanders are often killed as well. In the reified language of war and law, their deaths are 'collateral damage').

(ie, 'the fog of war') and resource constraints. In such a factual environment, it is difficult, if not impossible, to engage in the same rigorous right-based analysis that human rights law requires in times of peace. As a result, IHL accepts that military decisions are often adopted on the basis of crude 'rules of thumb' (such as treating all enemy soldiers as lawful targets), that a broad 'margin of discretion' is to be accorded to the military, and that institutional oversight of the latter's operations tends to be limited.

Although human rights law has an important role to play even in the course of a full-scale armed conflict as a harm-mitigating methodology with particular relevance to individualized measures applied during the conflict (eg, detention and trial of enemy combatants, confiscation of specific private property), an attempt to alter the basic attributes of the 'armed conflict' paradigm through the application of human rights law may result in problematic normative overreaching. In other words, such an attempt may lead to a law-application exercise divorced from the actual conditions and needs of warfare and is likely to attract limited support from important constituencies. As a result, a 'reconfigured armed conflict' paradigm may have only little impact on state conduct.

Viewed from this perspective, one may regard with a certain degree of apprehension attempts by human rights bodies to assess the lawfulness of counter-terrorist military operations *predominantly* pursuant to human rights standards. For example, when reviewing the lawfulness of two military operations conducted by Russian forces in Chechnya against Chechen rebels, which led to collateral loss of civilian lives, the ECtHR opined:

Article 2, which safeguards the right to life and sets out the circumstances when deprivation of life may be justified, ranks as one of the most fundamental provisions in the Convention, from which in peacetime no derogation is permitted under Article 15. Together with Article 3, it also enshrines one of the basic values of the democratic societies making up the Council of Europe. The circumstances in which deprivation of life may be justified must therefore be *strictly construed*. The object and purpose of the Convention as an instrument for the protection of individual human beings also requires that Article 2 be interpreted and applied so as to make its safeguards practical and effective.

Article 2 covers not only intentional killing but also the situations in which it is permitted to 'use force' which may result, as an unintended outcome, in the deprivation of life. However, the deliberate or intended use of lethal force is only one factor to be taken into account in assessing its necessity. Any use of force must be no more than 'absolutely necessary' for the achievement of one or more of the purposes set out in sub-paragraphs (a) to (c). This term indicates that *a stricter and more compelling test of necessity must be employed than that normally applicable when determining whether State action is 'necessary in a democratic society' under paragraphs 2 of Articles 8 to 11 of the Convention*. Consequently, the force used must be strictly proportionate to the achievement of the permitted aims.[79]

In other words, not only has the Court refused to afford the Russian military a high degree of discretion in applying the necessity and proportionality standards,

---

[79] *Isayeva v Russia*, Judgment of 24 February 2005, at 172–173 (ECtHR) (emphasis added). See also *Isayeva, Yusupova, and Bazayeva*, Judgment of 24 February 2005, at 168–169 (ECtHR).

the Court held that military operations that are likely to result in collateral damage should be subject to a stricter standard of care than the standard applicable under peacetime conditions. This approach to necessity and proportionality appears to conflict with the traditional, much more deferential, standard that IHL employs—that is, the standard of reasonableness.[80] More fundamentally, perhaps, IHL has never viewed the occurrence of collateral damage as indicative of a *prima facie* violation of law that has to be explained and strictly justified by the existence of a 'compelling' necessity (supported by 'convincing evidence').[81] Applying this high standard of responsibility, the ECtHR found that Russia failed to adopt sufficient measures of care to prevent harm to the civilian population present in the theatre of operations, in both of the reviewed cases, and that it did not adequately prove the existence of responsibility-mitigating factors (such as the use of civilians as 'human shields' by the Chechen rebels).[82]

Another, more recent example of a human rights-dominated approach to an armed conflict situation can be found in the *Goldstone Report* issued by a Human Rights Council fact-finding committee. The report, which examined Israel's counter-terrorism military operation in Gaza (2008–2009), seems to apply, by and large, the 'mixed' paradigm in the same way the paradigm has been applied by the ECtHR (notwithstanding the committee's explicit reliance on IHL sources). For example, when analysing the duty to provide 'effective warning' to civilians located in areas where military operations take place,[83] the committee wrote:

Article 57 (2) (c) requires the warning to be effective. The Mission understands by this that it must reach those who are likely to be in danger from the planned attack, it must give them sufficient time to react to the warning, it must clearly explain what they should do to avoid harm and it must be a credible warning. The warning also has to be clear so that the civilians are not in doubt that it is indeed addressed to them. As far as possible, warnings should state the location to be affected and where the civilians should seek safety. A credible warning means that civilians should be in no doubt that it is intended to be acted upon, as a false alarm or hoax may undermine future warnings, putting civilians at risk.[84]

Applying such a high standard of required precautions, the committee found most of the warnings issued by Israel to the civilian population in Gaza to be inadequate.[85] Interestingly enough, the committee did refer to the dangerous and confusing circumstances prevailing in Gaza during the operation, not to lighten the

---

[80] NATO Bombing Report, *supra* note 78, at 50.

[81] *Isayeva, Yusupova, and Bazayeva, supra* note 79, at 179. The Court suggests, moreover, that facts (including facts supporting legal defences) need to proved at a level of proof which is 'beyond reasonable doubt'. *Isayeva, supra* note 79, at 177; *Ilsayeva, Yusupova, and Bazayeva, supra* note 79, at 173.

[82] *Isayeva, supra* note 79, at 179–198; *Isayeva, Yusupova and Bazayeva, supra* note 79, at 174–197.

[83] *AP I*, Art 57(2)(c) ('Effective advance warning shall be given of attacks which may affect the civilian population, unless circumstances do not permit'.).

[84] *Report of the United Nations Fact Finding Mission on the Gaza Conflict*, 15 September 2009, UN Doc. A/HRC/12/48 (2009) at 528 (*Goldstone Report*).

[85] Ibid, at 535–540. Israel claimed to have made 165,000 telephone calls warning civilians of impending attacks, distributed leaflets, and issued radio broadcasts to that effect, and fired warning shots at targets before their destruction (in order to enable civilians to flee).

burden imposed on the Israeli military as the language of Article 57(2) seems to suggest, but rather to underscore Israel's duty to provide clearer warnings:

The effectiveness of the warnings has to be assessed in the light of the overall circumstances that prevailed and the subjective view of conditions that the civilians concerned would take in deciding upon their response to the warning.[86]

Another example of the imposition of burdens of proof and justification on a military conducting counter-terrorism operations can be found in the committee's treatment of the 'al-Daya' incident—the targeting of a populated civilian house by the Israeli Air Force, a case which Israel claimed to have been an operational mistake (allegedly, the attack was intended to target a nearby weapons storage facility). While the committee accepted that a mistake may have occurred and that Israel's responsibility for the attack under IHL cannot be established,[87] it nonetheless held that Israel should incur international responsibility under human rights law for the unfortunate consequences:

The firing of the projectile was a deliberate act in so far as it was planned, by Israel's admission, to strike the al-Daya house. The fact that target selection had gone wrong at the planning stage does not strip the act of its deliberate character. The consequences may have been unintended; the act was deliberate. Taken together with further facts (such as the failure to deliver an effective warning) and the nature of the 'intransgressible obligation' to protect civilian life, the Mission considers that, even if a fault element is required, the available information demonstrates a substantial failure of due diligence on the part of Israel. As such, the Mission considers Israel to be liable for the consequences of this wrongful act.

The Mission finds that Israel's lack of due diligence in this case also constitutes a violation of the right to life as set out in article 6 of the International Covenant on Civil and Political Rights, to which Israel is a party. The right to life includes the obligation to respect life and the positive obligation to protect life. The Human Rights Committee has stated that States parties should take measures not only to prevent and punish deprivation by criminal acts, but also to prevent arbitrary killing by their own security forces. No exception is made for acts during war.[88]

Once again, the approach taken by the committee appears to be informed by strong human rights sensibilities—that need to adopt every feasible measure to protect individuals from governmental power (a duty regarded by the commission as an 'intransgressible obligation'). The result of this analysis, however, leads to a reversal of the *lex specialis* rule: IHL with its greater tolerance for operational mistakes committed during the fog of war is cast aside, and human rights law, which arguably imposes a more exacting standard of care, is selected as the principal legal framework for the imposition of liability.

To be clear, it is certainly plausible (even probable) that the Russian and Israeli militaries have violated the laws of war on more than one occasion during their respective counter-terrorism operations in Chechnya and Gaza. Still, the

---

[86] Ibid, at 540.
[87] Ibid, at 858 ('In the absence of information necessary to determine the precise circumstances of the incident, the Mission can make no findings on possible violations of international humanitarian law or international criminal law.').　　　　　　　　　　　　　　　　[88] Ibid, at 861–862.

introduction of a high standard of legal responsibility and a concomitant heavy burden of proof, may lead to counter-productive results: the widening gap between normative developments and military needs and practices would lead states to challenge the adequacy of the existing international legal framework, as applied by certain international institutions, and colour international law in 'utopian' colours.[89] In other words, even if one accepts the moral and ideological imperatives underlying the redefining of the 'armed conflict' paradigm as a 'mixed' paradigm dominated to a large extent by human rights law, the articulation of the new standard is not fully supported by actual state practice[90] and conflicts with important political state interests. Hence, assertions that a human rights-dominated 'mixed' paradigm constitutes a basis for legal responsibility under *lex lata* ought to be approached with a degree of caution.

3. Conclusions

The perceived rise in the level of the threat generated by terror groups has led to re-evaluation of the legal frameworks suitable for the conduct of the fight against terror: should states follow the 'law and order' or 'armed conflict' paradigm? Further, what version of these paradigms should be followed: the traditional 'law and order' paradigm or the 'revised law and order' paradigm? IHL governing international or non-international armed conflicts?

This chapter proposes to regard the choice between competing paradigms as reflective of a number of legal and political phenomena:

(a) a historical dialectic affected by the changing evaluations of the magnitude and imminence of the threat of terrorism—the catastrophic events of 9/11 have spurred attempts to dramatically revise the 'law and order' paradigm and develop an even more aggressive legal framework in the form of the 'armed conflict' paradigm. Subsequently, as the 'dust had sunk', cooler heads may have prevailed. Hence, a counter-movement towards reaffirmation of core human rights values can be observed, both in the context of the 'law and order' and 'armed conflict' paradigms. It remains to be seen whether in the long run, this counter-movement will be viewed as 'under-reaction' to the threat of terrorism, in the same way that some post-9/11 measures are often regarded today as 'over-reactions'.

(b) An institutional struggle—whereas the 'law and order' paradigm channels a good part of the fight against terror to ordinary legal procedures, the 'armed conflict' paradigm empowers the executive branch and liberates it from meaningful judicial and legislative oversight. Hence, the choice between

---

[89] See Koskenniemi, *supra* note 8, 172.

[90] For an assessment of actual state practice on matters addressed by the *Goldstone Report* see Kemp, 'International Law and Military Operations in Practice' (2009), <http://www.jcpa.org/> [last accessed 3 May 2010] (Hamas, the Gaza War, and Accountability under International Law/Col Richard Kemp).

paradigms, as well as between paradigm variants, may boil down to a choice among visions of proper governance that is inevitably informed by the actual level of trust conferred upon the different branches of government by different constituencies.[91]

(c) A struggle over a professional/ideological vocabulary—perhaps the most interesting aspect of the paradigmatic competition discussed above— involves the attempt to produce through law-selection a narrative of the fight against terror, which adopts as its starting point certain ideological assumptions about power and justice. At a first level, the attempt to redefine the fight against terror as an armed conflict invokes the images of war as a rallying cry against terror. This narrative also imports some assumptions about war—a struggle between collectives requiring the grant of broad discretionary powers to the military and limited judicial review. It also denotes a greater tolerance for operational mistakes and collateral damage.

The introduction of a 'mixed' paradigm—a development which is hard to challenge on doctrinal and moral grounds—opens up a space for a counter-move by human rights advocates, which may considerably offset the freedom of action promised by the 'armed conflict' paradigm. Such a move entails the reading in of basic assumptions about the exercise of government powers, limiting as much as possible harm to individual interest by governmental action, into the laws of war. The challenge that this approach will have to confront, sooner or later, is whether it can bridge the gap between law and social reality, namely, whether in the long run it could impact state practices, which currently appear to be out of synch with a human rights-dominated 'mixed' counter-terrorism paradigm.

---

[91] For a comparable analysis of an institutional struggle over global governance, see Benvenisti. 'Reclaiming Democracy: The Strategic Uses of Foreign and International Law by Foreign Courts', 102 *AJIL* (2008) 241.

3

The Role of Human Rights and International Humanitarian Law in New Types of Armed Conflicts

Marco Sassòli*

1. Introduction

Every event in life and in history is new compared to previous events. Yet even the most revolutionary event consists of some unchanged facts and even the most repetitive event has necessarily some new aspects, if only its temporal environment. The nature and circumstances of armed conflicts, as all other categories in history and all social phenomena, constantly develop, but the human mind also detects some similarities with previous armed conflicts. The claim that some situations are genuinely completely new never survives critical historical analysis.[1]

International Humanitarian Law (IHL) applies to armed conflicts, protecting, mainly through rules of behaviour addressed to belligerents, those who do not or no longer directly participate in the hostilities against attacks and arbitrary treatment. It also limits the amount of violence permissible to the amount necessary to weaken the military potential of the enemy. International Human Rights Law (IHRL) provides everyone subjective rights, mainly against the state. It applies in and outside armed conflicts, but was not specifically made for armed conflicts. A discussion of the role of IHL and IHRL in new types of armed conflicts must start with an analysis of those conflicts. In Part 2 I will provide an overview of current types of conflicts often considered to be new (2.A), such

* I would like to thank very warmly my research assistants, Lindsey Cameron and Anne Laurence Brugère, for their thorough research and useful comments on many issues dealt with in this chapter and for having revised it.

[1] Herrmann and Palmieri, 'Les nouveaux conflits: une modernité archaïque?', 85 *International Review of the Red Cross* (2003) 23–44. von Clausewitz, *On War* (Penguin Classics: 1982) at 121 wrote: 'War is, therefore...chameleon-like in character, because it changes its colour in some degree in each particular case.' In that same passage he also identifies elements which he considers present in all wars. Keegan, *A History of Warfare* (1994) at 386–391, argues that war is 'always an expression of culture' and identifies similarities across cultures and through time. See also Hobsbawm, *Nations and Nationalism since 1780* (1994) at 163.

as asymmetric conflicts, the 'war on terror', failed states and (UN) peace operations. This will be followed by a brief description of the two archetypes of armed conflicts for which IHL was made (2.B): international armed conflicts between states and non-international armed conflicts between governmental forces of one state and rebels which want to seize power over the whole or a part of that state. As the characteristics of new types of conflicts do not correspond in many respects to those of the mentioned archetypes, I will add some general thoughts on the applicability of existing rules to 'new' phenomena (2.C). The main purpose of the overview of allegedly 'new' types of armed conflicts (under 2.A) will be to describe what aspects and issues relevant for the application of IHL and IHRL are considered to be new in those situations and to summarize the discussions about the rules of IHL and IHRL applicable to those new aspects. This discussion will show that in several 'new situations' the same IHL and IHRL issues arise. I will therefore deal with those issues in the main part of this essay (Part 3) in a systematic way rather than separately for each 'new' type of conflict. My aim is to apply the existing rules of IHL and IHRL to those issues, focusing on the relationship between the two branches. Those issues arising in several types of 'new conflicts' are in particular: the classification of a situation as an (international or non-international) armed conflict (3.A.1); the question whether entities other than States are bound by the two branches (3.A.2); the extraterritorial applicability of IHRL (3.A.3); the difficulties linked to coalition operations (3.A.4); the relevance of UN mandates (3.A.5). If both IHL and IHRL apply, most importantly the issue arises in new types of armed conflicts even more acutely than in traditional ones which of the two branches prevails. This issue will be discussed in general, including the meaning of the *lex specialis* principle which is generally considered to indicate the priority between two concurring rules of IHL and IHRL (3.B). More importantly, the relationship between the two branches will be discussed regarding two questions which are both crucial in new types of conflicts and for which IHL and IHRL appear to foresee differing rules: when may a 'fighter'[2] be attacked and killed (3.C.1) and when and under what procedural safeguards may a 'fighter' be detained (3.C.2). This contribution can therefore not provide an overview of all contemporary substantive challenges of and controversies on IHL and IHRL. It puts the emphasis on those where either the very applicability of IHL or IHRL (or of both) is controversial (3.A) or on which the answer provided by the two branches possibly differs (3.B and C).

---

[2] In this chapter, I use the term 'fighter' for a member of an armed group with a fighting function (see for a discussion *infra*, text accompanying notes 201 and 212) and for members of governmental armed forces. Similarly, the International Institute of Humanitarian Law, *The Manual on the Law of Non-International Armed Conflict. With Commentary* (2006), employs the term 'fighter' to qualify 'members of armed forces and dissident armed forces or other organized armed groups, or [those] taking an active (direct) part in hostilities' (1.1.2), while 'Civilians are all those who are not fighters' (1.1.3).

2. The Allegedly 'New' Situations and the Situations for which the Existing Rules were Made

A. The allegedly new situations and the controversies surrounding them

In this Part, I will simply list the different legal issues arising in several allegedly new types of conflicts. This list will show that many questions—such as what is an armed conflict, who is bound by IHL and IHRL, who may be attacked and detained on what basis under IHL and IHRL and, if both apply, which of the two prevails—arise in such conceptually and legally diverse situations as UN peace operations, the 'war on terror', and failed States (which in reality are in turn often overlapping and describing the same situation). A discussion of some of the issues listed, namely those for which either the very applicability of IHL or IHRL is controversial or in which the solutions offered by the two branches appear to contradict each other, will be made in the next Part, issue by issue and not according to the situation in which they appear.

1. Asymmetric conflicts

The more asymmetric a conflict is, the more difficult it is for both sides to respect IHL (without losing the conflict) and also the more difficult it is for the outside world to monitor and enforce the respect of IHL.[3] Some even consider that 'violations of IHL are indeed a classic response to asymmetric inferiority'.[4] At least when the US is involved, every conflict is asymmetric because of the incredible technological superiority and military strength of US armed forces. In non-international armed conflicts, those fighting against the government are, at least in the initial phase, nearly by definition inferior in power and would have no chance to overcome governmental armed forces in an open battle between clearly distinguished fighters, which is the situation for which IHL is best suited.

In such asymmetric conflicts, both sides are convinced that they cannot win the war without violating or at least 'reinterpreting' IHL. Concerning the 'war on terror', an official US commission of inquiry has concluded that the US could not defeat the 'enemy' if captured enemies had to be treated according to IHL as interpreted by the ICRC.[5] Implicitly, the claim was that the necessary

---

[3] See Pfanner, 'Asymmetrical Warfare from the Perspective of Humanitarian Law and Humanitarian Action', 87 *International Review of the Red Cross* (2005) 149–174; Geiss, 'Asymetric Conflict Structures', 88 *International Review of the Red Cross* (2006) 757–777; Schmitt, 'Asymmetrical Warfare and International Humanitarian Law', 62 *Air Force L. Rev.* (2008) 1–42; Bassiouni 'The New Wars and the Crisis of Compliance with the Law of Armed Conflict by Non-State Actors', 98 *J. Crim. L. and Criminology* (2008) 711–810.

[4] Boothby, '"The end justifies the means" Should this be the philosophy?', in Heintschel von Heinegg and Epping (eds), *International Humanitarian Law Facing New Challenges: Symposium in Honour of Knut Ipsen* (2007) 49, at 50.

[5] Schlesinger (Chairman), *Final Report of the Independent Panel to Review DoD Detention Operations* (2004) at 85, <http://www.defenselink.mil./news/Aug2004/d20040824finalreport.pdf> [last accessed 12 April 2010].

intelligence information about terrorist networks can only be obtained by treating those who are believed to have such information inhumanely. IHRL is by definition made for asymmetric relations, the relation between the state and the individual. States consider however (implicitly) that the contemporary asymmetric conflicts are not sufficiently asymmetric to deal with them in accordance with IHRL, rationalizing their position *inter alia* by arguments that IHL—reinvented, rethought, or reinterpreted—must take precedence as *lex specialis* over IHRL in such conflicts.

As for the enemy in asymmetric conflicts, it most often consists of armed groups. As will be shown below, it is controversial whether and to what extent IHRL applies to armed groups. IHL is addressed to armed groups (but it is controversial as to why). However, the more detailed and demanding IHL of non-international armed conflicts becomes, the more the question arises whether its rules are realistic, ie whether they could be respected by an armed group willing to comply with IHL without losing the war. In addition, the implementation mechanisms and incentives addressed to armed groups are weaker than those addressed to states.[6]

In addition, armed groups are often classified as 'terrorist', because they regularly resort to terrorist acts. This first raises the question how terrorist acts should be defined. If every act committed against state forces is 'terrorist', as some suggest, this weakens IHL and the willingness of armed groups to comply with IHL.[7] Second, armed groups actually often do resort to deliberate attacks against civilians and to clearly prohibited indiscriminate attacks. In my view, that behaviour is not simply due to a lack of humanity and motivated by hatred, but is based on a very rational calculation. 'Terrorist groups' believe that their only chance to overcome their enemy, who is so superior in equipment, technology, and often manpower, is by demoralizing the enemy's (or even their 'own') civilian population through terrorist acts.

Furthermore, in asymmetric armed conflicts, most rules of IHL are in fact addressed to only one side and those of IHRL are—according to the wording of the treaties—only addressed to states. Only one side has prisoners, only one side has an air force and only one side could possibly use its own civilian population as shields or launch suicide attacks. Whereas under IHL reciprocity is not a legal justification for violations,[8] positive reciprocity, ie the wish that the enemy would respect the rules in a similar situation in which the roles were reversed, certainly plays an important role as a non-legal factor contributing to the respect of IHL. A combatant treats captured enemy combatants humanely because he or she hopes

---

[6] See generally Sassòli, 'Possible Legal Mechanisms To Improve Compliance By Armed Groups With International Humanitarian Law And International Human Rights Law', Paper submitted at the Armed Groups Conference, Vancouver, 13–15 November 2003, <http://www.genevacall.org/resources/testi-reference-materials/testi-other-documents/sassoli-13nov03.pdf> [last accessed 12 April 2010].

[7] See Sassòli and Rouillard, 'La définition du terrorisme et le droit international humanitaire', *Revue québécoise de droit international (Hors-série), Études en hommage à Katia Boustany* (2007) 29, at 41–44.

[8] See Vienna Convention on the Law of Treaties (adopted 23 May 1969, entered into force 27 January 1980) 1155 UNTS 331 (VCLT), Art 60(5).

that he would also be treated humanely if captured. Such motivation is largely lacking in asymmetric conflicts.

Beyond that, the very philosophy of IHL is challenged by such conflicts. The St Petersburg Declaration of 1868 has laid down that 'the only legitimate object which States should endeavour to accomplish during war is to weaken the military forces of the enemy'.[9] While the aim of a conflict is to prevail politically, acts of violence for that purpose may only aim at the military. This basic philosophy is beside the point in asymmetric wars. The stronger side is often not confronted by 'military' forces at all and the weaker side can never hope to defeat the military potential of the enemy. It can often win the war by failing to lose it. Finally, the weaker side in an asymmetric conflict often lacks the necessary structures of authority, hierarchy, communication between superiors and subordinates, and processes of accountability, all of which are necessary to enforce IHL and even more conspicuously IHRL rules. Legally, as will be discussed below, one may even consider that IHL does not apply at all to conflicts in which the enemy does not fulfil the necessary minimum criteria of organization. As for IHRL, even in the most asymmetric conflict, the positive obligation of the state to protect the human rights of persons on its territory including against armed groups is of no great value in practice, as a government confronted by an armed conflict is by definition unable to ensure the respect of rules by the enemies it is fighting.

2. Failed states

All law needs a minimum of structure of authority within the society to which it applies. International law is still centred on states. IHRL is fundamentally addressed to states and it must be implemented by states, for the benefit of individuals under their jurisdiction, including against other individuals threatening their rights. IHL is also addressed to individuals, but its implementation depends heavily on 'parties' of armed conflicts: states and, in non-international armed conflicts, organized armed groups. This raises problems in failed states, where formal structures of authority have collapsed and informal structures are non-transparent, transient, and based upon interpersonal relations rather than rules.[10] In such situations, the question discussed below, whether IHL applies only to conflicts between parties with a minimum of organization, arises. Furthermore, questions relating to the applicability and application of IHL and IHRL to armed groups arise. Finally, it is simply much more difficult in practice for third parties (such as humanitarian organizations) to convince, train, and monitor every (perhaps drug-addicted) child soldier concerning the respect for IHL, than if a commander exists who can commit his subordinates to respect IHL, instruct them,

---

[9] 'Declaration Renouncing the Use, in Time of War, of Explosive Projectiles Under 400 Grammes Weight, St. Petersburg, 29 November/11 December 1868', in de Martens (ed), *Nouveau recueil général de traités et autres actes relatifs aux rapports de droit international*, 1ère sèrie, Vol XVIII (1843–75) at 474–475; reproduced in Schindler and Toman, *The Laws of Armed Conflicts* (2004) at 91.

[10] See Thürer, 'The "Failed State" and International Law', 81 *International Review of the Red Cross* (1999) 731–761.

monitor their respect, repress violations, and receive and deal with allegations of non-respect.

3. The 'war on terror'

Following the terrorist attacks of 11 September 2001 on New York City and Washington DC, the Bush administration declared that the US was engaged in a global 'war on terror'.[11] On 6 October 2001, it launched a military campaign against Afghanistan, whose *de facto* government, the Taliban, harboured the Al Qaeda terrorist group, which had planned and executed the 11 September 2001 attacks. The 'war on terror' also included attacks and arrests directed at suspected members of Al Qaeda or other 'terrorists' elsewhere around the world. The initial line of argument made by the Bush administration to justify indefinite detention without trial of suspected terrorists in Guantánamo and in other, often undisclosed, locations may be summed up as follows.[12] First, the US was engaged in an international armed conflict—the 'war on terror'. This was, secondly, one single worldwide armed conflict against a non-state actor (Al Qaeda) and its associates. That armed conflict started at some point in time in the 1990s and will continue until victory. Thirdly, while the Bush administration claimed in this conflict all the prerogatives that IHL of international armed conflicts confers upon a party to such a conflict, in particular to attack enemy combatants without necessarily trying to arrest them and to detain them without any judicial decision, it denied these detainees protection by most of that law, arguing that their detention was governed neither by the rules applying to combatants nor by those applicable to civilians. It argued that no trial or individual decision was needed to detain such 'unlawful combatants' until the end of active hostilities in the 'war on terror'. Fourthly, 'unlawful combatants' were not dealt with under domestic criminal legislation, nor were they considered to benefit from IHRL. The Obama administration has abandoned the terms 'war on terror' and 'unlawful combatants'. While its position is still under review, it continues however to argue that an armed conflict exists (and the laws of war apply) between the US, on the one hand, and Al Qaeda, the Taliban, and 'associated' forces on the other hand. More importantly, it considers that those who provide 'substantial support' to those enemies may be attacked

---

[11] *National Strategy for Combating Terrorism* (September 2006), <http://www.globalsecurity.org/security/library/policy/national/nsct_sep2006.htm> [last accessed 12 April 2010].

[12] See for a legal explanation of the US position: The White House, *Memorandum of February 7th, 2002*, Appendix C to *Independent Panel to Review DoD Detention Operations* (see *supra* note 5); Dworkin, Crimes of War Project, *Excerpts from an Interview with Charles Allen, Deputy General Counsel for International Affairs, U.S. Department of Defence* (16 December 2002), <http://www.crimesofwar.org/onnews/news-pentagon-trans.html> [last accessed 12 April 2010]; Bellinger, 'Legal Issues in the War on Terrorism—A Reply to Silja N. U. Vöneky', 8 *German Law Journal* (2007) 847–860. See for a critical assessment of the position of the Bush administration: Sassòli, 'Use and Abuse of the Laws of War in the "War on Terrorism"', 22 *Law and Inequality* (2004) 195, at 198–203; Fitzpatrick, 'Speaking Law to Power: The War Against Terrorism and Human Rights', 14 *EJIL* (2003) 241, at 249–251; Paust, 'War and Enemy Status after 9/11: Attacks on the Laws of War', 28 *Yale J. Int'l L* (2003) 325–335; and Moore, 'International Humanitarian Law and the Prisoners at Guantanamo Bay', 7 *Intl J Hum Rts* (2003) 1–27.

and detained under the laws of war, just as enemy combatants could under IHL of international armed conflicts.[13]

Under IHL, the line of argument of the US raises several issues. First it is controversial whether the 'war on terror' may be dealt with under IHL (or, which is for me a separate question, whether it should be dealt with *de lege ferenda* under IHL) as one single armed conflict, or whether it has to be split up into different situations, some of them being international armed conflicts, some non-international armed conflicts, and some not armed conflicts at all. Such classification discussed in detail below obviously affects the applicable IHL and whether IHL, IHRL, or both apply. In any case, components of the 'war on terror' that are armed conflicts are by definition asymmetrical, involve armed groups as the enemy, and happen often in failed states, raising all the problems for IHL and IHRL mentioned above and dealt with below.

If all or parts of the 'war on terror' constitute an international armed conflict, under IHL, there are two categories of persons: civilians and combatants. In the conduct of hostilities, only combatants and civilians directly participating in the hostilities (while so participating) may be attacked, while civilians are protected against attacks. Once in the hands of the enemy, there are equally two categories of protected persons under the Geneva Conventions,[14] who are subject to two very different legal regimes: combatants, who become prisoners of war (POWs) protected by Geneva Convention III (*GC III*); and civilians, protected by Geneva Convention IV (*GC IV*). The Bush administration argued that the persons it targeted in the 'war on terror' and that it held in Guantánamo are neither combatants nor civilians but 'unlawful combatants'. Critics object that according to the text, context, and aim of Conventions III and IV, no one can fall between the two and thus be protected by neither of the two.[15]

The Bush administration also argued that the Taliban, who were members of the armed forces of the *de facto* government of Afghanistan, are not POWs because they have not effectively distinguished themselves from the civilian population and have not conducted their operations in accordance with the laws and customs of war.[16] Such behaviour would indeed be contrary to two conditions which 'militias...volunteer corps...including resistance movements' have to fulfil collectively

---

[13] See US District, Court District of Columbia, *In Re: Guantánamo Bay Detainee Litigation, Respondents' Memorandum Regarding the Government's Authority Relative to Detainees Held at Guantánamo Bay*, Misc No 08-442 TFH (2009), <http://www.usdoj.gov/opa/documents/memo-re-det-auth.pdf> [last accessed 12 April 2010].

[14] Convention [No I] for the Amelioration of the Condition of the Wounded and Sick in Armed Forces in the Field, 12 August 1949 (entered into force 21 October 1950) 75 UNTS 31; Convention [No II] for the Amelioration of the Condition of the Wounded, Sick and Shipwrecked Members of Armed Forces at Sea, 12 August 1949 (entered into force 21 October 1950) 75 UNTS 85; Convention [No III] relative to the Treatment of Prisoners of War, 12 August 1949 (entered into force 21 October 1950) 75 UNTS 135; Convention [No IV] relative to the Protection of Civilian Persons in Time of War, 12 August 1949 (entered into force 21 October 1950) 75 UNTS 287.

[15] See for a detailed argument: Sassòli, 'Query: Is There a Status of "Unlawful Combatant"?' in Jaques (ed), *Issues in International Law and Military Operations* (vol 80 US Naval War College International Law Studies 2006) at 57–67.   [16] See *supra* note 12.

to obtain POW status.[17] Those conditions are not explicitly prescribed for 'members of the armed forces of a party to the conflict',[18] but some argue that they constitute an implicit requirement for such regular forces.[19]

In case of doubt whether persons having committed a belligerent act are combatants, they must be treated as POWs 'until such time as their status has been determined by a competent tribunal'.[20] The Bush administration initially argued that in the case of those detained in Guantánamo, there is no doubt. Later the Bush administration set up Combatant Status Review Tribunals to determine whether a Guantánamo detainee is an enemy combatant or a harmless civilian to be released.

If the law of non-international armed conflicts covers some or all persons held in the 'war on terror', the distinction between combatants and civilians is irrelevant for them (because there is no combatant status in that law). That law provides only for guarantees of humane treatment and, in case of prosecution for criminal offences, for judicial guarantees for the benefit of all those who do not or who no longer actively participate in hostilities. The US Supreme Court held in *Hamdan v Rumsfeld* that the Military Commissions set up under a presidential order did not meet the requirements of Article 3 common to the Geneva Conventions.[21] As in all non-international armed conflicts, the question discussed below would arise whether enemy fighters could be attacked, like combatants in international armed conflicts, at any time until they surrender, whether they could be attacked, like civilians under IHL, only when and for such time as they directly participate in hostilities (which raises the question what constitutes direct participation in hostilities), or whether IHRL requires that they only be attacked when absolutely necessary to preserve human life and when an arrest is not feasible. As for the admissibility of detaining 'terrorists', if the 'war on terror' or some of its components were non-international armed conflicts, the question discussed below arises whether such 'terrorists' may be detained, as the Obama administration argues, like combatants in international armed conflicts, without any individual decision or procedural safeguard until the end of active hostilities, or only under the much more elaborate procedural and substantive requirements of IHRL.

When it comes to IHRL, the Bush administration has argued that enemy combatants are not covered by human rights but exclusively by the 'laws of war'.[22] If both branches apply, a question arises as to which of the two prevails on a certain issue when they contradict each other. As will be shown below, this is generally discussed in the framework of the *lex specialis* principle, the meaning of which is controversial, in particular concerning the crucial question when enemies may be

---

[17] See Art 4(A)(2) of *GC III* (see *supra* note 14).   [18] Ibid Art 4(A)(1).

[19] Wedgwood, 'Al Qaeda, Terrorism, and Military Commissions', 96 *AJIL* (2002) 328, at 335; Lietzau 'Combating Terrorism: Law Enforcement or War?' in Schmitt and Beruto (eds), *Terrorism and International Law, Challenges and Responses* (2002) 75–84.

[20] Art 5(2) of *GC III* (see *supra* note 14).   [21] 548 US 557, 126 S Ct 2749 (2006).

[22] Response of US to request for Precautionary Measures—*Detainees in Guantanamo Bay, Cuba*, 11 April 2002, Inter-American Commission on Human Rights 41 ILM (2002) 1015.

deliberately targeted and on what legal basis and under which procedure they may be detained.

Many persons are attacked or detained by the US and other states in the 'war on terror' outside their territory, eg attacked in Pakistan, Afghanistan, or Yemen or detained in Guantánamo (Cuba) or in Afghanistan. This raises the controversial question discussed below whether IHRL obligations apply to persons who are under the jurisdiction but not on the territory of a state and the distinct question what level of control over a territory on which a person is found or over the person him- or herself is necessary to bring that person under the jurisdiction of a state.

Under IHRL, the possibility to detain persons who are not suspected of a crime, for simple reasons of public security, is controversial, except when derogation is made in emergency situations. In any case, such persons must be detained based on a domestic law and they must be treated humanely. As will be shown below, it is however controversial whether access to *habeas corpus* is a non-derogable right.

4. Peace operations

Since the inception of UN peacekeeping operations, a controversy existed whether, when, and which IHL applied to such operations.[23] Classic peacekeeping operations were based on the consent of the parties and were independent and impartial. They were created under what has been called Chapter 'VI½' of the UN Charter (therefore peaceful dispute resolution 'plus') and the use of force in such operations was (eg in Cyprus or on the Golan Heights) limited to self-defence. Together, these conditions made the question as to whether IHL applied to such operations somewhat academic. However, over time this model has evolved and there are many permutations of peace operations. As of the early 90s, there have been peace operations (eg in Somalia and Bosnia and Herzegovina) with the consent of the host state (therefore still based in Chapter VI of the UN Charter) but given the power to use force beyond self-defence, eg in defence of the mandate ('robust' peacekeeping operations). The degree of force that can be used in self-defence has also expanded over time. In addition, many recent peace operations have been authorized under Chapter VII of the UN Charter and have a broad mandate to use force (eg in Sudan and Democratic Republic of the Congo). Classic peace operations (such as Cyprus) were also under the exclusive command and control of the UN; however, many peace operations today are authorized by the UN Security Council but their

---

[23] See, on the whole debate whether IHL applies to UN operations: Greenwood, 'International Humanitarian Law and United Nations Military Operations', 1 *YIHL* (1998) 3–34; Emanuelli, *Les actions militaires de l'ONU et le droit international humanitaire* (1997) 3–43; Shraga, 'The United Nations as an Actor Bound by International Humanitarian Law' in Condorelli *et al* (eds), *Les Nations Unies et le droit international humanitaire, Actes du Colloque international à l'occasion du cinquantième anniversaire des Nations Unies, Genève 19, 20, 21 octobre 1995* (1996) at 317–337; Schindler, 'United Nations Forces and International Humanitarian Law' in Swinarski (ed), *Studies and Essays on International Humanitarian Law and Red Cross Principles in Honour of J. Pictet* (1984) 521, at 523. See also Zwanenburg, *Accountability of Peace Support Operations* (2005) at 131–203; and Saura, 'Lawful Peacekeeping: Applicability of International Humanitarian Law to United Nations Peacekeeping Operations', 58 *Hastings L.J.* (2007) 479–531.

command is delegated to another international organization (such as NATO in Afghanistan). Additional concepts such as 'peace support operations' and 'stability operations' have appeared. Many of them are not conducted by the UN, but normally are authorized by the UN Security Council. All of them are called 'peace operations'.[24] The traditional academic debate over the applicability of IHL to UN peace-keeping operations has therefore spilled over and put into question the issue that is much more important in practice: the applicability of IHL to military operations conducted by other international organizations, be they regional organizations, such as the African Union, or even the North Atlantic Treaty Organization (NATO). Some may even call any (UN authorized) coalition operation a 'peace operation'.[25] If the full applicability of IHL to all those is put into doubt, few contemporary armed conflicts would be fully governed by the existing IHL treaties.

I will deal hereafter with the most important conceptual issue implied in this debate, ie whether and how international organizations are addressees of IHL and IHRL—or if those branches apply via states members of the organization or contributing to the operation. Other challenges to the applicability of IHL are based upon the mandate and purpose of peace operations. Such operations are certainly a noble reason for conducting hostilities. This should normally not matter for the applicability of IHL. The reason is the fundamental distinction and complete separation between, on the one hand, *jus ad bellum*, that is the law on the legality of the use of force and, on the other hand, the *jus in bello*, that is the humanitarian rules to be respected when force is used.[26] Nevertheless, in debates about when IHL fully applies to UN forces, some argue that this depends on the mandate of such forces,[27] which is clearly a *jus ad bellum* argument. More generally, underlying the reluctance of the UN to be bound by the full corpus of IHL rules, there is in my view also the idea that UN forces, which represent international legality and the international community, and which enforce international law, cannot be bound by the same rules as their enemies.

---

[24] A Roberts and R Guelff (eds), *Documents on the Laws of War* (2000) at 26, indicate that the term applies to UN run and UN authorized peace operations. They refer to 'peacekeeping operations, whether conducted under UN *or other* auspices…' (emphasis added). The *Brahimi Report* considers the 'NATO-led operations' in Kosovo which facilitate the functioning of UNMIK in the context of peace operations. *Report of the Panel on United Nations Peace Operations* (21 August 2000), UN Doc A/55/305, S/2000/809, at para 104 (hereinafter *Brahimi Report*).

[25] UN Department of Peacekeeping Operations, *United Nations Peacekeeping Operations: Principles and Guidelines* (the 'Capstone Doctrine') (2008) at 8: 'The spectrum of contemporary peace operations has become increasingly broad and includes both United Nations-led peace operations, as well as those conducted by other actors, *normally* with the authorization of the Security Council' (emphasis added), <http://pbpu.unlb.org/PBPS/Library/Capstone_Doctrine_ENG.pdf> [last accessed 12 April 2010]

[26] See generally Sassòli, '*Ius ad bellum* and *Ius in Bello*—The Separation between the Legality of the Use of Force and Humanitarian Rules to be Respected in Warfare: Crucial or Outdated?', in Schmitt and Pejic (eds), *International Law and Armed Conflict: Exploring the Faultlines, Essays in Honour of Yoram Dinstein* (2007) at 241–264, with references.

[27] UK Ministry of Defence, *The Manual of the Law of Armed Conflict* (2004) para 14.5: 'A PSO [Peace Support Operations] force can become party to an armed conflict, and thus subject to the law of armed conflict: (a) where it was mandated from the outset to engage in hostilities with opposing armed forces as part of its mission…'.

Even if IHL could as such fully apply to the UN (or to contributing states regarding the conduct of their contingents), it would only do so if and when the UN (or the respective contingent) is engaged in an armed conflict. For this, it is not sufficient that UN forces are deployed on a territory where others are fighting an armed conflict. This raises the general issue, dealt with below, of the material field of application of IHL. What is an international armed conflict? What is the minimum threshold of a non-international armed conflict? Can a peace operation, conducted on the territory of a state with the consent of its government, be classified as a non-international armed conflict, directed at an armed group fighting against that government, or does IHL of international armed conflicts apply? Those two alternatives have an impact on two issues dealt with below: the admissibility of attacks directed against enemies and the procedures necessary to detain such enemies—and for those and other purposes on the relationship between IHL and IHRL. In any case, under both IHL and IHRL the question arises whether and under what safeguards persons arrested by the international forces may be transferred to the host government. Finally, whether IHL of international or of non-international armed conflicts is considered to apply, peace operations are most often confronted with non-state armed groups, raising all the issues dealt with below relating to the applicability and application of IHL and IHRL to armed groups. Such confrontations are in addition nearly always asymmetrical and happen often in weak, failing, or failed states, raising all the issues mentioned above.

In addition, even if the peace operation is engaged in an armed conflict, the questions dealt with below arise as to how far IHRL applies, even in armed conflicts, as *lex specialis* to police operations and how police operations are to be distinguished from hostilities.

One of the main practical reasons for the reluctance of contributing and member states to recognize that IHL applies to peace forces is that they correctly perceive that if IHL (of international armed conflicts) applied to hostilities between those forces and armed forces opposed to them, both would be combatants and therefore lawful targets of attacks. Contributing states obviously hope that their forces will not be attacked. Even when recognizing the applicability of IHL, those states therefore argue that members of their forces are not combatants. The ICC Statute even classifies them in many situations as 'civilians'.[28] Another problem relative to the status of members of UN forces is created by the 1994 Convention on the Safety of United Nations and Associated Personnel.[29] That convention basically prohibits attacks on UN personnel and makes any such attacks crimes that must be prosecuted by all states. This convention is incompatible with IHL as far as an international armed conflict against such UN forces is concerned because, under IHL, a combatant cannot be punished for having attacked another combatant. Article 2 of that convention says that it 'will not apply to an UN operation

[28] Art 8(2)(b)(iii) and (e)(iii) of the ICC Statute (Rome Statute, UN Doc A/CONF.183/9 17 July 1998, entered into force 1 July 2002).
[29] Convention on the Safety of United Nations and Associated Personnel (adopted 9 December 1994, entered into force 15 January 1999), UNGA Res 49/59, 49 UN GAOR Supp no 49 at 299, UN Doc A/49/49.

authorized by the Security Council as an enforcement action under chapter VII [of the UN Charter] in which any of the personnel are engaged as combatants against organized armed forces and to which the law of international armed conflicts applies'. This can mean that IHL of international armed conflicts fully applies to UN enforcement actions in which any of the personnel are engaged as combatants against organized armed forces (which in turn may happen because they have the mandate to do that or because the enemy attacks them). Article 2 can, however, also mean that the convention will not apply only when, first, these conditions are fulfilled and, second, IHL of international armed conflicts applies.

Finally, when a territory (such as Kosovo or East Timor) is placed under the authority of UN forces or a UN administration, the question arises whether and on what basis IHRL and the rules of IHL on occupied territories apply.[30] IHL of international armed conflicts, including the rules on military occupation, does not apply when UN forces are present based on the consent of the sovereign of the territory in question (which was the case in both examples mentioned). Nonetheless, in those circumstances, it may be wise to apply IHL by analogy since it provides a framework to address many of the situations with which peacekeepers will be confronted.[31] Beyond that, may a UN presence, if not consented to by the territorial state, ever be classified as military occupation?

B. The traditional armed conflicts for which international humanitarian law (IHL) was made

1. International armed conflicts between regular forces of states

The archetype of conflicts for which IHL of international armed conflicts was made are hostilities between regular armed forces of states, trying to impose their political will by weakening the military potential of the enemy so as to, if necessary, occupy the enemy territory. In this environment the principle arose that acts of violence may only aim to overcome the military forces of the enemy.[32] Once its military forces were neutralized, even the politically, psychologically, or economically stronger enemy could no longer resist.[33] This presupposes, however, the readiness of belligerent states to occupy, if necessary, their enemy's territory. Indeed, otherwise one belligerent, having destroyed all military objectives, could 'run out of legitimate targets' while neither having been able to impose its will upon the government of the enemy state nor to replace that government.

---

[30] Wills, 'Occupation Law and Multi-National Operations: Problems and Perspectives', 77 *B.Y.B.I.L.* (2006) 256–332; Kolb *et al*, *L'application du droit international humanitaire et des droits de l'homme aux organisations internationales: Forces de paix et administrations civiles transitoires* (2005); Chesterman, *You the People: The United Nations, Transitional Administration and State Building* (2004).

[31] Sassòli, 'Legislation and Maintenance of Public Order and Civil Life by Occupying Powers', 16 *EJIL* (2005) 661, at 689 and 691—693.

[32] As stated in the St Petersburg Declaration, *supra* note 9.

[33] This reasoning is qualified as 'oversimplistic' by Schmitt, 'Targeting and Humanitarian Law: Current Issues', 33 *Israel Y.B.Hum.Rts.* (2003) 59, at 68.

This archetype never corresponded to all situations to which IHL applied, not even at the time of the drafting of the main IHL treaties. The existence of '*francstireurs*' was already known when the 1907 Hague Conventions were adopted and led to the famous 'Martens clause'.[34] The 1949 Geneva Conventions were adopted to deal with the humanitarian problems experienced in the Second World War. That war was largely fought between regular armies, but also involved organized and unorganized resistance movements. Finally, the 1977 Additional Protocol I (*AP I*) was adopted precisely to adapt IHL to new realities, *inter alia* the guerrilla warfare experienced in the decolonization wars and the Vietnam War.

Many, but not all[35] contemporary international armed conflicts constitute a reality far removed from the archetype. Sometimes one side has no regular armed forces at all (arguably Afghanistan in 2001), or its fighters consist only of persons who could be classified under IHL as civilians because they do not fulfil the requirements for combatant status (eg Hamas in Gaza). In other cases, the technological, material, and manpower superiority of one side is so great that the regular armed forces of the enemy do not have the slightest chance in open hostilities over control of territory (Iraq in 2003). In other cases, the more powerful side is not willing to engage in ground operations, but wants to win the conflict exclusively through air power (Serbia in 1999). More generally, whether seen from the perspective of the UN as a collective security system or analysed in the framework of an alleged hegemonic world order of coalitions of the willing, most international armed conflicts between states can no longer be perceived as conflicts between equals. Even in the past, only few conflicts were fought between equally powerful states. What is new today is that in most contemporary conflicts the parties are unequal both from the point of view of the means at the disposal of the two sides and from a moral point of view. On the one side there is the international community and those who represent it, or at least who claim to represent it; on the other side there is the—generally one single—'outlaw' State (in recent years for instance Yugoslavia or Iraq). The weaker side has not the slightest chance to win the war by invading the enemy's territory.

2. Civil wars

As for IHL of non-international armed conflicts, the archetypal situations for which it was adopted were hostilities on the territory of a state between its armed forces and armed forces of a rebel group wishing to become the government of the state or to form a new state. When states adopted the first treaty rule applicable to such conflicts, Common Article 3 to the four Geneva Conventions[36] in 1949, they had the Spanish Civil War fresh in their minds. The archetype appears even

---

[34] Kalshoven and Zegveld, *Constraints on the Waging of War* (2001) at 22. See also Nahlik, 'L'extension du statut de combattant à la lumière du Protocole I de Genève de 1977', 164 *Recueil des cours* (1979) 171, at 195–196.

[35] Recall the war between Russia and Georgia in 2008 or the war between Eritrea and Ethiopia in 2000.   [36] Art 3 common to Conventions I–IV, *supra* note 14.

explicitly in Additional Protocol II of 1977 (*AP II*),[37] the most recent and detailed treaty covering non-international armed conflicts and the only one covering exclusively such conflicts. Indeed this Protocol only applies to armed conflicts between governmental and dissident or rebel forces, and even in that case only if the rebel forces control part of the territory of the State concerned.[38] Conflicts between several non-state armed groups or in failed states are not covered.

Many contemporary non-international armed conflicts are far removed from this archetype. Often, armed groups fight against each other and not against governmental forces. Often the fighting spills over into neighbouring countries (such as the fighting between Rwandan government and rebel forces in the Congo), or even consists exclusively of hostilities between a state and an armed non-state actor on the territory of other states (such as Operation Enduring Freedom between the US and its Allies on the one hand and Al Qaeda and its associates in Afghanistan on the other). I will show later that as far as the 'war on terror' is an armed conflict, it could only be classified under IHL as a conflict not of an international character, arguably conducted all over the globe, but it certainly does not correspond to what the drafters of Article 3 of the Geneva Conventions had in mind. As for the aims of non-governmental parties in relation to contemporary non-international armed conflicts, it is often not power over the existing (or a new) state that drives the conflict, but rather ethnic or religious hatred, looting, or even the destruction of the existing international system.

C. Some general thoughts on applying the 'old law' and 'new situations'

When applying the existing law to allegedly new situations, a distinction must be made between the question whether the existing rules cover the new situation and the question whether they are adequate for that situation. This distinction between *lex lata* and *lex ferenda* is admittedly much more relative in international law than in domestic law.[39] International law is largely a self-applied system, in which the main addressees, states, are simultaneously the legislators. At least for customary rules, every violation is also state practice, which, if followed by others, may give rise to a new rule. A strict distinction between statements about the existing law (which constitute state practice) and statements about the desirable law (which would not count) is artificial.[40] Nevertheless, law must have a minimum stability to keep its normative character, its claim to regulate, not simply to describe, behaviour. The mere fact that the addressees of a rule consider that in a certain situation that rule is inadequate to what they perceive as the normative needs cannot make

---

[37] Protocol [No II] Additional to the Geneva Conventions of 12 August 1949, and relating to the Protection of Victims of Non- International Armed Conflicts, 8 June 1977 (entered into force 7 December 1978) 1125 UNTS 609 (*AP II*). [38] Ibid, Art 1.

[39] Weil, 'Towards Relative Normativity in International Law?', 77 *AJIL* (1983) 413, at 415.

[40] Sassòli, *Bedeutung einer Kodifikation für das allgemeine Völkerrecht—mit besonderer Betrachtung der Regeln zum Schutze der Zivilbevölkerung vor den Auswirkungen von Feindseligkeiten* (1990) at 121–122.

the rule disappear, in particular as long as no consensus on a new desirable rule exists.

1. Determining whether an existing rule applies to a 'new situation'

The determination of the *lex lata* applicable to a given question boils down to an issue of interpretation of the existing rules. Treaty rules not only cover the situations which were envisaged when they were drafted, but all situations falling under their wording, understood according to their purpose and object.[41] The *travaux préparatoires*, which may reveal the historical purposes of the legislator, are only a complementary means of interpretation.[42] As for customary law, its traditional rules, deduced from state behaviour and *opinio iuris* in previous cases, by definition cover future cases which always differ in some respect from the preceding ones that have created the customary rules.

For IHL, the first issue of interpretation that arises is whether it applies at all in a given situation. As IHL applies only to armed conflicts, the issue is whether a given situation is an armed conflict. If it is, it must in addition be determined whether that conflict is of an international or not of an international character, as the rules applicable to those two kinds of conflicts differ. For IHRL, the situation does not have to be classified to determine its applicability, but the (extra-)territorial and personal reach of its rules are controversial.

Once IHL and/or IHRL apply, every rule is obviously subject to interpretation. Whether a certain person is a combatant or a civilian, whether the rules on occupied territories apply to a certain place, whether a certain person is or is not directly participating in the hostilities, are all issues of interpretation. To claim that a situation is 'new' is not very helpful in this exercise. By definition, except in case of retroactive legislation, the facts to which an existing rule is applied are always new. The novelty of the situation is simply often a pretext for violating the existing rules. Many of those violating the law claim or genuinely consider that their situation is so new that the rules they violate do not or should not apply. In particular in the fields of IHL and IHRL, when interpreting rules to determine whether they apply to given facts, the alternative, ie the legal situation resulting from their non-applicability, must also be taken into account in an effort of systematic interpretation. The result that no rule applies in a certain situation or protects a certain person is certainly not compatible with the object and purpose of the two branches.

2. Determining whether the existing law should be adapted to new situations

Even if the existing rules, when appropriately interpreted, apply to a given situation and provide an answer to the questions raised, it may legitimately be asked whether those rules *should* be modified to cover new realities more adequately.

---

[41] VCLT, *supra* note 8, Art 31.   [42] Ibid, Art 32.

Some scholars, politicians, and journalists claim that IHL as it stands was developed at another time and is not adequate for the new challenges raised by contemporary kinds of conflicts. It should therefore be adapted to 'new realities'.[43] As for human rights, they have been qualified as a suicide pact if fully and invariably applied to protect 'terrorists'.[44] Any discussion of these serious challenges is rendered difficult by two problems.

First, I am not aware of many concrete proposals by those labelling the Geneva Conventions 'outdated' or human rights 'inadequate' as to which provisions of IHL or IHRL treaties should be amended with what new wording.[45] For someone like me, who has the preconceived idea that IHL, correctly understood, is adequate for those contemporary situations that are indeed armed conflicts and who believes that human rights are precisely made to protect criminals and outlaws, it is therefore difficult to respond or to be inspired about what should be discussed. More importantly, if scholars and politicians say that IHL or IHRL is not adequate without immediately adding which rules *are* adequate in what situation, this has catastrophic results in the field. When told by his or her superior that the existing rules are no longer adequate, every soldier, policeman, or interrogator, even when he or she has been correctly trained in IHL and IHRL, may consider inadequate those rules (eg to take feasible precautions in attack or not to torture) when pressed hard by the enemy or the need to avoid terrorist attacks. The mere statement that the existing rules are not adequate without a clear instruction on what rules must be complied with puts the practitioner in the field in a very difficult situation. As a defence attorney of a US private accused of having tortured someone to death in Afghanistan has put it: 'The President of the United States doesn't know what the rules are! The secretary of defense doesn't know what the rules are. But the government expects this Pfc. to know what the rules are?'[46]

---

[43] See eg about the speech made by the (then) British Defence Secretary John Reid, on 3 April 2006, at Banqueting House, Royal Palace of Whitehall, 'International Law hinder UK troops—Reid', *The Guardian* (4 April 2006), <http://www.guardian.co.uk/politics/2006/apr/04/uk.military> [last accessed 12 April 2010]; certain remarks of US Defence Secretary Donald Rumsfeld at a press conference of 8 February 2002, US Department of Defence, <http://www.defenselink.mil/transcripts/transcript.aspx?transcriptid=2624> [last accessed 12 April 2010] and White House, 'Press Briefing by Ari Fleischer' of 28 January 2002, <http://www.whitehouse.gov/news/releases/2002/01/20020128-11.html> [no longer available]; Montgomery, 'Geneva Convention's Gentility, Treaty Stresses Civil Treatment of Prisoners', *Washington Post* (2002) F01; Posner, 'War, International Law, and Sovereignty: Re-evaluating the Rules of the Game in a New Century: Terrorism and the Laws of War', 5 *Chicago J. Int'l L.* (2005) 423–434; Wedgwood, 'The Supreme Court and the Guantánamo Controversy', in P Berkowitz (ed), *Terrorism, the Laws of War, and the Constitution: Debating the Enemy Combatant Cases* (2005) 159, at 173–177; Schondorf, 'Extra-State Armed Conflicts: Is there a Need for a New Legal Regime?', 37 *N.Y.U.J. Int'l Law & Pol.* (2004) 1, at 61–75.

[44] See for example, for US constitutional rights, Posner, *Not a Suicide Pact: The Constitution in a Time of National Emergency* (2006) and for human rights other than the prohibition of torture generally Ignatieff, *The Lesser Evil: Political Ethics in an Age of Terrorism* (2004) 136–143.

[45] Eric Posner, *supra* note 43, eg simply writes that the laws of war 'might sensibly be applied...though most likely in a highly modified form'. In my view the most interesting and precise, although still very tentative, proposals are made by Schondorf, *supra* note 43, at 61–75.

[46] See Golden, 'Abuse Inquiry Yields Little Justice', *International Herald Tribune* (13 February 2006) at 1–2.

Second, the claim that the rules are inadequate may either mean that they apply, but are not adequate, or that they do not apply but that they (or new, adapted rules) should apply. While both possible arguments are interlinked, it is important to distinguish them. If someone criticizes Swiss family law because it does not adequately cover my cat (indeed it does not contain any provision about domestic animals), the *de lege lata* reply is easy: in law, my cat is not part of the family, but simple moveable property belonging to one family member, governed by property laws. Similarly, if most aspects of the 'war on terror' are not adequately covered by IHL, this is so simply because legally they are not armed conflicts and they are therefore not governed by IHL but rather by IHRL, international and domestic criminal law, domestic rules on law enforcement, and international rules on judicial cooperation in criminal matters. This is however not the end of the matter. The criticism directed against Swiss family law may also mean that the relation between me and my cat should, *de lege ferenda*, be governed by family law, because in the social reality of contemporary families, cats may have as important a role as humans. For IHL, this would mean, for example, that it should cover all aspects of the struggle between terrorist groups and states, instead of splitting it into several legal sub-categories to which different rules apply, as existing IHL does in my view.

3. An Attempt to Apply Existing Rules of IHL and of International Human Rights Law (IHRL) to the Allegedly 'New' Situations

The preceding section has demonstrated that in conceptually very different 'new conflict' situations, the same legal issues arise. I will discuss these issues as far as they either concern the very applicability of IHL or IHRL or the priority to be given to the solutions offered by one or the other branch, where those solutions appear to contradict each other.

A. The applicability of IHL and of IHRL

1. Material field of application

(a) International human rights law

IHRL protects human beings in all situations. Its rules were developed in regard to problems individuals face in peacetime, above all when confronting their own state. Formally, however, there is no limitation on their material field of application. They apply in peacetime and in times of armed conflict. Their applicability during armed conflicts has been re-affirmed time and time again by the Security Council, the UN General Assembly, the now-defunct UN Human Rights Commission and its Special Rapporteurs, as well as by the International Court of Justice (ICJ). The ICJ affirmed that 'the protection offered by human rights conventions does not cease in case of armed conflict, save for the effect of provisions for derogation...'.[47] Article 15 of the European Convention on Human Rights contains a clause permitting states '[i]n time of war or other public emergency threatening the life of the nation' to take measures derogating from some of the rights protected by the Conventions, but only 'to the extent strictly required by the exigencies of the situation, provided that such measures are not inconsistent with...other obligations under international law'. Moreover, the derogating state must inform the Council of Europe of the measures taken and their justification. Non-derogable rights, or the 'core', include the right to life as well as protection against torture, the prohibition of slavery, and the prohibition of retroactive criminal laws. Other international human rights instruments contain similar rules, but their list of non-derogable rights is more extensive.[48]

(b) International humanitarian law

(i) *IHL applies to armed conflicts which have to be classified*

IHL applies only to armed conflicts and its treaty rules, which are largely codified in the Geneva Conventions and Additional Protocols, distinguish and strictly separate two categories of armed conflicts: international armed conflicts and non-international ones. For a situation to be classified as an international armed conflict between states, the necessary level of violence is lower and the number of treaty rules applicable in such a conflict is much larger than for non-international armed conflicts. For violence with a non-state actor to amount to an armed conflict (not of an international character), its intensity must be much greater. In addition, the number of treaty rules applicable to such conflicts is much more limited. As for customary international law, a recent comprehensive study undertaken under the auspices of the International Committee of the Red Cross (ICRC) has found a large body of customary rules, the majority of which apply to both international and non-international armed conflicts.[49] That study has neither clarified the distinction between international and non-international armed conflicts, nor has it defined the lower threshold at which violence amounts to an armed conflict (for non-international armed conflicts).

Traditionally, when states were confronted with armed conflicts, the first line of defence against the restraints of IHL to which some of them resorted was denying it applied. They insisted that they were not engaged in hostilities, but in law enforcement. Although they were reluctant to admit it, those states could not deny that IHRL and domestic constitutional guarantees applied to the situation. This, for example, was for decades the position of the Turkish government, which considered that the situation in Eastern Turkey was not an armed conflict, but simple

---

[47] *Legal Consequences of the Construction of a Wall in the Occupied Palestinian Territories* Advisory Opinion, ICJ Reports (2004) 136, at 178, paras 102–106 and *Legality of the Threat or Use of Nuclear Weapons* Advisory Opinion, ICJ Reports (1996) at 226, para 25.

[48] See Art 4 International Covenant on Civil and Political Rights (adopted 16 December 1966, entered into force 23 March 1976), 999 UNTS 171 (ICCPR) and Art 27 of the American Convention on Human Rights (adopted 22 November 1969, entered into force 18 July 1978), 1114 UNTS 143 (ACHR).

[49] Henckaerts and Doswald-Beck (eds), *Customary International Humanitarian Law* (2005).

law enforcement against PKK terrorists.[50] This was also the position of the Russian government concerning Chechnya.[51]

One of the few genuinely new challenges of IHL is the reverse phenomenon: states try to 'overclassify' a situation as an armed conflict in order to apply IHL even where it does not apply. As mentioned above, after September 11, 2001, the Bush administration declared that it was engaged in a single worldwide international armed conflict against a non-state actor (Al Qaeda) or perhaps also against a social or criminal phenomenon, terrorism. The Obama administration continues to argue that it is engaged in an armed conflict against Al Qaeda and its associates. Such 'overclassification' is not a privilege of the United States, but in discussions with military from Latin America and Central Asia it has been my experience that they try to invoke the existence of an armed conflict to justify more robust methods in fighting social unrest.

Many humanitarians who were previously convinced that IHL should be applied as broadly as possible[52] had to realize that such an 'overapplication' of that law has at least four negative effects. First, as will be shown below, if applicable as *lex specialis*, IHL may deprive persons of the better protection they would benefit from under the law of peace, in particular under IHRL against the use of force and deprivation of freedom.[53] Second, not astonishingly, when applied to a situation for which it was not made, IHL appears inadequate. Therefore, it is applied selectively. Indeed, third, while the Bush administration claimed in the 'war on terror' all the prerogatives that IHL of international armed conflicts confers upon a party to such a conflict, it denied the enemy the protection afforded by most of that law. Fourth, this pick-and-choose approach inevitably weakens the willingness to respect IHL entirely, unconditionally, and independently of conflicting contrary interests even in situations where IHL actually and uncontroversially applies. Many consider that the cases of torture in Abu Ghraib would not have been possible without the corrupting influence of the selective application of IHL in Guantánamo, although for the former—contrary to the latter—the Bush administration never denied the full applicability of *GC III* and *IV*.[54]

(ii) *The definition of international armed conflicts*
International armed conflicts are covered by the four Geneva Conventions (and *AP I*). Common Article 2 to the Conventions states that they 'shall apply to all cases of declared war or of any other armed conflict which may arise between

---

[50] For an example of this position, consistently re-affirmed by Turkish government officials, see the text of a report in English by the Turkish news agency Anatolia, 'Turkish premier re-iterates determination to combat terrorism', 11 May 2008 (reproduced by BBC Monitoring Europe).

[51] Panfilov, 'Managing Freedom of Speech' *The Moscow Times* (27 August 2002). See also J Russell, *Chechnya—Russia's 'War on Terror'* (2007) at 74.

[52] Such as those following the arguments of Jean Pictet, International Committee of the Red Cross, *Commentary, IV, Geneva Convention Relative to the Protection of Civilian Persons in Time of War* (1958) at 36.

[53] See *infra* notes 219–231 and 277–290, respectively, and accompanying text.

[54] See, for example, Greenberg and Dratel (eds), *The Torture Papers: The Road to Abu Ghraib* (2005).

two or more of the High Contracting Parties'.[55] Only states can be parties to the Conventions. Al Qaeda and/or terrorism are not states. Therefore, the Conventions do not apply to a conflict with such non-state actors like Al Qaeda and amorphous concepts like 'terrorism'. As for customary international law, there is no indication confirming what seemed to be the view of the Bush administration, ie that the concept of international armed conflict under customary international law is broader.[56] State practice and *opinio juris* do not apply the law of international armed conflict to conflicts between states and some non-state actors. On the contrary, and in conformity with the basics of the Westphalian system, states have always distinguished between conflicts against one another, to which the whole of IHL applied, and other armed conflicts, to which they were never prepared to apply those same rules, but only more limited humanitarian rules.

(iii) *The definition of non-international armed conflicts*

As for non-international armed conflicts, covered by Common Article 3 and *AP II* in treaty law, it must be determined when a situation constitutes an armed conflict and whether every situation which fulfils those criteria but is not fought between states is perforce a non-international armed conflict.

As for the lower threshold of a non-international armed conflict, *AP II* excludes 'situations of internal disturbances and tensions, such as riots, isolated and sporadic acts of violence and other acts of a similar nature, as not being armed conflicts'.[57] Relevant factors that contribute to an armed conflict include: intensity, number of active participants, number of victims, duration and protracted character of the violence, organization and discipline of the parties, capacity to respect IHL, collective, open, and coordinated character of the hostilities, direct involvement of governmental armed forces (vs. law enforcement agencies), and *de facto* authority by the non-state actor over potential victims.[58] The International Criminal Tribunal for the Former Yugoslavia (ICTY) originally put a particular emphasis on the protracted character of the conflict (or the violence) and the extent of organization of the parties.[59] It was followed by states defining in the ICC Statute the field of application of war crimes in non-international armed conflicts other than those consisting of violations of Article 3 common to the Geneva Conventions.[60] Yet the protracted character cannot be the decisive criterion[61] because it is not foreseeable

---

[55] Art 2 common to the Conventions (*supra*, note 14). Art 1(3) of *AP I* refers to this provision, but Art 1(4) expands the field of application to national liberation wars, a provision vehemently opposed by the US Protocol [No I] Additional to the Geneva Conventions of 12 August 1949, and relating to the Protection of Victims of International Armed Conflicts, 8 June 1977 (entered into force 7 December 1978) 1125 UNTS 3.　　　[56] See Lietzau, *supra* note 19, at 80.

[57] *AP II*, Art 1(2), *supra* note 37.

[58] See Moir, *The Law of Internal Armed Conflict* (2002) at 30–52. and Quéguiner, 'Dix ans après la création du Tribunal pénal international pour l'ex-Yougoslavie: évaluation de l'apport de sa jurisprudence au droit international humanitaire', 85 *International Review of the Red Cross* (2003) 271, at 278.

[59] *Prosecutor v Tadic* (Jurisdiction), IT-94-1 (2 October 1995), para 70, and *Prosecutor v Delalic, Mucic, Delic, and Landzo* (Trial Judgment), IT-96-21-T (16 November 1998), (Čelebići Camp), para 184.　　　[60] See Art 8(2)(f) of the ICC Statute, *supra* note 28.

[61] See detailed criticism by Quéguiner, *supra* note 58, at 278–281.

at the outset of a conflict. It is difficult to imagine that the obligation to respect IHL does not arise at the very beginning of the conflict but only from the time when it turns out to be protracted. The Inter-American Commission on Human Rights has indeed applied IHL to a conflict which lasted only two days.[62] In the meantime, the ICTY has taken this criticism into account and it has defined the necessary intensity as follows:

The criterion of protracted armed violence has...been interpreted in practice...as referring more to the intensity of the armed violence than to its duration. Trial Chambers have relied on indicative factors relevant for assessing the 'intensity' criterion, none of which are, in themselves, essential to establish that the criterion is satisfied. These indicative factors include the number, duration and intensity of individual confrontations; the type of weapons and other military equipment used; the number and calibre of munitions fired; the number of persons and type of forces partaking in the fighting; the number of casualties; the extent of material destruction; and the number of civilians fleeing combat zones.[63]

For IHL of non-international armed conflicts to apply, in addition to such a minimum level of intensity, at least two non-state armed groups fighting each other or one group fighting the government must have a minimum degree of organization discussed below in relation to the question when armed groups are addressees of IHL.[64]

In failed states, the main problem is not whether the minimum intensity of violence is fulfilled, but whether those fighting have the minimum degree of organization required.

Concerning the 'war on terror', some authors also take the views of the parties into consideration, arguing that concerns about state sovereignty, which historically accounted for the high threshold of application of IHL in non-international armed conflicts, do not matter where the government accepts or invokes IHL.[65] Both the Bush administration and Al Qaeda considered themselves involved in a war.[66] In my view, however, the legal classification of a conflict depends upon the facts themselves and not upon the classification of the facts by those subject to the law.

Until now, terrorist acts by private groups have not customarily been viewed as creating armed conflicts.[67] The United Kingdom stated when it ratified *AP I*: 'It is

---

[62] *Abella v Argentina*, Case No 11.137, Report no 55/97, Inter-American Commission on Human Rights, OEA/Ser/L/V/II.98, Doc 38 (6 December 1997), <http://www.cidh.org> [last accessed 12 April 2010].

[63] *Prosecutor v Ramush Haradinaj, Idriz Balaj and Lahi Brahimaj* (Trial Judgment), IT-04-84-T (3 April 2008) para 49. See for an even more detailed analysis, based upon a vast review of the jurisprudence of the ICTY and of national courts, *Prosecutor v Ljube Boškoski and Johan Tarčulovski* (Trial Judgment), IT-04-82-T (10 July 2008), paras 177–193.

[64] See *infra*, notes 80–86 and accompanying text.

[65] Jinks, 'September 11 and the Laws of War', 28 *Yale J. Int'l L.* (2003) 1, at 31–38.

[66] Ibid, at 35–38; Mohamedou, 'Non-Linearity of Engagement: Transnational Armed Groups, International Law, and the Conflict between Al Qaeda and the United States', *Harvard Program on Humanitarian Policy and Conflict Research* (2005), <http://www.hpcr.org> [last accessed 12 April 2010]

[67] Green, *The Contemporary Law of Armed Conflict* (2000) at 56 ('[A]cts of violence committed by private individuals or groups which are regarded as acts of terrorism...are outside the scope of "IHL" '). See also the ICTY in *Delalic et al, supra* note 59, para 184.

the understanding of the United Kingdom that the term "armed conflict" of itself and in its context denotes a situation of a kind which is not constituted by the commission of ordinary crimes including acts of terrorism whether concerted or in isolation.'[68] The British and Spanish campaigns against the IRA and ETA have not been treated as armed conflicts under IHL.[69] Admittedly, those campaigns arose on the territory of only one state. However, I do not understand why a situation which is not an armed conflict (not of an international character) when it arises on the territory of only one state should be an armed conflict (not of an international character) when it spreads over the territory of several states.

On the second issue, whether a conflict can be classified as non-international although it spreads over the territory of many states, the Bush administration argued that the war against Al Qaeda was not covered by Common Article 3.[70] This reasoning was not followed by the US Supreme Court in *Hamdan v Rumsfeld*, holding that every armed conflict which 'does not involve a clash between nations' is not of an international character, and that the latter phrase 'bears its literal meaning'.[71] In my view the Supreme Court is correct, although the wording of the IHL treaties may be ambiguous. On the one hand, Common Article 3 refers to 'armed conflicts not of an international character' and Article 1 of *AP II* refers to 'armed conflicts which are not covered by Article 1 of... Protocol I,' two indications that every armed conflict not qualifying as international is perforce non-international. On the other hand, Common Article 3 refers to conflicts 'occurring in the territory of one of the High Contracting Parties'. According to the aim and purpose of IHL, this must be understood as simply recalling that treaties apply only to their state parties. If this wording meant that conflicts opposing states and organized armed groups and spreading over the territory of several states were not 'non-international armed conflicts', there would be a gap in protection, which could not be explained by states' concerns about their sovereignty. Those concerns made the law of non-international armed conflicts more rudimentary. Yet concerns about state sovereignty could not explain why victims of conflicts spilling over the territory of several states should benefit from less protection than those affected by conflicts limited to the territory of only one state. In addition, Articles 1 and 7 of the Statute of the International Criminal Tribunal for Rwanda extend the jurisdiction of that tribunal to enforce, *inter alia*, the law of non-international armed conflicts, to the neighbouring countries. This confirms that even a conflict spreading across borders remains a non-international armed conflict. Such a teleological interpretation is more difficult for *AP II*, as it goes against its clear wording, stating that the treaty applies to armed conflicts 'which take place in the territory of a High Contracting Party between *its* armed forces... and armed groups',[72] which excludes non-international armed conflicts abroad. In conclusion,

---

[68] Reservation by the United Kingdom to Art 1(4) and Art 96(3) of *AP I*, available online at <http://www.icrc.org/ihl.nsf> [last accessed 12 April 2010].

[69] McCoubrey and White, *International Law and Armed Conflict* (1992) at 318.

[70] See The White House, *Memorandum, supra* note 12.

[71] See *Hamdan v Rumsfeld, supra* note 21; see Jinks, *supra* note 65, at 38–41.

[72] Art 1(1) of *AP II* (emphasis added), *supra* note 37.

'internal conflicts are distinguished from international armed conflicts by the parties involved rather than by the territorial scope of the conflict'.[73]

Applying the abovementioned definitions and minimum thresholds, a sustained 'war' between one or several states on the one side, and a trans-national terrorist group on the other side, may fall under the concept (and IHL) of a non-international armed conflict.[74] Some consider that the conflict between Al Qaeda and the US and other conflicts against groups labelled by the state concerned as terrorist are such armed conflicts.[75] Others conclude that beyond Afghanistan, the 'war on terror' is not an armed conflict at all.[76] In my view, determining who is correct depends exclusively upon the facts, ie the quantity and quality of violence, which are controversial in the Al Qaeda conflict, and upon the possible legal consequences of a classification. After the Madrid and London attacks in 2004 and 2005, the UK and Spanish governments did not consider themselves involved in an armed conflict (and for example did not bomb as military objectives the apartments where those responsible were hiding).

2. *Personal field of application*

As branches of international law, both IHL and IHRL are obviously primarily addressed to states. What is more controversial is whether and to what extent they equally have other addressees.

(a) Armed groups

For IHL of non-international armed conflicts, it is undisputed that it binds, under the explicit wording of Common Article 3 of the four Geneva Conventions of 1949, 'each party to the conflict,' ie the non-state armed group as much as the governmental side.[77] For IHRL this is much more controversial. Even prominent human rights defenders advance good reasons why armed groups should not be seen as addressees of human rights.[78] On the other hand, there exists an increasing soft

---

[73] Zegveld, *Accountability of Armed Opposition Groups in International Law* (2002) at 136.

[74] See Inter-American Commission on Human Rights, *Report on Terrorism and Human Rights* (22 October 2002), OEA/Ser L/V/II.116 Doc 5 rev 1 corr, para 7, <http://www.cidh.oas.org/Terrorism/Eng/toc.htm> [last accessed 12 April 2010]; Bassiouni, 'Legal Control of International Terrorism. A Policy-Oriented Assessment', 43 *Harv. Int'l L.J.* (2002) 83, at 100.

[75] See eg Jinks, *supra* note 65, at 21–31. See for a detailed and nuanced analysis: Quenivet, 'The Applicability of International Humanitarian Law to Situations of a (Counter-) Terrorist Nature', in Arnold and Hildbrand (eds.), *International Humanitarian Law and the 21ˢᵗ Century's Conflicts* (2005) at 31–57.

[76] See Pejic, 'Terrorist Acts and Groups: A Role for International Law?', 75 *B.Y.B.I.L.* (2004) 71, at 85–88.   [77] Zegveld, *supra* note 73, at 9–38, with further references.

[78] Rodley, 'Can Armed Opposition Groups Violate Human Rights Standards?', in Mahoney and Mahoney (eds), *Human Rights in the Twenty-First Century* (1993) at 297–318. See also para 47 of the *Report of the consultative meeting on the draft Basic principles and guidelines on the right to a remedy and reparation for victims of violations of international Human Rights and humanitarian law* (27 December 2002), UN ESCOR, 59th Sess, UN Doc E/CN.4/2003/63. Martin Scheinin, in his Preliminary Report on the idea of establishing a World Human Rights Court significantly envisages that 'other entities but states, including multinational corporations, religious communities, and indigenous or minority groups may by unilateral declaration recognize the binding jurisdiction of the Court', but he does not mention armed groups, although all other non-state entities mentioned

law in the human rights field—pronouncements of international and non-governmental bodies, some judicial decisions, and a growing part of scholarly writings that claim that non-state actors or specifically armed groups have human rights obligations.[79] It is however evident that IHRL needs much more practical translation and adjustment to the special problems raised by armed groups involved in armed conflicts than do the rules of behaviour mandated under IHL, which were made for such situations and such actors.

For both IHL and IHRL, the armed group(s) involved must have a minimum degree of organization. This issue is mainly discussed in IHL, in relation to the minimum degree of organization of an armed group necessary to render hostilities between that group and governmental forces a non-international armed conflict, but since IHRL is only claimed to apply to armed groups to the extent appropriate and that they are able to respect it, this discussion may also inform the discussion for IHRL. Within the human rights community, the debate is primarily centred on whether armed opposition groups exercise government powers, which suggests an implicitly high degree of organization of a group in order to be bound by human rights law.[80] Article 1(1) of *AP II* sets a relatively high threshold for a group to be an addressee of it (and which at least one anti-governmental armed group must meet to make *AP II* applicable). The group must 'under responsible command, exercise such control over [a High Contracting Party's] territory as to enable [it] to carry out sustained and concerted military operations and to implement this Protocol'. The criteria a group must fulfil to make Common Article 3 (and presumably the parallel customary law) applicable are lower, but controversial, as the text itself does not clarify anything. The UN Security Council and the former UN Human Rights Commission have applied IHL to thirty very fragmented groups in a situation of chaos in Somalia.[81] On the other hand, the international *ad hoc* criminal tribunals and the Inter-American Commission on Human Rights are more restrictive and put emphasis on a minimum degree of organization of a group.[82]

On this question of what degree of organization an armed group must have to make hostilities between that group and governmental forces a non-international armed conflict (and the group therefore an addressee of IHL), the ICTY writes:

[A]rmed conflict can exist only between parties that are sufficiently organized to confront each other with military means. State governmental authorities have been presumed to

---

could also be reached through the national implementation system of states (see Scheinin, 'Towards a World Human Rights Court, Interim Research Paper submitted within the framework of the Swiss Initiative to Commemorate the 60th Anniversary of the Universal Declaration of Human Rights' (2008) at 7, <http://www.udhr60.ch/report/hrCourt_scheinin.pdf> [last accessed 12 April 2010].

[79] See for an affirmative view: A Clapham, *Human Rights Obligations of Non-State Actors* (2006); Clapham, 'Human Rights Obligations of Non-State Actors in Conflict Situations', 88 *International Review of the Red Cross* (2006) 491, at 494–507; Matas, 'Armed opposition groups', 24 *Manitoba L.J.* (1997) 621, at 630–634; Zegveld, *supra* note 73, at 38–55; International Council on Human Rights Policy, 'Ends & means: Human Rights approaches to armed groups' (2000), <http://www.reliefweb.int/library/documents/2001/EndsandMeans.pdf> [last accessed 12 April 2010], at 59–62.

[80] See Zegveld, *supra* note 73, at 281. However Clapham, *Human Rights Obligations of Non-State Actors, supra* note 79, at 279–285, expressly disagrees with her.

[81] See Zegveld, *supra* note 73, at 138–141.   [82] Ibid, at 134–138.

dispose of armed forces that satisfy this criterion. As for armed groups, Trial Chambers have relied on several indicative factors, none of which are, in themselves, essential to establish whether the 'organization' criterion is fulfilled. Such indicative factors include the existence of a command structure and disciplinary rules and mechanisms within the group; the existence of a headquarters; the fact that the group controls a certain territory; the ability of the group to gain access to weapons, other military equipment, recruits and military training; its ability to plan, coordinate and carry out military operations, including troop movements and logistics; its ability to define a unified military strategy and use military tactics; and its ability to speak with one voice and negotiate and conclude agreements such as cease-fire or peace accords.[83]

Applying those criteria to the 'war on terror', it transpires from judicial enquiries following terrorist attacks in Madrid and London that their authors were perhaps not linked to Al Qaeda by anything other than reading the same websites and harbouring the same hatred against Western societies as Al Qaeda apparently does.[84] In fact, an assessment of all intelligence the US possesses on terrorism points to decentralized groups that spring up independently and that operate independently and without any connection to Al Qaeda. The burgeoning number of groups gathers strategy, tactics, and inspiration from more than 5,000 radical Islamic websites. Even the director of the CIA predicted in April 2006, '[n]ew jihadist networks and cells, *sometimes united by little more than their anti-Western agendas*, are increasingly likely to emerge' (emphasis added).[85]

In asymmetric conflicts and failed states, in many cases the fighters involved will not fulfil the minimum requirements of organization required by the ICTY. This would not only mean that IHL (and IHRL) does not apply to them, but also that the more organized governmental side or international forces involved are not bound by IHL. The only way to avoid this conclusion would be a functional approach, considering any group to be subject to some rules formulated in terms of absolute prohibitions (such as the prohibition of torture), while not necessarily also to rules requiring a minimum degree of organization (such as the respect of judicial guarantees). This approach may be appropriate once an armed conflict already exists. However it defies logic if it is used to determine whether at least two groups have the necessary degree of organisation to make the situation an armed conflict, as IHL cannot only partly apply in a situation. For that purpose, I argue, it is preferable to require from an armed group the minimum degree of organization necessary to comply with all rules of IHL of non-international armed conflicts—which are anyway mostly formulated in prohibitory terms. The claim that customary IHL of non-international armed conflicts largely

[83] *Haradinaj, supra* note 63, para 60. See also for a more detailed analysis: *Boškoski, supra* note 63, paras 194–206.

[84] See McLean, 'Indictments are near in '04 attacks, Report says Madrid will charge 30-40', *International Herald Tribune* (10 April 2006) at p 3; Langellier, 'Al-Qaida n'est pas lié aux attentats de Londres', *Le Monde* (11 April 2006) at p 8.

[85] See Mazzetti, 'Spy Agencies Say Iraq War Worsens Terrorism Threat', *New York Times* (24 September 2006) at p A1, citing the leaked 'National Intelligence Estimate' of 2006, a 30-page document synthesizing intelligence from 16 different US intelligence agencies. See also De Young, 'Spy Agencies Say Iraq War Hurting U.S. Terror Fight', *Washington Post* (24 September 2006) at p A1.

corresponds to customary IHL of international armed conflicts[86] has however an unintended negative side-effect in this respect: the more rules are binding upon an armed group, the more often a group must be considered not to have the minimum degree of organization necessary to comply with those rules, which would in turn mean that IHL does not apply at all, if no group fulfils those criteria.

(b) Individuals

Once IHL applies because the material threshold is met, as a minimum, its criminalized rules apply to every act committed with a nexus to the conflict,[87] even if the perpetrator of the act does not belong to any party to the conflict and acts outside any structure of authority. As for IHRL, some of its violations are equally criminalized as international crimes and as such bind individuals. The remainder of IHRL is traditionally addressed to states, but under different theories and to a controversial extent it is claimed to bind equally everyone who exercises governmental authority or even every organ of society.[88] Some instruments also prescribe duties for individuals.[89] In addition, states not only have an obligation to respect human rights, but also to protect those rights of individuals under their jurisdiction against other individuals.[90] This must *inter alia* be implemented through legislative measures which are by definition binding upon all individuals found under the jurisdiction of the state. Some treaties contain obligations to criminalize certain conduct through domestic legislation. Some states have in addition provided victims of IHRL violations tort claims against those responsible.[91] Several international initiatives try to specify international legal obligations and best practices relating to private military and security companies and to extraction companies working in conflict areas (whose employees are, obviously, individuals).[92] Finally, such companies are more or less voluntarily subject to codes of conduct.[93] Those

---

[86] See Henckaerts and Doswald-Beck, *supra* note 49.

[87] *Tadić* (Jurisdiction), *supra* note 59, para 70, and *Prosecutor v Jean-Paul Akayesu* Judgment, ICTR-96-4-A (1 June 2001), paras 425–446.

[88] See Clapham, *Human Rights Obligations of Non-State Actors, supra* note 79, at 70–73.

[89] See Art 29 of the Universal Declaration on Human Rights (adopted 10 December 1948) UNGA Res 217 A(III), Arts 27 and 28 of the African Charter of Human and Peoples' Rights (adopted 27 June 1981, entered into force 21 October 1986) 21 ILM (1982) 58, OAU Doc CAB/LEG/67/3 rev 5.

[90] See, for example, *Mahmut Kaya v Turkey*, ECtHR (2000-III), especially paras 85–101; *Osman v United Kingdom*, ECtHR (1998-VIII).

[91] See for the US the Alien Torts Claims Act, 28 USC, para 1350.

[92] See *Montreux Document on Pertinent International Legal Obligations and Good Practices of States related to Operations of Private Military and Security Companies during Armed Conflict*, Montreux, 17 September 2008, <http://www.eda.admin.ch/etc/medialib/downloads/edazen/topics/intla/hum-law.Par.0056.File.tmp/Montreux%20Document.pdf> [last accessed 12 April 2010]. In Canada, a specially constituted Advisory Group, based on a series of National Roundtables with industry leaders, government, and academics, produced a report on Corporate Social Responsibility (CSR) and the Canadian Extractive Industry in Developing Countries (29 March 2007) (it also specifically dealt with issues raised by mining in conflict zones). The report recommended the establishment of a Canadian CSR Framework based on the agreed recommendations of all parties. However the Canadian government has not yet taken any steps to implement the recommendations.

[93] The OECD Guidelines for Multinational Enterprises (Revision 2000) include principles stating that 'enterprises should... [r]espect the human rights of those affected by their activities consistent

codes are often based upon IHL and IHRL provisions, translated into the specificities of private companies.

(c) International organizations

International organizations may be bound by IHL and IHRL whether because their internal law says so, because they have undertaken to respect those bodies of law, or because customary law is the same for states and international organizations.[94] Human rights are one of the purposes of the UN and IHL can be seen as guaranteeing those rights in armed conflicts. However, it is controversial whether the rules of the UN Charter on the respect of human rights are equally addressed to the organization itself. In addition, the relevant provisions in the Charter are vague and specific internal instructions or decisions to fully comply with IHL or IHRL are rare.[95] For IHL, the UN Secretary-General's Bulletin on Observance by United Nations Forces of IHL includes and summarizes many—but not all—rules of IHL and instructs UN forces to comply with them when engaged as combatants in armed conflicts.[96] Are the missing rules (*inter alia* those on combatant status and treatment of protected persons in occupied territories) never binding upon UN forces?

As for treaties, only a draft amendment to the ECHR envisages that an organization, the EU, can become a party to an IHRL treaty.[97] International organizations are not presently able to become parties to other IHL and IHRL treaties and there are a good number of rules which could not be respected by an international organization but only by a state having a territory, laws, and courts or tribunals.[98] As for customary law, the majority view in the doctrine on IHL and IHRL is that as international organizations have (limited) legal personality, they are bound by the same rules as states if they engage in the same activities

---

with the host government's international obligations and commitments'; and 'abstain from any improper involvement in local political activity') <http://www.oecd.org/dataoecd/56/36/1922428. pdf> [last accessed 12 April 2010]. See in addition, the Voluntary Principles for Security and Human Rights, drawn up based on an initiative by the US, UK, Norwegian, and Dutch governments along with NGOs and representatives from the extractive and energy sectors. See <http:// www.voluntaryprinciples.org> [no longer available]. Some trade associations of private military companies have their own voluntary codes of conduct. See for example, <http://ipoaworld.org/eng/ codeofconduct.html> [last accessed 12 April 2010].

[94] See, for a discussion of the applicability of human rights law to international organizations: Cameron, 'Human Rights Accountability of International Civil Administrations to the People Subject to Administration', 1 *Human Rights and International Legal Discourse* (2007) 267, at 271–283.   [95] See Kälin and Künzli, *Universeller Menschenrechtsschutz* (2008) at 100.

[96] UN Secretary-General, 'Observance by United Nations Forces of International Humanitarian Law', (6 August 1999), UN Doc ST/SGB/1999/13.

[97] Art 59(2) European Convention for the Protection of Human Rights and Fundamental Freedoms, 213 UNTS 222 (European Convention on Human Rights, as amended) (ECtHR) according to Protocol 14, which has not yet entered into force.

[98] United Nations Office of Legal Affairs, 'Question of the possible accession of intergovernmental organizations to the Geneva Conventions for the protection of war victims: Memorandum to the Under-Secretary General for Political Affairs' (Selected Legal Opinions of the Secretariats of the United Nations and related Intergovernmental Organizations), 153 *U.N. Juridical Y.B.* (1972) esp para 3.

as states.[99] The real question is however whether they are bound by precisely the same customary obligations as states.[100] The UN long insisted that it was bound only by the 'principles and spirit' of IHL[101]—which is a rather vague instruction for fighting forces. This formulation has changed over time to become the 'principles and *rules*' of IHL,[102] but as the UN denies that it is bound by many of the detailed rules of IHL, I have also some doubts whether it is bound by customary IHL as customary law flows from the behaviour and *opinio juris* of its addressees. For IHRL, as international organizations have no territory, the question as to when a person is under the jurisdiction of the organization arises.

Even if and as far as international organizations are not bound by IHL and IHRL, those who actually act for them may be bound as individuals (by criminalized rules of IHL) or because they are organs of (contributing) states which are bound. Troop contributing states are parties to IHL and IHRL treaties, but they would certainly not like to be parties to an armed conflict and it is controversial whether and when an operation can also be attributed to them if an organization has command and control. A recent judgment of the ECtHR suggests that in such a case the sending state will not have jurisdiction for the purposes of its obligations under IHRL.[103] This judgment seems to run counter to explicit statements by states and to practice.[104] In my view, here as elsewhere

---

[99] Brownlie, *Principles of Public International Law* (1998) at 690; Bothe, 'Peacekeeping', in Simma (ed), *The Charter of the United Nations: A Commentary* (2002) 648, at 695; Zwanenburg, *supra* note 23, at 151–158. Zwanenburg argues, 'it is a small step from accepting application of international humanitarian law to organized armed groups to accepting its application to international organizations', at 158; Emanuelli, *Les Actions Militaires de l'ONU et le Droit International Humanitaire*, *supra* note 23, at 41–43. As for international organizations and human rights, see in particular Tomuschat, 'International Law: Ensuring the Survival of Mankind on the Eve of a New Century', 281 *Recueil des Cours de l'Académie de Droit International* (1999) at 134.

[100] See Kälin and Künzli, *supra*, note 95, at 99.

[101] This phrase is used for example in the UN model participating States agreement. See UN Doc A/46/185 (23 May 1991) 28. See also 'Question of the possible accession', *supra* note 98, at 154.

[102] See the 'Capstone Doctrine', *supra* note 25, at 15–16: 'United Nations peacekeepers must have a clear understanding of the principles and rules of international humanitarian law and observe them in situations where they apply. The Secretary General's Bulletin on the Observance by United Nations Forces of International Humanitarian Law...sets out the fundamental principles and rules of international law that may be applicable to United Nations peacekeepers.'

[103] See *Behrami et al v France et al*, ECtHR (2007), Admissibility. In this case, the question of attribution was not clearly distinguished from the abovementioned question whether a Security Council resolution overrides the substantive human rights obligations of a State, but in its global reasoning the ECtHR suggested that such resolutions have precisely that effect (ibid, para 149). The two questions were distinguished in the *Al Jedda* case by the UK House of Lords, see *R (On the Application of Al-Jedda) (FC) v Secretary of State for Defence* [2007] UKHL 58, per Lord Bingham, para 38, <http://www.publications.parliament.uk/pa/ld/ldjudgmt.htm> [last accessed 12 April 2010], which rejected on the facts the claims of the government under the first question but answered the second question affirmatively (per Lord Bingham, paras 22–24 (attribution) and para 39 (whether Security Council Resolutions prevail); Lord Rodger dissenting on the question of attribution, see esp para 99).

[104] UNCHR, 'Germany' UN Doc CCPR/CO/80/DEU/Add.1 (5 January 2005), (Follow-up response by State Party to the Human Rights Committee); UNCHR, 'Concluding Observations of the Human Rights Committee Poland' (fifth periodic report), (2 December 2004), UN Doc CCPR/CO/82/POL para 3. Other states parties have answered questions regarding the actions of their national forces in peacekeeping missions without contending that the ICCPR does not apply beyond their State borders or in that context (for Italy, see UN Doc CCPR/C/SR.1707, para 22; Belgium,

everything depends on the facts.[105] It may well be that a state contributes troops to a peace operation in such a way that it no longer has control over what those troops do and that the exclusive command and control is with the UN, with another international organization, or with a third state. In fact, this is the situation the drafters envisaged in Articles 43–47 of the UN Charter, which have remained a dead letter. In reality, contributing states retain a very large degree of control over their forces. UN peace forces remain subject to the disciplinary system of the sending state. Everyone familiar with NATO operations knows of the national caveats.[106] If UN Security Council Resolutions and NATO rules allow a contributing state to opt out of a certain kind of operation, out of any given operation, or out of certain methods to implement them, then that state has enough control over the acts of its own troops to be responsible for their conformity with its IHL and IHRL obligations. The case of joint control by a state and an international organization can be dealt with similarly to that, dealt with below, of joint control by several States.[107]

   If the operation or at least the conduct of their contingent can be attributed to contributing states, in both IHL and IHRL the problem dealt with below arises that different contributing states may have different treaty obligations.[108] For IHRL, in addition, the question arises whether and to what extent contributing states are bound extraterritorially by their treaty obligations.[109] If the operation cannot be attributed to contributing states, under IHL they are still bound to 'ensure respect' for IHL obligations.[110] It is however unclear what this obligation implies in case of peace operations.

   International organizations have member states with (often differing) treaty obligations. This raises the additional question as to when member states are responsible for the conduct of their international organization. They certainly have the obligation to 'ensure respect' of IHL by their organization. They are in addition responsible for activities they entrusted their organization to perform, if such delegation circumvented their own obligations in respect of those activities.[111] As for IHRL, it has been held that ztates which entrust an international organization with a certain task must ensure that persons benefit from a protection of their rights equivalent to that the states would be bound to offer. The corresponding case-law

---

UN Doc CCPR/C/SR.1680, para 22; Canada, UN Doc CCPR/C/SR.1738 (7 March 1999) paras 29, 32.)

[105] See for a similar approach Cerone, 'Human Dignity in the Line of Fire: the application of international human rights law during armed conflict, occupation, and peace operations', 39 *Vanderbilt J Transnatl L* (2006) 1447, at 1457 and 1508.

[106] See NATO Parliamentary Assembly, 'Resolution 336 on Reducing National Caveats' (15 November 2005) <http://www.nato-pa.int/default.asp?SHORTCUT=828> [last accessed 12 April 2010].

[107] See Draft Arts 28 and 29 of the Draft Articles on the Responsibility of International Organizations, ILC, *Report of the International Law Commission on the Work of its 58th Session* (1 May–9 June, 3 July–11 August 2006), UN Doc A/61/10, ch VII.

[108] See *infra* notes 142–150 and accompanying text.

[109] See *infra* notes 114–123 and accompanying text.

[110] Art 1 common to the four Geneva Conventions, *supra* note 14.

[111] See Draft Art 28 on the Responsibility of International Organizations, *supra* note 107, at 283.

always concerned however cases in which the individual was on the territory of the respondent state.[112] If the UN authorized an operation to use force, for both IHL and IHRL the question dealt with below finally arises whether, in what circumstances, and how far the mandate given by the UN Security Council prevails, under Article 103 of the UN Charter, over IHL and IHRL obligations of member states or contributing states.[113]

3. Territorial field of application

IHL by definition applies to state organs, ie armed forces, fighting both inside and outside the territory of the state.[114] Some of its rules (eg on the protection of prisoners of war and protected civilians) protect only those who are in the power of a state, while other rules (such as those on the conduct of hostilities) protect everyone, including, eg the civilian population of the adverse party against indiscriminate attacks or fighting enemy soldiers against acts of perfidy or the use of prohibited weapons. For IHRL, its territorial field of application raises much more controversies.

(a) The extraterritorial applicability of IHRL

Peace forces and armed forces involved in the 'war on terror' do not act on their own territory. They are therefore bound by IHRL only if its obligations bind a state even when acting beyond that state's territory. Article 1 of both the American Convention on Human Rights and the European Convention on Human Rights (ECHR) clearly state that the states parties must secure the rights listed in those conventions to everyone within their jurisdiction. Under the jurisprudence of the European Court of Human Rights (ECtHR) this includes an occupied territory,[115] and in one case even a *de facto* regime abroad which could not have survived without the military, economic, and political support of the responding state.[116]

On the universal level, under the International Covenant on Civil and Political Rights a party undertakes 'to respect and to ensure to all individuals within its territory *and* subject to its jurisdiction the rights recognized...'.[117] This wording and the negotiating history lean towards understanding territory and jurisdiction as cumulative conditions.[118] The United States and Israel therefore deny that the

---

[112] *Waite and Kennedy v Germany*, ECtHR (1999-I) at 393; *Bosphorus Hava Yollari Turizm v Ticaret Anonim Sirketi v Ireland*, ECtHR (2005-VI) para 155.

[113] See *infra* notes 136–141 and accompanying text.

[114] See however for the issue whether IHL of non-international armed conflicts applies extraterritorially, *supra* notes 70–72 and accompanying text.

[115] *Loizidou v Turkey*, ECtHR (1996-VI) 2216, at 2235–2236, para 56, and *Cyprus v Turkey*, ECtHR (2001-IV), para 77.

[116] *Ilascu and others v Moldova and Russian Federation*, ECtHR (2004-VII), para 392.

[117] Art 2(1) of the Covenant on Civil and Political Rights, *supra* note 48 (emphasis added).

[118] See Dennis, 'Application of Human Rights Treaties Extraterritorially in Times of Armed Conflict and Military Occupation', 99 *AJIL* (2005) 119, at 123–124.

Covenant is applicable extraterritorially.[119] The International Court of Justice,[120] the UN Human Rights Committee,[121] and other states[122] are however of the opinion that the Covenant equally applies in an occupied territory.[123] From a teleological point of view it would indeed be astonishing that persons whose rights can neither be violated nor protected by the territorial state lose any protection of their fundamental rights against the state which can actually violate and protect their rights.

(b) The degree of control necessary to be under the jurisdiction of a state

If IHRL applies extraterritorially, the next question that arises is when a person can be considered to be under the jurisdiction of a state.[124] The Inter-American Court and Commission for Human Rights have tended to adopt broad views of what may give rise to a state having extraterritorial jurisdiction. The widely-cited case of *Alejandre v Cuba* illustrates that physical control over territory exercised through having 'boots on the ground' is not necessary for jurisdiction to arise in the Inter-American system. In that case, the Commission held that the applicants came within Cuban jurisdiction when Cuba's airplanes fired on another airplane flying in international airspace.[125]

As for the European Court of Human Rights, from its strictest test articulated in *Bankovic*—that a state must exercise effective control over territory by being physically present on that territory in order to have jurisdiction[126]—the ECtHR has moved, over the past decade, to applying a standard that does not always require 'boots on the ground'. In *Issa*, the ECtHR looked for effective territorial control. It found, on the facts, that Turkish forces in northern Iraq did not exhibit that level of control and therefore, in its decision on the merits, held that in fact the Iraqi

---

[119] See for the government of Israel, *Legal Consequences of the Construction of a Wall*, *supra* note 47, at paras 102 and 110; Roberts, 'Prolonged Military Occupations: the Israeli-Occupied Territories since 1967', 84 *AJIL* (1990) 44, at 71–72. It seems that the Israeli High Court of Justice recognizes the extraterritorial applicability of IHRL (see Ben-Naftali and Shany, 'Living in Denial: the Application of Human Rights in Occupied Territories', 37 *Is. L.R.* (2003–04) 17, at 87–95). For the US see Bellinger, *supra* note 12, at 877. The Coalition Provisional Authority Administrator in Iraq, Ambassador L Paul Bremer is reported to have stated in a letter to Amnesty International that 'the only relevant standard applicable to the Coalition's detention practices is the Fourth Geneva Convention of 1949'. See Amnesty International, 'Iraq: Memorandum on concerns related to legislation introduced by the Coalition Provisional Authority' (4 December 2003), AI-Index MDE 14/176/2003.

[120] *Legal Consequences of the Construction of a Wall*, *supra* note 47, paras 107–112; *Armed Activities on the Territory of the Congo (Dem Rep Congo v Uganda)* (Merits), ICJ Reports (2005) 116, paras 216–217.

[121] UNCHR, 'Concluding Observations of the Human Rights Committee: Israel. 18/08/98', UN Doc CCPR/C/79/Add.93, para 10; UNCHR 'General Comment 31' in 'Note by the Secretariat, Compilation of General Comments and General Recommendations adopted by Human Rights Treaty Bodies' (2004), UN Doc HRI/GEN/1/Rev.7, UN Doc CCPR/C/21/Rev.1/Add.13, para 10.

[122] UK, Ministry of Defence, *The Manual of the Law of Armed Conflict* (2004), paras 11–19.

[123] See also references in Kälin, *Report on the situation of human rights in Kuwait under Iraqi Occupation*, UN Doc E/CN.4/1992/26, at paras 50–59 (16 January 1992).

[124] Cerone, *supra* note 105, at 1491–1492.

[125] Case No 11.589, Report no 86/99, Inter-American Commission on Human Rights, OEA/Ser.L/V/II.106 Doc 3 rev at 586 (1999), para 25.

[126] *Bankovic et al v Belgium et al*, ECtHR (2001-XII), Admissibility, 333, paras 70–71.

applicants' claim was inadmissible.[127] In a very recent case, however, the ECtHR has held that jurisdiction can flow from facts not unlike those in *Alejandre v Cuba* (or indeed, in *Bankovic*). *Pad v Turkey* involved a skirmish on the Turkish-Iranian border in which seven Iranians were killed by Turkish helicopter gunships. The Court held that

> it is not required to determine the exact location of the impugned events, given that the Government had already admitted that the fire discharged from the helicopters had caused the killing of the applicants' relatives…Accordingly, the Court finds that the victims of the impugned events were within the jurisdiction of Turkey at the material time.[128]

This conclusion is clearly at variance with *Bankovic*, where 'the Court found that jurisdiction could not arise by the mere fact of dropping bombs on individuals.'[129] It would be specious if, in future, the Court were to distinguish *Pad* exclusively on the grounds that Turkey had not formally contested that it had jurisdiction over the applicants' relatives.

Conceivably, for all treaties, jurisdiction could arise through a state's extra-territorial exercise of control over persons. Before *Pad*, however, the ECtHR also looked for effective control over territory, identifying the following indicators of such control: (1) the number of soldiers on the ground; (2) the size of the area controlled; (3) the degree of control exercised (ie whether checkpoints, etc were established); and (4) the duration of the exercise of control.[130] The first and third factors are valid indicators to measure something as nebulous as 'control'; however, with all due respect to the Court, the second and fourth factors bring little to the analysis. All other things being equal, it is difficult to imagine why it would make a difference whether foreign forces controlled a vast area or only a village. The fourth factor, the duration of control, may be helpful for a Court reviewing actions long after the fact, but it fails to provide states and their forces or agents with a clear indication of when they begin to be responsible for respecting (and possibly even protecting) the human rights of the people in their care.

In my view, a solution could be found through a functional approach, distinguishing the degree of control necessary according to the right to be protected.[131] Such a 'sliding scale' approach, explicitly rejected by the ECtHR in *Bankovic*,[132] would reconcile the object and purpose of IHRL to protect everyone with the need not to bind states by guarantees they cannot deliver outside their territory and the protection of the sovereignty of the territorial state (which may be encroached upon by international forces protecting human rights against anyone

---

[127] *Issa v Turkey* (App No 31821/96) (Merits), ECtHR (2004-II), paras 76–82.

[128] *Pad and others v Turkey*, ECtHR (2007-VI), Admissibility, para 54.

[129] Mole, '*Issa v. Turkey*: Delineating the Extra-territorial effect of the European Convention on Human Rights', 1 *E.H.R.L.R.* (2005) 86, at 87.

[130] *Issa, supra* note 127, para 75. In this the Court was drawing on its prior case law regarding Cyprus.

[131] Cerone, *supra* note 105, at 1494–1507, frames the discussion in terms of a 'range' of applicable rights and in terms of the 'level of obligation' binding states acting extra-territorially.

[132] *Bankovic, supra* note 126, paras 75–76.

other than themselves).[133] This functional approach would for example mean that international forces have to respect the right to life of a person simply by omitting to attack that person as soon as those forces could affect that right by their attack. On the other hand, it is only while they physically detain a person that they would have to respect the procedural guarantees inherent in the right to personal freedom, but not if they hand an arrested person over to the custody of another state. The applicability of IHRL obviously does not yet determine whether its guarantees or those of IHL prevail in a given situation. All on the contrary, the *lex specialis* issue only arises if both branches apply to a certain situation.

(c) Admissibility of extraterritorial derogations

Under normal circumstances, a state's ability, mentioned above, to derogate from its obligations under IHRL is limited to situations in which the security of the state itself is in jeopardy.[134] Can this requirement be met when a state's forces are involved in an operation abroad? Concerning the UK in Iraq, Lord Bingham of Cornhill wrote in *Al Jedda* that '[i]t is hard to think that these conditions could ever be met when a State had chosen to conduct an overseas peacekeeping operation, however dangerous the conditions, from which it could withdraw'.[135] In my view, one cannot simultaneously hold a state accountable because it has a certain level of control abroad and deny it the possibility to derogate because there is no emergency on that state's own territory. An emergency on an occupied territory or a territory where the state has a certain limited control must be sufficient.

4. *The impact of a UN mandate on the applicability of IHL and IHRL*

IHL applies independently from whether or not an armed conflict is justified under the UN Charter.[136] Normally, the legality or illegality of an exercise of jurisdiction does not matter for the applicability of IHRL either.[137] The ECtHR held that the responsibility of a state also arose 'when as a consequence of military action— *whether lawful or unlawful*—it exercises effective control of an area outside its national territory'.[138] Theoretically, UN Security Council Resolutions could, under Article 103 of the UN Charter, prevail over IHL and IHRL obligations

---

[133] See the very nuanced discussion by Wilde, 'Triggering State Obligations Extraterritorially: The Spatial Test in Certain Human Rights Treaties', in Arnold and Quénivet (eds), *International Humanitarian Law and Human Rights: Towards a New Merger in International Law* (2008) 133, at 144–152.

[134] Art 15 ECHR (*supra* note 97) refers to 'time of war or other public emergency threatening the life of the nation...'; Art 4 of the ICCPR (*supra* note 48) refers to 'time of public emergency which threatens the life of the nation and the existence of which is officially proclaimed...'; Art 27 of the ACHR (*supra* note 48) refers to 'time of war, public danger, or other emergency that threatens the independence or security of a State Party...'.

[135] *R (On the Application of Al-Jedda) (FC) v Secretary of State for Defence*, *supra* note 103.

[136] See *supra* note 26 and accompanying text.

[137] See however Schabas, 'Lex specialis? Belt and Suspenders? The Parallel Operation of Human Rights Law and the Law of Armed Conflict and the Conundrum of jus ad bellum', 40 *Is. L.R.* (2007) 592, at 607–610.

[138] *Loizidou*, *supra* note 115, at 2235–2236, para 52 (emphasis added). See also General Comment No 31, *supra* note 121, para 10.

of states. In my view, any such derogation must however be explicit. In *Al Jedda*, the UK House of Lords considered that UN Security Council Resolution 1546, authorizing 'internment where...necessary for imperative reasons of security' qualified the UK's obligations under Article 5 of the ECHR.[139] In my view, the wording of this Resolution is not explicit enough to be considered to mandate UN member states not to provide such internees with the procedural guarantees they are obliged to offer under IHRL. UN Security Council Resolutions must be interpreted whenever possible in a manner compatible with the rest of international law. The mandate of the Security Council to maintain international peace and security includes the possibility to authorize the use of force. How such force may be used is however governed by other branches of international law, in particular IHL, but also, to an extent to be discussed below, by IHRL. No one would claim that a UN Security Council Resolution urging states to prevent acts of terrorism implicitly authorizes torture or summary executions. Beyond that, it is often argued that even the Security Council must comply with *jus cogens*.[140] In practice, even if the organization is bound, most organizations lack internal judicial review procedures in which an individual could invoke his or her rights and domestic courts are barred by the organization's absolute immunity to enforce those rights against the organization. This leaves the possibility that member states simply do not implement Resolutions that are at variance with *jus cogens* because the obligation of member states to comply the UN Security Council Resolutions does not comprise such Resolutions.[141]

5. The problems resulting from joint operations, shared jurisdiction and differing treaty obligations

Even if IHRL applies extraterritorially and if every state contributing to a peace operation is bound by its IHL and IHRL obligations, in case of coalition operations additional questions arise. Can the degree of control necessary to exercise jurisdiction under IHRL result from cumulative contributions by different states, including the host state? In such a case, does every contributing state have jurisdiction? These questions have been raised but not exhaustively examined before the ECtHR. In *Hussein v Albania et al,* the Court held that the applicant Saddam

---

[139] *Al Jedda, supra* note 103, paras 26–39 (per Lord Bingham), paras 125–129 (per Baroness Hale), paras 130–135 (per Lord Carswell), and para.151 (per Lord Brown). Lord Rodger agrees in principle in *obiter* at para 118. The Law Lords held that Art 5 rights may be 'displaced' or 'qualified' by UN SC Res 1546 but insisted that the infringement be limited. Lord Bingham held that they must 'ensure that the detainee's rights under article 5 are not infringed to any greater extent than is inherent in such detention' (para 39). Lord Carswell proposed specific 'safeguards' to be implemented during such detention 'so far as is practicable and consistent with the needs of national security and the safety of other persons' (para 130).

[140] See Case T-315/01 *Kadi v Council and Commission* [2005] ECR II-3649, para 230 and Case T-306/01 *Yusuf and Al Barakaat International Foundation v Council and Commission* [2005] ECR II-3533, para 281; Separate Opinion of Judge Lauterpacht in the *Case concerning Application of the Convention on the Prevention and Punishment of the Crime of Genocide (Bosnia and Herzegovina v Yugoslavia)* (Provisional Measures), ICJ Reports (1993) 325, at 440–441, paras 100–102.

[141] *Kadi, supra* note 140, para 230; *Yusuf, supra* note 140, para 281; the Swiss Supreme Court in *Nada v SECO*, BGE 133 II 450 (2007), consideration 7.

Hussein had failed to furnish sufficient proof that the respondent states had control over Iraq or over him at the time of his detention (or arrest) from which jurisdiction would flow.[142] The Court seemed to suggest that jurisdiction would not automatically exist for states participating in a 'coalition with the US, when the impugned actions were carried out by the US, when security in the zone in which those actions took place was assigned to the US and when the overall command of the coalition was vested in the US'.[143] Given the last-mentioned specificities, there is no *prima facie* reason to exclude that collective control could suffice to establish jurisdiction. A case that provides more guidance on this issue is *Hess v United Kingdom*, which dealt with an application by Rudolph Hess' wife for his release from Spandau Prison.[144] At the relevant time, the prison was under the control of the four Allied powers in Germany following the Second World War. The Commission, in determining whether the prison came within the UK's jurisdiction, accepted *a priori* the premise that the ECHR could apply to the activities of British forces in Berlin. However, it took into account the fact that decision-making power regarding the prison was by unanimous agreement between all four Allied powers. As such, it held that:

…the United Kingdom acts only as a partner in the joint responsibility which it shares with the three other Powers. The Commission is of the opinion that the joint authority cannot be divided into four separate jurisdictions and that therefore the United Kingdom's participation in the exercise of the joint authority and consequently in the administration and supervision of Spandau Prison is not a matter 'within the jurisdiction' of the United Kingdom, within the meaning of Art. 1 of the Convention.[145]

This holding would seem to exclude the possibility of jurisdiction flowing from collective control during a multi-lateral operation. However, as one author has observed, the Commission was particularly troubled by the lack of executive decision-making power of the UK in regard to the prison.[146] Logically, if a state participating in a multi-lateral operation nevertheless retains executive decision-making power over its forces and personnel, there is no reason to deny jurisdiction.

Moreover, any agreement between states participating in a multi-lateral operation affecting that kind of decision-making power could fall afoul of a state's obligations. In *Hess*, the Commission wrote:

The conclusion by the respondent Government of an agreement concerning Spandau prison of the kind in question in this case *could raise an issue under the Convention* if it were entered into when the Convention was already in force for the respondent Government. The agreement concerning the prison, however, came into force in 1945.[147]

To take as an example the right to life and the prohibition of arbitrary detention, I would conclude as follows: no contributing state may make a deliberate causal contribution to a violation of the right to life of any person. However, a

---

[142] *Hussein v Albania et al*, ECtHR (2006), Admissibility, at 3.   [143] Ibid, at 4.
[144] *Hess v United Kingdom* (1975) 18 Yearbook 146 (EComHR).   [145] Ibid, at 176.
[146] Kamchibekova, 'State Responsibility for Extra-Territorial Human Rights Violations', 13 *Buff. Hum. Rts. Law Rev.* (2007) 87, at 125.   [147] *Hess, supra* note 144, at 176 (emphasis added).

contributing state that is not an occupying power does not exercise the level of jurisdiction over a person that would oblige it to protect that person's right to life against other coalition partners or the host state.[148] As for detainees, even a state which is not an occupying power must offer any person it actually detains, independently of whether it also arrested that person or not,[149] the rights that detainee has during that phase of detention; however, such rights may also be respected by measures actually taken by another coalition partner or the host state.

In my view, the same analysis must be made when different coalition partners and a host state are bound by differing treaty obligations.[150] Every state has to comply with its own obligations concerning its own contribution. In addition, a state actually detaining a person must protect the rights of that person even against states not bound to grant such rights.

B. The simultaneous application of IHL and IHRL in general

According to the preceding section, both IHL and IHRL apply to many issues arising in new types of conflicts. This raises the general question how those two branches interact where both apply, an issue which will be dealt with in this section, while the next section will be dedicated specifically to two questions, which are in my view most important in practice and on which the two branches seem to offer contradictory answers: the admissibility of killing and detaining an enemy fighter in a conflict not of an international character. It was indeed shown above that nearly all new types of conflicts must be correctly classified as not of an international character—simply because the fighting does not arise between forces attributable to different states.

1. The relationship between IHL and IHRL

It is generally accepted that the problems of application and interpretation caused by the overlapping of IHL and IHRL are resolved by the maxim *lex specialis derogat legi generali*. The International Court of Justice has said that '[t]he test of what is an arbitrary deprivation of life . . . falls to be determined by the applicable *lex specialis*,

---

[148] A state that is an occupying power, however, has the positive obligation to protect the right to life of persons within its jurisdiction against third parties. The ICJ held that Uganda, as an occupying power in Congo, had an obligation 'to protect the inhabitants of the occupied territory against acts of violence, and not to tolerate such violence by any third party'. See *Congo v Uganda, supra* note 120, at paras 178–179.

[149] See on the irrelevance of who arrested a detainee, UK, 'In the Matter of the All Party Parliamentary Group on Extraordinary Rendition and in the Matter of the Human Rights Responsibility Arising from the Military Detainee Handovers in Iraq, Joint Opinion' (28 July 2008), paras. 10 and 15(2), <http://www.extraordinaryrendition.org/index.php?option=com_docman&task=cat_view&gid=30&Itemid=27> [last accessed 13 April 2010].

[150] While all States are parties to the four Geneva Conventions, not all are parties to the Additional Protocols and, furthermore, not all are parties to treaties dealing with specific weapons such as the Convention on the Prohibition of the Use, Stockpiling, Production and Transfer of Anti-Personnel Mines and on their Destruction (adopted 18 September 1997, entered into force 1 March 1999) 2056 UNTS 211.

namely, the law applicable in armed conflict which is designed to regulate the conduct of hostilities'.[151] The Inter-American Commission on Human Rights, for its part, has affirmed that 'in a situation of armed conflict, the test for assessing the observance of a particular right [protected by the American Declaration of the Rights and Duties of Man], may, under given circumstances, be distinct from that applicable in a time of peace. For that reason, the standard to be applied must be deduced by reference to the applicable *lex specialis*.'[152] As for the Human Rights Committee, it writes that 'more specific rules of international humanitarian law may be specially relevant for the purposes of the interpretation of Covenant rights'.[153]

The European Court of Human Rights has never made any pronouncements on the relationship between the two branches. This is because the ECtHR applies only the ECHR and never refers to IHL, even when it is adjudicating the application of human rights during an armed conflict, and even when the issue it is deciding is also governed by IHL.[154]

While the applicability of the maxim is clear, its precise meaning gives rise to controversy. Some argue that IHL always prevails, or at least, it prevails in every situation for which it has a rule. Others, applying the rule of interpretation used to decide between competing or contradictory human rights rules, argue that in any circumstance one must apply the rule that provides the greatest level of protection.[155] In my view, this approach neglects the fact that IHL is a compromise between the elementary considerations of humanity—thus, the protection of the individual—and military necessity. As such, it is preferable to apply the more detailed rule, that is, that which is more precise vis-à-vis the situation and the problem to be addressed (not forgetting that some protection provided by human rights law may disappear due to derogations, in which case the protection provided by IHL may again be more precise). Before this understanding can be illustrated and applied to the most crucial issues arising and 'new' types of armed conflicts, the meaning of the principle *lex specialis derogat legi generali* must be discussed.

2. Meaning of the lex specialis principle

The utility, scope, and meaning of the *lex specialis* principle are subject to many unresolved controversies, in particular as far as IHL and IHRL are concerned.[156]

---

[151] *Legality of the Threat or Use of Nuclear Weapons, supra* note 47, at 240, para 25.

[152] *Coard v United States*, Case no 10.951, Report no 109/99, IACommHR, 29 September 1999, paras 38–44; see also *Detainees in Guantanamo Bay, Cuba*—Request for precautionary measures (12 March 2002) IACommHR 41 ILM (2002) 532.

[153] General Comment No 31, *supra* note 121, para 11.

[154] See Sassòli, 'La Cour européenne des droits de l'homme et les conflits armés' in Breitenmoster *et al* (eds), *Liber Amicorum Luzius Wildhaber, Human Rights, Democracy and the Rule of Law* (2007) at 709.

[155] See Gaggioli and Kolb, 'A Right to Life in Armed Conflicts? The Contribution of the European Court of Human Rights', 37 *Israel Y.B. Hum. Rts.* (2007) 115, at 122.

[156] See most recently McCarthy, 'Legal Conclusion or Interpretative Process? Lex Specialis and the Applicability of International Human Rights Standards' in Arnold and Quénivet, *supra* note 133, at 101–118.

I have tried elsewhere to explore what the principle *lex specialis derogat legi generali* means in general and in particular concerning IHL and IHRL.[157] In my view, the principle is a useful tool of interpretation, but it does not indicate an inherent quality in one branch of law or of one of its rules. Rather, it determines which rule prevails over another in a particular situation.[158] Each case must be analysed individually.[159]

Several factors must be weighed to determine which rule, in relation to a certain problem, is special. Specialty in the logical sense implies that the norm that applies to certain facts must give way to the norm that applies to those same facts as well as to an additional fact present in the given situation. Between two applicable rules, the one which has the larger 'common contact surface area'[160] with the situation applies. The norm with the scope of application that enters completely into that of the other norm must prevail, otherwise it would never apply.[161] It is the norm with the more precise or narrower material and/or personal scope of application that prevails.[162] Precision requires that the norm addressing a problem explicitly prevails over the one that treats it implicitly, the one providing more details over the other's generality,[163] and the more restrictive norm over the one covering the entire problem but in a less exacting manner.[164]

A less formal factor—and also less objective—that permits determination of which of two rules apply is the conformity of the solution to the systemic objectives of the law.[165] Characterizing this solution as '*lex specialis*' perhaps constitutes misuse of language. The systemic order of international law is a normative postulate founded upon value judgments.[166] In particular when formal standards do not indicate a clear result, this teleological criterion must weigh in, even though it allows for personal preferences.[167]

---

[157] Sassòli, 'Le droit international humanitaire, une lex specialis par rapport aux droits humains?' in A Auer *et al* (eds), *Les droits de l'homme et la constitution, Etudes en l'honneur du Professeur Giorgio Malinverni* (2007) at 375–395.

[158] Koskenniemi, 'Fragmentation of International Law: Difficulties arising from the Diversification and Expansion of International Law, Report of the Study Group of the International Law Commission', UN Doc A/CN.4/L.682, para 112 (2006); Krieger, 'A Conflict of Norms: The Relationship between Humanitarian Law and Human Rights Law in the ICRC Customary Law Study', 11 *J.C. & S.L.* (2006) 265, at 269, 271; Alston *et al*, 'The Competence of the UN Human Rights Council and its Special Procedures in relation to Armed Conflicts: Extrajudicial Executions in the "War on Terror"', 19 *EJIL* (2008) 183, at 192; ILC *Report of the International Law Commission on the Work of its 56th Session* (3 May–4 June, 5 July–6 August 2004) UN Doc A/59/10, para 304.

[159] Lindroos, 'Addressing Norm Conflicts in a Fragmented System: The Doctrine of Lex Specialis', 74 *Nord. J Int'l L.* (2005) 27, at 42.

[160] These terms were first used by Mary Ellen Walker, LLM Student at the Geneva Academy of International Humanitarian Law and Human Rights in my 2007–2008 IHL course.

[161] Larenz, *Methodenlehre der Rechtswissenschaft* (6th edn, 1991) 267–268.

[162] Bobbio, 'Des critères pour résoudre les antinomies', in Perelman (ed), *Les antinomies en droit: études* (1965) 237, at 244.

[163] See for examples Ali Sadat-Akha, *Methods of Resolving Conflicts between Treaties* (2003) at 124.

[164] See eg the ECtHR concerning the relationship between Arts 13 and 5(4) of the ECHR, *Brannigan and McBride v UK*, ECtHR (1993) Ser A, No 258, at 57, para 76.

[165] Koskenniemi, *supra* note 158, at para 107.   [166] Krieger, *supra* note 158, at 280.

[167] Bobbio, *supra* note 162, at 240–241. See also Jenks, 'The Conflict of Law-Making Treaties', 30 *BYBIL* (1953) at 450.

The principle traditionally deals with antinomies between conventional rules. Whether it also applies to the relationship between two customary rules is less clear. Theoretically, this is not the case, if one adopts a traditional understanding of customary law. The customary rule applicable to a certain problem derives from the practice and *opinio iuris* of states in relation to that problem. In relation to the same problem, there cannot be a customary 'IHRL' and another customary 'IHL' rule. One always focuses on the practice and the *opinio iuris* manifested in relation to problems as similar as possible to the one to be resolved. This appears to be the approach of the ICRC, which refers, in its Customary Law Study, to a vast array of practice in IHRL including outside of armed conflicts.[168] In practice, however, when one looks for a customary rule, one often refers today to a text, whether a treaty or another instrument codifying customary law or one that instigated the development of a customary rule,[169] or even a doctrinal text. Then, one specific problem could be covered by two contradictory texts, both deduced from state practice. The choice between these two texts is, in my opinion, governed by the same principles as the choice between two treaty rules. If the state practice clarifying which of the two rules prevails in the given situation is not sufficiently dense, one must discover by the usual methods which of the two rules, derived from the practice analysed from different perspectives, constitutes the *lex specialis*.

3. *Possible relations between IHL and IHRL in practice*

The ICJ enumerates three possible situations: 'some rights may be exclusively matters of international humanitarian law; others may be exclusively matters of human rights law; yet others may be matters of both these branches of international law'.[170] In the following, I propose six possible relationships,[171] with examples, although I admit that the lines between two neighbouring categories may be blurry.

(a) IHL deals with questions not covered by IHRL
First of all, IHL has certain rules that are vital to the protection of victims of armed conflicts that cannot—even implicitly—be deduced from human rights. Thus a crucial question in 'new' types of armed conflicts is who has the right to directly participate in hostilities and what constitutes such participation.[172] One would have to have a great deal of imagination to deduce from the right to life and security of the person of civilians and combatants a right for only certain persons (who distinguish themselves from the civilian population) to commit hostile acts. This issue is thus exclusively governed by IHL.

---

[168] Henckaerts and Doswald-Beck, *supra* note 49, at 299–383.

[169] Sassòli, *Bedeutung, supra* note 40.

[170] *Legal Consequences of the Construction of a Wall, supra* note 47, para 106.

[171] See for another categorization, specific to occupied territories, which leads to very similar results, Ben-Naftali and Shany, *supra* note 120, at 100–109.

[172] See Arts 44(1)–(3) and 51(3) of *AP I, supra* note 55.

(b) IHL prevails over an applicable rule of IHRL

According to Convention III, members of enemy armed forces may be interned as prisoners of war for the simple reason that they are combatants, without any individual judicial or administrative decision. This justification for a deprivation of liberty prevails over the human rights rule and over national law, which require a judicial decision or the possibly non-derogable right to *habeas corpus* discussed below.[173] Even in this uncontroversial case, the *lex specialis* does not result from a strictly formalistic application of the rules. The text of Convention III does not exclude a judicial proceeding. It simply provides that prisoners of war may be interned,[174] without specifying a procedure for doing so. Looking only at the text one could even conclude that IHRL is more precise, but the systemic context leads clearly to the conclusion that IHL prevails. Prisoners of war are not interned for reasons related to their person or behaviour, but solely for the reason that they belong to enemy armed forces and in order to impede their direct participation in hostilities. When it is uncontroversial that the individual is a member of the armed forces, an individual procedure would be out of place, since no individual element or factor plays any role whatsoever. It is probably because it gave priority to this *lex specialis*, which was respected, that the European Commission on Human Rights did not deem it necessary to assess whether the detention of Cypriot prisoners of war by Turkey was a violation of Article 5 of the ECHR,[175] although that provision does not list any exception that could be interpreted as a 'renvoi' to IHL.

In my view, the *lex specialis* permitting detention of POWs without judicial supervision cannot be applied by analogy to other cases of detention of persons who are not prisoners of war and who therefore benefit neither from supervisory mechanisms more appropriate to armed conflict (for example, ICRC visits), nor from a status that carries with it a detailed regime and treatment. Thus, as discussed below in relation to arrested enemy fighters in armed conflicts not of an international character, persons detained by 'peace forces' and/or in the 'war on terror' and rightly or wrongly denied POW status must benefit from a right to *habeas corpus*.[176]

(c) IHL specifies a rule of IHRL more precisely

In many ways, IHL informs human rights. It translates them into rules of behaviour for belligerents, while taking into account the special context of armed conflicts and integrating limitations in a detailed and specific manner. In some respects it indicates the limitations that are admissible in situations of armed conflict, which would have to be clarified by courts if IHL did not exist. Thus, the International Covenant on Civil and Political Rights (ICCPR) and the American Convention prohibit arbitrary detention and the ICCPR prohibits arbitrary deprivation of life. IHL specifies, in each case, what is arbitrary,[177] but only insofar as it has rules on

---

[173] See *infra*, notes 277–290 and accompanying text.   [174] *GC III*, art 21, *supra* note 14.

[175] *Cyprus v Turkey*, (1976) 4, at 532–533, para 313 (EComHR).

[176] See *infra*, notes 291–297 and accompanying text.

[177] See *Coard*, *supra* note 152, para 42; Koskenniemi, *supra* note 158, paras 96 and 104; J Pauwelyn, *Conflict of Norms in Public International Law, How the WTO Law Relates to other Rules of International Law* (2003) at 410.

the issue in question. Thus it has rules on attacks against combatants, incidental civilian losses, detention of prisoners of war or civil internees. However, it has no rules for the deprivation of life in a police operation directed against civilians[178] or on reasons justifying the detention of a person in a non-international armed conflict.[179]

Moreover, in IHRL, the legitimacy of an attack depends on the necessity and proportionality of the attack in view of the legitimate goals pursued. Nothing indicates that this evaluation must be made only in regard to the *jus in bello* objective and without regard to the legitimacy of the conflict in *jus ad bellum*. On this point, however, IHL is explicit and uncontroversial: the *jus in bello* must be distinguished and absolutely separated from the *jus ad bellum* and no element of *jus ad bellum* may interfere in the application or interpretation of the *jus in bello*.[180] One may therefore consider that the IHL separation between *jus ad bellum* and *jus in bello* implies that, when assessing the legitimacy of a use of force (eg of a police operation in an occupied territory) under IHRL, the legality of the conflict itself may not be taken into account. The opposite[181] would mean that every police operation in an illegally occupied territory is unlawful, which would be incompatible with the IHL obligation of any occupying power to maintain law and order.[182]

(d) IHRL specifies or interprets a rule of IHL

For some issues, even in armed conflicts, IHRL constitutes the *lex specialis*. For example, IHL prescribes, with variable normative density, judicial guarantees for prisoners of war, protected civilians being prosecuted by an occupying power, and for all persons being prosecuted for crimes related to a non-international armed conflict. Article 3 common to all four Geneva Conventions simply requires a 'judgment...affording all the judicial guarantees which are recognized as indispensable by civilized peoples'. IHRL specifies, as *lex specialis*, what those guarantees are. Even the ICRC gives this example to affirm that 'international humanitarian law contains concepts the interpretation of which needs to include a reference to human rights law'.[183] Even where judicial guarantees of IHL are much more precise, for example when Article 105 of Convention III requires that '[p]articulars of the charge or charges on which the prisoner of war is to be arraigned...shall be communicated to the accused...in good time before the opening of the trial', one must turn to the case-law of human rights bodies in order to know what details must be given and when those details may be modified.[184] Since they are not

---

[178] See *infra*, notes 197–200 and accompanying text.
[179] See *infra*, notes 258–276 and accompanying text.   [180] See *supra* note 26.
[181] See Schabas, *supra* note 137, at 593 and 607–610.
[182] See Art 43 of the Hague Regulations: Convention (IV) Respecting the Laws and Customs of War on Land and its Annex: Regulations Concerning the Laws and Customs of War on Land, The Hague, 18 October 1907, reproduced in Schindler and Toman, *supra* note 9, at 60–87.
[183] Henckaerts and Doswald-Beck, *supra* note 49, vol I, at xxxi.
[184] *D Monguya Mbengue v Zaire* (Comm no 16/1977) 2 Selected Decisions of the Human Rights Committee 80 (25 March 1983); *Case of Chichlian and Ekindjian v France*, EComHR Report 16 March 1989 (case ended through a friendly settlement and therefore struck out of the list on 29 November 1989); Koering-Joulin, 'La chambre criminelle et les droits reconnus par la Convention

derogable under IHL, in my view one must refer not only to the non-derogable core of human rights guarantees but to their entirety—all the while taking account of the fact that IHRL adapts more flexibly to a particular situation.

Similarly, IHRL and the rich jurisprudence flowing from human rights bodies help to define what constitutes torture or inhuman treatment.[185] Since the prohibition of inhuman treatment is absolute in both branches, there is no reason not to apply this jurisprudence to both. Torture, in contrast, had to be interpreted differently in IHL and IHRL, since the latter is traditionally only addressed to the state, whereas IHL is also addressed to armed groups and individuals in regard to acts having a nexus to an armed conflict. It made sense for IHL to reject the condition of the presence of a state agent or another person invested with authority for an act to amount to torture.[186]

However, it remains difficult to know whether the decisions of human rights implementing bodies may be applied to armed conflicts, without other precautions, even if those decisions were not issued in the context of an armed conflict. The ICRC frequently refers to the case law of IHRL bodies in its study of customary IHL in order to identify the content of fundamental guarantees for persons who find themselves in the power of the enemy. It justifies this approach as follows: 'this was done, not for the purpose of providing an assessment of customary human rights law but in order to support, strengthen and clarify analogous principles of humanitarian law'.[187] However, in case of reference to human rights case-law, it must be taken into account that the limitations admissible under IHRL provisions often permit the content of the obligation to be adapted according to the context. The case law defining the maximum length of detention without being brought before a judge in times of peace may not, for example, be applied to a chaotic situation of armed conflict. Human rights implementing bodies themselves adapt their requirements to the situation.[188]

Interpreting IHL in light of IHRL presupposes that one has verified whether the human rights rule is indeed applicable in the situation covered by IHL, taking into account the limitations and derogations admissible under human rights law.[189] In my view, in this context it would be too formalistic to take account only of derogations that have been declared by the state in question. One should rather take into account all derogations that could have complied with the requirements of proportionality and necessity, even if they were not actually made. The state concerned could, by hypothesis, have not bothered to derogate because it did not consider it necessary since the issue was governed by IHL as *lex specialis*.

---

européenne des droits de l'homme à l' «accusé» avant le jugement' in *Mélanges offerts à Georges Lavasseur, Droit pénal, droit européen* (1992) at 214–215; Poncet, 'La protection de l'accusé par la Convention européenne des droits de l'homme' in *Études de droit comparé, Mémoires publiés par la faculté de droit de Genève* (1977) at 136–137.

[185] Krieger, *supra* note 158, at 275.
[186] *Prosecutor v Kunarac* (Judgment) ICTR-96-23-T and IT-96-23/1 (22 February 2001), para 496. [187] Henckaerts and Doswald-Beck, *supra* note 49, vol I, at 299.
[188] Krieger, *supra* note 158, at 285. [189] Ibid at 279 and 281.

There is a drawback to using IHRL to clarify or interpret IHL—a drawback that is more pronounced when it comes to using the case-law from their implementing bodies. Indeed, such recourse means that the principles of universality of IHL and of the equality of belligerents before IHL[190] are abandoned. A European state engaged in an armed conflict against an Asian state would thus interpret the judicial guarantees prescribed by IHL according to the detailed jurisprudence of the European Court of Human Rights, whereas its enemy would not be enjoined by those specifications.

(e) IHRL has revised a rule of IHL

The development of IHRL largely occurred subsequent to the Geneva Conventions of 1949. It may therefore not be excluded that some human rights prevail over some rules of inter-state behaviour adopted in 1949.[191] For example, Article 118 of Convention III prescribes that prisoners of war must be repatriated without delay at the end of active hostilities. The *travaux préparatoires* and an interpretation according to the system of IHL indicate that this obligation does not depend in any way on the will of the prisoners to be repatriated.[192] Meanwhile, the principle of non-refoulement is recognized as a rule of *jus cogens*[193] and must prevail as the *lex superior* over the IHL obligation to repatriate, which is an inter-state rule and which is not *jus cogens*. Even beyond this clear-cut case linked to pure normative hierarchy, some IHL rules are probably no longer compatible with current human rights conceptions, even though the special context of armed conflicts themselves would not require any change to the rule. For example, has the requirement of a bi-annual review of a decision to intern a civilian for imperative reasons of security[194] been surpassed by a requirement of revision after much shorter intervals, which flow from the right to liberty? Some would go even further and require, in conformity with IHRL, judicial review of such detention and not, as IHL prescribes, merely review by a competent administrative body.[195]

---

[190] See Sassòli, 'Ius ad bellum', *supra* note 26, at 246–248.

[191] Even the ICRC admits: 'Since the adoption of the Geneva Convention there has been a significant development in international human rights law relating to the procedures required to prevent arbitrary deprivation of liberty' (Henckaerts and Doswald-Beck, *supra* note 49, vol I, at 349). One of the authors of the ICRC study is even more forthright, affirming, 'international humanitarian law rules, although very advanced by 1949 standards, have now fallen behind the protections provided by HR treaties' (Doswald-Beck, 'Human Rights and Humanitarian Law: Are there some Individuals Bereft of All Legal Protection?', 98 *ASIL PROC.* (2004) at 356).

[192] See Sassòli, 'The Status, Treatment and Repatriation of Deserters under International Humanitarian Law', *YB. Int'l Inst. Hum. L.* (1985) at 31–35.

[193] See eg the decision ATF 108 Ib 411 et 109 Ib 72 of the Swiss Federal Tribunal.

[194] See Arts 43 and 78 of *GC IV, supra* note 14.

[195] Ibid. See UNCHR, 'General Comment 29' (24 July 2001) in 'Note by the Secretariat, Compilation of General Comments and General Recommendations adopted by Human Rights Treaty Bodies' (2004) UN Doc HRI/GEN/1/Rev.7, UN Doc CCPR/C/21/Rev.1/Add.11, regarding Art 4 ICCPR. See in particular para 16.

(f) IHRL deals, even in armed conflicts, exclusively with questions not covered by IHL

Where one of two applicable branches has no rule on a specific issue, the other one obviously constitutes the *lex specialis*.[196] Even for persons it protects against the enemy—for example in cases of military occupation or non-international armed conflict—IHL contains no rules protecting rights such as freedom of expression or political rights. I do not believe that this is a qualified silence, such that IHL as the *lex specialis* abolishes these rights automatically and entirely in such situations. Instead, they are issues that remain exclusively governed by IHRL. The rights in question cannot be abrogated or limited except in accordance with the human rights rules on the limitations of each right or derogation in case of a state of emergency.

Another issue on which IHL does not contain any specific rules and which is of great practical importance in 'new' types of conflicts, is the admissible degree of use of force against civilians who do not directly participate in hostilities. Article 27 of Convention IV simply requires that they be 'respected' and IHL of international and non-international armed conflicts prohibits 'attacks' against such persons.[197] What does that mean for civilians who commit crimes or disturb public order? On this point, it is crucial to distinguish between military operations and police operations.

The conduct of hostilities—military operations—directed against members of armed groups or armed forces (or against civilians who directly participate in hostilities) is governed by IHL. On the other hand, even in an armed conflict, public order is re-established by police operations directed against civilians (suspected of crimes or threatening public order). Those operations are governed by national law and IHRL. While military operations aim to weaken the military potential of the enemy, police operations enforce the law or re-establish public order. Police operations are subject to a greater number of restrictions. For example, force must not be used except as a last resort and only when non-violent methods have not been successful. The use of firearms is an extreme measure[198] in police operations, while in the conduct of hostilities, the use of firearms by and against combatants is normal. In police operations, precautionary measures aiming to avoid or minimize risks to human life not only have to be taken in regard to third parties ('civilians', in IHL terminology) but also in regard to the person who is the target of the operation.[199] The principle of proportionality, applicable in both IHL and IHRL, thus has a different content or meaning under each branch.[200] In military operations, the IHL understanding of proportionality constitutes the *lex specialis*; in police operations,

---

[196] See *The Mavrommatis Palestine Concessions*, 1924 PCIJ Ser A, No 2, at 31; Lindroos, *supra* note 159, at 56; Rousseau, 'De la compatibilité des normes juridiques contradictoires dans l'ordre international', 39 *Revue générale de droit international public* (1932) 133, at 177.

[197] See Art 51(2) of *AP I* (*supra* note 55) and Art 13(2) of *AP II* (*supra* note 37).

[198] See Art 9 of the Basic Principles on the Use of Force and Firearms by Law Enforcement Officials, adopted by the 9th UN Congress on the Prevention of Crime and Treatment of Offenders (27 August to 7 September 1990) UN Doc A/CONF.144/28/Rev.1 at 112 (1990) (hereinafter Basic Principles).   [199] See ibid Arts 4 and 5.

[200] Krieger, *supra* note 158, at 280–281.

it is the IHRL understanding that does. Obviously, this distinction between police operations and military operations is particularly difficult in 'new' types of armed conflicts. It is nevertheless essential to apply to the use of force in police operations only the *lex specialis* rules of IHRL—which, moreover, are non-derogable because they protect the right to life—and not IHL, which has no rules on this point but only on the distinct question of the conduct of hostilities.

C. Unresolved problems in armed conflicts not of an international character

As explained above, nearly all new types of conflicts are, under IHL, if they are armed conflicts at all, not of an international character. IHL treaty rules for such conflicts are more rudimentary than those for international armed conflicts, which would leave more space for IHRL under the *lex specialis* principle. Customary rules are allegedly largely the same, but certainly not concerning combatant status. This absence of combatant status has important implications for when a person may be attacked or detained.

Before these issues on which the two branches diverge are discussed, it must however be stressed that even in non-international armed conflicts, on most issues, IHL and IHRL lead to similar results, one or the other providing more details. If applicable, both branches prohibit the killing of civilians and detainees, torture, the taking of hostages, require humane treatment of detainees and the respect of judicial guarantees in any trial. Both branches prohibit the starving of civilians and forcible displacements and both branches require that the wounded and sick are collected and cared for. Furthermore, it is uncontroversial that rules on who may use the red cross emblem, on what weapons are unlawful in hostilities, and on what constitutes perfidy must be found in IHL, while the freedom of press, the right to work, or social security are governed by IHRL.

The only issues on which the two branches appear to offer divergent solutions, and which are of great practical importance in all 'new' types of conflicts enumerated above (and in traditional non-international armed conflicts as well) are when a fighter may be attacked and when and under what procedures a fighter may be detained. I use the term 'fighter' for a member of an armed group with a fighting function and for members of governmental armed forces.[201] Indeed, neither Article 3 common to the Geneva Conventions nor *AP II* refers to 'combatants' because states did not want, in non-international armed conflicts, to confer on anyone the right to participate in hostilities and its corresponding combatant immunity. While the prohibition of attacking harmless civilians is the same in both branches, and while IHL does not contain any rules on when and why harmless civilians may be arrested and detained, the regime applicable to fighters seems to differ under the two branches, in particular if, as the contemporary tendency goes and the factual similarity seems to require, rules of IHL of international armed conflicts are applied by analogy to non-international armed conflicts.

---

[201] See *infra* notes 210–212 and accompanying text for a discussion.

1. Circumstances in which a fighter may be deliberately killed

(a) The rule applicable to combatants in international armed conflicts

In international armed conflicts, members of armed forces belonging to a party to the conflict are combatants. Combatants may be attacked at any time until they surrender or are otherwise '*hors de combat*' and not only while they are actually threatening the enemy. As for the proportionality requirement, it applies to attacks directed at legitimate targets, including combatants, but only to protect civilians incidentally affected.[202] Attacks against combatants are not subject to a proportionality evaluation between the harm inflicted on the combatant and the military advantage drawn from the attack.

(b) The treaty rules applicable to non-international armed conflicts

IHL of non-international armed conflicts prohibits 'violence to life and person, in particular murder' directed against 'persons taking no active part in hostilities', including those who have ceased to take part in hostilities.[203] Specifically addressing the conduct of hostilities, Article 13 of *AP II* prohibits attacks against 'civilians... unless and for such time as they take a direct part in hostilities'.[204] One may deduce from these rules and from the absence of any mention of 'combatants' that everyone is a civilian in a non-international armed conflict and that no one may be attacked unless he or she directly participates in hostilities. However, first, it would then be astonishing that Article 13 uses the term 'civilian' instead of a broader term such as 'person'.[205] Secondly, if everyone is a civilian, the principle of distinction, which is a fundamental principle of IHL, becomes meaningless and impossible to apply.[206] Thirdly, Common Article 3 confers its protection on 'persons taking no active part in hostilities, including members of armed forces who have laid down their arms or are otherwise hors de combat'. The latter part of the phrase suggests that for such members of armed forces[207] it is not sufficient to no longer take an active part in hostilities to be immune from attack. They must take additional steps and actively disengage. Fourthly, on a more practical level, to prohibit government forces from attacking clearly identified fighters unless (and only while!)

---

[202] Art 51(5)(b) of *AP I* (*supra* note 55).

[203] See Art 3 common to the Geneva Conventions and Art 4 of *AP II* (*supra* note 37).

[204] The ICRC has drawn up, following a five-year process of research and reflection in consultation with experts, an interpretative guidance on the notion of 'direct participation in hostilities' under IHL (see 'Interpretive guidance on the notion of direct participation in hostilities under international humanitarian law', 90 *International Review of the Red Cross* (2008) 991–1047). This process has clearly demonstrated profound divergences over the question when enemy fighters may be killed in a non-international armed conflict. See Reports of the 2003 meeting (hereinafter DPH 2003 Report), the 2004 meeting (hereinafter DPH 2004 Report) and the 2005 meeting (hereinafter DPH 2005 Report), available at: <http://www.icrc.org/web/eng/siteeng0.nsf/htmlall/participation-hostilities-ihl-311205?opendocument> [last accessed 21 May 2008].

[205] University Centre for International Humanitarian Law, 'Expert Meeting on the Right to Life in Armed Conflict and Situations of Occupation' (September 2005) <http://www.adh-geneva.ch/events/expert-meetings.php> [last accessed 21 May 2008] (UCIHL Report) at 34.

[206] DPH 2005 Report, *supra* note 204, at 64; Kretzmer, 'Targeted Killing of Suspected Terrorists: Extra-Judicial Executions or Legitimate Means of Defence?', 16 *EJIL* (2005) 171, at 197–198.

[207] Under Common Art 3, the term 'armed forces' includes rebel armed groups (see Sassòli, 'Terrorism and War', 4 *JICJ* (2006) 959, at 977).

the latter engage government forces is militarily unrealistic as it would oblige the latter to react rather than to prevent, while facilitating hit-and-run operations by the rebel group. These arguments may explain why even the ICRC Commentary to *AP II* considers that '[t]hose belonging to armed forces or armed groups may be attacked at any time'.[208]

There are two ways to conceptualize this conclusion. First, 'direct participation in hostilities' can be understood to encompass the simple fact of remaining a member of the group[209] or of keeping a fighting function.[210] Secondly, one may consider that fighters are not 'civilians' (benefiting from the protection against attacks unless and for such time as they directly participate in hostilities).[211] However, both constructions raise difficult questions in practice. How do government forces determine membership in an armed group while the individual in question does not commit hostile acts? How can membership in the armed group be distinguished from simple affiliation with a party to the conflict for which the group is fighting—in other words, membership in the political, educational, or humanitarian wing of a rebel movement? One of the most convincing avenues envisaged is to allow attacks only against a person who either actually directly participates in hostilities or has, within the armed group, the specific function to commit continuously acts that constitute direct participation in the hostilities.[212]

(c) Customary IHL

Customary IHL is not less ambiguous than treaty provisions on the crucial question when fighters in non-international armed conflicts may be attacked. According to the ICRC Customary Law Study, in both international and non-international armed conflicts, '[a]ttacks may only be directed against combatants'.[213] The

---

[208] Sandoz *et al* (eds), *Commentary on the Additional Protocols of 8 June 1977 to the Geneva Conventions of 12 August 1949* (1987), para 4789.

[209] DPH 2005 Report, *supra* note 204, at 48–49.

[210] Israeli Supreme Court sitting as the High Court of Justice, *Public Committee against Torture in Israel v Government of Israel et al*, HCJ 769/02, 11 December 2005, para 39 (hereinafter *Public Committee against Torture*). The Court uses a larger concept of direct participation than I would adopt, including eg voluntary human shields (for my position, see Sassòli, 'Human Shields and International Humanitarian Law', in Fischer-Lescano *et al* (eds), *Peace in Liberty, Festschrift für Michael Bothe zum 70. Geburtstag* (2008) at 567–578.

[211] Interpretative Guidance, *supra* note 204, at 1002–1003; DPH 2005 Report, *supra* note 204, at 43–44. This seems to have been the position of the Prosecution in the *Strugar* case: '[I]n a non-international armed conflict, the label of "combatant" which carries with it the right to participate in the armed conflict and prisoner of war status would not specifically apply. Nonetheless, the Prosecution submits that it is necessary to distinguish between individuals who are actually conducting hostilities on behalf of a party, i.e. members of the armed forces and other organised armed groups, and civilians who are not conducting hostilities' (*Prosecutor v Pavle Strugar* (Appeal Judgment) IT-01-42 (17 July 2008) 64, note 427). The Appeals Chamber itself was more ambiguous because it found on the one hand that it had been impossible to establish a nexus between the person targeted (a driver of the Dubrovnik Municipal Crisis Staff) and any possible direct participation in the hostilities 'at the time of the offence [ie the attack]' (ibid para 184), but it had previously analysed what the victim did in the weeks preceding the attack (ibid para 182).

[212] Interpretative Guidance, *supra* note 204, at 1006–1009; DPH 2005 Report, *supra* note 204, at 64; Melzer, *Targeted Killing in International Law* (2008) at 321; Kretzmer, *supra* note 206, at 198–199, goes in a similar direction.

[213] Henckaerts and Doswald-Beck, *supra* note 49, 'Rule 1', at 3.

Commentary explains however (in a rather circular reasoning) that the term combatant in non-international armed conflicts simply 'indicat[es] persons who do not enjoy the protection against attacks accorded to civilians'.[214] It adds that while 'State armed forces may be considered combatants...practice is not clear as to the situation of members of armed opposition groups'.[215] As for the US, the Obama administration still considers that in the armed conflict against Al Qaeda, the Taliban, and 'associated forces', those who provide substantial support to the enemy 'may be attacked (and, *a fortiori,* captured) at any time' without any need to directly participate in the hostilities.[216]

(d) Arguments for and against an analogous application of the rule applicable to international armed conflicts

On the one hand, the general tendency is to bring the law of non-international armed conflicts closer to that of international armed conflicts, which has also the positive side effects of rendering moot controversies on whether a given conflict is international or non-international and on what law to apply in conflicts of a mixed nature. There is, in addition, no real difference between a non-international armed conflict such as the fighting between Sri Lankan government forces and the LTTE in northern Sri Lanka in 2008 and the international armed conflict between Eritrea and Ethiopia in 1999. To require soldiers in the former conflict to capture enemies whenever this is feasible (but not in the latter) is unrealistic on the battlefield. In addition, the decision when an enemy may be shot at must be taken by every soldier on the ground in a split second and cannot be left to commanders and courts. Clear instructions must exist. Whenever possible, the training of soldiers must be the same in view of international and non-international armed conflicts in order to create automatisms which work under the stress of the battle.

On the other hand, strong arguments call into question the appropriateness of applying the same rule as in international armed conflicts. As discussed above, many non-international armed conflicts are fought against or between groups that are not well structured. It is much more difficult to determine who belongs to an armed group than who belongs to governmental armed forces. Positive IHL of non-international armed conflicts does not even prescribe explicitly, as the law of international armed conflicts does, that fighters must distinguish themselves from the civilian population. Persons join and quit armed groups in an informal way, while members in governmental armed forces are incorporated and formally dismissed. As armed groups are inevitably illegal, their members will do their best not to appear as such. Claiming that fighters may be shot at on sight may therefore put many civilians in danger,[217] whether they are sympathizers of the group, members of the 'political wing', belong to the same ethnic group, or simply happen to be

---

[214] Ibid, at 3.   [215] Ibid, at 12. Similarly, ibid, at 17.
[216] See *In Re: Guantánamo Bay Detainee Litigation, Respondents' Memorandum, supra* note 13.
[217] Orakhelashvili, 'The Interaction between Human Rights and Humanitarian Law: Fragmentation, Conflict, Parallelism, or Convergence?', 19 *EJIL* (2008) 167.

in the wrong place at the wrong time. In addition, while in international armed conflicts a clear distinction exists between law enforcement by the police against civilians and conduct of hostilities by combatants against combatants, there is no equivalent clear distinction in non-international armed conflicts. Insurgence in a non-international armed conflict always also constitutes a crime under domestic law. Criminals should be dealt with by courts and may not be 'punished' by instant extrajudicial execution.

The arguments in favour of a different rule in non-international armed conflicts obviously mainly apply to armed groups and they could therefore be seen as requiring a distinction between governmental forces and armed groups rather than between international and non-international armed conflicts. The problem is that IHL, if it wants to have the slightest chance to be respected, must be the same for both sides of a conflict. The principle of the equality of the belligerents before IHL applies also in non-international armed conflicts.[218]

(e) The rule of IHRL

As the rule of IHL on this issue is unclear, it seems normal to apply the rule of IHRL. Human rights treaties prohibit arbitrary deprivation of life. The ECHR specifies that not to be arbitrary, the killing must be 'absolutely necessary:

(a) in defence of any person from unlawful violence;

(b) in order to effect a lawful arrest or to prevent the escape of a person lawfully detained;

(c) in action lawfully taken for the purpose of quelling a riot or insurrection.'[219]

In its case-law outside armed conflicts, the ECtHR has admitted the lawfulness of killing a person who the authorities genuinely thought was about to detonate a bomb, but found insufficient planning of the operation to violate the right to life.[220] By and large, other universal and regional human rights bodies take the same approach.[221] The UN Basic Principles on the Use of Force and Firearms by Law Enforcement Officials provide an authoritative interpretation of the principles authorities must respect when using force in order not to infringe the right to life. Those principles limit the use of firearms to cases of 'self-defence or defence of others against the imminent threat of death or serious injury, to prevent the perpetration of a particularly serious crime involving grave threat to life, to arrest a person presenting such a danger and resisting their authority, or to prevent his or her escape, and only when less extreme means are insufficient to achieve these objectives.' The intentional lethal use of firearms is only admissible 'when strictly unavoidable in order to protect life'. In addition, law enforcement officials 'shall . . . give a clear warning of their intent

---

[218] Bugnion, 'Jus ad Bellum, Jus in Bello and Non-International Armed Conflict', 6 *YIHL* (2003) 167–198; Sassòli, '*Ius ad bellum*', *supra* note 26, at 254–257.

[219] ECHR, *supra* note 97 Art 2(2).

[220] *McCann v United Kingdom*, ECtHR (1995) Ser A, No 324, paras 200–205.

[221] See, for example, *Las Palmeras Case*, Inter-American Court of Human Rights (2002) Ser C, No 96.

to use firearms, with sufficient time for the warning to be observed, unless to do so would unduly place the law enforcement officials at risk or would create a risk of death or serious harm to other persons, or would be clearly inappropriate or pointless in the circumstances of the incident'.[222] It must however be stressed that the Basic Principles are addressed to officers 'who exercise police powers, especially the powers of arrest or detention'. Military authorities are included, but only if they exercise police powers,[223] which could be interpreted as meaning *e contrario* that the rules do not bind military authorities engaged in the conduct of hostilities. If IHRL is to provide an answer as to when a fighter may be killed, it is thus imperative to know an answer to the question discussed above when military authorities, in a situation of armed conflict, are or should be exercising police powers.[224]

The preceding description of the IHRL regime applicable to deliberate killings is largely based upon the practice of human rights bodies relating to peacetime. There are few precedents of human rights bodies in armed conflicts. Theoretically, IHRL is the same in international and non-international, and outside of, armed conflicts. The right to life is in addition not subject to derogations, except, under the ECHR, in case of 'lawful acts of war'.[225] The classic case in which a human rights body has assessed the right to life in the context of an armed conflict is the *Tablada* case. In that case, a group of fighters attacked an army base in Argentina. The Inter-American Commission on Human Rights held that 'civilians...who attacked the *Tablada* base...whether singly or as a member of a group thereby...are subject to direct individualized attack to the same extent as combatants' and lose the benefit of the proportionality principle and of precautionary measures.[226] It then exclusively applied IHL (of international armed conflicts) to those attackers. Only civilian bystanders and attackers who surrendered were considered to benefit from the right to life. The Commission did not raise the issue whether the fighters should have been arrested rather than killed whenever possible.

In the *Guerrero* case, the Human Rights Committee found Colombia to have arbitrarily deprived persons who were suspected—but even by the subsequent enquiry not proven—to be kidnappers and members of a 'guerrilla organization', of their right to life. The police waited for the suspected kidnappers in the house where they had believed the victim of a kidnapping to be held, but which they found empty. When the suspected kidnappers arrived, they were shot without warning, without being given an opportunity to surrender and

---

[222] See Basic Principles, *supra* note 198, Arts 9 and 10.

[223] In the Basic Principles, *supra* note 198, a footnote added to the term 'law enforcement officials' clarifies this by referring to the commentary to Art 1 of the Code of Conduct for Law Enforcement Officials.   [224] See *supra*, text accompanying notes 198–200.

[225] ECHR, *supra* note 97, Art 15(2). It has been argued that this only refers to international armed conflicts (see Doswald-Beck, 'The right to life in armed conflict: does international humanitarian law provide all the answers?', 88 *International Review of the Red Cross* (2006) 881, at 883 (hereinafter, Doswald-Beck, 'Answers']). In any case, no state has ever tried to derogate based upon this exception.   [226] *Abella (Tablada)*, *supra* note 62, para 178.

despite the fact that none of the kidnappers had fired a shot, but simply tried to flee.[227]

The jurisprudence of the ECtHR in cases involving the right to life in the non-international armed conflict in Chechnya includes statements which appear to require that, in the planning and execution of even a lawful action against fighters, any risk to life and the use of lethal force must be minimized.[228] These statements were not limited to the protection of the life of civilians, but in most cases the actual victims were civilians.[229] Most recently, however, the ECtHR held in the *Khatsiyeva* case that even assuming that the victims of a Russian aerial bombardment were armed, it was not convinced that the killing constituted a use of force which was not more than absolutely necessary because the appropriate care in assessing the situation and in planning the attack had not been taken.[230] From an IHL perspective this may obviously be considered as implying that the mere fact of being armed may not yet lead to the conclusion that a person targeted is a fighter. The details which the Court criticized the governmental forces for not having assessed[231] show however that the mere fact that they had been fighters would not have been sufficient to make their attack legitimate. In all other cases in which human rights bodies and the ICJ applied the right to life in armed conflicts not of an international character, the persons killed were either *hors de combat* or not alleged to have been fighters.[232] However, fighters are very often killed, eg bombed while they are not *hors de combat*. Nevertheless, no such case has been brought before an IHRL monitoring body. Some observers have deduced from the absence of any such case-law that such killings do not violate the right to life, a case being brought before the Inter-American system by a surviving relative of a FARC member being 'unthinkable'.[233]

(f) An attempt to apply the *lex specialis* principle

The limited body of case-law is thus not conclusive on the question as to what IHRL requires from government authorities using force against fighters. As both the answer of IHRL and that of IHL is ambiguous, it is not easy to apply the *lex specialis* principle

First, it must however be emphasized that there is a good deal of common ground between the two branches of law. In a 'battlefield-like' situation, arrest is virtually always impossible without putting the government forces into disproportionate danger. Under IHRL, a fighter presents a great threat to life even if that

---

[227] UNCHR, *Suarez de Guerrero v Colombia* (Comm No R.11/45) (31 March 1982), UN Doc Supp No 40 (A37/40) (*Guerrero*).

[228] *Isayeva v Russia*, ECtHR (2005-I), paras 175–176; *Khatsiyeva and others v Russia*, ECtHR (2008-V), paras 133–140.

[229] Quénivet, 'The Right to Life in International Humanitarian Law and Human Rights Law' in Arnold and Quénivet, *supra* note 133, at 341, concludes (writing before the *Khatsiyeva* decision mentioned, *supra* note 228, was rendered) that a careful examination of the jurisprudence of the ECtHR proves that the Court does not use the principle of necessity.

[230] *Khatsiyeva and others*, *supra* note 228, at paras 137–138.   [231] Ibid, para 136.

[232] See an overview by Melzer, *supra* note 212, at 169–173 and 384–392.

[233] UCIHL Report, *supra* note 205, at 36.

threat consists of attacks against armed forces. The immediacy of that threat might be based not only on what the targeted fighter is expected to do, but also on his or her previous behaviour.[234] Therefore, even under IHRL, in such situations, lethal force could be used. On the other hand, the life of a fighter who is *hors de combat*, is equally protected by both branches.

It is where the solutions of the two branches actually contradict each other that the applicable rule must be determined under the *lex specialis* principle. The quintessential example of such a contradiction is the FARC leader shopping in a supermarket in government-controlled Bogotá. Many interpret IHL as permitting authorities to shoot to kill since he is a fighter. Under IHRL he must be arrested and a graduated use of force must be employed, but this rule is based upon precedents which arose in peacetime and IHRL is always more flexible according to the situation. In addition, IHRL too 'must be realistic in the sense of not categorically forbidding killing in the context of armed conflict or otherwise making compliance with the law and victory in battle impossible to achieve at once'.[235]

In my view, some situations contain more specificities of the situation for which the IHL rule was made and some situations more facts for which IHRL were typically made. There is a sliding scale[236] between the lone FARC member mentioned above and the soldier in Franco's forces during the battle of the Ebro. It is impossible and unnecessary to provide a 'one size fits all' answer; as shown above, the *lex specialis* principle does not determine priorities between two rules in the abstract, but offers a solution to a concrete case in which competing rules lead to different results. The famous dictum by the ICJ that '[t]he test of what constitutes an arbitrary deprivation of life...must be determined by the applicable *lex specialis*, namely the law applicable in armed conflicts'[237] should not be misunderstood. It has to be read in the context of the opinion,[238] in which the ICJ had to determine the legality *in abstracto* of the use of a certain weapon.

While the answer must be flexible, it is necessary to determine factors which make either the IHL of international armed conflicts rule or the IHRL rule prevail. The existence and extent of government control over the place[239] where the killing occurs points towards IHRL as *lex specialis*.[240] For government forces acting on their own territory, control over the place where the attack occurs is not a requirement for IHRL to apply,[241] but simply a factor making it prevail over IHL.

---

[234] DPH 2005 Report, *supra* note 204, at 52.

[235] Abresch, 'A Human Rights Law of Internal Armed Conflict: the European Court of Human Rights in Chechnya', 16 *EJIL* (2005) 741, at 750.

[236] UCIHL Report, *supra* note 205, at 38; several experts in DPH 2005 Report, *supra* note 204, at 51–52.   [237] *Legality of the Threat or Use of Nuclear Weapons*, *supra* note 47, para 25.

[238] Alston, *supra* note 158, at 183–209 and 192–193.

[239] If the very person targeted is under government control, both branches prohibit any summary execution.

[240] Doswald-Beck, 'Answers', *supra* note 225, at 897; UCIHL Report, *supra* note 205, at 36; Kretzmer, *supra* note 206, at 203; Droege, 'The Interplay between International Humanitarian Law and International Human Rights Law in Situations of Armed Conflict', 40 *Is. L.R.* (2007) 310, at 347.

[241] See for the responsibility of a state for human rights violations committed on a part of the territory of a state that is not under government control ECtHR, *Ilascu*, *supra* note 116, para 333.

IHL was made for hostilities against forces on or beyond the frontline, ie in a place that is not under the control of those who attack them, while law enforcement concerns persons who are under the jurisdiction of those who act. In traditional conflict situations this corresponds to the question of how remote the situation is from the battlefield,[242] although new types of conflicts are characterized by the absence of frontlines and battlefields. What then constitutes sufficient control to warrant IHRL predominating as the *lex specialis*? In my view, the mere presence of a solitary rebel or even a group of rebels on a stable part of the territory of a state does not yet indicate that the government is in fact not fully in control of the place and that it may therefore act under IHL as *lex specialis*. The question is rather one of degree. If a government could effect an arrest (of individuals or groups) without being overly concerned about interference by other rebels in that operation, then it has sufficient control over the place to make IHRL prevail as *lex specialis*.

This criterion of government control leaves the solution more open in an area situated on the territory of the state whose government is fighting the rebels, but which is neither under firm rebel nor under firm government control (such as regions of central Peru at the time of the *Sendero Luminoso* insurgency).[243] Here, the impossibility to arrest the fighter,[244] the danger inherent in an attempt to arrest the fighter,[245] and the danger represented by the fighter for government forces and civilians as well as the immediacy of this danger[246] may lead to the conclusion that IHL is the *lex specialis* in that situation. These factors are interlinked with the elements of control described above. In addition, where neither party has clear geographical control, in my view, the higher the degree of certainty that the target is actually a fighter, the more easily the IHL approach appears as *lex specialis*.[247] Attacks are lawful against persons who are actually fighters, while law enforcement is by definition directed against suspects.

Even where IHRL prevails as the *lex specialis*, in the context of armed conflict, IHL remains in the background and relaxes the IHRL requirements of proportionality and warning once an attempt to arrest has been made unsuccessfully or is not feasible. By the same token, even where IHL prevails, IHRL remains in the background. Some argue that it requires an enquiry whenever a person has been deliberately killed.[248]

---

[242] Droege, *supra* note 240, at 347.   [243] UCIHL Report, *supra* note 205, at 37.

[244] *Public Committee against Torture*, *supra* note 210, para 40; Doswald-Beck 'Answers', *supra* note 225, at 891.   [245] *Public Committee against Torture*, *supra* note 210, para 40.

[246] Kretzmer, *supra* note 206, at 203.

[247] *Guerrero*, *supra* note 227, paras 13.1–13.3; *Public Committee against Torture*, *supra* note 210, para 40; Ben-Naftali and Michaeli, ' "We must Not Make a Scarecrow of the Law": A Legal Analysis of the Israeli Policy of Targeted Killings', 36 *Cornell Int'l LJ* (2003–04) 233, at 290.

[248] Thus for the killing of what it terms civilians directly participating in hostilities, see *Public Committee against Torture*, *supra* note 210, para 40. See, for human rights law, precisely in situations of non-international armed conflicts, *Kaya v Turkey*, ECtHR (1998-I), paras 86–91 (where it was controversial whether the killed person was or was not an armed rebel and the Court criticizes that the enquiry did not determine this issue); *Ergi v Turkey*, ECtHR (1998-IV) 1778, para 85; *Isayeva, Yusupova and Bazayeva v Russia*, ECtHR (2005-I), paras 209–213. Philip Alston, Special Rapporteur on Extrajudicial, Summary or Arbitrary Executions, even argues that such an obligation exists under humanitarian law (see UNCHR, *Report to the Human Rights Commission of the Special Rapporteur on Extrajudicial, Summary or Arbitrary Executions* (2006) UN Doc E/CN.4/2006/53,

If such a flexible approach to determine the *lex specialis* is accepted, the question arises whether it is valid both for members of armed groups and of government forces. Both parties must be equal as far as the applicable IHL is concerned, but they are not equal as far as IHRL is concerned.[249] Even if IHRL binds armed groups, it can only require from them certain conduct towards persons who are in an area under their control, as such actors do not have any jurisdiction over a territory.[250] A government has the alternative of law enforcement and of applying domestic criminal law, and therefore to plan an operation in such a way so as to maximize the possibility of being able to arrest persons,[251] while the question whether armed groups may legislate to make government action illegal or whether they may enforce government legislation is controversial, as will be shown below.[252]

It is therefore not unreasonable to consider armed groups to be bound only by IHL (and domestic law which in any case renders any killing by them unlawful), while government forces are bound by both IHL and IHRL, the latter prevailing in some situations and to a certain extent as *lex specialis*, and obviously by their own domestic law. The fact that rebels do not have IHRL obligations limiting attacks on security forces does not mean that there are no limits on such attacks. While police forces cannot be considered to be civilians (as is the case in international armed conflicts), if they are engaged in law enforcement consisting of searching for and arresting rebels,[253] attacks upon police units not involved in a non-international armed conflict but in normal peacetime police work would violate the IHL prohibition to attack civilians.[254]

The most important problem with our solution is whether it is practicable in actual armed conflicts. Can it be applied by every single soldier? The answer must be precise instructions and rules of engagement for every operation and every sortie. In addition, on the international level, guidelines might be developed in discussions between IHL experts, human rights experts, law enforcement practitioners, and representatives of the military.

2. On what legal basis and according to what procedure may a fighter be detained?

(a) The IHL rule applicable to combatants in international armed conflicts
During armed conflicts as in peacetime, persons may be detained in view of a trial for a crime or based upon conviction for a crime. What is more specific to armed

---

paras 25–26). I would limit that obligation to possible violations. To require an enquiry every time an enemy soldier is killed on the battlefield is unrealistic.

[249] Doswald-Beck 'Answers', *supra* note 225, at 890.

[250] Even Clapham, *Human Rights Obligations of Non-State Actors*, *supra* note 79, at 284. considers that human rights obligations apply to them only 'to the extent appropriate to the context'.

[251] Doswald-Beck 'Answers', *supra* note 225, at 890; UCIHL Report, *supra* note 205, at 35.

[252] See *infra* notes 296–297 and accompanying text.

[253] See also *Report of the International Commission of Enquiry on Darfur to the UN Secretary-General* (25 January 2005) para 422, available at: <http://www.un.org/news/dh/sudan/com_inq_darfur.pdf> [last accessed 13 April 2010].

[254] Nepal Human Rights Commission, 'Minimum immediate steps for CPN-(Maoist) to respect International Humanitarian Law and Human Rights Principles' in *Annual Report 2004* (Chapter 8, Section 8.3) at 99–100.

conflicts is that enemies may also be interned without criminal charge as a pre-ventative security measure. In international armed conflicts this is the essence of POW status. Prisoners of war may be interned without any further procedure until the end of active hostilities.[255] IHL also allows for internment of a civilian 'for imperative reasons of security';[256] however, it requires an assessment to determine if a civilian poses a threat to security. Thus, Convention IV mandates procedures to be followed for reviewing the internment of civilians, designating the type of review body—either an administrative board or court—and providing for appeal and periodic review.[257]

(b) The uncertain answer of IHL treaties applicable to non-international armed conflicts

IHL treaty rules applicable to non-international armed conflict prescribe how persons deprived of liberty for reasons related to the armed conflict must be treated[258] and they prescribe judicial guarantees for those who are prosecuted for offences relating to the conflict[259] (such as individual non-state actor participation in the conflict, which always constitutes a crime under the domestic law of the state affected by the conflict). Those treaty rules do not clarify for which reasons and by which procedures a person may be interned for security reasons.[260] Yet the drafters of *AP II* recognized the possibility of internment taking place in non-international armed conflicts, as demonstrated by the specific reference to intern-ment in Articles 5 and 6.[261]

(c) Customary IHL

According to the ICRC Study, based upon state practice which arguably can-not be divided into practice under IHL and practice under IHRL,[262] customary IHL prohibits the arbitrary deprivation of liberty in both international and non-international armed conflicts.[263] This rule is interpreted through significant refer-ence to IHRL. The Study states that the basis for internment must be previously established by law and restates an 'obligation to provide a person deprived of lib-erty with an opportunity to challenge the lawfulness of detention'.[264]

(d) Arguments for and against an analogous application of the rule applicable to international armed conflicts

IHL of non-international armed conflicts indicates that internment occurs in non-international armed conflict,[265] but it contains no indication of how it is to be reg-ulated. One could therefore apply on this issue IHL of international armed conflict

---

[255] Art 21 of *GC III*, *supra* note 14.
[256] *GC IV*, Art 78(1) (in occupied territory) and, with a slightly different wording, Art 42 (for an alien on the territory of a party), *supra* note 14.   [257] Ibid Arts 43 and 78(2).
[258] Art 5 of *AP II*, *supra* note 37.   [259] Ibid Art 6.
[260] Bellinger, *supra* note 12, at 874.   [261] Arts 5 and 6(5) of *AP II*, *supra* note 37.
[262] See text accompanying notes 168 and 169.
[263] Henckaerts and Doswald-Beck, *supra* note 49, at 344–352.   [264] Ibid, at 348–351.
[265] Arts 5 and 6 of *AP II*, *supra* note 37.

to non-international armed conflicts by way of analogy.[266] For members of an armed group with a fighting function, the closest possible analogy with the regulation of international armed conflicts is that with POWs, who may be detained without any legal procedure until the end of active hostilities.[267] The ICRC Customary Law Study indicates the appropriateness of applying by analogy the standards of Convention III to those designated as 'combatants' in non-international armed conflict.[268] As for the US, the Obama administration considers that in the armed conflict against Al Qaeda, the Taliban, and 'associated forces', those who provide substantial support to the enemy may be detained like prisoners of war in an international armed conflict.[269] Most arguments in favour of and against such an analogy are similar to those mentioned above in relation to the admissibility to attack fighters. Some arguments are however specific to the detention issue. In favour of POW treatment, it must be mentioned that Article 3 of Convention III encourages parties to non-international armed conflicts 'to bring into force by special agreements, all or part of the other provisions of the present Convention'. If the parties so agree, they could therefore apply to fighters the rules of Convention III, which do not require any individual procedure to decide upon the internment. As special agreements to the detriment of war victims are void under IHL,[270] application of POW status was therefore not considered as detrimental to fighters. Even without an agreement, a government could obtain the same result, ie POW status of fighters, by resuscitating the concept of recognition of the belligerency of an armed group, which has fallen into disuse.[271]

Arguments against this analogy are first that upon arrest it is more difficult to identify fighters than soldiers of armed forces of another state. The correct classification can be made by a tribunal, which will only have its say if the arrested person is not classified as a POW.[272] Second, while in international armed conflicts POWs must be released and repatriated at the end of active hostilities, that moment in

---

[266] See Procedural Principles and Safeguards for Internment/Administrative Detention in Armed Conflict and Other Situations of Violence, Annex 1 to 'International Humanitarian Law and the Challenges of Contemporary Armed Conflicts' (ICRC document prepared for the 30th International Conference of the Red Cross and Red Crescent, 30IC/07/8.4, at 11), <http://www.icrc.org/Web/eng/siteeng0.nsf/htmlall/ihl-30-international-conference-101207/$File/IHL-challenges-30th-International-Conference-ENG.pdf> [last accessed 13 April 2010], (originally published as Pejic, 'Procedural Principles and Safeguards for Internment/Administrative Detention in Armed Conflict and Other Situations of Violence', 87 *International Review of the Red Cross* (2005) at 377–391) (ICRC Guidelines).

[267] See for a position rejecting such an analogy UN Commission on Human Rights, UNCHR, 'Situation of Detainees at Guantánamo Bay, Report of the Chairperson-Rapporteur of the Working Group on Arbitrary Detention, Leila Zerrougui; the Special Rapporteur on the independence of judges and lawyers, Leandro Despouy; the Special Rapporteur on torture and other cruel, inhuman or degrading treatment or punishment, Manfred Nowak; the Special Rapporteur on freedom of religion or belief, Asma Jahangir; and the Special Rapporteur on the right of everyone to the enjoyment of the highest attainable standard of physical and mental health, Paul Hunt' (2006) UN Doc E/CN.4/2006/120 para 24.   [268] Henckaerts and Doswald-Beck, *supra* note 49, at 352.

[269] See *In Re: Guantánamo Bay Detainee Litigation, Respondents' Memorandum, supra* note 13.

[270] Art 6 of *GC III, supra* note 14.

[271] Henckaerts and Doswald-Beck, *supra* note 49, at 352; Moir, *supra* note 58, at 41.

[272] Art 5 of *GC III* prescribes status determination tribunals only for persons a detaining power wants to *deny* POW status.

time is more difficult to determine in a non-international armed conflict,[273] and repatriation is logically impossible in traditional non-international armed conflicts limited to the territory of one state. Even when the end of active hostilities is determined, no obligation for a government to release rebels at that moment exists in IHL.[274]

In an article I co-authored with Laura Olson, we suggested that even for enemy fighters, the analogy should be made with the regime established for civilians interned for imperative security reasons, rather than with the regime of POWs.[275] Indeed, the rules applicable to international armed conflict generally apply only to protected person categories, such as prisoners of war or civilians, while no such categories exist in non-international armed conflict and what counts is each individual's conduct. The precise nature of that conduct can only be established through a procedure. When making this suggestion, we had to admit that 'the practicality of this approach, however, does not make it legally binding'.[276]

(e) The IHRL Rule

IHRL stipulates that a person may only be deprived of liberty 'on such grounds and in accordance with such procedure as are established by law'.[277] All treaties prohibit arbitrary arrest or detention.[278] The Human Rights Committee underlines that '[t]he drafting history...confirms that "arbitrariness", is not [simply] to be equated with "against the law", but must be interpreted more broadly to include inappropriateness, injustice, lack of predictability and due process of law'.[279] The arrest and detention must be reasonable and necessary.[280]

Only Article 5 of the ECHR specifically and exhaustively enumerates the admissible reasons for depriving a person of his/her liberty. Pursuant to Article 5(1)(c), these include not only detention on remand, but also, as an alternative, instances 'when [the detention] is reasonably considered necessary to prevent his committing an offence...'. Under the jurisprudence of the ECtHR, the latter alternative could be seen as implicitly allowing for internment, ie administrative detention, to hinder an individual from committing a concrete and specific offence.[281] In that situation, however, the person must also be brought (under

---

[273] When are active hostilities against the Taliban over? Only once the last Taliban hidden in a mountain cave is arrested?

[274] Art 6(5) of *AP II* simply *encourages* the widest possible amnesty.

[275] See Sassòli and Olson, 'The Relationship between International Humanitarian and Human Rights Law where it Matters: Admissible Killing and Internment of Fighters in Non-International Armed Conflicts', 90 *International Review of the Red Cross* (2008), 599 at 624–627.

[276] Ibid, at 626.

[277] Art 9(1) ICCPR. See also Art 5(1) ECHR, Art 7 ACHR, and Art 6 ACHPR.

[278] Art 9(1) ICCPR, Art 5 ECHR, Art 7(3) ACHR, and Art 6 ACHPR.

[279] *Mukong v Cameroon* (1994), 5 Selected Decisions of the Human Rights Committee, at 86.

[280] UNCHR, *H van Alphen v the Netherlands* (Comm no 305/1988) (1990) UN Doc A/45/40 (vol II) at 115, para 5.8 and UNCHR, *Spakmo v Norway* (Comm no 631/1995) (1999) UN Doc A/55/40 (vol II) at 26, para 6.3. See also UNCHR, 'General Comment No 8, Right to liberty and security of persons (Art 9): 30/06/82' (1982) in 'Note by the Secretariat, Compilation of General Comments and General Recommendations adopted by Human Rights Treaty Bodies' (2004) UN Doc HRI/GEN/1/Rev.7, paras 1 and 4.

[281] See *Guzzardi v Italy*, ECtHR (1981) Ser A, No 39, 3, at 333, para 102.

Article 5(3)) 'promptly before a judge or other officer authorized to exercise judicial power and shall be entitled to *trial* within a reasonable period or to releases pending *trial*' (emphasis added). Therefore, a majority of writers conclude that Article 5(1)(c) covers only detention in the framework of criminal proceedings and does not allow internment (except in a state of emergency).[282] The jurisprudence of the ECtHR is however not clear on this issue and certain *obiter dicta* seem to indicate the contrary.[283]

Internment of enemy fighters would therefore certainly be admissible even without a trial under the ICCPR, while the jury is still out for the ECHR. Under both instruments, however, two procedures must be complied with for a person to be lawfully deprived of his/her liberty. First, an arrested person must be promptly informed of the reasons for arrest.[284] Second, any person deprived of liberty 'shall be entitled to take proceedings before a court, in order that that court may decide without delay on the lawfulness of his detention and order his release if the detention is not lawful'.[285]

As such, the right to personal freedom is subject to possible derogations in case of a situation threatening the life of the nation. Under the American Convention on Human Rights however, judicial guarantees essential for the protection of non-derogable rights may not be subject to derogations. The Inter-American Court of Human Rights has therefore found that the access to *habeas corpus* and *amparo* proceedings are non-derogable rights.[286] Similarly, the Human Rights Committee considers that the right to have any arrest controlled by a judicial body may never be derogated from because it constitutes a necessary mechanism of enforcement for such non-derogable rights as the prohibition of inhumane and degrading treatment and the right to life.[287] The ECtHR accepted in the past that certain violations of the right to a judicial remedy provided for in Article 5(4) ECHR were covered by the right to derogation under Article 15 ECHR.[288] The Court would however not necessarily decide so today, as international practice has in the meantime developed towards recognizing the non-derogable nature of *habeas corpus*. As a possible first step in this direction, the Court held that a period of 14 days before being brought before a judicial authority, together with lack of access to lawyer and of a possibility to communicate with family and friends, was contrary to the Convention despite a derogation by the state concerned.[289] As for customary IHRL, it is widely claimed that the right to *habeas corpus* is non-derogable.[290]

---

[282] See Harris *et al*, *Law of the European Convention on Human Rights* (1995) at 115–121, esp at 117 (in human rights terms 'internment' is more commonly referred to as 'preventive detention'); see also Ovey and White, *Jacobs and White: European Convention on Human Rights* (2002) at 108–110.

[283] *Lawless v Ireland (No 3)*, ECtHR (1979–80) Ser A, No 3, 27, at 51–53, para 14 of section entitled 'The Law'. [284] Art 9(2) ICCPR, Art 5(2) ECHR. See also Art 7(4) ACHR.

[285] Art 9(4) ICCPR, Art 5(4) ECHR. See also Art 7(6) ACHR, and Art 7(1)(a) ACHPR.

[286] *Habeas Corpus in Emergency Situations (Arts 27(2) and 7(6) of the American Convention on Human Rights*, Inter-American Court of Human Rights (1987) Ser A, No 8.

[287] See 'General Comment 29', *supra* note 195, para 16.

[288] *Ireland v United Kingdom*, ECtHR (1978) Ser A, No 25, paras 202–224.

[289] *Aksoy v Turkey*, ECtHR (1996), 2260, paras 78, 83, and 84.

[290] For a list of practice pointing to the non-derogability of *habeas corpus*, see Henckaerts and Doswald-Beck, *supra* note 49, at 350–351 and accompanying footnotes (including General

Although not based upon IHRL, for the detainees held by the US in the 'war on terror', access to *habeas corpus* proceedings was granted by the US Supreme Court in 2004,[291] was again eliminated by Congress in 2006, and was again imposed by the US Supreme Court on constitutional grounds in 2008.[292]

(f) An attempt to apply the *lex specialis* principle

When comparing the rules of IHL of non-international armed conflicts on procedural guarantees for persons arrested with those of IHRL, the former do not exist while, except for the admissible extent of derogations, the latter are clear and well developed by jurisprudence. As far as persons detained by a state are concerned, the extraterritorial application of IHRL to those persons is also less controversial than for other issues. The IHRL rules must therefore prevail. They are more precise and more restrictive. The ICRC Customary Law Study appears to adopt this approach when it interprets the alleged IHL rule prohibiting the arbitrary deprivation of liberty through the lens of IHRL.[293] Unlike a person to be targeted, for whom a flexible approach was advocated above, a detainee is moreover clearly under control of those who detain him or her. It may be added that the result is not so different from that of an application by analogy of the guarantees foreseen by Convention IV for civilians in international armed conflicts, the only difference being that under IHRL a court must decide, while under IHL an administrative body is sufficient.[294]

The only exception where IHL must prevail, as it was specifically made for armed conflicts and foresees a rule, exists when either an agreement between the parties or a unilateral recognition of belligerency makes the full regime of POWs applicable. In that case detained fighters have the disadvantage of a lack of access to *habeas corpus* (although there must inevitably exist a procedure to determine whether an arrested person is or is not an enemy fighter benefiting from POW status), but they have the advantage of a detailed regime governing their detention, of immunity against prosecution, and of a right to be released at the end of active hostilities.

The main difficulty with this approach too is whether it is realistic to expect states and non-state actors, interning possibly thousands, to bring all internees before a court without delay during armed conflict. If it is not, such an obligation risks making it extremely difficult to conduct war effectively and, thus, could lead to less compliance with the rules in the long term, eg summary executions disguised as battlefield killings. Pragmatically, this may be an argument to prefer

---

Comment 29, para 16, *supra* note 195). See also Cassel, 'Pretrial and preventative detention of suspected terrorists: options and constraints under international law', 98 *J. Crim L. and Criminology* (2008) 811, at 829 and notes 104–106; ICRC Guidelines, *supra* note 266, at 387.

[291] *Hamdan v Rumsfeld, supra* note 21.

[292] See *Boumediene et al v Bush et al* 128 S Ct 2229 (12 June 2008), Nos 06-1195 and 06-1196, which could be evidence that states consider habeas corpus to cover even persons they consider enemy fighters in what they consider an armed conflict.

[293] See Henckaerts and Doswald-Beck, *supra* note 49, at 344–352.

[294] Pictet, *supra* note 52, at 260 and 369.

the IHL rule on internment of civilians,[295] but legally this is difficult to justify if IHRL applies at all.

A second concern derives from the differences between state and non-state actors, which have equal obligations under IHL but not under IHRL. The question of whether a non-state actor may establish a court remains controversial.[296] The requirements that there be a legal basis and procedures established by law for internment raise the same concern. Neither IHRL nor IHL applicable to non-international armed conflict provide a specific legal basis for internment—which is required by IHRL. While a state can so provide in its domestic law, how is the non-state actor to establish this basis in law? Could a non-state actor also derogate from IHRL? Parties to armed conflicts intern persons, hindering them from continuing to bear arms, so as to gain the military advantage. If, under IHRL, the non-state actor cannot legally intern members of government forces it is left with no option but either to release the captured enemy fighters or to kill them. The former is unrealistic, the latter a war crime.[297] If rules applicable to armed conflict make efficient fighting impossible, they will not be respected, thus undermining any protection the law provides. These may be reasons for not applying the same *lex specialis* reasoning to armed groups even if IHRL were considered to bind non-state armed groups.

4. Conclusion

New types of conflicts are not so new that existing IHL and IHRL rules could not be applied through normal legal reasoning. Often the new situations are not armed conflicts under the existing definition of IHL and therefore only IHRL applies, limited by controversies over its active personal and territorial field of application. If they are genuine armed conflicts, most of the time they are armed conflicts not of an international character because they are not fought between states. In such situations, the relationship between IHL and IHRL is particularly controversial and difficult to determine. Nevertheless, both IHL and IHRL lead in most cases to the same results. In the few situations in which the results differ, legal reasoning allows for differentiated solutions on when and on which issues the solution of one or the other branch prevails. The real question is however whether those solutions are realistic, in particular for those engaged on the ground. In an ideal world, armed forces and armed groups could apply one set of rules; they would always know who a person they are confronted with is; they would deal under IHL with enemy fighters, while the police would deal in full respect of IHRL with everyone else. This ideal world does not exist in new types of conflicts. Their only relatively new feature is precisely that the full spectrum of laws applies to everyone involved: IHL,

---

[295] As we suggested elsewhere, see *supra* note 275.

[296] Somer, 'Jungle justice: passing sentence on the equality of belligerents in non-international armed conflict', 89 *International Review of the Red Cross* (2007) at 655–690.

[297] Art 8(2)(e)(x) of the Statute of the International Criminal Court. See also Henckaerts and Doswald-Beck, *supra* note 49, at 161.

made for armed conflicts but leaving some questions open, in particular in non-international armed conflicts; IHRL, made for the relations between a state and its citizens, but also applicable to (or at least containing values that must protect) people confronted with agents of a state abroad; and the domestic law of the territorial state and of the home state of international forces. It is also normal that there is no general answer on how those laws interrelate and which one prevails. Everything depends on where on the spectrum a certain contact is situated. Most often, in addition, those acting in the field do not know where on the spectrum they are standing. Therefore, the relationship between IHL and IHRL depends on many variables, and the identity and weight of those variables is in addition controversial among lawyers.

Many will consider the nuanced line I suggest, which in addition on some important issues is unable to provide solutions and only lists arguments, to be unrealistic. In my view, military operations in 'new situations', difficult to classify and often covering the full spectrum from hostilities to law enforcement, require those involved at an increasingly lower level to apply, simultaneously, complicated and controversial rules. However, they are not and they should not be left alone. This is true for government armed forces, but even more so for armed groups; otherwise every hope that they respect IHL vanishes. All those involved need the best possible training and clear instructions for every sortie. In addition, international lawyers and practitioners should meet, not to reaffirm the theory or to conclude that the old rules are not adequate for the new situation, but to operationalize the interplay between the existing rules agreed upon by states, including explaining the few issues on which there are genuine divergences of view, the (often rather limited) practical impact of those divergences, and the possible solutions. Although it must sound like heresy to state representatives obsessed with sovereignty, such a process must include representatives of armed groups and deal with the specific difficulties such groups are confronted with. This is the new frontier of IHL. One common feature of 'new' types of conflicts is the increased involvement of non-state armed groups. If IHL does not develop on that frontier, it will become slowly, but increasingly, irrelevant. It will turn into a specific branch of IHRL. This branch of IHRL will be, and the rest of it is, traditionally addressed only to states and therefore leaves half of the victims, ie those in the power of armed groups, without any protection. Modern theories and innovative practice try to overcome this limitation, but to define exactly the IHRL rules addressed to armed groups—and to obtain their respect—is an even greater challenge than it is for IHL.

4

Norm Conflicts, International Humanitarian Law, and Human Rights Law

*Marko Milanović**

1. Introduction

Much has been written on the relationship between international humanitarian law (IHL) and international human rights law (IHRL). So much so, in fact, that it is hard to find something new, not to mention useful, to say. This chapter will therefore not attempt to reinvent the wheel or shift paradigms. Rather, it will seek to assess the state of our efforts to explain the relationship between these two bodies of law, and then determine its prospects and limitations.

At the outset it must be said that this is not an abstract academic endeavour, but rather a pragmatic and practical project designed to have a real-life impact. Together with the related question of the extraterritorial application of human rights treaties, the IHL/IHRL project serves several purposes. The first, and broadest, is the affirmation of an idea: the law applicable in war is no longer solely a law between sovereigns who agree out of grace and on the basis of reciprocity to limit themselves in their struggles in order to reduce the suffering of innocent people. Rather, human beings embroiled in armed conflict retain those rights that are inherent in their human dignity, which are more—not less—important in wartime than in peacetime, and which apply regardless of considerations of reciprocity between warring parties.

Consequently, a more radical purpose of the project (perhaps not universally shared even among its adherents) is to shift the balance between effectiveness and humanitarianism struck by states during the drafting of the major IHL treaties more in the direction of humanitarianism. In other words, what we as participants in this project really want to do by examining the relationship between IHL and IHRL law is to further humanize IHL.[1] We do this partly by using human rights norms to fill the gaps or areas left unregulated or very sparsely regulated by IHL,

* I would like to thank Dapo Akande, Ken Anderson, David Feldman, Charles Garraway, Francesco Messineo, Jelena Pejic, and Tobias Thienel for their helpful comments. Email: marko. milanovic@gmail.com. An earlier version of this chapter was published in 14 *Journal of Conflict & Security Law* (2009).

[1] See generally Meron, 'The Humanization of Humanitarian Law', 94 *AJIL* (2000) 243.

for example with regard to non-international armed conflicts, and partly by trying to change some outcomes that are in fact determined by IHL through the introduction of human rights rules and arguments into the equation.

Finally, a more down to earth purpose of the project is the enforcement of IHL through human rights mechanisms.[2] Thus, even if human rights substantively added nothing to IHL, ie if the relationship between IHL and IHRL was such that IHRL in wartime brought no fewer, but also no more, protections for individuals than IHL, there would still be a point in regarding IHL and IHRL as two complementary bodies of law. IHL, now (jurisdictionally) framed in human rights terms, could be enforced (or attempts could be made to enforce it) before political bodies, such as the Human Rights Council or UN political organs more generally, or through judicial and quasi-judicial mechanisms, such as the International Court of Justice, the European Court of Human Rights, the UN treaty bodies, or domestic courts.[3]

In brief, we wish to (boldly) take human rights to places, be they extraterritorial situations or those of armed conflict, or both, where, as a matter of practical reality, no human rights have gone before. Saying openly that we are participating in a project with pragmatic and transformative ends in mind, rather than engaging in some sort of abstract discovery of the law, does not mean that we as lawyers are doing so illegitimately, or that we are usurping the legislative prerogatives of states. It is the states themselves that have affirmed the complementary application of IHL and human rights law, both in the texts of the relevant human rights treaties[4] (that were after all concluded in the aftermath of the most inhumane abuses committed during an armed conflict, the Second World War), and in their official pronouncements in international fora. States have also greatly contributed to the humanization of IHL through the adoption of the 1977 Additional Protocols to the 1949 Geneva Conventions, for example through their provisions on fundamental humanitarian guarantees, or through greater limitations on reprisals.[5] As is often the case, states may not have abided in practice with their commitments as they should have, but this does not mean that these commitments were not made.

---

[2] See eg Verdirame, 'Human Rights in Wartime: A Framework for Analysis', *EHRLR* (2008) 689, at 691.

[3] A most effective example is the extensive litigation in UK domestic courts under the Human Rights Act 1998 arising from the occupation of Iraq, several cases of which will be referred to throughout this chapter.

[4] See the derogation clauses in the major human rights treaties, two of which explicitly mention 'war' as a situation in which derogations might be appropriate—Art 4, International Covenant on Civil and Political Rights, 99 UNTS 171 (ICCPR); Art 15, European Convention for the Protection of Human Rights and Fundamental Freedoms, 213 UNTS 222 (ECHR); and Art 27, American Convention on Human Rights, 1144 UNTS 123 (ACHR). See also Art 72 of Additional Protocol I to the Geneva Conventions (*AP I*), which refers to 'other applicable rules of international law relating to the protection of fundamental human rights during international armed conflict', as well as the second preambular paragraph of Additional Protocol II (*AP II*), stating that 'international instruments relating to human rights offer a basic protection to the human person'.

[5] For a general overview, see Droege, 'Elective Affinities? Human Rights and Humanitarian Law', 90 *International Review of the Red Cross* (2008) 501, at 503 *et seq*.

That said, there are limits to what legitimate methods of interpretation can do to harmonize IHL and IHRL. Further, for human rights-based arguments to be even remotely persuasive in regard to situations of armed conflict, and to avoid the impression of a fluffy, utopian human-rightist disregard for the realities of international relations, these arguments must meet certain requirements. First, it is immediately apparent from even a cursory examination of the case-law on the application of human rights treaties extraterritorially or in times of armed conflict that courts greatly fear over-complexity and their own institutional incompetence, whether perceived or real. A paradigmatic example would be *Bankovic*[6]—that rightfully much maligned case[7]—which was at least in part the product of the European Court's apprehensiveness regarding its lack of both expertise and a reliable factual record in order to apply IHL through IHRL to a situation as politically sensitive as was the NATO bombing of Yugoslavia. Therefore, we have to be able to offer courts and other relevant bodies some relatively clear, workable rules on both threshold applicability issues and on substantive issues that can arise from the joint application of IHL and human rights law.

Second, it must also be realized that there is a price to be paid for the joint application of IHL and IHRL. Though it may be our goal to further humanize IHL, in order to do so we must also be prepared to water down IHRL to make its application possible and practical. To the extent that war and armed conflict are accepted as a reality—as they must be, if this project is to make any sense—human rights norms cannot be applied in a business as usual kind of way, with their interminable casuistry and balancing of this and that. Considerations of effectiveness must always be taken into account. This may be a somewhat obvious point, but it must be made nonetheless.

Yet it must also be stressed that though human rights have to be watered down to be applied jointly with IHL, they must not be watered down too much. Not only would this defy the whole purpose of the exercise, but it would also potentially compromise the values safeguarded by the human rights regime in peacetime.[8] For instance, allowing the state to kill combatants or insurgents *under human rights law* without showing an absolute necessity to do so, or to detain preventively during armed conflict, might lead to allowing the state to do the same outside armed conflict, with one precedent leading to another, and then another, and yet another. The potential of emergencies or states of exception to balloon out

---

[6] *Bankovic and Others v Belgium and Others* (2001) 11 BHRC 435.

[7] On *Bankovic* and the extraterritorial application of human rights treaties generally, see the contributions in Coomans and Kamminga (eds), *Extraterritorial Application of Human Rights Treaties* (2004); Milanovic, 'From Compromise to Principle: Clarifying the Concept of State Jurisdiction in Human Rights Treaties', 8 *HRLRev.* (2008) 411; Ben-Naftali and Shany, 'Living in Denial: The Application of Human Rights in the Occupied Territories', 37 *Is. L.R.* (2003–04) 17.

[8] See also the insightful critique by Schabas, '*Lex Specialis?* Belts and Suspenders? The Parallel Operation of Human Rights Law and the Law of Armed Conflict, and the Conundrum of *Jus ad Bellum*', 40 *Is. LR* (2007) 592, who argues that if IHL and IHRL are to be reconciled, IHRL must develop an IHL-like indifference to the *jus ad bellum* lawfulness of war, as well as allow the 'collateral' of civilians regardless of the overall legality of the use of force, and that this abandonment of pacifism is too high a price to pay for harmony.

and become the norm rather than the exception has of course long been recognized. This is, *inter alia*, why there are derogation clauses in human rights treaties, and why they impose such strict requirements on any derogation. In other words, there must be caution in applying IHL together with human rights, as it is human rights that might lose something in the process.[9] After all, for all its humanitarian ethos, IHL is still a discipline about killing people, albeit in a civilized sort of way.[10]

Having taken these considerations into account, we can move on to their implications for the relationship between IHL and IHRL. First, in order to be able to provide judges and other decision-makers with workable rules that they may then apply, and (more importantly) that they would be *willing* to apply, the focus of our debate must be shifted from the relationship between the two regimes as such, to the relationship between the particular norms belonging to the two regimes that control specific factual situations. Secondly, since this relationship is of course but one of many that contribute to the wider phenomenon of the fragmentation of international law,[11] we must be prepared to fully employ the toolbox that the doctrine of international law provides us with for avoiding or resolving conflicts of norms. Thirdly, we must place the *lex specialis* maxim, whose exact nature remains unclear, inside that toolbox. Having done so, we will realize that *lex specialis* must be abandoned as a sort of magical, two-word explanation of the relationship between IHL and IHRL, as it confuses far more than it clarifies. Finally, we must be prepared to concede that there are some situations—perhaps not many, but by no means practically irrelevant—where the international lawyer's craft and tools will fail, and where no legal solution can be provided. Such situations of unresolvable conflict or antinomy can be solved only in the manner in which they were created—through the political process. I will address these issues in turn.

2. A Relationship between Norms, not between Regimes

The relationship between IHL and IHRL, and the fragmentation phenomenon more broadly, are often examined from a high altitude perspective of a relationship between two or more legal regimes. Though there may be some use in such inquiries, they are more often than not unhelpful. When it comes to the relationship between IHL and IHRL in particular, they can not only

---

[9] A further risk is that injecting human rights discourse into warfare would actually serve to legitimize war as a phenomenon—see Verdirame, *supra* note 2, at 692.

[10] This fear, whether entirely conscious or not, that human rights might be compromised by giving too much way to effectiveness and to the realities of armed conflict might provide at least a partial explanation for the European Court's reluctance so far to explicitly take IHL into account in its cases on Chechnya, together with related fears regarding institutional incompetence. See also Abresch, 'A Human Rights Law of Internal Armed Conflict: The European Court of Human Rights in Chechnya', 16 *EJIL* (2005) 741. For an overview of the Chechen cases, see Leach, 'The Chechen Conflict: Analysing the Oversight of the European Court of Human Rights', (2008) *EHRLR.* 732.

[11] See eg Cassimatis, 'International Humanitarian Law, International Human Rights Law, and the Fragmentation of International Law', 56 *ICLQ* (2007) 623.

be unhelpful—viz the *lex specialis* mantra—but misleading and even dangerous as well. To see how this can be the case, we need only turn to the most
remarked upon examples of such high altitude pronouncements, those of the
International Court of Justice.

As is well known, the Court's first foray into the matter took place in the *Nuclear
Weapons* Advisory Opinion, where it remarked that:

[i]n principle, the right not arbitrarily to be deprived of one's life applies also in hostilities.
The test of what is an arbitrary deprivation of life, however, then falls to be determined by
the applicable *lex specialis*, namely, the law applicable in armed conflict which is designed
to regulate the conduct of hostilities. Thus whether a particular loss of life, through the use
of a certain weapon in warfare, is to be considered an arbitrary deprivation of life contrary
to Article 6 of the Covenant, can only be decided by reference to the law applicable in
armed conflict and not deduced from the terms of the Covenant itself.[12]

It is of note that the Court in *Nuclear Weapons* did not *really* examine the relationship between IHL and IHRL as regimes. It examined the relationship between
one particular IHRL norm, the right to life, and, at that, the right to life as it is
formulated in Article 6 ICCPR (which is worded differently to Article 2 ECHR,
for instance), and the relevant rules of IHL. It was these *specific rules* that were held
to be *lex specialis*, in that they could help interpret the 'arbitrary' part of Article 6
ICCPR in times of armed conflict. Though the Court pronouncement was thus
framed in terms of one particular problem and one particular set of norms, it
nonetheless understandably provoked an academic extrapolation to the relationship between IHL and IHRL as a whole. The *Nuclear Weapons* Opinion was thus
understood as saying that IHL defines what IHRL means in wartime, with IHRL
guaranteeing no less, but also no more, rights to individuals affected by armed
conflict than does IHL.[13]

Our discussions have of course evolved since then, and so has the ICJ, whose next
pronouncement in the *Wall* Advisory Opinion was decidedly broader in nature:

More generally, the Court considers that the protection offered by human rights conventions does not cease in case of armed conflict, save through the effect of provisions for
derogation of the kind to be found in Article 4 of the International Covenant on Civil and
Political Rights. As regards the relationship between international humanitarian law and
human rights law, there are thus three possible situations: some rights may be exclusively
matters of international humanitarian law; others may be exclusively matters of human
rights law; yet others may be matters of both these branches of international law. In order
to answer the question put to it, the Court will have to take into consideration both these
branches of international law, namely human rights law and, as *lex specialis*, international
humanitarian law.[14]

---

[12] *Legality of the Threat or Use of Nuclear Weapons*, Advisory Opinion of 8 July 1996, ICJ Reports
(1996) 226, para 25.

[13] See eg Doswald-Beck, 'International humanitarian law and the Advisory Opinion of
the International Court of Justice on the Legality of the Threat or Use of Nuclear Weapons', 37
International Review of the Red Cross (1997) 35.

[14] *Legal Consequences of the Construction of a Wall in the Occupied Palestinian Territory*, Advisory
Opinion of 9 July 2004, ICJ Reports (2004) 136, para 106.

As opposed to *Nuclear Weapons*, the Court here does refer to IHL as *lex specialis* to IHRL, ie it considers not only some particular norms, but one regime to be special to the other. The problem with such a characterization is not just that it is overly broad, but also that the concept of *lex specialis* is vague and can mean at least two radically different things, as I will explain below.[15] (It should be noted, in that regard, that when the Court in *Congo v Uganda* quoted its dictum from the *Wall* case,[16] it dropped the reference to *lex specialis*. Whether this omission was intentional is anyone's guess but let us hope that it was.) On a purely practical level, the three categories outlined by the Court do not work at all, if only because the Court does not say anything about which rules fall within which category, and on what basis. If you are, say, a British judge asked to rule under the Human Rights Act whether the preventive security detention of persons by British troops in Iraq violates Article 5 ECHR, the ICJ's dicta will provide you with precisely zero guidance.

To say, therefore, that the two 'spheres of law are complementary, not mutually exclusive',[17] may be perfectly true, but is nonetheless equally unhelpful in providing practical solutions to actual cases. The complementarity claim is only an answer to the equally broad counter-claim that the two regimes are mutually exclusive. To the extent that the latter was for many years the default position—and admittedly it was so, as a matter of actual practice—the complementarity claim does have a purpose. But beyond that, it does not solve anything. It is the relationships between specific IHL and IHRL norms that need examining.[18]

As I stated above, dwelling too much on the relationship between regimes, instead of on the relationship between the relevant norms, is not only unhelpful, but can also be dangerous. Indeed, it can be particularly dangerous if we refer to IHL as *lex specialis* to IHRL as a whole. Consider, for instance, the Bush administration's legal strategy in its 'war on terror'. It denied that persons detained in Guantánamo were entitled to protection under human rights law on the basis of two separate arguments. First, it contended that the relevant human rights treaties did not apply extraterritorially. Second, it claimed that even if they did, they were displaced by IHL, which applied as *lex specialis* to the putative global armed conflict between the US and Al Qaeda.[19] Even if IHRL did apply formally, it granted no more protection than IHL. Because the detainees were 'unlawful combatants', they enjoyed no protection under IHL; because the absence of a rule, ie an unrestrained freedom for the state to act, is also a rule, IHRL brought nothing to the table, and the Guantánamo detainees had no rights under international law. Now, admittedly, this argument of the departed administration was a succession of non

---

[15] See also Krieger, 'A Conflict of Norms: The Relationship between Humanitarian Law and Human Rights Law in the ICRC Customary Law Study', 11 *JC & SL* (2006) 265, at 269.
[16] *Case Concerning Armed Activities on the Territory of the Congo (DRC v Uganda)*, Judgment of 19 December 2005, para 216.
[17] Human Rights Committee, General Comment No 31, CCPR/C/21/Rev.1/Add.13 (26 May 2004) para 11.   [18] See Krieger, *supra* note 15, at 271.
[19] See Hampson, 'The Relationship between International Humanitarian Law and Human Rights Law from the Perspective of a Treaty Body', 90 *International Review of the Red Cross* (2008) 549, at 550 *et seq*.

sequiturs, but it was nonetheless made using the same language in which the gentler souls among us argue for a complementary relationship between IHL and IHRL, *lex specialis* and all.[20]

We are past that stage where there is much use in general inquiries as to the relationship between IHL and IHRL as regimes. Moreover, those who continue to oppose the joint application of IHL and IHRL will not be persuaded to the contrary no matter what generalities we or the ICJ might produce. If this is so, then why bother? It is enough to say that the complementary nature of the relationship between IHL and IHRL is confirmed by numerous pronouncements by states and international political bodies,[21] by international courts and tribunals,[22] by the text of derogation clauses of human rights treaties and, above all else, by the object and purpose of the treaties.[23] If human rights accrue to human beings solely by virtue of their humanity, why should these rights then evaporate merely because two states, or a state and a non-state actor, have engaged in an armed conflict? More limited these rights might be, but they cannot be completely extinguished or displaced if their basic universality premise, that they are immanent in the human dignity of every individual, is accepted.[24] And though it is of course quite possible for this premise to be contested on ideological grounds, in *legal* terms that premise is hard-coded into the relevant international human rights instruments. In other words, it is the *law* that human rights are universal and that they accrue to every human being, war or no war. Nothing more needs to be said, and indeed nothing more *can* be said on the matter.

It is to specific practical problems and their solutions that we must turn. Before doing that, however, we must take stock of the tools that are at our disposal to avoid or resolve norm conflicts.

3. Norm Conflict Avoidance and Norm Conflict Resolution

A. Defining norm conflict

To provide a norm conflict perspective on the relationship between IHL and IHRL (an expression that I will continue to use merely as convenient shorthand, with all of the caveats stated above), I must first give both a definition of norm

---

[20] See, more generally, Alston, Morgan-Foster, and Abresch, 'The Competence of the UN Human Rights Council and its Special Procedures in relation to Armed Conflicts: Extraterritorial Executions in the "War on Terror"', 19 *EJIL* (2008) 183.

[21] See eg Tehran Conference, General Resolution XXIII, 'Respect for Human Rights in Armed Conflicts', UN Doc A/Conf.32/41 (13 May 1968); UNGA Res 2444 (1968); UNGA Res 2647 (1970); UNSC Res 237 (1967), UNSC Res 1649 (2005), UNSC Res 1882 (2009).

[22] See eg *Nuclear Weapons, supra* note 12; *Wall, supra* note 14; *Serrano-Cruz Sisters v El Salvador* (Preliminary Objections), 23 November 2004, Inter-Am Ct HR Series C, No 118, para 112.

[23] See also McGoldrick, 'Human Rights and Humanitarian Law in the UK Courts', 40 *Is. L.R.* (2007) 527, at 531.

[24] See also Ben-Naftali and Shany, *supra* note 7, at 41–42; Verdirame, *supra* note 2, at 691–692.

conflict and some other conceptual clarifications.[25] The notion of conflict will be defined broadly: a relationship of conflict exists between two norms if one norm constitutes, has led to, or may lead to, a breach of the other.[26] With regard to IHL and IHRL norms specifically, the notion of conflict could be defined even more broadly—a norm conflict would exist whenever the application of the two norms leads to two opposite results, for example if IHL provided that a particular use of force was lawful, while IHRL made it unlawful.

A further distinction must be made between apparent and genuine norm conflicts, and consequently between conflict avoidance on the one hand, and conflict resolution on the other. An apparent conflict is one where the content of the two norms is at first glance contradictory, yet the conflict can be avoided, most often by interpretative means. In instances in which all techniques of conflict avoidance fail, a genuine, as opposed to an apparent, conflict will emerge.[27] These true norm conflicts are those that cannot be avoided, but which it might be possible to resolve. Unlike avoidance, which interprets away any incompatibility, norm conflict resolution requires one conflicting norm to prevail or have priority over the other. Moreover, for a genuine conflict to be truly resolved in a case of conflicting obligations it is necessary for the wrongfulness on the part of the state for failing to abide by the displaced norm to be precluded as a matter of state responsibility. It is only if the state bears no legal cost for disregarding one of its commitments in favour of another that a norm conflict has truly been resolved.[28]

An examination of a norm conflict situation will usually proceed in two steps. The first is an inquiry into whether it is possible to avoid a norm conflict by interpreting the two potentially conflicting norms so as to make them compatible. Second, if avoidance is impossible, the conflict might be resolved by assigning priority to one norm over the other. However, as I will show, a third outcome is also possible, and is in fact far from unlikely—that a norm conflict will not only be unavoidable, but also unresolvable. In such situations, which are a consequence of the diffuse and decentralized nature of the international legal system, there can only be a political solution to the conflict between two equal norms.[29] Regrettably, despite our best efforts, a number of the potentially conflicting norms of IHL and IHRL might end up in this third category.

But before venturing into this third category, I will examine the utility of the various tools of norm conflict resolution and avoidance. I will start with methods of norm conflict resolution, even if only to show how impracticable they are in addressing IHL and IHRL norm conflicts.

---

[25] In doing so I will refer the readers to my more exhaustive treatment of the subject in Milanovic, 'Norm Conflict in International Law: Whither Human Rights?', 20 *Duke J. Comp. & Int'l L.* (2009) 69, available at SSRN at <http://ssrn.com/abstract=1372423>, and the authorities cited therein.

[26] Pauwelyn, *Conflict of Norms in Public International Law* (2003) 176.

[27] See Pauwelyn, *supra* note 26, at 272.

[28] See more generally Milanovic, *supra* note 25, at 6 *et seq.*

[29] See also Pauwelyn, *supra* note 26, at 418 *et seq.*

B. Methods of norm conflict resolution

Purely practically speaking, international law is not, and it might never be, a legal system in which a hierarchy based on the sources of norms plays an important role. Although, for example, a treaty will usually prevail over a customary rule, this is so only because the customary rule is *jus dispositivum*, and applies only so long as states do not agree otherwise[30]—and the same goes for treaties. Of course, IHL and IHRL norms that can be in a state of apparent conflict can emanate from both custom and treaties, the custom usually being derived in large part from the treaties to which many but not all states concerned may be parties. There are four principal ways of resolving norm conflict, which, as stated above, requires the assigning of priority to one norm over another: (1) *jus cogens*; (2) Article 103 of the UN Charter; (3) conflict clauses in treaties; and (4) *lex posterior*.

There is probably no concept that has attracted so much scholarly attention, yet so little practical application, as *jus cogens*. And by little, I mean zero. There has not been, to my knowledge, a single case where *jus cogens* was unambiguously the basis for a court ruling that a conflicting rule of international law was null and void.[31] There are several reasons why this is so. First, as a general point, rigid hierarchy does not sit well with the overarching structure of international law, which is still largely the product of consensual law-making between states. Secondly, despite what some of its more fervent adherents might claim, the number of rules that undisputedly belong to the category of *jus cogens* (for instance, the prohibition of torture, genocide, or slavery) is quite limited.[32] Thirdly, states are not nearly so foolish as to conclude treaties or engage in some other sort of international law-making that is openly contrary to *jus cogens* norms.

Finally, *jus cogens* is a blunt instrument, which allows for no balancing of conflicting interests, but mandates a single result on the basis of hierarchy. In cases lacking similar political and moral certainty—and that would be almost all of them—the use of such an instrument would pose an understandably unappealing prospect for most judges. It should likewise be noted in that regard that Article 53 of the Vienna Convention on the Law of Treaties (VCLT), which solidified the status of *jus cogens* as positive law, provides not that a particular *norm* that conflicts with a rule of *jus cogens* is void, but that the *treaty* which so conflicts, all of it, would be void.[33] Now, assuming the general validity of Article 53 VCLT, imagine if we were to say that an IHRL rule prevails over an IHL rule contained in one or more of the Geneva Conventions because it has the

---

[30] See International Law Commission, 'Fragmentation of International Law: Difficulties Arising from the Diversification and Expansion of International Law', UN Doc A/CN.4/L.682 (13 April 2006), hereinafter 'ILC Study', para 79 *et seq*. See also Verdross, '*Jus Dispositivum* and *Jus Cogens* in International Law', 60 *AJIL* (1966) 55, at 58.

[31] This of course does not stop judges from injecting liberal references to *jus cogens*, peremptory or intransgressible norms or whatnot in a number of judgments. I am not saying that this is a bad thing—far from it, symbolically at least—but that does not mean that *jus cogens* as a concept has an actual, practical role in the result of the case.

[32] See Higgins, 'A Babel of Judicial Voices? Ruminations from the Bench', 55 *ICLQ* (2006) 791, at 801.   [33] See also Art 64 VCLT.

status of *jus cogens*—this would mean the voidness of the Geneva Conventions, not just of that particular rule.

Aside from *jus cogens*, there is one other quasi-hierarchical rule of norm conflict resolution that does have practical relevance—Article 103 of the UN Charter. It provides that:

[i]n the event of a conflict between the obligations of the Members of the United Nations under the present Charter and their obligations under any other international agreement, their obligations under the present Charter shall prevail.

Most importantly, this priority rule extends to state obligations under binding resolutions of the UN Security Council.[34] Depending on the situation, the Council can thus inject rules of its own making into the IHL/IHRL calculus, rules that arguably have priority over all others save for *jus cogens*. A good example would be the *Al-Jedda* case before English courts,[35] where a dual Iraqi/British national was held in security detention by British forces in Iraq. He was so held not under any authority of the UK as an occupying power, both because he was a British national and because the occupation had arguably already been terminated at the time. Rather, he was held on the basis of an authorization of preventive detention by the Security Council in its Resolution 1546 (2004), with the House of Lords deciding that this authorization prevailed over Article 5 ECHR, which does not allow for detention on preventive grounds, by virtue of Article 103 of the Charter.[36]

As for conflict clauses, they are used in treaty practice to explicitly give priority to one treaty over another,[37] though not nearly often enough.[38] Obviously, no such clauses exist in the relevant IHL and IHRL treaties. The closest we come to them are the derogation clauses in human rights treaties, which allow for the temporary suspension of certain rights during an emergency to the extent strictly required by the exigencies of the situation.[39] By limiting the content of applicable human rights law, as it were, derogations can potentially resolve many conflicts with IHL. However, as a practical matter, such derogations are rarely used, particularly in an extraterritorial context, since their use by a state would be interpreted as a concession that the IHRL treaty in question in principle applies extraterritorially to a given situation, and would thus open up the state's actions to judicial scrutiny, even if a curtailed one.[40] Consequently, for example, the UK has not derogated from

---

[34] See *Questions of Interpretation and Application of the 1971 Montreal Convention arising from the Aerial Incident at Lockerbie*, Provisional Measures, Order of 14 April 1992, ICJ Reports (1992) 114, at 126, para. 42.

[35] *R (Al-Jedda) v Secretary of State for Defence* [2007] UKHL 58, [2008] 1 AC 332, [2008] 2 WLR 31, 12 December 2007 (hereinafter *Al-Jedda*).

[36] See *Al-Jedda* (per Lord Bingham) para 39. See also *Al-Jedda* (per Baroness Hale) paras 126 and 129, and *Al-Jedda* (per Lord Carswell) para 136.

[37] Indeed, Art 103 of the Charter is in effect a special, proto-constitutional type of prospective conflict clause.

[38] See eg Arts 237(1) and 311 of the UN Convention on the Law of the Sea. On conflict clauses in treaties, see generally Borgen, 'Resolving Treaty Conflicts', 37 *Geo Wash Int'l L Rev* (2005) 573, 584–587; ILC Study, paras 267–271.   [39] See *supra* note 4.

[40] See also McGoldrick, *supra* note 23, at 555–556.

either the ECHR or the ICCPR in respect of the conflicts in Iraq and Afghanistan, thereby creating, rather than resolving, a host of difficult problems.[41]

Finally, there is that equally magical sibling of *lex specialis* (on which more in a moment), *lex posterior*. In domestic legal systems, which are after all a model for us as to how *any* legal system is supposed to work, if the legislature passes a statute which contradicts a prior statute, the latter in time will prevail, even if it does not contain a clause saying so explicitly. We justify this rule basically by inferring the relevant intent on the part of the single, uniform legislature, operating within a unified hierarchical system, which is not supposed to issue contradictory commands to citizens. However, whatever its validity in domestic law, this assumption manifestly does not hold true in the international system.[42] This is why (what goes for) the international *lex posterior* rule[43] can hardly ever apply to conflicting multilateral law-making treaties, even assuming that they could be deemed to relate to the same subject matter, which is a prerequisite for the rule's application. When it comes to the IHL and IHRL treaties in particular, not only is there the obvious problem that the law-making in the two areas temporally occurred in several waves, so that it is somewhat absurd to treat these treaties as successive to each other in a *lex posterior* sense, but there is also not the slightest hint of state intent that the relationship between the two bodies of law should be governed by this rule.

In conclusion, the only two rules of norm conflict resolution that are of practical relevance for the relationship between IHL and IHRL are Article 103 of the Charter and the derogation clauses of human rights treaties. As is also the case more generally, it is the methods of norm conflict avoidance which are far more useful in practical terms.

C. Methods of norm conflict avoidance

Every legal system, but particularly the international one, can simultaneously tend towards fragmentation, because it tries to accommodate a number of widely diverging values and interests, and towards harmonization, because without a measure of unity a legal system would soon stop being one and thus divide into several particular regimes. The latter tendency is especially evident in case law, as judges are generally more or less keen on preserving the integrity of the system to which they perceive themselves as belonging. Avoidance of norm conflict hence usually is (and should be) the first recourse.[44] When two norms can be interpreted harmoniously, they generally are—we in fact do norm conflict avoidance all the time.

---

[41] Some doubts have been expressed as to whether derogations would be available in an extraterritorial context where the 'life of the nation' using the derogation is not itself threatened, for instance by Lord Bingham in *Al-Jedda*. I consider that they would be, but I will not further examine that point here.

[42] 'There is no single legislative will behind international law. Treaties and custom come about as a result of conflicting motives and objectives—they are "bargains" and "package-deals" and often result from spontaneous reactions to events in the environment.' ILC Study, para 34.

[43] See Arts 30 and 59 VCLT.

[44] To give two domestic law examples, consider the constitutional avoidance canon in US constitutional law, whereby a statute will be interpreted so far as possible to not pose a constitutional

For the purposes of this chapter, I propose to (entirely informally) trace the various forms of avoidance on a broad spectrum, ranging from 'consistent' at one end to 'forced' at the other, with 'creative' being somewhere in the middle. Let me explain each more fully.

Consistent avoidance happens when the language, object and purpose, and other structural elements of the two potentially or apparently conflicting norms can be reasonably reconciled without much effort. An example has been given by the ICJ in *Nuclear Weapons*—Article 6 ICCPR prohibits 'arbitrary' deprivations of life, while IHL can tell us what 'arbitrary' means in times of armed conflict. Such a method of interpretation is warranted, *inter alia*, by the principle of systemic integration set out in Article 31(3)(c) VCLT, which requires that other applicable rules of international law be taken into account when interpreting a treaty.

In many cases, the 'fit' between the two norms will be far from perfect. This will usually, but not always, require one of the norms to be 'read down' from what its ordinary meaning would initially suggest, or from how it is ordinarily applied, so as to accommodate the other. For example, I would argue that Security Council Resolutions that purport to limit certain human rights have to do so in clear and unambiguous terms.[45] But it is not always other norms of international law that need to be read down to accommodate the growing demands of human rights. In *Al-Adsani*,[46] for instance, the European Court held by nine votes to eight that Article 6 ECHR should be read consistently with international rules on state immunity, even in cases of alleged torture.[47] I would again emphasize the point that there is a price to be paid if the IHL/IHRL project is to work. A large part of human rights law as interpreted in peacetime will have to be read down, to a greater or lesser extent, in order to be effectively applied in wartime and so be realistic rather than utopian. To again take arbitrary deprivations of life as an example, we cannot reasonably judge in the same way situations in which the state has a peacetime monopoly on the use of force and must plan police operations so as to absolutely minimize any possible loss of life and combat situations where a state is embroiled in internal or international armed conflict.

This brings me to *creative avoidance*, which, to put it bluntly, involves a court simply making things up. Such creativity can be employed for good ends or bad, in ways which are legally and logically acceptable or not. One example is the *Bosphorus* line of cases before the European Court, in which the Court held that the transfer by states of competencies to international organizations that would be immune from judicial process both internally and before the

---

question or conflict, thus potentially leading to its unconstitutionality—see eg *INS v St Cyr*, 533 US 289, 299–300 (2001); *Crowell v Benson*, 285 US 22, 62 (1932); or section 3(1) of the UK Human Rights Act 1998, mandating that '[s]o far as it is possible to do so, primary legislation and subordinate legislation must be read and given effect in a way which is compatible with [ECHR] rights'.

[45] See Milanovic, *supra* note 25, at 37 *et seq.*

[46] *Al-Adsani v United Kingdom*, ECtHR, App No 35763/97, 21 November 2001.

[47] See also *Jones v Ministry of Interior Al-Mamlaka Al-Arabiya AS Saudiya (the Kingdom of* Saudi Arabia*)* [2006] UKHL 26, [2006] 2 WLR 1424.

Court itself would not be a violation of the ECHR so long as the organization in question provided an equivalent level of protection of human rights.[48] This was, in effect, a reading down of the ECHR for the sake of enhanced international cooperation through various international organizations, above all the EU. Opinions can differ on whether the Court's approach was justified (I think it was), but indisputably it was entirely made up, as the equivalent protection doctrine flowed neither from any provision of the ECHR nor from any general principle of international law.[49]

Another, much less palatable, example would be the *Behrami* case.[50] There the European Court simply invented an attribution rule whereby acts of peacekeepers on UN Security Council-authorized missions were attributable solely to the UN even if particular states, rather than the UN, had operational command and control. The Court did so, contrary to practically unanimous authority, at least partly in order to avoid an apparent norm conflict between Resolution 1244 (1999), whose vague provisions the states concerned interpreted as authorizing preventive detention without judicial review, and Article 5 ECHR, with Article 103 of the Charter and the approach of English courts in *Al-Jedda* looming in the background.[51] In that regard, perhaps the ultimate form of creative avoidance was employed by the European Court of Justice in *Kadi*, where it asserted that the EU legal system was independent of international law, and that UN Security Council Resolutions on terrorist sanctions are unable to penetrate this independent system and could thus not prevail over EU fundamental rights guarantees by virtue of Article 103 of the Charter.[52]

Finally, there is what I term *forced avoidance*, ie situations where a court is faced with a result that it deems undesirable (for example, a conflict with a *jus cogens* norm, or an unresolvable norm conflict), yet which it cannot avoid through normal means because the text of the relevant provisions simply cannot allow it under any reasonable interpretation. A court then might resort not just to innovation, but to a wholesale rewriting of a particular provision or rule. By and large, such methods are illegitimate, or at the very least improper.[53] To paraphrase Lord Bingham's view of such practices in the context of the Human Rights Act 1998, they do not constitute 'judicial interpretation, but judicial vandalism'.[54] Examples will follow.

---

[48] *M & Co v Federal Republic of Germany*, App No 13258/77, 64 ECommHR Dec & Rep 138 (1990); *Waite and Kennedy v Germany*, App No 26083/94, 30 ECtHR 261 (1999); *Beer and Regan v Germany*, App No 28934/95, ECtHR (1999); *Bosphorus Hava Yolları Turizm ve Ticaret Anonim Şirketi v Ireland*, App No 45036/98, 2005-VII ECtHR 109, 42 EHRR 1.

[49] See more generally, *supra* note 25, at 54 *et seq.*

[50] *Behrami and Behrami v France, Saramati v France, Germany and Norway*, App Nos 71412/01 and 78166/01, Grand Chamber, Decision, 2 May 2007.

[51] See more generally Milanovic and Papic, 'As Bad as it Gets: The European Court of Human Rights' *Behrami and Saramati* Decision and General International Law', 58 (2009) *ICLQ* 267.

[52] Joined Cases C-402/05 P and C-415/05 P, *Kadi & Al Barakaat International Foundation v Council and Commission*, Judgment of 3 September 2008.

[53] See Pauwelyn, *supra* note 26, at 244 *et seq.*

[54] *R (Anderson) v Secretary of State for the Home Department* [2002] UKHL 46, [2003] 1 AC 837, para 30.

D. Unresolvable norm conflicts

Though the international and domestic legal systems have in common both an inbuilt imperative for norm conflict avoidance and many techniques of conflict avoidance, there is a point where the similarities end. In domestic systems, all norm conflicts must eventually be either avoided or resolved, since all forms of legislation at whatever level of governance ultimately fit within a single normative hierarchy. In the international system the avenues of norm conflict resolution are, as we have seen, at best rudimentary. It therefore knows conflicts which are both unavoidable and unresolvable.[55] A more appropriate domestic analogy, if one is needed, would be with private, rather than with public law. Just as I can conclude two equally valid contracts whereby I commit to sell the same thing to two different people, and then have to face a choice as to which obligation to fulfil and which to breach and hence suffer the consequences, so a state can enter into two mutually contradictory, yet equally valid commitments from which the only escape is a political one. It can do so, moreover, not just bilaterally, but through multi-lateral law-making treaties.

Take, for example, the *Matthews* case before the European Court, dealing with the elections in Gibraltar for the European Parliament.[56] On the one hand, the ECHR, as interpreted and applied by the European Court, qualified the European Parliament as a legislature in respect of which states had to organize free elections. On the other, a treaty concluded between EU members prohibited the UK from extending the franchise for the European Parliament to Gibraltar. The Court thus found the UK responsible for violating the ECHR, irrespective of its other treaty obligations. This did not mean, however, that the treaty prohibiting the extension of the franchise to the inhabitants of Gibraltar was invalid, or that the ECHR prevailed over it in some hierarchical sense. Both treaties were formally of equal stature, and no norm conflict resolution was possible; the UK could not fulfil its obligations under either treaty without violating the other, thereby incurring state responsibility. Only a *political* solution was possible for this norm conflict, based on a political preference for the ECHR among the other EU member states, and an eventual extension of the franchise.[57]

Or take an even better known case, *Soering*.[58] There the European Court interpreted Article 3 ECHR as setting out a *non-refoulement* obligation, prohibiting the UK from transferring a person to the US if a real risk of that person being subjected to inhuman or degrading treatment in the US was established. At the other end was a perfectly valid extradition treaty between the UK and the US, which obliged the UK to extradite Soering, and which specified no exception to that obligation such as that devised by the European Court. There was, in other

---

[55] But see Droege, *supra* note 4, at 524, (arguing that in cases of genuine norm conflict, one of the norms must prevail). With respect, there is no 'must' here. That it is desirable to resolve conflicts is certainly true—but it is by no means possible in all circumstances.

[56] *Matthews v United Kingdom*, App No 24833/94, 28 ECtHR 361 (1999).

[57] For a fuller account of *Matthews*, see Milanovic, *supra* note 25.

[58] *Soering v United Kingdom*, 161 ECtHR (Ser A) (1989).

words, a norm conflict between the ECHR and the UK/US extradition treaty, and that was that. Now, one could argue, for instance, that the *non-refoulement* obligation invented by the Court in *Soering* had the status of *jus cogens*, and that it thus invalidated the conflicting extradition treaty—but this would be quite a stretch, to put it mildly.[59] Or, one could forcibly 'read in' an exception into the UK/US treaty, even though there was no such exception—but such a judicial rewriting of a treaty would in my view almost invariably be illegitimate. In reality what we had in *Soering* was an unresolvable norm conflict. The political solution to this conflict was that the US did not press the issue, and that it reached an accommodation with European states generally whereby it would provide assurances that a person whose extradition was being sought would not be tried for a capital offence.

I must emphasize at this point that the fact that the norm conflicts in *Matthews* and *Soering* were unresolvable does not mean that the two *cases* were unresolvable. In both cases the Court was asked the only question that it had the jurisdiction to answer—whether the ECHR was violated. In both cases it responded affirmatively. In both cases another treaty would have been violated had the state fulfilled its ECHR obligations, but in both cases this simply did not matter for answering the question that was put before the Court, as all avenues of norm conflict avoidance and resolution were exhausted. The only way that the Court could have avoided the norm conflict in *Soering*, for instance, was by ruling that there was no *non-refoulement* obligation arising under Article 3 ECHR, or by giving this obligation a rather pathetic content. And, of course, in its interpretation of the ECHR the Court made a variety of legal, policy, and value choices that rendered such a course undesirable, if not impossible. This shows that avoidance of norm conflict is not some sort of absolute priority, but is a value like any other, which will sometimes prevail, and sometimes not.

To bring this discussion of unresolvable norm conflicts a bit closer to home and the relationship between IHL and IHRL, I will now turn to *Al-Saadoon*, a case that ran its course through English courts at a most hectic pace,[60] and is at the time of writing pending before the European Court. The applicants in that case were individuals detained by UK troops in Iraq. They were initially held as security detainees on the basis of Resolution 1546. While they were detained on this basis, the Article 5 ECHR prohibition on preventive detention could be deemed to have been overridden by virtue of Article 103 of the Charter, per *Al-Jedda*.[61] But, at one point the legal basis for the applicants' detention changed. They were no longer held as security detainees, but were charged with specific crimes by the

---

[59] That the prohibition of torture is *jus cogens* does not automatically entail that the prohibition of other forms of ill-treatment is also *jus cogens*. Even if it is, this would not automatically entail that the derived *non-refoulement* obligation would also have such status. Likewise, that all of these norms are absolute—which they are—does not mean that they all necessarily must be *jus cogens*, since peremptory norms must be 'accepted and recognized [as such] by the international community of States as a whole' (Art 53 VCLT).

[60] *R (Al-Saadoon and Mufdhi) v Secretary of State for Defence* [2009] EWCA Civ 7, (hereinafter *Al-Saadoon CA*); *R (Al-Saadoon and Mufdhi) v Secretary of State for Defence* [2008] EWHC 3098 (hereinafter *Al-Saadoon HC*). [61] *Al-Jedda, supra* note 35.

Iraqi judiciary.[62] Their detention by British forces continued, but at this point with the consent and at the behest of the Iraqi government, in effect in a sort of pre-trial detention that is in principle permitted by Article 5(1)(c) ECHR.

As the expiry of their UN mandate and the withdrawal of UK forces from Iraq drew nearer, the Iraqi authorities requested the transfer of the applicants to Iraqi custody. The applicants challenged their impending transfer, first before the UK domestic courts and then before the European Court, arguing, *inter alia*, that there was a serious risk that they would be subjected to the death penalty by hanging if they were transferred to Iraqi custody, and that this triggered the UK's *non-refoulement* obligations under the ECHR.

To make this argument, the applicants of course first had to establish that the ECHR applied to them extraterritorially. In *Al-Skeini*[63] the UK government conceded that the ECHR applies to persons detained by UK forces in Iraq.[64] It thus had to come up with something new to deny the extraterritorial applicability of the ECHR in *Al-Saadoon*, and that it did. It argued that the applicants were held by UK forces at the order of an Iraqi court, and that the UK had a legal obligation to abide by the ruling of that court and transfer them to Iraqi authorities since UK forces were present in Iraq with Iraq's consent. Because it had no independent legal authority to detain the *Al-Saadoon* applicants, so argued the government, they were not within the UK's jurisdiction within the meaning of Article 1 ECHR.

In its decision, the Divisional Court did not accept this argument, ruling that the applicants were indeed within the UK's jurisdiction.[65] It held, however, that the ECHR *non-refoulement* principle had to be qualified (pursuant to a Court of Appeal precedent[66] that the Divisional Court thought was wrongly decided, but had to follow anyway), because the UK had a legal obligation to transfer the

---

[62] *Al-Saadoon HC, supra* note 60, at paras 24–31.

[63] *R (Al-Skeini and Others) v Secretary of State for Defence* [2007] UKHL 26, [2007] 3 WLR 33, [2007] 3 All ER 685, (hereinafter *Al-Skeini HL*); *R (Al-Skeini and Others) v Secretary of State for Defence* [2005] EWCA Civ 1609, [2007] QB 140, (hereinafter *Al-Skeini CA*).

[64] For commentary on the UK courts' reasoning regarding the extraterritorial applicability issues in *Al-Skeini*, see R Wilde's note in 102 *AJIL* (2008) 628, as well as Thienel, 'The ECHR in Iraq. The Judgment of the House of Lords in *R (Al-Skeini) v Secretary of State for Defence*', 6 *JICJ* (2008) 115.

[65] *Al-Saadoon HC, supra* note 60, at paras 82.

[66] *R (B) v Secretary of State for Foreign and Commonwealth Affairs* [2004] EWCA Civ 1344, [2005] QB 643, hereinafter *B*, was essentially *Soering* in an extraterritorial setting. The applicants were asylum-seekers in Australia, who were allegedly held in a detention centre in appalling conditions. They escaped and sought refuge in a British consulate, claiming that under Art 3 ECHR the UK could not release them to Australian authorities as they would be subjected to inhuman or degrading treatment. The Court of Appeal held that because the applicants were present on Australian sovereign territory, and the UK had an international legal obligation to surrender them to Australia, the UK's Art 3 *non-refoulement* obligation had to be qualified from what it would normally be under *Soering* (*B*, para 84):

> In a case such as *Soering* the Contracting State commits no breach of international law by permitting an individual to remain within its territorial jurisdiction rather than removing him to another State. The same is not necessarily true where a State permits an individual to remain within the shelter of consular premises rather than requiring him to leave. It does not seem to us that the Convention can require States to give refuge to fugitives within consular premises if to do so would violate international law. So to hold would be in fundamental conflict with the importance that the Grand Chamber attached in *Bankovic* to principles of international law. Furthermore, there must be an implication

applicant to Iraq.[67] On appeal, the Court of Appeal agreed entirely with the government's argument, finding that the ECHR did not apply because the UK had no independent legal authority to detain the applicants.[68] The applicants promptly moved to the European Court, and obtained a provisional measures order prohibiting their transfer to Iraqi authorities. And, for the first time in many years, the UK government decided to disobey such an order by the European Court, and transferred the applicants to Iraqi custody.[69]

Let us now examine *Al-Saadoon* from a norm conflict perspective. Accepting the UK's argument, it had an obligation to transfer the applicants to Iraq.[70]

> that obligations under a Convention are to be interpreted, insofar as possible, in a manner that accords with international law.

Therefore (*B*, paras 88–89):

> We have concluded that, if the *Soering* approach is to be applied to diplomatic asylum, the duty to provide refuge can only arise under the Convention where this is compatible with public international law. Where a fugitive is facing the risk of death or injury as the result of lawless disorder, no breach of international law will be occasioned by affording him refuge. Where, however, the receiving State requests that the fugitive be handed over the situation is very different. The basic principle is that the authorities of the receiving State can require surrender of a fugitive in respect of whom they wish to exercise the authority that arises from their territorial jurisdiction; see Art 55 of the 1963 Vienna Convention. Where such a request is made the Convention cannot normally require the diplomatic authorities of the sending State to permit the fugitive to remain within the diplomatic premises in defiance of the receiving State. Should it be clear, however, that the receiving State intends to subject the fugitive to treatment so harsh as to constitute a crime against humanity, international law must surely permit the officials of the sending state to do all that is reasonably possible, including allowing the fugitive to take refuge in the diplomatic premises, in order to protect him against such treatment. In such circumstances the Convention may well impose a duty on a Contracting State to afford diplomatic asylum.
>
> It may be that there is a lesser level of threatened harm that will justify the assertion of an entitlement under international law to grant diplomatic asylum. This is an area where the law is ill-defined. So far as Australian law was concerned, the applicants had escaped from lawful detention under the provisions of the Migration Act 1958. On the face of it international law entitled the Australian authorities to demand their return. We do not consider that the United Kingdom officials could be required by the Convention and the Human Rights Act to decline to hand over the applicants unless this was clearly necessary in order to protect them from the immediate likelihood of experiencing serious injury.

The Court of Appeal in *B* was faced with an apparent norm conflict, and decided to forcibly avoid it by reading down the *non-refoulement* obligation under Art 3 ECHR. The problem with its reasoning is of course that there was in fact a norm conflict in *Soering* between the ECHR and a valid extradition treaty, yet this was not enough for the European Court to read down the ECHR, thus leading to an unresolvable norm conflict. Not to mention that the Court of Appeal's actual reading down is as absurd as it is forced, since crimes against humanity can never be committed against individuals in isolation, but only in the context of a widespread or systematic attack on a civilian population—see, eg Art 7 of the Rome Statute of the International Criminal Court. This condition would hardly be satisfied even in places like Iraq or Iran, let alone in Australia.

[67] *Al-Saadoon HC, supra* note 60, at paras 89–96.

[68] *Al-Saadoon CA, supra* note 60, at paras 32–40.

[69] See Thienel, 'Cooperation in Iraq and the ECHR: An Awful Epilogue', *Invisible College* blog, 21 January 2009, available at <http://invisiblecollege.weblog.leidenuniv.nl/2009/01/21/cooperation-in-iraq-and-the-echr-an-awfu> [last accessed 12 April 2010]

[70] This obligation would derive from the customary obligation of all states not to interfere with the sovereignty and jurisdiction of other states—see, *mutatis mutandis, Asylum (Colombia v Peru),* ICJ Reports (1950) 275.

Accepting the applicants' argument, the UK had an ECHR obligation not to do so. In other words, there was a genuine norm conflict *à la Soering* at hand, and no consistent form of avoidance was available, nor could this norm conflict be resolved on the basis of some hierarchical rule. The Court of Appeal in particular thus had to resort to more imaginative forms of avoidance, ranging somewhere between the 'creative' and the 'forced' on my tentative scale. It first held that the ECHR simply did not apply extraterritorially, thus nipping the norm conflict in the bud, because the UK held the applicants solely on the basis of Iraqi legal authority and because it had an obligation to transfer them to Iraq. It then held, relying on its earlier precedent in *B*,[71] that even if the ECHR did apply, and if there in principle was an applicable *non-refoulement* obligation, that obligation had to be qualified, because the applicants were held on Iraqi soil and on Iraqi legal authority.[72]

The first of the Court's methods of avoidance is entirely unconvincing—there is no principled reason why the applicability of the ECHR should depend on the existence of other international obligations.[73] The UK undoubtedly had an obligation to extradite in *Soering*, but that had no bearing on the applicability of the ECHR. The Court's second method of avoidance is somewhat more credible. It is possible to argue that *Soering* is distinguishable in that the applicant in that case was held on UK territory, while the applicants in *Al-Saadoon* were held on Iraqi territory, and that respect for Iraqi sovereignty therefore warrants a more attenuated application of the ECHR. Such an approach remains questionable, however, because of the values that the *non-refoulement* rule is meant to protect—the prohibition of all kinds of ill-treatment.

It of course remains to be seen how the European Court will view the whole matter. The most recent item in this unfolding drama indeed came from the European Court. In its admissibility decision in *Al-Saadoon* it quite correctly decided that the Court of Appeal's first method of norm conflict avoidance was inappropriate, and that the ECHR applied extraterritorially to the applicants. However it reserved its judgment on the second method of avoidance for the merits of the case.[74]

If this second method of avoidance fails to convince, as I think it does, it is clear that in *Al-Saadoon* the UK brought itself into a situation of unresolvable norm conflict.[75] That conflict only had a political solution: the UK could have flatly refused to surrender the applicants to Iraq; it could have tried to negotiate with Iraq and obtain guarantees that the applicants would not be subjected to the death penalty—though Iraq could of course have refused to negotiate; or, it could have disobeyed its ECHR obligations and surrendered the applicants to Iraq. The UK, as we know, chose the third option.[76] The fact that most of us, however, might think

---

[71] *B, supra* note 66.   [72] *Al-Saadoon CA, supra* note 60, paras 41–51.

[73] I have argued at length elsewhere why the concept of Art 1 jurisdiction is not predicated on legal authority, but on factual authority and control over territory and (possibly) individuals—see Milanovic, *supra* note 7.

[74] *Al-Saadoon and Mufdhi v United Kingdom* (dec), App No 61498/08, 30 June 2009.

[75] See also Cross and Williams, 'Between the Devil and the Deep Blue Sea: Conflicted Thinking in the *Al-Saadoon* Affair', 58 *ICLQ* (2009) 689.

[76] The norm conflict has been openly acknowledged by the UK government—see Letter dated 26 January 2008 from the Minister of State for the Armed Forced to the Chairman of the Joint

that it should have gone for the second or first options, however, does not mean that this choice was *legally* warranted. The choice was an entirely political one—but it is one for which the UK has almost certainly incurred state responsibility for violating the ECHR, both in regard to the substance of the *non-refoulement* claim and in regard to the European Court's interim measures order.

4. Is *lex specialis* a Rule of Conflict Avoidance or of Conflict Resolution?

Having examined the tools that we have at our disposal for avoiding or resolving norm conflicts, I will now turn to discovering the proper place of *lex specialis* in the toolbox. That is to say, despite all that has been written on *lex specialis* and the relationship between IHL and IHRL, the meaning of the maxim remains entirely unclear. In the framework that I have set out above, we are still unsure whether *lex specialis* is a rule of norm conflict avoidance or a rule of norm conflict resolution, and this has extraordinary consequences for the practical utility of this rule. In my view, *lex specialis* can only be a tool of conflict avoidance, and not a particularly impressive one at that, as I will now try to explain.

That *lex specialis* can mean two essentially different things has long been recognized,[77] but the importance of this distinction has sometimes been downplayed or overlooked.[78] To see how the distinction between avoidance and resolution remains fundamental, we need only look at a familiar IHL/IHRL example—the lawfulness of preventive detention.

IHL either authorizes or considers as lawful at least two forms of preventive detention during international armed conflicts.[79] First, under Article 21 of the Geneva Convention III (*GC III*), prisoners of war may be subjected to internment, ie they may be detained on purely preventive grounds, so that they do not rejoin the hostilities. IHL does not require that the detaining power prove it is *necessary* to detain POWs—it simply presumes that this is the case, and POWs may be detained until the cessation of active hostilities. Second, under Articles 41–43 and 78 of Geneva Convention IV (*GC IV*), civilians, like combatants, can also be

Committee for Human Rights, available at <http://www.parliament.uk/documents/upload/Ainsworth_Saadoon260109.pdf>. Relying on the Court of Appeal's ruling that the applicants were not within the UK's jurisdiction, and having regard of the expiry of the UK forces' mandate on 31 December 2008, the letter states, *inter alia*, that the government was 'faced with the option of breaching the Rule 39 measure or acting unlawfully in international law.' Of course, the former was no less a violation of international law, particularly in the light of the European Court's decision that the applicants were at all times within the UK's jurisdiction.

[77] See eg Lindroos, 'Addressing Norm Conflicts in a Fragmented Legal System: The Doctrine of *Lex Specialis*', 74 *Nord. J. Int'l L.* (2005) 27, esp at 46; Prud'homme, '*Lex Specialis*: Oversimplifying a More Complex and Multifaceted Relationship?', 40 *Is. L.R.* (2007) 355, at 366 *et seq*; Droege, *supra* note 5, at 523–524; Krieger, *supra* note 15, at 268–270.; ILC Study, paras 56–57, and the authorities cited therein. [78] See ILC Study, *supra* note 77, paras 88–97.

[79] See generally J Pejic, 'Procedural Principles and Safeguards for Internment/Administrative Detention in Armed Conflict and Other Situations of Violence', 87 *International Review of the Red Cross* (2005) 375.

subjected to internment, 'if the security of the Detaining Power makes it absolutely necessary'. IHL therefore poses a stricter requirement for the internment of civilians than of combatants, as it requires a positive showing of necessity.

When it comes to IHRL, different instruments regulate detention in different ways. Article 9(1) ICCPR provides that:

[e]veryone has the right to liberty and security of person. No one shall be subjected to arbitrary arrest or detention. No one shall be deprived of his liberty except on such grounds and in accordance with such procedure as are established by law.

Unlike Article 9(1) ICCPR, which sets out a standard prohibiting *arbitrary* detention, Article 5(1) ECHR is much more specific:

Everyone has the right to liberty and security of person. No one shall be deprived of his liberty save in the following cases and in accordance with a procedure prescribed by law.

The list that elaborates on the 'save in the following cases' clause comprises six possible situations, none of which can be reasonably interpreted to allow for preventive security detention. Article 5 was quite deliberately drafted exhaustively, in order to prevent overly expansive interpretations intrusive on personal liberty of something like the ICCPR arbitrariness standard.

To briefly pose the problem: if somehow, unfathomably, France decided to declare war and invade the UK, would the detention of French POWs on UK soil constitute a violation of Article 5(1) ECHR, in the absence of a UK derogation? Less fancifully, but with the added problem of extraterritoriality, was the detention of thousands of persons by the UK as an occupying power in Iraq after the April 2003 invasion also a violation of Article 5(1), prior to the June 2004 Security Council authorization in Resolution 1546 that could prevail over the ECHR? Indeed, not only is this question not fanciful, but it is one of many that have been raised in *Al-Sweady*, a case currently pending before the English High Court.[80]

The answer to this question depends on what we think the nature of the *lex specialis* rule is. If it was just a rule of norm conflict avoidance, we could interpret the Article 9(1) ICCPR arbitrariness standard taking into account the rules of IHL, and we could say that preventive detention in times of international armed conflict in accordance with IHL was not arbitrary. (This, of course, is precisely what the ICJ did in *Nuclear Weapons* with regard to the same standard in relation to deprivation of the right to life.) But, if *lex specialis* was merely a method of avoidance, we would be powerless if the same issue was examined under Article 5(1) ECHR. That provision allows for no 'window' through which IHL could enter; no reasonable interpretation of its text that would reach a compatible result is possible. In the absence of a derogation, it is only if the European Court *forcibly* read Article 5 ECHR as if it set out an arbitrariness standard in the likes of Article 9 ICCPR that conflict avoidance would be possible. However, not only would such rewriting of

---

[80] See more at <http://www.publicinterestlawyers.co.uk/cases/cases.php?id=67> [last accessed 12 April 2010].

the treaty be judicial vandalism, not interpretation, as Lord Bingham so aptly put it, it would also have nothing to do with *lex specialis*.

If, on the other hand, *lex specalis* was not a rule of norm conflict avoidance, but of norm conflict resolution, then and only then could we say that IHL *prevails* over the ECHR in some quasi-hierarchical sense (presumably because states intended it to do so), and that it precludes the UK's responsibility for failing to abide by the express requirements of Article 5. But there is *simply no evidence* that *lex specialis* is in fact a rule of conflict resolution. No treaty says so. It has certainly never been used as such in an IHL/IHRL context, least of all by the ICJ, which only used to interpret general IHRL standards such as arbitrariness in light of IHL.[81] Neither the texts of the relevant treaties nor the official positions of states support an inference of a state intent to override the express language of human rights treaties by having regard to the nebulous *lex specialis* principle,[82] which is for that matter, unlike *lex posterior*, not even mentioned in the VCLT. If anything, the text of the human rights treaties makes it clear that states are supposed to use derogations to avoid conflicts with IHL.[83] Moreover, that states have so far not fully complied with their IHRL obligations in armed conflict hardly counts as an inference of such intent, as they do not fully comply with their IHL obligations either. Perhaps in *some* cases it might be possible to infer an intent by contracting parties to apply the more specific treaty *against the express terms* of a more general treaty, but this is most certainly not the case with IHL and IHRL.[84]

More fundamentally, *lex specialis* as a rule of conflict resolution rests on an unstated assumption—that for any given situation at any given point in time there is one, and there can *only* be one, expression of state consent or intent as to how that situation is to be regulated.[85] But that assumption is manifestly unfounded. As we have seen above, states, like people, are perfectly capable of assuming contradictory commitments. And just as *lex specialis* is unable to resolve conflicts such as those in *Matthews*, *Soering*, or *Al-Saadoon*, so it is unable to resolve conflicts between IHL and IHRL. In international law *lex specialis* is nothing more than a sub-species of harmonious interpretation, a method of norm conflict avoidance.[86] All it can do is assist in the interpretation of general terms and standards in either IHL or IHRL

---

[81] Perhaps the closest to doing so was the Inter-American Commission on Human Rights, which was overruled on that point by the Inter-American Court. See further McCarthy, 'Human Rights and the Laws of War under the American Convention on Human Rights', *EHRLR* (2008) 762, esp at 767 *et seq.*

[82] See also ILC Study, para 104, where the ILC considered that *lex specialis* in the context of the *Nuclear Weapons* case only affected the assessment of the Art 6 ICCPR arbitrariness standard. The ILC does not consider a scenario where no such malleable standard was available.

[83] See *Wall*, *supra* note 14.

[84] But see Krieger, *supra* note 15, at 272; Droege, *supra* note 5, at 524.

[85] See Pauwelyn, *supra* note 26, at 388.

[86] See Akehurst, 'The Hierarchy of the Sources of International Law', 47 *British Year Book of International Law* (1974–75) 273 stating that '*lex specialis* is nothing more than a rule of interpretation'; Pauwelyn, at 410. Confusingly, *lex specialis* is sometimes also invoked to describe the relationship between general (customary) international law and treaties, to the effect that treaties usually override custom. But, as stated above, this is only so because most customary (and treaty) rules apply so long as states do not agree otherwise. See further Lindroos, *supra* note 77, at 49 *et seq.* As we have seen in *Al-Saadoon*, however, a conflict between treaty and custom is nonetheless perfectly possible.

by reference to more specific norms from the other branch. It can hence help us determine whether particular deprivations of life or liberty during an armed conflict are arbitrary or not. It can also work both ways; for instance, the more detailed IHRL norms on fair trial and a developed human rights jurisprudence can help us interpret the more general Common Article 3 requirement for trials satisfying 'judicial guarantees which are recognized as indispensable by civilized peoples'.[87]

But it can do no more than that.[88] Above all it cannot create hierarchies where they do not exist. And precisely because the use of the term *lex specialis* to describe the relationship between IHRL and IHL creates a false impression of facility, its use should be avoided.[89] The joint application of two bodies of law indeed requires a great deal of avoidance and creativity, involving a host of different legal, policy, and value judgments. To some extent, these judgments will be governed by our impression of which norm is more 'special' in regard to the subject matter, parties, level of detail, etc.—but that is only one factor out of many. And it is because *lex specialis*, like other rules of norm conflict avoidance, must operate within the permissible bounds of interpretation, and may not stray into a disregard for perfectly clear, yet conflicting rules, that in a number of areas the relationship between IHL and IHRL may actually be that of unresolvable norm conflict. I will now turn to an examination of some of these.

5. Areas of Potentially Unresolvable Norm Conflict

A. Preventive detention and judicial review of detention

We have just examined one area of potentially unresolvable norm conflict—detention. Let us further compare three situations of detention, all actual situations occurring in Iraq, and each of them an actual ('Al-') court case, either pending or completed: *Al-Sweady*, *Al-Jedda*, and *Al-Saadoon*. In *Al-Jedda*, a genuine norm conflict between a Security Council authorization and Article 5(1) ECHR was resolved in the former's favour by Article 103 of the Charter. In *Al-Saadoon*, the Security Council-authorized security detention was transformed into a somewhat unorthodox form of pre-trial detention that is in principle compatible with Article 5(1) ECHR. In *Al-Sweady*, we have a pure conflict between IHL and IHRL. In regard to the ICCPR, that conflict can be avoided through the harmonious interpretation of the Article 9 ICCPR arbitrariness standard. In regard to Article 5 ECHR, in the absence of a derogation nothing can be done to either avoid or resolve the conflict, short of resorting to illegitimate, forceful means of avoidance.

---

[87] This is in effect what the US Supreme Court did in *Hamdan v Rumsfeld*, 548 US 557 (2006) note 66. See further Milanovic, 'Lessons for Human Rights and Humanitarian Law in the War on Terror: Comparing *Hamdan* and the Israeli *Targeted Killings* Case', 89 *International Review of the Red Cross* (2007) 373, 389 *et seq*. See also Krieger, *supra* note 15, at 274.

[88] See also Thienel, 'The Georgian Conflict, Racial Discrimination and the ICJ: The Order on Provisional Measures of 15 October 2008', 9 *HRL Rev.* (2009) 465, at 467–469.

[89] Similarly on the ineffectiveness and conceptual vagueness of *lex specialis*, see Prud'homme, *supra* note 77.

Does the UK's failure to derogate from Article 5 ECHR mean that all the persons it detained as an occupying power in Iraq before the passing of Resolution 1546, or as an occupying power in Afghanistan, were detained unlawfully, IHL notwithstanding? The answer to that question is regrettably a resounding yes as far as the ECHR is concerned. And this is entirely the UK's fault, since it made a conscious political choice not to use the method of avoidance provided for by the ECHR itself, preferring to deny that the ECHR applied at all. There is moreover nothing absurd about such a result, nor does it lead to some sort of *non liquet*. A court dealing with the matter can answer any of the questions asked of it. Was the detention authorized or at least permitted by IHL? Yes. Was it nonetheless contrary to the ECHR? Again, yes. That the law is in a state of antinomy is simply not the court's problem, after it has weighed up all the options at its disposal to either avoid or resolve that conflict.[90]

In addition to the grounds of detention, another possible area of unresolvable conflict is that of judicial review of the lawfulness of detention. Here the ICCPR and the ECHR are exactly the same: both of them demand such review, and allow for no exceptions from that rule. Thus, Article 5(4) ECHR provides that:

[e]veryone who is deprived of his liberty by arrest or detention shall be entitled to take proceedings by which the lawfulness of his detention shall be decided speedily by a court and his release ordered if the detention is not lawful.

While Article 9(4) ICCPR stipulates that:

[a]nyone who is deprived of his liberty by arrest or detention shall be entitled to take proceedings before a court, in order that that court may decide without delay on the lawfulness of his detention and order his release if the detention is not lawful.

When it comes to IHL, because with respect to POWs it requires no showing of necessity that they be detained, subsequent to a determination of their status under Article 5 of *GC III*, it also requires no judicial process of reviewing their detention. In respect of interned civilians, for whose preventive detention a necessity must be shown, Article 43(1) of *GC IV* does require periodic review 'by an appropriate court *or administrative board*'.

The IHRL norm that 'everyone' or 'anyone' must be able to challenge his detention before *a court*, period, cannot be reconciled, absent a derogation, with the IHL norms that the detention of POWs need not be reviewed at all, while the detention of civilians can be reviewed even by a mere administrative board. The only possible accommodation that IHRL can make for IHL in this respect is to read standards such as 'speedily' or 'without delay' more loosely in armed

---

[90] This is in fact precisely what happened in one of the interstate cases initiated by Cyprus against Turkey before the now defunct European Commission on Human Rights, in which a majority of the Commission held that the preventive detention of POWs by Turkey violated Art 5 ECHR in the absence of a derogation—see *Cyprus v Turkey*, App Nos 6780/74 and 6950/75, Report of the Commission, adopted on 10 July 1976. Françoise Hampson finds such a result to be absurd, apparently on policy grounds—see Hampson, *supra* note 19, at 565–566. Legally speaking, however, though it might be quite undesirable to have an unresolvable norm conflict, there is nothing absurd about it, particularly when Turkey could have used a derogation to avoid it.

conflict, but the core of the unambiguously expressed norm cannot just go away. Now, if one takes a more formal or narrow definition of norm conflict, then one could say that there is no conflict here between IHL and IHRL, as nothing prohibited the state from assuming a further set of IHRL obligations that are stricter than its IHL obligations.[91] Substantively, however, and above all *practically* speaking, we are faced with an unresolvable norm conflict, because one branch of the law regards a situation as perfectly lawful, while the other does not.

Moreover, not even a derogation might be able to completely avoid a conflict between IHRL and IHL in respect of detention. Recall that a state may take measures of derogation only 'to the extent strictly required by the exigencies of the situation, provided that such measures are not inconsistent with its other obligations under international law'.[92] Therefore, even if during an armed conflict a state party derogated from Article 5 ECHR or Article 9 ICCPR to allow for preventive detention without judicial review, in a manner completely consistent with IHL, this would not necessarily suffice to make that derogation stand; the measures taken still need to be 'strictly required', as a matter of some sort of objective external assessment.

For example, a derogation restating the blanket IHL position that combatants may *always* be preventively detained may be challenged, say, if the armed conflict is quite protracted and the burden of detention consequently grows greater, the security risk posed by the POWs is small, and less restrictive means for preventing their return to hostilities than internment are available. Or, in respect of the internment of civilians in occupied territory, a state which derogates from the ICCPR or the ECHR to allow for the review of their detention by mere administrative boards, but is in reality quite capable of creating independent courts that could do the reviewing, ultimately might not be able to rely on its derogation no matter what IHL might say.[93]

B. Necessity in targeting

The detention example of unresolvable norm conflict is far-reaching enough, but my next example, that of targeting, is no less important. In IHL, the traditional position has been that combatants may be targeted so long as they are not *hors de combat*,[94] and this position holds true with some temporal limitations even for civilians taking a direct part in hostilities.[95] In other words, one belligerent party does not need to prove any kind of necessity to kill combatants belonging to the other belligerent party in order to be able to do so law-

---

[91] See Cassimatis, *supra* note 11, at 633. [92] See Art 15 ECHR, Art 4 ICCPR.

[93] See Human Rights Committee, General Comment No 29, CCPR/C/21/Rev.1/Add.11, para 16, where the Committee asserts, perhaps too broadly, that states may never derogate from the requirement for judicial review of detention.

[94] See Dinstein, *The Conduct of Hostilities under the Law of International Armed Conflict* (2004) at 27–29 and 145; Lubell, 'Challenges in Applying Human Rights Law to Armed Conflict', 87 *International Review of the Red Cross* (2005) 737, at 745–746. [95] See Art 51(3) of *AP I*.

fully. 'Those who belong to armed forces or armed groups may be attacked at any time.'[96]

When it comes to IHRL, there are significant variations among the relevant treaties when it comes to conditions under which a state may deprive individuals of life. Article 6(1) ICCPR stipulates that '[n]o one shall be arbitrarily deprived of his life', while Article 4(2) thereof prohibits derogations from this prohibition under any circumstances. Article 2 ECHR prohibits any intentional deprivation of life, save 'when it results from the use of force which is no more than absolutely necessary: (a) in defence of any person from unlawful violence; (b) in order to effect a lawful arrest or to prevent the escape of a person lawfully detained; (c) in action lawfully taken for the purpose of quelling a riot or insurrection'. On the other hand, Article 15(2) does allow derogations from the right to life (only) 'in respect of deaths resulting from lawful acts of war', thus opening a window for IHL.

The ICCPR and the ECHR again pose somewhat different interpretative problems. The arbitrariness standard of the ICCPR allows for an easier reconciling with IHL, as the ICJ did in *Nuclear Weapons*. As for the ECHR, Article 2(2)(c) would govern situations of internal armed conflict, yet any deprivation of life would still have to be 'absolutely necessary', while Article 15(2) would apply to situations of international armed conflict.[97] But again, even with Article 15(2) in the picture, the derogation still needs to be 'strictly required by the exigencies of the situation' under Article 15(1).

This brings me to the potentially unresolvable norm conflict with IHL. Both the ICCPR and the ECHR can easily be interpreted as requiring a showing of necessity before *any* intentional deprivation of life,[98] while, as we have seen, IHL purposefully does not require such a showing in respect of combatants or civilians taking a direct part in hostilities.[99] The IHRL necessity standard may be relaxed somewhat to take into account the fact of armed conflict, but it is hard to see how it can be totally extinguished, as IHL warrants, as soon as an armed conflict takes place and solely on the basis of the person's status.

To see this norm conflict at work we need only take a look at the *Targeted Killings* judgment of the Supreme Court of Israel.[100] The Court's prime desire in that case was to give a level of clear guidance to the Israeli armed forces and secret services as to the conditions under which they can target a suspected terrorist.[101] One of the

---

[96] Sandoz *et al*, Commentary on the Additional Protocols of 8 June 1977 to the Geneva Conventions of 12 August 1949 (1987) 1453.

[97] It is worth noting that no ECHR state party has ever made a derogation under Art 15(2). For a similar analysis of this example, see Hampson, *supra* note 19, at 564–565.

[98] See eg *McCann and Others v United Kingdom*, ECtHR, App No 18984/91, Judgment of 27 September 1995, paras 149–150.

[99] See also McCarthy, *supra* note 81, at 773 *et seq*; Krieger, *supra* note 15, at 280–281.

[100] The Public Committee against Torture in *Israel et al v The Government of Israel et al*, Supreme Court of Israel sitting as the High Court of Justice, Judgment, 11 December 2006, HCJ 769/02, available at <http://elyon1.court.gov.il/Files_ENG/02/690/007/a34/02007690.a34.pdf> [last accessed 12 April 2010], (hereinafter *Targeted Killings*).

[101] Before examining the targeting question, the Court had to resolve two preliminary questions: first, it (somewhat questionably) held that the conflict between Israel and Palestinian groups in the occupied territories should be qualified as an international armed conflict; second, it held that the

conditions that it imposed was that a terrorist may not be targeted if the incidental damage caused to nearby civilians is disproportionate to the direct military advantage anticipated by the elimination of the said terrorist.[102] This is of course the IHL proportionality principle, whose purpose is to allow the use of lethal force but to minimize the collateral damage arising from its use.[103]

But the Court imposed a further condition—a terrorist may not be targeted if less harmful means can be employed, ie if he can be captured and put on trial. In the Court's own words, '[t]rial is preferable to use of force. A rule-of-law state employs, to the extent possible, procedures of law and not procedures of force.'[104] Now, it is not entirely clear whether the Court derived this rule from IHRL or from domestic constitutional law, but it is clear that it was a human rights norm that it was applying.[105] It used the kernel of a human rights rule—ie that necessity must be shown for any intentional deprivation of life, to restrict the application of an IHL rule—that in armed conflict no necessity need be shown for the killing of combatants or civilians taking a direct part in hostilities. This does not mean, of course, that when applied to a specific set of facts the legally different IHL and IHRL norms will ultimately produce different results. What it means is that in *every* case some measure of justification will have to be offered as to why the killing of a particular individual was necessary on the facts of that case, and that this justification cannot be exhausted merely by invoking the person's status under IHL.

The Court's holding was not based on *lex specialis* or any other form of mechanical reasoning. It made a policy and value judgment that in the context of the prolonged Israeli occupation of Palestinian territories the traditional IHL answer was no longer satisfactory, and it had a legal basis in human rights law to say so.[106] When one adversary possesses overwhelming strategic and tactical superiority; in the context of an occupation, especially a prolonged one; during a limited insurgency or non-international armed conflict; in situations, in other words, which lend themselves more easily to non-lethal approaches, the imposition of an IHRL necessity requirement becomes more and more attractive.[107]

---

suspected terrorists designated as targets can be qualified as civilians taking a direct part in hostilities—see *Targeted Killings*, paras 6–18, 33–40.

[102] *Targeted Killings, supra* note 100, para 40.   [103] See Art 51(5)(b) of *AP I*.
[104] *Targeted Killings, supra* note 100, para 40.
[105] The Court thus cited the *McCann* judgment of the European Court—see *supra* note 98.
[106] 'Arrest, investigation, and trial are not means which can always be used. At times the possibility does not exist whatsoever; at times it involves a risk so great to the lives of the soldiers, that it is not required. However, it is a possibility which should always be considered. It might actually be particularly practical under the conditions of belligerent occupation, in which the army controls the area in which the operation takes place, and in which arrest, investigation, and trial are at times realizable possibilities. Of course, given the circumstances of a certain case, that possibility might not exist. At times, its harm to nearby innocent civilians might be greater than that caused by refraining from it. In that state of affairs, it should not be used' *Targeted Killings*, para 40 (citations omitted). See also Milanovic, *supra* note 87, at 390–392.
[107] See in that regard the excellent recent study by Sassòli and Olson, 'The Relationship between International Humanitarian and Human Rights Law where it Matters: Admissible Killing and Internment of Fighters in Non-International Armed Conflicts' 90 *International Review of the Red Cross* (2008) 599, at 613–614, who come to a similar conclusion when it comes to the dependence of the IHRL rule on the level of state control. Where regretfully I part way with them is in their assertion

It is questionable, however, whether this necessity requirement could be effectively applied in a more traditional battlefield setting. There is perhaps no other area of potential conflict where the infusion of IHRL with IHL could lead to a greater slide into utopia, and a consequent slide into irrelevance. It might be better to have *some* rules which are effective than rules which satisfy our moral intuitions but are honoured only in their breach. If the IHRL necessity requirement is to be applied at all in such situations, *contra* IHL, it will in any event have to be read down significantly to be effective, flexible, and practicable.[108] But again, even if IHRL is read down so far that it would *never* consider as arbitrary a killing of a combatant who is not *hors de combat*, per IHL, this would not be because of the *lex specialis* principle, but because of a policy judgment that IHRL has to be (forcibly) read down far enough to be effective.

C. Transformative occupation

My final example of potentially unresolvable conflict between IHRL and IHL will be that of occupation. Suppose that the UK becomes the belligerent occupant of a territory that has Sharia as part of its domestic law, for instance Iran. The Penal Code of Iran prescribes stoning as a punishment for adultery, and even has a stunning provision which stipulates that '[t]he size of the stone used in stoning shall not be too large to kill the convict by one or two throws and at the same time shall not be too small to be called a stone'.[109] Since the UK is in effective overall control and thus possesses jurisdiction over a part of Iranian territory, the ICCPR and ECHR are applicable.[110] Both treaties require the UK to ensure or secure the human rights of all individuals within its jurisdiction, even against violations by other actors. A punishment of stoning for adultery undoubtedly qualifies at the very least as inhuman treatment under either of these treaties.

As for IHL, Article 43 of the Hague Regulations provides that '[t]he authority of the legitimate power having in fact passed into the hands of the occupant, the

that the *lex specialis* principle has something to do with this outcome. Similarly, see also Doswald-Beck, 'The Right to Life in Armed Conflict: Does International Humanitarian Law Provide All the Answers?', 88 *International Review of the Red Cross* (2006) 881; Prud'homme, *supra* note 77, at 391.

[108] Some scholars have resorted to a different, yet with respect ultimately unconvincing approach to avoiding this norm conflict, by claiming that IHL like IHRL also imposes a necessity requirement for civilians taking a direct part in hostilities, and possibly even combatants—see Melzer, *Targeted Killing in International Law* (2008) at 228 and 336 *et seq*, esp at 397; Droege, *supra* note 4, at 526. See also Abresch's review of Melzer's book, in 20 *EJIL* (2009) 449. Another step in this direction was made in the recently published ICRC Interpretative Guidance on the Notion of Direct Participation in Hostilities under International Humanitarian Law, available at <http://www.icrc.org/Web/eng/siteeng0.nsf/htmlall/direct-participation-report_res/$File/direct-participation-guidance-2009-icrc.pdf>, at 77 *et seq*. [last accessed 12 April 2010]. For commentary, see Akande, 'Clearing the Fog of War? The ICRC's Interpretive Guidance on Direct Participation in Hostilities', *EJIL: Talk!*, 4 June 2009, available at <http://www.ejiltalk.org/clearing-the-fog-of-war-the-icrcs-interpretive-guidance-on-direct-participation-in-hostilities/>.

[109] Art 104, Penal Code of Iran, available at <http://www.wluml.org/english/newsfulltxt.shtml?cmd[157]=x-157-555118> [last accessed 12 April 2010].

[110] Per *Loizidou v Turkey* (1995) 20 EHRR 99; Wall, *supra* note 14; *Congo v Uganda*, *supra* note 16; *contra Al-Skeini HL*.

latter shall take all the measures in his power to restore, and ensure, as far as possible, public order and safety, while respecting, unless absolutely prevented, the laws in force in the country'. Article 64 of *GC IV* is even more pertinent for our example, stipulating that '[t]he penal laws of the occupied territory shall remain in force, with the exception that they may be repealed or suspended by the occupying power in cases where they constitute a threat to its security or an obstacle to the application of the present Convention'.

The example that I have given is at least that of an apparent norm conflict. On the one hand, IHRL commands the UK to take all possible measures to prevent the stoning of adulterers in the territory that it has occupied. On the other hand, because it considers occupation to be a temporary situation which requires deference to the displaced sovereign, IHL prohibits the UK from changing the laws of the occupied country, particularly its penal laws.[111] Can these two contradictory obligations somehow be reconciled?[112]

To do that, we would either have to read down the IHL obligation, or the IHRL obligation. When it comes to IHL, Article 43 of the Hague Regulations is a somewhat easier target—it prohibits the occupant from altering the domestic law of the occupied territory unless it is 'absolutely prevented' from doing so. We can therefore say that the UK's IHRL obligation to put a stop to any inhuman treatment does, in fact, 'absolutely prevent' it from respecting Iran's domestic law.[113] Article 64 of *GC IV* is less malleable—the domestic penal law must be kept in force, with only two possible exceptions. Does maintaining stoning for adultery constitute a threat to the security of the UK, the occupying power? Hardly. Is it an obstacle to the application of the Convention itself? Well, no, not really. There is no other obligation of the UK derived from the Convention that it could not fulfil while allowing the courts of the *ancien régime* to go about their brutal business. In reality, therefore, Article 64 can only be read down forcibly, if it is in effect rewritten to accommodate a change in domestic laws which are incompatible with the occupant's IHRL obligations.

If IHL cannot consistently and reasonably be read down to accommodate IHRL, how about IHRL? We could say something like this: the UK's positive obligation to secure or ensure respect for human rights in occupied territories even by non-state actors is one of due diligence. It requires the state only to do all that it reasonably can to prevent violations.[114] Because in this particular instance doing so would require the UK to violate some of its other obligations under international law, the UK's positive obligation should be read as not requiring the UK to do so.

This is a textually and conceptually perfectly reasonable reading down of IHRL. But recall what I have said above—though a price must be paid if IHRL is to

---

[111] See generally Dinstein and Sassòli, 'Legislation and Maintenance of Public Order and Civil Life by Occupying Powers', 16 *EJIL* (2005) 661.

[112] On transformative occupations generally, see Roberts, 'Transformative Military Occupation: Applying the Laws of War and Human Rights', 100 *AJIL* (2006) 580; G Fox, *Humanitarian Occupation* (2008).

[113] See Sassòli, *supra* note 111, at 676; Thienel, *supra* note 64, at 126–127.

[114] See *Al-Skeini CA*, *supra* note 63, para 196.

be applied jointly with IHL, that price must not be too steep. I personally—and I suspect most other international lawyers—would never read down IHRL to accommodate stoning for adultery, even if as a technical matter it may be perfectly appropriate to do so.

This, however, is simply because of a policy and value judgment that I have made on the issue, because I *care* more about human rights than about consistency in international law in this particular instance. It is the values enshrined in the IHRL treaties that would make their reading down forced and inappropriate. Legally, then, there is an unresolvable norm conflict, with no norm having priority over the other. The UK would have a political choice to make as to which obligation to keep, and which to breach, and that is that. Yes, we would all like it to choose the ICCPR and the ECHR over *GC IV* in this particular instance, particularly because it is likely that it would not suffer many ill consequences for its breach of the latter, but we would do so because of our own value judgment and a political calculation that this is how things should be, not because the law warrants this choice.

This example is particularly instructive because of how potentially far-reaching it could be. First, unlike the previous examples of targeting and detention, it does not deal merely with a state's negative obligations towards individuals, whose rights it must not violate through the actions of its own organs or agents, but with its positive obligation to secure or ensure respect for human rights even by other actors. Second, in my previous examples a state would not incur any responsibility for having to abide by a stricter IHRL standard as opposed to a looser IHL standard, though as a practical matter its liberty to act might be significantly curtailed. In this example, however, conflicting IHRL and IHL obligations meet head on, and one cannot be fulfilled without violating the other. Finally, the example again demonstrates the distinction between interpretation and legislation, and the need to maintain it. As a matter of policy, we do not want to *entirely* abandon the rule that the occupant must not alter the legal system of the occupied territory—by and large, this is a good rule[115]—we just want to carve out a human rights exception to that rule. Absent a legislative change, however, this can probably be done only by either violating or doing violence to *GC IV*.

6. Conclusion

Improved enforcement and further humanization of IHL through the application of IHRL is the ultimate goal of this entire project—to bring states that created these treaties to the logical, legal, and moral conclusions that are mandated by their texts, but even more so by their fundamental normative underpinnings, and the values that inspire them. As we have seen, to have any hope of advancing this goal we must be practical and be prepared to apply IHRL standards in a more

---

[115] Generally on the evolution of the conservationist premise of belligerent occupation as a temporary condition during which the order imposed by the displaced sovereign should not be varied see Bhuta, 'The Antinomies of Transformative Occupation', 16 *EJIL* (2005) 721.

flexible fashion. Yet we also need to drop the pretence, inspired by a false analogy with domestic public law, that states have in their infinite wisdom created two legal regimes which mesh together perfectly. They simply do not, either in the texts of the treaties, or in the values and policy considerations behind them.[116] Frequently, their relationship is that of conflict.

To address these norm conflicts, we have a variety of tools at our disposal. The most helpful are those of norm conflict avoidance, which are interpretative in nature. Among these tools, but not among the most useful, is *lex specialis*. To again take preventive detention as an example, if faced with a pure IHL/IHRL case arising from Iraq, such as *Al-Sweady*, the European Court might in the end forcibly read down Article 5 ECHR as if setting an arbitrariness standard that could accommodate IHL like Article 9 ICCPR. However, this would not be as a consequence of the *lex specialis* principle, but rather because it weighed the competing policy considerations so as to warrant such a result even in the absence of a derogation.[117] As is so often the case with legalese Latin, *lex specialis* is descriptively misleading, vague in meaning, and of little practical use in application. It should be discarded as a general matter, and it should especially not be used to describe the relationship between IHL and IHRL as a whole.[118]

More often than not, IHL treaties and human rights treaties can be reconciled and interpreted harmoniously. But there will be instances—there *are* instances—where this quest for harmony will fail, when the two bodies of law cannot be reconciled, when all legitimate methods of norm conflict avoidance and resolution will be exhausted, and when ultimately a political choice will have to be made as to which of the conflicting norms should be given priority over the other.

That choice can rarely, if ever, be made by a court—sometimes it is only the legislator who produced the antinomy who can provide the remedy for it. The more forced the methods of avoidance, the less legitimate they are; the line between interpretation and legislation may often be a fine one, but it is nonetheless still there.[119] And when all methods of norm conflict avoidance and resolution fail, there is nothing shameful in admitting defeat and saying that in this or that particular instance IHL and IHRL cannot be reconciled. Just as a UK court can, after giving its best, ultimately say that a particular Act of Parliament is incompatible with the Human Rights Act, so can it say, in *Al-Sweady* for instance, that the internment of POWs and civilians during the occupation of Iraq was lawful under IHL, but unlawful under the ECHR.[120]

It is, of course, not an easy thing for a court to say, nor should it be. No wonder then that courts rarely, if ever, openly acknowledge the possibility of unresolvable conflict. To take *Al-Skeini* as the prime example, it is often far easier for courts to deny that IHRL applies at all, based on entirely arbitrary criteria (viz that the ECHR applies to a person killed in the custody of UK troops in Basra, but not to

---

[116] See also Schabas, *supra* note 8.   [117] See also Lindroos, *supra* note 77, at 42.
[118] See also Prud'homme, *supra* note 77.
[119] For a discussion on the frequently complex and ambiguous nature of this boundary, see A Kavanagh, 'The Elusive Divide between Interpretation and Legislation under the Human Rights Act 1998', 24 *OJLS* (2004) 259.   [120] But see Ben-Naftali and Shany, *supra* note 7, at 103.

persons killed by UK troops on patrol[121]), and switch IHRL on when it becomes morally intolerable not to do so, and off when it becomes impracticable, rather than address hotly disputed substantive issues which may expose unresolvable norm conflicts. However, norm conflicts are in themselves not so undesirable that they must be avoided or resolved at any cost. They are immanent to the international legal system, due to its decentralized, non-hierarchical nature, and the consensual character of its law-making processes.[122] They occur as much in peacetime as in wartime, intra-territorially as extra-territorially—for instance, in *Soering* and *Matthews*. Indeed, exposing an unresolvable norm conflict may ultimately prove to be *more* productive then forcibly avoiding it, as nothing will give a better incentive to states to improve the normative framework within which we must operate. And, of course, a good place for states to start would be for them to use mechanisms which are already in place, such as derogations.

---

[121] See also Hampson, *supra* note 19, at 570.
[122] See also Lindroos, *supra* note 77, at 28.

III
VARIATIONS

5

PathoLAWgical Occupation: Normalizing the Exceptional Case of the Occupied Palestinian Territory and Other Legal Pathologies

Orna Ben-Naftali

1. Introduction

There is no groundbreaking news in the assessment that more law does not necessarily make for better law.[1] Clichés, however, often have an irritating tendency to reflect some truth. Indeed, at times, more laws—arming to the teeth trailing troops of lawyers, legal advisers, judges, and scholars—operate to obfuscate rights and deny justice. The legal discourse developed over the past four decades with respect to the Israeli control of the Occupied Palestinian Territory (OPT) provides an excellent example of this specific truth. Due, no doubt, to the unprecedented decision of the Israeli Supreme Court, operating in its capacity as a High Court of Justice (HCJ),[2] to open its gates to petitions emanating from the OPT[3] and to determine such petitions in the light of Israeli administrative (and, to the extent that the Jewish settlers were involved, constitutional) law,[4] international

---

[1] See eg Judge Alex Kozinski: 'In the end, we do not believe that more law makes for better law', in *Hart v Massanari*, 266 F 3d 1155, 1180 (9th Cir 2001). This notion can be traced to Cicero's dictum 'The more law, the less justice' (*De officiis* I, 10, 33).

[2] Art 15(c) of the Basic Law: Judicature, 1984, 38 LSI (1983–84) 101, at 104 provides that the Supreme Court of Israel may also sit as a High Court of Justice (hereinafter HCJ), and 'when so sitting, it shall hear matters in which it deems it necessary to grant relief for the sake of justice and which are not within the jurisdiction of another court'.

[3] This decision was first made in 1972. See HCJ 337/71, *The Christian Society for the Holy Places v The Minister of Defense* 26(1) PD 574 at 354–357. For an English summary see 2 *Israel Year Book on Human Rights* (1972).

[4] HCJ 1661/05 *Regional Council Gaza Beach v The Knesset*, at paras 78–80. The HCJ decided that the Israeli Basic Laws (which comprise the nascent Constitution of Israel), including the Basic Law: Human Liberty and Dignity apply *in personam* to Israelis in the occupied territories, leaving open the question of the application of these laws to the Palestinian residents of the same territories. For a discussion of the application of different law to different people in the OPT, see *infra* text between notes 99 and 110.

humanitarian law (IHL),[5] and even international human rights law (IHRL),[6] this regime has become the most legalized occupation in world history, generating a multitude of judicial decisions as well as vast scholarly interest. It does not, alas, follow that law has operated to limit power. Indeed, the opposite is true: more often than not, law has enabled power (of both the state and its judiciary), cloaking the otherwise naked force used to sustain and deepen the occupation with a mantle of legitimacy.[7] Judicial review exercised by the HCJ, has rejected some 99 percent of the petitions challenging the legality of various decisions and actions of the occupying power;[8] scholarly work has tended, in the main, to follow the footsteps of the judiciary engaging in a (reactive) critique of specific judicial decisions rather than

---

[5] IHL comprises the following documents: Hague Convention Respecting the Laws and Customs of War, 18 Oct 1907, Annex, 36 Stat 2277; TS 539 (hereinafter *Hague IV or Hague Regulations*); Geneva Convention Relative to the Protection of Civilian Persons in Time of War, 12 August 1949, 75 UNTS 287 (hereinafter *GC IV*); Protocol Additional to the Geneva Conventions of 12 August 1949, and relating to the Protection of Victims of International Armed Conflicts, 8 June 1977, 1125 UNTS 3 (hereinafter *AP I*). The HCJ, recognizing the customary nature of *Hague IV*, has applied its provisions routinely. It is yet to determine the *de jure* applicability of *GC IV* (since the official Israeli position has been that the West Bank and Gaza Strip were not 'a territory of' a High Contracting Party before being occupied by Israel) and enforceability (since the official Israeli position has been that *GC IV* does not reflect customary international law and given that Israel employs a dualistic approach to the incorporation of international law), but has, in fact, applied it, relying on the state's benevolent willingness to adhere to its 'humanitarian' provisions. The official Israeli position was rejected by the ICJ in *Legal Consequences of the Construction of a Wall in the Occupied Palestinian Territory,* Advisory Opinion, ICJ Reports (2004) 136, at para 101 (hereinafter *Construction of a Wall*). For a review and critical appraisal of these issues, see Kretzmer, *The Occupation of Justice: The Supreme Court of Israel and the Occupied Territories* (2002) 35–56. Israel is not a party to *AP I*, and is a persistent objector to some of its provisions. Nevertheless, the HCJ has applied its Art 51, having deemed it to be customary, in HCJ 769/02 *The Public Committee against Torture in Israel v The Government of Israel* (hereinafter *Targeted Killings Case*), *available at* <http://elyon1.court.gov.il/files_eng/02/690/007/a34/02007690.a34. pdf> [last accessed 18 April 2010]. For a critical discussion of the case, see *infra* text between notes 218 and 262.
[6] While Israel's official position is that IHRL does not apply, the HCJ has occasionally applied it as a complementary source to IHL since 2002. See HCJ 7957/04 *Mara'abe v The Prime Minister of Israel* available online at <http://elyon1.court.gov.il/files_eng/04/570/079/a14/04079570.a14.pdf> [last accessed 18 April 2010]. For a comprehensive and critical review of the Israeli position and an analysis of relevant case law, see Ben-Naftali and Shany, 'Living in Denial: The Co-application of Humanitarian Law and Human Rights Law to the Occupied Territories' 37 *Is. LR* (2004) 17–118. For a critical analysis of the convergence of IHRL and IHL in situations of occupation in general and insofar as the HCJ jurisprudence is concerned in particular, see Gross, 'Human Proportions: Are Human Rights the Emperor's New Clothes of the International Law of Occupation?', 18(1) *EJIL* (2007) 1–35.
[7] Shamir, '"Landmark Cases" and the Reproduction of Legitimacy: The Case of Israel's High Court of Justice', 24 *Law and Society Review* (1990) 781–805. Shamir argues that the small number of the petitions that were accepted are 'Landmark Cases' which served mainly to legitimize the Israeli democracy, its independent judiciary and, significantly, the rejection of the vast majority of Palestinian petitions.
[8] The data gathered by Shamir, ibid, encompassing judgments rendered by the HCJ between the years 1967–1986, reveal that over this period only 1 percent of Palestinian petitions have been accepted by the HCJ. Data I gathered up to 2005 generate the same statistics, with the exception of the years during which the Oslo process was ongoing (1993–96), where the percentage of Palestinian petitions accepted by the HCJ reached to 3 percent.

in a (proactive) analysis of the nature and the legality of the occupation regime as such.[9]

The most legalized occupation in the world has entered its fifth decade. Given that the notion of limited duration governs and informs the law of occupation,[10] the time has come to consider the role that law has played in facilitating and prolonging it. A similar sense informs the (rhetorical) question with which Professor David Kreztmer concluded his seminal study of the role played by the HCJ in the shaping and sustaining of this occupation:[11]

Is it possible that in the medium or long term, the very lack of restraint that would have resulted from the absence of judicial review would have made the occupation less palatable to Israeli elites, and that the pressure to end the occupation by political settlement which began after the *Intifada* started in 1987, would have felt much easier?

Legal practice in general, and human rights advocacy in particular, is neither 'medium or long term', nor is it driven by self-reflection on its own systemic, structural, or legitimating implications. Its proper objective is—and should remain— seeking immediate relief for violation of specific rights of an individual client.[12] Contemplating the nature, structure, and ramifications of a regime and the role law has played in its shaping is—and should be—both the privilege and the responsibility of scholars. This chapter reflects my attempt to take this responsibility seriously. Drawing on, and revising when appropriate, previously published (collaborative and individual) pieces, it takes an additional step of weaving them together into an argument which is, I hope, coherent albeit as yet incomplete.

The argument rests on two, inter-related propositions: first, that the Israeli control of the OPT is an illegal occupation, the defining feature of which is the blurring of boundaries, both physical and legal, which has culminated in the reversal of the relationship between the rule and the exception (Part 2).[13] The second proposition focuses on the normative implications of this regime. It suggests that once law is implicated in the shaping of such a regime, law itself becomes infected, and

[9] Kretzmer, *supra* note 5, was the first comprehensive study to focus on the case-law of the HCJ and offer a critical appraisal of its jurisprudence. A search in Lexis-Nexis on the Israeli occupation of the OPT generates hundreds of entries concerned with various Israeli actions and positions as an occupying power. Similar results were obtained from Westlaw. An article I published with two colleagues in 2005 was the first article to focus on the nature and structure and the regime, as distinct from the legality of any specific measure undertaken by the occupying power. See Ben-Naftali, Gross, and Michaeli, 'Illegal Occupation: The Framing of the Occupied Palestinian Territory', 23(3) *Berkeley J. Int'l L.* (2005) 551–614; Reprinted in Kattan (ed), *The Palestine Question In International Law* (2008) (hereinafter *Illegal Occupation*). For a revised version of this article, written in 2007 and entitled 'The Illegality of the Occupation Regime: The Fabric of Law in the Occupied Palestinian Territory', see Ophir, Givoni, and Hanafi, (eds) *The Power of Inclusive Exclusion: Anatomy of Israeli Rule in the Occupied Palestinian Territories* (2009).
[10] Ben-Naftali, '"A La Recherche du Temps Perdu": Rethinking Article 6 of the Fourth Geneva Convention in the Light of the Construction of the Wall Advisory Opinion', 38(1–2) *Is. LR* (2005) 211–229.   [11] Kretzmer, *supra* note 5, at 198.
[12] Sfard, 'The Human Rights Lawyer's Existential Dilemma: The Occupation of Justice, The Supreme Court of Israel and the Occupied Territories by David Kretzmer', *38 Is. LR* (2005) 154–169, at 166–168.   [13] This is the proposition first advanced in *Illegal Occupation, supra* note 9.

is likely to operate in a manner that will defy its normative purpose on both an individual and a systemic level: its application to individual cases (through judicial review) would typically entail a 'dynamic' interpretation designed to advance the interests of the occupying power at the expense of the occupied people and it will contribute to and facilitate the formation of an environment (indicative of a state policy) of tolerance towards systematic violations of human rights. This tolerance, in turn, may transform grave such violations from war crimes into crimes against humanity (Part 3). This 'patholawgy', it is suggested, provides the proper context for understanding both the manner with which the military operation in Gaza ('Operation Cast Lead', 27 December 2008–18 January 2009) was exercised and the consequential *Report of the United Nations Fact Finding Mission on the Gaza Conflict* (Part 4).[14]

2. Anatomy of the Regime

A. General

1. *The argument*[15]

In this Part three inter-related propositions are advanced: (a) an occupation regime may be illegal (regardless of whether it was occasioned by a lawful use of force or by aggression);[16] (b) the continued Israeli control over the OPT is an illegal occupation; and (c) the defining feature of this illegal regime is its indeterminacy. This indeterminacy functions to legitimize what would otherwise be clearly illegal, obfuscating the boundaries between occupation/non-occupation; between annexation/non-annexation; between the temporary and the indefinite and, indeed, between the rule and the exception. In this manner, the international regime of occupation—a regime designed to ensure that the fabric of life in an occupied territory remains as intact as possible and premised

---

[14] *Report of the United Nations Fact Finding Mission on the Gaza Conflict*, A/HRC/12/48 (25 September 2009) at paras 1824–1828 and 1405–1409 (hereinafter the *Goldstone Report*). Available online at <http://www2.ohchr.org/english/bodies/hrcouncil/specialsession/9/FactFindingMission.htm> [last accessed 18 April 2010].

[15] This argument was first made in *Illegal Occupation, supra* note 9. An updated yet more condensed version of the article is forthcoming under the title Ben-Naftali, Gross, and Michaeli, 'The Illegality of the Occupation Regime: The Fabric of Law in the Occupied Palestinian Territory,' in Ophir, Givoni, and Hanafi (eds), *The Power of Inclusive Exclusion: Anatomy of Israeli Rule in the Occupied Palestinian Territories* (2009). The argument detailed in Part 2 of the present text is a shorter version of both these publications.

[16] The view that an occupation generated by the use of force in self-defence is, at least initially, legal was expressed, *inter alia*, by Cassese: 'self-determination is violated whenever there is a military invasion or belligerent occupation of a foreign country, except where the occupation—*although unlawful*—is of a minimal duration or is solely intended as a measure of repelling, under Art. 1 of the UN Charter, an armed attack initiated by the vanquished Power and consequently is not protracted', Cassese, *Self-Determination of Peoples* (1995) 238–239 (emphasis added). For a critical discussion of this nexus between the initiation of occupation and its legality see *infra* text between notes 30 and 34. For a comprehensive discussion of this point and related references, see *Illegal Occupation, supra* note 9, at 557–559.

on as quick as possible a return to the normal order of the international society (built normatively around sovereign states each exercising effective control over the people within its territory) has been manipulated in a manner that legitimizes the dispossession of Palestinians while advancing the political agenda of Israeli expansionism.

2. The definition of the phenomenon of occupation

The phenomenon of occupation is currently defined as 'the effective control of a power (be it one or more states or an international organization, such as the United Nations) over a territory to which that power has no sovereign title, without the volition of the sovereign of that territory'.[17]

There are three notable features to this widely accepted definition: first, it is expansive, thus covering varied types of occupation. The rationale behind this expansiveness is clear: the moment an occupation exists, the normative regime of occupation—which comprises a host of humanitarian and, to some extent human rights law—applies. Bearing in mind that occupying powers are notoriously reluctant to abide by these rules, their first line of defence being denial that the specific situation qualifies as an occupation,[18] the broad definition is designed to curb any such defiance. Israel's rejection of the applicability of *GC IV* to the situation, underscores the point.[19]

The second notable feature of the definition is that it incorporates the principle of the inalienability of sovereignty. This principle is the most basic tenet of the law of occupation: it indicates that occupation does not confer title[20] and it recognizes that the situation of occupation is exceptional, as it deviates from the normal order of sovereign states insofar as it reflects the suspension of the link between sovereignty and effective control. It is this exceptionality, in turn, which defines both the substantive and the temporal nature of the relationship between the occupying power and the sovereign.[21] Taken together then, these principles demarcate the boundaries of the phenomenon in relation to the normal order of the international state system.

The third notable feature of this definition is that it conceives of an occupation in factual terms: it is a phenomenon that exists once effective control is exercised by a foreign power without the volition of the occupied people. Clearly, if the phenomenon was merely factual, an occupation—as distinct from its normative consequences—could not have been legal or illegal. Such a conception is, however, incomplete. As explained below, the phenomenon of occupation is not only factual; it is also normative, and thus susceptible to an assessment of its legality.

---

[17] Benvenisti, *The International Law of Occupation* (2nd ed, 2004) 4. For a discussion of the evolutionary development of the law of occupation, see *Illegal Occupation, supra* note 9, at 561–567.

[18] Baxter, 'Some Existing Problems of Humanitarian Law', 14 *Revue de Droit Pénal Militaire et de Droit de la Guerre* (1975) 297–303, at 288.   [19] See *supra* note 5.

[20] This principle is discussed in *infra* text and between notes 28 and 42.

[21] See *infra* text and between notes 158 and 172.

3. *The criteria for the determination of the legality of an occupation regime*

The underlying principle of the international legal order rests on a presumption of sovereign equality between States.[22] Under current international law, said sovereignty is understood as vested in the people, giving expression to the right to self-determination.[23] Analytically, the phenomenon of occupation presents this order with the challenge of the extra-ordinary: the severance of the link between sovereignty and effective control entailed in an occupation, suspends this order as it relates to the occupied territory.[24] This exceptional situation cannot thus be defined as either a fact or a norm, because it exists only by virtue of the suspension of the norm.[25] It partakes in both. The international law of occupation enters the picture signifying both the need to distinguish between order and chaos and the need to distinguish between orders: between the rule and the exception. In distinguishing between order and chaos, its function is to manage the situation; to eliminate chaos through control of the exceptional situation. In distinguishing between orders, its function is to create an orderly space which is defined by its exceptionality, by its suspension of the rule.

It is submitted that the legal validity of the phenomenon of occupation, as it relates to the function of managing the situation, is to be measured in relation to three inter-related fundamental legal principles.

(a) Sovereignty and title in an occupied territory is not vested in the occupying power. The roots of this principle emanate from the principle of the inalienability of sovereignty through actual or threatened use of force. Under contemporary international law, and in view of the principle of self-determination, said sovereignty is vested in the population under occupation;[26]

---

[22] Enshrined in Art 2(1) of the UN Charter.   [23] Benvenisti, *supra* note 17, at 28.

[24] This notion of suspension was already recognized in the first attempt to codify the international law of occupation, in the Final Protocol and Project of an International Declaration Concerning the Laws and Customs of War, 27 August 1874, reprinted in Schindler and Toman (eds), *The Laws of Armed Conflict: A Collection of Conventions, Resolutions and other Documents* (3rd edn, 1988) 25.

[25] The tension between the rule and the exception formed one of the basic tenets of Carl Schmitt's critique of the liberal state and, indeed, of the very rule of law. See Schmitt, *Political Theology: Four Chapters on the Concept of Sovereignty* (Schwab trans, 1988). A critical discussion of Schmitt's concept of 'the exception' is offered in *infra* text and between notes 162 and 172.

[26] Traditionally, sovereignty was attached to the state which held title to the territory prior to occupation. Currently, the focus has shifted to the rights of the population under occupation. See Benvenisti, 'The Security Council and the Law on Occupation: Resolution 1483 on Iraq in Historical Perspective', 1 *Israel Defense Forces Law Review* (2003) 19–38, at 28. For a review of the recognition of the Palestinian right to self-determination, see Cassese, *supra* note 16, at 238–239. It is further important to note that Israel itself seems to have recognized this right, albeit implicitly, at least since the Oslo Accords of 1993, as can be inferred from both the text and the context of the Declaration of Principles signed between Israel and the PLO in 1993. See 'Declaration of Principles on Interim Self-Government Arrangements', 13 September 1993, 32 ILM (1993) 1525–1544. In the *Construction of a Wall*, the Palestinian right to self-determination was explicitly recognized, the Court opining that 'the existence of a "Palestinian people" is not longer an issue', and noting that Israel itself has recognized this right. *Construction of a Wall, supra* note 5, at para 118. It is significant in this context to note that the Court further opined that Israel has right to exist within the Green line, at paras 71 and 162.

(b) The occupying power is entrusted with the management of public order and civil life in the territory under its control. In view of the principle of self-determination, the people under occupation are the beneficiaries of this trust. The dispossession and subjugation of these people is thus a violation of this trust; and

(c) The occupation is temporary.[27] It may be neither permanent nor indefinite.

The violation of each of these principles, as distinct from the violation of a specific norm which reflects an aspect of these principles, renders an occupation illegal. Further, these principles inter-relate: the substantive constraints on the managerial discretion of the occupant elucidated in principles (a) and (b) respectively, generate the conclusion that it must necessarily be temporary, and the violation of the temporal constraints expressed in principle (c) cannot but violate principles (a) and (b), thereby generating the normative corruption of the regime. This occupation is illegal. This is the nature of the Israeli occupation of the OPT. Section B: 'Intrinsic dimensions of the Israeli occupation', substantiates this argument.

It is further submitted that the legal validity of the phenomenon of occupation in its functioning to create an orderly space that is nevertheless distinct from the normal political order of sovereign equality between states, is to be measured by its exceptionality: once the boundaries between the exception and the rule are blurred, the occupation becomes illegal. The nexus between the two functions is clear: an occupation that is illegal from the perspective of managing an otherwise chaotic situation is also illegal in that it obfuscates the distinction between the rule and its exception. Yet, the distinction between the two forms of illegality is important: the former is grounded in the intrinsic principles of the law of occupation; the latter is extrinsic to this law and delineates its limits. The Israeli occupation of the OPT is illegal both intrinsically and extrinsically. Section C: 'Extrinsic dimensions of the Israeli occupation', substantiates this argument. Section D: 'The matrix of illegal occupation' focuses on the third proposition, describing the indeterminacies of this occupation as reflecting both its essential feature and its legitimizing mechanism.

B. Intrinsic dimensions of the Israeli occupation

The Israeli occupation of the OPT violates the three basic tenets of the normative regime of occupation and is, therefore, intrinsically illegal. This section discusses the basic principles informing the normative regime and then applies them to the Israeli occupation.

---

[27] See *Construction of a Wall, supra* note 5, Separate Opinion of Judge Elaraby, at para 3.1; Separate Opinion of Judge Koroma, at para 2.

1. *The suspension of sovereignty: occupation does not confer title*

'The foundation upon which the entire law of occupation is based,' writes Benvenisti, 'is the principle of inalienability of sovereignty through the actual or threatened use of force. Effective control by foreign military force can never bring about by itself a valid transfer of sovereignty.'[28] The rule of non-recognition, forbidding states to recognize title thus acquired, is the normative consequence of this principle.[29]

This basic tenet of the law of occupation rests on and reflects the well-established general international legal principle that the acquisition of territory by force does not confer a valid title to the territory. This principle holds, even if force is used legally (ie in self-defence or pursuant to a decision of the Security Council under Chapter VII of the Charter of the United Nations) and even if the status of the territory under consideration is disputed.[30]

This principle is articulated in all relevant documents: Article 43 of the Hague Regulations limits the occupant's authority to maintaining public order and civil life, while 'respecting, unless absolutely prevented, the laws in force in the country'. This proviso precludes the annexation of the territory by the occupant.[31] This preclusion was further made clear in Article 47 of *GC IV*, which emphasized that annexation of an occupied territory during wartime, before any peace treaty had been concluded, does not deprive the protected persons of the rights guaranteed by the Convention, ie annexation does not alter the status of either the territory or its population.[32] The latest affirmation of the principle can be found in Article 4 of *AP I*, restating that neither occupation of a territory nor the application of the Protocol's provisions shall affect the legal status of the territory under dispute.[33]

Indeed, even if the occupation has been occasioned by a legal use of force, it cannot confer legal title. Thus, the UN Declaration on Principles of International Law Concerning Friendly Relations and Co-operation among States does not distinguish between legal and illegal use of force when it states that '*no* territorial acquisition resulting from the threat or use of force shall be recognized as legal'.[34] Despite Israel's adamant claim that the 1967 war was pursued in self-defence, the same rationale underlies the UN Security Council's Middle East Resolution 242 which reiterated the inadmissibility of the acquisition of territory by war.

---

[28] Benvenisti, *supra* note 17, at 5.

[29] Sharma, *Territorial Acquisition, Disputes and International Law* (1997) at 148.

[30] Eritrea-Ethiopia Claims Commission, Partial Award, Central front, Ethiopia's Claim 2, judgment of 28 April 2004, at paras 28–29.

[31] Schwarzenberger, *International Law as Applied by International Courts and Tribunals* (3rd edn, 1957) at 166–167.

[32] Pictet (ed), *The Geneva Conventions of 12 August 1949: Commentary IV Geneva Convention Relative to the Protection of Civilian Persons in Time of War* (1958) 275–276. Pictet emphasizes the fact that the reference to annexation in the article cannot be considered as implying recognition of it as a means to acquire territory and that the contrary is true.

[33] Sandoz, Swinarski, and Zimmermann (eds), *Commentary on the Additional Protocols of 8 June 1977 to the Geneva Conventions of 12 August 1949* (1987) 73–74.

[34] See the Declaration on Principles of International Law Concerning Friendly Relations and Co-operation Among States in Accordance with the Charter of the United Nations, GA Res 2625, UN GAOR, 25th Sess, Supp No 28, at 121, UN Doc A/8028 (1970) (emphasis added).

One conclusion to be drawn from the above is that the legality of an occupation—or lack thereof—cannot be grounded on a determination that an occupation has been occasioned as a result of a war of self-defence. Thus, even if the Israeli narrative of a war fought in self-defence in 1967 was accepted as the shared assumption of the conflict, it is irrelevant to both the determination of the legality of the continued occupation and to the principle of the inalienability of sovereignty.

Another conclusion is that the Israeli annexation of East Jerusalem— gradually expanding its boundaries from 6.5 to 71 square kilometres—is illegal.[35] This illegality was affirmed by both the Security Council and the General Assembly, with the consequence that under international law the area is still considered occupied.[36] The ICJ's *Construction of the Wall* Advisory Opinion confirms this conclusion.[37]

Complementing the principle that use of force of any kind cannot confer legal title to territory, is the principle of self-determination, which informs not only the United Nations decisions regarding Israel's annexation of occupied East Jerusalem, and its settlements in the OPT,[38] but also the Security Council's vision of 'a region where two states, Israel and Palestine, live side by side within secure and recognized borders'.[39] The rationale underlying this determination is that if peoples, according to Common Article 1(1) of the International Covenants on Human Rights, have the right to 'freely determine their political status',[40] then sovereignty belongs to the people, and no valid title can be transferred in disregard of the will of the population of the territory.[41] This point was wholeheartedly approved by the ICJ in the *Construction of a Wall* Advisory Opinion with respect to the *de facto* annexation of vast Palestinian territories entailed by the establishment of the settlements and the construction of a wall by Israel.[42]

---

[35] Israel extended its law to East Jerusalem on 26 June 1967. See The Law and Administration Ordinance (Amendment No 11) Law, 21 LSI 75 (1967); The Municipalities Ordinance (Amendment No 6) Law, 21 LSI 75 (1967). It formally annexed that area on 30 June 1980, See The Basic Law: Jerusalem, Capital of Israel, 34 LSI 209 (1980).

[36] See SC Res 478, UN SCOR, 35th Sess, 2245th mtg at 14, UN Doc S/INF/36 (1980); GA Res 35/169E, UN GAOR, 35th Sess, Supp No 48, at 208–209, UN Doc A/35/48 (1981); SC Res 673, UN SCOR, 46th Sess, 2949 mtg at Res & Dec 7, UN Doc S/INF/46 (1991). Israel based its claim to sovereignty over East Jerusalem essentially on its right to fill the sovereignty vacuum which existed since the termination of the Mandate, an argument which generated a debate among Israeli international lawyers, and failed to gain the support of the international community. On the debate within Israel, See eg Dinstein, 'The Future Redemption of Zion in International Law', 27 *Hapraklit* (1971) 5–11 (in Hebrew); Blum, 'The Redemption of Zion in International Law', *Is. LR* (1968) 315–324 (in Hebrew); for a discussion on the legal status of Jerusalem, see Quigley, 'The Future of Jerusalem: A symposium: Sovereignty in Jerusalem', 45 *Cath. UL Rev.* (1996) 653–941, at 765. Similar reactions followed Israel's annexation of the Golan Heights, a Syrian territory occupied by Israel during the Six-Day war of 1967. See the Golan Heights Law, 36 LSI 7 (5742-1981/2); SC Res 497 (1981); GA Res 36/226A (1981); GA Res 39/146A (1984).

[37] *Construction of a Wall, supra* note 5, at paras 74–75 and 120–122.

[38] GA Res 37/88C, UN GAOR, 37th Sess, Supp No 51, at 93, UN Doc A/37/51 (1982–83); SC Res 465, UN SCOR, 35th Sess, 2203d mtg at 5, UN Doc S/INF/36 (1980).

[39] SC Res 1397, UN SCOR, 4489th mtg, UN Doc S/RES/1397 (2002).

[40] See *Declaration on the Granting of Independence to Colonial Countries and Peoples*, GA Res 1514, 15 UN GAOR Supp (No 16) at 66, UN Doc A/4684 (1960).

[41] Imseis, 'On the Fourth Geneva Convention and the Occupied Palestinian Territory', 44 *Harv. Int'l LJ* (2003) 65–138, at 97; Benvenisti, *supra* note 17, at 183.

[42] *Construction of a Wall, supra* note 5, at paras 118–122.

An occupation, thus, suspends sovereignty insofar as it severs its ordinary link with effective control, but it does not, indeed cannot, alter sovereignty. Effective control must be exercised in a manner that reflects the obligations of the occupying power as a trustee.

2. Trust matters: an occupation is a form of trust

Implicit in the principle that occupation does not confer title, and that the occupant is vested with the authority, in the words of Article 43 of the Hague Regulations 'to take all the measures in his power to restore, and ensure, as far as possible, public order and safety/civil life, while respecting, unless absolutely prevented, the laws in force in the country', is the notion of trusteeship.[43] Occupied territories, thus, 'constitute...a sacred trust, which must be administered as a whole in the interests both of the inhabitants and the legitimate sovereign or the duly constituted successor in title'.[44] This trust, however, is of a particular nature.

The framework of the trust consists of two features: the security needs of the occupying power on the one hand, and the maintenance of civil life on the other hand. It thus carries with it a potential conflict of interests between those of the population and those of the occupant. In the nineteenth-century context, where governmental involvement in the life of the population was minimal, this framework produced two primary rules: the occupant was mainly burdened with the negative duty of refraining from infringing on the most basic rights of the inhabitants, while the latter were burdened with a duty of obedience to the occupant.[45]

With the continued evolution of the law of occupation, the scale began to tip to the side of the inhabitants. *GC IV* seems to reject the idea that the occupied population was under any international legal obligation to obey the occupant.[46] In parallel, the Convention expands considerably the protection due to the inhabitants, setting obligations to respect their persons, honour, family life, religious convictions, customs, and their right to be humanely treated at all times; women should be especially protected; discrimination is prohibited.[47] It also prohibits the infliction of physical suffering, corporal punishment, medical experiments, collective punishment, pillage, reprisals, the taking of hostages, deportations, and retroactive criminal legislation and punishment. The right of the occupant to compel the inhabitants to work is restricted. The Convention further imposes positive duties on the occupant with regard to the protection of children, ensuring food and medical supplies,[48] maintaining hospitals, providing for certain due process

---

[43] Roberts, 'What is a Military Occupation?', 55 *BYBIL* (1984) 249–305, at 295.
[44] *Construction of a Wall, supra* note 5, Separate Opinion of Judge Koroma, at para 2.
[45] Baxter, 'The Duty of Obedience to the Belligerent Occupant', 27 *BYBIL* (1950) 235–266.
[46] For example the terms 'war rebellion' and 'war treason' were not incorporated in the Convention. Furthermore, while providing the occupant with the right to take measures against protected persons who carry out acts detrimental to the security of the occupant, it nevertheless preserves most of their rights under the Convention. See Baxter, ibid, at 261 and 264.
[47] *GC IV*, Arts 27, 75.   [48] Ibid, Arts 55, 59-62.

rights, and rights of imprisoned persons.[49] It also restricts the right of the occupant to detain protected persons and stipulates substantial protection for detainees.[50]

This expanded protection of the inhabitants culminates in the currently prevailing view that international human rights law applies concurrently with international humanitarian law to occupied territories: the latter is the *lex specialis*, but the former is resorted to either in cases of lacunae or for interpenetrative purposes.[51] Indeed, the longer the occupation, the heavier is the weight to be accorded to the human rights of the occupied population.[52]

The inseparability of human rights guarantees from the concept of trust rests at the heart of the ICJ Advisory Opinion concerning the *Legal Consequences of the Continued Presence of South Africa in Namibia*.[53] The Court construed the relationship between South Africa and Namibia as a 'sacred trust',[54] and found South Africa's continued infringement of the rights and wellbeing of the inhabitants of Namibia, to destroy 'the very object and purpose of that relationship'.[55] In the light of this finding, it held that the termination of the Mandate by the UN General Assembly was valid and determined that the continuing presence of South Africa in Namibia—a presence which thereafter was a foreign occupation[56]—is illegal.[57]

It is interesting to note in this context that the Court reiterated this position in its *Construction of a Wall* Advisory Opinion. In the part of the Opinion dealing with the status of the OPT, the Court narrates the history of the conflict, the roots of which are described as follows: 'Palestine was part of the Ottoman Empire. At the end of the First World War, a class "A" Mandate for Palestine was entrusted to Great Britain by the League of Nations...'[58] The Court recalled that in its 1950 Opinion on the *International Status of South West Africa*,[59] it held that 'two principles were considered to be of paramount importance' with respect to territories that were placed under the Mandate system, 'the principle of non-annexation and

---

[49] Ibid, Arts 32, 33, 34, 49, 65, 67, 51, 52, 50, 55, 59–62, 66, 69, 71–73, 76, 77.

[50] Ibid, Arts 79–135.

[51] See *Construction of a Wall, supra* note 5, at paras 105–113; See also *Legality of the Threat or Use of Nuclear Weapons*, Advisory Opinion, ICJ Reports (1996) 226, at 249 (hereinafter *Nuclear Weapons* Advisory Opinion). See generally, Ben-Naftali and Shany, *supra* note 6; Gross, *supra* note 6.

[52] Cohen, *Human Rights in the Israeli-Occupied Territories 1967–1982* (1985) 29; Roberts, 'Prolonged Military Occupation: The Israeli Occupied Territories Since 1967', 84 *AJIL* (1990) 44–103, at 97.

[53] *Legal Consequences for States of the Continued Presence of South Africa in Namibia (South West Africa) notwithstanding Security Council Resolution 276 (1970)*, ICJ Reports (1971) 16 (hereinafter *Continued Presence of South Africa in Namibia* Advisory Opinion).

[54] Ibid. While the special context of the relationship between South Africa and Namibia was the Mandate system established by the League of Nations, the reasoning of the Court nevertheless seems to be of general applicability as emphasized by the fact that the Court interpreted the traditional concept of trust, found in the Mandate system, in light of recent legal developments, namely self-determination and independence of the people and basic human rights. Furthermore, the Court construed South Africa's presence in Namibia following the revocation of the Mandate as an occupation.

[55] Ibid, at 47.

[56] Roberts, *supra* note 43, at 293–294 (referring to this specific type of occupation).

[57] *Continued Presence of South Africa in Namibia* Advisory Opinion, *supra* note 53, at 54.

[58] *Construction of a Wall, supra* note 5, at para 70.

[59] *International Status of South-West Africa*, ICJ Reports (1950) 128.

the principle that the well-being and development of... peoples [not yet able to govern themselves] form[ed] "a sacred trust of civilization" '.[60]

The Court returned to this point in a later part of the Opinion, concerned with determining the relevant international legal rules applicable to the issue at hand. Recalling its 1971 Opinion on the *Continued Presence of South Africa in Namibia,* the Court stated that 'current developments in international law in regard to non-self governing territories... made the principle of self-determination applicable to all [such territories] ... these developments leave little doubt that the ultimate objective of the sacred trust... was the self-determination of the people concerned'.[61] The Court thus construed the concept of 'a sacred trust', the origins of which are rooted in the Mandate system, as the common denominator of all situations where people are not self-governing, occupation included. This construction is facilitated by the historical fact that Palestine was a Mandate territory, and that the roots of the Israeli–Palestinian conflict rest in the dissolution of the Mandate. This construction, in turn, enables the Court to emphasize not only the principle of self-determination, but also the related notion of a 'sacred trust' as applicable to the OPT.[62]

It is nevertheless clear that the trust, especially one emanating from a belligerent type of occupation rather than from a Mandate, does not abrogate the security interests of the occupying power.[63] *GC IV* explicitly subjects some of the guarantees afforded to the population to military necessity and conditions.[64] Furthermore, the occupant is allowed to take measures against protected persons in the form of promulgating penal laws,[65] assigning residence[66] and internment.[67] The balance between humanitarian and human rights concerns—pouring content into the notion of trust, on the one hand—and military necessity—delimiting but never substituting this trust, on the other hand—is thus the hallmark of the current law of occupation.

---

[60] Ibid, at 131; *Construction of a Wall, supra* note 5, at para 70.

[61] *Continued Presence of South Africa in Namibia* Advisory Opinion, *supra* note 53, at paras 52–54; cited in *Construction of a Wall, supra* note 5, at para 88.

[62] Note that some of the judges who appended separate opinions took issue with this analogy. See *Construction of a Wall, supra* note 5, Separate Opinion of Judge Higgins, at para 2; Separate Opinion of Judge Kooijmans, at para 33.

[63] It is interesting to note that Allan Gerson referred to the Israeli occupation as a 'Trustee Occupation'. His thesis was that this type of occupation occurs when the legal status of the territory prior to the occupation was short of full sovereignty, the occupation was not generated by a war of aggression, and the occupant was seeking to positively develop the area, the occupant should be seen as a trustee responsible for promoting the population right of self-determination, and should, therefore, not be constrained by the law requiring the preservation of the status quo. See Gerson, 'Trustee Occupant: The Legal Status of Israel's Presence in the West Bank', 14 *Harv. Int'.LJ* (1973) 1–49. This typology, however, is problematic from the perspective of law and fact alike: from a legal perspective, as discussed in the text above, the concept of trust underlies the law of occupation in general; from a factual perspective, it is unclear whether Israel's occupation generated from a war of self-defence, and even if it did, it is clear that it has not assumed the role of trustee fostering the Palestinian right to self-determination, as indeed was acknowledged by Gerson himself already in 1978, See, Gerson, *Israel, The West Bank and International Law* (1978) 78–82.

[64] *GC IV*, Art 27, second paragraph of Arts 49, 51, 53.   [65] Ibid, Art 64.

[66] Ibid, Art 78.   [67] Ibid, Art 42.

The working assumption behind this arrangement is that an occupation is of a relatively short duration. The restriction on the occupant's authority to amend the laws of the country so as to make necessary reforms, which might be called for throughout the years, underscores this point. In long-term occupations, the result may well be the stagnation of all aspects of life—economic, political, cultural, and social—with harsh consequences for the population. It is, in fact, hard to reconcile such an outcome with the occupant's general duty to ensure civil life in the occupied territory.[68] Furthermore, the longer the occupation lasts, the higher the likelihood of an uprising by the population, acting in pursuit of its right to self-determination. This, in turn, is likely to generate stricter security measures by the occupant, to the detriment of the population. The net result would thus be less, rather than more, weight given to the humanitarian and human rights concerns of the population, and, unless the uprising is successful, a further frustration of the right to self-determination, that is, a sacrifice of the trust at the altar of security. Such indeed is the sorry story of the Israeli occupation of the OPT.[69]

The story of the Israeli occupation had been framed by law even before it became a fact of power: much like a would-be parent carefully furnishing a nursery long before a child is born, the then Military Advocate-General (MAG)—and eventually Chief Justice of the Israeli Supreme Court—Meir Shamgar, had designed already in the early 1960s the legal framework within which the Israeli Defense Forces (IDF) was to exercise its power as an occupant. Thus, by June 1967, there was a cadre of trained military lawyers, accompanying the forces and ready to put the normative regime of occupation into effect.[70] The objective, said Shamgar, was to guarantee respect for the legal rights of the occupied population.[71] The means was innovative: to subject the actions of the IDF to judicial review, by allowing the occupied people to appeal to the highest judicial authority in Israel, the HCJ. The effect, alas, has been the judicial blurring of both physical and normative boundaries generating the legalization and legitimization of the dispossession of the occupied Palestinians. The fact that the initial military directive applying *GC IV* was cancelled and replaced by a thesis that the Convention does not apply (and that already in 1967, the territories were being considered as 'administered' rather than 'occupied', with the reference to 'Judea and Samaria' replacing the reference to 'the West Bank') is suggestive of what has come to pass. The story of the occupation, then, is inseparable from the story of law. It is also inseparable from the settlement enterprise.

The settlements generate both the dispossession of, and the discrimination against the Palestinians, thereby signifying Israel's breach of the trust entailed in the normative regime of occupation. In order to substantiate this argument, the

---

[68] Benvenisti, *supra* note 17, at 147; Roberts, *supra* note 52, at 52.

[69] As emphasized by Judge Elaraby. *Construction of a Wall, supra* note 5, Separate Opinion of Judge Elaraby, at para 3.1.

[70] See Eldar and Zertal, *Lords of the Land: The Settlers and the State of Israel 1967–2004* (2004) 439–453. It is notable that Israel was quite familiar with the notion of a military government, having effected it with respect to its Arab citizens between October 1948 and December 1966.

[71] Ibid, at 451.

remaining part of this subsection discusses the genesis of the settlements and the debate concerning their legality, and proceeds to focus on various aspects which their construction and maintenance entail, ranging from the confiscation of land to the existence of two separate legal systems in the area, operating along ethnic lines. While God, or the Devil, may well be in the details, for the purposes of this discussion, the focus is not on specific violations of the law of occupation occasioned by any particular action, violations that have indeed attracted attention elsewhere in the relevant literature. The main concern is rather with identifying the basic architecture of this occupation regime.

Immediately following the 1967 war, the Labor Government then in power initiated the settlement project based ostensibly on security considerations.[72] When the Likud Party, headed by Menachem Begin, formed a government in 1977, the security motive gave way to an ideological claim to the entire OPT, based on historical and religious grounds. The settlements enterprise thus became 'holy work', which Prime Minister Shamir, who took office after Begin in 1983, vowed to pursue.[73] That year, the Ministry of Agriculture and the World Zionist Organization (a quasi-governmental organization entrusted with furthering the political objectives of Zionism) jointly prepared a master-plan for the development of the settlements designed 'to achieve the incorporation (of the West Bank) into the (Israeli) national system'.[74] A comparison between its details and current ground realities indicate a high degree of geographical, if not demographical, materialization.[75] This has been achieved by land expropriation from the Palestinians coupled with economic incentives to the settlers.[76] As a result of this policy, there are at present some 121 settlements in the West Bank with over 289,600 settlers. The much ado about the 'disengagement' from the Gaza Strip involved the dismantlement

---

[72] See Benvenisti, *The West Bank Data Project: A Survey of Israel's Policies* (1984) 30–36; Shehadeh, *Occupier's Law: The West Bank and the Rule of Law* (1985) 15–49.

[73] Cited in Quigley, 'Living in Legal Limbo: Israel's Settlers in Occupied Palestinian Territory', 10 *Pace International Law Review* (1998) 1–29, at 6.

[74] Ibid. Note further that the first settlement plan prepared by the World Zionist Organization stated clearly that the objectives of the settlements were to make it difficult for the Palestinian population 'to form a territorial continuity and political unity when it is fragmented by Jewish settlements', cited in Kretzmer, *supra* note 5, at 76.

[75] Reproduced in Benvenisti, *supra* note 72, at 19–28.

[76] B'tselem, The Israeli Information Center for Human Rights in the Occupied Territories, Land Grab: Israel's Settlement Policy in the West Bank, available online at <http://www.btselem.org/Download/200205_Land_Grab_Eng.pdf> (hereinafter *Land Grab*) [last accessed 18 April 2010]. The settlers and other Israeli citizens working or investing in the settlements are entitled to significant financial benefits, such as generous loans for the purchase of apartments, part of which is converted to a grant, significant price reductions in leasing land, incentives for teachers, exemption from tuition fees in kindergartens, and free transportation to school, grants for investors, infrastructure for industrial zones, etc, incentives for social workers, and reductions in income tax for individuals and companies. The Ministry of the Interior provides increased grants for the local authorities in the territories relative to those provided for communities within Israel. Ibid. Additional data about the number of settlers and settlement is available on the website of the Israeli Central Bureau of Statistics: <http://www.cbs.gov.il/reader/shnaton/templ_shnaton.html?num_tab=st02_04&CYear=2009>. And on NGOs websites: <http://www.btselem.org/english/settlements/statistics.asp>; <http://www.peacenow.org.il/site/en/peace.asp?pi=61&docid=4372> [last accessed 18 April 2010].

of a mere 16 settlements and the evacuation of less than 10,000 settlers. Nearly 200,000 additional settlers live in the neighbourhoods of the expanded area of East Jerusalem. The population growth in the settlements is three times that of Israel.[77] At present, as noted by the *Goldstone Report*, Israel's Ministry of Housing and Planning is planning 'a further 73,000 settlement homes to be build in the West Bank. The building of 15,000 of these homes has already been approved, and, if all plans are realized, the number of settlers in the occupied Palestinian territory will be doubled.'[78]

The land upon which the settlements are built in the West Bank, when considered in tandem with adjacent confiscated land, settlements' by-pass roads, and other land controlled by the military, amounts to some 40 percent of the West Bank.[79] The settlements, and the bypass roads connecting them to each other as well as to Israel, have fragmented the West Bank into numerous discontinued zones; East Jerusalem is severed from the rest of the West Bank; Gaza is isolated.[80] The OPT has thus been dismembered.

The legal debate concerning the Israeli settlements has focused primarily on Article 49, paragraph 6 of *GC IV*, which prohibits the occupant from transferring parts of its own civilian population into the territory it occupies.[81] The Israeli government has always maintained that the prohibition does not include voluntary transfer by citizens to occupied territories because it was informed by, and should be interpreted in the light of, the policies practiced by Germany during the Second World War, policies to which the Israeli policy cannot be compared.[82]

---

[77] *Human Rights Situation in Palestine and Other Occupied Arab Territories*, Report of the Special Rapporteur of the Commission on Human Rights, John Dugard, on the situation of human rights in the Palestinian territories occupied by Israel since 1967, UN A/HRC/7/17 (21 January 2008) para 30 (hereinafter *2008 Human Rights Situation in Palestine and Other Occupied Arab Territories*); see *Question of the Violation of Human Rights in the Occupied Arab Territories, Including Palestine*, Report of the Special Rapporteur of the Commission on Human Rights, John Dugard, on the situation of human rights in the Palestinian territories occupied by Israel since 1967, UN E/CN.4/2004/6 (8 September 2003) (hereinafter *2003 Report on the Situation of Human Rights in the Palestinian Territories*); *Question of the Violation of Human Rights in the Occupied Arab Territories, Including Palestine*, Report of the Special Rapporteur of the Commission on Human Rights, John Dugard, on the situation of human rights in the Palestinian territories occupied by Israel since 1967, UN A/HRC/4/17 (29 January 2007) para 32 (hereinafter *2007 Report on the Situation of Human Rights in the Palestinian Territories*).   [78] *Goldstone Report, supra* note 14, at para 95.

[79] *2008 Human Rights Situation in Palestine and Other Occupied Arab Territories, supra* note 77, at para 30.

[80] *Question of the Violation of Human Rights in the Occupied Arab Territories, Including Palestine*, Update to the mission report on Israel's violations of human rights in the Palestinian territories occupied since 1967, submitted by Giorgio Giacomelli, Special Rapporteur, to the Commission on Human Rights at its fifth special session, UN E/CN.4/2001/30 (21 March 2001) para 26; ibid, at paras 30–40. For a discussion of the politics of the geography and planning of the settlements, see Segal and Weizman, 'The Mountain Principle of Building in Heights', in Segal, Tartakover, and Weizman (eds), *A Civilian Occupation: The Politics of Israeli Architecture* (2003) 75–93, at 79.

[81] Such transfer further constitutes a grave breach of *AP I*. See Art.85(4)(a) of *AP I*.

[82] For the Israeli position see <http://www.mfa.gov.il/mfa/go.asp?MFAH0jyz0> [last accessed 18 April 2010]; Levy, 'Israel Rejects Its Own Offspring: The International Criminal Court', 22 *Loy. L.A. Int'l & Comp. L. Rev.* (1999) 207–249, at 230–231; Henckaerts, 'Deportation and Transfer of Civilians in Time of War', 26 *Vanderbilt Journal of Transnational Law* (1993) 469–519, at 472.

This position is inconsistent with the ICRC's commentary on the Fourth Convention, according to which the intent of the drafters was to maintain a general demographic status quo in occupied territories.[83] Further pronouncement by the parties to the Convention rejected the Israeli interpretation, by declaring the settlements to reflect a breach of Article 49.[84] This is the context for understanding the different version of this prohibition adopted in Article 8(2)(b)(viii) of the Rome Statute, which criminalizes such transfer whether it is undertaken directly or indirectly. This provision might well render Israel's incentive policy as an 'indirect transfer', and largely explains Israel's decision not to ratify the Statute.[85]

Given, however, that the Israeli government built the settlements and given further the financial incentives provided to settlers, the settlement project is a 'direct transfer', and thus falls within the scope of the original prohibition of Article 49(6).[86] The ICJ had an opportunity to opine on this matter in its Advisory Opinion on the *Construction of a Wall*, as the 'wall's sinuous route has been traced in such a way as to include within that area the great majority of the Israeli settlements in the occupied Palestinian Territory (including East Jerusalem)'.[87] Noting that 'since 1977, Israel has conducted a policy and developed practices involving the establishment of settlements in the Occupied Palestinian Territory contrary to the terms of Art. 49 paragraph 6', the ICJ concluded that 'the Israeli settlements in the Occupied Palestinian Territory (including east Jerusalem) have been established in breach of international law'.[88]

Israel's extensive confiscation of Palestinian land, carried out to satisfy the needs of the continuing expansion of the settlements,[89] might also amount to a grave breach under Article 147 of *GC IV*. Article 147 prohibits 'extensive appropriation of property, not justified by military necessity and carried out unlawfully

---

[83] Pictet, *supra* note 32, at 283.

[84] See Declaration of the Conference of the Parties to the Fourth Geneva Convention, 5 December 2001, available online at
<http://domino.un.org/UNISPAL.NSF/fd807e46661e3689852570d00069e918/8fc4f064b9be5 bad85256c1400722951?OpenDocument> [last accessed 18 April 2010]; Glahn, *Law Among Nations: An Introduction to Public International Law* (7th edn, 1996) 675–676.

[85] See statement to that effect made by the then Legal Advisor to the Israeli Foreign Ministry Allen Baker, on 3 January 2001 available online at <http://www.mfa.gov.il/MFA/ MFAArchive/2000_2009/2001/1/International+Criminal+Court+-+Press+Briefing+by+I.htm> [last accessed 18 April 2010]. Israel signed the Statute on 31 December 2001, attaching a declaration conveying its disappointment of what was termed by it the 'politicization' of the Statute by the insertion of 'formulations tailored to meet the political agenda of certain states. On 28 August 2002 Israel informed the UN Secretary-General of its intention not to ratify the Statute. On the status of ratifications of the Rome Statute, including declarations made by Israel, see <http://www.amicc.org/ icc_ratifications.html#> [last accessed 18 April 2010].

[86] See Drew, 'Self–determination, Population Transfer and the Middle East Peace Accords', in Bowen (ed), *Human Rights, Self-Determination and Political Change in the Occupied Palestinian Territories* (1997) 119–168, at 144–146.   [87] *Construction of a Wall, supra* note 5, at para 119.

[88] Ibid, at para 120. The Court reached this conclusion based *inter alia* on UN Security Council Resolution 446 (1979).

[89] Such expropriation has continued during and after the Oslo process. On the expropriation methods, See generally, Shehadeh, *From Occupation to Interim Accords: Israel and the Palestinian Territories* (1997) 3–35; Imseis, *supra* note 41, at 102.

and wantonly'.[90] Such action is criminalized by Article 8(2)(a)(iv) of the Rome Statute.

The method and effect of this expropriation merit attention: following a determination by the HCJ that private land could not be confiscated for the establishment of civilian settlements,[91] the Israeli government moved quickly to define ever greater portions of the occupied territories as 'state land'. Such definition was facilitated by the lack of a comprehensive land ownership registration in the OPT which made it quite difficult for individuals to prove their land ownership, as well as by a governmental decision to designate all uncultivated rural land as 'state land'.[92] The effect of these practices has been two-fold: first, the *de facto* dispossession of individual Palestinians; second, the dispossession of the Palestinian population of land reserves that should primarily have served its interests. Instead, these lands are administered by the Israel Land Administration, a body set up under Israeli Law to administer state land in Israel proper, and now being used for settlements.[93]

Israel has also used control over planning to restrict the growth of Palestinian towns and villages, while expanding the settlements.[94] This control has been exercised by omission, that is, by refraining from 'preparing updated regional outline plans for the West Bank. As a result, until the transfer of authority to the Palestinian Authority (and, to this day, in area "C"), two regional plans prepared in the 1940's by the British Mandate continue to apply...'[95] Subsequent 'special partial outline plans' for some four hundred villages, far from alleviating the problem of inadequate planning schemes, underscored its rationale as they constituted demarcation plans which prohibited construction outside existing lines. This administrative and legal structure has then been used both to justify the rejection of Palestinians' applications for building permits on private land, and to issue demolition orders for houses that were constructed without permits.[96] Thus, the law that vested the occupant with the power to ensure the welfare of the occupied population has been used by the former to advance its own interests to the detriment of the latter.

Different phenomena are associated with the settlements, such as inequality in the allocation of water resources coupled with acute water shortage in

---

[90] Note that the *Construction of a Wall*, does not cite Art 147 of *GC IV* as relevant to the case at hand. This is due to the Court's interpretation of Art 6 as precluding the applicability of all but 43 of the Convention's 159 Articles including Art 147. This interpretation is unconvincing, even absurd, as is discussed in *infra* text between notes 122 and 135.

[91] HCJ 390/79 *Dewikat v Government of Israel*, 34(1) PD 1; See Kretzmer, *supra* note 5, at 85–89.

[92] For a detailed account of these practices and the complex set of legal mechanisms that enable them, see *Land Grab, supra* note 76; Shehadeh, *supra* note 72, at 22–41; see Kretzmer, *supra* note 5, at 89–94.   [93] See Kretzmer, *supra* note 5, at 95.

[94] Israel transferred the planning authority from the Jordanian Ministry of the Interior to the Commander of the IDF Forces in region. Following the Oslo Accords Israel retained this authority over area 'C', comprising some 60 percent of the West Bank territory and some 600,000 Palestinians. See *Land Grab, supra* note 76.   [95] Ibid.

[96] Ibid; Amnesty International, Demolition and Dispossession: The Destruction of Palestinian Homes, MDE 15/059/1999 (8 December 1999), available online at <http://www.amnesty.org/en/library/asset/MDE15/059/1999/en/3072a0ae-e065-11dd-9086-4d51a30f9335/mde150591999en.pdf> [last accessed 18 April 2010].

the Palestinian villages[97] and acts of violence committed by settlers against the Palestinian population which receive no proper response from the Israeli security forces.[98] It is, however, the legal terrain wrought by the occupation which merits special attention in the context of the present analysis. There are separate legal systems operating concurrently in the West Bank, effectively dividing the population along ethnic lines: Jewish settlers are extra-territorially subject to Israeli civilian law, whereas the Palestinians are subject to the Israeli military law and to local law.[99] Two methods are used to generate this situation: first, the application of Israeli law *in personam* to Israeli citizens and Jews in the OPT; second, the partial application of Israeli law, on a supposedly territorial basis, to the Jewish settlements in the OPT.

The personal application of Israeli law works in a myriad of ways. For example, Emergency Regulations issued by the Israeli government, and renewed regularly through legislation,[100] determine that Israeli courts will have jurisdiction over criminal offences committed by Israeli citizens, (and in general by people who are present in Israel) in the OPT, even if the offence took place in areas under the control of the Palestinian Authority.[101] Further, the law extending the Emergency Regulations determines that for certain statutes, people who live in the OPT will

---

[97] The average Palestinian in the West Bank residing in communities connected to a water network consumes 60 litres of water per day. The consumption of water by people not thus connected, while unknown, is certainly lower. The average consumption per capita in Israel as well as in the settlements is almost six times higher, that is, 350 litres a day. In practical terms this discrepancy means that settlements enjoy an unlimited supply of running water which allows for swimming pools and green lawns, while their neighbouring Palestinians often lack drinking and bathing water See Lein, 'Not Even A Drop: The Water Crisis in Palestinian Villages Without a Water Network' (2001); Lein, 'Thirsty for a Solution: The Water Crisis in the Occupied Territories and Its Resolution in the Final Status Agreement' (2002), available online at <http://www.btselem.org/Download/200107_Not_Even_A_Drop_Eng.doc> [last accessed 18 April 2010]; Lein, 'Disputed Waters: Israel's Responsibility for the Water Shortage in the Occupied Territories', (1998), available online at <http://www.btselem.org/Download/199809_Disputed_Waters_Eng.doc> [last accessed 18 April 2010].

[98] See SC Res 471 of 5 June 1980, UN SCOR 35th Sess, 2226th mtg UN Doc S/RES/36 (1980); SC Res 904 of 18 March 1994, UN SCOR 49th Sess, 3351 mtg, UN Doc S/RES/50 (1994), calling on Israel to assume its obligation to protect the civilian population and to take measures, including the confiscation of arms, to prevent illegal acts of violence by Israeli settlers; *Human Rights in Palestine and Other Occupied Arab Territories, Goldstone Report supra* note 14, at paras 1824–1828 and 1405–1409; See B'tselem website on this issue: <http://www.btselem.org/english/settler_violence/index.asp> [last accessed 18 April 2010]; Dudai, 'Free Rein: Vigilant Settlers and Israel's Non-Enforcement of the Law' (2001), available online at <http://www.btselem.org/Download/200110_Free_Rein_Eng.doc> [last accessed 18 April 2010]. This violence is particularly prevalent in Hebron, a city where 180,000 Palestinians live, and where a population of approximately 450 Jewish settlers is effectively allowed to humiliate, threaten, and exercise violence against Palestinian property and people. See, Swissa, 'Hebron, Area H2: Settlements Cause Mass Departure of Palestinians', (2003), available online at <http://www.btselem.org/Download/200308_Hebron_Area_H2_Eng.pdf> [last accessed 18 April 2010]; *2007 Report on the Situation of Human Rights in the Palestinian Territories, supra* note 77, at para 34; See Yesh Din—Volunteers for Human Rights, 'A Semblance of Law. Law Enforcement upon Israeli Civilians in the West Bank' (2006), available online at <http://www.yesh-din.org/report/ASemblanceofLaw-Eng.pdf> [last accessed 18 April 2010].

[99] Imseis, *supra* note 41, at 106.

[100] Law for the Extension of Emergency Regulations (Judea, Samaria and the Gaza Strip—Judging for Offences and Legal Aid) 1971.

[101] Other regulations allow Israeli courts in civil suits to engage with matters relating to residents of the OPT. Civil Procedure Regulations (Issuing of Documents to the Occupied Territories) 1969.

be considered residents of Israel, if they are Israeli citizens *or* are 'entitled to immigrate to Israel under the Law of Return' (ie Jews and family members of Jews).[102] These statutes, 17 in total, include the Income Tax Ordinance, the Social Security Law 1968, and the National Health Care Law 1994.[103] The net result is that there is a different set of rights and duties applying to different groups in the OPT along ethnic lines. Finally, of particular interest in this context, is the extension, on a personal basis, of Israel's Election Law, which determines that Israelis who reside in territories held by the IDF will be able to vote in their place of residence.[104] This provision is significant, especially when considered against the lack of absentee ballot in Israel.[105] Its effect is to allow Israeli settlers in the OPT to take part in choosing the government which rules these territories as an occupying power, whereas the Palestinian residents of the very same territories, who are also subject to the actions of this very same government, do not partake in choosing it.[106]

Whereas the personal application of Israeli law to Israelis—and in some cases, to non-Israeli Jews—in the OPT is effected through Emergency Regulations issued by the Israeli government and extended by the Israeli legislature, territorial application occurs through Orders issued by the Israeli Military Commander in the territories.[107] These Orders give special status to Jewish settlements in the OPT by applying certain aspects of Israeli law in various spheres, such as education, to those territorial units, giving them the privileges enjoyed by localities within Israel. The same mechanism further prohibits Palestinians from entry into the settlements unless they possess a special permit, a permit from which Israelis are exempt. Israelis are defined for this purpose as (1) residents of Israel; (2) residents of the territories who are Israeli citizens, or allowed to immigrate to Israel under the Law of Return; and, (3) people who are not residents of the territories, but have a valid visa to Israel. This definition extends the privilege of entering the settlements beyond Israeli citizens and Jews to tourists who are neither Israelis nor Jewish.[108]

---

[102] The Law of Return 1950 gives, in Art 1, the right to immigrate to Israel to Jews (defined in Art 4B as a person who is the offspring of a Jewish mother, or converted to Judaism, and is not a member of another religion), and also to children, grandchildren, and spouses of Jews, and to spouses of children and grandchildren of Jews, unless they were born Jews and willingly converted to another religion (Art 4A).

[103] This law does not apply in areas under the control of the Palestinian Authority, a fact that has no practical effect as Israelis and Jews do not reside in these areas.

[104] Art 147 of the Election Law (Consolidated Version) 1969.

[105] Israeli law does not allow Israeli citizens, with the exception of diplomats and similar official groups of people, to vote outside the geographic boundaries of Israel. (See Art 6 of the Election Law [Consolidated Version] 1969.)

[106] For an analysis of the Israeli legislation applying Israeli law on a personal basis to Israelis in the territories, see Rubinstein, 'The Changing Status of the 'Territories' (West Bank and Gaza): From Escrow to Legal Mongrel', 8 *Tel Aviv University Studies in Law* (1998) 59–79, at 68–72. For a discussion of the significance of the difference in suffrage, See Yiftachel, 'Ethnocracy': The Politics of Judaizing Israel/Palestine', 6 *Constellations* (1999) 364–390, at 377.

[107] Order regarding Management of Regional Councils (No 783) and Order regarding Management of Local Council (No 892). cited in *Land Grab, supra* note 76.

[108] Order Concerning Security Instructions (Judea and Sameria) (No 378) 1970—Announcement on a Closed Area (Israeli settlements), cited in *Land Grab, supra* note 76. For a discussion of the military legislation applying Israeli law on the settlements on a territorial basis, see Rubinstein, *supra* note 106, at 72–79.

Given this last qualification, the supposedly territorial application of said laws may also be seen as personal. The net result is the creation of two separate legal regimes, based on a combination of personal and territorial factors.

It should finally be noted that in a decision concerning the rights of Israeli settlers evacuated from the Gaza Strip, the HCJ decided that the Israeli Basic Laws (which comprise the nascent Constitution of Israel), including the Basic Law: Human Dignity and Liberty apply *in personam* to Israelis in the occupied territories, leaving open the question of the application of these laws to the Palestinian residents of the same territories.[109]

This partial application of Israeli law to the OPT, observed leading Israeli constitutional law scholar, Amnon Rubinstein, already in 1988, has generated the blurring of the boundaries between Israel and the territories, as well as the drastic change in the status of the territories from 'escrow' to 'legal mongrel': Once perceived as an 'escrow' under the rules of international law—that is, as a trust—'they have gradually been incorporated in practice into the realm of Israel's rule'.[110] The substitution of the 'legal mongrel' for the 'escrow' clearly signifies the breach of trust by the occupier, and the veiled annexation of the territories. Given that the violation of trust and the veiled annexation breach the two basic tenets of the normative regime of occupation, it would be more appropriate to conclude that the transition effected was from an 'escrow' to an 'illegal mongrel'.

It follows from the above that the legal structure of the occupation regime has been *designed* to—and in fact *does*—serve the interests of the settlers more than it does the interests of the occupied population. Indeed it does so at the latter's expense. It thus breaches the obligations of the occupant under Article 43 of the Hague Regulations, and contravenes the basic tenet of trust inherent in the law of occupation.[111] Inasmuch as the justness of an occupation is determined, as suggested by Michael Walzer in the context of the American occupation of Iraq, by its political direction and the distribution of benefits it provides,[112] the occupation of the OPT appears to be neither legal nor just.

The unjustness of the political geography created by the complex legal system of the occupation is most poignant in its tragic effect on the daily life of the occupied population.[113] The construction of the Wall signifies the culmination of policies that have devastated daily life. The ICJ's reading of this situation is quite pertinent:

[T]he route chosen for the wall gives expression *in loco* to the illegal measures taken by Israel with regard to Jerusalem and the settlements, as deplored by the Security

---

[109] *Regional Council Gaza Beach, supra* note 4, at paras 78–80; See also HCJ 3278/02 *The Center for the Defense of the Individual v Commander of the IDF in the West Bank*, 57(1) PD 385.

[110] Rubinstein, *supra* note 106, at 67.

[111] It is worthwhile to note here that the Israeli Supreme Court contributed to the undermining of Art 43, when it allowed large scale changes in local law and included the settlers as part of the local population for the purposes of Art 43. See Kretzmer, *supra* note 5, at 187.

[112] See Walzer, *Arguing About War* (2004) 162–165.

[113] *Question of the Violation of Human Rights in the Occupied Arab Territories, Including Palestine*, Report of the Special Rapporteur of the Commission on Human Rights, John Dugard, on the situation of human rights in the Palestinian territories occupied by Israel since 1967, UN E/CN.4/2006/29 (17 January 2006) para 34.

Council...There is also a risk of further alterations to the demographic composition of the Occupied Palestinian Territory...inasmuch as it is contributing to the departure of Palestinian population from certain areas...That construction, along with the measures taken previously, thus severely impedes the exercise by the Palestinian people of its right to self-determination...[114]

The destruction of the fabric of life of the Palestinian residents of the OPT is evident. It is equally clear, however, that an occupying power is not required to forsake its own security interests. Indeed, Israel contends that the Palestinians, having responded to Israel's offer to end the conflict with the *al-Aqsa intifada* comprising indiscriminate terrorist attacks—attacks constituting crimes against humanity[115]—against Israeli citizens, are responsible for their situation.[116] Israel argues further that 'many of the Palestinian terrorist groups perpetrate their atrocities not to put an end to Israel's presence, but rather to frustrate any political progress that may do just that'.[117] Israel's thesis thus rests on an attempt to sever the nexus between the occupation and the *Intifada* and, indeed, between its obligations as an occupying power and its right and duty to protect its own citizens and security.

In order to assess this issue, it is necessary to inquire into the last tenet of the normative regime, its temporal dimension.

3. *ChronoLAWgy: an occupation is temporary*

The two basic principles discussed above generate the third principle of occupation, its temporariness. Indeed, the very essence of occupation decrees so. Thus, writes Graber:

The modern law of belligerent occupation is anchored in the concept that occupation differs in its nature and legal consequences from conquest. It is therefore not surprising that the early definitions of the modern concept of occupation are chiefly concerned with the main aspects of this difference, namely the *temporary nature* of belligerent occupation as contrasted with the permanency of conquest, and *the limited, rather than the full powers* which belligerent occupation entails for the occupant.[118]

It is in this light that one should understand the various provisions in the documents detailing the law of occupation that have, *ab initio*, imposed constraints on the managerial powers of the occupant, evidencing the temporary nature of its

---

[114] *Construction of a Wall, supra* note 5, para 122.

[115] See Amnesty International, *Without Distinction—Attacks on Civilians by Palestinian Armed Groups* (10 July 2002). Available from: <http://www.amnesty.org/en/library/info/MDE02/003/2002> [last accessed 18 April 2010]

[116] See, for example, Israel's Response to the *Report Submitted by the Special Rapporteur on the Right to Food*, submitted to the Commission on Human Rights, 60th Sess, E/CN.4/2004/G/14 (6 November 2003) paras 5 and 6.

[117] Question of the Violation of Human Rights in the Occupied Arab Territories, Including Palestine, Note Verbale Dated 16 December 2002 from the Permanent Representative of Israel to the United Nations Office at Geneva Addressed to the Secretariat of the Commission of Human Rights, Commission of Human Rights, 59th Sess, E/CN.4/2003.G/21, (23 December 2002) at section 2.

[118] Graber, *The Development of the Law of Belligerent Occupation 1863-1914—A Historical Survey* (1949) at 37 (emphasis added).

control. Article 43 of the 1899 and 1907 Hague Conventions imposed a duty on the occupant to respect, unless 'absolutely prevented', the laws in force in the country. This understanding of the provisional, non-sovereign status of the occupant is reaffirmed by Article 55 of the 1907 Fourth Hague Convention stating that the occupant is merely to administer and safeguard public buildings, real estate, and the agriculture estates belonging to the state.[119]

The idea of occupation as a temporary form of control underlies the provisions of *GC IV*. Due, however, to the shift in emphasis of the Convention from the rights of the ousted sovereign, to the welfare of the occupied population, the temporal restrictions on the occupying authority are more implicit than explicit when compared to earlier codes. Thus, for instance, the non-recognition of annexation, stipulated in Article 47 of *GC IV*, is informed by, but does not explicitly state, the temporal nature of occupation.[120] This may also be said with regard to paragraph 6 of Article 49 prohibiting the settlement of the occupant's nationals in the occupied territory: informed by Second World War experience with the mass transportation of population, the provision was also designed to ensure that the sociological and demographic structure of the territory will be left unchanged.[121]

Further indication of the temporary nature of the occupation and its limitation to the preservation of the status quo is found in Article 54 of *GC IV* stipulating that the status of judges and public officials in the territory shall not be altered. This proscription reaffirms the maintenance of the country's judicial and administrative structure, which is expected to go on functioning without hindrance, and enhances the conclusion that the occupant authority is temporary and non-sovereign. Article 64 contains a similar provision with respect to the laws in place and, as suggested by the Convention's Commentary, 'expresses, in a more precise and detailed form, the terms of Art. 43 of the Hague regulations, which lays down that the Occupying Power is to respect the laws in force in the country "unless absolutely prevented"'.[122]

Article 6 of *GC IV* relates most directly to the temporal limits of occupation and thus merits special attention. It provides in paragraph 3:

In the case of occupied territory, the application of the present Convention shall cease one year after the general close of military operations; however, the Occupying Power shall be bound, for the duration of the occupation, to the extent that such Power exercises the functions of government in such territory, by the provisions of the following Articles 1 to 12, 27, 29 to 34, 47, 49, 51, 52, 53, 59, 61 to 77, 143 . . .

The ICJ considered this provision in the *Construction of a Wall* Advisory Opinion. The Court opined that:

[a] distinction is also made in the Fourth Geneva Convention between provisions applying during military operations leading to the occupation and those that remain applicable

---

[119] Gasser, 'Protection of the Civilian Population', in Fleck (ed), *The Handbook of Humanitarian Law in Armed Conflict* (1995) 209–292, at 246 (hereinafter *Handbook*).

[120] Pictet, *supra* note 32, at 274; Benvenisti, *supra* note 17, at 99.

[121] Pictet, ibid, at 283. This prohibition could also be understood as designed to prevent a situation wherein citizens of the occupying power reside in the occupied area and are subject to a different legal regime.   [122] Pictet, ibid, at 335.

throughout the entire period of occupation . . . Since the military operations leading to the occupation of the West Bank in 1967 ended a long time ago, only those Articles of the Fourth Geneva Convention referred to in Article 6, paragraph 3, remain applicable in that occupied territory.[123]

It is submitted that this textual interpretation, leading to the conclusion that long-term occupations reduce the responsibilities of occupying powers vis-à-vis the occupied civilian population, is an absurd conclusion: it is unwarranted by the text and is further incongruent with the purpose and legal practice of the normative regime of occupation, confusing a problem with a solution.[124]

Textually, Article 6 refers to a 'general close of military operations'. It does not refer to military operations 'leading to the occupation'.[125] The latter is a judicial insertion. The realities of the occupation in general, and in particular the circumstances surrounding the construction of the Wall (itself a military operation), attest to the fact of ongoing military operations. Thus, even a literal reading of the text of Article 6 should have revealed its inapplicability on its own terms. Indeed, Article 6 lends itself to an entirely different reading.

According to the language of Article 6, in an occupation that lasts longer than one year after the close of military operations, only 23 of the 32 articles comprising Section III of the Convention which deals with occupied territories would continue to apply.[126] The nine articles that would cease to apply include, for instance, the obligation incumbent on the occupying power to 'facilitate the proper working of all institutions devoted to the care and education of children'[127] and 'the duty of ensuring the food and medical supplies of the population'.[128] It is unreasonable to assume that the drafters of the Convention intended for children to be deprived of proper schooling or for the population to be deprived of medical supplies and food in long-term occupations, as such an intention would defy the Convention's main objective. The only reasonable conclusion, therefore, is that the working assumption behind Article 6 was that the situation of an occupation is bound to be relatively short and that responsibilities of this kind would be transferred to local authorities in a process leading to the end of the exceptional situation of occupation. The *travaux préparatoires* and the Commentary confirm this assumption.[129] Once reality defies the assumption, however, the rationale

---

[123] *Construction of a Wall, supra* note 5, at para 125. At para 126 the Court proceeded to identify Arts 47, 49, 52, 53, and 59 of the Fourth Geneva Convention as relevant to the question at hand. For a similar interpretation see Dinstein, 'The International Legal Status of the West Bank and the Gaza Strip—1998', 28 *Israel Yearbook on Human Rights* (1998) 37–51, at 42–44.

[124] For a critical review of this aspect of the Advisory Opinion see Ben-Naftali, *supra* note 10.

[125] *Construction of a Wall, supra* note 5, at para 125. Note that in para 135, in the context of addressing the term 'military operations' in Art 53 in order to determine the existence of military exigencies, the Court said that such exigencies 'may be invoked in occupied territories even after the general close of military operations that *led to their occupation*' (emphasis added).

[126] While 43 of the 159 Articles of the Conventions continue to apply, the emphasis is on Arts 47–78 comprising the relevant Section III.   [127] *GC IV*, Art 50

[128] Ibid, Art 55

[129] See 2A Final Record of the Diplomatic Conference of Geneva 1949, at 623–625; Pictet, *supra* note 32, at 63; Roberts, *supra* note 52, at 52–56. Roberts advances four arguments for the inapplicability of Art 6.

informing Article 6 disappears and, insofar as law is to make sense, it should no longer apply.

Subsequent developments in both law and legal practice lend support to this proposed reading of the provision: once it became clear that the drafters' assumption regarding the short duration of occupations was not supported by reality, and that this provision may be construed by occupying powers as limiting their responsibilities under the Convention precisely in situations where the latter should be expanded, the provision was abrogated: Article 3(b) of *AP I* provides for the application of the Protocol's provisions until the termination of the occupation.[130]

The argument that Article 6 of *GC IV* limits the Convention's scope of applicability was never raised before Israeli Courts, and indeed the Israeli HCJ had applied provisions that would have otherwise become inapplicable in light of the language of Article 6.[131] This practice characterizes other prolonged occupations,[132] thereby lending support to the proposition that Article 3(b) of *AP I* enjoys customary status.

Further, the Court's determination regarding the limited scope of applicability of *GC IV* is incongruent with—and defies the rationale behind—its determination regarding the applicability of various human rights instruments together with humanitarian law in occupied territories. This co-application is designed to offer greater protection to the civilian population. It is this incongruence which explains the odd conclusion of the Court that Israel had violated some of its human rights obligations but not the very same obligations—only far clearer and specifically designed for the situation of occupation—as they appear in *GC IV*.[133] The implication is that human rights law came into play to fill a lacuna in the Geneva Convention, whereas, in fact, the latter contains relevant provisions. The lacuna, therefore, is constructed only to be filled by another, and less suitable, normative source. This does not make much sense.

It follows from the above that a proper reading of Article 6 should have generated the conclusion that this provision has, as Roberts suggested, 'correctly identified a problem', the problem of a prolonged occupation, but not a proper solution.[134] It is regrettable that the Court confused the solution with the problem. Had it engaged in a discussion of the temporal assumption informing *GC IV*, it

---

[130] Sandoz, Swinarski, and Zimmermann, *supra* note 33, at 66; Roberts, *supra* note 52, at 56. Admittedly, the language of Art 3(b) is unclear, and could be construed as suggesting that it applies *GC IV* subject to its own terms. For this construction see Dinstein *supra* note 123, at 37 and 43. Such a reading, however, defies both the drafters' intention and the teleological test of international humanitarian law.

[131] eg Art 78 of *GC IV* was applied by the HCJ in HCJ 7015/02 *Ajuri v IDF Commander in Judea and Samaria* 56(6) PD 352 (hereinafter *Ajuri*).   [132] Roberts, *supra* note 52, at 55.

[133] See eg Art 50 protecting children's right to education does not apply but this very same right as it appears in Art 28 of the Convention on the Rights of the Child (CRC) and Arts 10, 13 and 14 of the International Convention on Economic Social and Cultural Rights (ICESCR), does apply. Similarly, Arts 55 and 56, which stipulate the duty of the occupant to ensure the population's health through provision of food and medical supplies and the maintenance of medical and hospital establishments, has no applicability while similar duties, far less specific, clear and legally binding, enshrined in Arts 11 and 12 of the ICESCR (the right to adequate standard of living and the right to health respectively) and Arts 24 and 27 of the CRC (the rights to health and adequate standard of living and development respectively) apply.   [134] Roberts, *supra* note 52, at 57.

could have produced not merely a better reading of Article 6, but further shed light on the temporal limitations of an occupation. The remaining part of this Section offers such a discussion.

While there is overwhelming evidence for the proposition that the normative regime of occupation requires that it be temporary, no explicit time limit is set for its duration.[135] The absence of such exact time limits has been explained, indeed explained away, by Justice Meir Shamgar as being reflective of 'a factual situation', generating the conclusion that 'pending an alternative political or military solution this system of government could, from a legal point of view, continue indefinitely'.[136]

A legal point of view, however, is not merely reflective of a factual situation, nor does it sanction the substitution of 'indefinite' for 'temporary'. A temporary situation definitely has an end. An indefinite situation may, or may not, have an end. The two situations are very different. In order to appreciate the point, it is useful to reflect momentarily on the human condition: it is largely controlled by our awareness that our existence is temporary; had we conceived of our existence as indefinite, it is quite likely that the human condition would have altered significantly. 'Under the heaven', we are free to believe that there is 'a time for every purpose', but on earth, we know and understand time as a limited resource.[137] Time affects us individually and socially and it is our awareness of the temporary nature of the human existence which shapes, *inter alia*, our social institutions, including our law.

Law, far from reflecting time as a natural indefinite, allocates, distributes, and mediates time as a 'commodity, the supply of which is not inexhaustible'.[138] Law shapes our perceptions of the realities of time as an historical, social, cultural, and political construct.[139] Law thus defines not only the supposedly natural time of birth and of death, of childhood and of adulthood, but also incorporates certain assumptions about individual and collective time to delineate rights and duties.[140] Indeed, the very principle of legality as well as foundational legal presumptions, signify embedded conceptions of demarcated time without which they, and law itself, would be meaningless.[141]

---

[135] See *Construction of a Wall, supra* note 5, Separate Opinion of Judge Elaraby, at para 3.1; Separate Opinion of Judge Koroma, at para 2.

[136] Shamgar, 'Legal Concepts and Problems of the Israeli Military Government—The Initial Stage', in Shamgar (ed), *Military Government in the Territories Administered by Israel 1967–1980* (1982) 13–60, at 43.   [137] *Ecclesiastes* 3:1.

[138] Renquist, 'Successful Lawyers Pay the Price', 82 *A.B.A.J.* (1996) 100–101.

[139] On the ways time is conceived by law see generally, Greenhouse, 'Just in Time: Temporality and the Cultural Legitimation of Law', 98 *Yale L.J.* (1989) 1631–1651; French, 'Time in the Law', 72 *U. Colo. L.R.* (2001) 663–748; Rakoff, *A Time for Every Purpose: Law and the Balance of Life* (2002); Rubenfeld, *Freedom and Time: A Theory of Constitutional Self-Government* (2001).

[140] eg Statutes of limitations; jurisdictional time limits; civil and criminal procedure laws; the laws of evidence, intellectual property protections; the rule against perpetuities and sentencing are but examples that immediately come to mind and all embody legal assumptions about human interaction with time.

[141] eg The principle of *nullum crimen sine lege*, that is, of non-retroactivity is meaningful only due to the centrality of the concept of time. Similarly, any legal presumption would have been rendered meaningless where it not for the temporal dimension which allows for its refutation.

Law, then, is preoccupied with time. Given that the distribution of limited resources is a major legal function, the construction of time as a limited resource implies that law is interested in the distribution of time. Time, however, unlike other natural commodities, is *construed* as limited. As such, it cannot be distributed *in abstracto,* but only in relation to a concrete action. Indeed, it is the very conception of time as a limited resource that endows the concrete action with meaning and requires time allocation relative to competing interests. An example may illustrate this point: administrative detention is a concrete action which involves two competing interests: the public safety interest on the one hand, and the human right to liberty, on the other hand. As time is understood as a limited resource, the individual cannot be detained indefinitely and it is for this reason that a reasonable time limit is set on the action: if administrative detention were permitted indefinitely, liberty would have lost its meaning. Any other interpretation would be unreasonable.

It is equally unreasonable to place the concrete situation of occupation within an indefinite time frame. If occupation 'could, from a legal point of view, continue indefinitely', the interests it is designed to protect—the interest of the occupied people in reaching the point in time where they regain control over their life and exercise their right to self-determination, and the interest of the international system in resuming its normal order of sovereign equality between states—would be rendered meaningless. This, indeed, is the rationale behind the temporary—as distinct from the indefinite—nature of occupation.[142]

The notion of 'reasonable time' thus underlies any concrete limits set by law on the duration of an action. The very same rationale holds for setting limits on the duration of actions which are not defined in concrete temporal terms. The conclusion that actions not defined in concrete temporal terms somehow transform the temporary into the indefinite is unreasonable. Indeed, in such situations, the concrete time limit is determined by the legal construct of 'reasonable time', deriving from the legal principle of 'reasonableness'.[143] What is a reasonable time for an action depends on the nature, purpose, and circumstances of the action.[144]

---

[142] Applying this rationale to the analogous, for the purpose of this discussion, situation of a Mandate, a situation where no time limits have been explicitly set, Judge Ammoun concluded that: 'Mandates must have an end or are revocable'. See *Continued Presence of South Africa in Namibia,* Advisory Opinion, *supra* note 53, Separate Opinion of Vice-President Ammoun, at 72–73.

[143] The principle of reasonableness is a general principle of international law. Its application has generated the conclusion that a right cannot be exercised in a wholly unreasonable manner causing harm disproportionate to the right's holder interests. See Cheng, *General Principles of Law: As Applies by International Courts and Tribunals* (1987) at 121–123; see also, *World Trade Organization Appellate Body: Report of the Appellate Body in United States—Standards for Reformulated and Conventional Gasoline,* reprinted in 35 ILM (1996) 603–634, at 626.

[144] eg The Uniform Negotiable Instruments Law sets standards for the measurement of 'reasonable time'. See Speidel and Nicks, *Negotiable Instruments and Check Collections (The New Law) in a Nutshell* (4th edn, 1993) 60–61, 148–149, 152; Similarly, 'reasonable time' for taking an action is contemplated in the Uniform Commercial Code (Colorado) as depending 'on the nature, purpose and circumstances of such action'. See <http://www.law.du.edu/russell/contracts/ucc/4-1-204.htm.> [last accessed 18 April 2010]. It is interesting to note that the Israeli Supreme Court has itself resorted to the principle of reasonable time in order to determine the time limits of a judicial institutionalization order. See Crim A 3845/02 *Anonymous v the District Adult Psychiatric Committee.* This

Given the preceding discussion regarding the inalienability of sovereignty, the nature of the relationship between the occupied population and the occupying power as a form of trust, and the related rationale for the temporary nature of an occupation, it is clear that the purpose of the regime of occupation is to manage the situation in a manner designed to bring about political change and to generate a resumption of the normal order of international society. Relevant international norms further decree that this change should come about by peaceful means[145] and realize the principle of self-determination. The stand taken by the ICJ, the General Assembly, and the Security Council with respect to the illegality of South Africa's post-Mandate presence in Namibia all serve to emphasize the point.

The purpose of occupation would therefore be frustrated if its normative regime would be construed as indefinite in duration, as that construction may well generate political stagnation rather than the desired change. Such an interpretation, then, is unreasonable, and the observation that the law of occupation, essentially designed for a relatively brief period, arguably lends itself to it, should not obscure its unreasonableness relative to the purpose of that law. Israel's indefinite occupation frustrates the purpose of this regime.

It is not only the purpose of the regime of occupation, but also its essential nature that may well be defied if it is allowed to continue indefinitely: the occupied population under foreign control does not enjoy the full range of human rights, if only because it is deprived of citizenship and the rights attached to that status. The prolongation of such a situation may well be in the interests of an occupying power who may rely on the provisions of the law relative to the maintenance of the status quo, as well as to its security concerns, to the detriment of the population. Given that the occupant is likely to treat its own citizens in a manner vastly different from the manner with which it treats the occupied population, the result may well be the *de facto* institutionalization of Apartheid of some sort.[146] Such a scenario, while ostensibly legal in terms of a 'rule-book' conception of the rule of law, is manifestly illegal in terms of a 'right' conception of the rule of law.[147] Indeed, in making the very rule of law a casualty of an indefinite occupation, it corrupts the law.[148]

The achievement of the purpose of a peaceful political change is a major policy issue. Matters of policy necessitate planning designed to achieve the desired result. Such planning, especially in respect of complicated and bitterly contested

determination relied on a similar decision by the US Supreme Court, *Jackson v Indiana* 406 US 715, 738 (1972).

[145] Art 2(3) of the UN Charter.   [146] Roberts, *supra* note 52, at 52.

[147] To use Dworkin's reference to a formal and a substantive conception of the rule of law: the former is interested in the enforceability of law regardless of its content, that is, in order; the latter is interested in the substance, nature, and justification of the order, determined by the balance thereby achieved between the individual and society; between liberty and security. See generally, Dworkin, *A Matter of Principle* (1985) 11.

[148] '…the rule of law is one casualty of the conflict in the occupied Palestinian Territory, but the main casualties are the people of Palestine and of Israel'. See *Question of the Violation of Human Rights in the Occupied Arab Territories, Including Palestine*, Report of the Special Rapporteur of the Commission on Human Rights, John Dugard, on the Situation of Human Rights in the Palestinian Territories Occupied By Israel Since 1967, UN A/57/366 (29 August 2002) at para 31.

political issues that are not within the absolute control of one party, as is the Israeli-Palestinian conflict, is neither a trivial nor an immediate matter; it is a long-term process; it may be incremental; it may, indeed, fail. It is possible, however, to evaluate whether such a policy was in the making *ex-ante*. This evaluation requires the examination of the circumstances of the specific occupation.

The most relevant circumstances to be examined in this respect are whether the occupying power has annexed the occupied territory or has otherwise indicated an intention to retain its presence there indefinitely. The examination of Israel's annexation of East Jerusalem, the expropriation of vast portions of Palestinians land to establish settlements in the OPT, to construct the by-pass roads, and to erect the Wall, all suggest such an intention.[149] The ICJ's conclusion on this issue is quite pertinent:

Whilst the Court notes the assurance given by Israel that the construction of the wall does not amount to annexation and that the wall is of a temporary nature ... it nevertheless cannot remain indifferent to certain fears expressed to it that the route of the wall will prejudge the future frontier between Israel and Palestine, and the fear that Israel may integrate the settlements and their means of access. The Court considers that the construction of the wall and its associated regime create a 'fait accompli' on the ground that could well become permanent, in which case, and notwithstanding the formal characterization of the wall by Israel, it would be tantamount to *de facto* annexation.[150]

Had the ICJ entertained the notion that the space between the 'temporary' and the 'permanent' is inhabited by the 'indefinite', its conclusion would have been that said construction does not indicate a *de facto* annexation that may happen in the (permanent) future, but rather an annexation that has been effected in the (indefinite) present. When the above-described actions are coupled with the huge investments entailed in the 'settlement enterprise', inclusive of the Wall[151] as well as with the observation that they realize expansionist ideas within Israel,

---

[149] The Special Rapporteur of the UN Commission on Human Rights concluded that 'the construction of the Barrier within the West Bank, and the continued expansion of settlements, which, on the face of it have more to do with territorial expansion, *de facto* annexation or conquest, raise serious doubts about the good faith of Israel's justifications in the name of security', See *2003 Report on the Situation of Human Rights in the Palestinian Territories, supra* note 77, at 7 and 15.

[150] *Construction of a Wall, supra* note 5, at para 121.

[151] While it is virtually impossible to calculate the total investment, as it runs the whole gamut from military expenditure to monetary incentives to settlers, some figures are sufficiently telling for the present discussion: during the last decade, the Israeli government invested $2.5 billion in constructing new houses in the OPT, 50 percent of which was public, compared with 25 percent public financing inside the green line; during the same period, the Government allocated to municipalities an average of NIS 5,428 per settler a year compared to 3,807 per citizen in Israel. See Svirski, *Governmental Funding of Israeli Settlement In Judea and Samaria and the Golan Heights in the Nineties: Municipalities, Housing and Roads Construction* (2002) (in Hebrew) available online at <http://www.adva.org/UserFiles/File/mimun%20memshalti%20be%20esha%20&%20golan.pdf> [last accessed 18 April 2010]. Just the cost of constructing the by-passed roads in the OPT since Oslo has been estimated at more than $265 million. See Ze'ev Schiff, *The March of Folly of the By-Pass Roads,* Ha'Aretz, B.1, (15 February2002). According to data of the Ministry of Finance for the end of 2008, Israel has spent a total of approximately NIS 8.3 billion (about $1.9 billion) on the construction of the fence. The cost per kilometre is NIS 12 million (and NIS 15 million per kilometre of wall). Available online at <http://www.peacenow.org.il/site/he/peace.asp?pi=61&docid=4372&pos=2> [last accessed 18 April 2010].

the only reasonable conclusion is that Israel, far from treating the OPT as a negotiation card to be returned in exchange for peace, has intended to—and *de facto* did—annex[152] a substantial part thereof, thus frustrating the desired political change.

The question remains whether Israel's security concerns justify the settlements and the chain of actions generated by their establishment. Israel claims that its actions are justified by legitimate security concerns, especially in the light of suicide bombing, and that they are simply temporary measures evidencing no intention to alter political boundaries.[153] This argument, however, is untenable on the basis of both substantive law and evidence.

As a matter of substantive law, while it is clear that the law of occupation recognizes the legitimate security concerns of the occupying power, such recognition does not extend to all means and methods used to arguably further this security. Indeed, it does not extend to settlements: Paragraph 6 of Article 49 of *GC IV* contains no exception to its prohibition of settlements on the grounds of such security considerations, and the latter, therefore, do not render the settlements a valid security measure.[154] Even if, for the sake of argument, one dissociates the construction of the Wall from the settlements, and examines the legality of this one measure in isolation, it would be hard to legally sustain the security claim in view of two factors. First, the principle of proportionality:[155] the harm its construction entails for the Palestinian population is disproportionate relative to the security Israel may thereby achieve.[156] This point is strengthened when the second factor is added: the

[152] Unlike the *de jure* annexation of East Jerusalem, the actions described in the text lack the official act of annexation, but nevertheless amount to a *de facto* annexation, effected without giving the Palestinians the rights of citizenship, made visibly and materially clear by the planned path of the Wall. As noted by the Special Rapporteur of the UN Commission on Human Rights, John Dugard, '[L]anguage is a powerful instrument'. This explains why words that accurately describe a particular situation are often avoided. Focusing merely on the barrier, the Special Rapporteur observed that 'the Barrier that Israel is presently constructing within the territory of the West Bank...goes by the name of "Seam Zone"; "Security Fence" or "Wall". The word "annexation" is avoided as it is too accurate a description and too concerned about the need to obfuscate the truth...the fact must be faced that what we are presently witnessing in the West Bank is a visible and clear act of territorial annexation under the guise of security...Annexation of this kind goes by another name in international law: conquest.' See *2003 Report on the Situation of Human Rights in the Palestinian Territories*, *supra* note 77, at 6 and 8.　　　　[153] *Construction of a Wall, supra* note 5, at para 116.

[154] Ibid, at para 135.

[155] The concept of military necessity is not without its limits. One of those notable limitations is the customary principle of proportionality, the meaning of which is that the loss of life and damage to property not be out of proportion to the expected military advantage. See Parkerson, 'United States Compliance with Humanitarian Law Respecting Civilians During Operation Just Cause', 133 *Mil. L. Rev.* (1991) 31–140, at 47. It thus imposes the obligation to balance between the desired aim and the damage inflicted, thereby subjecting the means and methods used to the standard of reasonableness. See also the opinion of the Special Rapporteur voiced in his 2003 Report: 'The Special Rapporteur finds it difficult to accept that the excessive use of force that disregards the distinction between civilians and combatants, the creation of a humanitarian crisis by restrictions on the mobility of goods and people, the killing and inhuman treatment of children, the widespread destruction of property and, now, territorial expansion can be justified as a proportionate response to the violence and threats of violence to which Israel is subjected.' *2003 Report on the Situation of Human Rights in the Palestinian Territories, supra* note 77, at 15.

[156] *Construction of a Wall, supra* note 5, at paras 135–136; cf HCJ 2056/04 *Beit Sourik Village Council v The Government of Israel*, 58(5) PD 817, at paras 48 and 82–85 (hereinafter *Beit Sourik*

Wall does not actually separate Palestinians from Israelis; rather, it separates them from other Palestinians. Given that the construction of the Wall is inseparable from the construction of the settlements and the by-pass roads, the legal grounds for the Israeli argument are tenuous at best.

An occupation regime that substitutes the 'indefinite' for the 'temporary' has ceased to be, and to be conceived as, temporary. Such an occupation, as the discussion pertaining to its purpose, nature, and circumstances demonstrates, has exceeded its reasonable duration. Such an occupation violates the basic principle of temporariness underlying the normative regime of occupation.

The above does not suggest that the occupation is permanent. The 'disengagement' from the Gaza Strip shows that a political decision can generate the dismantling of settlements. Political will may also lead to the end of occupation. The discussion does suggest, however, that in substituting an 'indefinite' for a 'temporary' occupation, Israel has violated the normative regime of occupation. It is instructive to note in this context, that following the political decision to withdraw military forces from, and dismantle the settlements in, the Gaza Strip, the HCJ emphasized the temporary—as distinct from the indefinite—nature of occupation in order to deny the settlers' claim to remain in the settlements.[157] This decision is normatively sound. The fact that it was never made in order to question the legality of the settlements' enterprise in the preceding decades demonstrates that the temporary/indefinite indeterminacy is being used to legitimize power, not to contain it: the temporary nature of occupation was resurrected to replace the 'indefinite' construction only when a political will to pull out was reached.

In conclusion, the very same actions which indicate that the occupation can no longer be regarded as temporary, also disclose the violation of the substantive constraints imposed by the law of occupation on the managerial discretion of the occupying power: they amount to a *de facto* annexation of large portions of the occupied territory; they entail gross violations of humanitarian and human rights norms and defy both the principle of the inalienability of sovereignty and the principle of trust. The violation of the time constraints cannot but violate the two other basic tenets of the law of occupation, and the latter necessarily generate the conclusion that an occupation must be temporary. The Israeli occupation having thus violated the three basic principles underlying the normative regime of occupation is a conquest in disguise. It is, therefore, intrinsically illegal.

Village Case). Note that the HCJ's discussion of the proportionality requirement is ostensibly both more analytical and more specific than that of the ICJ: the HCJ applies that requirement to each and every segment of the Wall which was appealed and further inquires into the existence of alternative, less harmful means, through which the stated security objective may be met. Nevertheless, the HCJ's application of proportionality mixes various contexts of proportionality, importing into the context of occupation a proportionality analysis that is more befitting administrative law within a representative democracy. For a discussion of this move and its effects see Gross, 'The Construction of a Wall between Jerusalem and the Hague: The Enforcement and Limits of Humanitarian Law and the Structure of Occupation', 19 *LJIL* (2006) 393–440, at 405–411 and 419–423.

[157] *Regional Council Gaza Beach v The Knesset, supra* note 4, at paras 8–9, 115, 126.

C. Extrinsic dimensions of the Israeli occupation

Structurally, the law of occupation bears strong resemblance to an emergency regime. This regime, the roots of which date back to the Roman-Commissarial model, rests on three precepts: exceptionality; limited scope of powers; and temporary duration.[158] In this discourse, then, a situation of emergency is separated and distinguished from the ordinary state of affairs, as it signifies an occurrence which does not conform to the rule: the ordinary state of affairs is the general norm—this is what makes it 'normal'; the emergency is the exception—this is why its duration must be limited and generate no permanent effects. This is also the reason due to which the norm is regarded as superior to the exception: the existing legal order defines the terms under which it is suspended, and the powers granted in such a situation are to be used for the purpose of an expeditious return to normalcy.[159]

The basic tenets of the normative regime of occupation largely conform to this constitutional model, transporting it to the international arena: the normal order is based on the principle of sovereign equality between states that are, at least to some extent, presumed to be founded on the ideas of self-government and self-determination. The severance of the link between sovereignty and effective control, and life under foreign rule—both features of occupation—constitute an exceptional situation. The law of occupation recognizes it as an exception to be managed so as to ensure expeditious return to normalcy. This is why the occupant has only limited powers in terms of both scope and time, and is not permitted to act in a manner designed to generate permanent results.

Indeed, the conclusion of modern studies of emergency situations concerned with the derogation from human rights law thereby occasioned have concluded that: '[a]bove and beyond the rules…one principle, namely, the principle of provisional status, dominates all others. The right of derogation (of human rights) can be justified solely by the concern to return to normalcy.'[160] This conclusion holds true and equally applies to occupation.

A reversal of the relationship between the norm and the exception generates, as of necessity, the terminus of every normative system.[161] Carl Schmitt's political theology, wherein the norm becomes subservient to the exception, is both a

---

[158] See Mommsen, *The History of Rome*, (1958) 325–326; For later references to this classical model, See eg Machiavelli, *The Discourses* (L Walker trans, 1970) 194 and 198; Rousseau, *The Social Contract and Discourses* (Cole trans, 1993) 293–296.

[159] For the essential features of the traditional model of emergency powers, Gross, 'Exception and Emergency Powers: The Normless and Exceptionless Exception: Carl Schmitt's Theory of Emergency Powers and the "Norm-Exception" Dichotomy', 21 *Cardozo L. Rev.* (2000) 1825–1868, at 1836–1839.

[160] *Study of the Implications for Human Rights of Recent Development Concerning Situations Known as State of Siege or Emergency*, UN ESCOR, 35th Sess, Agenda Item 10, 69 UN Doc E/CN.4/Sub.2/1982/15 (1982) (N Questiaux). Also See Gross and Aolain, 'To Know Where We Are Going, We Need To Know Where We Are: Revisiting States of Emergency', in Leonard (eds), *Human Rights: An Agenda for the* 21st *Century* (1999) 79–144.

[161] Marramo, 'Schmitt and the Categories of the Political: The Exile of the Nomos: For a Critical Profile of Carl Schmitt', 27 *Cardozo L. Rev.* (2000) 1567–1588.

precedent and a warning at point: 'the rule,' said Schmitt, 'proves nothing; the exception proves everything: it confirms not only the rule but also its existence, which derives only from the exception'.[162] The state of emergency, which in German is called 'state of exception' (*Ausnahmezustand*), is one where the rule of man prevails over the rule of law[163] and where the Leviathan reigns supreme.[164] The result is a Hobbesian state of war—indeed the clearest case of an exception— where, bereft of any rights, the only meaningful distinction for a person to make is between the reified constructs of 'friend' and 'foe'.[165] This situation signifies the destruction of both the normative regime of the exception, and of the general rule. From a normative perspective it is thus as meaningless as it is indefensible.[166]

One lesson to be drawn from the above is the importance of retaining a clear distinction between the rule and the exception, lest the exception becomes a new rule, and generates a new conception of reality. This is important because in this new conception of reality, one's security habitually, uncritically, overrides one's enemy's human rights.[167] Indeed, the reversal of the relationship between the rule and the exception operates as a legitimizing device: it encourages a discourse of various specific violations of human rights carried out in the name of security, to be perceived as exceptional, thereby obfuscating the fact that said violations have become the rule, not the exception.

The Schmittian exception, reflects Agamben in his book *Homo Sacer*, has generated the conditions of possibility for the concentration camp, a space created once the exception—the temporary suspension of the rule—becomes the rule.[168] This space, where the extraordinary and the provisional condition becomes the ordinary and permanent, says Agamben, is not limited to Nazi concentration camps. It is paradigmatic to every situation where the political machinery of the modern

---

[162] Schmitt, *supra* note 25, at 15.

[163] Bielefeld, 'Carl Schmitt's Critique of Liberalism: Systematic Reconstruction and Countercriticism', 10 *CJLJ* (1997) 65–75, at 68.

[164] Schmitt was fascinated with Hobbes and regarded himself as his heir, ending his commentary on Hobbes' Leviathan with the words: 'You shall no longer teach in vain, Thomas Hobbes' See Schmitt, *The Leviathan in the State Theory of Thomas Hobbes: Meaning and Failure of a Political Symbol* (Schwab and Hilfstein trans, 1996). On the affinity between Schmitt and Hobbes, see Dyzenhaus, 'Now the Machine Runs Itself: Carl Schmitt on Hobbes and Kelsen', 16 *Cardozo L. Rev.* (1994) 1–19; McCormick, 'Fear, Technology, and the State: Carl Schmitt, 'Leo Strauss, and the Revival of Hobbes in Weimar and National Socialist Germany', 22 *Political Theory* (1994) 619–652.

[165] For Schmitt's 'friend'/'enemy' distinction see Schmitt, *The Concept of the Political* (J Harvey Lomax trans, 3rd edn, 1996) 25–37. For an analysis, See Norris, 'Carl Schmitt on Friends, Enemies and the Political', 112 *Telos* (1998) 68–88. On the odd history of Schmitt's reception in the Anglo-American academia see Richter, 'Carl Schmitt: The Defective Guidance for the Critique of Political Liberalism', 21 *Cardozo L. Rev.* (2000) 1619–1644.

[166] This was the political theology of the Third Reich. On Schmitt's defence of the President's action in July 1932 in *Prussia v Reich*, which was based on his construction of emergency, see Dyzenhaus, *Legality and Legitimacy: Carl Schmitt, Hans Kelsen and Hermann Heller in Weimar* (1997) 70–85.

[167] Harold Lasswell noted that 'an insidious outcome of continuing crisis is the tendency to slide into a new conception of normality that takes vastly extended control for granted, and thinks of freedom in smaller and smaller dimensions', see Lasswell, *National Security and Individual Freedom* (1950) 29, quoted in Gross, *supra* note 159, at 155.

[168] Agamben, *Homo Sacer: Sovereign Power and Bare Life* (Heller-Roazen trans, 1988) 166–168.

nation state finds itself in a continuous crisis and decides to take it upon itself to defend the biological life of the nation, collapsing human rights into citizens' rights,[169] subsuming humanity into citizenry and making the former the 'exceptionless exception'.[170] In such a situation, the enemy, stripped of human rights, is stripped of his humanity. Having been excluded from the body-politic, he has only his own body as a political tool and it is through this political body that he interacts with the body-politic that has thus reified him.[171] This may well be the typology of the suicide bomber. It does not justify his actions which, when directed against civilians, amount to war crimes and may amount to crimes against humanity,[172] but it does contextualize them.

It is in order to contain the eruption of a Schmittian 'friend–enemy' politics that the international rule of law recognized the situation of occupation as an exception and created a normative regime designed to ensure that the effective control of the occupying power is exercised in a manner that is temporary, respectful of the humanitarian needs and the human rights of the occupied population and leading to an expeditious return to normalcy based on sovereign equality. An occupation that fails to do this is substantively and intrinsically (in terms of the law of occupation), as well as structurally and extrinsically (in terms of the international legal order which provides the normative framework within which the law of occupation operates) illegal. The Israeli occupation of the OPT has thus failed.

D. The matrix of an illegal occupation

The discussion above suggests that obfuscation, indeterminacy, and the blurring of boundaries are the defining features of the Israeli control of the OPT. Indeed, the indeterminate nature of the regime has operated to legitimize that which would have otherwise been determined as illegal. Thus, while Israel has consistently argued that the OPT are not occupied territories, the State's attorneys have sought to justify Israel's actions in the territories which restrict the rights of Palestinians on the basis of the law of occupation.[173] Similarly, the HCJ, while never confirming the applicability of *GC IV* to the territories, has nevertheless decided to apply its 'humanitarian' provisions in a manner that has allowed the IDF to exercise the powers of a belligerent occupant but which rejected the vast majority of Palestinian petitions.[174] In this manner, Israel has been able to enjoy

---

[169] Ibid, at 126–131 and 174–176. Agamben, noting the very ambiguity of the title *'Declaration des droits de l'Homme et du Citoyen'* refers in this context to Arendt's discussion of the paradox wherein 'the Conception of human rights, based upon the assumed existence of a human being as such, broke down at the very moment when those who professed to believe in it were for the first time confronted with people who had indeed lost all other qualities and specific relationships—except that they were still human'. See Arendt, *The Origins of Totalitarianism* (1979). Thus, in the nation-state system, human rights that are considered inalienable have become meaningless once they cannot be attached to the citizens of a nation-state. The refugee, the person who was supposed to be the 'human rights' person *par excellence* has thus become the paradigm of 'bare life'.

[170] A term coined by Gross in his analysis of Schmitt's theory of the exception. See Gross, *supra* note 159. [171] Agamben, *supra* note 168, at 187–188

[172] *Supra* note 115. [173] See *supra* text between notes 85 and 97.

[174] *Supra* note 5; see *supra* text between notes 69 and 72.

the credit for applying IHL while at the same time violating its essential tenets. This occupation/non-occupation indeterminacy is complemented by its twin annexation/non-annexation indeterminacy: Israel acts in the territories as a sovereign insofar as it settles its citizens there and extends to them its laws on a personal and on a mixed personal/territorial bases; yet insofar as the territories have not been formally annexed and insofar as this exercise of sovereignty falls short of giving the Palestinian residents citizenship rights, Israel is not acting as a sovereign. In this manner, Israel enjoys in the OPT both the powers of an occupant and the powers of a sovereign while the Palestinians enjoy neither the rights of an occupied people nor the rights of citizenship. This indeterminacy thus allows Israel to avoid, for the most part, the wrath of the international community for having illegally annexed the territories, while pursuing the policies of 'greater Israel'[175] without jeopardizing its Jewish majority.

Finally, the blurring of the boundaries between the temporary and the indefinite and, indeed, between the rule and the exception has donned a mantle of legitimacy on this occupation, and has made possible the continuous interplay of occupation/non-occupation; annexation/non-annexation. This mantle, however, much like the Emperor's New Clothes, should not obfuscate our vision of the naked illegality of this regime. The implication of law in the shaping and sustaining of the regime is the focus of Part 3.

3. The Paths of Law

A. General

The main proposition advanced in this part is that once law becomes implicated in the reversal of the relationship between the rule and the exception, law itself becomes infected, and is likely to operate in a manner that will defy its normative purpose on both an individual and a systemic level: its application to individual cases would typically entail a 'dynamic' interpretation designed to advance the interests of the occupying power at the expense of the occupied people (3.B) and it will contribute to and facilitate the formation of an environment (indicative of a state policy) of tolerance towards systematic violations of human rights. This tolerance, in turn, may transform grave such violations from war crimes into crimes against humanity. These paths of law, far from restraining executive power, contribute to the spreading of its unlawful exercise and to the dissemination of a culture of impunity (3.C).

---

[175] On the 'Greater Israel' (*Eretz Isreal*/Land of Israel) ideology and its implications see Kimmerling, 'Between the Primordial and Civil Definitions of the Collective Identity: The State of Israel or Eretz Israel', in Cohen, Lissak, and Almagor (eds), *Social Dynamics: Essays in Honor of Shmuel Eisenstadt* (1984) at 262–283; Kimmerling, 'Boundaries and Frontiers of the Israeli Control System—Analytical Conclusions', in Kimmerling (ed), *The Israeli State and Society: Boundaries and Frontiers* (1989) 265–284, at 277.

B. The interpretive turn: crafting blind spots

1. General

The judicial review exercised by the HCJ approved a wide range of executive measures designed to sustain and expand the Israeli control of the OPT.[176] Simultaneously, it has instilled and perpetuated both the self-perception and the external image of Israel[177] as a law-abiding 'defensive democracy'[178] fighting 'with one hand tied behind her back'.[179] This is no mean feat. Occasional judicial slapping of the executive hand probably has a share in this perception.[180] In the main, however, the (unholy) alliance between *raison d'état* and law has been grounded in an ostensibly 'dynamic' and certainly creative interpretation of international legal rules advanced by the HCJ.

Various interpretative methodologies have been employed to this end, but their underlying logic falls neatly within the matrix of the regime discussed above. Due to space constraints, I will exemplify this proposition in reference to only two judicial texts: *Ajury v IDF Commander*[181] (revolving around the distinction between [permissible] assignment of residence and [prohibited] deportation or forcible transfer), and *The Public Committee against Torture in Israel v The Government of Israel*, (revolving around the legality of 'Targeted Killing').[182]

The choice to focus on these decisions emanates from their persuasive power: both texts were authored by then Chief Justice Aharon Barak, the dominant figure of the Court for over a quarter of a century and a highly esteemed jurist internationally. The *Ajury* case, the focus of 3.B.2 below, was the first judgment the Court has ever rendered that was based entirely on international law. The *Targeted Killings* judgment, discussed in 3.B.3 below, was the last decision Justice Barak delivered before retiring from the Court and is considered to have contributed significantly to the development of IHL. Both texts were released in Hebrew and in English and generated wide interest in Israel and abroad. Indeed, both command respect: a well-crafted structure, a thorough normative analysis of international legal rules

---

[176] See Kretzmer, *supra* note 5, who provides a comprehensive and critical analysis of the major decisions.

[177] The external perception is created, *inter alia*, by the publication of some landmark decisions, (notably those are based on a sophisticated application of international law coupled with an evocative narrative about the subjection of the executive to legal restraints even in the face of terror), in English, simultaneously with their publication in Hebrew. It is interesting to note that while Arabic, not English, is both an official language in Israel and the language of the petitioners, the judgments are not translated into Arabic.   [178] *Ajuri*, *supra* note 131, at para 41.

[179] HCJ 5100/94 *The Public Committee against Torture in Israel v The State of Israel*, 53(4) PD 817, at 845.

[180] eg HCJ 85/87 *Arjub v IDF Commander in Judea and Samaria* 42(1) PD 353, recommending the amelioration of the military court system by establishing an appeal instance; *Ajuri*, *supra* note 131, right to hearing before implementing an 'assigned residence' order; HCJ 3799/02 *Adallah v GOC Central Command IDF*, prohibiting the use of 'human shields'. Available online at <http://www.adalah.org/features/humshields/decision061005.pdf>[last accessed 18 April 2010]; *Beit Sourik Village Case*, *supra* note 156, placing some restrictions on the Construction of the Wall; *Targeted Killings Case*, *supra* note 5, forbidding the targeted killings of civilians who do not participate in the conduct of hostilities.   [181] *Ajuri*, *supra* note 131.

[182] *Targeted Killings* case, *supra* note 5.

and a finely-wrought narrative generate reasoned decisions that are intellectually engaging and substantively challenging. Most significantly, in both, the position of the executive was not fully endorsed.

2. *The* Ajuri *case*[183]

The *Ajuri* judgment, rendered in 2002, revolved around a petition of three residents of the West Bank against the legality of orders issued by the military commander of the IDF in Judea and Samaria (aka 'the West Bank') which assigned their place of residence for two years to the Gaza Strip.[184]

The unanimous judgment, written by Chief Justice Barak,[185] begins with an outline of the relevant narrative framework which provides the background for the military orders:

Since the end of September 2000, fierce fighting has been taking place in Judea, Samara and the Gaza strip...It is an armed struggle...Israel's fight is complex. The Palestinians use, *inter-alia*, guided human bombs...The forces fighting against Israel are terrorists; they are not members of a regular army, they do not wear uniforms; they hide among the civilian Palestinian population...they are supported by part of the civilian population, and by their family and relatives...In its struggle against terrorism, Israel has undertaken—by virtue of its right to self-defence—special military operations...In these operations, IDF forces entered many areas that were in the past under its control by virtue of belligerent occupation and which were transferred pursuant to agreements to the (full or partial) control of the Palestinian Authority...many reserve forces were mobilized; heavy weapons, including tanks, armoured personnel carriers, assault helicopters and aeroplanes, were used.[186]

The central question before the Court was whether the contested orders were a valid exercise of the authority of the military commander to assign residence under Article 78 of *GC IV*, or an invalid such exercise which amounts to forcible transfer or deportation, measures prohibited under Article 49 of the Convention.[187]

The Court's response to the question is structured deductively along three phases: the normative framework for the determination of the authority of the military commander to issue orders assigning residence; the analysis of the applicable law in order to determine the conditions for the exercise of said authority and its scope; and the application of the law to the specific facts pertaining to the three petitioners.

The applicable normative framework, says the Court, is the laws of belligerent occupation, comprising the rules of the 1907 Hague Regulations and *GC IV*. The

---

[183] *Ajuri, supra* note 131.

[184] Language is a powerful tool in the construction of consciousness. The area the international community refers to as the 'West Bank' is referred to in Israel as 'Judea and Samaria' to emphasize the historical claim to the land.

[185] The panel consisted of nine judges and was presided by Chief Justice Barak. The Supreme Court, both as an appellate court and the High Court of Justice, is normally constituted of a panel of three justices. The Supreme Court may sit as a panel of a larger uneven number of justices than three in matters that involve fundamental legal questions and constitutional issues of particular importance. See Art 26 of the Israeli Courts Act. [186] *Ajuri, supra* note 131, at paras 2–3.

[187] Ibid, at para 13.

former apply by virtue of their customary nature; the latter by virtue of the long-standing practice reflecting the decision of the government of Israel to act according to its humanitarian parts.[188] The authority of the military commander derives from these rules and they determine the extent of the permitted restriction on human rights as a result of a forcible assignment of residence.[189]

The issue before the Court is governed entirely by Article 78 of *GC IV*. This provision concerns assigned residence. This provision allows an occupying power, if it considers it necessary for imperative security reasons, to take safety measures concerning protected persons. Such measures include, at the most, assigned residence or internment and are subject to a certain procedure. Article 78, says the Court, constitutes *lex specialis*. As such, the measures indicated therein are permitted even if a general provision prohibits them. It follows that Article 49, which prohibits forcible transfer or deportation, is irrelevant to the case at hand. The order at issue was an order to assign residence, and Article 78 'provides a comprehensive and full arrangement', in this respect: it is 'both a source for the protection of the right of a person whose residence is being assigned and also a source for the possibility of restricting this right'.[190]

Having thus determined the normative framework, the Court proceeded to analyse Article 78 in the light of the two main arguments made by the petitioners in respect of it. The first argument related to the area within which assigned residence may be permissible. The petitioners argued that the new place of residence should be within a single territory subject to belligerent occupation, and that since the Gaza Strip is situated outside that territory, the assignment of their residence from the West Bank to Gaza is impermissible under Article 78 and amounts to deportation prohibited under Article 49. The Court, having accepted that the area to which a protected person is assigned is indeed a parameter that distinguishes between Article 49 and Article 78, had to determine whether the West Bank and Gaza form one territory or two separate territories. It decided that the fact that the territories were conquered from different states and are managed by two distinct military commanders does not suffice to conclude that they are separated territories: both areas form one territorial unit. This conclusion was based on two grounds: first, a teleological reading of Article 78 generates the conclusion that it restricts the validity of assigned residence to one territory, characterized by 'societal, linguistic, cultural, social and political unity' so as to minimize the harm caused to the person whose residence is being assigned, and that the West Bank and Gaza are thus united under one belligerent occupant. Second, both Israel and the Palestinian Authority view the West Bank and the Gaza Strip as a single territorial unit, as is evidenced,

---

[188] Ibid, The Court noted that the legal arguments supporting the Israeli position regarding the applicability of *GC IV* 'are not simple', but saw no need make a decision on the issue. The Court further noted that alongside the international legal rules, 'the fundamental Israeli of administrative law, such as the rules of natural justice, also apply. Indeed, every Israeli soldier carries in his pack both the rules of international law and the basic principles of Israeli administrative law...'

[189] Ibid, at para 16.   [190] Ibid, at para 17.

inter alia, in clause 11 of the Israel-Palestinian Interim Agreement on the West Bank and the Gaza Strip.[191]

The second argument of the petitioners concerned the considerations governing the military commander's exercise of authority. The Court accepted their position that the prevention of a danger from the person whose residence is being assigned, a danger that the assignment is to avert, is the essential and indeed necessary condition for exercising this authority. The Court based this view on a teleological interpretation of the Convention in general and of Article 78 in particular, an interpretation which emphasizes the particularly severe nature of this exceptional measure. It further opined that such an interpretation is in accordance with our 'Jewish and democratic values'.[192] The exceptionality of the measure further decrees that the authority is to be exercised only if there is convincing administrative evidence that if residence is not assigned there is a reasonable possibility that the person will present a real danger to the security of the territory and that the measure meets the standard of proportionality.[193] Nevertheless, the Court proceeded to opine, once it is clear that the authority was exercised as a preventive measure to avoid danger from a specific person, the military commander is authorized to also take into account the consideration of deterring others. Such reading of the scope of the authority, said the Court, is consistent with the Convention which regards assigned residence as a legitimate measure for the security of the territory, and is especially required by harsh ground realities, realities which call for a dynamic interpretation of the law.[194]

The orders assigning the residence of two of the three petitioners were issued due to the assistance they extended to 'terrorist Ahmed Ali Ajuri' to whom 'much terrorist activity is attributed...including sending suicide bombers with explosive belts'.[195] Having thus analysed the law, the Court proceeded to determine whether the military commander had used his authority accordingly with respect to each of them. Amtassar Ajuri, an unmarried woman aged 34, is the sister of Ahmed Ali Ajuri. The Court was satisfied that she was aware of her brother's forbidden activities, knew that he was armed, and had hidden an assault rifle in the apartment and further aided him by sewing explosive belts. Kipah Ajuri, a 38-year-old married man and the father of three children, is the brother of Ahmed Ali Ajuri. He too knew of his brother's activities and further aided him by acting as a look-out and, on occasion, bringing food to his brother's group. In the case of both, the Court found that the decision to assign their residence was a reasonable exercise of authority, as both pose a grave danger to the security of the area. The Court found, however, that the activities of the third petitioner, Abed Asida, a 38-year-old married man and brother of the 'terrorist' Nasser Asida, consisting of knowledge about his brother's activities, driving him and another person to a hospital after they were injured by an explosive, and occasionally lending his brother his car, fell short of the level of danger required for adopting the measure

---

[191] Ibid, at paras 20–22.   [192] Ibid, at para 24.   [193] Ibid, at para 25.
[194] Ibid, at para 27.   [195] Ibid, at para 31.

of assigned residence, and that therefore assigning residence in this case exceeded 'the zone of reasonableness'.[196]

The judgment concludes with two closing remarks. The first emphasizes the importance of a dynamic interpretation in the face of the new reality of 'living bombs' Israel is facing, a reality the drafters of Article 78 never anticipated.[197] The second remark provides a narrative—often repeated in judgments pertaining to the OPT—and directed at both the Israeli public and the world, about the role of law in war. The Court, noting that Israel is undergoing a difficult period due to terror, where both Israelis and the Arab population suffer, proceeds to assign the blame: 'all this because of acts of murder, killing and destruction perpetrated by terrorists', and concludes as follows:

The State of Israel is a freedom-seeking democracy. It is a defensive democracy acting within the framework of its right to self-defence—a right recognized by the Charter of the United Nations... It is a war carried out within the law and with the tools that law makes available... The well-known saying that 'In battle laws are silent'... does not reflect the law as it is nor as it should be... This is the price of democracy. It is expensive but worthwhile...[198]

The *Ajuri* case, as mentioned above, is noteworthy for being the first judgment that deals with a security issue to have been determined entirely on the basis of an in-depth analysis of IHL, and particularly on the basis of *GC IV*. From this perspective, while the Court still refrained from a clear determination regarding the applicability of *GC IV* as a matter of a legal obligation, the decision appears nevertheless to be a positive development insofar as the incorporation of international law into the Israeli legal discourse is concerned.[199] Appearances, however, are notoriously deceptive[200] and thus the assessment of the nature of this development depends on the objectives it is designed to achieve, primarily, whether its purpose is to ensure that the exercise of power is limited, rather than facilitated by law. The interpretative and narrative methodologies employed by the Court in the *Ajuri* case shed a dim light on the purposes that the resort to IHL was designed to, and did in fact, achieve.[201]

The Court, as described above, employed a dynamic as well as a teleological method of interpretation of Article 78. The justification for a dynamic interpretation was articulated as follows: 'we doubt whether the drafters of the provisions of Art. 78... anticipated protected persons who collaborated with terrorists and living bombs. This new reality requires a dynamic interpretation...'.[202] In reality, however, the drafters of *GC IV* did anticipate that protected persons would participate

---

[196] Ibid, at paras 31–39.   [197] Ibid, at para 40.   [198] Ibid, at para 41.

[199] It is instructive to note that this change is probably related to developments in international criminal law, and especially with the establishment of the International Criminal Court, the exercise of universal jurisdiction, and an appreciation of the implication of the principle of complementarity.

[200] In reference to the language used by Judge Krylov in his Dissenting Opinion in *Conditions of Admission of a State to Membership in The United Nations*, Advisory Opinion, ICJ Reports (1948) 57, at 107.

[201] The following analysis is based on the critical review of the judgment in Ben-Naftali and Micaheli, 'The Call of Abraham—Between Deportation and Assigned Residence: A Critique of the Ajouri Case', 9 *Hamishpat* (2004) 107–140 (in Hebrew).   [202] *Ajuri, supra* note 131, at para 40.

in hostilities against an occupying power, and it is precisely due to this anticipation that the Convention contains certain provisions, including Article 78, which authorize the latter to take security measures against protected persons who perpetrate or otherwise assist in such hostilities.[203] It does not follow that a dynamic interpretation is unwarranted, but the dubious justification given for advancing it informs, and indeed provides the Ariadne's thread for the understanding of the interpretive path paved by Justice Barak.

There is little doubt that a dynamic interpretation designed to align normative provisions with the nature of present warfare, is often necessary. This indeed was the methodology employed by the International Criminal Tribunal for the former Yugoslavia (ICTY) in the *Tadić* case.[204] The ICTY resorted to a dynamic interpretation in order to broaden the protection afforded to the civilian population, thus providing for an interpretation that is both teleological and dynamic. The HCJ, by contrast, employed it in order to broaden the scope of the discretion of the occupying power at the expense of the protection offered to the occupied population,[205] while at the same time casting a blind eye on the main reality the drafters of the Convention did not anticipate: a prolonged occupation the end of which is indefinitely deferred and the cause and effect relationship that may exist between this reality and Palestinian resistance.[206] It is not inconceivable that had the drafters contemplated such a situation, they would have changed the balance of power between the occupant and the protected persons in favour of the latter insofar as the limitations the Convention imposes on resisting an occupation

[203] Art 5 of *GC IV* provides 'Where, in the territory of a Party to the conflict, the latter is satisfied that an individual protected person is definitely suspected of or engaged in activities hostile to the security of the State, such individual person shall not be entitled to claim such rights and privileges under the present Convention as would, if exercised in the favour of such individual person, be prejudicial to the security of such State. Where in occupied territory an individual protected person is detained as a spy or saboteur, or as a person under definite suspicion of activity hostile to the security of the Occupying Power, such person shall, in those cases where absolute military security so requires, be regarded as having forfeited rights of communication under the present Convention. In each case, such persons shall nevertheless be treated with humanity, and in case of trial, shall not be deprived of the rights of fair and regular trial prescribed by the present Convention. They shall also be granted the full rights and privileges of a protected person under the present Convention at the earliest date consistent with the security of the State or Occupying Power, as the case may be.' Art 68 provides 'Protected persons who commit an offence which is solely intended to harm the Occupying Power, but which does not constitute an attempt on the life or limb of members of the occupying forces or administration, nor a grave collective danger, nor seriously damage the property of the occupying forces or administration or the installations used by them, shall be liable to internment or simple imprisonment, provided the duration of such internment or imprisonment is proportionate to the offence committed...'.

[204] The ICTY cancelled, in effect, the condition stipulated in Art 4 of *GC IV* according to which the nationality of the protected person should be different from the nationality of the occupying power, on the grounds that the drafters of the Convention did not anticipate the situation where ethnicity rather than nationality is the source of the conflict. See Opinion and Judgment, *Tadić* (ICTY-94-1-A), Appeal Chamber, 15 July 1999, at para 168; Judgment, *Aleksovski* (IT-95-14/1-A), Appeal Chamber, 24 March 2000, at paras 151–152; Judgment *Delalić et al* (IT-96-21-A), Appeal Chamber, 20 February 2001, at paras 82–84.

[205] By permitting the military commander to base its decision to assign residence on considerations of general deterrence in addition to the danger from the individual whose residence is being assigned, see text between notes 183 and 198.

[206] See discussion at *supra* text between notes 122 and 135.

are concerned.[207] The net result of the above is that the dynamic interpretation employed by the HCJ is incongruous with the teleological interpretation of *GC IV*, the main purpose of which is to protect the civilian population, as is indeed otherwise acknowledged by the Court.[208]

The teleological interpretation of Article 78 ostensibly employed by the Court becomes all the more problematic when it is considered in the light of another ground reality, namely, the lesser control Israel exercised over the Gaza Strip even prior to its withdrawal from the area, when compared to its control over the West Bank. The Court, as was discussed above, resorted to a teleological interpretation to conclude that Gaza and the West Bank are indeed one territory, stating that

... *[t]he purpose underlying the provisions of art. 78*...and which restricts the validity of assigned residence to one territory, lies in the societal, linguistic, cultural, social and political unity of the territory, *out of a desire to restrict the harm caused by assigning* residence to a foreign place.[209]

This conclusion is less clear-cut than it appears to be: a teleological interpretation of *GC IV* is indeed driven by a wish to offer the occupied people as broad a protection as possible. Meeting this objective, however, calls for a strict, rather than a wide interpretation of the scope of the territory, so as to minimize the harm to a protected person who is being removed from his home, family, and work, that is, from his life. Between the Gaza Strip and the West Bank, there is no territorial continuity and they are separated by Israeli-controlled borders. While they are connected nationally and linguistically, their different history accounts for significant differences in social, cultural, economic, and political terms. It was thus not unreasonable to assume that the alienation the petitioners would have felt in Gaza would not have been that different from what they would have felt in an altogether foreign country. This point becomes all the more poignant when considered in the light of the original purpose of Article 78, a purpose the Court was silent about: the clear rationale behind authorizing the occupying power to assign the residence of a protected person who presents a security danger, was to allow it to exercise greater and more effective control over that person's actions.[210] The assignment of the petitioners from the West Bank to Gaza, a territory over which even before its withdrawal Israel has exercised far less effective control, seems to defy that purpose. Indeed, if the idea was to isolate the petitioners from being in contact with hostile factors, then greater support is lent to their position that Gaza is a separate territory and that therefore the measure amounts to deportation rather than to assignment of residence.

The point becomes ever clearer when one takes a closer look at the application of the law to the facts of the case as they relate to the sister and the brother of Ahmed Ali Ajuri. The Commentary to Article 78 clarifies that in order for a protected person to be considered as presenting such a grave danger as to sanction assigned residence 'the State must have good reason to think that the person concerned, by

---

[207] Pictet, *supra* note 32, at 35–36.
[209] Ibid, at para 22 (emphasis added).
[208] *Ajuri, supra* note 131, at para 24.
[210] Pictet, *supra* note 32, at 256.

his *activities, knowledge or qualifications*, represents a real threat to its present or future security'.[211] It is clear from the judgment that the activities the siblings performed, and not any particular knowledge or qualifications, justified the security concern: indeed, the activities required neither special skills nor knowledge. It is equally clear that the tasks they had performed related directly to their essential role as brother and sister. It does not, of course, follow that because Ahmed Ali is their brother they are allowed to violate the law without consequences, but it does provide the proper context for their actions. It is against this context that the question regarding the security danger they pose, a danger justifying the assignment of their residence, should be evaluated. Ostensibly, the answer is apparent: it is reasonable to assume that if they assisted their brother in the past in a manner that endangered security, they are likely to continue to do so, unless otherwise prevented. Appearances, however, are indeed deceptive and often attest to blind-spots rather than to clear vision: the brother, Ahmed Ali, had been killed by the IDF on 6 August 2002, that is, about a month before the judgment was rendered. This fact was known to, but nevertheless ignored by, the Court.[212] Given that assisting their brother was the reason for their predicament, his death renders both the likelihood that they will pose a danger in the future and the proportionality of assigning their residence quite improbable, generating the conclusion that the assignment of their residence is, in reality, deportation or forcible transfer.

It follows from the above analysis that the dynamic interpretation, far from establishing a normative limit to the exercise of power by the occupant, has enabled it, supplying the Israeli narrative with a normative umbrella. This narrative indeed effects more than a 'dynamic interpretation'; it controls the dynamics of the conflict as understood by the Court itself. Thus, for instance, the narrative within which the Court frames its judicial review indicates, at both the beginning and the end of the judgment, that Israel is acting pursuant to its right to self-defence.[213] This indication is stated as a fact. It is, however, a normative proposition that is as debatable as it is irrelevant to the case at hand: it is debatable primarily because Israel is the belligerent occupant, exercising effective control over the OPT; it is unnecessary because the question whether or not power is exercised in self-defence has no relevance to the question whether the power (the authority to order the assignment of residence) has been exercised according to the rules of IHL. The first question is a *jus ad bellum* issue; the second, a *jus in bello* issue. The judicial reference to the right to self-defence, consciously blurring the boundaries between the two otherwise distinct legal arenas, indeed served no normative purpose in the judgment; its only implication was to advance a particular narrative, the Israeli narrative with which the Court identifies and which it exports to the international community.

---

[211] Ibid, at 258 (emphasis added).

[212] Both the petition of Amtassar Ajuri and the Respondent's brief referred to this fact. The point was noted by Amnesty International, see Amnesty International, Forcible transfers of Palestinians to Gaza constitutes a War Crime (3 September 2002), available online at <http://www.amnesty.org/en/library/asset/MDE15/134/2002/en/c977d660-faed-11dd-8917-49d72d0853f5/mde151342002en.pdf> [last accessed 18 April 2010].   [213] *Ajuri, supra* note 131, at paras 3 and 41.

The repetitive reference in the judgment to the 'terrorists' whom Israel is fighting equally serves no normative purpose and is designed to advance the Israeli narrative in the rhetorical battleground: as the Court itself admits, IHL recognizes only two statuses: a combatant and a non-combatant, a civilian. Both may perform illegal acts, and be engaged in terrorist activities, but it does not follow that there is either a third status, a terrorist, or that the 'war on terror' is otherwise exempt from the normative constraints imposed by IHL. The Court is well aware of that.[214]

The articulation of the dominant Israeli narrative finds further expression in the Court's assignment of blame for the 'harsh reality in which the State of Israel and the territory are situated' to the 'inhuman phenomenon of "living bombs"'[215] and in its sympathetic characterization of Israel as a 'defensive democracy'.[216] Competing narratives, ascribing the harsh reality to the continuation of the occupation, and regarding Israel as an aggressive 'ethnocracy',[217] are not a hard to find. The problem does not emanate from the fact that judges in Jerusalem share and empathize with the Israeli narrative, but rather from the fact that a national narrative controls the Court's 'dynamic interpretation' of IHL. The result is that an order designed to punish and deter is read as a preventive security measure and an impermissible order of deportation or forcible transfer is being legitimated as a permissible order to assign residence.

3. *The* Targeted Killings *case*[218]

In The *Targeted Killings* judgment, the HCJ examined the legality of Israel's 'preventive targeted killings' of members of militant Palestinian organizations. Its unanimous conclusion reads:

> The result of the examination is not that such strikes are always permissible or that they are always forbidden. The approach of customary international law applying to armed conflicts of an international nature is that civilians are protected from attacks by the army. However, that protection does not exist regarding those civilians 'for such time as they take a direct part in hostilities' (§51(3) of *The First Protocol*). Harming such civilians, even if the result is death, is permitted, on the condition that there is no other means which harms them less, and on the condition that innocent civilians are not harmed. Harm to the latter must be proportional.[219]

'Preemptive targeted killings' is a term used by Israel to describe one of the measures it employs to combat terrorist attacks directed against its citizens and soldiers.[220] Palestinians regard this measure as a type of state assassination, aimed

---

[214] Ibid, at para 41 '... not every effective measure is also a lawful measure'.

[215] Ibid, at para 27. [216] Ibid, at para 41. [217] See eg Yiftachel, *supra* note 106.

[218] *Targeted Killings, supra* note 5. The analysis of the judgment provided in this section reproduces the case-note I co-authored in its respect, see Ben-Naftali and Michaeli, 'The Public Committee against Torture in Israel v. Government of Israel', 101(2) *AJIL* (2007) 459–465.

[219] *Targeted Killings, supra* note 5, at para 60. The main judgment was written by President (emeritus) Barak. President Beinisch and Vice President Rivlin concurred and appended Individual Opinions.

[220] Note that Israel refers to attacks against both Israeli civilians and soldiers as 'terrorist' attacks. The HCJ, as was noted in the discussion of *Ajuri, supra* note 131, uses the same narrative. From a

at suppressing their opposition to the continuous occupation.[221] The first such acknowledged strike occurred on 9 November 2000.[222] As of the date of the judgment, 338 Palestinians had been killed as a result of this policy; 128 of them, including 29 children, were innocent bystanders.[223] These data underscore the controversial nature of the policy.

A previous attempt to subject the policy of targeted killings to judicial review failed when the Court accepted the state's position that the matter is not justiciable.[224] This position was reversed in the instant case.[225]

The starting point of the judgment is that since September 2000, a continuous situation of armed conflict exists between Israel and 'various terrorist organizations'.[226] In the Court's view, this armed conflict is of an international character because it 'crosses the borders of the state'.[227] Therefore, the applicable normative framework is the international law of armed conflicts. This law is part of IHL and includes the laws of belligerent occupation.[228] Substantial parts of this law are customary and, as such, part of Israeli law.[229] IHL is the *lex specialis,* to be supplemented, in cases of lacuna, by human rights law.[230] Israeli law requires soldiers of the IDF to act pursuant to the laws of armed conflict. If they act contrary to these laws 'they may be, *inter-alia,* criminally liable for their actions'.[231]

IHL, said the Court, is based on a balance between human rights and military requirements, thus reflecting 'the relativity of human rights and the limits of military needs'.[232] The principle of distinction, differentiating between two categories of people, combatants and civilians, is a central consideration in this balance: combatants are legitimate military targets; civilians are not.[233] IHL, at present, does not recognize a third category of 'unlawful combatants'.[234] The Palestinian militants fail to meet the qualifying conditions set in the Hague Regulations and in the Geneva Conventions for combatants. Consequently, they are civilians. They are not, however, entitled to the full protection granted to civilians who do not take a direct part in the hostilities.[235]

---

legal perspective, however, soldiers are legitimate targets and attacks against them, in the context of armed conflicts, do not constitute terrorist acts.

[221] For a brief review of 'targeted killings' in the context of the *Intifada,* see eg Ben-Naftali and Michaeli, 'We Must Not Make a Scarecrow of the Law: A Legal Analysis of the Israeli Policy of Targeted Killings', 36(2) *Cornell Int'l L.J.* (2003) 233–292, at 241–247. For the Court's description of the factual background see *Targeted Killings, supra* note 5, at paras 1–2.

[222] See Report by Amnesty International, Israel and The Occupied Territories: *State Assassinations And Other Unlawful Killings,* 21 February 2001, available online at <http://www.amnesty.org/en/library/asset/MDE15/005/2001/en/818d1e6d-dc4b-11dd-a4f4-6f07ed3e68c6/mde150052001en.pdf> [last accessed 18 April 2010].

[223] For relevant and updated data, see, <http://www.btselem.org/english/statistics/Casualties_Data.asp?Category=17&region=TER> [last accessed 18 April 2010].

[224] HCJ 5872/01, *Barakeh v Prime Minster,* 56(3) PD 1.

[225] The Israeli Supreme Court is not bound by the *stare decisis* principle, see Art 20(2) of the Basic Law: Judicature, *supra* note 2, at 105.   [226] *Targeted Killings, supra* note 5, at para 16.

[227] Ibid, at para 18.   [228] Ibid, at para 20.   [229] Ibid, at para 19.

[230] Ibid, at paras 18–21.   [231] Ibid, at para 19.   [232] Ibid, at para 22.

[233] Ibid, at paras 23–26 discusses the definitions of each status and its respective scope of protection.   [234] Ibid, at para 28.

[235] Ibid, at para 26.

According to the norm reflected in Article 51(3) of *AP I*, which the Court considered part of customary international law, civilians who take a 'direct part in hostilities' do not lose their status as civilians. However, 'for such time' as they take part in the hostilities they become legitimate objects of attack, without enjoying the rights of the latter.[236] The interpretation of this provision should be dynamic, adapting the rule to new realities.[237]

Article 51(3) of *AP I* comprises three cumulative components: (i) 'hostilities'; (ii) 'direct part'; and (iii) 'for such time'. The Court interpreted 'hostilities', as acts intended to cause damage to the army or to civilians. A civilian takes a direct part in hostilities when he engages in, or prepares himself for, such acts.[238] Noting the lack of an agreed upon customary standard for (ii) and (iii), the Court concluded that 'there is no escaping going case by case, while narrowing the area of disagreement'.[239] It thus offered guidelines and examples in respect of these two elements.

A civilian takes a 'direct part' in hostilities when he is physically engaged in them and when he plans, decides on, and sends others to be thus engaged. At one end of the spectrum, a civilian bearing arms who is on his way to (or from) the place where he will use (or had used) them, clearly takes a direct part in hostilities. At the other end, are cases of indirect support, including selling of supplies and financing hostile acts. In between are the hard cases, where the function the civilian performs determines the directness of the part he takes in the hostilities (eg collecting intelligence, servicing weapons, and functioning as a 'human shield', are direct acts of participation).[240]

A similar methodology is followed in respect of the third element, 'for such time': at one end of the spectrum, there is a civilian taking part in the hostilities once or sporadically, thereafter detaching himself from such activity. He is not to be attacked for his past participation. At the other end is the active member of a terrorist organization for whom the rest between hostilities is but 'preparation for the next hostility'.[241] He is a civilian who has lost his immunity. The wide spectrum in between are 'grey' cases, which require a case-by-case examination. The test involves four elements. First, targeting decisions must be grounded in well-based and thoroughly verified information regarding the identity and activities of the individual. Second, no attack is permitted if a less harmful means exists. This requirement, grounded in the principle of proportionality, reflects that 'trial is preferable to use of force'.[242] Its practicality is related to the status of the territories

---

[236] Ibid, at para 30. Combatant status brings with it a host of privileges, which include, *inter alia*, rights to medical treatment and religious services, food, clothing, and adequate conditions of detention. See Geneva Convention Relative to the Treatment of Prisoners of War, 12 August 1949, 75 UNTS 135, Arts 21–22, 25, 26, 27, 33–37 respectively (hereinafter GC III). Most importantly, combatant status entails the right to legal immunity from prosecution for the (legal) actions which they have performed during the war, which otherwise would have been criminal offences. This customary rule is universally accepted. See Jinks, 'The Declining Significance of POW Status', 45 *Harv. Int'l L.J.* (2004) 367–442, at 376, footnote 38.   [237] *Targeted Killings, supra* note 5, at para 28.
[238] Ibid, at para 33.
[239] Ibid, at para 34 (regarding 'direct') and at para 39 (regarding 'for such time').
[240] Ibid, at paras 34–37.   [241] Ibid, at para 39.   [242] Ibid, at para 40.

as occupied. Third, a retroactive independent examination must be undertaken regarding, *inter alia*, the precision of the identification of the target. In appropriate cases compensation for harm to innocent civilians should be paid. Finally, every effort should be made to minimize harm to innocent civilians; any such collateral damage must be proportional.[243]

Proportionality, opined the Court, is a general principle of customary international law. Its application in international armed conflicts requires a proper proportion between the military advantage of an attack and the damage caused to innocent civilians harmed by it.[244] Thus, shooting at 'a terrorist sniper shooting at soldiers or civilians from his porch'[245] is proportionate, even if innocent civilians are harmed. An instance that fails the proportionality test is the aerial bombarding of a building where 'scores of its residents and passersby are harmed'.[246] In between fall the hard cases, necessitating a case-by-case determination.

The Court proceeded to reject the State's preliminary argument regarding injusticiability, on the following grounds: (a) cases involving impingement on human rights are justiciable; (b) the disputed issues are legal; (c) the disputed issues are examined by international tribunals; and (d) judicial review will intensify the objectivity of the *ex post* examination of the conduct of the army.[247] Focusing on the scope of judicial review of military decisions to perform acts of targeted killings, the Court differentiated between questions regarding the applicable law, which fall within its expertise, and operational decisions, which fall within the professional expertise of the executive.[248]

In conclusion, the Court situated the decision within the context of previous judgments where it reviewed military measures, stating that

[e]very struggle of the State—against terrorism or any other enemy—is conducted according to rules and law...There are no 'black holes'...The state's struggle against terrorism is not conducted 'outside' the law. It is conducted 'inside' the law, with tools that the law places at the disposal of democratic states.[249]

The *Targeted Killings* judgment is the first ever comprehensive judicial attempt to clarify the legal status of, and the rules applicable to, civilians taking direct part in hostilities, embodied in Article 51(3) of *AP I*.[250] It is, thus, potentially invaluable to the development of the contemporary law of armed conflict, which has

---

[243] Ibid, at paras 38–40.   [244] Ibid, at paras 41–45.   [245] Ibid, at para 46.
[246] Ibid.
[247] Ibid, at paras 47–54. Note that justiciability is a preliminary matter: when a court discusses the issue, it normally does so before proceeding to the merits of a case as indeed the discussion may obviate the need to thus proceed. In the present case, however, the order is reversed: having analysed the question on the merits, the judgment proceeds to discuss the issue of justiciability. On the significance of this reversal, see Ben-Naftali, 'A Judgment in the Shadow of International Criminal Law: the Decision of the Israeli High Court of Justice on the Legality of Targeted Killings', 5(2) *JICJ* (2007) 322–331.   [248] *Targeted Killings, supra* note 5, at paras 55–59.
[249] Ibid, at para 61. The discussion of the legal limits imposed on a democracy extends to at para 62.
[250] Even the ICTY has refrained from thoroughly addressing the phrase 'taking direct part in hostilities'. See Opinion and Judgment, *Tadić* (ICTY-94-1-T), Trial Chamber, 7 May 1997, at para 16.

been characterized by lack of consensus on the issue,[251] and overwhelmed by the progressive erosion of traditional distinctions between civilians, combatants, terrorists, guerilla fighters, and civilian contractors.[252]

This potential contribution, however, is hampered by the Court's failure to properly reconcile the two main instruments comprising the legal framework of the decision, ie the Geneva Conventions and *AP I*.[253] This is evident already at the outset of the decision, where the Court refrains from clearly defining their applicability in relation to the characterization of the nature of the conflict.

As noted above, the Court defined the conflict as an international armed conflict primarily on the ground that it 'crosses the borders of the state'.[254] In international law, however, it is not the *border* that determines the nature of a dispute but rather the *identity* of the parties. Thus, the first paragraph of Common Article 2 of the 1949 Geneva Conventions, defines an international armed conflict as 'a conflict arising between two or more states'. Consequently, all other conflicts are rendered non-international. Arguably, the application of this provision should have generated the conclusion that the conflict is non-international, as the Palestinian Authority is not a state.[255]

A legal basis for the proposition that the conflict under discussion is of an international nature exists in Article 1(4) of *AP I*. This provision extends the applicability of the rules of international conflicts beyond the traditional inter-state context to conflicts between states and other actors, such as national liberation movements. However, given that Israel is not a party to *AP I* and has persistently objected to this very expansion,[256] the Court could not rely on it and chose to avoid referring to it altogether.

It follows that the Court's assertion that the Israeli–Palestinian conflict is of an international nature lacks a normative basis and is unclear at best. So are the

---

[251] For the various views on the subjects see ICRC, *Third Expert Meeting on the Notion of Direct Participation in Hostilities*, 23–25 October 2005, available online at <http://www.icrc.org/Web/eng/siteeng0.nsf/htmlall/participation-hostilities-ihl-311205/$File/Direct_participation_in_hostilities_2005_eng.pdf> [last accessed 18 April 2010]; See also, ICRC, Interpretive Guidance on the notion of direct participation in hostilities under IHL (2009).

[252] See Queguiner, *Direct Participation in Hostilities Under International Humanitarian Law* (Humanitarian Policy and Conflict Research Working Paper, 2003); Schmitt, 'Humanitarian Law and Direct Participation in Hostilities by Private Contractors or Civilian Employees', 5(2) *Chicago Journal of International Law* (2004) 511–546.

[253] Note that *AP I* was designed to integrate the 'Geneva' law and the 'Hague' law. *Nuclear Weapons* Advisory Opinion, *supra* note 51.   [254] See *supra* text between notes 225 and 231.

[255] Cf *Hamdan v Rumsfeld*, 126 S Ct 2749 (2006). On the complex issue of the status of the Palestinian Authority, see eg McKinney, 'The Legal Effects of the Israeli-PLO Declaration of Principles: Steps Toward Statehood for Palestine', 18 *Seattle U.L. Rev.* (1994) 93–128; Dajani, 'Stalled Between Seasons: The International Legal Status of Palestine During the Interim Period', 26 *Denv. J. Int'l L. & Pol'y* (1997) 27–92. Note further that had the Court engaged in the discussion, it would have had to relate to Israel's position regarding the non-applicability *de jure* of *GC IV* to the territories occupied since 1967, a confrontation it had always chosen to avoid. See *supra* note 5; see also *supra* text between notes 69 and 72.

[256] Greenwood, 'Terrorism and Humanitarian Law—The Debate Over Additional Protocol I', 19 *Israel Yearbook on Human Rights* (1989) 187–209; Burris, 'Re-examining the Prisoner of War Status of PLO Fedayeen', 22 *The North Carolina Journal of International Law and Commercial Regulation* (1997) 943–1008, at 976.

consequences of this determination: has the Court thus effectively 'sneaked' the host of provisions of *GC IV* and of *AP I* into the Israeli system through the back door? Are all customary rules of international armed conflict now applicable to the Israeli-Palestinian conflict? If not, what distinguishes those rules that are applicable from those that are not?

This indeterminacy concerning the applicability of *GC IV* and *AP I* ultimately generated further confusion into the already eroded distinction between civilians and combatants: it accounts for the fact that the judgment, while denying that there is a third status of 'unlawful combatants', nevertheless *de facto* recognizes such status, equating it with civilians who take a direct part in the hostilities. Such 'civilians/unlawful combatants' are bereft of either immunity (of civilians) or privileges (of combatants).[257] This result emanates from the Court's blurring the distinct logic informing the normative frameworks of *GC IV* and of *AP I* insofar as the definitions of 'combatants' and 'civilians' are concerned: *GC IV* stipulates strict qualifying conditions for 'combatants', which Palestinian fighters do not meet, primarily because 'they have no fixed emblem recognizable at a distance, and they do not conduct their operations in accordance with the laws and customs of war'.[258] This restrictive definition of 'combatants' is directly related to the broad protection offered to civilians under the Geneva law: there is no provision equivalent to Article 51(3) of *AP I* in the Geneva Conventions. While the purpose of *AP I* is identical to the Geneva regime, ie to maximize humanitarian protection in terms of both immunities (to civilians) and privileges (to combatants), its logic is different: recognizing that 'there are situations in armed conflicts where, owing to the nature of the hostilities', an armed combatant cannot distinguish himself, it offers a less restrictive definition of 'combatants'.[259] This definition of 'combatants' is, in turn, directly related to the lesser protection offered to civilians who take part in the hostilities under Article 51(3) of *AP I*. Palestinian fighters meet the flexible criteria for 'combatants' stipulated in Article 44(3) of *AP I*. Israel, however, has objected persistently to this expansion of the definition and is, therefore, not bound by it. Indeed, the Court, employing the restrictive definition of the Geneva framework to combatants, dismissed without much ado the notion that the Palestinian militants are combatants. This is a proper application

---

[257] See *supra* text between notes 232 and 246. The judgment further refers to civilians 'who take direct part in hostilities' as 'unlawful combatants', while at the same time denying that the latter exist as a status. See *Targeted Killings, supra* note 5, at para 26: 'The result is that an unlawful combatant is not a combatant, rather a 'civilian'. However, he is a civilian who is not protected from attack as long as he is taking a direct part in the hostilities...civilians who are unlawful combatants are legitimate targets for attack, and thus surely do not enjoy the rights of civilians who are not unlawful combatants, provided that they are taking a direct part in the hostilities at such time. Nor...do they enjoy the rights granted to combatants. Thus, for example, the law of prisoners of war does not apply to them.' See also the title of Section 6: 'Civilians who are unlawful combatants', paras 29–31.

[258] Ibid, at para 24. For the Geneva definition of combatants, see eg Art 2(4) of the *GC III*.

[259] Art 44(3) of *AP I* recognizes such situations and provides that such person shall nevertheless retain his status as a combatant, 'provided that, in such situations, he carries his arms openly: (a) during each military engagement, and (b) during such time as he is visible to the adversary while he is engaged in a military deployment preceding the launching of an attack in which he is to participate'.

of the relevant legal framework. At the same time, however, the Court did not recognize them as 'civilians' entitled to the broader protection offered by that framework, but rather applied to them the lesser protection offered to civilians under Article 51(3) of *AP I*. This is a problematic application of the law: applying simultaneously the framework of the Geneva Conventions to define 'combatants' and the framework of *AP I* to define 'civilians', while formally valid is substantively flawed.

Indeed, civilians who take direct part in hostilities lose their immunity for such time. This is prescribed both by Article 51(3) of *AP I* and customary law. The interpretation of the scope of this provision cannot, however, be made in a normative vacuum and should be related to the relevant normative framework within which it is placed. Thus, a more expansive interpretation is called for within the context of *AP I*, but outside its context, whenever the definition of 'combatants' applicable to a situation is defined by the Geneva Conventions, the provision should be narrowly construed. Blurring the line between the frameworks of Geneva and *AP I* by denying the broader definition of combatants on the one hand, and giving a broad interpretation to the customary provision of Article 51(3) on the other hand, results in the creation of a broad category of 'unlawful combatants': persons who are entitled to neither the privileges of combatants nor the immunities of civilians. This, however, is a category which neither instrument recognizes; indeed, it is a category which defies the humanitarian purpose of both and which the judgment itself otherwise rejects.

The fate of 'unlawful combatants', aka 'civilians who take direct part in the hostilities',[260] is further worsened by the 'dynamic' interpretation the Court employs,[261] an interpretation that might complement *AP I*'s framework, but not the Geneva framework. Indeed, human rights law, an additional normative framework that the Court refers to but does not expressly apply,[262] could have been invoked in order to narrowly construe this element, especially given the context of a long-term occupation.

4. *The alchemy of rights*[263]

The discussion of both the *Ajuri* and the *Targeted Killings* cases thus illustrates the fate of law once it is implicated in maintaining a regime based on an inverse relationship between the norm and the exception: judicial review of executive actions, and measures designed to sustain the regime and squash opposition thereto, would not only tend to approve and thereby legitimate said measures, it will further reflect and advance the underlying logic of the regime itself. Through a sophisticated reading of the law, resort to 'dynamic' interpretations and to 'pick and choose' interpretative methodologies, it will acquire an alchemical quality which will transform a prohibited 'deportation/enforced transfer' into a permissible 'assignment of

---

[260] *Targeted Killings, supra* note 5, at para 26.   [261] Ibid, at para 28.
[262] Ibid, at para 18.
[263] In reference to Williams, *The Alchemy of Race and Rights: Diary of a Law Professor* (1991).

residence', and generate the very status of an 'illegal combatant', a status the existence of which it simultaneously denies.

These cases are but illustrations. While a complete review of the various interpretative means used to generate similar results is beyond the scope of the present article, it is nevertheless significant to note that the very introduction of international human rights law into the law of occupation, a development designed to produce greater protection to the occupied population, has been turned on its head by the HCJ. The universality of human rights has been construed by the Court as an invitation to recognize the human rights of the settlers (the legality of their presence in the occupied territory notwithstanding),[264] thereby creating a space for balancing the settlers' human right with the human rights of 'protected persons' under IHL,[265] in a manner that, as Professor Gross observed, 'upsets the built-in balance of IHL, which ensures special protection to people living under occupation, and widens the justification for limiting their rights beyond the scope of a strict interpretation of IHL'.[266]

Alchemy, however, is not the province of law and of jurists; it does not attest to Law's Empire,[267] but rather to its demise. When coupled with the subjection of the (international) norm to the (national) narrative, law becomes implicated not merely in individual cases but in the generation of a culture of impunity on the systemic level.

C. The policy spin: turning a blind eye

1. General

A culture of impunity may, but does not necessarily, signify disregard for law: it may well be that its progenitors are a regime characterized by the reversal of the relationship between the rule and the exception, and a *nomos*, a political space comprising both rules and the narrative which gives them meaning. Once the

---

[264] 'The authority to construct a security fence for the purpose of defending the lives and safety of Israeli settlers is derived from the need to preserve "public order and safety" (regulation 43 of The Hague Regulations). It is called for, in light of the human dignity of every human individual. It is intended to preserve the life of every person created in God's image. The life of a person who is in the area illegally is not up for the taking. Even if a person is located in the area illegally, he is not outlawed' *Targeted Killings* case, *supra* note 5 para 19.

'Israel's duty to defend its citizens and residents, even if they are in the area, is anchored in internal Israeli law. The legality of the implementation of this duty is anchored in public international law, as discussed, in the provisions of regulation 43 of The Hague Regulations' at para 23.

HCJ 3969/06 <http://elyon2.court.gov.il/files/06/690/039/N25/06039690.N25.htm> [last accessed 18 April 2010] at para 16 (in Hebrew).

[265] Ibid. See also HCJ 10356/02 *Hass v Commander of the IDF forces in the West Bank*, 58(3) PD 443, available online at <http://elyon1.court.gov.il/files_eng/02/970/104/r15/02104970.r15.pdf> [last accessed 18 April 2010]; HCJ 1890/03 *City of Bethlehem v The State of Israel—Ministry of Defence*, 59(4) PD 736; HCJ 7862/04 *Abu Daher v IDF Commander in Judea and Samaria*; *Mara'abe*, *supra* note 6; HCJ 1348/05 *Dr Shatia, Mayor of Salfi t v State of Israel*; *Regional Council Gaza Beach*, *supra* note 4; For an excellent analysis of the cases, see Gross, *supra* note 6, at 13–26.

[266] Gross, *supra* note 6, at 5.

[267] Dworkin, Law's Empire (1986); a conception of law highly distinct from Austine, *The Province of Jurisprudence Determined* (1994).

exceptional regime and the *nomos* are joined, a space is created where the exception and the rule, the fact and the norm, are indistinguishable.[268] The culture of impunity generated by this union does not signify disregard for law but rather that law itself has become meaningless as an instrument constraining power, and indeed functions to legitimize and perpetuate the regime. In this section, I would like to illustrate this proposition by focusing on one particular incident, the shooting of a blindfolded, handcuffed civilian detainee by the IDF, and the manner with which it was handled by the legal establishment in Israel.[269]

Shooting a blindfolded, handcuffed civilian detainee is a war crime. Such shooting was ordered by an officer of the IDF and executed by a soldier during a routine non-violent demonstration against the construction of the (illegal) Wall in the OPT.[270] The Israeli Military Advocate General (MAG), Avichai Mandleblitt, decided to charge both with 'conduct unbecoming'.[271]

The term 'conduct unbecoming' has an archaic ring to it, echoing bygone days where officers were gentlemen and only gentlemen could become officers;[272] where a certain, not necessarily specified but nevertheless clear code of honour was expected of members of a certain class, reflecting their ethically superior esprit de corps and, by implication, legitimizing their privileged status. Yielding

---

[268] The term '*nomos*' as used in the text encompasses its varied meanings for Cover, for Schmitt, and for Agamben. For Cover, it indicates a normative universe, comprising both rules and the narratives that give them meaning. See Cover, 'The Supreme Court 1982 term—Foreword: Nomos and Narrative', 97 *Harv. L. Rev.* (1983) 4–68. For Schmitt it meant that right as original violence, as difference, rather than universalistic rationality being the foundation of law. See C Schmitt, *Der Nomos der Erde im Völkerrecht des Jus Publicum Europaeum* (1988), discussed in Galli, 'Carl Schmitt's antiliberalism: its theoretical and historical sources and its philosophical and political meaning', 21 *Cardozo L. Rev.* (2000) 1597–1617, at 1601. Giorgio Agamben's analysis brings Schmitt's theory of the exception to its logical conclusion by stating that the concentration camp—as a paradigmatic structure—has become the modern political nomos: the space where the exception and the rule, the fact and the norm, are indistinguishable and law becomes meaningless. See Agamben, *supra* note 168, at 166–180.

[269] The discussion in this section reproduces, *mutatis mutandis*, the article I co-authored on the incident, see Ben-Naftali and Zamir: 'Whose 'Conduct Unbecoming'? The Shooting of a Handcuffed, Blindfolded Palestinian Demonstrator', 7(1) *JICJ* (2009) 155–175. Keren Michaeli's invaluable contribution to this article is thankfully acknowledged.

[270] *Construction of a Wall, supra* note 5, at 136.

[271] See HCJ 7195/08 *Abu Rahme et al v the MAG*, 2. (a petition against the MAG's decision) (hereinafter the *Petition*) available online at <http://www.acri.org.il/pdf/petitions/hit7195.pdf> [last accessed 18 April 2010] (in Hebrew). The judgment, which was rendered on 1 July 2009, is available online at <http://elyon1.court.gov.il/files/08/950/071/r09/08071950.r09.pdf> [last accessed 18 April 2010] (in Hebrew) (hereinafter *Abu Rahme* Judgment); Note that the 'conduct unbecoming' offence is stipulated in Art 130 of the Israel's Military Justice Law 5715–1955. In general, the jurisprudence of military courts in Israel indicates that such conduct denotes an act which dishonours the actor and is morally objectionable. See eg A/365/81 *Maj Binyamini v the Chief Military Prosecutor*; A/256/96 *Maj Bibas v the Chief Military Prosecutor*. It is usually inserted in an indictment together with other offences: eg a soldier who poured boiling water on a cat was charged both with 'cruelty to animals' and 'conduct unbecoming'. See A/107/03 *St Srg Kradi v Chief Military Prosecutor*.

[272] Such an offence still exists in military codes of justice, see eg Art 133 of the United States' Uniform Code of Military Justice: 'Any commissioned officer, cadet, or midshipman who is convicted of conduct unbecoming an officer and a gentleman shall be punished as a court-martial may direct.' See generally, Hillman, 'Gentlemen under Fire: The U.S. Military and "Conduct Unbecoming"', 26 *Law and Inequality Journal* (2008) 1–57.

to democratization processes, that class is currently far less specific, but old habits die hard. The offence of 'conduct unbecoming' still exists in many military codes, which have, probably grudgingly, been brought up to date, by inserting, for instance, an explanatory note to the effect that 'as used in this article, "gentleman" includes both male and female'.[273]

Common explanations of the nature of the offence tend to relate the conduct to personal disgrace which, if committed in a personal capacity 'seriously compromises the officer's character as a gentlemen', and, if committed in a professional capacity 'seriously compromises the person standing as an officer'.[274] Such disgrace is indicated by 'acts of dishonesty, unfair dealing, indecency, indecorum, lawlessness, injustice, or cruelty'. Examples of the offence include making a false official statement, using insulting language, cheating in an exam, being drunk in a public place, and public association with prostitutes.[275] Shooting a detainee clearly does not fit within the usual conception of 'conduct unbecoming an officer and a gentlemen'. Such conduct is indeed 'unbecoming', but from a broader human perspective which focuses on the human dignity of the victim rather than the honour of the perpetrator.[276]

The case raises a myriad of issues ranging from the proper response to civilian demonstrations against the illegal construction of the Wall[277] to obedience to a manifestly illegal order. For the purposes of the present discussion, however, the focus is limited to the designation of the shooting of a blindfolded and handcuffed detainee as 'conduct unbecoming' and to its implications.

Subsection 3.C.2 details the facts of the incident and proceeds to consider additional relevant data which suggest that the incident, far from being exceptional, in fact reflects routine, normal IDF practice. Subsection 3.C.3 proposes that the treatment of the detainee, from the moment of his apprehension and up to his shooting, is a war crime. Subsection 3.C.4 advances the argument that to the extent that such conduct reflects common and perhaps even systematic practice, the MAG's decision is even more problematic: it is indicative of a policy of tolerance towards military violence directed at non-violent civilian protest against the construction of the Wall. Such a policy might transform 'conduct unbecoming'—which as a matter of law is a war crime—into a crime against humanity. Subsection 3.C.5 concludes with a critical assessment of the *Abu Rahme* judgment rendered by the HCJ, a judgment which, while rejecting the MAG's position and ordering him to change the indictments to reflect the severe nature of the act, nevertheless failed to acknowledge both the routine nature of the act and the policy of tolerance towards such acts. This failure reflects, and indeed further exacerbates, the problem occasioned by the reversal of the relationship between the rule and the exception.

---

[273] Filbert and Kaufman, *Justice and Procedure in the Sea Services* (3rd edn, 1998) 112.
[274] Ibid.   [275] Ibid, at 115.
[276] On Human Dignity see Kamir, *Israeli Honor and Dignity: Social Norms, Gender Politics and the Law* (2004) 19–43 (in Hebrew).   [277] *Construction of a Wall, supra* note 5.

2. *The factual framework*

On 7 July 2008, during a routine demonstration against the construction of the Separation Wall in Nil'in, a village in the West Bank,[278] Israeli border policemen stopped, handcuffed, and blindfolded a 27-year-old Palestinian demonstrator, Ashraf Abu Rahme. He was taken to an army jeep, beaten, and driven to the village's entrance, where he was left for some two hours.[279] Thereafter, still handcuffed and blindfolded, a Lieutenant Colonel of the IDF led him by the arm to stand next to a jeep and, based on his acquaintance with Abu Rahme from previous demonstrations, asked him (in Hebrew) 'well, will you now stop participating in demonstrations against the IDF forces?' The detainee responded in Arabic in a manner that made it clear that he did not understand Hebrew. The officer then asked the soldier, who stood some two metres away: 'What do you say, shall we take him aside and "shoot rubber" at him?' The soldier responded, also in Hebrew: 'I have no problem shooting him'. The officer then instructed the soldier to load the bullet and the soldier responded that he had already done so. The soldier aimed his weapon at the demonstrator's legs and fired a rubber-coated steel bullet at him, hitting his left toe.[280]

The incident was filmed by Salaam Amira, a 15-year-old girl from Nil'in, from her home.[281] On 20 July B'tselem, the Israeli Information Center for Human Rights in the Occupied Territories, received and published the video-clip she shot.[282]

---

[278] Ni'lin is a Palestinian village located 17 kilometres west of Ramallah in the central West Bank. In May 2008, work began on the construction of the Separation Wall in the village's land. The route of the Wall—designed to secure the neighboring settlements—requires confiscation and destruction of agricultural lands, including the olive groves which are the main source of the villager's livelihood. Organized demonstrations against the construction of the Wall take place on a regular basis, involving the Palestinian villagers, Israelis, and internationals (mainly from the International Solidarity Movement). See <http://www.ynet.co.il/english/articles/0,7340,L-3579716,00.html> [last accessed 18 April 2010]. Note that the judgment describes the demonstration as 'violent'. See *Abu Rahme* Judgment, *supra* note 271, at para 3. It should be noted that the violence in these demonstrations is often generated by the security personnel.

[279] The *Petition* disclosed that Abu Rahme was beaten; the *Abu Rahme* Judgment, *supra* note 271, at para 3, notes that he was detained in view of his active engagement in disrupting orders and is silent on the fact that he was beaten.

[280] The so-called 'rubber bullets' are steel bullets, coated with thin rubber. They are used to disperse demonstrations based on the belief that such bullets are less lethal than live ammunition and that they are therefore appropriate for use in situations that pose no threat to the IDF soldiers' lives. Yet, they can be lethal, a fact acknowledged by the drafters of the Open-Fire Regulations, which stipulate, *inter alia*, a minimum range for firing them of 40 metres. In fact, 'rubber bullets' have caused the deaths of dozens of Palestinians, and it is probable that the fact that they are perceived as 'less lethal' generates a light trigger-finger. See <http://www.btselem.org/english/Firearms/Rubber_Coated_Bullets.asp> [last accessed 18 April 2010].

[281] The day following the release of the video, Salaam's father, Jamal, was detained by the IDF for 26 days, probably as a vengeful measure for the release of the video-clip, a connection acknowledged even by the military court which, having found no evidence to justify his continued detention, ordered his release. See <http://www.ynet.co.il/english/articles/0,7340,L-3583912,00.html> and <http://www.haaretz.com/hasen/spages/1016196.html> [last accessed 18 April 2010].

[282] The video-clip is available at <http://www.btselem.org/english/Firearms/20080819_HC_Suspends_Proceedings_In_Nilin_Shooting_Case.asp> [last accessed 18 April 2010].

Following the publication of the video-clip, B'tselem demanded that a military police investigation be opened and that the soldier, Staff Sergeant L, and the officer who turned out to be the battalion commander, Omri Borberg, be brought to justice. It was only then that the MAG ordered an investigation and the commander was transferred to a training officer position. In an interview, the Chief of Staff stated explicitly that he does not rule out the possibility that in the future the commander might resume his previous post.[283]

Following the investigation, the MAG decided to prosecute both the soldier and his then commander for 'conduct unbecoming'. A conviction for this offence does not result in any criminal record.[284] According to the military indictment, the commander intended merely to frighten the detainee (a justification hard to reconcile with the fact that he knew that the blindfolded detainee did not speak Hebrew), whereas the soldier understood that he had been ordered to shoot.[285] It is also important to note that ample evidence suggests various other questionable incidents under the command of Lt Col Borberg, which include shootings at Palestinian civilians involving both 'rubber bullets' and live ammunition, denying injured Palestinians access to medical care, and detainee beatings.[286]

On 19 August, Ashraf Abu Rahme and a coalition of human rights organizations filed an urgent petition to the HCJ against the MAG's decision, demanding that the indictment be altered to reflect the exceptional gravity of the offence.[287] The HCJ issued an interim injunction deferring both criminal proceedings and requiring the MAG to justify his decision.[288] On 28 September, the HCJ held a hearing on the petition and ordered the MAG to reconsider the indictment and to inform the court of its decision within 40 days.[289] On 4 November, following extensive consultations with the top echelons of the military and the government legal advisers, including the State Attorney General, the MAG decided to retain the original indictment and charge the officer and the soldier with no offence other than 'conduct unbecoming'.[290] On 1 July 2009, the Court rendered its judgment

---

[283] In an interview, the Chief of Staff stated explicitly that he does not rule out the possibility that in the future the commander might resume his previous post. Available online at <http://www.ynet. co.il/english/articles/0,7340,L-3581694,00.html> [last accessed 18 April 2010].

[284] Criminal Register and Rehabilitation Law 1981 (Regulations 1984).

[285] Cited in *Petition, supra* note 271, at Section E. 7-9. (a petition against the MAG decision); *Abu Rahme* Judgment, *supra* note 271, at para 3.   [286] *Petition, supra* note 271, at 7–10.

[287] *Petition*, ibid. The petitioning organizations are: B'tselem—The Israeli Information Center for Human Rights in the Occupied Territories (<http://www.btselem.org/English/About_BTselem/ Index.asp>); The Association for Civil Rights in Israel (ACRI) (<http://www.acri.org.il/eng/Story. aspx?id=15>); The Public Committee Against Torture in Israel (PCATI) (<http://www.stoptorture. org.il/en/odot>); and Yesh Din—Volunteers for Human Rights (<http://www.yesh-din.org/site/ index.php?page=about.us&lang=en>) [last accessed 18 April 2010].

[288] See HCJ interim-injunction available online at <http://elyon1.court.gov.il/files/08/950/071/ r01/08071950.r01.pdf> [last accessed 18 April 2010].

[289] See HCJ decision, available online at <http://elyon1.court.gov.il/files/08/950/071/ r04/08071950.r04.pdf> [last accessed 18 April 2010] (in Hebrew). See also <http://www.btselem. org/English/Firearms/2008106_Nilin_HCJ_Hearing.asp> and <http://www.ynet.co.il/articles/ 0,7340,L-3584653,00.html> [last accessed 18 April 2010].

[290] Available online at <http://www.btselem.org/english/firearms/20081104_nilin_state_ response.asp> [last accessed 18 April 2010].

in the case, directing the MAG to change the indictments to reflect the nature of the facts and the actions committed.[291]

The MAG's decision merits special attention not only because it trivializes a grave incident, but primarily because there is ample evidence suggesting that this incident reflects common and perhaps even systematic practice in the territories. Indeed, what is exceptional is that the incident was filmed and that the video-clip was distributed. The fact that during the time that elapsed between the incident and the mass distribution of the video-clip the MAG ordered no investigation demonstrates an inverse relationship between the IDF's concern for the honour of its soldiers and its respect for the human dignity of Palestinians under their control. This point is substantiated once the incident is placed in the wider context of the military response to Palestinian demonstrations against the continuous occupation in general and the construction of the Wall in particular.

Owing to the magnitude of the conflict, an overall evaluation of the Israeli response to the Palestinian opposition is beyond the scope of this chapter. After all, the context of such assessment is the prolonged occupation and more specifically the second Palestinian uprising (*Intifada*) that commenced in 2000. The conflict is complex, protracted, and wide in scope. For illustration, over the last eight years the astounding number of 4,829 Palestinians have been killed by the Israeli security forces.[292] Since 2005 the average number of Palestinians in the custody of Israeli security forces exceeds 8,000.[293] Cognizant of this difficulty, the following analysis confines itself merely to two facets of conduct of the IDF that are related directly to the treatment of Mr Abu Rahme: the exercise of the rules of engagement and the treatment of detainees.

The detention and shooting of Ashraf Abu Rahme is not an isolated incident. Indeed, participation in demonstrations against the Israeli occupation has proved to be a perilous activity, claiming the lives of over 100 Palestinian civilians, at least 10 of whom were protesting against the construction of the Wall.[294] As stated in the 2008 *Report of the Special Rapporteur on the Situation of Human Rights in the Occupied Palestinian Territories*, Israeli security forces use both rubber-coated steel bullets and live ammunition as a means to disperse demonstrations in the OPT.[295] In its 2007 Annual Report, B'Tselem stated that over 1,000 civilians

---

[291] *Abu Rahme* Judgment, *supra* note 271, at para 92 (A Procaccia, J). The Court further decided to revoke the order concealing the name of Sergeant L (Koroa Leonardo).

[292] According to the information gathered by B'tselem. Available online at <http://www.btselem. org/english/statistics/casualties.asp> [last accessed 18 April 2010]. During these eight years 727 Israeli civilians have been killed by Palestinians. These numbers do not include Palestinians killed or injured during the January 2009 operation in Gaza. On the numbers of Palestinians that have been killed by Israel in 2007 see also UN General Assembly, *Report of the Special Committee to Investigate Israeli Practices Affecting the Human Rights of the Palestinian People and Other Arabs of the Occupied Territories* (A/63/273), 13 August 2008, at paras 89–91.

[293] The data is supplied by the Israeli Government. Available online at <http://www.btselem.org/ english/statistics/detainees_and_prisoners.asp> [last accessed 18 April 2010].

[294] Available online at <http://www.btselem.org/english/statistics/casualties_data.asp?Category= 28&region=TER> [last accessed 18 April 2010].

[295] UN General Assembly, *Situation of human rights in the Palestinian territories occupied since 1967: note/by the Secretary-General* (A/63/326), 25 August 2008, at para 26.

protesting against the Wall have required medical attention since 2004 due to injuries from 'rubber' bullets, beatings, and tear gas inhalation and that 320 of them were injured during 2007 alone.[296] According to testimonies, most of the incidents involved no threat to the lives of the soldiers or policemen.[297] In a letter dated 31 August 2008, B'Tselem requested the Israeli General Attorney to review the escalating occurrence of ostensibly illegal shootings with rubber-coated steel bullets by the security forces. The letter draws attention to the fact that fired from a short range, rubber-coated steel bullets are lethal and in violation of the army's rules of engagement.[298]

The current rules of engagement themselves are subject to criticism from human rights organizations. Following incidents involving injury to Jewish-Israeli protesters,[299] the IDF's rules of engagement relating to the OPT were amended and now distinguish between demonstrations involving Israelis and those that do not. Although the IDF denies public access to the rules, media reports published relevant sections of these instructions.[300] These rules forbid the use of live ammunition or rubber bullets when Israeli protestors are present in a demonstration, unless the demonstration is violent and soldiers are faced with a 'clear and imminent' danger.[301] Palestinian demonstrations, on the other hand, are subject to more permissive rules, whereby the use of 'rubber' bullets is allowed when there is danger to the 'physical integrity' of soldiers.[302] According to B'Tselem, there has been a relaxation of the rules of engagement since the outbreak of the second *intifada*. Thus, during operations involving arrests of Palestinians suspected of terrorist activities, soldiers are allowed to shoot live ammunition at anyone fleeing the area without confirming the identity of the person first. Warning shots towards houses are also permitted even when civilians are present therein.[303] Another example are the 'death zones' around the Gaza perimeter fence where fire is opened automatically against any person approaching the fence.[304] These rules have resulted in the deaths of at least 16 people who were neither armed nor involved in hostilities.

It is estimated that over 2,000 Palestinians not taking part in hostilities have been killed since 2000.[305] The permissive character of the rules of engagement partly accounts for the high number of civilian casualties. The problem is exacerbated by the fact that the rules that do exist are consistently violated. The reasons for these violations are varied, and probably include, at least to some

---

[296] Available online at <http://www.btselem.org/Download/200712_Annual_Report_eng.pdf> at 27 [last accessed 18 April 2010].

[297] For example, Amnesty International reports that soldiers standing on rooftops of Palestinian houses shoot at Palestinian children throwing stones. Available online at <http://www.amnesty.org/en/library/asset/MDE15/033/2007/en/dom-MDE150332007en.html> at section 'Bullets Greet Anti-Wall Protesters' [last accessed 18 April 2010].

[298] Available online at <http://www.btselem.org/Download/20080831_12759_Letter_to_Mazuz_Concerning_use_of_rubber_coated_steel_bullets.doc> [last accessed 18 April 2010] (in Hebrew).   [299] Ibid.

[300] <http://www.nrg.co.il/online/1/ART1/590/452.html> [last accessed 18 April 2010] (in Hebrew).   [301] Ibid.

[302] Ibid.   [303] *Supra* note 296, at 6.   [304] Ibid, at 7.   [305] *Supra* note 292.

extent, the confusion surrounding them.[306] The finger on the trigger has become unbearably light.

The incident at hand should also be assessed in the context of the treatment accorded to Palestinian detainees by Israeli security forces. A 2009 report published by the Public Committee against Torture reveals the extent of violence and humiliation to which Palestinian detainees are subject from the moment of capture to post-trial imprisonment.[307] Numerous testimonies give evidence of widespread abuse of handcuffed Palestinians which begins immediately upon arrest and consists of brutal beatings and humiliation (such as their placement on the hot floor of military vehicles to serve as a foot rest for soldiers).[308] In a study conducted by UAT (Uniting against Torture) the ill treatment of detainees upon arrest is actually considered 'milder' than the treatment meted out in subsequent detention facilities.[309] A report published by B'Tselem and Hamoked—Center for the Defense of the Individual, on the treatment of Palestinian detainees indicates that at least 49 percent of the persons interviewed reported being beaten (most commonly by punching and kicking) whilst handcuffed and blindfolded;[310] 34 percent reported being cursed at (usually with respect to the detainee's family members) and humiliated (incidents include ridicule during strip searches);[311] 23 percent reported being deprived of basic needs such as food, water, medication, and visits to the toilet.[312]

The abuse of Ashraf Abu Rahme is thus clearly not an exceptional incident. It is part of a systematic pattern of conduct by the IDF against Palestinian civilians. It should finally be stressed that security considerations, the all-too-automatic justification for violations of human rights, are irrelevant to the case at hand (and, indeed, were so far not advanced) as well as to similar cases involving the use of force against Palestinian demonstrators.[313]

---

[306] An internal review undertaken by the IDF in 2006, found deficiencies in military training programmes concerning rules of engagement that brought about misconceptions and misunderstandings of the rules on the part of soldiers. Thus, for instance, confusion existed regarding the circumstances calling for the use of rubber bullet as opposed to those permitting live ammunition. Available online at <http://www.ynet.co.il/articles/0,7340,L-3235501,00.html> [last accessed 18 April 2010] (in Hebrew).

[307] Available online at <http://www.stoptorture.org.il/files/no_defense_heb.pdf> [last accessed 18 April 2010].   [308] Ibid, 7–10.

[309] Available online at <http://www.stoptorture.org.il/files/UAT_Report2007.pdf> at 30 [last accessed 18 April 2010]. Although the Israeli Supreme Court decreed that some of the GSS interrogating techniques amount to torture and are therefore illegal, they are still employed on a regular basis. On 2 November 2008, human rights organizations submitted a petition on contempt of court, due to the continued use of torture. The petition is available online at <http://www.stoptorture.il/en/node/1332> [last accessed 18 April 2010].

[310] Available online at <http://www.btselem.org/English/Publications/Summaries/200705_Utterly_Forbidden.asp> at 33 [last accessed 18 April 2010].   [311] Ibid.

[312] Ibid.

[313] Note that the demonstrations are considered illegal in the sense that they are not permitted by the IDF. Indeed, it would seem that from an Israeli perspective, the law allows not merely the deprivation of rights of Palestinians, but also deprives them of the right to protest this deprivation peacefully. From the perspective of international human rights law as indicated by the Special Rapporteur, Palestinian residents are entitled to protest against the construction of the Wall. Available online

3. *The normative framework: IHL and international criminal law*

The treatment of Mr Abu Rahme, from the moment of his apprehension and up to his shooting, makes for a textbook example of a war crime. It was undertaken in the context of an armed conflict; against a civilian; and it constitutes inhumane and cruel treatment, or at a minimum an outrage upon personal dignity.

IHL provides the primary normative framework applicable to this case. *Prima facie,* it is necessary to determine whether the conflict is of an international or a non-international character in order to determine the applicable rules. Arguably, the conflict between Israel and the Palestinians of the OPT is a non-international armed conflict. This is so for two reasons: first, Article 2(a) of the Fourth Geneva Convention defines an international armed conflict as a conflict between states;[314] the OPT is not a state. Secondly, Israel is not a party to *AP I,* the only instrument which transforms a conflict between a state and a non-state entity into an international conflict.[315] Nevertheless, the wider context of the conflict, namely, the occupation of the OPT by Israel, has imported the application of *GC IV* via Article 2(b) therein,[316] and with it the determination by the HCJ that the conflict qualifies as an international armed conflict.[317] For the purposes of the case at hand, however, the classification of the armed conflict as international or non-international is immaterial since the conduct under examination is, as shall be argued, prohibited and criminalized in both kinds of conflict.

The protection of human dignity is the hallmark of IHL in both international and non-international armed conflict. In the context of the former, Article 27 of *GC IV* reflects this notion. This provision is considered the 'basis of the Convention, proclaiming as it does the principles upon which the whole of the "Geneva Law" is founded' and 'the principle of respect for the human person and the inviolable character of the basic rights of individual men and women'.[318] Article 27 reads in its relevant part:

Protected persons are entitled, in all circumstances, to respect for their persons, their honour... They shall at all times be humanely treated, and shall be protected especially against all acts of violence or threats thereof...

The reference to the obligation to treat protected persons humanely, writes Pictet, is 'in truth, the "leitmotiv" of the four Geneva Conventions'; it is to be construed broadly 'as applying to all aspects of man's life'; it is absolute in character, valid in all circumstances and at all times, and 'remains fully valid in relation to persons in prison or interned... It is in such situations, where human values appear to be in

---

at <http://www.unhcr.org/refworld/country,,,,PSE,4562d8cf2,48e5e2be2,0.html> at para 27 [last accessed 18 April 2010].

[314] *GC IV* Art 2(a).

[315] *AP I* Art 1(4). The analysis of the *Targeted Killing* Judgment discussed, *inter alia,* the non-international character of the conflict. See *supra* text between notes 225 and 231.

[316] *Construction of a Wall, supra* note 5, at para 101.

[317] *Public Committee Against Torture in Israel v Government of Israel* HCJ 769/02 (2006) at para 18 available online at <http://elyon1.court.gov.il/files_eng/02/690/007/a34/02007690.a34.pdf> [last accessed 18 April 2010]; see Cassese, *International Law* (2nd edn, 2005) 420.

[318] Pictet, *supra* note 32, at 200.

greatest danger, that the provision assumes its full significance.'[319] Focusing on the obligation to respect the honour of protected persons, Pictet emphasizes that the fact that the protected person 'is an enemy cannot limit his right to consideration and to protection', and exemplifies acts that fail the obligation to treat a person humanely, such as slander, calumny, and insults.[320]

Article 32 of *GC IV* specifies the principle stated in Article 27, by clarifying that the prohibition on taking measures 'of such a character as to cause physical suffering' extends to 'any... measures of brutality'. Two points merit emphasis in this context: first, the similarity between this provision and the prohibition set forth in Article 27 of *GC IV* on 'acts of violence'.[321] Secondly, the drafters substituted a causal criterion ('of such a character as to cause') for a criterion of intention ('likely to cause', which appeared in the original draft).[322] The idea was, thus, to expand the scope of the prohibition.

In the context of a non-international armed conflict, Common Article 3 of the Geneva Conventions, a 'Convention in miniature',[323] reiterates the principle according to which 'persons not taking active part in the hostilities shall in all circumstances be treated humanely' and that acts consisting *inter alia* of cruel treatment and 'outrages upon personal dignity, in particular humiliating and degrading treatment', are prohibited.[324]

Mr Abu Rahme qualifies as a 'protected person'.[325] He was apprehended following his participation in a demonstration, was handcuffed and blindfolded, beaten, and driven to the village's entrance, where he was left for two hours. In this state he was thereafter shot and injured in his toe. The conduct of the IDF personnel towards Abu Rahme violated his humanity, dignity, and person. Under international customary law, such conduct violates the basic IHL principles described above and constitutes a war crime.

Both 'inhumane treatment' and 'degrading treatment' are part of the corpus of international criminal law. Their constitutive elements have been identified in the jurisprudence of the ICTY and the International Criminal Tribunal for Rwanda (ICTR), a jurisprudence that is used here as an authoritative guide.[326]

International criminal law does not distinguish between 'inhuman' and 'cruel' treatment as the degree of physical or mental suffering required to prove either one of those offences is the same.[327] Thus, 'inhumane treatment', which is considered as a grave breach by Article 147 *GC IV*,[328] is (a) an intentional act or omission, that is

---

[319] Ibid, 205.   [320] Ibid, 202.
[321] Art 27 provides: 'Protected Persons... shall at all times be humanely treated, and shall be protected especially against all acts of violence or threats...'. See also Pictet, *supra* note 318, at 224.
[322] Pictet, *supra* note 32, at 222.   [323] Ibid, 34   [324] Art 3(1)(c) *GC IV*.
[325] According Art 4 of *GC IV*, Mr Abu Rahme qualifies as a 'protected person' since he is in the hands of the occupying power (Israel) of which he is not national.
[326] While the decisions of the ICTY and ICTR are binding only on the defendants brought before them, they serve as a source supporting the existence of customary norms within Art 38(1)(d) of the ICJ Statute.
[327] Judgment, *Naletilić and Martinović* (IT-98-34-T), Trial Chamber, 31 March 2003, at paras 245–246.
[328] Pictet, *supra* note 32, at 596; See also Judgment, *Delalić et al* (IT-96-21-T), Trial Chamber, 16 November 1998, at paras 516–534.

an act which, judged objectively, is deliberate and not accidental; (b) which causes serious mental harm or physical suffering or injury or constitutes a serious attack on human dignity; and (c) committed against a protected person.[329] Similarly, 'cruel treatment' under Common Article 3 was defined as (a) an intentional act or omission; (b) which causes serious mental or physical suffering or injury or constitutes a serious attack on human dignity, and (c) committed against a person taking no active part in the hostilities.[330]

In the same vein, the elements of crimes for both Article 8(2)(a)(ii) of the Statute of the International Criminal Court (infliction of *inhuman* treatment in an international context), and Article 8(2)(c)(i) (violence to life and person, in particular *cruel* treatment in a non-international context) are identical.[331] They require that the 'perpetrator inflicted severe physical or mental pain or suffering upon one or more persons'.[332]

'Inhuman treatment' was further characterized by the Trial Chamber in *Blaškić* as follows:

[I]nhuman treatment is intentional treatment which does not conform with the fundamental principle of humanity...acts characterized in the Conventions and Commentaries as inhuman, or which are inconsistent with the principle of humanity, constitute examples of actions that can be characterized as inhuman treatment...[T]he category 'inhuman treatment' included not only acts such as torture and intentionally causing great suffering or inflicting serious injury to body, mind or health but also extended to other acts contravening the fundamental principle of humane treatment, in particular those which constitute an attack on human dignity.[333]

Another guiding tool to interpret the concept of 'inhuman and cruel treatment' is the case-law of international human rights bodies,[334] as employed by the ICTY itself.[335] According to the European Court of Human Rights:

Ill-treatment must attain a minimum level of severity...The assessment of this minimum is, in the nature of things, relative; it depends on all the circumstances of the case, such as the nature and context of the treatment, the manner and method of its execution, its duration, its physical or mental effects and, in some cases, the sex, age and state of health of the victim.[336]

---

[329] Judgment, *Blaškić* (IT-95-14-A), Appeals Chamber, 29 July 2004, at para 665.

[330] *Blaškić*, ibid, at para 595; Judgment, *Limaj, Bala and Musliu* (IT-03-66-T), Trial Chamber, 30 November 2005, at para 231; Judgment, *Strugar* (IT-01-42-T), Trial Chamber, 31 January 2005, at para 261.

[331] Zimmermann, 'Article 8—War Crimes, para 2(c)–(f)', in Triffterer (ed), *Commentary on the Rome Statute of the International Criminal Court—Observers' Notes, Article by Article* (2nd edn, 2008) 475–502, at 490.

[332] Elements of Crimes, Adopted by the Assembly of States Parties, ICC ASP/1/3 (2002) 130 (hereinafter *Elements of Crimes*).

[333] Judgment, *Blaškić* (IT-95-14-T), Trial Chamber, 3 March 2000, at para 155.

[334] Droege, 'In truth the leitmotiv: the prohibition of torture and other forms of ill treatment in international humanitarian law', 89 *International Review of the Red Cross* (2007) 515–543, at 520–524; Dörmann, with contributions by Doswald-Beck and Kolb, *Elements of War Crimes Under the Rome Statute of the International Criminal Court: Sources and Commentary* (2003) 66–69.

[335] *Delalić, supra* note 328.

[336] *Kudła v Poland*, ECtHR, App No 30210/96 (26 October 2000) at paras 90–94.

The notion that since the physical effect of the shooting was merely an injury to a toe, the shooting fails to meet the standard of serious pain accompanying serious physical injury[337] is not supported by relevant international jurisprudence. The Appeals Chamber of the ICTY in the *Braanin* case rejected a similar argument, holding that 'acts inflicting physical pain amount to torture even when they do not cause pain of the type accompanying serious injury'.[338] This is *a fortiori* the case when the conduct considered falls short of torture.[339] When coupled with the severe mental effect of being detained for hours while blindfolded and then shot at from short range is bound to have—an effect akin to that of a mock execution which has been considered torture[340]—the appropriate classification of the conduct is not 'unbecoming'; rather it is inhumane and cruel.

At a minimum, the treatment of Mr Abu Rahme constitutes 'other acts contravening the fundamental principle of humane treatment, in particular those which constitute an attack on human dignity'.[341] While an attack on human dignity is an element of the crime of inhumane/cruel treatment under customary law, it should be noted that under the normative framework of the ICCSt, it is not. Rather, a conduct amounting to an attack on human dignity falls under the crime of 'committing outrages upon personal dignity, in particular humiliating and degrading treatment' laid out in Article 8(2)(c)(ii) with respect to international armed conflicts and in Article 8(2)(b)(xxi) with respect to non-international armed conflicts. Like the crime of 'inhumane and cruel treatment', these provisions, as well as their respective elements of crimes, are identical. The elements required are that 'the perpetrator humiliated, degraded or otherwise violated the dignity of one or more persons' and that 'the severity of the humiliation, degradation or other violation was of such degree as to be generally recognized as an outrage upon personal dignity'.[342]

The foregoing elements correspond to the customary definition of the crime as articulated by the ICTY:

[T]he crime of outrages upon personal dignity requires: (i) that the accused intentionally committed or participated in an act or an omission which would be generally considered to cause serious humiliation, degradation or otherwise be a serious attack on human dignity, and (ii) that he knew that the act or omission could have that effect.[343]

---

[337] HCJ 7195/08 *Abu Rahme et al v the MAG*, at 27 (The State's response to the petition).

[338] Judgment, *Brdanin* (IT-99-36-T), Trial Chamber, 28 November 2003, at para 521.

[339] For further discussion on the differences between 'torture' and 'inhuman treatment' see De Vos, 'Mind the Gap: Purpose, Pain, and the Difference between Torture and Inhuman Treatment', 14 *Human Rights Brief* (2007) 4–9; Mettraux, 'Crimes Against Humanity in the Jurisprudence of the International Criminal Tribunals for the Former Yugoslavia and for Rwanda', 43 *Harv. Int'l L.J.* (2002) 237–316, at 289–291.

[340] See Commission on Human Rights, *Torture and Other Cruel, Inhuman or Degrading Treatment or Punishment: Report of the Social Rapporteur*, UN ESCOR, E/CN.4/1986/15 (19 February 1986) at para 119. [341] *Blaškić, supra* note 333.

[342] *Elements of Crimes, supra* note 332, at 140.

[343] Judgment, *Kunarac, Kovac, and Vuković* (IT-96-23 and 96-23/1-A), Appeals Chamber, 12 June 2002, at para 161.

The threshold of humiliation is high. Thus, 'the humiliation to the victim must be so intense that the reasonable person would be outraged'.[344] There is no requirement, however, that the injury to the victim be physical or be long-lasting.[345] Furthermore, any assessment as to the level of humiliation of the victim should take into account not only the victim's subjective evaluation but also objective criteria.[346]

In light of the above, the treatment of Mr Abu Rahme qualifies as degrading and humiliating treatment: it does not take a particularly active imagination to understand the vulnerable state in which he found himself both physically and mentally even before his injury and the fear he must have felt throughout the experience. Such treatment thus qualifies as an 'outrage on his personal dignity as a human being'.

4. *Policy of tolerance towards systematic violence and its implications*

The MAG, as noted above, decided to charge the officer who gave the shooting order and the soldier who executed it, with 'conduct unbecoming', a charge highly unbecoming a conduct that amounts to a war crime.[347] In responding to the petition against this decision,[348] the MAG detailed his reasoning. The deposition emphasizes the importance the MAG attributes to taking forceful steps against violations of the Army Rules of Conduct by soldiers. In the present case, however, the MAG believes that the circumstances and evidence do not merit a more severe charge since the shooting resulted from a 'misunderstanding' between the officer and the soldier. The investigation, proceeds the MAG, does not reveal an intention to hurt Abu Rahme nor was there any evidence of cruelty on the part of the soldiers involved to support a harsher charge. When these considerations are coupled with the slight physical injury, and with the disciplinary steps taken,[349] the charge of 'conduct unbecoming' should be maintained.[350] The view advanced by the MAG, thus, is that the IDF employs a vigorous policy against illegal conduct of soldiers towards Palestinians and that the manner with which this case was handled did not constitute an exception thereto, since, in the specific circumstances, both the disciplinary and criminal proceedings against the soldiers are appropriate.

It is submitted that the MAG's position is untenable as a matter of both fact and law: the analysis of the incident advanced in subsection 3 generates the conclusion

---

[344] Judgment, *Aleksovski* (IT-95-14/1-T), Trial Chamber, 25 June 1999, at paras 56–57.
[345] Judgment, *Kunarac, Kovac and Vukovič* (IT-96-23 and 96-23/1-A) Trial Chamber, 22 February 2001, at para 501.   [346] *Kunarac, Kovac, and Vukovič, supra* note 343, at para 162.
[347] Note that military manuals often refer to actions that are considered 'war crimes' in international law as domestic offences or violations of military discipline. Israel's Military Justice Law is no exception: it does not refer to war crimes, but it does include offences better suited for the conduct under consideration, such as the offences stipulated in Arts 65 (Maltreatment); 72 (Excess of authority to the extent of endangering life); 85 (Illegal use of arms); and 115 (Offences in connection with arrest). For further discussion on the abovementioned offences see *Petition, supra* note 271, at 15–16.   [348] *Petition, supra* note 271.
[349] HCJ 7195/08 *Abu Rahme et al. v the MAG*, at 5 & 11 (State's complementary notice and response by affidavit). Available online at <http://www.acri.org.il/pdf/petitions/hit7195mashlima.pdf> [last accessed 18 April 2010] (in Hebrew).   [350] Ibid.

that the conduct qualifies as a war crime. When coupled with relevant data suggesting that the investigation and prosecution policies of the IDF leave much to be desired, the MAG's decision becomes all the more problematic: indeed, the handling of the Abu Rahme incident is not an exception; it is the rule. It attests to a highly deficient enforcement system put in place by the IDF with respect to illegal violence against Palestinians in the OPT and reflects a consistent policy of tolerance towards such violence. Insofar as effective penal sanctions for war crimes are a necessary component of the duty to suppress such conduct, as indicated by Article 146 *GC IV*,[351] an inadequate legal response towards systematic violence against Palestinian civilians might indicate that said violence constitutes a 'state policy' which renders the systematic attack against civilians a crime against humanity.

Under international criminal law, as stipulated in Article 7 of the ICCSt, an act committed as part of a widespread or systematic attack against any civilian population is executed in pursuance of a state policy and amounts to crimes against humanity.[352] To the extent that the treatment of Mr Abu Rahme, far from being an isolated and an exceptional incident, actually conforms to a pattern of similar incidents, the inadequate legal response to this and to numerous similar occurrences, might establish that it has been committed in pursuance of a state policy, thus constituting a crime against humanity.

The customary category of 'crimes against humanity' is codified in Article 7 of the ICCSt. The provision enumerates 11 acts, the common denominator of which is that they constitute a 'serious attack on human dignity'[353] and gross violations of human rights law. Some such acts, if they take place during an armed conflict, also constitute war crimes.[354] In order for such violations to qualify as 'crimes against humanity', they must be 'committed as part of a widespread or systematic attack directed against any civilian population, with knowledge of the attack'.[355]

To qualify as 'widespread' an attack may either refer to a single attack the effect of which was extremely widespread, or to the cumulative effect of a number of attacks.[356] A 'systematic' attack refers to the organized nature of the violent acts and the improbability of their random occurrence.[357] It must reflect—and

---

[351] Art 146 of *GC IV* provides: 'The High Contracting Parties undertake to enact any legislation necessary to provide effective penal sanctions for persons committing, or ordering to be committed, any of the grave breaches of the present Convention defined in the following Article.'

[352] Art 7(1) ICCSt provides: 'For the purpose of this Statute, "crime against humanity" means any of the following acts when committed as part of a widespread or systematic attack directed against any civilian population, with knowledge of the attack.'

[353] Cassese, *International Criminal Law* (2nd edn, 2008) 98.

[354] For the development of the crime against humanity and for the connection between war crimes and crime against humanity see eg Akhavan, 'Reconciling Crimes Against Humanity with the Laws of War', 6 *JICJ* (2008) 21–37.   [355] Art 7 ICCSt.

[356] International Law Commission, *Report of the International Law Commission on the Work of Its Forty-Eighth Session,* from 6 May to 26 July 1996, UN GAOR, 48th Sess, Supp No 10, UN Doc A/51/10 (1996) at 94–95, quoting *Blaškić, supra* note 333, at para 206; Judgment, *Kayishema and Ruzindana* (ICTR-95-1-T),Trial Chamber, 21 May 1999, at para 123.

[357] *Kunarac, Kovac, and Vukovic, supra* note 345, at para 429. See also Judgment, *Akayesu* (ICTR-96-4-T), Trial Chamber, 2 September 1998, at para 580 ([Systematic means] 'thoroughly organised and following a regular pattern on the basis of a common policy involving substantial public or private resources'); *Blaškić, supra* note 333, at para 203; *Tadić, supra* note 250, at para 648; ILC 43rd

advance—a pattern of misconduct[358] that regularly 'interferes with the life and existence of a person or his relationships with his social spheres, or interferes with his assets and values, thereby offending against his human dignity as well as humanity as such'.[359]

The treatment of Mr Abu Rahme should be examined in the context of the IDF's reactions to Palestinian demonstrators and Palestinian detainees that serve as the backdrop of the incident. That context has been described in 3.C.2 above and is sufficient to establish a pattern of a 'cumulative effect of a number of attacks'. As suggested in 3.C.3, the act qualifies as 'other inhumane acts of a similar character intentionally causing great suffering, or serious injury to body or to mental or physical health'.[360]

The requirement of a 'widespread' or 'systematic' attack emphasizes the collective nature of crimes against humanity, thereby distinguishing them from isolated or sporadic acts which, at most, may amount to war crimes. Ensuring the gravity of the category of crimes against humanity, Article 7(2) of the ICCSt elaborates that the term 'attack directed against any civilian population' means a course of conduct involving the multiple commission of acts referred to in paragraph 1 against any civilian population, pursuant to or in furtherance of a *state or organizational policy* to commit such attack.

The significance of the 'policy' element in the context of Article 7(2) of the ICCSt cannot be underestimated. It was specifically inserted to secure the grave nature of the crime.[361] The 'policy' element is understood to require that 'the State or organization actively promote or encourage such an attack against a civilian population' and that:

[s]uch a policy may, in exceptional circumstances, be implemented by a *deliberate failure to take action*, which is *consciously* aimed at encouraging such attack. The existence of such a policy cannot be inferred solely from the absence of governmental or organizational action.[362]

It is against this normative position that the decision of the MAG as to the charge brought against the soldiers assumes its primary significance: an act might amount to a crime against humanity if it is part of an attack that is encouraged by a state's failure to take action with respect to such acts.[363] It is at

---

Sess, at 266 ('The systematic element relates to a constant practice or to a methodical plan to carry out such violations'); ILC 48th Sess, ibid.

[358] *Blaškić, supra* note 333, at para 251.

[359] Harlan Veit (Jud Süss) Germany, Court of Assizes (Schwurgericht) of Hamburg, 29 April 1950, 52 cited in Cassese, *supra* note 353, at 100, footnote 3.

[360] Art 71(k) the ICCSt; *Elements of Crimes, supra* note 332, at 124.

[361] This was done in response to concerns regarding the disjunctive nature of the 'systematic' and 'widespread' elements. See von Hebel and Robinson, 'Crimes within the Jurisdiction of the Court', in Lee (ed), *The International Criminal Court: The Making of the Rome Statute* (1999) 79–126, at 97; Sadat and Carden, 'The New International Criminal Court: An Uneasy Revolution', 88 *Geo. L.J.* (2000) 381–474, at 431–432.

[362] *Elements of Crimes, supra* note 332, at 116, footnote 6 (emphasis added).

[363] It should be noted that it is unclear whether the policy element constitutes part of the customary definition of crimes against humanity. According to the ICTY it is not. See *Kunarac, Kovac, and*

this point that the Israeli policy regarding investigations of abuse becomes relevant, indeed crucial. This is so because a systematic abdication by the Israeli authorities of their obligation to bring charges against personnel inflicting injuries on civilians that do not take part in hostilities might qualify as a 'deliberate failure to take action, which is consciously aimed at encouraging such attack[s]'.[364]

The nexus between this policy and the wide scope of abuse is quite clear: illegal behaviour of an individual soldier and his commander is not the only cause for the high number of Palestinians killed and injured who were not taking part in hostilities and posed no danger to security forces. The primary reason for these deaths and injuries is Israeli policy, set by the army's top echelon, which includes illegal easing of the military's rules of engagement, approval of operations that constitute disproportionate attacks, and *failure to carry out independent investigations* in cases.[365]

Numerous complaints brought forward by various NGOs are yet to generate a proper response designed to rectify the situation.[366] Reports by highly reputable NGOs concerning the mistreatment of detainees have so far generated merely an acknowledgement by the IDF regarding lack of rules and guidelines regulating the handling of detainees in the period between their arrest and arrival at detention centres.[367] Indeed, doubts as to the internalizing of the illegality of abuses by the military system have been voiced even in decisions of the Military Appeals Tribunal.[368]

In general, investigations and indictments are scarce. Many investigations are hampered by a myriad of shortcomings: the time gap between reported incidents and the decision to open an investigation means that physical evidence has disappeared and that suspects and witnesses are harder to trace; the military police employs only a handful of interpreters; and many investigations are overseen by reserve commanders and are therefore frequently handed down from one officer to another.[369] Statistics gathered by Yesh Din—Volunteers for Human Rights, a human rights organization dedicated to the enforcement of law in the OPT—substantiate this assessment:[370] between 2000 and 2007, out of 427 investigations conducted in relation to incidents of violence against Palestinians only 35 resulted in indictments, 33 of which ended in convictions; out of 239 investigations of

Vuković, supra note 343, at para 98, at footnote 114 (construing the case-law supporting the need for the element as either 'merely highlight[ing] the factual circumstances of the case at hand' or dismissing it on the ground that it 'has been shown not to constitute an authoritative statement of customary international law').

[364] *Elements of Crimes, supra* note 332, at 116, footnote 6.   [365] *Supra* note 296, at 5.
[366] *Supra* note 309, at 31.   [367] *Supra* note 307, at 33.
[368] A/28/04 *St Srg B S v the Chief Military Prosecutor*, available online at <http://www.courts.co.il/SR/army/irur-28-04.htm> at para 16 [last accessed 18 April 2010] (in Hebrew).
[369] *Supra* note 310, at 60.
[370] These statistics are based on the IDF Spokesperson's response to Yesh Din's questions, 28 October 2007. See <http://www.yesh-din.org/site/images/ds1eng.pdf> at 2, footnote 5 [last accessed 18 April 2010].

illegal shooting incidents only 30 reached the stage of indictment and only 16 indictments resulted in convictions.[371]

The judiciary plays some part in the culture of impunity: on top of the dearth of investigations and indictments, the sentences meted out by military tribunals do not reflect the severity of the crimes and rarely exceed four months' imprisonment.[372] A petition filed by B'Tselem and the ACRI against the MAG concerning the latter's decision to refrain from investigations into the deaths of many Palestinian civilians is still pending before the HCJ, nearly six years since proceedings commenced.[373]

Noting that 'investigations and, if appropriate prosecutions of those suspected of serious violations are necessary if respect for human rights and humanitarian law is to be ensured and to prevent the development of a climate of impunity',[374] the *Report of the United Nations Fact Finding Mission on the Gaza Conflict* proceeded to review the Israeli system of investigations and prosecution in order to assess whether Israel meets its international duty in this respect.[375] It concluded that the Israeli system does not comply with the universal principles of independence, effectiveness, promptness, and impartiality.[376] Of particular relevance to the present discussion is the finding that 'action against members of security forces who commit violence, including killings, serious injuries and other abuses, against Palestinians is very rare. Information available to the Mission points to a systematic lack of accountability of members of the security forces for such acts.'[377] A major factor contributing to this failure is the 'change of policy instituted in 2000 determining that full criminal investigations are possible only after "operational debriefings" have been carried out', a policy the practical implication of which is that 'in practice criminal investigations do not begin before six months after the events in question. By that time evidence may be corrupted or no longer available.'[378]

The MAG's decision to charge the soldiers responsible for the treatment of Mr Abu Rahme with 'conduct unbecoming' lends credence to the conclusion of the *Goldstone Report* that 'there are serious doubts about the willingness of Israel to carry out genuine investigations in an impartial, independent, prompt and effective way, as required by international law' and that Israel's system 'presents inherently discriminatory features that have proven to make the pursuit of justice for Palestinian victims very difficult'.[379] Indeed, it fits neatly into a pattern of inadequate sanction policy, and reflects a policy of tolerance towards IHL violations.

---

[371] Available online at <http://www.yesh-din.org/site/index.php?page=criminal4&lang=en> [last accessed 18 April 2010].   [372] *Supra* note 307, at 30–31.

[373] HCJ 9594/03, *B'Tselem v MAG*. The text of the petition is available online at <http://www.acri.org.il/Story.aspx?id=1014> [last accessed 18 April 2010].

[374] *Goldstone Report supra* note 14, at para 1570.   [375] Ibid, at paras 1586–1600.

[376] Ibid, at paras 1612–1630.

[377] Ibid, at para 1622. In this part the Report discusses Israel's obligation to prevent, investigate, and punish violations of human rights in the West Bank.   [378] Ibid, at para 1627.

[379] Ibid, at para 1629.

It also brings Israel closer to the threshold set in Article 7 ICCSt than it might realize.[380]

The MAG's insistence on designating the shooting of the handcuffed, blindfolded detainee as merely 'conduct unbecoming' itself qualifies as 'conduct unbecoming an officer and a gentlemen', in the sense that it disgraces both the military esprit de corps and the integrity of the legal profession. When coupled with the poor record of law enforcement, it is indicative of a policy of tolerance towards grave breaches of IHL and may itself amount to complicity in crime.[381]

While an analysis of the complicity of the legal profession in the commission of international crimes is beyond the scope of the present article[382] it is nevertheless necessary to note that Government lawyers in general and military lawyers in particular shoulder a responsibility that extends beyond serving the immediate interests of their formal clients. Their responsibility is to uphold the law, not to bend it; to foster an atmosphere that condemns, rather than condones, criminal behaviour; their responsibility is towards the general public, its interests and values,[383] and, in relevant cases, towards the international community.[384] In this context, the role played over the past few years by the legal advisers to the Bush Administration in the horrid road leading to Abu Ghraib is not a beacon to follow; it is a bonfire of vanities to avoid.[385] The shadow cast by the *Goldstone Report* over the role played by the legal advisers to the Israeli government in the context of the military operations conducted in Gaza during the period from 27 December 2008 and 18 January 2009, underscores the point.[386] The reason for this emphasis on the responsibility of legal advisers was well articulated by the Nuremberg International Military

---

[380] It should finally be noted that, for a crime against humanity to be established, the offender must be aware of the link between his action and the widespread or systematic practice, cognizant generally of the larger context—an attack against civilian population—to which he adds his specific offensive. The perpetrator may believe that such 'collegiality' would shield him from future liability. It is also quite conceivable that given the systematic practice with which his act coheres, he sees it as nothing extraordinary. This misconceived awareness, however, is precisely why international criminal law articulated this requirement.

[381] The different kinds of criminal responsibility are articulated in Arts 25(3) and 28 of the ICCSt. See Militello, 'The Personal Nature of Individual Criminal Responsibility and the ICC Statute', *JICJ* (2007) 941–952. On the complicity of lawyers in international crimes, see, Trials of War Criminals Before the Nuremberg Military Tribunal Under Control Council Law No 10, Vol 3 (1951) at 31 (hereinafter *The Justice Case*). In *The Justice Case*, high ranking bureaucrats in the Nazi Ministry of Justice and seven individuals who served as judges and lawyers were indicted for a conspiracy to commit war crimes and crimes against humanity. See generally, Lippman, 'Law, Lawyers and Legality in the Third Reich: The Perversion of Principle and Professionalism', 11 *Temple Int'l & Comp. L.J.* (1997) 199–307.

[382] Sands, *Torture Team: Deception, Cruelty and the Compromise of Law* (2008) esp at 211–278.

[383] See, *The Role of the Legal Adviser of the Department of State, A Report of the Joint Committee Established by the American Society of International Law and the American Branch of the International Law Association* (July 1990) (American Society of International Law, 1 October 1990) rep in 85 *AJIL* (1991) 358–373.

[384] See eg Ciammaichella, 'A Legal Adviser's Responsibility to the International Community: When is Legal Advice a War Crime', 41 *Val. UL Rev.* (2007) 1143–1164.

[385] See Greenberg and Dratel (eds), *The Torture Papers: The Road to Abu Ghraib* (2005); Mestrovic, *The Trials of Abu Ghraib: An Expert Witness Account of Shame and Honor* (2006).

[386] *Goldstone Report, supra* note 14, at paras 1183–1191.

Tribunal decisions concerning legal advisers who betray their role: an officer who 'sold' his intellect and scholarship to power, said the Tribunal, was engaged in 'the prostitution of a judicial system for the accomplishment of criminal ends', an engagement that 'involves an element of evil to the State which is not found in frank atrocities which do not sully judicial robes'.[387]

5. *The* Abu Rahme *judgment*

The HCJ concluded that the MAG's decision to charge the officer who gave a patently illegal order and the soldier who executed it with the offence of 'conduct unbecoming' is exceedingly unreasonable. Accordingly, it vitiated the decision and ordered the MAG to exercise his discretion as to which criminal indictments would best fit the nature and character of their respective actions.[388]

The decision is proper from a normative perspective and sends the right ethical message to its target audience, the Israeli public. Indeed, the judgment was not translated into English; the decision is justified on the basis of the fundamental principles and of Israeli administrative,[389] criminal,[390] and constitutional law,[391] as well as on the basis of its 'Jewish and democratic values'.[392] The Individual Opinions of Justices Rubinstein and Meltzer refer to the ethical code of the IDF[393] as well as to Jewish Law,[394] the writings of Israel first Prime Minister, David Ben-Gurion, and to Israeli poetry[395] as additional sources of both normative and eth(n)ical behaviour.

---

[387] *The Justice Case, supra* note 381, at 1086. This pronouncement was made in respect of the role played by Schlegelberger who headed the Nazi Ministry of Justice. See also *US v von Leeb* (U.S. Military Tribunal 1948) (hereinafter *The High Command Case*) rep in Trials of War Criminals Before the Nuremberg Military Tribunals Under Control Council Law No 10, Vol 11 (1950) 462, at 490–495 (convicting Rudolph Lehman, Chief the Legal Department of the Oberkommando der Wehrmacht for his criminal connection to the Barbarossa Jurisdiction Order, the Commando Order, and the Night and Fog Decree for either drafting or formulating the policy behind these illegal orders); *US v Göring* (IMT 1946) in Trials of the Major War Criminals Before the International Military Tribunal Vol 1 (1947) 223, at 286 (convicting Joachim von Ribbentrop who served as Hitler's Foreign Policy Adviser, of war crimes for his memorandum justifying Nazi 'preemptive strikes' against Norway, Denmark, and the Low Countries).

[388] *Abu Rahme* Judgment, *supra* note 271, at para 92. The main judgment was written by Justice Ayala Procaccia. Justices Elyakim Rubinstein and Hanan Meltzer appended Individual Opinions. On 21 July 2009 a revised indictment was issued, charging the officer with the criminal offence of threats under the Israeli criminal law and the staff sergeant with illegal use of weapons under the Israeli military law. See m/5/08 *Military Prosecutor v Lt General Omri Borberg and Staff Sergeant Koroa Leonardo*, (on file with the author). The case is still pending. It is interesting to note that whereas the judgment emphasized that the behaviour of the officer amounted to torture and cruel inhuman and degrading treatment, the MAG chose not to revise the judgment to include this offence as well.

[389] *Abu Rahme* Judgment, *supra* note 271, at paras 66–84.

[390] See for example, ibid, at paras 35–38, and at para 43.

[391] See for example, ibid, at para 40.   [392] Ibid, at para 90.

[393] Ibid, at para 11 of Rubinstein's Individual Opinion.

[394] Ibid, at paras 14–18. Rubinstein further indicates that the conduct at issue, amounts to *'Hillul Hashem'*, defamation of God. It is noteworthy in terms of his understanding of the 'imagined community' to whom the judgment is addressed, as indeed otherwise there seems to be little reason to engage God in the matter.

[395] Both Rubinstein and Meltzer refer to, and the latter quotes from the poetry of Nathan Alterman, the late distinguished Israeli poet and publicist, who, horrified by abuses of military power

An analysis of the issue in the light of international law is conspicuously absent from the judgment. This is not an oversight[396] but a conscious decision, alluded to in the Individual Opinion of Justice Meltzer:

This is the place to emphasize that even from the perspective of the Respondents... indicting them for... conduct unbecoming... would prove to be counter-productive in the final analysis. The reason for that is that it is possible, once the military court renders its final judgment, for someone to argue that given the nature of the indictment, they would not be able to avail themselves of the 'double jeopardy' defense under international criminal law, and I shall not expand on this point, though it brings us to a brief discussion of comparative law.[397]

The discomfort this passage generates notwithstanding,[398] the fact remains that international criminal law, and most particularly, the spectre of the exercise of universal jurisdiction, have assisted the Court in reaching its decision.[399] From this perspective, international law is present in the judgment in a significant way, albeit by omission.

A discussion of the root problem, however, is not only absent from the judgment, but the text produces a narrative that replicates, and *ipso facto* augments, that problem. The text presents the incident as an exceptional event.[400] In reality, as was described in 3.C.2 above, inhuman, cruel, and degrading treatment of Palestinians, far from being exceptional, is quite common, and the only exceptionality in this incident is that it was filmed and widely publicized. Indeed, the judgment further obfuscates the ever greater divide between the normative (detailed in the numerous and diversified sources on which the judgment relies to assert

---

in 1948, wrote condemning and widely publicized poems heralding the value of 'purity of arms' and behaviour restrained by law. See eg Meltzer J, Individual Opinion, at paras 11 and 14.

[396] The petition referred extensively to international law, and the Judgment acknowledges that the petitioners argued that 'international law regards inhuman and degrading behavior as grave breaches obliging the State to prosecute and to punish the perpetrators', but otherwise refrains from basing its decision on international law.

[397] Meltzer J, Individual Opinion, at para 7. It is instructive to note that the comparative discussion, *ibid* at paras 8–10 is designed to show that Israel fares better than other states insofar as the functioning of its military prosecution works and that according to the standard established by the European Court of Human Rights, *Ocalan v Turkey* (2003) 37 EHRR 10, detaining civilians, blindfolding them etc, does not amount to inhumane behaviour. The fact that this description does not exhaust the treatment accorded to Mr Abu Rahme notwithstanding, the judge further mentions in the context of this comparative analysis that the relationship between state and individual responsibility is a subject currently examined in international criminal law discourse.

[398] The ICCst provides at para 10 of the preamble and in Art 1 that the Court established under the Statute 'shall be complementary to national criminal jurisdictions'. See also Arts 15, 17, 18 and 19 ICCst. See generally, Rojo, 'The Role of Fair Trial Considerations in the Complementarity Regime of the International Criminal Court: From "No Peace without Justice" to "No Peace with Victor's Justice"?', 18 *LJIL* (2005) 829–869; *Goldstone Report, supra* note 14, at paras 1804–1835.

[399] Ben-Naftali and Zamir, *supra* note 271.

[400] *Abu Rahme* Judgment, at para 73: 'The severity of the event from a normative and a value perspective is great and exceptional.' It should be noted that the petitioning human rights organizations equally referred to the event as exceptional. This is noteworthy since much of the data suggesting that the incident is far from exceptional is painstakingly gathered by them. See *supra* text between notes 365 and 373. The explanation for this apparent discrepancy is as clear as it is indicative of the paradox inherent to their activities: the price of defending the interests of a particular client is collaboration with the system they otherwise oppose. See Sfard, *supra* note 12.

the ethical underpinnings of the IDF and, indeed, of Israel) and the descriptive (evidence pertaining to widespread violations, coupled with a systematic lack of enforcement of the law, detailed in 3.C.3 and 3.C.4, which is entirely missing from the judgment). This normative/descriptive obfuscation fits neatly within the matrix of the occupation regime.[401] Indeed, the characterization of the incident as exceptional (and the consequential exceptional decision to intervene in the discretion exercised by the MAG), is generated by and further generates the reversal of the relationship between the rule and the exception.

This reversal operates to numb public sense and sensibilities and provides the proper context for appreciating, *inter alia*, the following concern articulated in the *Goldstone Report*:

Video footage uploaded to the internet by Israeli border police, and filed under 'comedy' offers an insight into how wanton abuse is perceived by members of the security forces themselves. The Mission has received reports of other, similar occurrences, giving rise to the concern that *an increased level of force and the dehumanization have become normalized in the practice of the security forces.*[402]

4. Concluding Comments: Eyes Wide Shut

...a line has been crossed, *what is fallaciously considered acceptable 'wartime behavior' has become the norm.* Public support for a more hard-line attitude towards Palestinians generally, lack of public censure and lack of accountability all combine to increase the already critical level of violence against protected population.[403]

The *Goldstone Report* clarifies that the road to Gaza on 27 December 2008 was not paved with good intentions. It is a road as long and winding, as illegitimate and as illegal as the indefinite occupation and the various means and measures[404]— all ostensibly legal in the Israeli reading of international law[405]—undertaken over

---

[401] See *supra* text between notes 172 and 176.

[402] *Goldstone Report*, *supra* note 14, at para 1397 (emphasis added).

[403] Ibid, at para 1433 (emphasis added).

[404] eg attacks on government buildings and persons, detailed in chapter VII; failure to take feasible precaution to protect the civilian population, detailed in chapter IX; indiscriminate and indeed deliberate attacks against the civilian population, detailed in chapters X and XI; attacks on the foundation of life, including destruction of industrial infrastructure, food production, water installation, sewage treatment, and housing, indicative of a deliberate and systematic policy to target industrial sites and water installations, detailed in Chapter XII; the deliberate application of disproportionate force to create maximum disruption in the life of many people as a legitimate means to achieve military and political goals are some of the factual findings. Normatively, they violate the basic principles of IHL, and indicate an intention to inflict collective punishment and could amount to persecution, ibid, at paras 1332–1335.

[405] 'Israel's operations in the Occupied Palestinian Territory have had certain consistent features...The military operations from 27 December to 18 January, did not occur in a vacuum, either in terms of proximate causes in relation to the Hamas/Israeli dynamics or in relation to the development of Israeli military thinking about how best to describe the nature of its military objectives....while many of the tactics remain the same, the reframing of the strategic goals has resulted in a qualitative shift from relatively focused operations to massive and deliberate destructions...Major General Gadi Eisenkot, the Israeli Northern Command chief, expressed the premise of the doctrine: What happened in the Dahiya quarter in Beirut in 2006 will happen in every village

the years to sustain it. It is worthwhile quoting the pertinent paragraphs at some length:[406]

The Mission is of the view that Israel's military operation in Gaza between 27 December 2008 and 18 January 2009 and its impact cannot be understood and assessed in isolation from developments prior and subsequent to it. The operation fits into a *continuum of policies aimed at pursuing Israel's political objectives with regard to Gaza and the Occupied Palestinian Territory as a whole. Many such policies are based on or result in violations of international human rights and humanitarian law.* Military objectives as stated by the government of Israel do not explain the facts ascertained by the Mission, nor are they congruous with the patterns identified by the Mission during the investigation. The *continuum* is evident most immediately with the policy of blockade that preceded the operations and that in the Mission's view amounts to collective punishment intentionally inflicted by the Government of Israel on the people of the Gaza Strip. When the operations began, the Gaza Strip had been for almost three years under a severe regime of closures and restrictions on the movement of people, goods and services. This included basic life necessities... Adding hardship to the already difficult situation in the Gaza Strip, the effects of the prolonged blockade did not spare any aspect of the life of Gazans. Prior to the military operation the Gaza economy had been depleted, the health sector beleaguered, the population had been made dependent on humanitarian assistance for survival and the conduct of daily life. Men, women and children were psychologically suffering from longstanding poverty, insecurity and violence, and enforced confinement in a heavily overcrowded territory. The dignity of the people of Gaza had been severely eroded. This was the situation in the Gaza Strip when the Israeli armed forces launched their offensive in December 2008. The military operations and the manner in which they were conducted considerably exacerbated the aforementioned effects... *An analysis of the modalities and impact of the December-January military operations also sets them, in the Mission's view, in a continuum with a number of other pre-existing Israeli policies with regard to the OPT.* The progressive isolation and separation of the Gaza Strip from the West Bank, a policy that began much earlier and which was consolidated in particular with the imposition of tight closures, restrictions on movement and eventually the blockade, are among the most apparent. Several measures adopted by Israel in the West Bank during and following the military operations in Gaza also further deepen Israel's control over the West Bank, including East Jerusalem, and point to a convergence of objectives with the Gaza military operations... Systematic efforts to hinder and control Palestinian self-determined democratic processes, not least through the detention of elected political representatives and members of government and the punishment of the Gaza population for its perceived support for Hamas, culminated in the attacks on government buildings during the Gaza offensive, most prominently the Palestinian Legislative Council. The cumulative impact of these policies and actions make prospects for political and economic integration between Gaza and the West Bank more remote.

Indeed, it is not only the *Goldstone Report* which is, as suggested by its authors, 'illustrative of the main patterns of violation';[407] it is the operation in Gaza itself that is thus symptomatic of a pathological structure of control.

---

from which Israel is fired on [...] We will apply disproportionate force on it... From our standpoint, these are not civilian villages, they are military bases. [...] This is not a recommendation. This is a plan. And it has been approved.' Ibid, at paras 1189–1191.

[406] Ibid, at paras 1674–1676 (emphases added).
[407] Ibid, at para 16.

The role international law—as interpreted by the Israeli executive, legislator, and judiciary—has played in the making and the sustaining of this structure has been the focus of this chapter. This role generated the normalization of the exception (Part 2) and the subversion of the very notion of the rule of law on both the individual (2.3.A) and the systemic (2.3.B) levels. It is thus not merely a pathological but a pathoLAWgical structure of control.

The Israeli reaction to the *Goldstone Report* thus far ranges from attempts to shoot the messengers[408] to a wholesale denial of the message,[409] its condemnation as a death-blow to the peace process,[410] and calls for the change of IHL.[411] The direction of the change would presumably be the legitimization of not only the existence but the expansion of the settlements and the various means necessary to secure the human rights of the settlers; the transformation of civilians and civilian objects into civilians who 'take direct part in hostilities' and 'supporting infrastructure';[412] 'civilian villages' into 'military bases';[413] and a new notion of proportionality that befits 'a-symmetrical wars', that is, the infliction of what hitherto has been perceived as 'disproportionate destruction and creating the maximum disruption in the lives of many people' as a 'legitimate means to achieve not only military but also political goals'.[414] It is not farfetched to assume that as these words are being written, an assembly of juridical mandarins trained in the Humpty Dumpty School of Law is busy translating such ideas into an internationally palatable language. After all, this is the fifth decade in which they have been doing that quite successfully. 'Practice,' as the cliché indicates, 'makes perfect'. It is equally true, however, that 'familiarity breeds contempt'.

---

[408] See <http://docs.google.com/Doc?id=dgpc4hc9_136d88g8fcg> [last accessed 18 April 2010]. See the response of Justice Richard Goldstone, 'Justice in Gaza', *The New York Times*, 17 September 2009, available online at <http://www.nytimes.com/2009/09/17/opinion/17goldstone.html> [last accessed 18 April 2010].

[409] See <http://www.ynetnews.com/articles/0,7340,L-3777382,00.html> [last accessed 18 April 2010]. For a more balanced criticism see Landau, 'The Gaza Report's Wasted Opportunity', *The New York Times*, 19 September 2009, available online at <http://www.nytimes.com/2009/09/20/opinion/20landau.html> [last accessed 18 April 2010]; generally see 'Crimes of War', 16 September 2009, available online at <http://www.economist.com/displayStory.cfm?story_id=14445878> [last accessed 18 April 2010]; Kaye 'The Goldstone Report', *The American Society of International Law*, 1 October 2009, available online at <http://www.goldstonereport.org/pro-and-con/critics/124-david-kaye-the-goldstone-report-asil> [last accessed 18 April 2010].

[410] See <http://www.haaretz.com/hasen/spages/1117893.html> and <http://www.ynetnews.com/articles/0,7340,L-3792963,00.html> [last accessed 18 April 2010].

[411] See <http://www.ynetnews.com/articles/0,7340,L-3795714,00.html, and <http://www.ynetnews.com/articles/0,7340,L-3792960,00.html> [last accessed 18 April 2010].

[412] *Goldstone Report, supra* note 14, at paras 1203–1216.   [413] Ibid, at para 1191.

[414] Ibid, at para 63. For the theoretical basis for this position, see Kasher and Yadlin, 'Assassination and Preventive Killing', 25 *School of Advanced International Studies Review* (2005) 41–57. For a critical review see Margalit and Walzer, 'Israel: Civilians & Combatants', *New York Review of Books*, 14 May 2009, available online at <http://www.nybooks.com/articles/archives/2009/may/14/israel-civilians-combatants> [last accessed 18 April 2010].

6

The Role of the European Court of Human Rights in Monitoring Compliance with Humanitarian Law in Armed Conflict

Andrea Gioia

1. Introduction

The European Convention for the Protection of Human Rights and Fundamental Freedoms (ECHR) was adopted in Rome on 4 November 1950 under the auspices of the Council of Europe. The ECHR's purpose was to give effect, through the adoption of a binding treaty instrument, to the Universal Declaration of Human Rights proclaimed by the UN General Assembly on 10 December 1948: the Convention thus predated the most important human rights treaties adopted under the auspices of the UN Organization itself, ie the two 1966 International Covenants dealing, respectively, with civil and political rights and with economic, social, and cultural rights. As a regional treaty, the ECHR aims at maintaining and further realizing human rights among the member states of the Council of Europe: all member states are party to the ECHR, and new members are expected to sign and ratify the Convention at the earliest opportunity. Although it served as a model for the adoption of similar treaty instruments in other regions of the world, it can still be argued that the ECHR is the international agreement providing for the highest level of protection of human rights at both the regional and the world level. In fact, since its entry into force, on 3 September 1953, the ECHR has been amended more than once in order to further enhance the system of human rights protection; moreover, a number of additional Protocols have been adopted in order to add new rights or to strengthen those envisaged in the ECHR itself: these additional Protocols do not necessarily bind all states party to the ECHR, but it is understood that member states of the Council of Europe should aim at becoming party to as many of them as possible.

The most notable feature of the ECHR is the establishment of a European Court of Human Rights in order to ensure the observance of the engagements undertaken by the states party to the Convention and its additional Protocols through binding decisions whereby the Court is empowered, if it finds that there has been a violation of the Convention (or of an additional Protocol), to afford 'just satisfaction' to the injured party, a term interpreted as allowing for the awarding of damages; moreover, the Court's jurisdiction is not limited to inter-state disputes but extends to applications from any person, non-governmental organization, or group of individuals claiming to be the victim of a violation of the ECHR (or of an additional Protocol) by a contracting party.

There can be little doubt that when the ECHR was adopted in 1950, it was commonly assumed that the Convention would mainly apply in times of peace. The possibility of its application in times of armed conflict was hardly considered at the time—although, as will be pointed out later, the text of the Convention makes it clear that the ECHR *does* apply in times of armed conflict also. Consequently, both the relationship between the ECHR and the older rules of 'international humanitarian law' (IHL)—a modern euphemism for the international law of war—and the possibility for the European Court of Human Rights to apply IHL were not given serious thought by legal writers. This was due also to the fact that the international law of war traditionally applied to international armed conflicts only, ie to inter-state wars: non-international armed conflicts, ie civil wars within a state, were traditionally deemed to be regulated by the international law of peace. One year before the adoption of the ECHR, Article 3 common to the four 1949 Geneva Conventions had, for the first time in history, created a set of minimal rules of IHL applicable to non-international armed conflicts, but the implications of that recent development for the traditional distinction between 'war' and 'peace' were probably not fully realized at the time.

The situation has changed since then, but it is only comparatively recently that the relationship between the ECHR and IHL has come to the attention of legal writers. Since 1950, armed conflicts, both international and non-international, involving states party to the ECHR have been mercifully rare. This is due in part to the fact that, until the end of the Cold War, the Council of Europe, the ECHR parent organization, was mostly a club of Western European states enjoying a comparatively high degree of internal stability and determined, after the horrors of two World Wars, to keep friendly relations between themselves. Since 1989, however, the Council of Europe has become a truly pan-European organization and, at the same time, signature and ratification of the ECHR has become a *de facto* requirement for membership. As a result, among the parties to the ECHR there are now more states with situations of internal instability and, at the same time, with unresolved international disputes between themselves. It comes as no surprise, therefore, that in his recent annual opening speeches, the President of European Court of Human Rights pointed out that 'Europe is not a happy island, sheltered from wars and crises', and that there is an 'obvious correlation between internal and international conflicts and the aggravation of risks for human rights'.[1]

---

[1] European Court of Human Rights, *Annual Report 2007* (2008) at 29; *Annual Report 2008* (2009) at 34.

In recent years, the relationship between IHL and international human rights law (IHRL) has become a fashionable topic in the legal literature.[2] However, despite its increased involvement with cases relating to situations of armed conflict, the European Court of Human Rights, much more so than the Inter-American Court of Human Rights,[3] has shown a remarkable reluctance to clarify the relationship between the ECHR and IHL and, indeed, has often preferred to ignore all explicit reference to IHL altogether, as if the existence of an armed conflict had no impact on the law applicable by the Court.[4] In this chapter, the relationship between the ECHR and IHL will be briefly clarified from a general point of view, and then the case-law of the European Court of Human Rights will be examined in order to ascertain whether or not the Court's tendency to ignore IHL has so far led to results incompatible with this latter branch of international law, thus contributing to that fragmentation of international law which is often denounced by international lawyers.[5]

---

[2] See, among others: Migliazza, 'L'Évolution de la Réglementation de la Guerre à la Lumière de la Sauvegarde des Droits de l'Homme', in Académie de Droit International, *Recueil des Cours*, Vol 137 (1972 III) 141; Cerna, 'Human Rights in Armed Conflict: Implementation of International Humanitarian Law Norms by Regional Intergovernmental Human Rights Bodies', in Kalshoven and Sandoz (eds), *Implementation of International Humanitarian Law* (1989) 31; Warner (ed), *Human Rights and Humanitarian Law. The Quest for Universality* (1997); Venturini, 'Diritto Umanitario e Diritti dell'Uomo: Rispettivi Ambiti di Intervento e Punti di Confluenza', 14 *Rivista Internazionale dei Diritti dell'Uomo* (2001) 49; Heintze, 'On the Relationship between Human Rights Law Protection and International Humanitarian Law', 86 *International Review of the Red Cross* (2004) 789; Watkin, 'Controlling the Use of Force: A Role for Human Rights Norms in Contemporary Armed Conflict', 98 *AJIL* (2004) 1; Lubell, 'Challenges in Applying Human Rights Law in Armed Conflict', 87 *International Review of the Red Cross* (2005) 737; Guellali, '*Lex Specialis*, Droit International Humanitaire et Droits de l'Homme: Leur Interaction dans les Nouveaux Conflits Armés', 111 *Revue Générale de Droit International Public* (2007) 539; Orakhelashvili, 'The Interaction between Human Rights and Humanitarian Law: Fragmentation, Conflict, Parallelism or Convergence?', 19 *EJIL* (2008) 161.

[3] For a comparative analysis, see, among others: Martin 'Application du Droit International Humanitaire par la Cour Interaméricaine des Droits de l'Homme', 83 *Revue Internationale de la Croix-Rouge* (2001) 1037; Pisciotta, 'La Tutela dei Diritti Umani in Tempo di Conflitti Armati Non Internazionali: La Giurisprudenza di Due Corti a Confronto', 89 *Rivista di Diritto Internazionale* (2006) 736.

[4] On the relationship between the ECHR and IHL and on the European Court's practice, see, among others: Reidy, 'La Pratique de la Commission et de la Cour Européennes des Droits de l'Homme en Maitière de Droit International Humanitaire', 80 *Revue Internationale de la Croix-Rouge* (1998) 551; Heintze, 'The European Court of Human Rights and the Implementation of Human Rights Standards During Armed Conflicts', 45 *GYIL* (2003) 60; Abresch, 'A Human Rights Law of Internal Armed Conflict: The European Court of Human Rights in Chechnya', 16 *EJIL* (2005) 741; Gaggioli and Kolb, 'A Right to Life in Armed Conflicts? The Contribution of the European Court of Human Rights', 37 *Israel Y.B. Hum. Rts.* (2007) 115; Sassòli, 'La Cour Européenne des Droits de l'Homme et les Conflits Armés', in S. Breitenmoser *et al.* (eds), *Droits de l'Homme, Démocratie et État de Droit. Liber Amicorum Luzius Wildhaber* (2007) 709.

[5] The risks ensuing from the fragmentation of international law have been the object of examination within the UN International Law Commission (ILC) since its fifty-second session in 2000. However, the ILC decided not to deal with the more interesting aspect of fragmentation, ie the possibility of conflicts between the decisions of different institutions applying international law in view of the modern proliferation of international courts, tribunals, arbitrations, etc, some with overlapping jurisdictions.

2. The Relationship between the ECHR and International Humanitarian Law (IHL)

A. The continued application of the ECHR in times of armed conflict

Inasmuch as IHL is a body of rules governing the conduct of states in times of armed conflict, both international and non-international, the first question to be answered when discussing the relationship between the ECHR and IHL is whether or not, and to what extent, the ECHR continues to apply when a state party is involved in such an armed conflict. Although, as was pointed out earlier, the ECHR was principally adopted in order to apply in times of peace, this does not automatically entail that the Convention becomes inapplicable in times of armed conflict. On the contrary, the fact that the ECHR continues to apply when a state party is involved in an armed conflict is now universally acknowledged. A clear textual argument pointing to the Convention's continued application in situations of armed conflict can in fact be derived from Article 15, relating to the possibility for a state to derogate from the Convention in emergency situations: although Article 15 clearly entails that the application of the ECHR in emergency situations may be subject to limitations, it also entails that, as a matter of principle, the Convention continues to apply in such situations and that these may include armed conflicts, both international and non-international.

Under Article 15(1),

in time of war or other public emergency threatening the life of the nation any High Contracting Party may take measures derogating from its obligations under [the] Convention to the extent strictly required by the exigencies of the situation, provided that such measures are not inconsistent with its other obligations under international law. (emphasis added)

It seems clear, therefore, that although 'emergency' situations are not necessarily situations where the state is involved in an armed conflict, they do include such situations: even if the term 'war' is taken to refer, as it did traditionally refer, to an international armed conflict only, the expression 'other public emergency' is wide enough to include both a situation of internal disturbances or tensions falling short of an armed conflict and a fully-fledged civil war. In any case, Article 15(3) implicitly requires a state wishing to avail itself of this right of derogation to make a specific declaration to that effect: that state is in fact required not only to 'keep the Secretary General of the Council of Europe fully informed of the measures which it has taken and the reasons therefor', but also to inform the Secretary General 'when such measures have ceased to operate and the provisions of the Convention are again being fully executed'. These provisions clearly implicate that even 'in time of war or other public emergency', unless a specific declaration is made by a state wishing to derogate from its obligations, the ECHR continues to apply in full. Moreover, even in a situation where a state *has* declared that it wishes to avail itself of the right to derogate from the Convention, Article 15(2) clarifies that there are certain fundamental human rights that cannot be derogated from: these are the right to life (Article 2), the prohibition of torture (Article 3), the prohibition of slavery and servitude (Article 4(1)), and the prohibition of punishment without law (Article 7). Indeed, with specific reference to the right to life, Article 15(2) makes it clear that, although this right is in principle absolute, derogations can be allowed 'in respect of deaths resulting from *lawful acts of war*' (emphasis added).

It may be interesting to recall that, faced with a similar provision (Article 4) in the 1966 International Covenant on Civil and Political Rights (CCPR), the International Court of Justice (ICJ), in its famous 1996 Advisory Opinion on the legality of the threat or use of nuclear weapons, clearly stated that 'the protection of the CCPR does not cease in times of war, except by operation of Article 4 of the Covenant whereby certain provisions may be derogated from in a time of national emergency'.[6] Moreover, in the more recent 2004 Advisory Opinion on the legal consequences of the construction of a wall in the Palestine occupied territories, the ICJ stated, in rather more general terms, that 'the protection offered by human rights conventions does not cease in case of armed conflict, save through the effect of provisions for derogation of the kind to be found in Article 4 of the International CCPR':[7] in so doing, the Court made it clear that even human rights treaties without similar provisions for derogation may be taken to continue to apply in times of armed conflict.[8]

For its part, the European Court of Human Rights has never been so explicit about the continued application of the ECHR in times of armed conflict. This may be due to the fact that, as will be pointed out later, no state party to the Convention has ever expressly and clearly admitted before the Court that it was involved in an armed conflict. However, in situations where a state party was in fact clearly so involved, such as the military occupation of northern Cyprus by Turkey (since 1974) or the conflict in Chechnya within the Russian Federation (since 1999), the Court proceeded on the assumption that the Convention continued to apply; moreover, in both situations, the ECHR continued to apply in full, since neither Turkey nor Russia made a declaration under Article 15. This may in part also explain the reluctance of the Court to explicitly refer to IHL. There seems to be no need to refer to specific cases here, since the Court's decisions relating to both situations, as well as others where the interested state was arguably involved in an armed conflict, will be discussed in detail in Part 3 of this chapter.

B. The extraterritorial application of the ECHR in times of armed conflict

A second preliminary issue that needs to be addressed when discussing the relationship between the ECHR and IHL relates to the Convention's application *ratione loci*: in fact, even if there is no doubt that, as a matter of principle, the

---

[6] *Legality of the Threat or Use of Nuclear Weapons*, ICJ Reports (1996) 226, para 25.

[7] *Legal Consequences of the Construction of a Wall in the Occupied Palestinian Territory*, ICJ Reports (2004) 136, para 106.

[8] See also *Case Concerning Armed Activities on the Territory of the Congo (Democratic Republic of the Congo v Uganda)*, to be published in ICJ Reports (2005), but currently available at <http://www.icj-cij.org/docket/files/116/10455.pdf>, para 216 [last accessed 24 March 2010].

ECHR continues to apply in times of armed conflict also, actions or omissions attributable to a state party to the Convention may occur, especially in the event of an international armed conflict, outside that state's territory. By its very nature, IHL tends to regulate the conduct of belligerent states irrespective of whether or not this conduct takes place within their respective territories: most rules of IHL apply to all situations where protected persons find themselves 'in the power' of the adverse party wherever this may happen and, moreover, to combat operations wherever they occur. The situation as far as human rights treaties are concerned is not so clear-cut, since these treaties are primarily designed to regulate the conduct of states vis-à-vis individuals within their territory or otherwise subject to their 'jurisdiction', a term that tends to refer to governmental power in its various forms. As far as the ECHR is concerned, it appears that, whereas there is no doubt that the Convention applies to a state party's conduct taking place not only in its own territory, but also in territory under its effective control, other cases of extraterritorial conduct which may be relevant in times of armed conflict cannot so easily be brought within its reach: this means in practice that the issue of the relationship between the ECHR and IHL is more likely to arise in respect of situations of internal armed conflict and of belligerent occupation of foreign territory.

1. Articles 1 and 56 ECHR

Under Article 1 ECHR, states parties are obliged to 'secure to everyone *within their jurisdiction*' the rights and freedoms defined in the Convention (emphasis added). The expression 'within their jurisdiction' is certainly not equivalent to the expression 'within their territory' and may include, for example, actions or omissions taking place on board ships or aircraft registered in a state party when on the high seas or in the international airspace, but also actions or omissions taking place in territories which, though not belonging to that state party's territory *stricto sensu*, are still subject to its effective governmental power, be that *de jure* or *de facto*. Apart from Article 1, there is, however, another provision in the ECHR which might have had a considerable impact on the Convention's application *ratione loci*. In fact, Article 56, explicitly dealing with the 'territorial application' of the ECHR, makes the Convention inapplicable to the territories for whose international relations a state party is responsible, unless that state expressly declares, at the time of ratification or at any time thereafter, that it wishes to extend the application of the Convention to all or any of such territories.[9] The drafting history of Article 56 clarifies that its provisions were specifically meant to apply to colonial territories ('dependent territories' in the strict sense); this notwithstanding, a contextual interpretation of Article 1 in the light of Article 56 might certainly have led to the conclusion that, since the Convention does not automatically apply to

---

[9] Indeed, even where a state makes such a declaration, the Convention only becomes applicable in the interested territories 'with due regard . . . to local requirements' (Art 56(3)); moreover, that declaration does not automatically entail 'the competence of the Court to receive applications from individuals, non-governmental organizations or groups of individuals as provided by Article 34 of the Convention', which requires a specific declaration of acceptance by the interested state (Art 56(4)).

non-metropolitan territories which are, however, *de jure* subject to a state party's governmental power, *a fortiori* it could not automatically apply to territories only *de facto* so subject, such as, most notably, territories which are militarily occupied as a result of an armed conflict. The fact that little or no attention was paid to Article 56 when interpreting Article 1, both in the Court's case-law and in the legal literature, is a clear indication of the more general tendency to interpret the ECHR, as well as other human rights treaties, in the manner most favourable to the individual rather than the state.[10]

It seems interesting to recall in this respect that, even more so than Article 1 ECHR, Article 2 CCPR may give rise to a restrictive interpretation as to the Covenant's application *ratione loci*, since it obliges each state party to ensure the rights provided for in the Covenant to 'all individuals within its territory *and* subject to its jurisdiction' (emphasis added); indeed, at least the USA and Israel have consistently argued that both conditions apply simultaneously and that, therefore, the Covenant does not apply extraterritorially. This notwithstanding, the ICJ has repeatedly stated that the CCPR is applicable in respect of acts done by a state in the exercise of its jurisdiction outside its territory and that, more generally, all international human rights instruments not containing specific territorial restriction clauses are so applicable, particularly in occupied territories.[11]

2. The application of the ECHR in occupied territories

There can little doubt that the case-law of the European Court of Human Rights relating to Turkey's military occupation of northern Cyprus since 1974 had some influence on the later pronouncements by the ICJ relating to the territorial scope of the CCPR and of other human rights treaties. Even if it did not expressly refer to the concept of belligerent occupation, in the *Loizidou* case the Court held, already in 1995, that the concept of 'jurisdiction' under Article 1 ECHR is not restricted to a state's national territory and that, on the contrary, a state's responsibility under the ECHR 'may also arise when as a consequence of military action—whether lawful or unlawful—that state exercises *effective control* over an area outside its national territory'; indeed, the Court further held that the obligation to secure, in such an area, the rights and freedoms set out in the Convention 'derives from

---

[10] The general rule of interpretation for treaties is that: '[a] treaty shall be interpreted in good faith in accordance with the ordinary meaning to be given to the terms of the treaty in their context and in the light of its object and purpose' (Art 31(1) 1969 Vienna Convention on the Law of Treaties, hereinafter VCLT). In the case of human rights treaties, pre-eminence is usually given to the object of the treaty, ie the protection of individual rights and freedoms, sometimes at the expense of both the textual and the contextual criteria.

[11] See *Legal Consequences of the Construction of a Wall in the Occupied Palestinian Territory*, see note 7, paras 107–113; *Case Concerning Armed Activities on the Territory of the Congo (Democratic Republic of the Congo v Uganda)*, to be published in ICJ Reports (2005), but currently available at <http://www.icj-cij.org/docket/files/116/10455.pdf>, para 216 [last accessed 24 March 2010]; *Case Concerning Application of the International Convention on the Elimination of All Forms of Racial Discrimination, Request for Provisional Measures*, to be published in ICJ Reports (2008), but currently available at <http://www.icj-cij.org/docket/files/140/14801.pdf>, para 109 [last accessed 24 March 2010].

the fact of such control whether it be exercised *directly, through its armed forces, or through a subordinate local administration*'.[12] As will be pointed out later,[13] this finding could be reinforced by having reference to the concept of belligerent occupation in modern IHL.

In a more recent case relating to Transnistria, a region in Moldova which it found to be under the 'overall control' of the Russian Federation, the Court did not confine itself to confirming that a state's jurisdiction within the meaning of Article 1 ECHR extends to another state's territory which is under its effective control, but went on to clarify that even the state whose territory is under the effective control of another state is not completely free from responsibilities under the ECHR in respect of that territory: on the contrary, the Court stated that

the undertakings given by a Contracting State under Article 1 of the Convention include, in addition to the duty to refrain from interfering with the enjoyment of the rights and freedoms guaranteed, positive obligations to take appropriate steps to ensure respect for those rights and freedoms within its territory.... Those obligations remain even where the exercise of the State's authority is limited in part of its territory, so that it has a duty to take all the appropriate measures which it is still within its power to take.[14]

In other words, even if the primary responsibility for ensuring respect for human rights lies with the state which has effective overall control over the interested territory, the territorial sovereign cannot adopt an 'acquiescent attitude' vis-à-vis violations of the ECHR therein committed, but has to 'take the diplomatic, economic, judicial or other measures that it is in its power to take and are in accordance with international law to secure to the applicants the rights guaranteed by the Convention'.[15] Had the Court applied IHL, it could have reinforced this finding by recalling that, under Article 1 common to the 1949 Geneva Conventions all states are under a duty not only to respect IHL, but also to ensure respect thereof.

On the other hand, even if the relevant case-law does not relate to occupied territory *stricto sensu*, it seems important to recall that the Court appears to be unwilling to hold a state party to the ECHR responsible for violations of the Convention occurring in territories which are under the effective control of multinational operations attributable to an international organization having legal personality, even if the relevant actions or omissions were committed by members of military contingents placed at the disposal of such an international organization by that state party. In fact, in the recent decision relating to the *Behrami* and *Saramati* cases the Grand Chamber of the Court recognized that Kosovo was under the 'effective control' of 'international civil (UNMIK) and security (KFOR) presences' as decided by the UN Security Council under Chapter VII of the UN Charter,[16]

---

[12] *Loizidou v Turkey* (Preliminary Objections), App No 15318/89, ECtHR Chamber (1995), para 62 (emphasis added).   [13] See *infra*, 3.A.
[14] *Ilaşcu and Others v Moldova and Russia*, App No 48787/99, ECtHR Grand Chamber (2004), para 313.   [15] Ibid, paras 328–331.
[16] *Behrami and Behrami v France* and *Saramati v France, Germany and Norway (Decision as to Admissibility)*, Apps Nos 71412/01 and 78166/01, ECtHR Grand Chamber (2007), paras 69–71.

but dismissed the applications because it considered that the impugned acts and omissions of UNMIK and KFOR were directly and exclusively attributable to the United Nations Organization and not to the participating states and that, therefore, the complaints were incompatible *ratione personae* with the provisions of the ECHR.[17] Indeed, in so doing the Court appeared to make no distinction between an entity, such as UNMIK, directly created by the UN Security Council as its own subsidiary organ, and another entity, such as KFOR, created within NATO and merely authorized by the Council to exercise certain functions under its authority.

3. Other situations where the ECHR may apply extraterritorially

In a situation amounting to an international armed conflict but where there is no 'effective control', of foreign territory, the extraterritorial application of human rights treaties, and of the ECHR in particular, is more problematic. On the basis of the Court's case-law, it could be argued that the ECHR would apply to conduct taking place within a state's military camps or detention facilities, but it appears unrealistic to expect the ECHR to apply to naval or aerial bombardment of foreign territory or to combat operations in the field.

In the *Banković* case relating to NATO's air strikes against Yugoslavia (Serbia-Montenegro) in 1999, the Grand Chamber of the Court declared the application inadmissible under Article 1 ECHR on the basis that, 'from the standpoint of public international law, the jurisdictional competence of a state is primarily territorial' and, therefore, Article 1 'must be considered to reflect this ordinary and essentially territorial notion of jurisdiction, other bases of jurisdiction being exceptional and requiring special justification in the particular circumstances of each case'.[18] In *Banković* the Court recognized, on the basis of its previous case-law, that the Convention does apply when 'the respondent state, through the effective control of the relevant territory and its inhabitants abroad as a consequence of military occupation or through the consent, invitation or acquiescence of the Government of that territory, exercises all or some of the public powers normally to be exercised by that Government';[19] it further recognized that 'other recognised instances of the extra-territorial exercise of jurisdiction by a State include cases involving the activities of its diplomatic or consular agents abroad and on board craft and vessels registered in, or flying the flag of, that State',[20] and there seems no reason why a military base or a detention facility operated by the state in foreign territory could not be added to such cases. This was recently confirmed by a Chamber of the Court in *Al-Saadoon and Mufdhi v United Kingdom*, a case relating to the applicants' detention in UK detention facilities in Iraq: in this case, the Court declared the applications partly admissible on the ground that the applicants, who had been arrested and detained in 2003 at the time when the UK was one of the occupying powers in

---

[17] Ibid, para 152.
[18] *Banković and Others v Belgium and Others (Decision as to Admissibility)*, App No 52207/99, ECtHR Grand Chamber (2001), paras 59–61. [19] Ibid, para 71.
[20] Ibid, para 73.

Iraq, had remained under UK jurisdiction until their physical transfer to the Iraqi authorities in 2008, ie well after the formal end of the military occupation.[21] But the fact remains that in *Banković* the Court clearly denied that, when Belgrade was subject to aerial bombardment by the respondent states, the applicants were under their jurisdiction for the purposes of Article 1 ECHR and, in so doing, rejected an interpretation of Article 1 whereby 'anyone adversely affected by an act imputable to a contracting state, wherever in the world that act may have been committed or its consequences felt, is . . . brought within the jurisdiction of that State for the purpose of Article 1 of the Convention'.[22]

On the other hand, in the more recent *Issa* case, relating to a 1995 Turkish military operation in northern Iraq lasting less than one month, a Chamber of the Court gave the impression that the ECHR could indeed apply to combat operations in foreign territory: although the application was declared inadmissible because there was not sufficient evidence that the Turkish armed forces conducted operations in the area where the alleged violations took place, the Chamber appeared to admit that, as a matter of principle, a state could be held responsible for violations of the ECHR not only in situations where, as a result of military action, it temporarily exercises 'effective overall control' over a territory, ie in situations of short-term military occupation, but also where it has 'authority and control' over persons in another state's territory 'through its agents operating—whether lawfully or unlawfully—in the latter State': according to the Court, 'accountability in such situations stems from the fact that Article 1 of the Convention cannot be interpreted so as to allow a State party to perpetrate violations of the Convention on the territory of another State, which it could not perpetrate on its own territory'.[23] The possibility that the *obiter dictum* in *Issa* could alter the findings made by the Court's Grand Chamber in *Banković* was, however, denied by the UK House of Lords in an important 2007 decision in the *Al-Skeini* case, relating to the applicability of the UK's Human Rights Act to British activities in Iraq. The Law Lords tied the extraterritorial meaning of the Human Rights Act to that of the ECHR, as interpreted by the European Court of Human Rights in the *Banković* decision, and came to the conclusion that the Act applied in relation to a UK-run detention facility, but

---

[21] *Al-Saadoon and Mufdhi v United Kingdom (Decision as to Admissibility)*, App No 61498/08, ECtHR Chamber (2009) paras 84–89. It must be admitted that the decision is somewhat ambiguous in that the Court heavily relied on the fact that the UK was an occupying power in Iraq at the time of the original arrest and detention and did not expressly deal with the issue of whether or not the occupation had in fact ended at the time of the applicants' transfer to the Iraqi authorities: the Court confined itself to stressing that 'given the total and exclusive *de facto*, and subsequently also *de jure*, control exercised by the United Kingdom authorities over the premises in question, the individuals detained there, including the applicants, were within the United Kingdom's jurisdiction' (para 88). On the other hand, the interpretation given in the text appears to be reinforced by the reference made by the Court to the UK House of Lords decision in *Al-Skeini* (ibid), which will be referred to later in the text.
[22] *Banković and Others v Belgium and Others (Decision as to Admissibility)*, App No 52207/99, ECtHR Grand Chamber (2001) para 75.
[23] *Issa and Others v Turkey* (Merits), App No 31821/96, ECtHR Chamber (2004) para 71.

not in relation to streets and private houses where UK soldiers were temporarily present.[24]

4. *The 'legal space' of the ECHR*

These recent cases relating to military activities in Iraq raise another issue connected with the territorial application of the ECHR, ie the possibility that the ECHR may apply extraterritorially to a state party's actions or omissions taking place in the territory of a state not party to the ECHR. In the already quoted *Banković* decision the Court had distinguished NATO's bombardment of Belgrade from Turkey's occupation of northern Cyprus by observing that, whereas both Turkey and Cyprus were party to the ECHR, at the time of NATO's air strikes Yugoslavia (Serbia-Montenegro) was not: the Court observed in this respect that

the Convention is a multi-lateral treaty operating, subject to Article 56 of the Convention, in an essentially regional context and notably in the legal space (*espace juridique*) of the contracting states... The Convention was not designed to be applied throughout the world, even in respect of the conduct of contracting states. Accordingly, the desirability of avoiding a gap or vacuum in human rights' protection has so far been relied on by the Court in favour of establishing jurisdiction only when the territory in question was one that, but for the specific circumstances, would normally be covered by the Convention.[25]

It could be argued that the later decisions relating to military operations in Iraq have in fact contradicted such a narrow characterization of the 'legal space' of the ECHR. Even leaving aside decisions by municipal courts, such as the UK House of Lords, in the already mentioned *Issa* decision the Chamber tried to avoid an open contradiction with *Banković*, but chose to interpret the concept of the 'legal space' of the ECHR in a manifestly different way by observing that persons who find themselves within the jurisdiction of a state party, such as Turkey, even if they are in the territory of a non-party state, such as Iraq, are within the 'legal space' of the Convention.[26] In the case of *Saddam Hussein v Albania et al*, where the applicant claimed that he was under the jurisdiction of a number of states party to the ECHR 'because they were the occupying powers in Iraq, because he was under their direct authority and control or because they were responsible for the acts of their agents abroad', the Court made no reference to *Banković* or to the fact that Iraq was not a party to the ECHR and dismissed the application principally on the ground that, although the respondent states 'allegedly formed part (at varying unspecified levels) of a coalition with the US,... the impugned actions were carried out by the

---

[24] *R (On the Application of Al-Skeini) v Secretary of State for Defence (Redress Trust Intervening)* [2007] UKHL 26.

[25] *Banković and Others v Belgium and Others (Decision as to Admissibility)*, App No 52207/99, ECtHR Grand Chamber (2001) para 80. It is ironic that, in this context, the Court recalled Art 56, thus appearing to confine its relevance to the possibility of extending the Convention's territorial scope to a non-European territory.

[26] *Issa and Others v Turkey* (Merits), see note 23, paras 56 and 74.

US,...security in the zone in which those actions took place was assigned to the US and...the overall command of the coalition was vested in the US'.[27]

Both these Iraq cases were not decided by the Court's Grand Chamber, but similar considerations apply to the recent Grand Chamber decision in the *Behrami* and *Saramati* cases, which was also referred to earlier:[28] in this decision, which related to peacekeeping operations in Kosovo, the Court's Grand Chamber ignored the fact that Serbia, to which Kosovo legally belonged, was still not a party to the ECHR at the time of the applicants' complaints and preferred to dismiss the applications on the ground that the impugned actions or omissions were attributable to the UN and not to the participating states. On the other hand, given that in all of the cases so far discussed the applications were dismissed, albeit on different grounds, it would still have been hasty to conclude that the Court's interpretation of the 'legal space' of the ECHR, as clarified in *Banković*, had been, or was about to be, abandoned. The situation has, however, changed as a result of the even more recent decision in *Al-Saadoon and Mufdhi v United Kingdom*, where a Court's Chamber, as was pointed out earlier, declared the applications partly admissible on the basis that the applicants were under the jurisdiction of the UK when detained in UK detention facilities in Iraq not only at the time when the UK was one of the occupying powers in Iraq, but also later and until the applicants were transferred to the Iraqi authorities, in 2008, at the request of the latter.[29] Although this decision was not very explicit about the 'legal space' of the Convention, the impression is that the Court has come to interpret *Banković* in the narrow sense that persons who find themselves within the jurisdiction of a state party are within the 'legal space' of the Convention, even if they are in the territory of a non-party state.

C. IHL as *lex specialis* vis-à-vis international human rights law (IHRL)

In an armed conflict situation governed by IHL where IHRL continues to apply, the question arises of the relationship between these two branches of international law. In the two important Advisory Opinions which were referred to earlier, the ICJ clearly stated that IHL is *lex specialis* vis-à-vis IHRL. In the 1996 Opinion on the legality of the threat or use of nuclear weapons, the Court made specific reference to the right to life as guaranteed in Article 6 CCPR, a right which cannot be derogated from even if a state avails itself of the derogation clause in Article 4 CCPR: according to the Court, the right not arbitrarily to be deprived of one's life applies also in hostilities, but 'the test of what is an arbitrary deprivation of life...then falls to be determined by the applicable *lex specialis,* namely, the law applicable in armed conflict which is designed to regulate the conduct of hostilities'.[30] In the

---

[27] *Saddam Hussein v Albania and Others (Decision as to Admissinility)*, App No 23276/04, ECtHR Chamber (2006).

[28] *Behrami and Behrami v France* and *Saramati v France, Germany, and Norway (Decision as to Admissibility)*, App Nos 71412/01 and 78166/01, ECtHR Grand Chamber (2007).

[29] *Al-Saadoon and Mufdhi v United Kingdom (Decision as to Admissibility)*, App No 61498/08, ECtHR Chamber (2009) paras 84–89.

[30] *Legality of the Threat or Use of Nuclear Weapons*, ICJ Reports (1996) 226, para 25.

more recent 2004 Opinion on the legal consequences of the construction of a wall in the Palestine occupied territories, the Court clarified, from a more general perspective, that:

As regards the relationship between international humanitarian law and human rights law, there are thus three possible situations: some rights may be exclusively matters of international humanitarian law; others may be exclusively matters of human rights law; yet others may be matters of both these branches of international law. In order to answer the question put to it, the Court will have to take into consideration both these branches of international law, namely human rights law and, as *lex specialis*, international humanitarian law.[31]

What exactly the speciality of IHL entails for IHRL is, however, a matter of considerable debate both in the practice of states and in the legal literature. A radical interpretation which appears to be favoured by the government of the United States[32] would make the speciality of IHL operate at a very general level, so that IHL would replace IRHL altogether in times of armed conflict. This interpretation, which is equally favoured by the government of Israel, appears to have been endorsed, as a matter of principle, by the Israeli Supreme Court in two important recent decisions, although the Court did at least allow resort to IHRL in order to fill existing gaps in IHL.[33] In fact, in the so-called 'targeted killings decision' of 2006, the Israeli Supreme Court sitting as the High Court of Justice, having determined that the armed conflict between Israel, on the one hand, and the various terrorist organizations active in 'Judea, Samaria and the Gaza Strip', on the other, constituted 'an international armed conflict', even irrespective of whether or not it took place in occupied territory, found that the normative system applicable to that armed conflict was IHL, this being 'the *lex specialis* which applies in case of an armed conflict'; the Court then referred to IHRL also, but only in order to point out that its role in situations of armed conflict is to 'supplement' IHL 'when there is a gap (lacuna) in that law' and, in this context, it made reference, *inter alia*, to the ICJ Advisory Opinion of 1996.[34] The Court gave no examples of how IHRL could fill the lacunae of IHL in the part of the decision dealing with the applicable law, but then, as will be seen in 3.B.3, it did proceed to 'supplement' the alleged IHL rules on the targeting of civilians taking a direct part in hostilities with IHRL obligations relating to the need for adequate information before each attack and for a subsequent investigation on the circumstances of that attack. In the 'internment' decision of 2008, the Court sitting as the Court of Criminal Appeals recalled the 2006 decision in order to confirm that the armed conflict between Israel and terrorist

---

[31] *Legal Consequences of the Construction of a Wall in the Occupied Palestinian Territory*, see note 7, para 106. See also *Case Concerning Armed Activities on the Territory of the Congo (Democratic Republic of the Congo v Uganda)*, see note 11, para 216.

[32] See 'Reply of the Government of the United States of America to the Five UNCH Special Rapporteurs on Detainees in Guantanamo Bay, Cuba', 45 ILM (2006) 742, paras IV, V, and VI.

[33] For a different interpretation of the stand adopted by the Israeli Supreme Court in this respect, see the discussion in: Ben-Naftali and Shany, 'Living in Denial', 37 *Is. L.R.* (2003–04) 17. This article, however, predates the decisions referred to in the text.

[34] *The Public Committee against torture in Israel et al v The Government of Israel et al*, Supreme Court of Israel sitting as the High Court of Justice (2006), available at <http://elyon1.court.gov.il/Files_ENG/02/690/007/a34/02007690.a34.htm>, paras 16–18 and 21.

organizations was an international armed conflict governed by IHL, whose customary provisions form part of the municipal law of Israel, and that, in addition, IHRL can be applied 'where there is a lacuna in the laws of armed conflict'.[35]

But the view that IHRL is completely superseded by IHL in times of armed conflict is hard to reconcile with the ICJ's Advisory Opinions. In the light of the World Court's opinions, it would seem indeed that, at the very least, each of the two branches of international law can be used to fill the lacunae which may be present in the other. It is only when both branches of the law apply to certain individual rights that IHL as a whole may properly be characterized as *lex specialis* vis-à-vis IHRL. But even in such cases, the speciality of IHL cannot simply entail that IHL replaces IHRL altogether, since this would be tantamount to a denial of the continued application of IHRL in times of armed conflict which was, on the contrary, reaffirmed by the ICJ. Therefore, it appears to be more correct to interpret the speciality of IHL as a means of addressing the relationship between *individual norms* belonging to the two different branches of the law *on a case-by-case basis*. In cases where there is an actual conflict of international obligations, in the sense that a norm cannot be complied with without violating another, then the special norm of IHL should prevail.[36] But fortunately a clear-cut conflict is unlikely to arise between a norm of IHL and a norm of IHRL. In most cases, the norms belonging to the two branches can indeed be applied simultaneously, so that the maxim *lex specialis derogat legi generali* may be replaced by the maxim *lex specialis completat legi generali*. In other words, in most cases the speciality of IHL simply entails that IHRL norms have to be interpreted in the light of IHL norms, precisely as the ICJ itself did when it stated that, in times of armed conflict, what is an 'arbitrary' deprivation of life under Article 6 CCPR falls to be determined by IHL, the relevant *lex specialis*. But, as will be pointed out in 3.C, the same could be said of the 'arbitrary' deprivation of liberty inasmuch as this is prohibited under Article 9 CCPR

In any case, even if, from the wider perspective of the international legal order as a whole, IHL is to be characterized as *lex specialis* vis-à-vis IHRL, it remains to be seen whether or not this general characterization is acceptable from the narrower perspective of a judicial institution, such as the European Court of Human Rights, specifically created in order to ensure compliance with certain IHRL rules, such as the ECHR and the Protocols thereto. There is no doubt that an international arbitral or judicial institution, such as the ICJ, which is called to settle an inter-state dispute on the basis of 'international law', may embark upon an examination of

---

[35] *A & B v The State of Israel*, Supreme Court of Israel sitting as the Court of Criminal Appeals (2008), available at <http://elyon1.court.gov.il/files_eng/06/590/066/n04/06066590.n044.pdf>, para 9.

[36] Some commentators have argued that, even in that situation, it would not be possible to affirm *a priori* that the IHR rule automatically prevails over the IHRL rule. According to this view, in determining which rule is the special rule several elements would have to be taken into account, such as the precision or clarity of the rule, its adaptation to the particular circumstances of the case, and the degree of protection it offers: see especially Gaggioli and Kolb, *supra* note 4, at 118–124, where the whole discussion is based on the assumption that the construction of the ICJ's opinions, whereby IHL as a whole is the more special law with respect with IHRL 'is difficult to accept' (at 119). But his view is difficult to reconcile with the Court's opinions, which indeed appeared to characterize IHL *as a whole* as the applicable *lex specialis* in situations of armed conflict.

the relationship between IHRL and IHL without having first to ascertain whether both branches of the law come within the applicable law; the same could be said of a state's municipal court, such as the Israeli Supreme Court, when it is called to decide a case on the basis of 'international law' as it applies in that state's domestic legal system. But when it comes to a court whose function is to ensure the observance of the engagements undertaken by the states party to a specific IHRL treaty, the preliminary question may be asked as to whether IHL comes within the law applicable by that court. Moreover, even if IHL *does* come within the applicable law, in a situation where certain rights are governed by both branches of the law, it remains to be seen whether, and to what extent, such an institution is prepared to interpret the relevant rule of IHRL in the light of the relevant rule of IHL, let alone allow the relevant rule of IHL to prevail in case of a conflict with an incompatible rule of IHRL. This is especially relevant where the European Court of Human Rights is concerned, since, as will be pointed out in Part 3 of this chapter, Articles 2 and 5 ECHR, unlike the corresponding Articles 6 and 9 CCPR, do not simply prohibit the 'arbitrary' deprivation of life and liberty, thus leaving the door open for the application of IHL as *lex specialis* in order to determine what is an arbitrary deprivation of life or liberty in the event of an armed conflict, but rather provide that any deprivation of life or liberty, in order to be regarded as lawful, must always fall within one of the exceptions to the prohibitions provided for in the ECHR itself.

D. The competence of the European Court of Human Rights to apply IHL

It comes as no surprise, therefore, that the issue of the competence of human rights bodies to apply IHL has been a matter of some discussion in the international legal literature, in the practice of states, and even in the practice of some such bodies. It is interesting to recall, in particular, the practice of the Inter-American human rights bodies, which in the past were confronted with situations of armed conflict more often than their European counterparts. The Inter-American system, which is largely modelled on the original structure of the ECHR, is still based on the existence of two human rights bodies, ie the Inter-American Commission on Human Rights and the Inter-American Court of Human Rights. The Inter-American Commission was first faced with situations of armed conflict and appeared to be prepared to apply IHL as *lex specialis*, both in order to interpret the relevant IHRL rule and as a *direct* source of specific normative standards applicable in times of armed conflict.[37] However, in two important 2000 decisions, the Inter-American Court proved to be far less enthusiastic about a direct application of IHL rules: although it admitted the possibility of resorting to IHL as a means

---

[37] See especially *Juan Carlos Abella v Argentina* (1997), relating to the attack of a military barracks by an armed group; *Coard and Al v United States*, Report No 109/99 (1999), relating to the US invasion of Grenada in 1983. But see also, more recently *Decision on Request for Precautionary Measures* (2002), relating to the status of the detainees in the US military base at Guantanamo Bay, 41 ILM (2002) 532.

of interpreting the relevant rule of IHRL, it very clearly stated that the American Convention gives it competence 'to determine whether the acts or the norms of the states are compatible with the Convention itself, and not with the 1949 Geneva Conventions'.[38] For its part, the European Court of Human Rights has never so far embarked upon a discussion of its competence to apply IHL. Indeed, the Court has only very rarely expressly referred to IHL, even as a means of reinforcing findings already made on the basis of the relevant rule of the ECHR. However, on the basis of the ECHR there appear to be no *legal* impediments for the Court to apply IHL, both as a means of interpretation of the relevant ECHR rule and, in some situations, even as a direct source of normative standards applicable in times of armed conflict.

Although, under Article 19 ECHR, the Court's specific function is 'to ensure the observance of the engagements undertaken by the High Contracting Parties in the Convention and in the Protocols thereto', it is sometimes the ECHR itself which allows and, indeed, directs the Court to apply external legal sources, including IHL, in order to perform this task. Mention may be made, in particular, of Article 15 ECHR: as was mentioned above, paragraph 1 of this Article allows a state party to take measures derogating from its obligations under the Convention 'in time of war or other public emergency', provided that such measures are not inconsistent with its other obligations under 'international law'. The Convention does not itself define 'war' or 'public emergency' and the Court's case-law demonstrates that, when a state makes a declaration under Article 15 ECHR, that state's unilateral qualification of a situation as 'war or other public emergency' is not binding on the Court, which may proceed to ascertain whether or not the same state is in fact entitled to avail itself of the right to derogate from the provisions of the ECHR. Moreover, there can be no doubt that 'international law' includes IHL in all situations where this is applicable, ie wherever a 'public emergency' actually amounts to an armed conflict, be it international ('war' in the traditional sense) or non-international. Consequently, irrespective of whether a state invokes Article 15 on the basis that it is involved in a 'war' or another 'public emergency', the Court may directly apply IHL in order to ascertain whether or not that situation actually amounts to an armed conflict and, if that is the case, whether or not the measures taken by that state are consistent with its other 'international law' obligations. Moreover, Article 15(2) lists a number of provisions that cannot be derogated from, including Article 2 relating to the right to life 'except in respect of deaths resulting from lawful acts of war': here again, the Convention does not itself define what is a 'lawful act of war', thus allowing for a direct reference to the relevant rules of IHL.

But even leaving aside the cases where the Court could, and indeed should, directly apply IHL, on the basis of a *renvoi* made by the ECHR itself, there is no reason why the Court should not otherwise apply IHL, if not as *lex specialis* automatically prevailing in the (unlikely) case where there is an actual conflict between an individual rule of IHL and an individual rule of the ECHR, at least in order to

---

[38] *Las Palmeras Case* (Preliminary Objections) (2000), para 33. The other decision referred to in the text is the *Bámaca-Velásquez Case* (2000).

interpret the relevant rule of the ECHR and apply it in the light of the relevant rule of IHL. In other words, even if Article 15 is not invoked by a state and, as a result, the ECHR applies in full, there is no legal impediment for the Court to ascertain whether or not that state is involved in an armed conflict and, in that case, to apply IHL as a means of interpreting the relevant ECHR rule. Although, as was pointed out in the preceding sub-paragraph and will be better explained in Part 3 of this chapter, the ECHR is arguably less open to the application of IHL than other human rights treaties—which, for example, prohibit the 'arbitrary' deprivation of life or liberty, and thus open the way for the application of IHL in order to determine what is such an 'arbitrary' deprivation in times of war—the fact remains that the Court itself has repeatedly recognized that, as an international treaty, the ECHR cannot be interpreted and applied in a vacuum and that, on the contrary, it should be interpreted as far as possible in harmony with other principles of international law. To take but one example, the Court most notably admitted that the international customary law of state immunity prevails over the right of access to court which is implicitly guaranteed by Article 6 ECHR,[39] but other decisions may be considered relevant as well.[40] In allowing for the application of general international law, the Court often referred to the general rules on the interpretation of treaties, as now codified in the 1969 Vienna Convention on the Law of Treaties (VCLT): although the general rule of interpretation requires a treaty to be interpreted in accordance with the 'ordinary meaning' to be given to its terms 'in their context and in the light of its object and purpose' (Article 31(1) VCLT), account must also be taken of 'any relevant rules of international law applicable in the relations between the parties' (Article 31(3)(c) VCLT).

If, therefore, there appears to be no legal impediment to the application of IHL as a means of interpreting the relevant rules of the ECHR in situations amounting to armed conflict, the question may arise of whether or not there are paramount reasons of *legal policy* for disregarding IHL in the context of the application of the ECHR. Most commentators (and I myself) agree that ignoring the IHL rules governing international armed conflicts would be a mistake and would lead to legal confusion: those rules are in fact well-developed and very detailed, and could not be ignored without openly disregarding the express intention of states. On the other hand, some commentators believe that the opposite is true in respect of the IHL rules governing internal armed conflicts: given the undoubtedly less-developed and often fragmented character of those rules, the main rationale that makes resort to IHL as *lex specialis* appealing—ie that its rules have greater specificity—would be missing in respect of internal armed conflicts.[41]

As will be pointed out in Part 3, the less-developed state of IHL governing non-international armed conflicts is probably one of the reasons for the European Court's marked reluctance to refer to that body of law. As a matter of principle,

---

[39] See *Golder v United Kingdom*, App No 4451/70, ECtHR Plenary (1975) paras 28–36; *Al-Adsani v United Kingdom*, App No 35763/97, ECtHR Grand Chamber (2001) paras 52–67;
[40] See, eg *Loizidou v Turkey* (Merits), App No 15318/89, ECtHR Chamber (1996) para 43; *Banković and Others v Belgium and Others (Decision as to Admissibility)*, App No 52207/99, ECtHR Grand Chamber (2001) paras 55–57.   [41] See esp Abresch, *supra* note 4, at 743–751.

however, the fundamental question arises of whether or not IHRL—and, in this context, the ECHR—provide satisfactory rules governing non-international armed conflicts. Even the most enthusiastic supporters of IHRL sometimes agree that it would be unrealistic and, indeed, dangerous to assume that IHRL is to be applied in exactly the same way irrespective of whether or not the interested state is involved in an armed conflict, eg by categorically forbidding killing in a combat situation or 'otherwise making compliance with the law and victory in battle impossible to achieve at once'.[42] That being the case, the question remains of whether or not 'realistic rules' governing internal armed conflicts must be exclusively derived from the legal standards of IHRL. In my opinion, resort to IHL would undoubtedly help in this respect and would, indeed, contribute to giving greater coherence to international law, thus avoiding its further fragmentation. Whereas it is true that the treaty rules of IHL governing internal armed conflict are less developed than those governing international armed conflict, there is now a sufficient consensus that the present state of customary IHL allows for the application to internal armed conflict of most of the rules applicable to international armed conflict.[43] Indeed, the European Court of Human Rights could make an important contribution in this respect.

3. The Practice of the European Court of Human Rights in Situations Amounting to Armed Conflicts

In light of its readiness to refer to other branches of international law in order to arrive at the correct interpretation of the relevant ECHR provisions, the Court's marked reluctance to refer to IHL has understandably surprised several commentators. Although it is not true that the Court never expressly referred to IHL, it is certainly true that the Court very rarely did so, and then only in order to reinforce a finding already made on the basis of the ECHR. Moreover, the Court only appears to have referred to IHL in respect of the Turkish occupation of northern Cyprus, ie a situation governed by the IHL rules applicable to international armed conflicts. This is in part due to the uncertainty about the existence of a non-international armed conflict in the other cases decided by the Court; however, in the recent cases relating to Chechnya, the Court was faced with a situation which clearly amounted to an armed conflict and yet it chose to make no explicit reference to the relevant rules of IHL. According to some commentators, these cases have made it clear that the Court's attitude is the outcome of a precise policy *not* to apply IHL and, indeed, to apply the ECHR in a manner which is 'at odds with IHL'.[44] In my opinion, a specific judicial policy not to apply IHL is unlikely to exist, and the Court's attitude can probably be explained otherwise: *inter alia*, by the comparatively more uncertain state of the IHL rules applicable to non-international armed

---

[42] Abresch, *supra* note 4, at 746.
[43] See esp Henckaerts and Doswald-Beck (eds), *Customary International Humanitarian Law, Vol. 1: Rules* (2005) at xxix.   [44] Abresch, *supra* note 4, at 742.

conflicts, and by the interested states' own reluctance to resort to Article 15 ECHR on the basis that they are involved in a civil war. I have already explained why I consider this attitude on the part of the Court as unfortunate, whereas others have hailed it as pointing to the fact that IHRL is more adequate than IHL in respect of the regulation of internal armed conflicts. Be that as it may, it seems to me that the Court's findings in the cases relating to situations that have been characterized as armed conflicts in the legal literature were not in fact incompatible with the relevant rules of IHL.

A. The existence of an armed conflict

As was pointed out above, there are certainly no legal impediments in the ECHR itself preventing the Court from ascertaining the existence of an armed conflict governed by IHL: on the contrary, at least when a state resorts to Article 15 ECHR in order to justify measures derogating from the provisions of the Convention, the Court is entitled to ascertain not only whether or not the emergency situation in which that state is allegedly involved actually exists, but also whether or not that situation amounts to an armed conflict. The fact that the Court never reached the second stage of this analysis may be due, in part, to the fact that no state ever invoked Article 15 on the basis that it was involved in a 'war'; neither did a state explicitly admit that the 'public emergency' it was allegedly involved in, even where this was due to riots or organized acts of 'terrorism', actually amounted to an armed conflict.[45] On the other hand, the Court is certainly not bound by the characterizations made by states on the basis of Article 15. It may well be argued that in fact no situation where Article 15 has been invoked so far actually amounted to an armed conflict, although some commentators have argued otherwise, at least in respect of Turkey's invocation of Article 15 because of 'terrorist actions amounting to threats to national security in South East Anatolia' (1990–2002).[46] Indeed, the cases where most commentators agreed that IHL might have been applied because of the existence of an armed conflict—ie those relating to Turkey's invasion and subsequent occupation of northern Cyprus and those relating to the situation in

---

[45] According to the list provided for at <http://conventions.coe.int/Treaty/Commun/ ListeDeclarations.asp?NT=005&CM=8&DF=4/10/2009&CL=ENG&VL=1> [last accessed 24 March 2010], the following states made declarations under Art 15 ECHR in respect of specific emergency situations: Albania, in respect of 'armed rebellion and terrorist attacks' (10.03.1997–24.07.1997); Armenia, in respect of 'threats to constitutional order' (04.03.2008–21.03.2008); France, in respect of 'disturbances and riots in New Caledonia' (08.02.1985–30.06.1985); Georgia, in respect of 'bird flu emergency' (03.03.2006–16.03.2006), and of an 'attempted *coup*' (09.11.2007–16.11.2007); Ireland, in respect of 'offences against public peace' (22.07.1957–09.03.1962), and of 'serious acts of terrorism' (21.10.1976–16.10.1977); Turkey, in respect of 'terrorist actions amounting to threats to national security in South East Anatolia' (06.08.1990–29.01.2002); United Kingdom, in respect of 'organized terrorism connected with the affairs of Northern Ireland' (23.03.1989–26.02.2001), in order to justify 'measures regarding Channel Dependencies' (12.11.1998–05.05.2006), and in respect of a general 'threat from international terrorism' (18.12.2001–16.03.2005) after the events of 11 September 2001.

[46] See eg Abresch, *supra* note 4, at 755. Turkey itself, however, denied that the situation amounted to an armed conflict governed by IHL.

Chechnya, within the Russian Federation—related to situations where the interested states, albeit for different reasons, had not availed themselves of the right of derogation provided for in Article 15. On the other hand, it was also pointed out above that even where Article 15 is not invoked there is no legal impediment for the Court to ascertain whether the interested state is involved in an armed conflict, in order to take IHL into account when applying the relevant rule of the ECHR. It has often been suggested that one explanation for the Court's reluctance to refer to IHL might be the political and, to some extent, legal difficulties surrounding the basic condition for its application, ie the existence of an armed conflict. From a purely political point of view, the reluctance of states to admit that their military forces abroad are involved in an international armed conflict, let alone one involving the belligerent occupation of foreign territory, or (indeed, even more so) that an internal situation amounts to a civil war is notorious, and it is understandable that the Court might wish to avoid tackling such diplomatically sensitive issues whenever this is not deemed absolutely necessary in order to reach a decision. From the legal point of view, the threshold triggering the application of IHL, most notably in the case of non-international armed conflicts, is not always easy to ascertain.

In the light of these considerations, it is perhaps not surprising that the only decision where the Court has so far explicitly referred to IHL is comparatively recent (January 2008) and relates to persons missing as a result of Turkey's invasion and subsequent occupation of northern Cyprus, a region explicitly characterized by the Court as 'a zone of international conflict where two armies are engaged in acts of war'.[47] In fact, according to the majority of legal opinion, no special threshold is required in order to trigger the application of IHL in a situation of international armed conflict: reference can be made, in particular, to Article 2 common to the four 1949 Geneva Conventions, whereby the Conventions apply 'to all cases of declared war or of any other armed conflict', even if the 'state of war' is not recognized by one party to the conflict.[48] The current debate on the legal concept of international armed conflict does not so much revolve around the existence of a threshold triggering its application, since the most hotly debated issue is now whether or not the IHL relating to international armed conflicts applies to an armed conflict between a state and a non-state entity, such as a terrorist organization. But, unlike the United States of America and Israel, no European state has so far invoked the application of IHL in order to derogate from the ECHR on the basis that the fight against international terrorism is to be legally qualified as 'war', and the Court has, therefore, been mercifully spared from the need to tackle this extremely controversial issue.

As for the IHL of belligerent occupation, the mere *fact* of effective control by a state over another state's territory, or part thereof, is sufficient in order to trigger its application. As was pointed out above, in the earlier *Loizidou* case the Court had not expressly referred to the IHL of belligerent occupation when it found that

---

[47] See *Varnava and Others v Turkey*, App Nos 16064/90, 16065/90, 16066/90, 16068/90, 16069/90, 16070/90, 16071/90, 16072/90 and 16073/90, ECtHR Chamber (2008) para 130. This decision, which was referred to the Grand Chamber, related to missing persons in northern Cyprus, and will be referred to below in greater detail.   [48] See Art 2(1).

Turkey could be held responsible under the ECHR and the Protocols thereto for violations committed in northern Cyprus not only by its own military forces, but also by the self-proclaimed Turkish Cypriot state:[49] the Court confined itself to observing that a state's responsibility may arise 'when as a consequence of military action—whether lawful or unlawful—that state exercises effective control over an area outside its national territory', and further added that the obligation to secure, in such an area, the rights and freedoms set out in the Convention 'derives from the fact of such control whether it be exercised directly, through its armed forces, or through a subordinate local administration'.[50] But there can be little doubt that the Court's findings could have been reinforced by having reference to the concept of belligerent occupation in IHL: reference can be made, in addition to Article 2 common to the four Geneva Conventions,[51] to Articles 42 and 43 of the Regulations annexed to 1907 Hague Convention IV (*Hague IV*)[52] and, especially, to Article 47 of 1949 Geneva Convention IV (*GC IV*).[53] Moreover, from a political point of view, it cannot be overlooked that the Court's characterization was undoubtedly made easier by UN Security Council Resolutions which had declared the attempt to create a secessionist state in northern Cyprus as 'invalid' and had expressly referred to 'the occupied part of the Republic of Cyprus'.[54] The same could be said of the more recent decision in the *Al-Saadoon* case, where the Court explicitly stated that 'during the first months of the applicants' detention, the United Kingdom was an occupying power in Iraq'.[55]

On the other hand, in this latter case, the Court understandably avoided addressing the issue of the exact moment when the regime of occupation ends, despite the fact that, in this respect also, it could have relied on relevant UN Security Council Resolutions.[56] Whereas the United Kingdom had clearly pointed out that, at the time when the applicants were handed over to the Iraqi authorities, in 2008, the occupation had ended, Iraq was a sovereign state exercising sovereign powers within its own territory over its own nationals, and the applicants had been handed over at

---

[49] *Loizidou v Turkey* (Merits), App No 15318/89, ECtHR Chamber (1996) para 56.

[50] *Loizidou v Turkey* (Preliminary Objections), App No 15318/89, ECtHR Chamber (1995) para 62.

[51] See Art 2(2), whereby the Conventions also apply 'to all cases of partial or total occupation of the territory of a High Contracting Party even if the said occupation meets with no armed resistance'.

[52] Under Art 42, 'territory is considered occupied when it is actually placed under the authority of the hostile army. The occupation extends only to the territory where such authority has been established and can be established.' Under Art 43, 'the authority of the legitimate power having in fact passed into the hands of the occupant, the latter shall take all the measures in its power to restore and ensure, as far as possible, public order and safety, while respecting, unless absolutely prevented, the laws in force in the country'.

[53] 'Protected persons who are in occupied territory shall not be deprived, in any case or in any manner whatsoever, of the benefits of the present Convention by any change introduced, as the result of occupation of a territory, into the institutions of government of the said territory, nor by any agreement concluded between the authorities of the occupied territories and the occupying Power, nor by any annexation by the latter of the whole or part of the occupied territory.'

[54] See, in particular, SC Res 541(1983) and SC Res 550 (1984). The Court made express reference to those Resolutions.

[55] See *Al-Saadoon and Mufdhi v United Kingdom (Decision as to Admissibility)*, App No 61498/08, ECtHR Chamber (2009) para 87.   [56] See, in particular, SC Res 1546 (2004).

the request of the competent Iraqi authority,[57] the Court confined itself to observing that the UK had maintained 'total and exclusive *de facto*, and subsequently also *de jure*, control' over the premises where the applicants were detained until their transfer to the Iraqi authorities and that, therefore, the applicants had been at all times until such transfer under the jurisdiction of the UK.[58] The issue of the precise moment when belligerent occupation ends is in fact one of the more controversial issues of IHL. Under Article 6 of 1949 *GC IV*, most of the Convention's provisions relating to occupied territory cease to apply 'one year after the general close of hostilities', but some important provisions continue to apply 'for the duration of the occupation' and, under Article 3 of 1977 Geneva Protocol I, all of the Protocol's provisions remain applicable until 'the termination of occupation'. But precisely when such termination takes place is often disputed, especially in the light of Article 47 of 1949 *GC IV*, whereby the Convention continues to apply in occupied territory notwithstanding 'any change introduced, as a result of the occupation of a territory, into the institutions of government of the said territory', or 'any agreement concluded between the authorities of the occupied territory and the Occupying Power'.

Similarly, in situations of internal armed conflict, in addition to the political complications due to the interested state's reluctance to admit that an armed conflict governed by IHL actually exists, the Court's task in ascertaining the existence of such an armed conflict would indeed be complicated by the different thresholds triggering the application of different international legal instruments. It is a well-known fact that, whereas Article 3 common to the four 1949 Geneva Conventions generically refers to an 'armed conflict not of an international character', 1977 Geneva Protocol II (*AP II*) exclusively applies to an armed conflict where 'dissident armed forces or other organized armed groups... under responsible command... exercise such control over a part of [a state's] territory as to enable them to carry out sustained and concerted military operations and to implement [the] Protocol'.[59] Moreover, although the 1977 Protocol explicitly states that it 'develops and supplements' Common Article 3 '*without modifying its existing conditions of application*',[60] it then further specifies that it shall not apply to 'situations of internal disturbances and tensions, such as riots, isolated and sporadic acts of violence and other acts of a similar nature, *as not being armed conflicts*'.[61] Consequently, the majority of legal opinion now agrees that, although the very high threshold required for the application of 1977 Geneva Protocol II is not required by either Common Article 3 or customary international law, there is a lower threshold below which disturbances and tensions within a state do not constitute an armed conflict governed by IHL.

It may be significant, in this last respect, that, although the Court never explicitly ascertained the existence of an internal armed conflict governed by IHL, it did appear to distinguish between situations of internal disturbances and tensions and situations of fully-fledged armed conflict and, in this latter case, to recognize that

---

[57] Ibid, paras 75–81.   [58] Ibid, paras 88–89.   [59] See Art 1(1).
[60] Ibid (emphasis added).   [61] See Art 1(2) (emphasis added).

exceptional measures may be justified even under the ECHR. Mention may be made, in particular, of the cases relating to alleged law-enforcement operations in Chechnya: on the one hand, the Court recalled that, as no martial law and no state of emergency had been declared in Chechnya, and no derogation had been made by Russia under Article 15 ECHR, such operations had to be judged against a '*normal legal background*'; on the other, it recognized that 'the situation that existed in Chechnya at the relevant time called for *exceptional measures* on behalf of the state in order to regain control over the Republic and to suppress the *illegal armed insurgency*'.[62] No such explicit language had ever been used in previous cases and, most notably, in those relating to south-east Anatolia in respect of which Article 15 had been invoked.

B. The right to life in armed conflict

As was pointed out above, the special nature of IHL vis-à-vis IHRL was first affirmed by the ICJ in respect of the right to life, as provided for in Article 6 CCPR: Article 6(1) CCPR states that 'every human being has the inherent right to life', that 'this right shall be protected by law' and that 'no one shall be *arbitrarily* deprived of his life' (emphasis added). Although, under Article 4 CCPR, no derogation from Article 6 is permitted in time of 'public emergency', the Court stated that the test of what is an arbitrary deprivation of life in time of armed conflict falls to be determined by 'the applicable *lex specialis*', ie IHL, 'which is designed to regulate the conduct of hostilities'.[63] However, it remains to be seen whether or not the reasoning applied by the ICJ in respect of the interpretation of Article 6 CCPR may apply to the interpretation of Article 2 ECHR as well.

In fact, unlike Article 6 CCPR, Article 2 ECHR does *not* refer to the 'arbitrary' deprivation of life: Article 2(1) states that 'everyone's right to life shall be protected by law' and then adds in rather more general terms that 'no one shall be deprived of his life intentionally save in the execution of a sentence of a court following his conviction of a crime for which this penalty is provided by law'. Article 2(2) ECHR goes on to list a number of exceptions to the prohibition by adding that deprivation of life may be regarded as lawful when 'it results from the use of force which is no more than absolutely necessary: (a) in defence of any person from unlawful violence; (b) in order to effect a lawful arrest or to prevent the escape of a person lawfully detained; (c) in action lawfully taken for the purpose of quelling a riot or an insurrection'. On the other hand, unlike the CCPR, the ECHR allows a state to derogate from the provisions relating to the right to life: when a state avails itself of the right of derogation provided for in Article 15 ECHR on the basis that it is involved in 'war or other public emergency', Article 15(2) specifically allows for derogations to Article 2 'in respect of deaths resulting from lawful acts of war'.

---

[62] See especially *Isayeva v Russia*, App No 57950/00, ECtHR Chamber (2005) paras 180 and 191; *Isayeva, Yusupova, and Bazayeva v Russia*, App Nos 57947/00, 57948/00, and 57949/00, ECtHR Chamber (2005), paras 125 and 178. The emphasis is added.

[63] *Legality of the Threat or Use of Nuclear Weapons*, ICJ Reports (1996) 226, para 25.

It appears, therefore, that the question of what may or may not be an 'arbitrary' deprivation of life is not left open to interpretation by the ECHR, since any deprivation of life, in order to be regarded as lawful, must always fall within one of the exceptions to the prohibition provided for in the ECHR itself. In situations where Article 15 ECHR is invoked, there can be no doubt that IHL may be applied in order to determine what constitutes a 'lawful act of war'; but, as was pointed out above, no state has ever invoked that provision on the basis that it was involved in an armed conflict. In situations where Article 15 is not invoked and the ECHR applies in full, it must be recognized that the possibility for the European Court of Human Rights to determine that there has been no violation of Article 2 wherever a deprivation of life is allowed under IHL is not immediately evident. Of course, the exception listed in Article 2(2)(c) may specifically be invoked not only in situations of non-international armed conflicts, but also in situations of belligerent occupation of foreign territory where the occupying power is faced with resistance on the part of the local population, and it can certainly be argued that, at least where the situation can be qualified as an 'insurrection', as opposed to a mere 'riot', IHL may be taken into account in order to determine whether a state's conduct can be qualified as 'action lawfully taken' in order to quell such an insurrection. But the fact remains that, even in such a situation, the use of force must be 'no more than absolutely necessary' to that end. These observations may in part explain the Court's marked reluctance to explicitly refer to IHL, even in cases where the applicants themselves had made that reference. On the other hand, it seems to me that the case-law of the European Court of Human Rights so far demonstrates that, in most cases, the application of the relevant rules of IHL would not have led to substantially different results.

1. Lawful targets in combat situations

In determining what effects, if any, the application of IHL as *lex specialis* might have on the right to life as provided for in IHRL instruments, it seems useful to recall that IHL essentially regulates the conduct of hostilities during armed conflict, and the treatment of civilians and persons *hors de combat* who find themselves in the power of a party to the conflict.[64] It seems clear from the language quoted above that the ICJ itself, when affirming the relevance of IHL for determining what is an arbitrary deprivation of life in times of armed conflict, essentially had in mind the first set of rules, inasmuch as it explicitly referred to the legal regulation of the 'conduct of hostilities'. In fact, whereas IHL does not substantially differ from IHRL as far as the killing of persons in the power of a party to the conflict is concerned,[65]

---

[64] Both branches of IHL—which were previously often referred to, respectively, as 'Hague Law' and 'Geneva Law'—were reaffirmed and developed by the 1977 Geneva Protocols additional to the 1949 Geneva Conventions. Contemporary writers tend to agree, with few exceptions, that most of these provisions reflect existing customary law.

[65] The 'wilful killing' of 'protected persons' (ie wounded, sick, and shipwrecked members of armed forces, prisoners of war, and civilians who find themselves in the power of a party to the conflict, or occupying power, of which they are not nationals) is considered as a 'grave breach' of the 1949 Geneva Conventions: see Art 59 of *GC I*, Art 51 of *GC II*, Art 130 of *GC III*, and Art 147 of

differences may indeed arise in respect of the killing of persons during 'the conduct of hostilities'. The use of lethal force in combat situations is regulated by specific IHL rules on targeting which may be seen as different from those applying to peacetime law-enforcement operations. On the other hand, the IHL rules on targeting are only clearly spelled out in respect of international armed conflicts: although the majority of contemporary legal writers tend to agree that, under customary international law, similar rules apply in respect of non-international armed conflicts as well, the existing rules of treaty IHL are either silent on the conduct of hostilities[66] or require a very high threshold for their application.[67] Moreover, it must be stressed that law-enforcement operations may take place in times of armed conflict as well: although there are situations, such as non-international armed conflicts or insurrections in occupied territory, where the distinction between law enforcement and combat may appear to be very thin or to vanish altogether, an effort should be made to keep the two types of operation distinct.

Although it is not possible here to examine the IHL rules on targeting in detail, it may briefly be recalled that IHL is based on the fundamental principle of distinction between combatants and the civilian population:[68] attacks can in principle be directed against combatants, ie regular and irregular members of the armed forces of the parties to the conflict,[69] unless they are *hors de combat*;[70] moreover, although civilians as such cannot be the object of attack, they lose such protection if and for such time as they take a direct part in hostilities.[71] In non-international armed conflicts, or in cases where the belligerent occupation of foreign territory meets with armed resistance, the distinction between combatants and the civilian population is not so clear-cut, but there can be no doubt that civilians taking a direct part in hostilities can be the object of attack.[72]

On the other hand, the differences between IHL and IHRL, including the ECHR, in respect of the protection of the right to life in combat situations should not be overestimated. On the contrary, I tend to agree that, on the whole, 'the differences of tools and reasoning' that exist between the two branches of international law 'do not lead to substantive divergences or even to incompatibilities'.[73] The IHRL principle that the use of force must be no more than absolutely necessary to pursue a legitimate aim may well in practice converge with the IHL principle whereby attacks may only be directed at combatants (or civilians taking a direct part in hostilities) and at 'military objectives', these latter being defined as 'those objects which by their nature, location, purpose or use make an effective contribution to military action and whose total or partial destruction, capture or

---

GC IV. See also Art 85(2) of 1977 *AP I*, relating to persons in the power of an adverse party. As for non-international armed conflicts, the murder of persons taking no active part in hostilities is prohibited by Art 3 common to the four 1949 Geneva Conventions and by Art 4 of 1977 *AP II*.

[66] See Art 3 common to the 1949 Geneva Conventions.

[67] See Art 1 of 1977 *AP II*, an instrument which does contain a number of rules on the conduct of hostilities, especially in Part IV thereof.   [68] See Art 48 of 1977 *AP I*.

[69] See Art 43 of 1977 *AP I*.   [70] See Arts 41 and 42 of 1977 *AP I*.

[71] See Art 51(2) and (3) of 1977 *AP I*.   [72] See Art 13(3) of 1977 *AP II*.

[73] Gaggioli and Kolb, *supra* note 4, at 138.

neutralization, in the circumstances ruling at the time, offers a definite military advantage'.[74] Once again, the distinction between law-enforcement and combat operations must be taken into account: whereas in a law-enforcement operation the principle that the use of force must be no more than absolutely necessary to pursue a legitimate aim may require the arrest of a person wherever this is possible and the use of force only as a last resort, to require the same in a combat situation would not only contradict IHL but would also be unrealistic.[75] It seems to me that, far from being 'at odds' with IHL,[76] the case-law of the European Court of Human Rights confirms this assumption: even if it made no explicit reference to IHL, it would seem that in fact the distinction between a law-enforcement operation and a real combat operation *was* taken into account by the Court when determining whether or not the use of force on the part of the respondent state had been lawful. Moreover, when assessing whether or not its case-law is actually 'at odds' with IHL, account must be taken of the fact that the Court rarely had to deal directly with the issue of the lawfulness of the killing of combatants, or of civilians taking a direct part in hostilities.

In the case of *McCann and Others v United Kingdom*,[77] which can be considered in many respects as 'the leading case' in its case-law, the Court clearly confirmed that the use of force must be absolutely necessary for the achievement of one of the purposes set out in Article 2(2) ECHR, and it reaffirmed this principle in all subsequent cases, including those where IHL might have been relevant. In *McCann*, the issue was whether or not the shooting of suspected terrorists could be considered as lawful in order to counter an anticipated terrorist attack, and therefore the right to life of the targeted persons was at the core of the decision. But it was clear that the situation did not amount to an armed conflict and that the targets of the attack were, therefore, neither combatants nor civilians taking a direct part in hostilities in the sense of IHL.

The same could be said of a number of subsequent cases relating to south-eastern Anatolia, inasmuch as the existence of an armed conflict in that region was not only denied by Turkey, but was also a matter of considerable debate in the legal literature. But even assuming that there *was* an armed conflict in south-eastern Anatolia, the Court was rarely faced with what might have been considered as a real combat situation, as opposed to a law-enforcement operation: for example, in *Oğur v Turkey* the Court had to deal with the shooting without warning of an alleged terrorist at a site belonging to a mine company where he was working.[78] Where the Court *was*

---

[74] Art 52(2) 1977 *AP I*.   [75] In this sense, see also Sassòli, *supra* note 4, at 722.

[76] Abresch, *supra* note 4, at 742.

[77] *McCann and Others v United Kingdom*, Case No 17/1994/464/545, ECtHR Grand Chamber (1995). The case related to a police operation designed to counter an expected IRA terrorist attack in Gibraltar, in the course of which three suspected terrorists were shot. The Court held that there had been a violation of Art 2 having regard to: the authorities' decision not to prevent the suspects from travelling into Gibraltar; their failure to make sufficient allowances for the possibility that their intelligence assessments might be erroneous; the automatic recourse to lethal force when the soldiers opened fire.

[78] *Oğur v Turkey*, App no 21594/93, ECtHR Grand Chamber (1999). See also *Mansuroğlu v Turkey*, App No 43443/98, ECtHR Chamber (2008).

arguably faced with a combat situation, as in the case of *Ahmet Özkan and Others v Turkey*, which related to an operation designed to search for members of PKK, it *did* accept that, in view of the 'serious disturbances in south-east Turkey involving *armed conflict* between the security forces and members of the PKK', the decision taken by Turkish security forces to respond to shots coming from a nearby village with intensive firing was justified under Article 2 ECHR.[79] In most of the other cases relating to south-eastern Anatolia, the issue was not the right to life of the targeted persons, but rather the incidental damage caused to innocent bystanders, the lack of proportionality in the use of force, or of adequate precautionary measures, and at least in some such cases the Court again accepted that the use of force was per se lawful, either to quell an unauthorized demonstration[80] or to conduct an operation designed to apprehend terrorists.[81]

As was pointed out above, the only cases where the Court was undoubtedly faced with a situation of armed conflict were those relating to northern Cyprus and Chechnya. In most of the cases relating to northern Cyprus, the right to life was not at issue in respect of targeting, but rather in respect of persons missing as a result of military operations, an issue which will be dealt with later;[82] moreover, some of the more recent cases clearly related to law-enforcement activities on the part of the occupying power well after the end of active hostilities.[83] On the other hand, in the cases relating to Chechnya, the Court made it even clearer than in those relating to south-eastern Anatolia that it regarded the targeting of 'combatants' as lawful. Thus, in the case of *Isayeva v Russia*, relating to the aerial bombardment of a village followed by the bombardment of escaping civilians, the Court accepted that, in a conflict situation such as existed in Chechnya, a military operation 'aimed at either disarmament or destruction of the fighters' is per se legitimate: therefore, in view of the fact that in the village attacked there was a large number of 'combatants', the Court accepted that the military operation was pursuing a legitimate aim, and a violation of Article 2 ECHR was only found because the Court did not accept that the operation 'was planned and executed with the requisite care for the lives of the civilian population'.[84] In the case of *Isayeva, Yusopova and Bazayeva v Russia*, relating to the aerial bombardment of a civilian convoy fleeing from Grozny, the Court

---

[79] See *Ahmet Özkan and Others v Turkey*, App no 21689/93, ECtHR Chamber (2004), paras 305–306 (emphasis added).

[80] See *Güleç v Turkey*, Case No 54/1997/838/1044, ECtHR Chamber (1998). This case related to the killing of the applicant's 15-year-old son, while he was going home from school, by a fragment of a bullet fired from an armoured vehicle during an operation designed to quell an unauthorized demonstration. The Court accepted that the use of force was justified under Art 2(2)(c), ECHR, but added that 'a balance must be struck between the aim pursued and the means employed to achieve it' (para 71). [81] See eg *Ergi v Turkey*, Case No 66/1997/850/1057, ECtHR Chamber (1998).

[82] See *infra*, at B.3.

[83] See *Kakoulli v Turkey*, App No 38595/97, ECtHR Chamber (2005), relating to the shooting of a Greek Cypriot by a Turkish soldier engaged in border policing in 1996; *Solomonou and Others v Turkey*, App No 36832/97, ECtHR Chamber (2008), and *Isaak v Turkey*, App No 44587/98, ECtHR Chamber (2008), both relating to the shooting of Greek Cypriots who had voluntarily entered the UN buffer zone and crossed the Turkish-Cypriot forces' ceasefire line during anti-Turkish demonstrations in 1996.

[84] *Isayeva v Russia*, App No 57950/00, ECtHR Chamber (2005), especially paras 180–181.

had more doubts as to the legitimacy of the attack because it was unclear if 'combatants' were in fact present in significant numbers among the convoyed civilians, but it still decided to assume that the attack *was* legitimate per se since it found that a violation of Article 2 could in any case be derived from the fact that this operation was, in its turn, planned and executed without the necessary degree of care for the lives of the civilian population.[85] In other more recent decisions the Court was less explicit about the legitimacy of the use of force and concentrated on violations of Article 2 vis-à-vis innocent civilians.[86]

It may be interesting to point out that, although the Court never explicitly referred to IHL it sometimes used a terminology evoking the IHL distinction between 'combatants' and the 'civilian population', and that it did so in respect of non-international armed conflicts, ie conflicts in respect of which, as was pointed out above, the distinction is not so clear-cut in IHL itself. Inasmuch as, in both international and non-international armed conflicts, civilians are protected from attack 'unless and for such time as they take a direct part in hostilities', the real issue is what is meant by direct participation in hostilities, especially in respect of the duration of such participation. This is a hotly debated issue both in the legal literature and in the practice of states relating to IHL: the question is whether civilians can exclusively be attacked during their participation in a specific combat action (or preparation of, or return from, such action), or whether they can be attacked also when not actually engaged in combat, at least where their participation in hostilities is not sporadic but regular.[87] The first approach necessarily entails that civilians lose and regain their protection against direct attack in parallel with the intervals of their direct participation in hostilities (the so-called 'revolving door' approach); the second approach allows for the attack of members of an organized armed group irrespective of whether or not they are actively engaged in a specific combat action (the so-called 'membership' approach).

The case-law of the European Court is sometimes said to favour the first and more restrictive approach,[88] but in my opinion the Court's attitude is in fact more nuanced. It is certainly true that in *McCann* the Court appeared to stress the point that a person cannot be attacked simply because of his or her participation in criminal, including terrorist, activities, but that case related to a law-enforcement operation in time of peace. As was pointed out above, the same could be said in respect of the cases relating to south-eastern Anatolia where the Court appeared

---

[85] *Isayeva, Yusupova, and Bazayeva v Russia,* App Nos 57947/00, 57948/00, and 57949/00, ECtHR Chamber (2005), especially paras 178–181.

[86] See eg *Mezhidov v Russia*, App No 67326/01, ECtHR Chamber (2008), relating to the killing of a number of the applicant's relations by a shell bursting in the courtyard of the building where they were living in the course of an attack directed at the village of Znamenskoye in Chechnya. In this case, Russia had denied that its forces had been involved in the attack and, therefore, gave no explanation for it, but the Court was of the opinion 'that the large-calibre shells mentioned in the expert report of 9 August 2000 could only be fired from heavy artillery pieces, and that such guns were presumably in the exclusive possession of the Russian armed forces' (para 60).

[87] The International Committe of the Red Cross (ICRC) has recently published an 'interpretative guidance' on this controversial issue. See ICRC, *Interpretative Guidance on the Notion of Direct Participation in Hostilities under International Humanitarian Law* (2009).

[88] See, in particular, Gaggioli and Kolb, *supra* note 4, at 144–149.

to confirm *McCann*, such as the already mentioned *Oğur* case or the case of *Gül v Turkey* relating to the shooting of a presumptive terrorist while he was sitting at home with his family.[89] But even assuming that there was an armed conflict in south-eastern Anatolia, it must be pointed out that both of these cases related to attacks on persons whose qualification as 'terrorists' by the respondent state was based on a mere presumption and was disputed by the applicants. The same can be said of the more recent case of *Mansuroğlu v Turkey*, relating to the presumed killing of an alleged terrorist during an anti-terrorist operation.[90] The issue of the need for adequate information before a person is attacked on the basis that he or she may be qualified as 'terrorist' or 'combatant' was squarely at issue in the more recent case of *Khatsiyeva and Others v Russia*, relating to helicopter attacks on a group of people cutting grass but allegedly armed in a district in Ingushetia bordering on Chechnya. In this case the Court accepted once again that 'the difficult situation...in the neighbouring region...called for exceptional measures on the part of the state to suppress the illegal armed insurgency'. This notwithstanding, the Court concluded that, even assuming that the attackers honestly believed that the targeted persons were in fact armed with machine guns, this fact alone could not justify the use of lethal force: it observed in this respect that between the pilots' report (stating that they could see a group of armed men) and the authorities' order to destroy them, there elapsed a very short time and the authorities in command made no attempt to seek any further details in order to enable them adequately to assess the situation and take an appropriate decision.[91] In other words, it could be argued that the Court left the door open for the targeting of armed civilians when, on the basis of sufficient information, it results that they are in fact 'combatants' or that, although they are not actually engaged in combat, they may fall within the category of 'civilians taking a direct part in hostilities'.

It seems to me that in practice the differences between the two approaches outlined above may not be as great as one might think on the basis of a purely theoretical analysis. Even if direct participation in hostilities on the part of a civilian is narrowly construed to exclusively consist of specific acts, including measures preparatory for the execution of such specific acts as well as the deployment to and the return from the location of their execution, it can be argued that in a non-international armed conflict members of organized armed groups belonging to a non-state party to the conflict cease to be civilians for all purposes, and lose protection against direct attack for as long as they assume their continuous combat function.[92] In other words, the 'revolving door' approach may be correct in respect of real civilians, but the 'membership' approach may still be correct in respect of members of the organized armed forces of a party to the conflict. On the other hand, even where the 'membership' approach is adopted, it might still be argued

---

[89] *Gül v Turkey*, App No 22676/93, ECtHR Chamber (2000).
[90] *Mansuroğlu v Turkey*, App No 43443/98, ECtHR Chamber (2008).
[91] See *Khatsiyeva and Others v Russia*, App No 5108/02, ECtHR Chamber (2008), paras 134–137.
[92] ICRC, *Interpretative Guidance on the Notion of Direct Participation in Hostilities under International Humanitarian Law, op cit*, at 17.

that the use of force against persons not actively engaged in combat must be exceptional, since membership of an organized armed group may not be as easy to prove as membership of a state's regular armed forces. It is significant in this respect that even the Israeli Supreme Court, in a recent decision relating to the targeting of terrorists in the Palestinian Territories which upheld a wide interpretation of the concept of direct participation, quoted *McCann* in order to point out that civilians taking a direct part in hostilities cannot be attacked if less harmful means, such as arrest and trial, can be employed and that, even though there may be circumstances where such means cannot be employed and an attack is warranted, 'careful verification is needed before an attack is made', so that 'the burden of proof on the attacking army is heavy'.[93]

2. *The principle of proportionality and the need for precautions in attack*

Under Article 2(2) ECHR, the use of force, in order to be legitimate, must be 'no more than absolutely necessary' to pursue a legitimate aim. Thus, once established that the use of force on the part of a state was per se legitimate, it remains to be seen whether or not it was also proportionate. Like the principle of necessity, the principle of proportionality is often seen as operating in a different way in IHL and in IHRL. But it could rather be argued that, when the interested state is involved in an armed conflict, just as the IHRL principle that the use of force must be necessary to pursue a legitimate aim may in fact converge with the IHL principle that attacks may be directed only at combatants and at military objectives, the IHRL principle that care must be taken to reduce casualties at a maximum may in fact converge with the IHL principle prohibiting 'indiscriminate attacks'. In principle, 'indiscriminate attacks' are defined as those 'of a nature to strike military objectives and civilians or civilian objects without distinction', either because they are not directed at a specific military objective or because they employ means or methods of combat which cannot be so directed or the effects of which cannot be limited;[94] moreover, among the types of attacks to be considered as 'indiscriminate', specific mention is made of 'an attack which may be expected to cause incidental loss of civilian life, injury to civilians, damage to civilian objects, or a combination thereof, which would be excessive in relation to the concrete and direct military advantage anticipated'.[95]

It could be retorted that, under IHRL, the principle of proportionality allows for no distinction between combatants and civilians, in the sense that the lives of combatants, including civilians taking a direct part in hostilities, must be taken into account when assessing proportionality, just as those of civilians, but such a strict interpretation of proportionality would fail to distinguish between law-enforcement operations and real combat situations: in a combat situation, requiring the life of combatants to be taken into account when assessing proportionality

---

[93] See *The Public Committee against torture in Israel et al v The Government of Israel et al, supra* note 34, para 40. it seems important to point out that the Court explicitly quoted the case-law of the European Court of Human Rights in this respect.   [94] See Art 51(4) of 1977 *AP I*.
   [95] See Art 51(5) (b) of 1977 *AP I*.

would not only be at odds with IHL but would also be unrealistic.[96] The case-law of the European Court of Human Rights might be seen as confirming this assumption, even if the relevant cases exclusively relate to non-international armed conflict, where the rules of IHL are less developed, and the Court chose not to explicitly refer to IHL. In the cases relating to south-eastern Anatolia, where the existence of an armed conflict was disputed, it appears that at least when the Court was faced with a real combat situation, as opposed to a law-enforcement operation, it never took the lives of 'combatants' into account when assessing proportionality: for example, in *Ahmet Özkan* the Court accepted that the Turkish security forces' tactical reaction to the initial shots fired at them from a nearby village, and consisting in 'intensive firing, including the use of RPG-7 missiles and various grenades that were fired at perceived points of fire in the village', could not be regarded as 'entailing a disproportionate degree of force'.[97] Even in *Gül*, where the Court was arguably faced with a mere law-enforced operation designed to search for alleged terrorists, the decision of the Turkish officers to open fire with automatic weapons, in reaction to the sound of a door bolt being drawn back in the mistaken view that they were about to come under fire by terrorists, was found to be 'grossly disproportionate' in view of the fact that the operation took place 'in a residential block inhabited by innocent civilians, women and children'.[98] Moreover, as was pointed out above, in this as in other cases relating to anti-terrorist operations in south-eastern Anatolia,[99] the qualification of the victim as a 'terrorist' was at issue. In the already mentioned cases relating to Chechnya, where the Court accepted, despite the absence of a state of emergency, that the situation called for exceptional measures by the state in order to regain control over the region and to 'suppress the illegal armed insurgency', the question was always that of the risk posed to the lives of innocent 'civilians'.

But, even leaving aside the issue of the relevance of the life of 'combatants' in order to assess proportionality, it could be argued, in addition, that the principle of proportionality is stricter in IHRL than in IHL, inasmuch as it requires reducing casualties to a minimum, whereas IHL only requires avoiding excessive incidental damage. But, since strict proportionality does not imply that 'incidental damages' are not acceptable, this perceived difference appears to be rather relative and I agree that, 'at the end of the day, the concrete operation of the principle of proportionality seems broadly equivalent in both branches' of international law.[100] In this respect also, the Court's case-law does not appear to be incompatible with IHL. For example, the Court's case-law appears to confirm that the means necessary for fighting against an 'insurrection' may not be the same as those sufficient for the quelling of a mere 'riot' or for conducting a law-enforcement operation even in situations where the state is arguably engaged in an armed conflict. Thus, in *Güleç* the Court found that the use of armoured vehicles (as opposed to truncheons, riot shields, water cannon, rubber bullets, or tear gas) was not an adequate means for

[96] See Sassòli, *supra* note 4, at 723.

[97] *Ahmet Özkan and Others v Turkey*, App No 21689/93, ECtHR Chamber (2004) paras 298 and 305.   [98] *Gül v Turkey*, App No 22676/93, ECtHR Chamber (2000) para 82.

[99] See also eg *Hamiyet Kaplan and Others v Turkey*, App No 36749/97, ECtHR Chamber (2005) paras 50–52.   [100] Gaggioli and Kolb, *supra* note 4, at 138.

quelling a riot.[101] Equally, in *Hamiyet and Others v Turkey* it was found that the use of firearms (as opposed to tear gas or paralyzing grenades) was excessive in order to arrest alleged terrorists who had been encircled in a house inhabited by innocent people.[102] On the other hand, in both *Isayeva* cases, the Court appeared to admit that measures necessary to fight against an insurrection could include, in principle, the deployment of army units equipped with combat weapons, including military aviation and artillery, and the issue in these latter cases was rather whether the use of such weapons in the concrete circumstances could be seen as proportionate in relation to the damage to the civilian population that might have been anticipated.[103] Indeed, the language used by the Court in assessing proportionality in this respect was sometimes similar to the terminology used in IHL: for example, in *Isayeva v Russia*, which related to the aerial bombing of a village with heavy combat weapons, the Court found that 'the massive use of indiscriminate weapons' stood in contrast with the aim of an operation allegedly designed to defend the lives of the village population which was said to have been taken hostage by a group of fighters.[104] Although the Court underlined in this respect that the bombardment had taken place not only 'without prior evacuation of the civilians' but also 'outside wartime',[105] in view of the fact that no state of emergency had been declared and the respondent state itself did not qualify the situation as an armed conflict regulated by IHL, it could be argued that the result might have been the same had the Court applied IHL: although under IHL it would not have been correct to speak of 'indiscriminate weapons' in respect of heavy combat weapons used in aerial bombardment, the attacks in question might still have been considered as 'indiscriminate attacks' since, in the concrete circumstances, the arms used could have had indiscriminate effects in view of the lack of proportion between the expected military advantage and the incidental damage to civilians which could have been anticipated.

In both *Isayeva* cases, the lack of proportionality was considered together with the lack of adequate precautionary measures designed to minimize the impact of an attack on the civilian population. The need for a state to take precautionary measures was clearly affirmed by the Court in *McCann*,[106] a case not relating to armed conflict, and is but one aspect of a more general tendency on the part of the Court, as well as of other human rights bodies, to strengthen the right to life by affirming that a state has not only the duty to refrain from arbitrary killings, but also a number of 'positive obligations' designed to safeguard the lives of persons under its jurisdiction. There can be no doubt that in times of armed conflict the

---

[101] *Güleç v Turkey*, Case No 54/1997/838/1044, ECtHR Chamber (1998) paras 70–71.

[102] *Hamiyet Kaplan and Others v Turkey*, App No 36749/97, ECtHR Chamber (2005) paras 51–52.

[103] See *Isayeva v Russia*, App No 57950/00, ECtHR Chamber (2005) paras 180–181; *Isayeva, Yusupova, and Bazayeva v. Russia*, App Nos 57947/00, 57948/00, and 57949/00, ECtHR Chamber (2005) paras 178–181.

[104] *Isayeva v Russia*, App No 57950/00, ECtHR Chamber (2005) para 189.

[105] Ibid, para 191.

[106] See *McCann and Others v United Kingdom*, Case No 17/1994/464/545, ECtHR Grand Chamber (1995) paras 202–214.

obligation to plan an operation involving the use of lethal force so as to reduce such use to the minimum tends to converge with the IHL principle requiring a belligerent state to take precautions in the choice of means and methods of attack, so that incidental damage to civilians and civilian objects is reduced to the minimum. On the other hand, this principle is only clearly spelled out in detailed rules of IHL in respect of international armed conflicts,[107] and the fact that the Court has repeatedly confirmed this principle in respect of non-international armed conflicts can thus be seen as an important contribution on its part towards a better legal regulation of such conflicts.

The need for adequate information before an attack is directed against persons not actually engaged in combat on the basis that they are 'civilians taking a direct part in hostilities' has already been addressed above. As for the need to plan a combat operation so that incidental damage to 'innocent' civilians is reduced to a minimum, several commentators have again pointed out that the language used by the Court was sometimes very similar to that used by the IHL rules relating to international armed conflicts. For example, in some of the cases relating to south eastern-Anatolia, the Court stated that under Article 2, read in conjunction with Article 1, ECHR, a state's responsibility may be engaged in all cases where state agents 'fail to take all feasible precautions in the choice of means and methods of a security operation mounted against an opposing group with a view to avoiding and, in any event, to minimising, incidental loss of civilian life'.[108] On the other hand, in some such cases, as well as in the Chechnya cases, the Court probably went even beyond what is required by IHL. For example, IHL requires a belligerent state to give an 'effective advance warning' of 'attacks which may affect the civilian population', and then only 'unless circumstances do not permit',[109] whereas in *Isayeva v Russia* the Court affirmed that Russia should have warned the local population of the probable arrival of rebels in their village, a circumstance that might have exposed the village to attacks.[110] In *Ergi v Turkey* the Court considered it necessary to ascertain whether an anti-terrorist operation conducted by Turkish security forces 'had been planned and conducted in such a way as to avoid or minimise, to the greatest extent possible, any risk to the lives of the villagers, *including from the fire-power of the PKK members caught in the ambush*',[111] whereas under IHL each belligerent is responsible for the damage to civilians caused by its own armed forces. But these obligations would certainly not contradict IHL obligations, and might rather be seen as complementing them, thus contributing to the further development of the law applicable to armed conflicts. In the more recent case of *Albekov v Russia*, the Court found that Russia should have warned the local population of an anti-personnel minefield allegedly laid by the rebels but

---

[107] See Arts 57 and 58 of 1977 *AP I*.

[108] See *Ergi v Turkey*, Case No 66/1997/850/1057, ECtHR Chamber (1998) para 79; *Ahmet Özkan and Others v Turkey*, App No 21689/93, ECtHR Chamber (2004) para 297.

[109] See Art 57, para 2(c), of 1977 *AP I*.

[110] See *Isayeva v Russia*, App No 57950/00, ECtHR Chamber (2005) para 187.

[111] *Ergi v Turkey*, Case No 66/1997/850/1057, ECtHR Chamber (1998) para 79 (emphasis added).

of which it was aware, an obligation which could have been reinforced by reference to IHL.[112]

3. *The obligation to investigate whenever people are killed or missing*

Perhaps the most important contribution of the Court's case-law to the development of the legal regulation of armed conflict consists in the articulation of another positive obligation strengthening the right to life, ie the duty to conduct a thorough and meaningful enquiry whenever a person is killed. Although this obligation is not expressly provided for in Article 2 ECHR, the Court clearly affirmed it in *McCann*[113] on the basis of a joint interpretation of Articles 1 and 2 ECHR, and always reaffirmed it in its subsequent case-law, including in cases relating to armed conflict situations. On the basis of the Court's case-law, the duty to investigate is quite far-reaching, and extends to cases where the use of lethal force was attributable to non-state agents, such as insurgents or 'terrorists'.[114] On the other hand, the Court appears to accept that, although the authorities must act of their own motion once the matter has come to their attention, and cannot leave it to the initiative of the next of kin either to lodge a formal complaint or to take responsibility for the conduct of any investigative procedures, the form of the investigation may have to vary depending on the circumstances.[115] But even if the obligation to conduct a meaningful investigation may have to be adapted in order to avoid requiring a state engaged in an armed conflict to go beyond prescriptions of due diligence,[116] the important point is that, as a matter of principle, this obligation applies in situations of armed conflict just as it does in times of peace. Indeed, in the cases relating to south-eastern Anatolia the Court often explicitly stated that 'neither the prevalence of violent armed clashes nor the high incidence of fatalities can displace the obligation under Article 2 to ensure that an effective, independent investigation is conducted into the deaths arising out of clashes involving the security forces, more so in cases...where the circumstances are in many respects unclear'.[117]

---

[112] See *Albekov and Others v Russia*, App No 68216/01, ECtHR Chamber (2008) paras 84–85; the Court held Russia responsible for the accidental deaths caused by a minefield, because of its 'failure to endeavour to locate and deactivate the mines, to mark and seal off the mined area so as to prevent anybody from freely entering it, and to provide the villagers with comprehensive warnings concerning the mines laid in the vicinity of their village' (para 90). As for IHL, Protocol II to the 1981 UN Convention on Prohibitions and Restrictions on the Use of Certain Conventional Weapons, which specifically relates to 'mines, booby-traps and other devices' was recently amended in order to apply to non-international armed conflicts also. In addition, the 1997 Ottawa Convention on the Prohibition on the Use, Stockpiling, Production and Transfer of Anti-Personnel Mines and on their Destruction applies to all circumstances and, therefore, to both international and non-international armed conflicts.

[113] See *McCann and Others v United Kingdom*, Case No 17/1994/464/545, ECtHR Grand Chamber (1995) para 161.

[114] See *Ergi v Turkey*, Case No 66/1997/850/1057, ECtHR Chamber (1998) para 82.

[115] See eg *Ahmet Özkan and Others v Turkey*, App No 21689/93, ECtHR Chamber (2004) para 310; *Isayeva v Russia*, App No 57950/00, ECtHR Chamber (2005) para 210.

[116] In this sense, see Gaggioli and Kolb, *supra* note 4, at 156.

[117] *Kaya v Turkey*, Case No 158/1996/777/978, ECtHR Chamber (1998, para 91. See also eg *Güleç v Turkey*, Case No. 54/1997/838/1044, ECtHR Chamber (1998) para 81; *Ergi v Turkey*, Case No 66/1997/850/1057, ECtHR Chamber (1998) para 85. The obligation to conduct a meaningful

In respect of the often 'unclear' circumstances of a person's death in cases relating to armed conflict, it must be pointed out that the Court never squarely had to deal with the death of a 'combatant' in the field: the Court's case-law exclusively relates to the death of 'innocent' civilians or of persons whose qualification as terrorists or 'combatants' was presumed by the attacking forces but was often at issue. Indeed, it might be argued that in a traditional situation of international armed conflict where two regular state armies are engaged in combat, it would be unrealistic to expect each belligerent to conduct a meaningful and thorough enquiry into the death of each enemy combatant in the field: it is significant, in this respect, that IHL only specifically provides for an obligation to officially enquire into the death of prisoners of war and of interned civilians.[118] On the other hand, it was pointed out above that even in the field combatants cannot be targeted when they are *hors de combat*: inasmuch as the killing of persons *hors de combat* is a 'grave breach' of IHL,[119] it might be argued that an obligation to investigate into 'unclear' deaths of enemy combatants can be derived from the general obligation incumbent on all belligerents to search for persons alleged to have committed, or to have ordered to be committed, such grave breaches, and to bring them to trial.[120] However that may be, it seems clear that the Court's case-law is especially relevant for situations of non-international armed conflict and, more generally, for situations where a state is engaged in combat with the armed forces of a non-state entity, such as an organization of insurgents or 'terrorists', and, more generally, for all situations where the distinction between combatants and civilians is not clear-cut and where it is, therefore, necessary to ascertain whether or not a civilian was lawfully targeted because he or she had taken a direct part in hostilities. It seems significant in this respect that even the Israeli Supreme Court, when interpreting the concept of direct participation as sometimes allowing for the targeted killing of terrorists when they are not actively engaged in hostilities, stressed the need for the targeting state not only to make sure that each attack is founded on well-based information on the targeted person, but also that it is followed by 'a thorough investigation regarding the precision of the identification of the target and the circumstances of the attack': indeed, the Israeli Court expressly quoted *McCann* when it added that such an investigation must be 'independent'.[121]

Moreover, although most of the cases examined by the Court related to the killing of persons during law-enforcement or combat operations in the field, either because these persons were directly targeted or because they suffered 'incidental damage', some important cases related to the fate of persons missing as a result of

enquiry was reaffirmed by the Court in the cases relating to Chechnya as well: see eg *Isayeva v Russia*, App No 57950/00, ECtHR Chamber (2005) paras 202–224; *Isayeva, Yusupova, and Bazayeva v Russia*, App Nos 57947/00, 57948/00, and 57949/00, ECtHR Chamber (2005) paras 201–225; *Khatsiyeva and Others v Russia*, App No 5108/02, ECtHR Chamber (2008) paras 141–153.

[118] See Art 121 of 1949 *GC III* and Art 131 of 1949 *GC IV*.

[119] See Art 85(3)(e) of 1977 *AP I*.

[120] See Art 49 of 1949 *GC I*, Art 50 of 1949 *GC II*, Art 129 of 1949 *GC III*, Art 146 of 1949 *GC IV*, and Art 85(1) of 1977 *AP I*.

[121] See *The Public Committee against torture in Israel et al v The Government of Israel et al*, *supra* note 34, para 40.

such operations. Indeed, in some such cases the Court found that the prolonged silence on the part of a state's authorities in respect of the fate of missing persons constituted not only a violation of the right to life under Article 2 ECHR, but also a violation of the prohibition on 'inhuman or degrading treatment' under Article 3 ECHR vis-à-vis the families of such persons.[122] In some cases relating to south-eastern Anatolia[123] and Chechnya,[124] the Court was faced with 'enforced disappearances', ie with the disappearance of persons who had been allegedly apprehended and detained by the respondent state, even though these circumstances were often unacknowledged: in these cases, the Court often found that the interested persons could be presumed killed while in detention and that, therefore, there had been a substantive violation of Article 2 in addition to the failure to conduct a thorough and meaningful enquiry.[125] On the other hand, in *Cyprus v Turkey*, a case decided in 2001, the Court was unable to establish that any of the missing persons had been unlawfully killed, but still found that a violation had occurred as a result of the failure of the authorities of the respondent State to conduct an effective investigation aimed at clarifying the whereabouts and fate of Greek-Cypriot missing persons who disappeared in life-threatening circumstances'.[126] Indeed, in the more recent case of *Varnava and Others v Turkey*, decided in 2008, the Court explicitly distinguished the situation in northern Cyprus from that in south-eastern Anatolia or Chechnya in order to do away with the applicants' need 'to give an evidential basis for finding that their relatives were taken into some form of custody by agents of the state',[127] and in so doing it decided to make what appears to be its first explicit reference to IHL.

---

[122] See eg *Cyprus v Turkey*, App No 25781/94, ECtHR Grand Chamber (2001) paras 156–157. But most of the cases quoted in the following two footnotes are also relevant in this respect.

[123] See eg *Kurt v Turkey*, Case No 15/1997/799/1002, ECtHR Chamber (1998); *Akdeniz and Others v Turkey*, App No 23954/94, ECtHR Chamber (2001); *Osmanoğlu v Turkey*, App No 48804/99, ECtHR Chamber (2008).

[124] See eg *Bazorkina v Russia*, App No 69481/01, ECtHR Chamber (2006); *Luluyev and Others v Russia*, App No 69480/01, ECtHR Chamber (2006); *Imakayeva v Russia*, App No 7615/02, ECtHR Chamber (2006); *Betayev and Betayeva v Russia*, App No 37315/03, ECtHR Chamber (2008); *Ibragimov and Others v Russia*, App No 34561/03, ECtHR Chamber (2008); *Gekhayeva and Others v Russia*, App No 1755/04, ECtHR Chamber (2008); *Sangariyeva and Others v Russia*, App No 1839/04, ECtHR Chamber (2008); *Utsayeva and Others v Russia*, App No 29133/03, ECtHR Chamber (2008); *Akhiyadova v Russia*, App No 32059/02, ECtHR Chamber (2008); *Musayeva v Russia*, App No 12703/02, ECtHR Chamber (2008); *Ruslan Umarov v. Russia*, App No 12712/02, ECtHR Chamber (2008). But there are several similar cases decided by the Court in the second half of 2008 and in 2009.

[125] Although the Court made no reference to IHL, it was pointed out above that IHL does not differ from IHRL in respect of the killing of persons who are in the power of a party to an armed conflict: see *supra* note 65. For these reasons, I find it hard to agree with the view that the application of IHL might have led to a lowering of the standard of protection: see eg Aleni, 'Diritti Umani e Diritto Umanitario nella Pronuncia della Corte Europea dei Diritti dell'Uomo nel Caso *Bazorkina*', 1 *Diritti Umani e Diritto Internazionale* (2007) 127, at 132.

[126] *Cyprus v Turkey*, App No 25781/94, ECtHR Grand Chamber (2001) paras 132–136.

[127] *Varnava and Others v Turkey*, App Nos 16064/90, 16065/90, 16066/90, 16068/90, 16069/90, 16070/90, 16071/90, 16072/90, and 16073/90, ECtHR Chamber (2008) para 130. The Court quoted the following cases: *Kurt v Turkey*, Case No 15/1997/799/1002, ECtHR Chamber (1998) para 99; *Akdeniz and Others v Turkey*, App No 23954/94, ECtHR Chamber (2001),para 84; *Sarli v*

The Court observed, in the first place, that 'a zone of international conflict where two armies are engaged in acts of war per se places those present in a situation of danger and threat to life' and that 'circumstances will frequently be such that the events in issue lie wholly, or in large part, within the exclusive knowledge of the military forces in the field': consequently, 'it would not be realistic to expect applicants to provide more than minimal information placing their relative in the area at risk'. Secondly, the Court recalled that 'international treaties, which have attained the status of customary law, impose obligations on combatant states as regards care of wounded, prisoners of war and civilians', and added that 'Article 2 of the Convention certainly extends so far as to require contracting states to take such steps as may be reasonably available to them to protect the lives of those not, or no longer, engaged in hostilities', so that 'disappearances in such circumstances... attract the protection of that provision'.[128]

Although the Court did not quote specific rules of the relevant 'international treaties',[129] there is no doubt that IHL safeguards 'the right of families to know the fate of their relatives,'[130] and that, 'as soon as circumstances permit, and at least from the end of active hostilities', each party to the conflict is under a duty to search for the persons who have been reported missing by the adverse party.[131] These provisions do not exclusively relate to persons who have been detained by a party to the conflict, in respect of whom there are specific duties to provide information.[132] The fact that IHL only specifically envisages the gathering of information designed to clarify the fate of missing persons[133] does not contradict the need that, under Article 2 ECHR, an effective investigation should also be directed at ascertaining the cause of any established death, as well as the responsibility therefor: in fact, a duty to investigate into 'unclear' deaths for such purposes might also be derived from the general IHL obligation incumbent on all belligerents to search for persons alleged to have committed, or to have ordered to be committed, grave breaches, and to bring them to trial, which was referred to above. On the

---

Turkey, App No 24490/94, ECtHR Chamber (2001); *Imakayeva v Russia*, App No 7615/02, ECtHR Chamber (2006) para 141.

[128] Ibid.

[129] See ibid. In a footnote, the Court quoted, without further specification, the four 1949 Geneva Conventions 'together with three additional amendment protocols, Protocol I (1977), Protocol II (1977) and Protocol III (2005)'.   [130] See Art 32 of 1977 *AP I*.

[131] See Art 33(1) of 1977 *AP I*.

[132] See Art 16 of 1949 *GC I*; Art 19 of 1949 *GC II*; Arts 122–123 of 1949 *GC III*; Arts 136 and 140 of 1949 *GC IV*; Art 33(2) of 1977 *AP I*.

[133] Thus the Court considered that Turkey's procedural obligation under Art 2 ECHR could not be discharged through its contribution to the investigatory work of the UN Committee on Missing Persons (CMP), which was set up to 'look into cases of persons reported missing in the inter-communal fighting as well as in the events of July 1974 and afterwards' and 'to draw up comprehensive lists of missing persons of both communities, specifying as appropriate whether they are still alive or dead, and in the latter case approximate times of death': the Court observed in this respect that, 'whatever its humanitarian usefulness', the CMP did not provide procedures sufficient to meet the standard of an effective investigation required by Art 2 ECHR, 'especially in view of the narrow scope of that body's investigations'. See *Cyprus v Turkey*, Appl No 25781/94, ECtHR Grand Chamber (2001) paras 27 and 135; *Varnava and Others v Turkey*, App Nos 16064/90, 16065/90, 16066/90, 16068/90, 16069/90, 16070/90, 16071/90, 16072/90, and 16073/90, ECtHR Chamber (2008) para 131.

other hand, the fact that all such obligations are only clearly spelled out in treaties relating to international armed conflicts, may explain why the Court decided thus to distinguish the situation in northern Cyprus from that in south-eastern Anatolia or Chechnya, where no explicit reference was made to IHL. But, at least under international customary law, it would seem that the legal regulation of non-international armed conflicts would not be different in this respect.

C. The right to liberty in armed conflict

Apart from the right to life, the special nature of IHL vis-à-vis IHRL might be affirmed in respect of the right to liberty also. In particular, it could be argued that the language used in Article 9 CCPR, which prohibits 'arbitrary detention', warrants the application, by way of analogy, of the same reasoning which the ICJ applied to the protection of the right to life: in other words, it could be argued that the test of what is an arbitrary detention in times of armed conflict falls to be determined by the applicable *lex specialis*, ie IHL. However, when the ECHR is taken into consideration, it must be pointed out in this respect also that Article 5 ECHR is not as immediately open to the application of IHL as *lex specialis*. In fact, unlike Article 9 CCPR, Article 5 ECHR does *not* refer to 'arbitrary' detention: Article 5(1) rather states that 'everyone has the right to liberty and security of person' and then gives an exhaustive list of cases where the deprivation of liberty can be considered lawful,[134] provided that such deprivation is 'in accordance with a procedure prescribed by law'. In other words, just as the question of what is an arbitrary deprivation of life, the question of what is an arbitrary detention is not left open by the ECHR, since any deprivation of liberty, in order to be regarded as lawful, must always fall within one of the cases provided for in the ECHR itself. Indeed, it could be argued that the list given in Article 5(1) leaves even less space to the application of IHL than the corresponding list given in Article 2(2) in respect of cases where the deprivation of life can be regarded as lawful. Moreover, Article 5(4) ECHR, like Article 9(4) CCPR, states in very general terms that every arrested or detained person is entitled to take proceedings by which the lawfulness of his (or her) detention shall be decided speedily by a court and his (or her) release ordered if the detention is not lawful.

On the other hand, just as Article 9 CCPR, Article 5 ECHR may be derogated from 'in time of war or other public emergency threatening the life of the nation',

---

[134] These cases are: 'a) the lawful detention of a person after conviction by a competent court; b) the lawful arrest or detention of a person for non-compliance with the lawful order of a court or in order to secure the fulfilment of any obligation prescribed by law; c) the lawful arrest or detention of a person effected for the purpose of bringing him before the competent legal authority on reasonable suspicion of having committed an offence or when it is reasonably considered necessary to prevent his committing an offence or fleeing after having done so; d) the detention of a minor by lawful order for the purpose of educational supervision or his lawful detention for the purpose of bringing him before the competent legal authority; e) the lawful detention of persons for the prevention of the spreading of infectious diseases, of persons of unsound mind, alcoholics or drug addicts or vagrants; f) the lawful arrest or detention of a person to prevent his effecting an unauthorised entry into the country or of a person against whom action is being taken with a view to deportation or extradition'.

provided that the interested state complies with its 'other obligations under international law', including its obligations under IHL. There can be little doubt that in fact the application of IHL as *lex specialis* might have a significant impact on the protection of the right to liberty in times of armed conflict, especially in respect of the possibility to detain a person indefinitely, without charges being filed against him or her, without a court hearing, and without entitlement to a legal consultant. But, as was pointed out above, there have been very few cases where derogations from Article 5 ECHR have been justified on the basis that the interested state was involved in 'war or other public emergency', and most such cases either did not amount to armed conflicts or amounted to non-international armed conflicts, in respect of which the rules of IHL are not as clear-cut. It is therefore understandable that, to my knowledge, the European Court of Human Rights never felt it necessary to refer to IHL when ascertaining violations of Article 5 ECHR.

1. *The detention of prisoners of war*

Under IHL applicable to international armed conflicts, 'combatants', ie members of the armed forces of one party to the conflict, falling into the power of the enemy are entitled to the status of 'prisoners of war' (POWs),[135] which is regulated in detail by 1949 Geneva Convention III (*GC III*). Inasmuch as they participated directly in hostilities as a matter of 'right',[136] POWs cannot be charged with a criminal offence for the mere fact of such direct participation; on the other hand, they can be 'interned' by the enemy until the end of active hostilities for the simple reason that they are combatants, irrespective of whether or not they are charged with any criminal offence and without any need for an individual court or administrative decision.[137] The only requirement under IHL is that, in case of doubt as to whether or not persons having fallen into the power of the enemy after committing 'a belligerent act' are entitled to the status of POWs, such persons are to be treated as a POWs 'until such time as their status has been determined by a competent tribunal'.[138]

The European Court of Human Rights was never faced with the question of the lawfulness of the detention of POWs during an international armed conflict. On the other hand, when examining the detention of POWs by the Turkish army as a result of the invasion of Cyprus in 1974, the European Commission of Human Rights *had* 'taken account of the fact' that both Cyprus and Turkey were party to the 1949 *GC III* and that Turkey had made its intention to respect the Convention clear to the International Committee of the Red Cross: as a result, the Commission had not 'found it necessary to examine the question of a breach of Article 5 ECHR with regard to persons accorded the status of POWs'.[139] This conclusion was all the more significant inasmuch as the Commission had found, on the one hand, that the detention of Greek Cypriot military personnel was per se a violation of

---

[135] See Art 4 of 1949 *GC III* and Arts 43–44 of 1977 *AP I*.
[136] See Art 43(2) of 1977 *AP I*.   [137] See Arts 21 and 118 of 1949 *GC III*.
[138] See Art 5 of 1949 of *GC III*.
[139] See *Cyprus v Turkey*, App Nos 6780/74 and 6950/75, EComHR (1976) para 313.

Article 5(1) ECHR and, on the other, that Article 15 ECHR could not be applied to measures taken by Turkey in the absence of a formal and public act of derogation on its part.[140] This had led a dissenting Commissioner to point out that, even in the absence of such a formal and public act, 'measures which are in themselves contrary to a provision of the ECHR but which are taken legitimately under the international law applicable to an armed conflict are to be considered as legitimate measures of derogation from the obligations flowing from the Convention'.[141]

2. *The detention of civilians having taken a direct part in hostilities*

Neither the Court, nor the European Commission before it, have ever directly examined the question of the lawfulness of the detention of civilians having taken a direct part in hostilities:[142] in the cases relating to armed conflict situations, the Court had to deal with the unacknowledged detention of missing persons[143] or with the detention of civilians on grounds other than their direct participation in hostilities. The lawfulness of the detention of civilians having taken a direct part in hostilities is a relevant question in respect of both international and non-international armed conflicts, but one to which the answer is not clear-cut in IHL itself. As was pointed out above, in case of doubt as to whether or not persons having fallen into the power of the enemy after committing 'a belligerent act' are entitled to the status of POWs, such persons are to be treated as POWs 'until such time as their status has been determined by a competent tribunal',[144] but this requirement exclusively applies to international armed conflicts: more generally, the provisions relating to POWs do not apply to non-international armed conflicts, unless the law applicable to international armed conflicts is brought into force 'by means of special agreements' between the parties to such conflicts.[145] Assuming that the interested persons are not entitled to the status of POW, there is no doubt that, since they did not participate directly in hostilities as a matter of 'right', they can be charged with a criminal offence for the mere fact of such direct participation; on the other hand, the possibility to 'intern' them until the end of active hostilities for the mere fact that they have taken a direct part in hostilities is not as immediately evident as in the case of POWs.[146]

---

[140] Ibid, paras 309–312 and 524–531.

[141] Ibid, Dissenting Opinion by Mr G Sperduti Joined by Mr S Trechsel on Article 15 of the Convention, para 7.

[142] According to one view, civilians taking a direct part in hostilities constitute an intermediate category between combatants and civilians: as such, they are often labelled as 'unlawful combatants' or as 'unprivileged combatants'. Under existing IHL treaties, such a third category does not exist, but the issue ultimately relates to definition: the real question under IHL is what is the legal status of the members of the armed forces of a non-state entity party to an armed conflict and, more generally, of civilians taking a direct part in hostilities, as opposed to that of other civilians.

[143] See some of the cases referred to *supra*, notes 122, 123, and 124.

[144] See Art 5 1949 of *GC III*.   [145] See Art 3 of 1949 *GC III*.

[146] It is a well-known fact that the theory whereby 'unlawful combatants', just as POWs, can be detained by the capturing state until the end of hostilities irrespective of whether or not they are charged with any criminal offence was put forward by the government of the United States in the so-called 'war on terror', which is allegedly an international armed conflict exclusively governed by international customary law. See esp *Reply of the Government of the United States of America to the*

The 1949 *GC IV does* allow for the administrative 'internment' of enemy civilians, if the security of the detaining state makes it absolutely necessary, but then specifies that interned persons have the right to have such action reconsidered by a competent court or administrative body designated by the detaining state, and that any decision confirming 'internment' has to be periodically reviewed.[147] These provisions, which were recently found to constitute international customary law by the Israeli Supreme Court,[148] are all the more important since, unless a civilian is caught in the act, the fact of direct participation in hostilities is often disputed; moreover, although the same provisions appear to justify the 'internment' of civilians on the basis of mere membership of an organization of 'insurgents' or 'terrorists', even irrespective of direct participation in hostilities, the Israeli Supreme Court itself pointed out that such membership may not be as easy to prove as membership of a state's armed forces.[149] In light of these considerations, there can be no doubt that the provisions of 1977 Geneva Protocol I represent an important development bringing IHL more in line with IHRL as far as the detention of civilians, including those having taken a direct part in hostilities, is concerned. In particular, Article 75(3) provides not only that 'any person arrested, detained or interned for actions related to the armed conflict' is to be promptly informed of the reasons why such measures were taken, but also that, unless they are charged with a criminal offence, such persons are to be 'released with the minimum delay possible and in any event as soon as the circumstances justifying the arrest, detention or internment have ceased to exist'.

On the other hand, the relevant provisions in both 1949 *GC IV* and 1977 Geneva Protocol I (*AP I*) exclusively apply to international armed conflicts: IHL treaty rules relating to non-international armed conflicts do not provide for specific guarantees against arbitrary detention, and merely contain certain fundamental rules relating to the humane treatment of persons *hors de combat*, including detained persons.[150] It could, therefore, be argued that IHRL should continue to apply in full in order to protect the right to liberty even during a non-international armed conflict, all the more so as far as Article 5 ECHR is concerned since the detention of civilians having taken a direct part in hostilities is not therein listed among the cases where the deprivation of liberty can be regarded as lawful. On the other hand, should a state resort to measures derogating from Article 5 ECHR on the basis that it is involved in a non-international armed conflict, it could be argued

---

Five UNCH Special Rapporteurs on Detainees in Guantánamo Bay, Cuba, dated 10 March 2006, in 45 ILM (2006), 742. This theory has apparently survived the US Supreme Court decision in *Boumediene v Bush*, 128 SCt 2229 (12 June 2008), affirming *habeas corpus* for Guantánamo Bay detainees: see Crook (ed), 'Contemporary Practice of the United States Relating to International Law', 102 *AJIL* (2008), 860, at 863 *et seq* and 873 *et seq.*

[147] See Arts 42–43 and 78 of 1949 *GC IV*. Art 147 of 1949 *GC IV* lists the 'unlawful confinement' of civilians among the 'grave breaches' of the Convention.

[148] *A & B v The State of Israel*, Supreme Court of Israel sitting as the Court of Criminal Appeals (2008), available at <http://elyon1.court.gov.il/files_eng/06/590/066/n04/06066590.n044.pdf> [last accessed 24 March 2010].

[149] Ibid, paras 21 and 22 *et seq*. The issue of direct participation had been more thoroughly analysed by the Court in the earlier 'targeted killings' decision, which was referred to *supra*, in B.1.

[150] See Art 3 common to the 1949 Geneva Conventions and Arts 4 and 5 of 1977 *AP II*.

that, at least under customary IHL, certain fundamental guarantees against the arbitrary detention of civilians, including members of an insurgent or 'terrorist' organization and all other civilians having taken a direct part in hostilities, should still be respected. Whether these guarantees correspond to those provided for in the 1949 *GC IV* or in the 1977 *AP I* may still be a controversial issue, but there can be no doubt that, should the European Court of Human Rights decide to abandon its 'ivory tower' attitude vis-à-vis IHL, it could make a substantial contribution towards the definitive consolidation of the provisions of Article 75(3) of 1977 *AP I* as customary rules applicable to all cases of armed conflict.

D. The protection of property and of private and family life during armed conflict

Some of the cases examined by the European Court of Human rights related to the protection of property, often in connection with the protection of private and family life. Under Article 1(1) of 1952 Protocol No 1 to the ECHR, every person is entitled to 'the peaceful enjoyment of his possessions', and deprivation of such possessions can only be effected 'in the public interest and subject to conditions provided for by law and by the general principles of international law'. Under Article 8 ECHR, 'everyone has the right to respect for his private and family life, his home and his correspondence', and interference with this right on the part of a public authority is only allowed if 'in accordance with the law' and if 'necessary in a democratic society in the interests of national security, public safety or the economic well-being of the country, for the prevention of disorder or crime, for the protection of health or morals, or for the protection of the rights and freedoms of others'.

In times of armed conflict, private property is often destroyed or damaged, and people are often obliged to leave their home. However, it is arguable that in situations different from actual combat operations, and especially in situations of military occupation of foreign territory, the application of IHL would not entail substantial derogations from IHRL, since pillage, the destruction of property, unless it is 'rendered absolutely necessary by military operations', and the confiscation of private property are prohibited;[151] family honour and rights must be respected also, and both the forcible transfer and the deportation of civilians, as opposed to the temporary evacuation of a given area when 'the security of the population or imperative military reasons so demand', are prohibited.[152]

---

[151] See Arts 33 and 53 of 1949 *GC IV* and Art 46 of the Regulations annexed to the 1907 *Hague IV*. There is a tendency to apply similar provisions, at least in respect of the destruction of private property, not only where a territory is effectively occupied, but also during an invasion of foreign territory which may or may not precede its effective occupation: see eg *Partial Award, Central Front, Eritrea's Claims 2, 4, 6, 7, 8 & 22*, Eritrea Ethiopia Claims Commission (2004), available at <http://www.pca-cpa.org/upload/files/Eritrea%20Central%20Front%20award.pdf>, paras 26–27. See also my comments in Gioia, 'The Belligerent Occupation of Territory', in de Guttry, Post, and Venturini (eds), *The 1998–2000 War Between Eritrea and Ethiopia. An International Legal Perspective* (2009) 351.

[152] See Art 49 of 1949 *GC IV*.

The cases relating to northern Cyprus are especially relevant for the law applicable in occupied territory. In the first such case, the European Commission of Human Rights had found that violations of both Article 8 ECHR and Article 1 of Protocol No 1 had occurred as a result, on the one hand, of the expulsion of Greek Cypriots from their homes and their transfer elsewhere and, on the other, of looting and robbery and, more generally, of the deprivation of Greek Cypriots' possessions on a large scale.[153] Although the majority of the Commissioners made no reference to IHL, at least one Commissioner pointed out that there existed specific rules of IHL designed to apply to such actions and which would probably have led to the same result.[154] As for the Court itself, no express reference was made to IHL in the relevant decisions, and indeed in some cases it was found that violations of IHRL had occurred where no specific IHL rule had been violated: for example, in the famous case of *Loizidou v Turkey* a violation of Article 1 of Protocol No 1 was found because the applicant had been consistently refused access to her property in northern Cyprus and this amounted to an unjustified interference with the peaceful enjoyment of her possessions.[155] In this respect, I agree that the relevant IHL rules on forcible transfers were not applicable, since Mrs Loizidou was already in southern Cyprus, and the majority of the other interested Greek Cypriots had fled there, when the Turkish invasion of northern Cyprus took place, and IHL does not grant a specific right to return to occupied territory.[156] On the other hand, the granting of such a right would not be incompatible with IHL, and the persistent interference with the peaceful enjoyment of private property might well be seen to amount to a *de facto* confiscation.[157]

When it comes to actual combat operations, however, the picture changes: the application of IHL as *lex specialis* would entail that attacks are lawful if directed at military objectives, ie 'those objects which by their nature, location, purpose or use make an effective contribution to military action and whose total or partial destruction, capture or neutralization, in the circumstances ruling at the time, offers a definite military advantage';[158] in addition, the prohibition of 'indis-

---

[153] See *Cyprus v Turkey*, App Nos 6780/74 and 6950/75, EComHR (1976) paras 208–211 and 486.

[154] Ibid, Dissenting Opinion by Mr G Sperduti Joined by Mr S Trechsel on Article 15 of the Convention. See also *Cyprus v Turkey*, App No 8007/77, EComHR (1983), Separate Opinion by Mr G Tenekides.

[155] See *Loizidou v Turkey* (Merits), App No 15318/89, ECtHR Chamber (1996) paras 58–64. This finding was later confirmed in *Cyprus v Turkey*, App No 25781/94, ECtHR Grand Chamber (2001) paras 178–189. See also *Xenides-Arestis v Turkey*, App No 46347/99, ECtHR Chamber (2005).

[156] See Sassòli, *supra* note 4, at 716. The contrary view had been taken by: Heintze, *supra* note 2, at 808.

[157] Indeed, the property of people who had fled northern Cyprus as a result of the Turkish invasion *had* been expropriated by the local de facto government whose actions were found by the Court to be attributable to Turkey, but such expropriation was found to be invalid.

[158] See Art 52 of 1977 *AP I*, which defines 'civilian objects' *a contrario*, as 'objects which are not military objectives'. Specific rules in the 1949 Geneva Conventions and in 1977 *AP I* relate to the protection of medical units, establishments, buildings, materials, and means of transport. Moreover, specific rules of Protocol I are devoted to the protection of cultural objects and places of worship (Art 53), of objects indispensable for the survival of the civilian population (Art 54), of the natural environment (Art 55), and of works and installations containing dangerous forces' (Art 56). As far as

criminate attacks' entails that not only the civilian population but also civilian objects may suffer 'incidental damage' from an attack directed at a military objective, provided that such damage is not 'excessive in relation to the concrete and direct military advantage anticipated'.[159] On the other hand, in the conduct of military operations precautionary measures are needed in order to make sure that, just as the civilian population, civilian objects are spared as much as possible.[160] The European Court of Human Rights never had to deal with the destruction of property as a result of combat operations during an international armed conflict: the relevant cases relate to internal situations where the existence of an armed conflict was disputed and where, as was pointed out above, the distinction between real combat situations and law-enforcement operations, albeit difficult, should still be made. Moreover, the IHL rules applicable to non-international armed conflicts are not as clear as those briefly outlined above, at least as a matter of treaty law: only the specific prohibition on the displacement of the civilian population, 'unless the security of the civilians involved or imperative military reasons so demand', was extended to non-international armed conflicts by the 1977 Protocol II additional to the 1949 Geneva Conventions.[161] It is, therefore, understandable that the Court never felt it necessary to refer to IHL when assessing violations of Article I of Protocol No 1 to the ECHR or of Article 8 ECHR.

In a number of cases relating to anti-terrorist operations in south-eastern Anatolia, the Court found that the deliberate destruction of property, and the consequent eviction of the applicants from their homes, on the part of Turkish security forces violated both Article 1 of Protocol No 1 and Article 8 ECHR[162] and, in one such case, that it even amounted to inhuman and degrading treatment under Article 3 ECHR because of the manner in which the applicants' homes were destroyed and their personal circumstances: in this latter respect, the Court recalled the non-derogable character of Article 3 and pointed out that, 'even if it were the case that the acts in question were carried out without any intention of punishing the applicants, but instead to prevent their homes being used by terrorists or as a discouragement to others, this would not provide a justification for the ill-treatment'.[163] Even if no reference was made by the Court to IHL, there can be little doubt that the application of IHL would not have led to substantially different results, at least in so far as the displacement of the civilian population is concerned: as for the deliberate destruction of property, it could be argued that, even if 1977

---

cultural property is concerned, mention must also be made of the specific 1954 Hague Convention and of its two Additional Protocols.

[159] See Art 51 of 1977 *AP I*.   [160] See Art 57 of 1977 *AP I*.

[161] See Art 17 of 1977 *AP II*. The only exceptions relate to objects indispensable to the survival of the civilian population (Art 14), works and installations containing dangerous forces (Art 15), and cultural objects and places of worship (Art 16).

[162] See *Akdivar and Others v Turkey*, Case No 99/1995/605/693, ECtHR Grand Chamber (1996) para 88; *Menteş and Others v Turkey*, Case No 58/1996/677/867, ECtHR Grand Chamber (1997) paras 70–73; *Selçuk and Asker v Turkey*, Case No 12/1997/796-998-999, ECtHR Chamber (1998) paras 86–87.

[163] See *Selçuk and Asker v Turkey*, Case No 12/1997/796-998-999, ECtHR Chamber (1998) paras 72–79.

Geneva Protocol II exclusively deals with the protection of the civilian population and does not explicitly refer to the protection of civilian objects as such,[164] the IHL rules applicable to international armed conflicts should equally apply, as customary rules, to non-international armed conflicts and that, indeed, the Court's case-law is an important contribution towards the definitive consolidation of such rules. Moreover, insofar as the destruction of property can be considered as amounting to inhuman and degrading treatment, such treatment is prohibited by Article 3 common to the 1949 Geneva Conventions.

On the other hand, in a more recent case where the Court was undoubtedly faced with a combat situation, ie an operation designed to search for members of PKK in the course of which the decision by Turkish security forces to respond to shots coming from a nearby village resulted in intensive firing, the Court found that Turkey was responsible under Article 8 ECHR for the burning of civilian homes even if it was unable to make any definitive findings 'as to which houses caught fire as a result of firing and which as a result of deliberate acts of the security forces'.[165] It has been pointed out in the legal literature[166] that, at least as far as the unintentional damage caused by intensive firing was concerned, IHL would have been violated only if such 'incidental damage' could be considered as 'excessive in relation to the concrete and direct military advantage anticipated' by the decision to respond to the shots, or if the necessary precautionary measures had not been taken. The Court exclusively dealt with these aspects in connection with the right to life,[167] but the IHL rules relating to combat operations are substantially the same in so far as the protection of both the civilian population and civilian objects are concerned. In this respect, even if it still made no reference to IHL, the Court showed a more coherent attitude in one of the cases relating to Chechnya, where the destruction of private property resulting from an attack which violated Article 2 ECHR was found to violate Article 1 of Protocol No 1.[168]

4. Conclusions

It is by now a well-established fact that IHRL treaties, including the ECHR, continue to apply in times of armed conflict, in so far as the victims thereof can be considered to be within the 'jurisdiction' of the states party to such treaties: with specific reference to the ECHR, the case-law of the European Court of Human Rights confirms that the Convention applies to a state party's conduct taking place not only in its own territory, but also in foreign territory under its effective control, such as territory subject to belligerent occupation; moreover, it can be argued

---

[164] See Part IV of 1977 *AP II*.

[165] *Ahmet Özkan and Others v Turkey*, App No 21689/93, ECtHR Chamber (2004) paras 150 and 404–408. [166] See Sassòli, *supra* note 4, at 720.

[167] See *Ahmet Özkan and Others v Turkey*, App No 21689/93, ECtHR Chamber (2004) paras 297 and 305–306.

[168] See *Isayeva, Yusupova, and Bazayeva v Russia*, App Nos 57947/00, 57948/00, and 57949/00, ECtHR Chamber (2005) paras 230–234.

that the ECHR applies also to a state party's conduct within its military camps or detention facilities abroad. On the other hand, the application of the ECHR to naval or aerial bombardment of foreign territory or to combat operations in the field appears to be more problematic, and it would probably be unrealistic to expect major developments in this direction. Moreover, the ECHR being a regional treaty, there is still room in the Court's case-law for excluding its application to a state party's conduct outside the Convention's 'legal space', ie within territory belonging to a state not party thereto, even if some recent cases might be interpreted as implicating a change of attitude on the part of the Court in this respect. Finally, a worrying development is the Court's readiness to exclude its jurisdiction *ratione personae* whenever a state party's conduct takes place in the framework of a multinational operation created by the United Nations Organization or operating under its authority.

The fact that IHRL treaties, including the ECHR, apply alongside with IHL, albeit with some differences regarding their respective fields of application *ratione loci*, should be seen as a positive development in the international law regulating armed conflict, at least from the perspective of war victims. In fact, IHL tends to emphasize individual criminal responsibility rather that state liability for damage caused by violations: although states are in principle obliged to compensate all damage caused by violations of IHL, the practical implementation of this obligation is still left to traditional inter-state mechanisms and is, therefore, often lacking and/or does not entail a right of action on the part of the interested individual.[169] The possibility for a person who suffered damage as a result of an act of war to apply to the European Court of Human Rights, or other competent IHRL bodies, in order to obtain 'just satisfaction'[170] from a state found in violation of IHRL is thus an important added value of contemporary international law.

At the same time, the relationship between IHRL and IHL must be clarified, especially if violations of both branches of international law are to be prevented as far as possible: states, through their military or other organs more directly involved in the conduct of hostilities in times of armed conflict, should at least have a coherent idea of their obligations under the applicable rules of international law. In this respect, the characterization of IHL as *lex specialis* vis-à-vis IHRL made by the ICJ appears to serve an important objective, inasmuch as it entails that, whenever an actual conflict of international obligations arises, IHL obligations should prevail as

---

[169] For example, the Eritrea-Ethiopia Claims Commission, established by Eritrea and Ethiopia in 2000 in order to decide through binding arbitration all claims for loss, damage, or injury that were related to the 1998–2000 armed conflict between the two states and resulted from violations of IHL or other violations of international law, could only examine claims submitted by each of the two states, both on its own behalf and on behalf of its nationals: see Art 5 of the Algiers Agreement of 12 December 2000, available at <http://www.pca-cpa.org/upload/files/Algiers%20Agreement.pdf> [last accessed 24 March 2010]. Even the UN Compensation Commission, which was established by the UN Security Council in 1991 under Chapter VII of the UN Charter in order to decide claims for compensation of damage caused by Iraq's invasion and occupation of Kuwait, could, as a rule, hear claims submitted by states both on their own behalf and on behalf of their nationals, and could only hear claims directly submitted by private juridical persons (not natural persons!) on an exceptional basis: see SC Res 687 (1991) Part E, SC Res 692 (1991) para 3, and Art 19 of Decision No 1, of 2 August 1991, of the Commission's Governing Council.   [170] See Art 41 ECHR.

a matter of principle. In practice, however, such conflicts are unlikely to arise and in most cases the function of IHL is rather to allow for the application of IHRL in a manner that takes into account the existence of an armed conflict (and, of course, vice versa). At the same time, as even the ICJ recognized, each of the two branches of international law can fill the lacunae present in the other: especially as regards the regulation of non-international armed conflict, IHRL treaties have an important role to play, given the unsatisfactory state of the applicable rules of IHL.

As far as the ECHR is concerned, there is no insurmountable legal obstacle to the application of IHL by the European Court of Human Rights. On the one hand, there are situations where the ECHR itself allows for a direct application of IHL: when a state resorts to Article 15 ECHR in order to justify measures derogating from its obligations under the Convention on the basis that it is involved in 'war or other public emergency', these measures must be consistent with that state's 'other obligations under international law', and the Court is therefore allowed (and, indeed, obliged) to apply IHL if it determines that the situation, whether the interested state admits it or not, amounts to an armed conflict. But even where Article 15 is not invoked and the ECHR applies in full, the general rules on treaty interpretation allow the Court to take IHL into account when interpreting and applying the provisions of the Convention. In theory, therefore, the European Court of Human Rights could play an important role not only in monitoring compliance with IHL, but also in clarifying the relationship between IHL and the IHRL and thus contributing to the convergence of the two bodies of law towards a more coherent legal regulation of the conduct of states during armed conflict.

It is, therefore, regrettable that the Court has so far largely ignored IHL when deciding cases where the interested state was clearly involved in an armed conflict. Commentators have attempted various explanations and justifications for this 'ivory tower' attitude on the part of the Court. In my opinion, the principal reason why the Court has never directly applied IHL is that no state has so far relied on Article 15 ECHR in order to justify derogations from the Convention on the basis that it was involved in an armed conflict: there have been cases where Article 15 was invoked in situations which the Court itself might have considered to amount to an armed conflict, but it is perhaps understandable that the Court may wish to avoid contradicting a different legal qualification made by the interested state. As for the Court's reluctance to take IHL into account when applying the relevant rules of the ECHR, I tried to point out that these rules, such as Article 2 relating to the right to life or Article 5 relating to the right to liberty, are not as immediately open to the application of IHL as the corresponding provisions in the CCPR which the ICJ had in mind when it characterized IHL as *lex specialis*, since they do not prohibit the 'arbitrary' deprivation of life or liberty and rather give an exhaustive list of cases where such deprivation can be considered as lawful. But the Court did refer to IHL in at least one case relating to Turkey's occupation of northern Cyprus, where no declaration had been made under Article 15 ECHR. In my opinion, therefore, the Court's reluctance to refer to IHL in other cases can further be explained by the fact that all of these cases related to situations of non-international armed conflict, ie situations where the state of IHL itself is uncertain both as regards the threshold triggering its application and in respect of the applicable rules. On the other hand, there is a large body of legal opinion, often substantiated by the case-law of the international criminal tribunals, whereby the majority of the rules codified in 1977 Geneva Protocol I correspond to customary rules applicable to both international and non-international armed conflicts and it is regrettable that the Court's 'ivory tower' attitude has so far prevented it from making a contribution in this respect.

At the same time, it must be recognized that, except perhaps in one case relating to the right to a fair trial in occupied territory,[171] the Court has so far never squarely contradicted IHL in its case-law. On the contrary, the Court has in some respects contributed to a better legal regulation of armed conflict, both international and non-international, as is demonstrated by the fact that its case-law is sometimes relied upon by national courts when filling perceived lacunae in IHL, as did the Israeli Supreme Court when it required 'careful verification' before a civilian is attacked on the ground that he or she directly participated in hostilities, as well as a thorough and independent investigation after the attack regarding the circumstances thereof and the precision of the identification of the target. The Court's case law relating to the right to life and to the protection of property is only convincing because it has so far never squarely contradicted the IHL rules on the targeting of combatants and of military objectives, just as its case-law relating to the right to liberty has never contradicted the IHL rules on the internment of POWs. Indeed, the language used in some of the most important cases might be seen as confirming that the Court *is* aware of the relevant rules of IHL and is unwilling to contradict them, even if it is not prepared to expressly refer to them in situations of non-international armed conflict, especially where no declaration was made under Article 15 ECHR.

On the other hand, the danger inherent in the Court's 'ivory tower' attitude is that some of the principles enunciated in its case-law might in the future lead to decisions contradicting IHL. It was pointed out above that some commentators already interpret the Court's case-law relating to the right to life as being 'at odds' with IHL and, indeed, hail this as the beginning of a 'new approach' whereby combat operations will be treated in the same way as law-enforcement operations. This attitude is often based on the perception that the protection provided to individuals

---

[171] In a case relating to northern Cyprus, the Court found that Turkey had violated Art 6 ECHR because the authorities of the 'Turkish Republic of Northern Cyprus', whose actions were found by the Court to be attributable to Turkey, operated a system of military courts which had jurisdiction to try cases against civilians in respect of matters categorised as military offences: see *Cyprus v Turkey*, App No 25781/94, ECtHR Grand Chamber (2001) paras 354–359. As was pointed out by Sassòli, *supra* note 4, at 717–718, IHL actually requires an occupying power to hand over persons accused of a breach of the penal provisions promulgated by it to its 'properly constituted, non-political military courts, on condition that the said courts sit in the occupied territory' (Art 66 of 1949 *GC IV*); more generally, the author rightly pointed out that the law of belligerent occupation exclusively authorizes an occupying power to constitute military courts in occupied territory because the creation of civilian courts would be tantamount to an illegal annexation of such territory. On the other hand, the author also pointed out that, inasmuch as the military courts of the *de facto* government of northern Cyprus were not, strictly speaking, those of the occupying power, Turkey could have been found in violation of IHL as well.

by IHL is less than that afforded under IHRL. In my opinion, however, this perception is largely mistaken, just as the view that IHRL should apply in times of armed conflict in exactly the same way as it applies in times of peace and without any adaptations is unrealistic and thus, ultimately, dangerous: IHRL extremists tend to forget that international law is the product of a society where sovereign states still play the leading role.

7

Cultural Heritage in Human Rights and Humanitarian Law

Ana Filipa Vrdoljak*

1. Introduction

The public outcry in response to the looting of the Baghdad Museum following the 2003 invasion of Iraq and the bombardment of the historic city of Dubrovnik in 1991 are contemporary examples of international condemnation of attacks upon cultural heritage during armed conflict and belligerent occupation. This international concern has manifested itself since the earliest codification of the laws of war which provided cultural heritage with a protection regime distinct from other civilian property, and stated categorically that violations shall be subject to legal sanctions. These general international humanitarian law instruments are augmented by a specialist multi-lateral framework which governs the protection of the cultural heritage in preparation for armed conflict, during armed conflict, and belligerent occupation. International humanitarian law was the first specialist field within international law to afford cultural heritage such exceptionalism. The rationale underlining this protection—its importance to all humanity—has evolved and spread beyond armed conflict and belligerent occupation.

The exceptionalism originally afforded cultural heritage in international humanitarian law arose from its perceived significance to humanity through its advancement of the arts and sciences, and knowledge. By the mid-twentieth century, and the rise of human rights in international law, this rationale was recalibrated to emphasize its importance to the enjoyment of human rights and promotion of cultural diversity. This shift in rationale manifested itself most clearly in the articulation and prosecution of war crimes, crimes against humanity, and genocide. Cultural heritage and its protection were no longer based on its exclusivity but its intrinsic importance to people and individuals, to their identity, and

* I am grateful for the funding provided for this project by the European Commission's Marie Curie FP6 Action (No MIF1-CT-2006-021861) hosted by the Law Department, European University Institute, Fiesole, Italy.

their enjoyment of their human rights. It has become fundamental in establishing cases of violations of international humanitarian law and international criminal law, and assessing the claims of victims of gross violations of human rights. Furthermore, this shift in rationale has been reinforced with a broadening notion of cultural heritage in the late twentieth century. No longer confined to tangible heritage like monuments, sites, and works of art of exceptional importance to all humanity, cultural heritage encompasses the intangible and the ephemeral, like language, traditional knowledge, songs, dance, deemed significant by a group (not necessarily a state).

In examining the protection of cultural heritage in this chapter, I focus on this shifting rationale to highlight the ever-present interplay and interdependence between international humanitarian law and human rights law. First, I outline the exceptional treatment of cultural heritage in general international humanitarian law instruments including those covering non-international armed conflicts, and its overlap with international human rights law. Then, I detail how this protection has been built upon by the specialist regime for the protection of cultural heritage during armed conflict and belligerent occupation developed under the auspices of UNESCO. Next, I analyse international criminal law jurisprudence from the International Military Tribunal, Nuremberg to the International Criminal Court for the former Yugoslavia, to show how efforts to prosecute violations of the laws and customs of war relating to cultural heritage have been intrinsic to the articulation and prosecution of crimes against humanity and genocide. Finally, I consider the evolving and potential future normative trends in this field in the light of recent developments with reference to obligations *erga omnes*, intentional destruction and the content of the obligation, and intangible heritage and cultural diversity.

2. International Humanitarian Law (IHL) and Cultural Heritage

From the 19th-century codification efforts to humanize the laws of war, international humanitarian law has bestowed singular treatment upon cultural heritage. It has afforded it protection over and above other civilian property and pronounced explicitly that violations of such obligations should be subject to legal sanctions. While these protective and punitive strands would be elaborated by international cultural heritage law and international criminal law, which I examine in Parts 3 and 4 respectively below, this basic feature remains intact in contemporary international humanitarian law.

As the reach of international humanitarian law was extended to non-international conflicts with the emergence of human rights in international law, the provisions relating to cultural heritage were likewise extended. This development together with the recalibration of other international humanitarian law and human rights provisions has reinforced the interdependence of the protection of cultural heritage (tangible and intangible) and the effective enjoyment of human rights by individuals and groups.

A. Early developments

Philosophers and scholars since antiquity have condemned attacks on sacred places and ceremonial objects.[1] This prohibition traversed cultures and religious traditions.[2] While Hugo Grotius wrote in 1625 that: 'the law of nations in itself [did] not exempt things that are sacred, that is, things dedicated to God or to the gods... in a public war anyone at all becomes owner, without limit or restriction, of what he has taken from the enemy'.[3] The practice of states from the Treaty of Westphalia of 1648 onwards evidenced peace treaties which implicitly condemned pillage by sanctioning the return of plunder.[4] With the rise of humanism during this period, the rationale of exceptionalism was gradually secularized with historic monuments and sites, and works of art and science protected because of their aesthetic beauty and scientific significance and not simply their religious importance.[5]

Writing during the Enlightenment, Emer de Vattel argued that certain buildings, sites, and objects 'of remarkable beauty' which were 'an honour to the human race and which do not add to the strength of the enemy' should be spared. He asked: 'What is gained by destroying them? It is the act of a declared enemy of the human race thus wantonly to deprive men of these monuments of art and models of architecture.'[6] Working during the same period, Jean-Jacques Rousseau likewise maintained that private property of civilians and public property not serving a direct military purpose, like places of worship or education and libraries, collections, and laboratories should be quarantined from hostilities. He wrote: 'War... is not a relation between men, but between states; in war individuals are enemies wholly by chance, not as men, not even as citizens, but only as soldiers; not as members of their country, but only as its defenders.'[7] This rationale of protecting certain cultural heritage of importance to humanity because of its significance to the arts and sciences, and the distinction made between private and public property

---

[1]   See Gentili, *De Juris Belli Libri Tres,* trans Kelse, (1598, reprinted 1933), Book III, ch 6, at 313–314; De Visscher, 'International Protection of Works of Art and Historic Monuments', in Department of State Publication 3590, International Information and Cultural Series 8, reprinted in Documents and State Papers, June 1949, 821, at 823–825; Nahlik, 'Protection internationale des biens culturels en cas de conflit armé', 120 *Receuil des Cours* (1967-I) at 61; Toman, 'The Protection of Cultural Property in the Event of Armed Conflict: Commentary on the Convention for the Protection of Cultural Property in the Event of Armed Conflict and its Protocol', signed on 14 May 1954 in The Hague, and on other instruments of international law concerning such protection, (1996) at 3–7; and O'Keefe, *The Protection of Cultural Property in Armed Conflict* (2006) at 5–13.

[2]   Ndam Njoya, The African Concept, in UNESCO, *International Dimensions of Humanitarian Law* (1988) at 8; Adachi, The Asian Concept, ibid, at 16; and Sultan, The Islamic Concept, ibid, at 38.

[3]   Grotius, *De Jure Belli Ac Pacis* (The Law of War and Peace), (1625) Book III, ch 1, § 4.

[4]   Nahlik, *supra* note 1 at 77. In particular, the Congress of Vienna of 1815 following the defeat of Napoleon: Müntz, 'Les annexions de collections d'art ou de bibliothèques et leur rôle dans les relations internationals', 8 *Revue d'histoire diplomatique* (1895) 481, and 9 *Revue d'histoire diplomatique* (1895); Treue, *Art Plunder: The Fate of Art in War and Unrest,* trans Creighton (1961) at 186–199; and Vrdoljak, *International Law, Museums and the Return of Cultural Objects,* (2006) at 23–29.

[5]   Przyłuski, *Leges seu statuta ac privilegia Regni Poloniae* (1553) at 875 cited in Nahlik, *supra* note 1, at 73, and Toman, *supra* note 1, at 4; and Gentilis, *Dissertatio de eo quod in bello licet* (1690) at 21, cited in Nahlik, *supra* note 1, at 75.

[6]   de Vattel, *Le Droit des Gens, ou Principes de la Loi Naturelle, appliqués à la Conduite et aux Affaires des Nations et des Souverains,* (1758, reprinted 1916), Book 3, ch 9, §168. See also §173.

[7]   Rousseau, *The Social Contract,* (1762, reprinted 1968) at 56–57.

figured prominently in the nineteenth century efforts to humanize and codify the rules of war at the international level.

The perceived exceptional nature of certain cultural heritage compared to other property manifested itself from the first codification initiatives in the mid-nineteenth century. The Instructions for the Government of Armies of the United States in the Field prepared by Francis Lieber (Lieber Code), promulgated as General Order No 100 by President Abraham Lincoln in 1863 during the US Civil War made the distinction between private and public property.[8] Article 34 provided that 'as a general rule' the property of churches, hospitals, charitable organizations, places of education and learning, museums of fine arts or science were deemed to be private property. During hostilities, 'classical works of art, libraries, scientific collections of precious instruments, such as astronomical telescopes, as well as hospitals' were to be protected against 'all avoidable injury' even if located in fortified areas (Article 35). Yet, it also provided that if such property of the enemy could be removed 'without injury', the ruler of the conquering force could order its seizure with ownership to be settled by the subsequent peace treaty. However, Article 36 also stated that: '[i]n no case shall they be sold or given away, if captured by the armies of the United States, nor shall they ever be privately appropriated, or wantonly destroyed or injured'. This provision would find little support in later codification of international humanitarian law which strictly forbade pillage either during hostilities or belligerent occupation. In 1868, Johann Caspar Bluntschli noted that while custom at the start of the century did not support the protection of cultural heritage during armed conflict, popular opinion increasingly viewed it as vandalism of 'eternal monuments to the peaceful development of nations', with no direct benefit to the warring parties.[9]

Public outcry at the destruction of Strasbourg's cathedral and library during the Franco-Prussian War of 1870–71 precipitated in part the international conference instigated by Jean Henri Dunant, the founder of the International Committee of the Red Cross, in mid-1874.[10] It resulted in the International Regulations on the Laws and Customs of War (Brussels Declaration), which although it never came into force, prefigured many elements which characterize protection of cultural heritage in contemporary international humanitarian law.[11] It provided that during belligerent occupation the property of municipalities and 'institutions dedicated to religion, charity and education, the arts and sciences even when State property' were to be treated as private property. The destruction, damage, or seizure of these institutions, historic monuments, or works of art and science were to be prosecuted by competent authorities (Article 8). The more general

---

[8] Prepared by Francis Lieber and promulgated as General Order No 100 by President Lincoln, 24 April 1863, reproduced in Schindler and Toman (eds), *The Laws of Armed Conflict. A Collection of Conventions, Resolutions and Other Documents,* (4th revised and completed edition, 2004) at 3.

[9] Reprinted as Bluntschli, *Le droit international codifié* (1895) at 602.

[10] Rolin-Jaequemyns, 'Essai complémentaire sur la guerre franco-allemande dans ses rapports avec le droit international', 2 *Revue de droit international* (1871) 288, at 302.

[11] International Declaration concerning the Laws and Customs of War, 27 August 1874, not ratified, 1 (supp) *AJIL* (1907) at 96; and Schindler and Toman, *supra* note 8, at 21.

term—'religious' buildings—was used at the behest of the Turkish delegation.[12] During bombardment and sieges, a commander was required to take 'necessary steps ... to spare, as far as possible' buildings dedicated to art, science, charitable purposes, and hospitals and where the wounded were housed as long as it was not being used at the time for military purposes (Article 17). However, the besieged were obliged to indicate the presence of such buildings by 'distinctive and visible signs communicated to other combatants' beforehand. In contrast to the Lieber Code, it prohibited conquering troops pillaging towns that had fallen under their control (Article 18).

The Laws of War on Land (Oxford Manual) adopted by the *Institut de droit international* on 9 September 1880 deliberately reflected the provisions of the Brussels Declaration 'not [seeking] innovations [but] content[ing] itself with stating clearly and codifying the accepted ideas of our age so far as this has appeared allowable and practicable'.[13]

B. 1899 Hague II and 1907 Hague IV Conventions and Regulations

The first binding international obligations for the protection of cultural heritage related to the rules of war emerged from the series of international conferences held at The Hague in 1899 and 1907.[14] Convention (II) with Respect to the Laws and Customs of War on Land and Annex, adopted in 1899 (1899 Hague II Convention) and Convention (IV) respecting the Laws and Customs of War on Land, adopted in 1907 (1907 Hague IV Convention) are only applicable in respect of international armed conflict and if all belligerents are party to the treaty.[15] Nonetheless, the International Military Tribunal at Nuremberg found that by 1939, the regulations (Hague Regulations) annexed to these Conventions were 'recognized by all civilized nations and were regarded as being declaratory of the laws and customs of war'.[16] The International Court of Justice[17] and the International Criminal

---

[12] See Toman, *supra* note 1, at 9.

[13] Preface to Institut de droit international, 'Les lois de la guerre sur terre. Manuel publié par l'Institut de droit international', 5 *Annuaire de l'Institut de Droit International* (1881–82) 157; and Schindler and Toman, *supra* note 8, at 29, in particular see Arts 32, 34, and 53.

[14] See Huber, 'La propriété publique en cas de guerre sur terre', *Revue Générale de Droit International Public* (1913) at 657.

[15] Convention (II) with Respect to the Laws and Customs of War on Land and its annex: Regulations concerning the Laws and Customs of War on Land, 29 July 1899, in force 4 September 1900, 187 *Parry's CTS* (1898–99) 429, 1 (supp) *AJIL* (1907) 129; and Schindler and Toman, *supra* note 8, at 55; and Convention (IV) respecting the Laws and Customs of War on Land, and Annex, The Hague, 18 October 1907, in force 26 January 1910, 208 *Parry's CTS* (1907) 77, 2 (supp) *AJIL* (1908) 90; and Schindler and Toman, *supra* note 8, at 55. See also Convention (IX) concerning Bombardment by Naval Forces in Time of War, 18 October 1907, in force 26 January 1910, in Schindler and Toman, *supra* note 8, at 1087, in which Art 4 is equivalent to Art 27 of the 1907 Hague IV Regulations.

[16] *Trial of the Major War Criminals before the International Military Tribunal, Nuremberg, 14 November 1945–1 October 1946*, (42 vols, 1947–49), vol I, at 253–254; and 41 *AJIL* (1947) 172, at 248–249.

[17] *Legality of the Threat or Use of Nuclear Weapons*, Advisory Opinion, ICJ Reports (1996) 226, at 256; and *Legal Consequences of the Construction of the Wall in the Occupied Palestinian Territory*, Advisory Opinion, ICJ Reports (2004) 136, at 172.

Tribunal for the former Yugoslavia (ICTY) have recognized and reaffirmed that these obligations form part of customary international law, that is, they are binding even on non-states parties.[18]

The 1907 Hague IV Convention in its preamble makes reference to its predecessor, the 1899 Hague II Convention and the 1874 Brussels Declaration.[19] It also notes that until a 'more complete code of the laws of war' was agreed upon in those instances falling outside the Convention, civilians and combatants remained protected by international law principles 'result[ing] from the usages established between civilized peoples, from the laws of humanity, and the requirements of the public conscience'.[20] In addition to the general provisions relating to the protection of civilian property, the regulations contain specialist provisions covering cultural property during siege and bombardment (Article 27) and belligerent occupation (Article 56).

During hostilities, 'all necessary steps should be taken to spare, as far as possible, buildings dedicated to religion, art, science, or charitable purposes, historic monuments, hospitals, and places where the sick and wounded are collected' as long as they are not used for military purposes, marked with the distinctive sign, and notified to the enemy (Article 27). This provision covers immovable heritage, with movables only protected if housed within such buildings. The inclusion of the term 'historic monuments' was made at the request of the Greek delegation to align the *ratione materiae* more closely with Article 56.[21] Pillage is prohibited during hostilities and belligerent occupation (Articles 28 and 47).

During occupation, the 'property of the communes, that of religious, charitable, and educational institutions, and those of arts and science', even if public property, is accorded protection as private property with no proviso made for military necessity. Destruction, intentional damage, or seizure perpetrated against these institutions, historical monuments, works of art or science, is forbidden and violations are to be made subject to legal proceedings (Article 56). The more neutral term— 'religious' buildings—was deliberately used rather than 'churches'.[22] Charles de Visscher noted that this immunity covered not only immovable and movable property of these institutions but also their assets including funds and security.[23] He added that it was granted because these objects and sites were 'dedicated to an ideal purpose'.[24]

---

[18] *Prosecutor v Dario Kordić and Mario Čerkez*, Trial Judgment, Case No IT-95-14/2-T, ICTY (26 February 2001) at 359–362; and *Prosecutor v Miodrag Jokić*, Trial Judgment, Case No IT-01-42/1-S, Trial Chamber I, ICTY, (18 March 2004) at 48.

[19] Fourth preambular recital, 1907 Hague IV Convention, *supra* note 15. See also Russian Circular Note proposing program of the first conference dated 30 December 1989, reprinted in J Brown Scott, *The Hague Conventions and Declarations of 1899 and 1907 accompanied by Tables of Signatures, Ratifications, and Adhesions of the Various Powers and Texts of Reservations,* (3rd edn, 1918) at xviii.   [20] Eighth preambular recital, 1907 Hague IV Convention, ibid.

[21] De Visscher, *supra* note 1 at 837. See Nahlik, 'Protection of Cultural Property', in UNESCO, *supra* note 2, at 205; and Nahlik, *supra* note 1, at 93–94.

[22] Rolin, *Le droit moderne de la guerre* (1920) vol. 1, at 535–540.

[23] De Visscher, *supra* note 1, at 828 citing the report of Baron Rolin Jaequemyns which stated that this provision circumscribing the power of the occupant 'apply *a fortiori* to the invader during the period preceding the establishment of regular occupation' (footnote 26).   [24] Ibid.

Finally, the Hague Regulations requirement that the occupying power take all measures they are able to return public order and safety 'while respecting, unless absolutely prevented, the laws in force in the country' necessarily relates to legislation covering cultural heritage (Article 43).[25] The International Court of Justice has stated that this duty meant that an occupying power could be held responsible not only for its own acts and omissions but also for failing to prevent others on that territory violating human rights and international humanitarian law.[26] However, during hostilities, they would only be liable for the acts and omissions of their own forces.

C. 1923 Hague Air Rules

The Hague Regulations remain the essence of the protection afforded cultural property in international humanitarian law to date. However, the lacunae in this protection and lack of implementation during the First World War drew attention to the need for the regime to be strengthened.[27] There were various efforts on this front during the course of the conflict. A draft international convention was prepared by Ernst Zitelmann in the wake of a conference held between Austrian, German, and Swiss legal scholars in early 1915.[28] It proposed the establishment of an international administration in Bern to maintain lists of monuments protected during armed conflict and occupation, with protection only being granted following acknowledgment of such status by the belligerents.[29]

In 1918, the *Nederlandsche Oudheidkundige Bond* (Netherlands Archaeological Society or NOB) circulated a report which stated that damage to monuments and cultural objects impacted not only upon their owners and relevant states but also 'humanity as a whole'.[30] It recommended the establishment of demilitarized zones around monuments and sites of cultural significance, giving them 'international status' and placing an obligation on the host state to ensure that they were not used for a military purpose.[31] Under this proposal, an occupying power had to positively protect monuments and sites, and cooperate with the local authorities to these ends. Significantly, states would undertake preparation during peacetime for the protection of cultural property during war.[32] Like the German-Swiss initiative, it too recommended the establishment of an international office to oversee

---

[25] 1907 Hague IV Convention, *supra* note 15. Cf Art 43, 1899 Hague II Convention.

[26] *Case Concerning Armed Activities on the Territory of the Congo (Democratic Republic of Congo v Uganda),* No 116, 19 December 2005, at 60.

[27] Berlia, *Report on the International Protection of Cultural Property by Penal Measures in the Event of Armed Conflict,* 8 March 1950 UNESCO Doc 5C/PRG/6, Annex I, at 3–4.

[28] Jerusalem, 'Monuments of Art in War-Time and International Law', in Clemen (ed), Protection of Art During War and the German and Austrian Measures Taken for their Preservation, Rescue and Research (1919) 135, at 140.

[29] See Zitelmann, Der Kreig und die Denkmalpflege: Zeitschrift für Völkerrecht, X (1916) S I.

[30] 'Pays-bas. La protection des monuments et objets historiques et artistiques contre les destruction de la guerre. Proposition de la Société néerlandaise d'archéologie', 26 *Revue générale de droit international public* (1919) 329, at 331.

[31] See De Visscher, *supra* note 1, at 838; and Berlia, *supra* note 27, at 4.

[32] De Visscher, *supra* note 1, at 839; and *supra* note 27, at 4.

compliance and oversight by neutrals. However, it made no conclusions regarding criminal prosecution for violations by national or international courts.[33] De Visscher observed that although these recommendations were not taken up immediately they had a significant influence on the work of the Commission of Jurists who prepared the subsequent Hague Rules Concerning the Control of Radio in Time of War and Air Warfare (Hague Rules).[34]

The Hague Rules drafted in 1923 for the first time provided for the delineation between general protection as contained in Article 27 of the 1907 Hague Regulations,[35] and special protection for monuments of greater historic importance.[36] This latter provision was the first detailed and specific legal regime for the protection of historic monuments during armed conflict.[37] This Italian initiative was prepared as a response to the aerial bombardment of Venice and Ravenna during the First World War and drew inspiration from the NOB report. It centred on two innovations: first, the creation of a 'neutralized zone' around 'important historical (and artistic) monuments' to make them immune from bombardment provided they were not used for military purposes, and a system of international inspection of such sites.[38] Also, the notion of military defence as a qualifier of such protection is replaced with the more restrictive military 'objective'.[39] Although the 1923 Hague Rules were not formally adopted they were accepted as broadly reflective of international law by the United Kingdom and Germany in the lead-up to the Second World War.[40]

D. 1949 Geneva Convention IV and Universal Declaration of Human Rights

The renewed efforts in the immediate post-Second World War period to further articulate rules for the protection of civilians during armed conflict and belligerent occupation led to the finalization of the various Geneva Conventions of 1949. Significantly, these international humanitarian law instruments, while reaffirming the protection of civilian property afforded in the 1899 and 1907 Hague Conventions, are silent on the protection of cultural property. However, the earlier Italian proposal of neutralized zones for the protection of cultural property was implemented in respect of protection of civilian populations in the Geneva

---

[33] De Visscher, *supra* note 1, at 835; O'Keefe, *supra* note 1, at 42–43.

[34] De Visscher, *supra* note 1, at 839; and 'Commission of Jurists to Consider and Report upon the Revision of the Rules of Warfare. General Report', 32 (supp) *AJIL* (1938) 1, at 23.

[35] Art 25 of the Hague Rules Concerning the Control of Radio in Time of War and Air Warfare, Adopted 19 February 1923, not in force, UK Misc No 14 (1924), Cmd 2201, 30 *Revue générale de droit international public* (1923) 1, and Schindler and Toman, *supra* note 8 at 315.

[36] Art 26, Hague Rules, ibid.

[37] De Visscher, *supra* note 1 at 839 and 841. See 'Commission of Jurists', *supra* note 34, at 23.

[38] 'Commission of Jurists', *supra* note 34, at 26–27; and De Visscher, *supra* note 1 at 842.

[39] Art 24, Hague Rules, *supra* note 35. While welcoming this change to the Hague Regulations, De Visscher was nonetheless scathing of the expansive interpretation given to military objective: *supra* note 1, at 839–840.   [40] O'Keefe, *supra* note 1, at 49.

framework.[41] The protection afforded to civilian property necessarily covers cultural heritage. Article 53 of the Geneva Convention relative to the Protection of Civilian Persons in Time of War (*GC IV*) prohibits 'destruction' of civilian real or personal property subject to the proviso of military necessity.[42] It is important to note that it only relates to destruction, thereby reaffirming that the occupying power may requisition or confiscate property for military purposes. However, pillaging is prohibited (Article 33).

In addition, provisions in *GC IV* which encompass human rights also facilitate the protection of cultural heritage. For example, Article 27 of *GC IV*, which reiterates Article 46 of the Hague Regulations, confirms that a protected person's honour, family rights, religious convictions and practices, and manners and customs shall be respected.[43] It is reaffirmed in the two Additional Protocols to Geneva Conventions finalized in 1977 with the deliberately broader wording: 'convictions and religious practices' used to encompass 'all philosophical and ethical practices'.[44] The ICRC commentary states that this respect of the person includes their physical and intellectual integrity.[45] Intellectual integrity is defined as 'all the moral values which form part of man's heritage, and appl[y] to the whole complex structure of convictions, conceptions and aspirations peculiar to each individual'.[46] The phrase 'respect for religious practices and convictions' covers 'religious observances, services and rites'.[47] This provision is augmented by Article 38(3) (hostile territory) and Article 58 (occupation) of *GC IV* concerning access to religious ministers, and books and other materials to facilitate the protected communities in their religious observances and practices.[48]

---

[41] 'Historical Note concerning the Draft Convention for the Protection of Cultural Property in the Event of Armed Conflict', UNESCO Doc CBC/7, at 5, at 11; and Committee of Governmental Experts Convened in Paris from 21 July to 14 August 1952 to Draw Up the Final Draft of an International Convention for the Protection of Cultural Property during Armed Conflict, Report of the Rapporteur, UNESCO Doc 7C/PRG/7, Annex I, at 5.

[42] 12 August 1949, in force 21 October 1950, 75 UNTS 287, and Schindler and Toman, *supra* note 8, at 575.

[43] Pictet, *Geneva Convention relative to the Protection of Civilian Persons in Time of War, Commentary* (1958) at 200; and Pilloup, 'La Déclaration universelle des Droits de l'Homme et les Conventions internationales protégeant les victimes de la guerre', *Revue internationale de la Croix-Rouge* (1949) at 252–258.

[44] Art 75 of Protocol Additional to the Geneva Conventions of 12 August 1949, and Relating to the Protection of Victims of International Armed Conflicts (*AP I*), 8 June 1977, in force 7 December 1978, 1125 UNTS 3, and Schindler and Toman, *supra* note 8, at 711; and Art 4(1) of Protocol Additional to the Geneva Conventions of 12 August 1949, and Relating to the Protection of Victims of Non-International Armed Conflicts (*AP II*), 8 June 1977, in force 7 December 1978, 1125 UNTS 609, and Schindler and Toman, *supra* note 8, at 775. See Sandoz *et al* (eds), *Commentary on the Additional Protocols of 8 June 1977 to the Geneva Conventions of 12 August 1949*, (1987) at 1370 and 5422: that this slight drafting modification was deliberate: see *Official Records of the Diplomatic Conference on the Reaffirmation and Development of International Humanitarian Law applicable in Armed Conflicts*, (1974–1977) OR, vol X, at 186–187, CDDH/405/Rev.1, at 35 and 36; OR vol XV, at 461, CDDH/407/Rev.1, at 43. The word 'religious' only qualifies 'practices', so that convictions including philosophical and political convictions, as well as religious ones, are also protected.

[45] Pictet, *supra* note 43, at 201.   [46] Ibid.   [47] Ibid, at 203.

[48] See Arts 15(5) concerning protection of civilian religious personnel and 69(1) of *AP I* which refers to 'other supplies essential to the survival of the civilian population of the occupied territory and objects necessary for religious worship'. The ICRC Commentary notes this is more broadly

These obligations in respect to religious practices are extended to prisoners of war under Article 18 of the Hague Regulations, and reiterated and extended to internees by the 1949 Geneva Conventions and Additional Protocols.[49] The ICRC commentary explains that it covers: 'those [practices] of a physical character, methods of preparing food, periods of fast or prayer, or the wearing of ritual adornment'.[50] In addition, Article 130 provides that internees when they die shall be 'honourably buried, if possible according to the rites of the religion to which they belonged . . .'.[51]

Article 27 of *GC IV* also refers to respect for the 'manners and customs' of protected persons which covers both individual and communal elements.[52] By way of explanation, the ICRC commentary notes: 'Everybody remembers the measures adopted in certain cases during the Second World War, which could with justice be described as "cultural genocide". The clause under discussion is intended to prevent a reversion to such practices.'[53] The overlap between genocide, international humanitarian law, and human rights is considered below in the light of ICTY jurisprudence.

The protection afforded children during armed conflict and belligerent occupation under international law extends to their cultural, and religious, heritage. During armed conflict, parties must take necessary measures to ensure that children under fifteen years that are orphaned or separated from their families, whether they are nationals or not, can exercise their religion and their education in 'a similar cultural tradition', where possible.[54] According to the ICRC, this provision is 'intended to exclude any religious or political propaganda designed to wean children from their natural milieu; for that would cause additional suffering to human beings already grievously stricken by the loss of their parents'.[55] The same obligations apply to neutral countries to which the children may be transferred.[56] During belligerent occupation, where local institutions are unable to do so, the occupying power must organize that persons of the same nationality, language, and religion as the child maintain and educate them, where the child is orphaned, separated from their parents, or cannot be adequately cared for by next of kin or friends (Article 50).[57] This provision, which is based on Article 18(2) of the International Covenant of Civil and Political Rights covering the right to freedom of thought, conscience, and religion and defined as a non-derogable right, was the subject of extended deliberation.[58] In respect of the equivalent provision in

defined than Art 58 of *GC IV* and the objects are not described because the civilian population itself determines what is of importance for their religious practices: Sandoz *et al, supra* note 44, at 812 and 2781.

[49] See Art 16 of the Geneva Convention relative to the Treatment of Prisoners of War, 27 July 1929, in force 19 June 1931, 118 LNTS 343; Arts 34–37 of Convention (III) relative to the Treatment of Prisoners of War, 12 August 1949, in force 21 October 1950, 75 UNTS 135. In respect of internees see Art 93, *GC IV*; and Art 5(1)(d), *AP II.*   [50] Pictet, *supra* note 43, at 406.
[51] Ibid, at 506. See also Art 76(3), 1929 Geneva Convention.   [52] Ibid.
[53] Ibid, at 204.   [54] Art 24, 1949 *GC IV.* See Pictet, *supra* note 43 at 186.   [55] Ibid.
[56] Ibid, at 188; and *Final Record of the Diplomatic Conference of Geneva of 1949*, (1963, 3 vols), vol II-A, at 638.   [57] *Final Record*, ibid, vol II-A, at 828.
[58] International Covenant on Civil and Political Rights, 16 December 1966, in force 23 March 1976, GA Res 2200A (XXI), 21 UN GAOR Supp (No 16) at 52, UN Doc A/6316 (1966), 999

AP II, it was noted that continuity of education is crucial to ensuring that children 'retain their cultural identity and a link with their roots' and it sought to prohibit practices where they were deliberately schooled in the cultural, religious, or moral practices of the occupying power.[59] As I explain below, this aim ties in with those raised during deliberations over the definition of genocide contained in the 1948 Genocide Convention.

Drafted, deliberated, and adopted by the international community at the same time as the Universal Declaration of Human Rights, it is not a coincidence that the 1949 Geneva Conventions have overlapping concerns with that instrument. There are several provisions contained within general human rights instruments which have been interpreted broadly to afford protection to cultural heritage during armed conflict and belligerent occupation. While some human rights treaties provide for derogation during 'states of emergency',[60] the UN General Assembly and the International Court of Justice have confirmed the continuing operation of certain non-derogable human rights norms during armed conflict.[61] In addition, in 2007 the Human Rights Council recognised the mutually reinforcing protection afforded cultural rights and cultural heritage by international humanitarian law and human rights.[62]

The equivalent human rights provisions to the international humanitarian law protections outlined above include: the right to privacy and family life;[63] the right to freedom of expression including receiving and imparting information and ideas;[64] the right to education and full development of human personality;[65] and the right to freedom of thought, conscience and religion and which was defined as a non-derogable right by the Human Rights Committee.[66] The Committee's

UNTS 171. See Sandoz *et al, supra* note 44, at 898–899; and OR vol III, at 300–301, CDDH/III/304, CDDH/III/324 and Corr 1 and CDDH/III/325; and General Comment No 22, Art 18 ICCPR, 30 July 1993. UN Doc CCPR/C/21/Rev.1/Add.4, at 1.

[59] Art 4(3) *AP II,* and Sandoz *et al, supra* note 44 at 1378 and 4552. See OR vol XV, at 79, CDDH/III/SR.46, at 11.

[60] Art 4 ICCPR; Art 27 of American Convention on Human Rights, 21 November 1969, in force 18 July 1978, OASTS No 36, 1144 UNTS 123; Art 15 of Convention for the Protection of Human Rights and Fundamental Freedoms (European Convention on Human Rights or ECHR), 4 November 1950, in force 3 September 1953, ETS 5, 213 UNTS 221. No derogation is permitted under the African Charter on Human and Peoples' Rights, 27 June 1981, in force 21 October 1986, OAU Doc CAB/LEG/67/3 rev 5, 1520 UNTS 217, but Art 27(2) which has been strictly interpreted by the African Commission on Human and Peoples' Rights.

[61] GA Res 2675 (XXV), 9 December 1970; and *Legality of Nuclear Weapons, supra* note 17, at 240; and *Wall in the Occupied Palestinian Territory, supra* note 17, at 173. See also Human Rights Committee, General Comment No 29, Art 4 ICCPR States of emergency, 31 August 2001, UN Doc CCPR/C/21/Rev.1/Add.11, at 3.

[62] HRC Res 6/1, 27 September 2007, Protection of cultural rights and property in situations of armed conflict, UN Doc A/HRC/RES/6/1.

[63] Art 12 of the Universal Declaration of Human Rights (UDHR), GA Res 217A(III), 10 December 1948; Art 17 ICCPR; and the European equivalent, Art 8 ECHR.

[64] Art 19 UDHR, Art 19(2) ICCPR, and Art 5 ECHR.

[65] Art 26(2) UDHR, Art 13(1) of International Covenant on Economic, Social and Cultural Rights (ICESCR), 16 December 1966, in force 3 January 1976, GA Res 2200A(XXI), 21 UN GAOR Supp (No 16), 49, and 993 UNTS 3, and Art 2 ECHR.

[66] Art 18 UDHR, Art 18(2) ICCPR, and Art 9 ECHR. See General Comment No 22, *supra* note 58, at 1.

General Comment No 22 defines right to freedom of thought, conscience, and religion broadly to encompass a holistic understanding of cultural heritage, including tangible (buildings of worship, ritual objects, distinctive clothing), intangible (language, rituals), and persons (religious leaders, teachers), and extends to include the freedom to establish schools, and produce and disseminate texts.[67]

This overlap between human rights and protection of cultural heritage during armed conflict and belligerent occupation is necessarily most pronounced in respect of those rights specifically related to culture, namely, the right to participated in cultural life,[68] and the so-called minority protection provision.[69] The International Court of Justice, the UN Committee on Economic, Social and Cultural Rights (CESCR), and the Human Rights Council have interpreted the application of the ICESCR generally (including the right to participate in cultural life) to extend to 'both territories over which a State party has sovereignty and to those over which that State exercises territorial jurisdiction'.[70] In respect of this obligation, states parties are required to report on:

the measures taken to protect cultural diversity, promote awareness of the cultural heritage of ethnic, religious or linguistic minorities and of indigenous communities, and create favourable conditions for them to preserve, develop, express and disseminate their identity, history, culture, language, traditions and customs.[71]

And:

[t]o ensure the protection of the moral and material interests of indigenous peoples relating to their cultural heritage and traditional knowledge.[72]

The latter reporting requirement reflects the protections contained in the UN Declaration on the Rights of Indigenous Peoples,[73] in particular Articles 11 (culture), 12 (religion), and 13 (language). However, explicit extension of the application of the 1949 Geneva Conventions to indigenous peoples contained in Article 11 of the 1993 draft Declaration was deleted from the final text of this instrument.[74]

Article 27 of the International Covenant on Civil and Political Rights covers cultural, religious, and language rights of minorities. The Human Rights Committee's General Comment No 23 states that this provision imposes positive obligations on states parties.[75] UN Special Rapporteur Francesco Capotorti also suggested that 'culture' must be interpreted broadly to include customs, morals, traditions, rituals, types of housing, eating habits, as well as the arts, music,

---

[67] Ibid, at 4.   [68] Art 27 UDHR, and Art 15 ICESCR.   [69] Art 27 ICCPR.

[70] *Wall in the Occupied Palestinian Territory, supra* note 17, at 180; UN Doc. E/C.12/1/Add 90; and HRC Res 6/19, 28 September 2007, Religious and cultural rights in the Occupied Palestinian Territory, including East Jerusalem, UN Doc A/HRC/RES/6/19.

[71] Guidelines on Treaty-Specific Documents to be Submitted by States Parties under Articles 16 and 17 of the International Covenant on Economic, Social and Cultural Rights, 13 January 2009, UN Doc E/C.12/2008/2 at 14, para 68.   [72] Ibid, at 71(c).

[73] GA Res 61/295, 13 September 2007, UN Doc A/RES/61/295.

[74] Draft UN Declaration on the Rights of Indigenous Peoples, approved by the Working Group on Indigenous Populations on 26 August 1994, UN Doc E/CN.4/Sub.2/1994/56, 34 ILM (1995) 541.

[75] General Comment No 23, UN Doc HRI/GEN/1/Rev.1, 38 (1994) at 6.1, 6.2, and 9.

cultural organizations, literature, and education.[76] The Committee has similarly endorsed a wide concept of culture including, for example, a particular way of life associated with the use of land resources, especially in relation to indigenous peoples.[77] The inter-war minority guarantees from which Article 27 traces its lineage, were part of the same tradition from which the articulation of the crimes against humanity of persecution and genocide in international criminal law emerged.

E. 1977 Additional Protocols I and II to the 1949 Geneva Conventions

The absence of specific reference to the protection of cultural heritage in the 1949 Geneva Conventions spurred the realization of the first specialist international humanitarian law instrument for the protection of cultural heritage: the 1954 Hague Convention. However, before moving to this specialist framework, it is important to acknowledge other developments in international humanitarian law in this field. Foremost among these, formal and explicit reaffirmation of the exclusivity of cultural heritage over and above other civilian property in binding international humanitarian law instruments for the first time since the 1907 Hague Regulations is contained in Additional Protocols I and II to the Geneva Conventions which were adopted in 1977 (*AP I* and *II*).[78] Furthermore, this protection was now afforded during non-international conflicts. Common Article 3 of the Geneva Conventions applies to armed conflict of 'non-international character occurring on the territory of one of the contracting parties'; while *AP II* refers to conflict between armed forces of High Contracting Parties and dissident armed forces or other organized armed groups which exercise control over part of territory (Article 1). The 1954 Hague Convention is likewise applicable to international and internal armed conflicts.[79]

AP I covering international armed conflicts defines general protection afforded civilian objects in Article 52. While there is a presumption of civilian use in respect of places of worship, schools, houses, and other dwellings, the ICRC commentary suggests that it is confined to physical objects and not intangible elements of civilian life.[80] However, as explained below, during the 1940s, the UN War Crimes Commission interpreted the equivalent provision contained in the Hague Regulations to cover intangible aspects of cultural heritage related to the use of such objects and sites.

Furthermore, *AP I* provides specific protection for cultural heritage. Article 53 is *lex specialis* in respect of historic monuments, works of art, and places of worship

---

[76] UN Doc E/CN.4/Sub.2/384/Rev.1 at 99–100.

[77] General Comment No 23, at 7, *supra* note 75.

[78] See OR, vol I, at 213, and CDDH/215/Rev.1, at 68–70, and OR vol XV, at 277–278. For summary of the negotiating history of Art 53, *AP I* and Art 16, *AP II*, see Toman, *supra* note 1, at 382–383.

[79] Art 19 of the Convention for the Protection of Cultural Property in the Event of Armed Conflict, 14 May 1954, in force 7 August 1956, 249 UNTS 240; and Schindler and Toman, *supra* note 8, at 999. which only refers to conflicts not of an international character: See Toman, *supra* note 1, at 386–387.

[80] See Sandoz *et al, supra* note 44, at 633–634; and Toman, *supra* note 1, at 384.

which 'constitute the cultural or spiritual heritage of peoples'. The same phase is used in Article 16 of *AP II* concerning non-international armed conflicts. There is some conjecture concerning their *ratione materiae*.[81] The provision relates to movable and immovable heritage, even if renovated or restored.[82] While Article 53 operates without prejudice to the obligations contained in 1954 Hague Convention and other relevant international treaties including the Hague Regulations,[83] it appears that the definition of cultural heritage covered by it is distinguishable from that covered by the 1954 Hague Convention. The ICRC commentary intimates that this phrase: 'the cultural *or* spiritual heritage of *peoples*', is deliberately distinguishable from 'of great importance to the cultural heritage of every people' contained in the preamble of the 1954 Hague Convention.[84] It suggests that the *ratione materiae* is broader in respect of the Additional Protocols for two reasons. First, the word 'peoples' was intended to 'transcend...national borders' and 'problems of intolerance which arise with respect of religions which do not belong to the country'.[85] However, the ICRC maintains that this provision only applies to 'a limited amount of very important cultural property, namely that which forms part of the cultural or spiritual heritage of "peoples" (i.e., mankind), while the scope of the Hague Convention is broader...'.[86] Second, the addition of the words 'or spiritual' encompasses 'the places referred to are those which have a quality of sanctity independently of their cultural value and express the conscience of the people'.[87] The ICRC study on customary international humanitarian law reaffirms this interpretation.[88] The ICRC position was referred to with approval by the ICTY Appeals Chamber in *Kordić and Čerkez*.[89] The Eriteria-Ethiopia Claims Commission likewise drew a distinction between Article 53 and the preamble of the 1954 Hague Convention, which they found to be broader.[90]

---

[81] Jiří Toman argues that the heritage protected by the Additional Protocols is broader because of the extension to include sites and objects of spiritual importance: *supra* note 1, at 388. Cf Roger O'Keefe, who considers it no more than a shorthand form of the definition contained in the 1954 Hague Convention: *supra* note 1, at 209.

[82] OR vol XV, at 277–278, CDDH/215/Rev.1, at 68–70.

[83] The Federal Republic of Germany, the United States, and Canada indicated that Art 53 did not displace existing customary international law encompassed in Art 27 1907 Hague IV Convention which covered various cultural and religious objects: OR vol VI, 224, 225, and 240. Resolution 20 adopted by the Diplomatic Conference at the same time as the Protocols urged states who had not yet done so to become party to the 1954 Hague Convention. Consequently, this was interpreted as intending not to alter the existing legal framework for the protection of cultural property during armed conflict: Sandoz *et al*, *supra* note 44, at 641, 2046.

[84] Sandoz *et al.*, *supra* note 44, at 646–647 and 1469–1470, 2063–2068, and 4844 (emphasis added).

[85] OR vol XV, at 220, CDDH/III/SR.59, at 68; and Sandoz *et al*, *supra* note 44, at 1469–1470, 4844.

[86] Henckaerts and Doswald-Beck, *Customary International Humanitarian Law*, (3 vols, 2005) vol 1, at 130.

[87] Ibid, at 646–647, 2063–2068. The 1954 Hague Convention also covers sites, monuments, and objects of religious importance: Art 1(1).

[88] Henckaerts and Doswald-Beck, *supra* note 86 at 130 and 132.

[89] *Prosecutor v Dario Kordić and Mario Čerkez*, Appeal Judgment, Case No IT-95-14/2, Appeals Chamber, ICTY (17 December 2004) at 91.

[90] Partial Award: Central Front. Eritrea's Claims 2, 4, 6, 7, 8, and 22, 43 ILM (2004) 1249, at 113.

Unlike the 1954 Hague framework, *AP I* provides immunity for cultural property without the military necessity proviso.[91] However, violation of the obligation not to use such objects and sites 'in support of the military effort' (Article 53(b)) may render it a military objective as defined under Article 52, to which the principle of proportionality is applicable.[92] Nonetheless, as under the 1954 Hague Convention, they cannot be the object of reprisals (Article 53(c)).

The inclusion of a simplified form of this cultural property provision in *AP II* covering non-international armed conflict was the subject of 'heated controversy'.[93] The primary concern of opponents was the perceived priority of other humanitarian concerns in such a condensed instrument.[94] Unlike *AP I*, this instrument, covering as it does acts within a state, makes a direct link between international humanitarian law and human rights in its preamble.[95] It was the first international humanitarian law instrument to use the phrase 'human rights'.[96] The protections afforded in *AP II* are viewed as encapsulating these core human rights which are viewed as non-derogable.[97] It is instructive then that the final text explicitly protects cultural heritage.

Contained in Part IV covering civilian populations, Article 16 provides a summarized version of the protection afforded in Article 53 of *AP I*. Its *ratione materiae* is identical. However, it is only made without prejudice to the operation of the 1954 Hague Convention, the only multilateral treaty in force (with the exception of the regional 1935 Washington Treaty) which would have overlapping jurisdiction in respect of non-international armed conflicts.[98] Like *AP I*, the immunity afforded makes no proviso for military necessity but this is removed when the object or site is 'used... in support of the military effort'. Therefore, like Article 53 of *AP I*, Article 16 prohibits the targeting of such cultural property and its use as a military objective.[99] Unlike its sister provision, Article 16 does not prohibit reprisals. But *AP II* does prohibit pillage (Article 4(2)(g)).

---

[91] Cf Art 27 Hague IV Convention referring to 'as far as possible'. If state is party to the 1954 Hague Convention and the Additional Protocol derogation under the specialist framework applies. However, if party to the Additional Protocols but not 1954 Hague Convention then no derogation permitted: Sandoz *et al, supra* note 44, at 647, 2071–2073.

[92] Sandoz *et al, supra* note 44, at 648, 2079; and Henckaerts and Doswald-Beck, *supra* note 86 at vol II, 779–790, §§282–354.

[93] OR, vol XV, at 107, CDDH/III/SR.49; and Sandoz *et al, supra* note 44, at 1466, 4828. Art 16 was adopted by 35 votes in favour, 15 against, and 32 abstentions: see OR vol VII, at 156–157, 162–163, CDDH/SR.53.   [94] OR vol VII, at 156–157, 162–163, CDDH/SR.53.

[95] First and second preambular recitals, *AP II*.

[96] Sandoz *et al, supra* note 44 at 1339, 4427. See *Conference of Government Experts on the Reaffirmation and Development of International Humanitarian Law Applicable in Armed Conflict, Geneva, 3 May–3 June 1972, (second session), Report on the work of the Conference* (2 vols with Annexes, 1972), vol I, at 120, 2.536–2.537 and 2.539. The fourth preambular recital of this Protocol extends the application of the Martens Clause to non-international armed conflicts.

[97] Sandoz *et al, supra* note 44 at 1340–1341, 4429–4430.

[98] Sandoz *et al, supra* note 44 at 1468, 4837: Referring to the failure to cite the 1970 UNESCO Convention and 1972 World Heritage Convention it states: 'These omissions have no material consequences on protection.' See also Toman, *supra* note 1, at 386.

[99] See Sandoz *et al, supra* note 44 at 1470, 4845.

The specific protection afforded cultural heritage in international humanitarian law from its earliest codification is reinforced by the concomitant explicit obligation to punish violations. Provisions covering cultural property during belligerent occupation in the 1874 Brussels Declaration and 1907 Hague Regulations specifically state that violations 'shall be made subject to legal proceedings'.[100] In respect of no other provision in these instruments is such an obligation explicitly laid down. The obligation is reaffirmed by Article 85 of *AP I* which provides for repression of grave breaches.[101] Grave breaches include attacking and causing extensive damage to 'clearly-recognized historic monuments, works of art or places of worship which constitute the cultural or spiritual heritage of peoples and to which special protection has been given by special arrangement, for example, within the framework of a competent international organization' which were not being used in support of military effort nor located in the immediate proximity of military objectives (Article 85(4)(d)). Special protection means not only that afforded under the 1954 Hague Convention, (and enhanced protection under the 1999 Second Protocol) but includes the lists established under the 1972 World Heritage and 2003 Intangible Heritage Conventions.[102] The chapeau of the Article 85 requires that the breach be committed wilfully and in violation of the Protocol or Conventions. If the object or site is marked or on a list that is adequately circulated this would satisfy the *mens rea* requirement.[103] Article 85(3)(f) includes among grave breaches and war crimes the perfidious use of emblem recognized by the Conventions or *AP I*.

Article 85(5) states that such grave breaches will be considered 'war crimes'.[104] The international and hybrid criminal tribunals established under the auspices of the United Nations since the 1990s have jurisdiction in respect of war crimes relating to civilian property generally and cultural heritage specifically.[105] Likewise,

---

[100] Art 8, 1874 Brussels Declaration; and Art 56, 1907 Hague IV Convention.

[101] The no grave breaches regime is explicitly applicable in respect of Art 16 of *AP II*, but it can be implied by referring back to Geneva Conventions Common Art 3 in Art 1(1) which requires suppression of violations including criminalisation and universal jurisdiction.

[102] Sandoz *et al, supra* note 44, at 1002–1003, 3517, footnote 37; Roucounas, 'Les infractions graves au droit humanitaire (Article 85 du Protocole additionale I aux Conventions des Genève)', 31 *Revue Hellénique de droit international* (1978) 57, at 113–114; and Toman, *supra* note 1 at 392.

[103] Sandoz *et al, supra* note 44, at 1002–1003, 3517; Roucounas, ibid, at 109.

[104] See Toman, *supra* note 1, at 392–393 (concerning the deliberations over the inclusion of this sentence).

[105] Art 3(d) (seizure of, destruction, or wilful damage done to institutions dedicated to religion, charity, education, the arts and sciences, historic monuments, and works of art and science), Statute of the International Criminal Tribunal for the Former Yugoslavia, GA Res 827, 25 May 1993, amended by GA Res 1166 (1998), 1329 (2000), 1411 (2002), 1431 (2002) 1481 (2003), 1597 (2005), and 1660 (2006) (ICTY Statute); Art 4 (serious violations of Common Art 3 of 1949 Geneva Conventions and *AP II*), Statute of the International Criminal Tribunal for Rwanda, SC Res 955, 8 November 1994 as adopted and amended to SC Res 1717, 13 October 2006; Arts 8(2)(b)(international conflicts), and 8(2)(e)(iv) (not international armed conflicts), Rome Statute of the International Criminal Court, 17 July 1998, in force 1 July 2002, UN Doc A/CONF. 183/9; 37 ILM 1002 (1998); 2187 UNTS 90; Art 3 (Serious violations of 1949 Geneva Conventions and *AP II* including pillage), Statute of the Special Court for Sierra Leone, in Agreement between the United Nations and the Government of Sierra Leone on the Establishment of a Special Court for Sierra Leone, SC Res 1315 of 14 August 2000, 2178 UNTS 138, 145; 97 *AJIL* (2000) 295; UN Doc S/2002/246, Appendix II; Art 9 (jurisdiction includes grave breaches of the 1949 Geneva Conventions), Agreement Between the United

and pursuant to obligations on High Contracting Parties contained in Part V, Section II of *AP I*, a number of domestic penal codes provide for the prosecution of such violations in national courts.[106]

Since the 1977 Additional Protocols, other instruments have been negotiated to limit the use of weapons and their impact on civilian populations and private property, which reference to cultural heritage. For example, the 1980 Convention on Prohibitions or Restrictions on the Use of Certain Conventional Weapons Which May be Deemed to be Excessively Injurious or to Have Indiscriminate Effects, with its three optional Protocols,[107] Protocol II Article 6(1)(b) refers to 'historic monuments, works of art or places of worship which constitute the cultural or spiritual heritage of peoples',[108] and Protocol III Article 2 extends protection to civilian objects not specifically cultural heritage.[109]

3. Specialist Regime for Cultural Heritage: The Hague Framework

As the *travaux préparatoires* of the 1954 Hague Convention and First Protocol clearly evidence, this specialist framework developed under the auspices of UNESCO after the Second World War was a product of its times. It cannot be fully understood without reference to the international humanitarian law instruments which preceded it, or by ignoring contemporaneous developments like the Nuremberg trials, the Genocide Convention, and Universal Declaration of Human Rights.

A response to the silence of the 1949 Geneva Conventions concerning cultural heritage specifically, the 1954 Hague framework borrowed from them to articulate the first specialist instrument for the protection of cultural heritage during armed conflict and belligerent occupation. The 1954 Hague Convention also traces its

---

Nations and the Royal Government of Cambodia Concerning the Prosecution under Cambodian Law of Crimes Committed During the Period of Democratic Kampuchea, GA Res 57/228B of 22 May 2003, UN Doc A/RES/57/228B (2003) Annex; Ar 6 (destruction and serious damage to property, not justified by military necessity and carried out unlawfully and wantonly), Law on the Establishment of Extraordinary Chambers in the Court of Cambodia for the Prosecution of Crimes committed during the period of Democratic Kampuchea, with the inclusion of amendments as promulgated on 27 October 2004 (NS/RKM/1004/006). This later law provides specific jurisdiction for the prosecution of persons violating obligations under the 1954 Hague Convention during the Khmer Rouge regime: Art 7.

[106] Also Arts 146 and 147 of *GC IV*. For enactment into domestic legislation: see Henckaerts and Doswald-Beck, *supra* note 86, at vol II, at 746–755, 105–172.

[107] 10 October 1980, in force 2 December 1983, 1342 UNTS 137, and Schindler and Toman, *supra* note 8, at 181.

[108] Protocol on Prohibitions or Restrictions on the Use of Mines, Booby-Traps and Other Devices (Protocol II), 10 October 1980, in force 2 December 1983, 1342 UNTS 137, and Schindler and Toman, *supra* note 8, at 191. Amended to cover non-international armed conflicts also, 3 May 1996, in force 3 December 1998, UN Doc CCW/CONF.I/16, and Schindler and Toman, *supra* note 8, at 196.

[109] Protocol on Prohibitions or Restrictions on the Use of Incendiary Weapons (Protocol III), 10 October 1980, in force 2 December 1983, 1342 UNTS 137, and Schindler and Toman, *supra* note 8 at 210.

lineage to the defunct inter-war efforts to establish a dedicated regime for cultural heritage, and this is especially evident in the inclusion of peacetime measures. However, the development came at a price, namely, the continued application of the military necessity proviso.

A. Roerich Pact and 1935 Washington Treaty

The damage inflicted on cultural heritage during the First World War highlighted the inadequacies of existing general international humanitarian law instruments like the 1899 and 1907 Hague Conventions especially in the face of new technologies which render war total and no longer able to be confined to a discrete area. The distinction between defended and undefended towns was no longer sustainable. Such destruction of objects and sites described as 'the common heritage of civilisation' was viewed as 'an outrage to humanity' and drove initiatives for the formulation of a specialist instrument.[110] Accordingly, as noted above, the first efforts occurred during the progress of the war, including the Zitelmann proposal and the NOB report which paved the way for the shift in the modalities of protection contained in the instruments prepared during the inter-war period.

The Treaty on the Protection of Artistic and Scientific Institutions and Historic Monuments (1935 Washington Treaty) which incorporated the principles contained in the Roerich Pact was the first specialist multi-lateral instrument for the protection of cultural property during armed conflict and peacetime.[111] This was primarily a Pan-American Union initiative drafted by Georges Chklaver and Nicholas Roerich.[112] The preamble of the Roerich Pact referred to the obligation of all nations to promote 'the advancement of the Arts and Science in the common interest of humanity' and that 'the Institutions dedicated to the education of youth, to Arts and Science, constitute[d] a common treasure of all the Nations of the World'.[113] The draft text was originally presented to the League of Nations' *Office International des Musées* (OIM). It subsequently found favour with the Pan-American Union which adopted it on 15 April 1935. The League had earlier rejected similar entreaties determining that it was 'both difficult and inopportune' to consider such a project when its efforts were devoted to the 'elimination of war.'[114]

---

[110] Phillipson, *International Law and the Great War* (1915) at 168.

[111] 15 April 1935, in force 26 August 1935, OASTS No 33, 167 LNTS 289, 30 (supp) *AJIL* (1936) 195; and Schindler and Toman, *supra* note 8, at 991.

[112] 6 *Revue de droit international* (Paris) (1930) 593; and Seventh International Conference of American States, *Minutes and Antecedents with General Index*, Montevideo, 1933, unpublished, Roerich Museum Archives, New York.

[113] Second and Third recitals, Preamble, Roerich Pact, ibid. See Chklaver, 'Projet d'une convention pour la protection des institutions et monuments consacrés aux arts et aux sciences', 6 *Revue de droit international* (Paris) (1930) 589 at 590: where he refers to monuments and buildings which constitute the 'common heritage of humanity'.

[114] LNOJ, 18th Year, No 12 (December 1937) at 1047. The OIM preferred to circulate recommendations to national authorities based on those produced by the NOB covering peacetime measures for the preparation of protection of cultural heritage during armed conflict: Vergier-Boimond, *Villes sanitaires et cités d'asile* (1939) at 122–123 and 318–319.

The preamble of the 1935 Washington Treaty defined its aim as the 'preserv[ation] in any time of danger of all nationally and privately owned immovable monuments which form the cultural treasures of peoples'. It remains binding on eleven American countries including the United States. The instrument covers immovable objects namely, historic monuments, museums, scientific, artistic, educational, and cultural institutions and related personnel, which are considered 'neutral',[115] and to be respected and protected by belligerents (Article 1). Movable objects are protected if located in such protected buildings. If the site or monument is used for military purposes the protection is lost (Article 5). However, the qualification of 'military necessity' itself is not mentioned in the instrument. The territorial state must pass necessary domestic legislation to effect such protection (Article 2), display a distinct flag over these institutions (which differs from the one provided under the 1907 Hague Regulations and 1954 Hague Convention) (Article 3),[116] and provide a list of relevant sites to the Pan-American Union (Article 4). The 1954 Hague Convention is supplementary to the Roerich Pact in the relations between High Contacting Parties.[117]

B. 1938 OIM Draft Convention and 1939 OIM Declaration

During the same period, the League of Nations' International Committee on Intellectual Cooperation (ICIC) commenced preparing an instrument for the protection of cultural heritage during armed conflict precipitated by the outbreak of the Spanish Civil War and Sino-Japanese War.[118] The OIM was charged with undertaking the necessary work and it commissioned Charles de Visscher to author a report having regard to the Committee of Jurists' work for the 1923 Hague Rules and the 1918 NOB survey.[119] His report was then presented to the ICIC that approved a meeting of legal and military experts.[120] The preliminary draft international convention with regulations (1938 OIM Draft Convention), prepared by Geouffre de Lapradelle, Nicholas Politis, De Visscher, and others, was 'confine[d]...to what seemed feasible in practice, rather than aim at a higher

[115] Art 2, 1935 Washington Treaty provides: 'The neutrality...shall be recognized in the entire expanse of territories subject to the sovereignty of each of the Signatory and Acceding States, without any discrimination as to the State allegiance of said monuments and institutions.'
[116] This flag is replaced by the distinctive sign contained in Art 16 of 1954 Hague Convention: Art 36(2) 1954 Hague Convention.
[117] Fourth preambular recital and Art 36(2), 1954 Hague Convention.
[118] LNOJ, 18th Year, No 12 (December 1937) at 1047. See Thomas and Thomas, 'International aspects of the Civil War in Spain 1936–1939', in Falk (ed), *The International Law of Civil War* (1971) at 111.
[119] See De Visscher, 'La protection internationale des objets d'art et des monuments historiques. Deuxième Partie. Les monuments historiques et les œuvres d'art en temps de guerre et dans les traités de la paix' 16 *Revue de droit international (3ème série)* (1935) at 246, and 35–36 *Mouseion* (1936) 1; Office International des Musées, *La protection de monuments et œuvres d'art en temps de guerre,* (1939); and 2 *Art et Archéologie. Receuil de législation comparée de droit international* (1940) at 47.
[120] Doc O.I.M.53.1926; Doc O.I.M.96.1937; and ICIC Res, LNOJ, 18th Year, No 12 (December 1937) at 1004.

mark…'.[121] The international conference called to negotiate this instrument in The Hague was cancelled because of the outbreak of the Second World War.[122] Instead, a Declaration Concerning the Protection of Historic Buildings and Works of Art in Time of War, pared down to the ten articles, was adopted by Belgium, Spain, Greece, the United States, and the Netherlands (1939 OIM Declaration).[123]

The OIM initiative's rationale for the protection of cultural property was encapsulated from its initial proposal. Bolivia raised the need for a multilateral specialist instrument which protected that which was 'a matter of importance to civilisation as a whole'.[124] The 1938 OIM Draft Convention's preamble provided:

Whereas the preservation of artistic treasures is a concern of the community of States and it is important that such treasures should receive international protection;

Being convinced that the destruction of a master piece, whatever nation may have produced it, is a spiritual impoverishment for the entire international community.[125]

Only this second preambular recital was retained in the 1939 OIM Declaration.

The OIM Draft Convention was applicable to 'disturbances' and 'armed conflicts' within a state (draft Article 10), with obligations, particularly those related to movable heritage and their removal for safekeeping, modified accordingly. The experts' commentary advised that as the proposed instrument was 'conceived in a spirit of international solidarity' it was 'only natural that it also envisage[d] the dangers which threatened monuments and works of art during civil disturbances.'[126] The 1939 Declaration made no such concession.

Neither the declaration nor the Draft Convention had a dedicated provision defining its *ratione materiae*. It referred only to 'historic buildings', 'monuments', and 'works of art' and by extrapolation covers both movable and immovable heritage.

The international obligation to protect such cultural property fell to states in whose territory it was located.[127] Accordingly, such states were duty bound to provide material protection to objects and sites against the destructive impact of war and 'insure such protection by all the technical means at their disposal' (Article 1). In their commentary, the experts noted that these obligations implied 'recognition of the principle that the preservation of artistic and historical treasures is a matter that concerns the world as a whole. The countries possessing artistic treasures are merely their custodians and remain accountable for them to the international community.'[128]

---

[121] LNOJ, 19th Year, No 11 (November 1938) at 936–991; and De Visscher, *supra* note 1, at 861. See *Report by the Directors' Committee of the International Museums Office to the International Committee on Intellectual Co-operation for the Year 1937/38, together with a Preliminary Draft International Convention on the Protection of Historic Buildings and Works of Art*, in LNOJ, 19th Year, No 11 (November 1938) at 937.

[122] UNESCO Doc CBC/7, at 3, at 8.

[123] De Visscher, *supra* note 1, at 859; 2 *Art et Archéologie. Receuil de législation comparée de droit international* (1940), supplement; Berlia, *supra* note 27, Annex I, at 5–7; and Deltenre, *General Collection of the Laws and Customs of War* (1943), at 755–759.

[124] LNOJ, Special Supplement No 161 (1936) at 57.

[125] LNOJ, 19th Year, No 11 (November 1938) at 936.   [126] Ibid.

[127] LNOJ, 19th Year, No11 (November 1938) at 937.   [128] Ibid, at 961.

The projected peacetime measures contained in the Draft Convention and inspired by the NOB report were incorporated, in abbreviated form, into the 1939 OIM Declaration. Signatories agreed to take 'all possible precautions' to spare cultural property during military engagements and that they were immune from reprisals. Territorial states were to refrain from using cultural property and its surroundings for purposes that would expose it to attack (Article 2). Their armed forces were to be instructed to respect such property and were prohibited from looting or damaging it during the armed conflict (Article 3). '[E]ssentially important' sites were to be marked as prescribed by Article 27 of the 1907 Hague Regulations by the competent governmental authorities and any abuse of the protective marking was to be prosecuted (Article 6). The obligation to respect remained for all cultural property, even if unmarked.

The 1939 Declaration retained the notion of 'neutrality' granted on the basis of removal of military advantage originally proposed by the NOB report and 1923 Hague Rules. The committee of experts commenting on the failure of the operation of the Hague Regulations noted: 'It was felt that the only possible way to protect monuments and works of art . . . was to meet the destructive effects of the war with defensive measures equally as effective, or, still better, to divest such monuments of anything likely to provoke their destruction.'[129] Accordingly, refuges established to house movable heritage were not to be put to use for a purpose nor located near a site which would render them military objectives (Article 4).[130] Further, in respect of 'certain monuments, groups of monuments or built-up areas, the safeguarding of which [was] of exceptional importance for the international community', states were encouraged to enter agreements for special protection during armed conflict (Article 5).[131]

During belligerent occupation, the occupying power was required to bring cultural property of 'artistic or historic interest' to the attention of its forces and counsel them that their preservation '[was] the concern of the entire international community' (Article 8). Also, existing national staff employed in respect of refuges, museums, or monuments were afforded the same protection as the civilian population and were to be retained 'unless there is any legitimate military reason for their dismissal'. The occupying power was to take all necessary action to preserve damaged cultural property, but could not go beyond 'strengthening' it.

Finally, the signatories agreed that any violations of the Declaration were to be examined by a Commission of Inquiry (Article 9). The Committee was composed of five persons from neutral countries having expertise in fine art, antiquities, being jurists with an international reputation. Two persons were nominated by the belligerent state alleging the breach and two nominated by the other belligerent,

---

[129] LNOJ, 19th Year, No 11 (November 1938) at 961.

[130] States not involved in the armed conflict were encouraged to assist those that were by providing refuge for their movable heritage during the hostilities: Art 7, 1939 OIM Declaration.

[131] The expert commentary noted a similar provision included in the Draft Convention was intended for those urban centres which have so many monuments that they could not satisfy the special protection requirements but nonetheless were 'of essential importance to the world at large': LNOJ, 19th Year, No 11 (November 1938) at 962.

with the fifth member who acted as chairperson nominated by these four. The Commission could also fulfil any other task entrusted to it by the belligerents designed to facilitate the aims of the Declaration.

At the outbreak of the war, US President Franklin D Roosevelt requested reassurances from Germany, France, and the United Kingdom that civilian populations and property would be spared.[132] Germany, France, the United Kingdom, and Poland responded affirmatively. Indeed, a joint French and British statement on 3 September 1939 advised that they 'solemnly and publicly affirm...to preserve, with every possible measure, the monuments of civilisation...they will exclude objectives which do not present a clearly defined military objective...'.[133] The belligerents largely adhered to these assurances until 1943.[134] The devastation wrought to civilians and their property thereafter by Axis forces became the subject of prosecutions before the post-war military tribunals, which are considered in Part 3 below.

C. 1954 Hague Convention, and First and Second Hague Protocols

In 1949, the fourth UNESCO General Conference adopted a Resolution acknowledging the need to protect 'all objects of cultural value, particularly those kept in museums, libraries and archives, against the probable consequences of armed conflict'.[135] Thereafter, the UNESCO Secretariat restarted the process of formulating a convention suspended because of the war which led to the adoption of the Convention for the Protection of Cultural Property in the Event of Armed Conflict five years later (1954 Hague Convention).[136]

The present day specialist international humanitarian law framework for the protection of cultural heritage during armed conflict and belligerent occupation includes the 1954 Hague Convention, the 1954 Hague Protocol,[137] and the 1999 Second Protocol.[138] Each instrument bears evidence of concessions made to encourage their uptake and ensure a minimum standard of conduct during hostilities and occupation.[139] The most significant compromise is the proviso of military

---

[132] OIM, *supra* note at 222.   [133] Ibid, at 225–226.

[134] Boylan, 'Review of the Convention for the Protection of Cultural Property in the Event of Armed Conflict (The Hague Convention of 1954)', (1993) UNESCO Doc CLT-93/WS/12, at 35–37.

[135] Res 6.42, in *Records of the General Conference of the United Nations Educational, Scientific and Cultural Organization, Fourth Session, Paris 1949, Resolutions* (1949) at 27.

[136] See UNESCO Doc CBC/7.

[137] Protocol for the Protection of Cultural Property in the Event of Armed Conflict, 14 May 1954, in force 7 August 1956, 249 UNTS 358; and Schindler and Toman, *supra* note 8, at 1027.

[138] Second Protocol to the Hague Convention for the Protection of Cultural Property in the Event of Armed Conflict, 26 March 1999, in force 9 March 2004, 38 ILM (1999) at 769; and Schindler and Toman, *supra* note 8, at 1037.

[139] UNESCO Doc 7C/PRG/7, Annex I, at 6. During the Diplomatic Conference to finalize the Second Protocol, China, Denmark, Ireland, United Kingdom, and the United States 'announced progress towards their participation in the Hague Convention': Summary Report, Diplomatic Conference on the Second Protocol to the Hague Convention for the Protection of Cultural Property in the Event of Armed Conflict, June 1999, at 2, at 8. China (2000), Denmark (2003), and the United States (2009) have become states parties.

necessity, which was retained in the 1999 Second Protocol negotiated two decades after the Additional Protocols to the 1949 Geneva Conventions.

The 1954 Hague Convention, and therefore the two Protocols, owes much to the legacy of the inter-war efforts. Its preamble acknowledges that it is 'guided by the principles' contained in the 1899 Hague II and 1907 Hague IV Conventions and the 1935 Washington Treaty.[140] The convention's rationale contained in the second and third preambular recitals tacitly replicates that of the stalled OIM Draft Convention:

Being convinced that damage to cultural property belonging to any people whatsoever means damage to the cultural heritage of all mankind, since each people makes its contribution to the culture of the world;

Considering that the preservation of the cultural heritage is of great importance for all peoples of the world and that it is important that this heritage should receive international protection...[141]

For the first time we have a reference to 'cultural heritage' rather than 'cultural property' in such an instrument.[142] It points to its intergenerational importance, an aspect reaffirmed by a Resolution adopted at the first meeting of the High Contracting Parties to the Convention which noted that 'the purpose of the Convention...is to protect the cultural heritage of all peoples for future generations'.[143]

The preamble also deliberately refers to 'peoples' rather than 'states'.[144] The original text contained the words used in a 1932 ICIC Resolution which stated that the 'preservation of the artistic and architectural heritage of mankind [was] a matter of interest to the *community of States*'.[145] This amendment together with the redrafted version of the current second preambular recital was proposed by the USSR delegation.[146] The *travaux* noted that armistice agreements and peace treaties after the conflict had provided for restitution of cultural property and the Nuremberg Tribunal has 'introduced the principle of punishing attacks on the cultural

---

[140] Fourth preambular recital, 1954 Hague Convention.

[141] Second and third preambular recitals, 1954 Hague Convention.

[142] UNESCO Doc 7C/PRG/7, Annex II, at 20.   [143] UNESCO Doc CUA/120, at 22.

[144] Cf UNESCO Doc 7C/PRG/7, Annex II, at 20. See Toman, *supra* note 1, at 42, and O'Keefe, *supra* note 1, at 95.

[145] LNOJ, 13th Year, No 11 (November 1932) at 1776. The OIM draft had read: 'Whereas the preservation of artistic treasures is a concern of the community of States and it is important that such treasures should receive international protection': LNOJ, 19th Year, No 11 (November 1938) at 936, Appendix 2, sub-appendix. The draft preamble of the 1954 Hague Convention had originally read: 'Considering that the preservation of the cultural heritage is the concern of the community of States and it is important that this heritage should receive international protection': 7C/PRG/7, Annex II, at 20. The USSR suggested the following amendment: 'Replace "is the concern of the community of States" by "is of great importance for all peoples of the world"': Doc CBC/DR/37.

[146] Ibid. The draft recital had read: 'Being convinced that damage to cultural property results in a spiritual impoverishment for the whole of humanity': 7C/PRG/7, Annex II, at 20. The OIM draft had read: 'Being convinced that the destruction of a master piece, whatever nation may have produced it, is a spiritual impoverishment for the entire international community': LNOJ, 19th Year, No 11 (November 1938) at 936, Appendix 2, sub-appendix.

heritage of a nation into positive international law'.[147] The Hague Convention was a response to the destruction caused by belligerents against enemy states and their own nationals during the Second World War. As I explain below, this rationale is concomitant with other instruments developed in response to those atrocities, including the Nuremberg Principles, the Genocide Convention, and Universal Declaration of Human Rights.

Like the 1949 Geneva Conventions, the 1954 Hague Convention applies to international and non-international armed conflicts.[148] In respect of internal armed conflict each of the parties to the conflict is bound to the Convention's obligations 'as a minimum' (Article 19(1)). The application of the Convention to non-international armed conflict is recognized as forming part of customary international law.[149] In respect of international armed conflicts, if one of the parties is not a High Contracting Party, the treaty obligations remain binding on the High Contracting Parties and any other party which declares that it accepts and applies the obligations (Article 18(3)). The *travaux* record that this 'refusal to regard non-contracting States purely and simply as third parties' was deliberate because of the 'moral obligation to respect the cultural property of an adversary not party to the Convention, such property belonging to the international community as well as the State concerned'.[150] In addition, it should be noted that the United Nations has indicated its willingness to be bound by this framework pursuant to the request contained in Resolution I of the Final Act of the Intergovernmental Conference in 1954.[151]

The definition of cultural property covered by the 1954 Hague Convention moves beyond the nature and purpose approach of earlier instruments. This elaborate definition covers publicly or privately owned, movable and immovable property 'of great importance to the cultural heritage of every people' including monuments, archaeological sites, groups of buildings, works of art, books, scientific collections, archives, buildings for their preservation including museums, libraries, archival depositories and refuges, and centres containing a large repository of cultural heritage (Article 1).[152] Read consistently with the preamble, the 'importance' of the cultural site or object should not be determined exclusively

---

[147] UNESCO Doc 7C/PRG/7, Annex I, at 5.

[148] Art 19, 1954 Hague Convention; and Art 22, 1999 Second Hague Protocol. The *travaux* of the First Protocol noted that: '[w]here property has changed hands on the national territory and has not been exported, the case is one for the national legislation alone': UNESCO Doc CL/717, Annex IV, 47. O'Keefe is of the opinion that the provisions relating to belligerent occupation (in particular 1954 Hague Protocol) do not extend to non-international armed conflict: *supra* note 1, at 98. Cf Prott, 'The Protocol to the Convention for the Protection of Cultural Property in the Event of Armed Conflict (The Hague Convention) 1954', in Briat and Freedberg (eds), *Legal Aspects of International Trade in Art*, (1996) 167 at 170.

[149] *Prosecutor v Duško Tadić*, Interlocutory Appeal on Jurisdiction Judgment, No IT-94-1-A, Appeals Chamber, ICTY, (2 October 1995) at 98 and 127.

[150] UNESCO Doc 7C/PRG/7, Annex I, at 5–6.

[151] *Intergovernmental Conference on the Protection of Cultural Property in the Event of Armed Conflict* (1954) at 3–5, Toman and Schindler, *supra* note 8 at 995; and Secretary-General's Bulletin on the Observance by UN Forces of International Humanitarian Law, 6 August 1999, UN Doc ST/SGB/1999/13, at 6.6.

[152] See Toman, *supra* note 1, at 45–56; and O'Keefe, *supra* note 1, at 101–111.

by the state where it is located. Rather it extends to 'people'.[153] This definition is applied to the two optional Protocols also.[154]

The 1954 Hague Convention together with its regulations elaborate obligations for the safeguarding and respect of cultural property by the High Contracting Parties which takes effect during peacetime, armed conflict, and belligerent occupation. The 'safeguarding' or positive measures to be implemented during peacetime and espoused by 1918 NOB report and 1923 Hague Rules finally find binding force in Article 3 of the Convention. It obliges High Contracting Parties 'to prepare in time of peace for the safeguarding of cultural property situated within their own territory against the foreseeable effects of an armed conflict, by taking such measures as they consider appropriate'.[155] The measures to be taken are left to the discretion of the High Contracting Party in the light of its financial and technical circumstances.[156] This lack of detail led to further elaboration of the obligation in the Second Protocol, including the preparation of inventories, emergency measures against fire or structural collapse, plans for the removal of movable cultural property or their adequate protection *in situ*, and nomination of competent authorities.[157] Other relevant measures required by the Convention itself include the issuing of military regulations or instructions and fostering in the armed forces 'a spirit of respect for the culture and cultural property of all peoples'.[158] Also, cultural property should be marked with the distinctive emblem.[159] Failure to undertake these obligations to safeguard in peacetime does not waive obligations to respect which arise when hostilities break out.[160]

The obligations to respect ('obligation not to do') arising during hostilities,[161] are triggered by a declaration of war or an armed conflict between two or more High Contracting Parties, even if not recognized as a state of war by one of them.[162] It

---

[153] O'Keefe argues it must be of national importance as importance is determined by the state party: *supra* note 1, at 103–104. While it is the responsibility of each state to identify which property is protected under the Convention, to read the definition narrowly is not only inconsistent with the spirit of the Convention as encapsulated in the preamble but also with subsequent developments in the field of cultural heritage law.   [154] Art 1, First Protocol; and Art 1(b), 1999 Second Protocol.

[155] See O'Keefe, *supra* note 1, at 111–120; Toman, *supra* note 1 at 59–66; and Boylan, *supra* note 134, at 61–73.

[156] UNESCO Doc 7C/PRG/7, Annex I, at 8; and A Noblecourt, *Protection of Cultural Property in the Event of Armed Conflict* (1958). The reports of the High Contracting Parties to the Convention provide detailed information about the preventive steps taken by individual states: see for example, Report on the activities from 1995 to 2004, UNESCO Doc CLT.2005/WS/6.

[157] Art 5, 1999 Second Protocol, and Guideline 27 of draft Guidelines for the Implementation of the 1999 Second Protocol to the Hague Convention of 1954 for the Protection of Cultural Property in the Event of Armed Conflict Developed by the Committee for the Protection of Cultural Property in the Event of Armed Conflict at its Second Meeting, 17–19 December 2007, UNESCO Doc CLT-07/CONF/212/3 Rev.2, at 12.

[158] Art 7(1), 1954 Hague Convention. Further, parties undertake to plan with their military personnel to secure cooperation with specialist civilian authorities: Art 7(2), 1954 Hague Convention and Art 82, *AP I*. For a survey of military manuals: see Henckaerts and Doswald-Beck, *supra* note 86, at vol II, Part 2, 782–786 and 793–796.   [159] Arts 6 and 16, 1954 Hague Convention.

[160] Art 4(5), 1954 Hague Convention.

[161] The *travaux* notes that the obligation to respect 'means abstention from endangering cultural property and the arrangements which ensure its safeguarding, and abstention from prejudicing them': UNESCO Doc 7C/PRG/7, Annex, at 8.   [162] Art 18, 1954 Hague Convention.

applies to total or partial occupation of the territory of the High Contracting Party even if there is no resistance. The obligation to respect includes, first, undertaking to respect cultural property situated within their *own* territory as well as within the territory of other High Contracting Parties, by refraining from any use of the property and its immediate surroundings for purposes which are likely to expose it to destruction or damage in the event of armed conflict.[163] Second, they must refrain from any act of hostility directed against such property. This obligation is subject to the proviso that it will be waived if 'military necessity imperatively requires'.[164]

As noted above, this qualification does not form part of the protection afforded under general international humanitarian law and its inclusion in the 1954 Hague framework was contested.[165] Despite recommendations to the contrary,[166] its application was reaffirmed in the Second Protocol.[167]

However, Article 6 of the Second Protocol provides that waiver on the basis of 'imperative military necessity' will only justify an attack on cultural property when and for as long as, by its function, it is a military objective, and there is no 'feasible alternative' available to gain a similar military advantage. This decision can only be made by an officer commanding a force the equivalent of a battalion or larger, or a smaller force 'where circumstances do not permit otherwise'. Regardless, 'an effective advance warning' should be given where possible in the circumstances'. This strict delimitation of 'imperative military necessity' overlaps substantially with the notion of 'military objective' as defined by *AP I*.[168] Consequently, judicial interpretations of military objective and loss of immunity arising under Article 52(2) of that Protocol and equivalent provisions in the governing statutes of international criminal tribunals are relevant.[169] Also, when launching an attack, a party must take the following precautions (without prejudice to existing international humanitarian law): feasible measures to ensure that the object to be attacked is not cultural property; feasible measures concerning method and means of attack to avoid or minimize incidental damage to cultural property; refrain from attacking where incidental damage to such property would be disproportionate to the

---

[163] Art 4(1), 1954 Hague Convention.   [164] Art 4(2), 1954 Hague Convention.

[165] See Toman, *supra* note 1, at 74–79; O'Keefe, *supra* note 1, at 121–128. Within the Legal Committee, the proposal to draft a provision along the lines of Art 11(1) was rejected. Instead, the following minute was added regarding interpretation of Art 4: 'The obligation to respect an item of cultural property remains even if that item is used by the opposing Party for military purposes. The obligation of respect is therefore only withdrawn in the event of imperative military necessity': CBC/DR/125, *Records*, at 221, at 1167.   [166] Boylan, *supra* note 134, at 17, at G.4.

[167] Art 6, 1999 Second Protocol. The Summary Report of the Diplomatic Conference noted: 'a few States wanted significant changes to the description of cultural property, considering that the draft weakened the provisions of the Hague Convention and was contrary to the provisions of the Additional Protocol I of the Geneva Convention'. Others had requested that the provision relating to loss of general protection be reformulated to coincide with the *AP I*, whilst others requested its removal all together: *supra* note 139, at 2, at 9 and 10.

[168] O'Keefe, *supra* note 1 at 252–257. For state practice see Henckaerts and Doswald-Beck, *supra* note 86, at vol 1, at 130 and 132 and vol 2, Part I, at 726, 730–745, 779–780, and 782–786.

[169] See *Prosecutor v Pavle Strugar*, Trial Judgment, Chamber II, ICTY, No IT-01-42-T, (31 January 2005) at 295. See O'Keefe, *supra* note 1, at 125–132; Toman, *supra* note 1 at 389–390; and Sandoz *et al*, *supra* note 44, at 648, 2079.

military advantage gained; and cancel and suspend an attack when aware that the target is cultural property or attack is excessive in relation to military advantage gained.[170] All parties must not locate movable heritage near military objectives (or must otherwise provide *in situ* protection) and remove military objectives from the vicinity of immovable heritage.[171]

The remaining obligations contained within Article 4 of the Hague Convention are not subject to the military necessity proviso. Consequently, High Contracting Parties undertake to refrain from acts of reprisal against cultural property and to prohibit, prevent, and stop the theft, pillage, and misappropriation of any acts of vandalism toward cultural heritage.[172]

The 1954 Hague Convention also elaborates upon the obligations arising during belligerent occupation originally contained in the unrealized 1938 OIM Draft Convention.[173] The occupying power must cooperate with and support the competent national authorities for the protection of cultural heritage. If it is necessary to take measures to preserve the cultural heritage damaged by hostilities, and the competent authorities are unable to undertake the work, then the occupying power shall take 'the most necessary measures of preservation' with their cooperation, where possible. The provision extends to informing insurgent groups of their obligation to respect cultural property. The obligation is clarified further by Article 9 of the Second Protocol.[174] It encompasses obligations espoused in the 1956 UNESCO Recommendation on International Principles Applicable to Archaeological Excavations.[175] It provides that the High Contracting Party must prevent and prohibit any illicit export, other removal, or transfer of ownership of cultural property;[176] archaeological excavations except when 'strictly required to safeguard, record or preserve' cultural property; and changes to the cultural property intended to hide or destroy 'cultural, historical or scientific evidence'. Archaeological excavations or changes to cultural property in occupied territory shall only (unless circumstances do not permit) be carried out in close cooperation with the competent national authorities of the occupied territory.

---

[170] Art 7, 1999 Second Protocol.

[171] Art 8, 1999 Second Protocol. This provision was modelled on Art 58 Additional Protocol I: Summary Report, *supra* note 139, at 3, at 13.

[172] The ICRC states that it is reflective of customary international law in respect of international and non-international armed conflicts: Henckaerts and Doswald-Beck, *supra* note 86, at vol 1, at 132–136 and vol 2, Part I, at 790–813.

[173] Art 5, 1954 Hague Convention; and Arts 8 and 9, Regulations of the 1938 OIM Draft Convention.

[174] The Greek delegation had unsuccessfully tried to incorporate such an obligation in the Convention proper in the 1950s during the original negotiations: *Records, supra* note 180, at 1912–1915.

[175] Art 32, Part VI of the 1956 UNESCO Recommendation, in *Records of the General Conference, Ninth Session, New Delhi 1956: Resolutions*, (1957) at 40.

[176] Arts 11 and 12 of the Convention on the Means of Prohibiting and Preventing the Illicit Import, Export and Transfer of Ownership of Cultural Property, 14 November 1970, in force 24 April 1972, 823 UNTS 231; and reports of the Intergovernmental Committee for Promoting the Return of Cultural Property to its Countries of Origin or its Restitution in Case of Illicit Appropriation: for example, GA Res 61/52 of 11 September 2006, UN Doc A/RES/61/52.

This protection afforded cultural heritage during occupation is augmented by the First Protocol concerning the removal and return of movable heritage. It draws upon the experience of the Allied Powers during and following the Second World War, in particular the principles contained in the 1938 OIM Draft Convention and Declaration of the Allied Nations against Acts of Dispossession Committed in Territories under Enemy Occupation or Control (1943 London Declaration).[177] It requires High Contracting Parties to prevent the export of cultural objects from territory under their control (para 1). High Contracting Parties (even those not party to the conflict) must take into their custody cultural property from occupied territory which enters their territory immediately or upon request of the occupied territory's authorities (para 2). The property on their territory removed in contravention of Article 1 shall be returned to the competent authorities of the territory immediately upon cessation of the occupation (para 3). Cultural property must never be kept as war reparations (para 3).[178] There is no time limit for lodging a claim for the return of such cultural objects.[179] The High Contracting Party obligated to prevent the exportation in the first place shall pay an indemnity to the holder in good faith which is subsequently returned (para 4). This provision is more limited than the post-1945 restitution scheme because it does not extend to neutral third party states.[180] In circumstances where cultural property is deposited by a High Contracting Party in the custody of another for safekeeping against hostilities it shall be returned at the cessation to the competent authorities of the territory (para 5). The initial inclusion of a draft provision covering restitution in the Convention proper proved highly contentious and was consequently relegated to an optional Protocol to placate certain states whom it was feared would not otherwise sign up to the Convention.[181]

The obligations contained in the 1954 Protocol have largely been replicated in Security Council Resolutions concerning Iraq during the first Gulf War in 1990 and the invasion in 2003 which provided for the taking into safekeeping and restitution of cultural heritage removed from that country.[182] They bound all UN member states and not only states parties to the First Protocol. Indeed, it sometimes led to the passage of domestic laws stricter than the international obligations contained in the Hague framework by countries not parties to these instruments.[183]

---

[177] 5 January 1943, 8 *Department of State Bulletin* (1943) 21.

[178] For a discussion of contrary Russian state practice: Henckaerts and Doswald-Beck, *supra* note 86, vol I, at 137–138 in which it notes that these acts of removal occurred prior to the operation of the First Protocol.

[179] See UNESCO Doc CL/717, Annex IV, 47; Nahlik, *supra* note 1, at 147; and Prott, *supra* note 148.

[180] See *Intergovernmental Conference on the Protection of Cultural Property in the Event of Armed Conflict—The Hague, 1954. Records of the Conference*, (1961) at 1630 and 1637.

[181] Ibid, at 1645–1690 and 1750–1756. See O'Keefe, *supra* note 1, at 196–201; Toman, *supra* note 1 at 333–356; O'Keefe, 'The First Protocol of the Hague Convention Fifty Years On', 9 *Art Antiquity and Law* (2004) 99, at 113; and Prott, *supra* note 148, at 163–173.

[182] SC Res 661, 6 August 1990, and SC Res 1483, 22 May 2003, at 7.

[183] See, for example, Iraq (United Nations Sanctions) Order 2003 (UK), which shifted the burden of proof from the prosecution to the defendant. He or she has prove to that they 'did not know and had no reason to suppose' that the object was removed illegally from Iraq after the relevant date: section 8(2) and (3).

The 1954 Hague framework revived and absorbed the notion of special protection for cultural property of 'very great importance' flagged by the OIM Draft Convention. The distinction made in the 1954 Hague Convention between general protection (Chapter I) and special protection (Chapters II of Convention and Regulations) is significant for the purposes of the prosecution of war crimes, that is, grave breaches of international humanitarian law. However, the criteria laid down for attracting special protection were so onerous that very few sites or properties were listed. By 1999, only one site (the Vatican) and refuges nominated by the Netherlands, Austria, and the Federal Republic of Germany had been listed.[184]

The Second Protocol introduced another category of protection: enhanced protection. Pursuant to Article 10, to attract such protection it must be: (a) cultural heritage of the 'greatest importance to humanity';[185] (b) protected adequately by any national legal and administrative measures recognizing its 'exceptional cultural and historic value and ensuring the highest level of protection';[186] and (c) not be used for military purposes or as a shield of military sites and the party controlling the property must declare that it will not be used as such. The guarding of sites by armed custodians or police responsible for public order is deemed not to be a military purpose.[187]

The Second Protocol establishes a committee which accepts nominations from High Contracting Parties, non-governmental organizations, and other parties,

---

[184] Summary Report, *supra* note 139, at 2, at 6; and Toman, *supra* note 1, at 108–109.

[185] The draft Article had referred to its importance to 'all peoples' but this was amended to 'humanity' to 'emphasiz[e] the common interest in safeguarding important cultural heritage': Summary Report, *supra* note 139 at 4. The draft Guidelines provide that when evaluating whether a property satisfied these criteria it must evaluate its 'exceptional cultural significance, and/or its uniqueness, and/or if its destruction would lead to irretrievable loss for humanity' (draft Guideline 32). Exceptional cultural significance is determined by the following criteria:

– it is an exceptional cultural property bearing a testimony of one or more period of the development of humankind at the national, regional or global level;
– it represents a masterpiece of human creativity;
– it bears an exceptional testimony to a cultural tradition or to a civilization which is living or which has disappeared;
– it exhibits an important interchange of human achievements, over a span of time or within a cultural area of the world on developments in arts and sciences;
– it has a central significance to the cultural identity of societies concerned.

Uniqueness is defined as there being no other 'comparable cultural property that is of the same cultural significance' having regard to age, history, community, representativity, location, size and dimension, shape and design, purity and authenticity in style, integrity, context, artistic craftsmanship, aesthetic value, and scientific value (draft Guideline 34). The criterion of 'irretrievable loss for humanity' is satisfied when damage or loss 'result[s] in the impoverishment of the cultural diversity or cultural heritage of humankind'. Properties listed on the World Heritage List and Memory of the World Register are presumed to satisfy these criteria.

[186] The draft Guidelines provide that the Committee must consider whether the national legal and administrative measures adequately identify and safeguard the property, are covered in military planning and training programmes, there are appropriate penal provisions, and (where appropriate) marking with the 1954 Hague Convention emblem (at 39). Such measures will only be considered adequate if effective in practice, that is, 'based on a coherent system of protection and achieve the expected results' (at 41). Peacetime provisions would also cover adequate protection against negligence, decay, or destruction.   [187] Art 8(4), 1954 Hague Convention.

and advises all parties of the request.[188] It can seek the advice of governmental and non-governmental experts.[189] The property may be listed even if it does not satisfy the criteria, provided the requesting party has asked for international assistance.[190] There is also the possibility for the emergency granting of enhanced protection during hostilities.[191] The protection is afforded when the property is listed by the Committee.[192] The Committee is required to inform the UNESCO Director-General of its decision, who in turn notifies the UN Secretary-General. The relevant cultural property and its surroundings attract the immunity.[193] The protection will be terminated or suspended if it is a military objective;[194] or cancelled or suspended by the Committee when it no longer meets the criteria of Article 10,[195] or its continuous and serious use for the advancement of a military purpose.[196]

Property ascribed enhanced protection may be the object of attack if this is the only feasible means of ceasing its use as a military objective, all feasible precautions as to choice of means and method are taken to terminate such use and avoid or minimize damage to it, and the attack can only be ordered at the highest operational level of command, and effective advance warning and reasonable time is given to the opponent to stop such use.[197] The last requirement may be discarded in circumstances of self-defence.

Finally, the Second Hague Protocol elaborates upon the duty to prosecute violations. This obligation predates the 1954 Hague Convention and is contained in the 1907 Hague Regulations, referred to above.[198] High Contracting Parties to the Second Protocol must introduce domestic penal legislation (establishing

---

[188] Art 11(1), (2) and (3), Second Protocol, and draft Guidelines 44 and 51.

[189] Arts 11(6) and 27(3), Second Protocol, and draft Guidelines 24 and 51.

[190] Art 11(8), Second Protocol, and draft Guideline 50.

[191] Art 11(9), Second Protocol, and draft Guideline 63. Such requests must at a minimum: identify the cultural property, provide a description, define its use with a declaration that it is not used for nor in the vicinity of military objectives; provide details of the responsible authorities, in the form required by the UNESCO secretariat, and duly signed by the Party's competent authority.

[192] Art 12, Second Protocol.   [193] Art 13, Second Protocol.

[194] Art 13(1)(b), Second Protocol.

[195] Suspension, being a provisional measure, can only be ordered by the Committee if the conditions contained in Art 10 are no longer fulfilled but may be at later date. This applies only to conditions specified in Art 10(b) and (c) concerning adequate domestic measures and non-military use respectively (draft Guideline 84). As cancellation is a definitive measure it is applied only when the conditions contained in Art 10(a) are no longer met and cannot be met at a later date (draft Guideline 87).

[196] Arts 12 and 14(2), Second Protocol. The Committee may suspend the enhanced protection if the property or its immediate surroundings are used as a military objective (draft Guideline 85). Cancellation may be ordered exceptionally where it is used in such a manner for six months or more and 'there is no evidence that the use will stop' (draft Guideline 88). During the Diplomatic Conference, some states proposed the closure of the loophole by making loss of protection arising only from use in 'direct and indirect support of military operations'. Whilst the ICRC noted that *AP I* was no longer limited to 'only a few unique objects: attack is now allowed only on military objectives, all other objects being protected. The protection accorded to these significant items should therefore be substantially higher than the general protection': Summary Report, *supra* note 139 at 4, at 18.   [197] Art 13(2), Second Protocol.

[198] Art 28, 1954 Hague Convention. USSR had unsuccessfully proposed a provision which drew inspiration from Art 146 of the 1949 Fourth Geneva Convention: *Records, supra* note 180, CBC/DR/71, at 390.

jurisdiction and appropriate penalties) concerning serious violations occurring within their territory or perpetrated by nationals.[199] Serious violations are defined as acts committed intentionally and in violation of the Convention or Second Protocol, namely, attacks on property under enhanced protection, using such property or its immediate surroundings in support of military action, extensive destruction or appropriation of cultural property covered by general protection, making such property the object of attack, and theft, pillage, or misappropriation of property under general protection.[200] Universal jurisdiction must be established for the first three of these serious violations.[201] If a party does not prosecute, then it must extradite to a country that can and which meets minimum standards in international law.[202] Further, a party may introduce legislative, administrative, or disciplinary measures which suppress the intentional use of cultural property in violation of the Convention or Second Protocol, and the illicit export, removal, or transfer of ownership of cultural property from occupied territory in violation of the Convention or Protocol.[203]

4. International Criminal Law and Cultural Heritage

In the year that the Geneva Conventions were adopted, UNESCO reopened the question of a specialist instrument for the protection of cultural property during armed conflict and belligerent occupation. An expert report prepared for the organization by Georges Berlia emphasized the importance of preventive and punitive measures.[204] Preventive measures were encapsulated in efforts such as the 1938 OIM Draft Convention which included obligations arising during peacetime to minimize the impact of hostilities. This approach was realized with the adoption of the Hague framework. Equally important were the punitive measures identified by Berlia. Written a few short years after the Nuremberg Judgment, he made reference not only to war crimes but extended his discussion to crimes against humanity and genocide.

Berlia's early identification of the link between the international protection of cultural heritage and these newly articulated international crimes is central to my contention that the mid-twentieth century with the Nuremberg Judgment,[205] and

---

[199] Arts 15(2) and 16(1), Second Protocol.

[200] Art 15(1), Second Protocol. The Summary Report of the Diplomatic Conference records drafters intended this provision to be consistent with Art 85, *AP I* and the Rome Statute. However, serious concerns were raised about the initial draft particularly by the ICRC which questioned the omission of intentional attacks and pillage as war crimes, *supra* note 139 at 6, at 26 and 27.

[201] Art 16(1)(c), Second Protocol.

[202] Arts 17 and 18, Second Protocol. It also provides for grounds for refusal of extradition (political crimes or racial, religious etc motivations) and provision of mutual legal assistance: Arts 19 and 20.   [203] Art 21, Second Protocol.

[204] Berlia, *supra* note 27, at 12.

[205] Affirmed by GA Res 95 (I), 11 December 1946. See also Principles of International Law Recognized in the Charter of the Nürnberg Tribunal and in the Judgment of the Tribunal, UN GAOR Supp (No 12) at 11, UN Doc A/1316 (1950); 1950 *UNYBILC* 374, vol II, and 44 *AJIL* (1950) 126.

the adoption of the Genocide Convention and the UDHR represented a shift in the dynamics within the international community.[206] The 1954 Hague Convention and all international instruments for the protection of cultural heritage which follow it must be understood within this context. It is a change encapsulated in the preamble of the 1954 Hague Convention. The rationale for the protection of cultural heritage is no longer its universal importance to humanity because of the advancement of the arts and sciences (though this important aim remains), rather it is more complex and relates to the significance of the heritage to peoples. This recalibration is reflected more broadly in recent multi-lateral instruments for the protection of cultural heritage,[207] and human rights.[208]

This shift is best understood by looking at these individual international crimes as they have been developed from the Hague Regulations to the present day and how cultural heritage has been deployed in the prosecution of alleged perpetrators of these crimes. In this final part, I examine the jurisprudence from the Nuremberg trials to the work of the ICTY in respect of war crimes against cultural property, the crime against humanity of persecution and finally, the crime of genocide.

A. Violation of the laws and customs of war

The first efforts to put the obligation to prosecute violations of the laws and customs of war relating to cultural heritage into practice occurred at the close of the First World War. In early 1919, Sub Commission III on the Responsibilities of the Authors of War and on Enforcement of Penalties for Violations of the Laws and Customs of War established during the Preliminary Peace Conference in Versailles had included 'pillage' and 'wanton destruction of religious, charitable, educational, and historic buildings and monuments' on its list of war crimes to be investigated and prosecuted;[209] thereby, in effect, pronouncing Articles 27, 28, and 56 of the Hague Regulations customary international law. France requested the extradition of sixteen persons from Germany to stand trial for violations pertaining to cultural property during the war, but no prosecutions were realized.[210] However, the 1919

---

[206] Convention on the Prevention and Punishment of the Crime of Genocide, UNGA Res 260A(III), 9 December 1948, in force 12 January 1951, 78 UNTS 277; and Universal Declaration of Human Rights, GA Res 217A(III), 10 December 1948, and 43(supp) *AJIL* (1949) 127.

[207] See Convention concerning the Protection of the World Cultural and Natural Heritage, 16 November 1972, in force 17 December 1975, 1037 UNTS 151; Universal Declaration on Cultural Diversity, 2 November 2001, UNESCO Doc 31C/Res 25, Annex I, 41 ILM (2002) 57; Convention for the Safeguarding of the Intangible Cultural Heritage, 17 October 2003, in force 20 April 2006, 2368 UNTS 1; Declaration concerning the Intentional Destruction of Cultural Heritage, 17 October 2003, UNESCO Doc 32C/Res 39; and Convention on the Protection and Promotion of the Diversity of Cultural Expressions, 20 October 2005, in force 18 March 2007, in UNESCO, *Records of the General Conference, 33rd session, Paris, 3–21 October 2005* (2 vols, 2005) vol I, at 83.

[208] See Declaration on the Rights of Persons Belonging to National or Ethnic, Religious and Linguistic Minorities, GA Res 47/135, 18 December 1992, UN Doc A/Res/47/135; 32 ILM (1993) 911; and Declaration on the Rights of Indigenous Peoples.

[209] Reproduced in 14 *AJIL* (1920) 95 at 114–115; and UNWCC, *History of the United Nations War Crimes Commission and the Development of the Law of War* (1948) at 34.

[210] Horne and Kramer, *German Atrocities 1914. A History of Denial* (2001) at 448.

List (prepared by delegations which included Italy and Japan) was revisited during the lead-up to the war crimes trials after 1944.

During the Second World War, the Allied Powers made successive announcements stating that they would hold Axis nationals who had violated the laws and customs of war to account at the end of the hostilities.[211] The 1943 London Declaration reiterated this warning and explicitly extended it to violations concerning civilian property. Also, they advised that such property would be subject to restitution whether it was held by nationals of Axis or neutral states.[212] The jurisdiction of the International Military Tribunal (IMT) extended to violations of the laws and customs of war including 'plunder of public or private property, wanton destruction of cities, towns or villages, or devastation not justified by military necessity'.[213]

The indictment of the major German war criminals at Nuremberg charged that as part of their 'plan of criminal exploitation', they had 'destroyed industrial cities, cultural monuments, scientific institutions, and property of all types in the occupied territories'.[214] Alfred Rosenberg had headed 'Einsatzstab Rosenberg', a programme which confiscated cultural objects from private German collections and occupied territories to fill the regime's own museums and institutions.[215] The IMT found that he had directed that the Hague Regulations 'were not applicable to the Occupied Eastern Territories'. It noted that he was 'responsible for a system of organised plunder of both public and private property throughout the invaded countries of Europe'.[216] Rosenberg was found guilty of this and other counts of the indictment and sentenced to death.

There was little further jurisprudence on war crimes concerning cultural property until the establishment of the International Criminal Tribunal for the former Yugoslavia in 1993. From the earliest phases of the Yugoslav wars, the various parties to the conflict deliberately targeted the cultural and religious property of the opposing parties.[217] Likewise, the international community under the auspices of

---

[211] See in particular, Declaration of the Four Nations on General Security (Moscow Declaration), 30 October 1943, 38 (supp) *AJIL* (1944) 7–8.

[212] Third preambular paragraph, 1943 London Declaration.

[213] Art 6(b) of the Charter of the International Military Tribunal, Nuremberg annexed to the Agreement by United Kingdom, United States, France and USSR for the Prosecution and Punishment of the Major War Criminals of the European Axis, 8 August 1945, 82 UNTS 279, and 39 (supp) *AJIL* (1945) 257.

[214] Count Three (War Crimes), Part E (Plunder of Public and Private Property), Indictment, in *Trial of the Major War Criminals, supra* note 16, at 11–30.

[215] Nicholas, *The Rape of Europa: The fate of Europe's treasures in the Third Reich and the Second World War* (1994).   [216] Nuremberg Judgment, *supra* note 16, at 95–96, and 237 *et seq.*

[217] *Report of the Secretary-General to the President of the UN Security Council, annexing the Interim Report of the Commission of Experts Established Pursuant to SC Res 780(1992)*, UN Doc S/1993/25274 (9 February 1993) (concluded that grave breaches and other violations of international humanitarian law had been committed in the territory of the former Yugoslavia including the destruction of cultural and religious property); Kéba M'Baye, *Final Report of the United Nations Commission of Experts Established Pursuant to SC Res. 780(1992)*, UN Doc S/1994 674 (27 May 1994) Annex XI: Destruction of Cultural Property Report, 66–68, at 285–297 (focused on Dubrovnik and the Mostar Bridge and only touched on the systematic nature of the destruction and damaging of cultural property); Fenwick, Annex XI.A: The Battle of Dubrovnik and the Law

the United Nations quickly resolved to investigate and prosecute those responsible for these acts. The adoption of the ICTY Statute by the international community during the progress of the armed conflict was observed to have both punitive and deterrent aims.[218]

The articulation of the crimes relating to the confiscation and destruction of cultural property in the ICTY Statute mimics Article 56 of the 1907 Hague Regulations rather than the Hague framework, even though all belligerents were Parties to the 1954 Convention and Protocol.[219] Article 3(d) of the Statute includes among the violations of the laws and customs of war:

[S]eizure, destruction or willful damage done to institutions dedicated to religion, charity and education, the arts and sciences, historic monuments and works of art and science.[220]

The ICTY has made clear that Article 3 is a catch-all provision which encompasses customary international law.[221] Under this provision, it must be shown that the international or internal armed conflict existed and had a close nexus with the alleged acts.[222] This provision covering non-international armed conflict reflects developments contained in the 1949 Geneva Conventions and 1954 Hague Convention.

There have been a number of indictments brought under Article 3(d), including Slobodan Milošević ('[w]ilful destruction or wilful damage done to historic monuments and institutions dedicated to education or religion' in violation of the laws or customs of war).[223] The most significant cases on this count pertain to the bombardment of the fortified city of Dubrovnik in early October 1991.[224] The leading cases involved Miodrag Jokić, a commander of the Yugoslav People's Army and responsible for the forces which attacked Dubrovnik on 6 October 1991, Pavle

---

of Armed Conflict; European Community Monitoring Mission, Cultural Heritage Report No 2, April 1995, at 2.

[218] Frulli, 'Advancing the Protection of Cultural Property through the Implementation of Individual Criminal Responsibility: The Case-Law of the International Criminal Tribunal for the former Yugoslavia', 15 *Italian Y.B. Int'l L.* (2005) 195, at 197.

[219] Yugoslavia was a High Contracting Party to the 1954 Hague Convention and 1954 Hague Protocol, and after its dissolution the successor states have become parties: Croatia (1992), Slovenia (1992), Bosnia and Herzegovina (1993), Serbia (2001), and Montenegro (2007). Serbia (2002), Slovenia (2004), Croatia (2006), and Montenegro (2007) are High Contracting Parties to the 1999 Second Protocol.

[220] While Art 3(d) ICTY Statute refers to 'seizure, destruction or damage', the Rome Statute's equivalent provision (Art 8(2)(b)(ix) refers only to 'attacks against' such property not including works of art).

[221] *Prosecutor v Anto Furundžija*, Trial Judgment, No IT-95-17, (10 December 1998) at 133. Art 3 was originally published as Annex to the Report of the Secretary-General Pursuant to para 2 of SC Res 808 (1993).

[222] *Strugar* Rule 98*bis* Motion, at 24; and *Prosecutor v Duško Tadić*, Appeal Judgment, No IT-94-1-A, Appeals Chamber, ICTY (2 October 1995) at 66–70.

[223] Milošević Amended Indictment 'Bosnia and Herzegovina' (22 November 2002), Count 21; and Second Amended Indictment 'Croatia' (28 July 2004), Count 19, Case No IT-02-54-T. There being an overlap between the counts under Arts 3(b) and 3(d) of the ICTY Statute.

[224] For detailed treatment see C Bories, *Les bombardements serbes sur la vieille ville de Dubrovnik: La protection internationale des biens culturels* (2005).

Strugar, his superior found to have 'legal and effective control' over the forces in the area during the relevant period, and Vladimir Kovačević.[225]

Several indictments issued by the ICTY reflect the overlap between this provision and protection afforded civilian objects generally in international humanitarian law.[226] The tribunal has affirmed that civilian objects enjoy a 'similar level of protection as a civilian population'.[227] The ICTY has repeatedly held that although acts under Article 3(d) overlap to a certain extent with the offence of unlawful attacks on civilian objects under Article 3(b), when the acts are specifically directed at the 'cultural heritage of a certain population', Article 3(d) is *lex specialis*.[228]

In *Kordić and Čerkez*, the Trial Chamber confirmed that the prohibition contained in Article 3(d) in respect of 'institutions dedicated to religion', in particular, is customary international law.[229] In that case, the defendants, who were Bosnian Croats, were found guilty of violations of the laws and customs of war arising from deliberate armed attacks against historic mosques in Bosnia and Herzegovina. The tribunal supported its finding of customary international law with reference to Article 27 of the 1907 Hague Regulations, Article 53 of 1977 *AP I*, and Article 1 of the 1954 Hague Convention.[230]

When determining which property falls within the protection afforded under Article 3(d), the tribunal has referenced definitions contained in conventions covering both during armed conflict and peacetime including the Roerich Pact,[231] and 1972 World Heritage Convention. In *Strugar,* the Trial Chamber placed significant weight on the Old Town's inscription on the World Heritage List. It observed that the List includes 'cultural and natural properties deemed to be of outstanding universal value from the point of view of history, art or science' and a reasonable trier of fact could conclude that it comes within the meaning of cultural property covered by Article 3(d).[232]

In respect of the *actus reus* (requisite material) element of this war crime, the tribunal has considered customary law concerning attacks on cultural property. Early in the life of the tribunal, the Trial Chamber in *Blaškić* took a restrictive view finding that they should not have been used for military purposes at the time of the acts nor located in the 'immediate vicinity of military objectives'.[233]

---

[225] The matter of *Prosecutor v Vladimir Kovačević*, Case No IT-01-42-2 was ordered by the ICTY to be transferred to and tried by the Republic of Serbia on 17 November 2006.

[226] Strugar Third Amended Indictment 'Dubrovnik' (10 December 2003), Counts 4, 5, and 6, Case No IT-02-42-PT; and Jokić Second Amended Indictment 'Dubrovnik' (27 August 2003), Counts 4, 5, and 6, Case No IT-01-42.

[227] *Prosecutor v Pavle Strugar*, Rule 98*bis* Motion, No IT-01-42-T, Trial Chamber II, ICTY (21 June 2004) at 62.

[228] *Strugar* Rule 98*bis* Motion.; *Prosecutor v Miodrag Jokić*, Trial Judgment, No IT-01-42/1-S, Trial Chamber I, ICTY (18 March 2004) at 46; *Dario Kordić and Mario Čerdez*, Trial Judgment, No IT-95-14/2-T (26 February 2001) at 36 and 360. Cf *Prosecutor v Dario Kordić and Mario Čerdez*, Appeal Judgment, Case No IT-95-14/2-A (17 December 2004) at 89–92 concerning educational institutions.   [229] *Kordić and Čerdez*, Trial Judgment, at 206.

[230] Ibid, at 359–362. See also Jokić, Trial Judgment, at 48.

[231] *Kordić and Čerkez*, Judgment, at 361.

[232] *Strugar* Rule 98*bis* Motion, at 80–81, and *Jokić*, Trial Judgment, at 49 and 51.

[233] *Prosecutor v Tihomir Blaškić*, Trial Judgment, No IT-1995-14-T, Trial Chamber, ICTY (3 March 2000) at 185.

It moved away from this interpretation in *Strugar,* where it rejected the notion that it must not be in the immediate vicinity of military objectives at the time of the attack or that this would justify an attack. The tribunal emphasized that it was the cultural property's use rather than its location which was determinative of loss of immunity.[234] Furthermore, the ICTY found it was presumed to enjoy the same general protection afforded to civilian objects, except where they had become military objectives because 'their nature, location, purpose or use make an effective contribution to military action and whose total or partial destruction, capture, or neutralisation, in the circumstances ruling at the time, offers a definite military advantage'.[235]

In respect of the *mens rea* requirement of this crime, it must be shown that the defendant committed the acted wilfully, that is, deliberately or with reckless disregard for the substantial likelihood of the destruction or damage of a protected cultural or religious property.[236] The perpetrator must act with the knowledge that the object is cultural property. For example, in *Strugar* this was evidenced by the fact that Dubrovnik was included on the World Heritage List, whilst in *Jokić* the tribunal noted that the 1954 Hague emblem was clearly visible.[237]

In respect of sentencing for war crimes against cultural property, the tribunal has stated that 'this crime represents a violation of values especially protected by the international community'.[238] In *Jokić,* the Trial Chamber found that the attack on Dubrovnik was exacerbated because it was a 'living city' and 'the existence of the population was intimately intertwined with its ancient heritage'.[239] It held that while 'it is a serious violation of international humanitarian law to attack civilian buildings, it is a crime of even greater seriousness to direct an attack on an especially protected site'.[240] A site once destroyed could not be returned to its original status.[241] Taking into account Jokić's remorse he was sentenced to seven years' imprisonment,[242] whilst Strugar was given eight years.[243]

---

[234] *Prosecutor v Pavle Strugar,* Trial Judgment, Chamber II, ICTY, No IT-01-42-T, (31 January 2005) at 310. Cf O'Keefe, *supra* note 1, at 321–322 arguing that this customary international provides that it is not solely use but nature, location, and purpose of cultural property which may render it a military objective.

[235] *Prosecutor v Radoslav Brđanin,* Trial Judgment, Case No IT-99-36-T, Trial Chamber II, ICTY (1 September 2004) at 596. The court also noted even non-state parties to *AP I,* including the United States, Turkey, and India, recognized the customary law nature of Art 52(2) *AP I* during the diplomatic conference called for the Second Hague Protocol in 1999: ibid, at footnote 1509.

[236] Ibid, at 599; and *Prosecutor v Pavle Strugar,* Appeals Judgment, No IT-01-42-A, Appeals Chamber, ICTY (17 July 2008) at 277–278.

[237] *Prosecutor v Miodrag Jokić,* Trial Judgment, No IT-01-42/1-S, Trial Chamber I, ICTY (18 March 2004) at 23 and 49; and *Strugar,* Trial Judgment, at 22, 183, 279, 327 and 329.

[238] *Jokić,* Trial Judgment, at 46.   [239] Ibid, at 51.   [240] Ibid, at 53.

[241] Ibid, at 52.

[242] Confirmed on appeal: *Prosecutor v Miodrag Jokić,* Judgment on Sentencing Appeal, No IT-01-42/1-A, Appeals Chamber, ICTY (30 August 2005).

[243] This sentence was reduced on appeal to seven and a half years imprisonment: *Strugar,* Appeals Judgment, and pardoned by Decision of the President on the application for pardon or commutation of sentence of Pavle Strugar, No IT-01-42-ES (16 January 2009).

B. Crime against humanity of persecution

The prohibition of crimes against humanity in international law stretches back to the early twentieth century and the investigation by the 1919 Commission of offences committed by Germany and her allies against their own nationals, particularly in Turkey and Austria.[244] Dissent from the United States meant no provision for the prosecution of these acts was incorporated in the peace treaty with Austria.[245] However, under Article 230 of its peace treaty with Allied Powers (Treaty of Sèvres), Turkey was obliged to recognize and cooperate with any tribunal appointed by the Allies to prosecute alleged perpetrators, by providing relevant information and surrendering persons 'responsible for the massacres committed during the continuance of the state of war on the territories which formed part of the Turkish Empire on 1st August 1914'.[246] There was also provision made for the restitution of property removed from these communities.[247] Significantly, whilst these acts occurred within the context of an international armed conflict, the provision targeted the acts of a state against its own nationals. However, British attempts to try the perpetrators before an international tribunal and Turkish endeavours in national courts met with limited success.[248]

As noted earlier, during the Second World War the Allied Powers, warned perpetrators of atrocities against civilians and civilian property that they would be held to account. Many atrocities of the Axis forces went beyond the established time and space parameters of existing international humanitarian law as defined by the Hague Regulations. They had occurred prior to the commencement of war and were often perpetrated by states against their own nationals within their own territory. Early Allied declarations concerning the punishment of these acts were tightly bound to the constraints of the Hague Conventions and made no reference to such acts. However, gradually it was accepted that the remit of the Nuremberg tribunal would not confine itself to the violation of the laws and customs of war committed against Allied combatants or occupied civilians, that is, war crimes. Rather, it was extended to include acts perpetrated against civilians that were stateless or Axis citizens on Axis territory.

This seminal leap in international law was encapsulated in Article 6(c) of the London Charter which extended the International Military Tribunal's jurisdiction to encompass crimes against humanity including 'persecutions on political, racial or religious grounds in execution of or in connection with any crime within the jurisdiction of the Tribunal, whether or not in violation of the domestic law

---

[244] 1919 Commission Report, *supra* note 209, at 114–115 and 122. Egon Schwelb later noted that most of the charges listed by the commission referred to the persecution of Armenian and Greek minorities by Turkish authorities: Schwelb, 'Crimes Against Humanity', 23 *BYBIL* (1946) 178, at 181.

[245] 1919 Commission Report, ibid, at 14; and 'Memorandum of Reservations Presented by the Representatives of the United States to the Report of the Commission on Responsibilities', Annex II, 4 April 1919, 14 *AJIL* (1920) 127, at 134.

[246] Treaty of Peace with Turkey, 10 August 1920, not ratified, Cmd 964 (1920), *British and Foreign State Papers*, vol 113, at 652, and 15 (supp) *AJIL* (1921)179.

[247] Art 144, Treaty of Peace with Turkey.

[248] Hughes, 'Recent Questions and Negotiations', 18 *AJIL* (1924) 229, at 237.

of the country where perpetrated'. Count Four of the Nuremberg Indictment detailed how 'Jews [were] systematically persecuted since 1933...from Germany and from the occupied Western Countries were sent to the Eastern Countries for extermination'.[249] The IMT held that confiscation and destruction of religious and cultural institutions and objects of Jewish communities amounted to persecution that was a crime against humanity.[250] The Allied Powers later remedied the drafting error for subsequent trials that had led the IMT to restrict its findings to acts committed during or in connection with the war.[251] Despite this significant limitation, the prosecution of crimes against humanity without reference to 'time and place and national sovereignty' heightened the Nuremberg Charter's importance for the promotion of international human rights.[252]

Alfred Rosenberg was found guilty of crimes against humanity including the plunder in 1941 of Jewish homes in Western Europe through his 'Einsatzstab Rosenberg'. The tribunal also held that as supreme authority in the Occupied Eastern Territories from mid-1941, he was instrumental in the persecution of the Jews and opponents of the Nazi regime.[253] Julius Streicher, who was not a member of the military, was found guilty on Count Four for his incitement of the persecution and extermination of Jews through propaganda including as publisher of the anti-Semitic newspaper, *Der Stürmer*. He was also found to have been responsible for the destruction of the Nuremberg synagogue in 1938.[254] Later, the District Court of Jerusalem found Adolf Eichmann guilty of crimes against humanity (and war crimes) arising from, among other things, the destruction of synagogues and other religious institutions which amounted to persecution.[255]

The international and hybrid criminal tribunals established under the auspices of the United Nations since the 1990s have invariably extended jurisdiction to the crimes against humanity of persecution.[256] The establishment of the ICTY a half century after Nuremberg reopened the question of persecution as it related to

---

[249] Ibid.   [250] Nuremberg Judgment, *supra* note 16, at 243–247.

[251] See Robinson, 'The International Military Tribunal and the Holocaust: Some Legal Reflections', 7 *Is. L.R.* (1972) 1 at 7–12; and Art II(1)(c), Control Council Law No 10, Punishment of Persons Guilty of War Crimes, Crimes against Peace and against Humanity, 20 December 1945, *Official Gazette of the Control Council of Germany*, No 3, 31 January 1946, at 50–55.

[252] Schwelb, *supra* note 245.   [253] Nuremberg Judgment, *supra* note 16, at 287–288.

[254] Nuremberg Judgment, *supra* note 16, at 294–295. See also Von Schirach, ibid, at 310–311, found guilty of Count Four. Cf *Flick* and *Farben* decided by the US Military Tribunal pursuant to Control Council Law No 10 where it held that acts against property did not constitute crimes against humanity: UNWCC, *Law Reports of Trials of War Criminals*, (15 vols, 1947–49) vol VI, at 1215–1216, and vol VIII, Part 2, at 1123–1133.

[255] *Attorney-General of the Government of Israel v Adolf Eichmann*, 361 ILR 5 (Dist Ct of Jerusalem, 1961) at 57.

[256] Art 3(h) ICTR Statute; Art 7(1)(h) (Persecution against any identifiable group or collectivity on political, racial, national, ethnic, cultural, religious, gender grounds as identified in para 3, or other grounds universally recognized as impermissible under international law, in connection with any act, referred to in this paragraph or any other crime within the jurisdiction of the Court) and 2(g) defines 'Persecution' as 'intentional and severe deprivation of fundamental rights contrary to international law by reason of the identity of the group or collectivity', Rome Statute; Art 2(h) Statute of the Special Court for Sierra Leone; Art 9 Statute of the Special Court for Cambodia; Art 3 (Religious Persecution) and Art 5 (Crimes Against Humanity including persecution) Law on the Establishment of Cambodian Extraordinary Chambers.

cultural heritage. During the first years of the Yugoslav conflicts, the International Law Commission in its 1991 Report on the Draft Code of Crimes Against Peace and Security related persecution on social, political, religious, or cultural grounds to 'human rights violations... committed in a systematic manner or on a mass scale by government officials or by groups that exercise de facto power over a particular territory...'.[257] The ILC noted that the systematic destruction of monuments, buildings, and sites of highly symbolic value for a specific social, religious, or cultural group amounted to persecution.[258] Moreover, this definition extended to intangible elements of heritage including the suppression of language, religious practices, and detention of community or religious leaders.

Under the ICTY Statute, crimes against humanity are covered by Article 5. This provision does not list acts against cultural property or civilian property per se nor does it define 'persecution'. However, the ICTY has held that the destruction or damaging of the institutions of a particular political, racial, or religious group is clearly a crime against humanity of persecution under Article 5(h).[259] Referring to its own earlier jurisprudence, the Nuremberg Judgment, and the 1991 ILC Report, the Trial Chamber in *Kordić and Čerkez* expounded that:

[t]his act, when perpetrated with the requisite discriminatory intent, amounts to an attack on the very religious identity of a people. As such, it manifests a nearly pure expression of the notion of 'crimes against humanity', for all humanity is indeed injured by the destruction of a unique religious culture and its concomitant cultural objects.[260]

The ICTY has stated that the attacks must be directed against a civilian population, be widespread or systematic, and perpetrated on discriminatory grounds for damage inflicted to cultural property to qualify as persecution.[261] This requirement is intended to ensure that crimes of a collective nature are penalized because a person is 'victimised not because of his individual attributes but rather because of his membership of a targeted civilian population'.[262] Similarly, cultural property is protected not for its own sake, but because it represents a particular group. While it is now generally accepted that the crimes of humanity, including acts of persecution, do not need to take place during armed conflict, it is a requirement under Article 5 of the ICTY Statute. The tribunal must find a nexus with the international or internal armed conflict in order to have jurisdiction.[263]

The Lašva Valley cases with the defendants Tihomir Blaškić, Dario Kordić, and Mario Čerkez serve to underscore the ICTY's jurisprudence concerning acts against cultural property being defined as the crime against humanity of

---

[257] *Report of the International Law Commission on the Work of its Forty-Third Session*, UN Doc A/46/10/suppl.10 (1991) at 268.   [258] Ibid.

[259] *Kordić and Čerkez*, Trial Judgment, at 207.   [260] Ibid, at 206 and 207.

[261] *Prosecutor v Zoran Kupreškić et al*, Trial Judgment, Case No IT-95-16-T, Trial Chamber, ICTY (14 January 2000) at 544; and *Prosecutor v Tihomir Blaškić*, Trial Judgment, Case No IT-95-14-T, Trial Chamber, ICTY (30 March 2000) at 207.

[262] *Prosecutor v Duško Tadić*, Opinion Trial Judgment, No IT-94-1-T, Trial Chamber, ICTY (7 May 1997) at 644.

[263] *Blaškić*, Trial Judgment, at 66 and 227; *Tadić*, Appeal Judgment, at 249, and *Prosecutor v Radislav Krstić*, Trial Judgment, Case No IT-98-33, Trial Chamber, ICTY (2 August 2001) at 480.

persecution. From November 1991 to March 1994, the primary political party in Croatia at the time, the Croatian Democratic Union (HDZ) espoused the right of secession of the 'Croatian nation inside its historical and natural borders'. The Croatian Democratic Union of Bosnia and Herzegovina (HDZ-BiH) was the main Bosnian Croatian party and it had an identical platform. In November 1991, the Croatian Community of Herceg-Bosnia proclaimed its right to exist separately in the territory of Bosnia and Herzegovina. The Croatian Defence Council (HVO) was the Community's supreme executive, administrative, and defence authority. These groups, with their military and police forces, organized and executed a campaign of persecution and ethnic cleansing, which included targeting Bosnian Muslim civilians, their property, and cultural heritage in the Lašva Valley.

In respect of the material element or *actus reus* of persecution under Article 5(h) of the ICTY Statute, the tribunal has found that it encompasses crimes against persons and crimes against property as long as it is accompanied by the requisite intent.[264] Under this provision, the tribunal has dealt with crimes against property in general and those specifically directed at cultural property. It has held that comprehensive destruction of homes and property may cause forced transfer or deportation and, if done discriminatorily, constitutes 'the destruction of the livelihood of a certain population' and therefore, persecution.[265] In *Blaškić*, the Trial Chamber convicted the defendant of the persecution which took 'the form of confiscation or destruction' by Bosnian Croat forces of 'symbolic buildings...belonging to the Muslim population of Bosnia-Herzegovina'.[266] It found that 'the methods of attack and the scale of the crimes committed against the Muslim population or the edifices symbolizing their culture sufficed to establish beyond reasonable doubt that the attack was aimed at the Muslim civilian population'.[267]

Further, the ICTY has held that a vital element of crimes under Article 5 is that they are part of 'a widespread or systematic attack against a civilian population'.[268] Acts should not be examined in isolation but in terms of their cumulative effect.[269] However, they do not need to be part of a pre-existing criminal policy or plan.[270] While the tribunal acknowledged that this element of the test may exclude certain acts against property of a group from the realm of criminal persecution, it has affirmed that destruction of cultural property, even a single act, with the requisite discriminatory intent may constitute persecution.[271] Further, it has emphasized the need that it be directed against 'civilian populations'.[272]

---

[264] *Blaškić*, Trial Judgment, at 233.
[265] *Kupreškić et al*, Trial Judgment, at 631 (involving the massacre and destruction of homes in Ahmići). [266] *Blaškić*, Trial Judgment, at 227–228.
[267] Ibid, at 425. [268] *Krstić*, Trial Judgment, at 535.
[269] *Kupreškić et al*, Trial Judgment, at 615.
[270] *Blaškić*, Appeal Judgment, at 120; and *Prosecutor v Dragoljub Kunarac et al.*, Appeal Judgment, Case No IT-96-23, Appeals Chamber, ICTY (12 June 2002) at 98.
[271] *Kordić and Čerkez*, Trial Judgment, at 196, 199, 205, and 207.
[272] *Kunarac et al*, Appeal Judgment, at 78, 87, and 90–92; *Prosecutor v Tihomir Blaškić*, Appeals Judgment, Case No IT-95-14-A, Appeals Chamber, ICTY (29 July 2004) at 103–116; and *Prosecutor v Milan Martić*, Appeals Judgment, Case No IT-95-11-A, Appeals Chamber, ICTY, (8 October 2008) at 310–314.

The Trial Chamber found that an act must reach the same level of gravity as the other crimes against humanity enumerated in Article 5. However, it has added that persecutory acts are not limited to acts listed in Article 5 or elsewhere in the ICTY Statute, 'but also include the denial of other fundamental human rights, provided they are of equal gravity or severity'.[273] The Appeals Chamber in *Blaškić* found that committing an act with the requisite intent is not sufficient, the act itself must 'constitute the denial or infringement upon a fundamental right laid down in customary international law'.[274] In *Kupreškić*, Trial Chamber stated: '[A]lthough the realm of human rights is dynamic and expansive, not every denial of a human right may constitute a crime against humanity.'[275] The test will only be met when there is a gross violation of a fundamental right.[276]

Persecution requires a specific additional *mens rea* element over and above that needed for other crimes against humanity, namely a discriminatory intent 'on political, racial or religious' grounds' (not necessarily cultural).[277] Although the *actus reus* of persecution may be identical to other crimes against humanity it was distinguishable because it was committed on discriminatory grounds. The ICTY has pointed out that persecution may be 'acts rendered serious not by their apparent cruelty but by the discrimination they seek to instil within humankind'.[278] There is no additional requirement of 'persecutory intent'.[279] It noted that the intent to discriminate need not be the primary intent but a significant one.[280] In addition, this discriminatory intent must be combined with knowledge of an attack on civilians and that the act forms part of that attack.[281]

The severity of sentences handed down to persons convicted under this count compared to war crimes illustrates the gravity with which it is held by the tribunal. For example, the Trial Chamber sentenced Tihomir Blaškić to 45 years' imprisonment after he was found guilty of crimes against humanity (and Article 3(d)) which included the destruction and plunder of property and, in particular, of institutions dedicated to religion and education;[282] while Dario Kordić received 25 years which was upheld on appeal and Mario Čerkez received 15 years' imprisonment reduced to six years on appeal.[283]

Several indictments brought before the ICTY for the wanton destruction or damage of cultural property related to religious or ethnic groups included charges of persecution and genocide. However, while such acts have been used to establish

---

[273] *Krstić*, Trial Judgment, at 535; and *Prosecutor v Radoslav Brdanin*, Appeals Judgment, Appeals Chamber, ICTY (3 April 2007) at 296–297.

[274] *Prosecutor v Tihomir Blaškić*, Appeals Judgment, Case No IT-95-14-A, Appeals Chamber, ICTY (29 July 2004) at 139.   [275] Kupreškić *et al*, Trial Judgment, at 618.

[276] Ibid, at 621.

[277] *Blaškić*, Trial Judgment, at 283; *Krstić*, Trial Judgment, at 480; and *Kordić and Čerkez*, Trial Judgment, at 211 and 212.   [278] *Blaškić*, Trial Judgment, at 227.

[279] *Blaškić*, Appeals Judgment, at 165.

[280] *Kupreškić*, Trial Judgment, at 431, 607, and 625.

[281] *Blaškić*, Appeals Judgment, at 121–128.

[282] *Blaškić*'s sentence was substituted on appeal to nine years: *Prosecutor v Tihomir Blaškić*, Appeal Judgment, Case No IT-95-14-A, Appeals Chamber, ICTY (29 July 2004).

[283] *Prosecutor v Dario Kordić and Mario Čerkez*, Appeal Judgment, Case No IT-95-14/2, Appeals Chamber, ICTY (17 December 2004).

the *mens rea* of a defendant, that is, the discriminatory intent required for proving genocide and persecution. The targeting of cultural property may amount to *actus reus* in respect of the crime of persecution, but as explained below, the tribunal has not included such acts within the definition of genocide under Article 4 of the ICTY Statute.

C. Genocide

Cultural heritage has been intimately connected to the prosecution of the crime of genocide in international law since it was first articulated in the 1940s. However, that relationship has been fraught and remains contentious. The reasons are complex and perennial. In this section, I examine the contestations concerning the 'cultural' elements of genocide during the negotiation of the 1948 Genocide Convention, and then I consider how the evidence of the destruction or damage of cultural property of the targeted group has played a vital role in establishing individual criminal responsibility for genocide before the ICTY and state responsibility in the 2007 decision of the International Court of Justice in *Application of the Convention on the Prevention and Punishment of the Crime of Genocide* (*Genocide* case).[284]

1. Nuremberg, 1948 Genocide Convention, and cultural genocide

The articulation of the crime of genocide in the mid-twentieth century evolved from existing international humanitarian law. Many acts perpetrated by the Nuremberg defendants as part of their genocidal programme had been outlawed by international law as evidenced by their inclusion on the 1919 List, like denationalization, pillage, confiscation of property, wanton destruction of religious, charitable, educational, and historic buildings and monuments.[285] The United Nations War Crimes Commission (UNWCC) maintained that crimes like 'denationalisation' were not legal, even if they were not specifically enumerated in the various Hague Conventions.[286] It pointed to the preamble of the 1907 Hague IV Convention which stipulates that if an act is not covered by the Convention, it must be considered in the light of principles derived from 'the laws of humanity and dictated by public conscience'.[287]

The term 'genocide' was only coined by Raphael Lemkin in 1943.[288] The UNWCC's earliest response to genocide, following Lemkin's lobbying, was the

---

[284] *Bosnia and Herzegovina v Serbia and Montenegro*, ICJ, Judgment of 26 February 2007, at <http://www.icj-cij.org/docket/files/91/13685.pdf> [last accessed 2 May 2010].

[285] 1919 Commission Report, *supra* note 209, at 114–115; and C.149, 4 October 1945, at 6, 6/34/PAG-3/1.1.0, United Nations War Crimes Commission 1943–1949, Predecessor Archives Group, United Nations Archives, New York (UNWCC Archive).

[286] C.148, 28 September 1945, 2–3, 6/34/PAG-3/1.1.0, UNWCC Archive.

[287] Eighth recital, Preamble, 1907 Hague IV Convention; and Ečer, Scope of the Retributive Action of the United Nations according to their Official Declarations, III/4, 27 April 1944, 6, box 9, reel 36, PAG-3/1.1.3, UNWCC Archive.

[288] Lemkin, *Axis Rule in Occupied Europe. Laws of Occupation, Analysis of Government, Proposals for Redress* (1944) ch 9.

re-articulation of the 'denationalisation of inhabitants of occupied territory'.[289] To this end, the UNWCC's Committee III (Legal) focused on provisions like Articles 27 and 56 of the Hague Regulations. It employed an expansive interpretation of Article 56,[290] by suggesting that the 'rationale' for this provision was the protection of spiritual values and intellectual life related to such institutions and objects.[291] Furthermore, the deliberate removal or destruction of cultural objects from the group was viewed as a fundamental component of this international crime.[292] When these provisions were interpreted in the spirit of the preamble of the Hague Convention, Committee III unanimously agreed that 'denationalisation' was forbidden by international law.[293] Committee III defined 'denationalisation' as a crime driven by policies adopted by an occupying power for the purpose of 'disrupting and disintegrating the national conscience, spiritual life and national individuality',[294] noting that it was committed not against individuals but against the group.[295]

Lemkin argued that while the various acts often perpetrated to achieve a genocidal purpose were largely outlawed by international law, there was a need to recognize the heinousness of the acts which he termed 'genocide', that is, the aim to destroy the physical and cultural elements of targeted groups. For this reason, it was more than simply mass murder because it resulted in 'the specific losses of civilization in the form of the cultural contributions which can only be made by groups of people united through national, racial or cultural characteristics'.[296]

The word genocide did not appear in the London Charter establishing the jurisdiction of the International Military Tribunal. However, Count Four of the indictment of the major war criminals, based on Article 6(c) of the Charter, charged them with 'deliberate and systematic genocide, viz., the extermination of racial and national groups, against civilian populations of certain occupied territories in order to destroy particular races and classes of people, and national, racial or religious groups…'.[297] However, the term 'genocide' was not explicitly used in the Nuremberg Judgment. Lemkin conceded that the method by which the crime was incorporated into the indictment, via the count on crimes against humanity,

---

[289] See Notes of Committee III meeting, 9 October 1945, box 5, reel 34, PAG-3/1.0.2, UNWCC.

[290] See Schwelb, Note on the Criminality of 'Attempts to Denationalise the Inhabitants of Occupied Territory', III/15, 10 September 1945, at 11; and Draft Report Committee III on the Criminality of 'Attempts to Denationalise the Inhabitants of Occupied Territory', III/17, 24 September 1945, at 8 and 9, box 9, reel 36, PAG-3/1.1.3, UNWCC Archive.

[291] C.149, 4 October 1945, at 8, 6/34/PAG-3/1.1.0.

[292] Including the deportation of children to the occupier's state to educate them; the interference in occupied people's religious traditions; removal of national symbols and names; compulsory or automatic granting of citizenship of the occupier; and colonization of the occupied territory by nationals of the occupier: III/17, 24 September 1945, at 6, 9/36/PAG-3/1.1.3, UNWCC Archive.

[293] III/17, 24 September 1945, at 8, 9/36/PAG-3/1.1.3.

[294] Report Sub-Committee, 2 December 1942, C.1, and Preliminary Report Chairman of Committee III, 28 September 1945, C.148, 2, box 6, reel 34, PAG-3/1.1.0, UNWCC Archive.

[295] See Criminality of Attempts to Denationalise the Inhabitants of Occupied Territory, 4 October 1945, C.149, at 6, box 6, reel 34, PAG-3/1.1.0, UNWCC Archive.

[296] Lemkin, *supra* note 288, at 84.

[297] Nuremberg Indictment, in *Trial Proceedings, supra* note 18, vol 1, at 11–30.

proved problematic.[298] He noted that whilst genocide usually occurred under the guise of armed conflict, any definition should not differentiate between acts taking place during peace or war time.[299]

Lemkin's broader notion of genocide, which included cultural elements, was affirmed by the second wave of prosecutions pursued under Control Council Law No 10, which did not require a nexus to be made between crimes against humanity and an armed conflict. The indictment in the case of *Ulrich Greifelt and Others,* before the US Military Tribunal at Nuremberg, covered the 'systematic program of genocide, aimed at the destruction of foreign nations and ethnic groups, in part by murderous extermination, and in part by the elimination and suppression of national characteristics'.[300] Likewise, in the *Artur Grieser* case, the Supreme National Tribunal of Poland used the term for the first time in a judgment denouncing 'physical and spiritual genocide' and attacks on smaller nations' right to exist and have 'an identity and culture of their own'.[301] The same court in the *Amon Leopold Goeth* case stated that 'the wholesale extermination of Jews and...Poles had all the characteristics of genocide in the biological meaning of this term, and embraced in addition, the destruction of the cultural life of these nations'.[302]

Two months after the Nuremberg Judgment, the UN General Assembly on 11 December 1946 unanimously adopted the Resolution on the Crime of Genocide (Genocide Resolution).[303] The Resolution augmented the view that genocide was a crime in international law before the Genocide Convention.[304] In its Advisory Opinion on *Reservations to the Convention on Genocide,* the ICJ found that the Convention encapsulated 'principles which are recognized by civilized nations as binding on States, even without any conventional obligations'.[305]

The Genocide Resolution states that genocide 'is a crime under international law', independent of crimes against humanity and without reference to a nexus to armed conflict.[306] The Resolution's preamble notes that genocide 'shocked the

---

[298] Lemkin, 'Genocide as a Crime under International Law', 41 *AJIL* (1947) 145, at 148.

[299] Lemkin, *supra* note 288, at 93.

[300] *US v Greifelt and Others* (US Military Tribunal, Nuremberg), 13 LRTWC (1949) 1, at 36–42, and 15 *Annual Digest* (1948) 653, at 654.

[301] *Poland v Greiser* (Supreme National Tribunal of Poland) 13 LRTWC (1949) 70 at 114, and 105, and 13 *Annual Digest* (1946) 387, at 389. The offences for which he was indicted included: 'Systematic destruction of Polish culture, robbery of Polish cultural treasures and germanization of the Polish country and population, and illegal seizure of public property' (ibid, 71).

[302] *Poland v Goeth* (Supreme National Tribunal of Poland), 7 LRTWC (1946) 4, at 9, and 13 *Annual Digest* (1946) 268.   [303] GA Res 96(I), 11 December 1946, *YBUN* (1946–47) at 255.

[304] See Justice Trial (*Josef Altstötter and Others*) (US Military Tribunal), 4 LRTWC (1946) 48 stated that: '[t]he General Assembly is not an international legislature, but it is the most authoritative organ in existence for the interpretation of world opinion. Its recognition as an international crime is persuasive evidence of the fact'; and *Reservations to the Convention on the Prevention and Punishment of the Crime of Genocide Case,* ICJ Reports (1951) 15, at 23, and *Barcelona Traction, Light and Power Co case (Belgium v. Spain),* ICJ Reports (1970) 3 at 32.   [305] Ibid, at 23.

[306] Para 1, GA Res 96(I). The range of groups covered by the Genocide Resolution—'racial, religious, political and other groups'—reflects the list contained in Art 6(c) of the London Charter except that that list was exhaustive. The initial draft of the Resolution was narrower and referred to 'national, racial, ethnical or religious groups', which is closer to the definition contained in Art II Genocide Convention: UN Doc A/BUR/50.

conscience of mankind [and] resulted in great losses to humanity in the form of cultural and other contributions represented by these groups'. The phrase recalls the humanitarian law origins of the proposed convention and the rationale propagated by Lemkin. It was a sentiment contained in the preamble of the 1954 Hague Convention. However, the Resolution went on to define genocide narrowly as 'a denial of the right to existence of entire human groups, as homicide is the denial of the right to live for individual human beings'.

Following a direction from the Economic and Social Council, the Secretary-General requested the Division of Human Rights to prepare a Draft Convention on the Prevention and Punishment of Genocide. The Secretariat draft categorized acts constituting genocide in three parts: physical, biological, and cultural.[307] Acts that fell within the cultural element of its definition included those designed to destroy the characteristics of the group including the forced removal of children to another group, systematic and forced exile of representatives of the targeted group, complete prohibition on the use of its language, systematic destruction of books in the language or those related to its religious practices, and 'systematic destruction of historical or religious monuments or their diversion to alien uses, or destruction or dispersion of documents or objects of historical, artistic, or religious interest and of religious accessories'.[308]

Of the legal experts consulted by the Secretariat, only Lemkin supported the inclusion of 'cultural genocide'. He argued a group's right to exist was justified morally but also because of 'the value of the contribution made by such a group to civilization generally'. He reiterated: 'If the diversity of cultures were destroyed, it would be as disastrous for civilization as the physical destruction of nations'.[309] The other legal experts, Donnedieu de Vabres and Vespasian V Pella maintained that these cultural elements 'represented an undue extension of the notion of genocide and amounted to reconstituting the former protection of minorities (which has been based on other conceptions) under the cover of the term of genocide'.[310] The division between the proponents and opponents of the inclusion of cultural elements in the definition of genocide was sustained as the Draft Convention progressed through various stages in the UN system.[311]

---

[307] Committee on the Progressive Development of International Law and its Codification, Draft Convention for the Prevention and Punishment of Genocide, prepared by the Secretariat, 6 June 1947, UN Doc A/AC.10/42 (Secretariat draft).

[308] Draft Art 3(e), UN Doc A/AC.10/42 at 3.

[309] See UN Doc E/447, 27; and Contribution of the Convention on the Prevention and Punishment of the Crime of Genocide to the Prevention of Discrimination and the Protection of Minorities, December 7, 1949, UN Doc E/CN4/Sub.2/80, at 22.   [310] Ibid.

[311] Ad Hoc Committee on Genocide, Report of the Committee and Draft Convention drawn up by the Committee, K Azkoul, Rapporteur, 24 May 1948, UN Doc E/794, 17: agreed to retain 'cultural genocide' but as a separate provision which was narrowly defined. Article III encompassed 'any deliberate act committed with the intent to destroy the language, religion, or culture of a national, racial or religious group'. It referred specifically to the prohibition on the use of language of the group; and the destruction or prevention of the use of libraries, museums, schools, historic monuments, places of worship, or other cultural institutions and objects of the group. Article III was adopted 4-0-3. The United States condemned its inclusion declaring such acts were more appropriately dealt with under the protection of minorities: UN Doc E/794, 18. Next, the discussion in the Sixth (Legal) Committee was confined simply to the question of whether the Convention should include cultural

The Genocide Convention was adopted by the General Assembly on 9 December 1948. The only element of the cultural component contained in the Secretariat's definition of genocide that remains in final text is the reference to the removal of children from the group.[312] As noted above, this provision ties in with protections included in the 1949 Geneva Conventions. Like the Genocide Resolution, the Genocide Convention defines genocide as a crime under international law independently of crimes against humanity and specifically affirms that it can be 'committed in time of peace or in time of war'. Freed of these strictures, the Convention has been viewed as an important instrument for safeguarding human rights norms.

Despite successive opportunities to extend the definition of genocide to include acts which cover those eliminate cultural elements of the original draft—the international community has consistently refused to do so. The parameters demarcated by Article II of the Convention have been reaffirmed repeatedly by the international community and international courts.[313]

2. ICTY and individual criminal responsibility for genocide

Following the 1948 Genocide Convention, Article 4 the ICTY Statute contains the same definition of genocide as Article II and does not require that the acts occur during an armed conflict to constitute the crime of genocide. The acts must have been perpetrated with a specific intent or *dolus specialis,* that is, with the intent 'to destroy, in whole or in part, a national, ethnic, racial or religious group as such...'.[314]

The ICTY has emphasized that there are two elements to the special intent requirement of the crime of genocide: (i) the act or acts must target a national, ethnical, racial, or religious group;[315] and (ii) the act or acts must seek to destroy all or part of that group. It has found that the *travaux préparatoires* of the Genocide Convention highlight that the list of groups contained in Article II 'was designed more to describe a single phenomenon, roughly corresponding to what was recognised, before the second world war, as "national minorities", rather than to refer to several distinct prototypes of human groups'.[316] Furthermore, the Trial

---

genocide. The Committee voted against the inclusion of the provision relating to cultural genocide (25-16-4): UN Doc A/C.6/SR.83 at item 30, at 206; and Daes, 'Protection of Minorities under the International Bill of Human Rights and the Genocide Convention', in *Xenion: Festschrift für Pan J Zepos anlasslich seines 65*, II, (1973) 35 at 69. Its inclusion was not effectively revived thereafter. In the Economic and Social Council: ECOSOC, UN Doc E/SR.218 and 219; and J Spiropolous, Genocide: Draft Convention and Report of the Economic and Social Council, Report of the Sixth Committee, December 3, 1948, UN Doc A/760; and finally, the General Assembly: UN Doc A/PV.178 and 179 (with the USSR effort to reintroduce a new Art III being defeated 14-31-10).

[312] Art 2(e), Genocide Convention.
[313] See Art 2, ICTR Statute; Art 6, Rome Statute; Art 9, Statute of the Special Court for Cambodia; and Art 4, Law on the Establishment of Cambodian Extraordinary Chambers.
[314] *Krstić*, Trial Judgment, at 480.   [315] Ibid, at 551–553.
[316] Ibid, at 556. Cf Crimes against humanity of persecution also includes political groups.

Chamber emphasized that it was not individual members of the group that were to be targeted but the group itself.[317]

In the case of *Radoslav Krstić*, where the defendant was charged with atrocities related to the fall of Srebrenica in mid-1995, the ICTY Trial Chamber took the opportunity to re-examine the question of whether acts directed at the cultural aspects of a group constituted genocide as a crime in international law. It noted that

[t]he physical destruction of a group is the most obvious method, but one may also conceive of destroying a group through purposeful eradication of its culture and identity resulting in the eventual extinction of the group as an entity distinct from the remainder of the community.[318]

The tribunal observed that, unlike genocide, persecution was not limited to the physical or biological destruction of a group but extended to include 'all acts designed to destroy the social and/or cultural bases of a group'.[319] The tribunal noted that some recent declarations and case-law interpreted the 'intent to destroy clause in Article 4' as relating to acts that involved cultural forms of destruction of the group.[320]

Nonetheless, the tribunal found that the drafters of the Genocide Convention expressly considered and rejected the inclusion of the cultural elements in the list of acts constituting genocide.[321] Indeed, it observed that despite numerous opportunities to recalibrate the definition of genocide, Article II of the Convention was replicated in the statutes of the two *ad hoc* tribunals for the former Yugoslavia and Rwanda, the 1996 Draft ILC Code of Crimes Against Peace and Security of Mankind,[322] and the Rome Statute for the establishment of the International Criminal Court.[323] The Trial Chamber in *Krstić* found these developments had not altered the definition of genocidal acts in customary international law and felt confined by the principle of *nullum crime sine lege*. The Appeals Chamber in *Krstić*

---

[317] Ibid, at 551–553.   [318] Ibid, at 574.   [319] Ibid, at 575.

[320] Including GA Res. 47/121, 18 December 1992 defining ethnic cleansing as 'genocide'.

[321] *Krstić*, Trial Judgment, at 576.

[322] Art 17, Draft Code of Crimes Against the Peace and Security of Mankind, 51 UN GAOR Supp (No 10) at 14, UN Doc A/CN.4/L.532, corr 1, corr 3 (1996). During the 1951 session, Jean Spiropoulos prepared a revised draft code (UN Doc A/CN.4/44) added the word 'including' at the end of the chapeau of the definition prior to the enumeration of the acts of genocide: 2 *U.N.Y.B.I.L.C.* (1951) at 136. Art II of the Genocide Convention was deliberately an exhaustive list of acts: UN Doc A/C.6/SR.81. At the 1989 session, the ILC noted that Special Rapporteur Doudou Thiam's definition of genocide which also included this wording was favourably received 'because unlike that in the 1948 Genocide Convention, the enumeration of acts constituting the crime of genocide proposed by the Special Rapporteur was not exhaustive'. *Report of the ILC on the Work of Its Forty-First Session*, GAOR, 41st session, Supp No 10, UN Doc A/44/10, (1989) 59, at 159. The final draft however effectively reproduced the definition of acts contained in Art II, Genocide Convention.

[323] The ILC, when drafting a code of crimes which it submitted to the ICC Preparatory Committee, concluded: 'As clearly shown by the preparatory work of the Convention, the destruction in question is the material destruction of a group either by physical or by biological means, not the destruction of the national, linguistic, cultural or other identity of a particular group.' *Report of the ILC on the Work of its Forty-Eighth Session*, GAOR, 51st session, Supp No 10 UN Doc A/51/10, (1996) 90–91. No suggestion to expand the list of acts contained in Art 2 of the Genocide Convention was raised during the deliberations for the Rome Statute.

confirmed that the Genocide Convention and customary international law limited genocide to the physical or biological destruction of the group, noting with approval that 'the Trial Chamber expressly acknowledged this limitation, and eschewed any broader definition'.[324]

Nonetheless, the Trial Chamber in the *Krstić* case used evidence of the destruction of mosques and the houses of Bosnian Muslims to prove the *mens rea* or the specific intent element of genocide. The Trial Chamber found that

an enterprise attacking only the cultural or sociological characteristics of a human group in order to annihilate these elements which give to that group its own identity distinct from the rest of the community would not fall under the definition of genocide... [H]owever...where there is physical or biological destruction there are often simultaneous attacks on cultural and religious property and symbols of the targeted group as well, attacks which may legitimately be considered as evidence of an intent to physically destroy the group.[325]

Judge Mohamed Shahabuddeen in the Appeals Chamber developed this reasoning further. In his partial dissenting decision, he argued that the *travaux* did not exclude 'an intent to destroy a group in a non-physical or non-biological way...provided that that intent is attached to a listed act, this being of a physical or biological nature'.[326]

It is sobering to recount the words of the prosecution in the *Krstić* Trial Chamber detailing the impact of the atrocities on the Srebrenica survivors: '[W]hat remains of the Srebrenica community survives in many cases only in the biological sense, nothing more.... [I]t's a community that's a shadow of what it once was.'[327] Judge Shahabuddeen observed that the Genocide Convention protected the group which 'is constituted by characteristics—often intangible—binding together a collection of people as a social unit'. He argued that if these characteristics are destroyed with an intent that is accompanied by an enumerated 'biological' or 'physical' act, it is not sustainable to argue that 'is not genocide because the obliteration was not physical or biological'.[328] The Appeal Chamber pronounced that genocide was 'crime against all humankind' because 'those who devise and implement genocide seek to deprive humanity of the manifold richness its nationalities, races, ethnicities and religions provide'.[329]

Krstić was found guilty of genocide (and the crime of humanity of persecution and violation of the laws and customs of war) and was sentenced to 46 years' imprisonment by the Trial Chamber. The Appeal Chamber reduced this sentence to 35 years when it found that he had aided and abetted these crimes rather than being a participant in a joint criminal enterprise.

---

[324] *Prosecutor v Radislav Krstić*, Appeals Judgment, Case No IT-98-33-A (19 April 2004) at 25.

[325] *Krstić*, Trial Judgment, at 580.

[326] *Krstić*, Appeals Judgment, dissenting judgment of Judge Mohamed Shahabuddeen, at 50.

[327] *Krstić*, Trial Judgment, at 592.

[328] *Krstić*, Appeals Judgment, dissenting judgment of Judge Mohamed Shahabuddeen, at 51.

[329] *Krstić*, Appeals Judgment, at 36. It reaffirmed this sentiment again in *Prosecutor v Milomir Stakić*, Appeals Judgment, Case No IT-97-24-A, Appeals Chamber ICTY (22 March 2006) at 20–24.

3. *ICJ* Genocide *case and state responsibility for genocide*

The *Genocide* case filed by Bosnia and Herzegovina against Yugoslavia (later Serbia and Montenegro) with the International Court of Justice in 1993 was an action for interim measures and reparations for Yugoslavia's violations of obligations under the 1948 Genocide Convention to which it was a state party. Unlike the actions before the ICTY concerning individual criminal responsibility, the action went to the 'criminal' culpability of a state in respect of the international crime of genocide.

In its submission during the Merits phase, the applicant, Bosnia and Herzegovina presented only two witnesses to the Court, one of which was the expert testimony of András J Riedlmayer in respect of the destruction of cultural, religious, and architectural heritage of Bosnia and Herzegovina.[330] Riedlmayer had previously given evidence before the ICTY in the *Milošević* case.[331] His evidence was used to prove the specific intent element of genocide, which distinguishes it from other international crimes especially those enumerated under crimes against humanity. The deployment of such evidence in this way reaffirmed an observation made by Lemkin more than a half-century ago, that the destruction of the cultural elements of a group is intimately tied to genocidal programmes and often preceded the final—biological and physical—stage.

Accepting that there was 'conclusive evidence of the deliberate destruction of the historical, cultural and religious heritage of the protected group',[332] the ICJ, like the ICTY before it, turned its mind to the definition of genocide and the place if any of the cultural elements within it. It found that:

the destruction of historical, cultural and religious heritage cannot be considered to constitute the deliberate infliction of conditions of life calculated to bring about the physical destruction of the group. Although such destruction may be highly significant inasmuch as it is directed to the elimination of all traces of the cultural or religious presence of a group, and contrary to other legal norms, it does not fall within the categories of acts of genocide set out in Article II of the Convention.[333]

The International Court embraced the ICTY's interpretation in *Krstić* that the definition of genocide had not evolved to include the cultural elements discarded in 1948. It reaffirmed the ICTY's position that the destruction of the historical, religious, and cultural heritage of a group only goes to proving the *mens rea* of the crime of genocide and not the *actus reus*.[334]

---

[330] In the case concerning the *Application of the Convention on the Prevention and Punishment of the Crime of Genocide*, CR 2006/22 Public sitting held on Friday 17 March 2006, at 10 am, at the Peace Palace, President Higgins presiding—Oral arguments on behalf of Bosnia and Herzegovina: András J Riedlmayer (expert called by Bosnia and Herzegovina) at <http://www.icj-cij.org/docket/files/91/10628.pdf> [last accessed on 24 March 2009].

[331] *Prosecutor v Slobodan Milošević*, Trial Proceedings, Case No IT-02-54, Trial Chamber, ICTY, (8 July 2003) at 23,785 (Reidlmayer).

[332] ICJ *Genocide* case, at 344. See also at 335–344 generally.

[333] ICJ *Genocide* case, at 191–201, especially at 194.

[334] ICJ *Genocide* case, at 344.

The ICJ also affirmed the decision of the ICTY Appeals Chamber in *Stakić* delivered in 2006 which determined that the Convention requires that the targeted group be positively defined. Again, the International Court invoked the rejection of the cultural genocide during the drafting of the Convention in support of its position.[335] By contrast, the ICTY Appeals Chamber did not dismiss the debate concerning the cultural elements of genocide. Instead, the tribunal recalled that Lemkin had argued that genocide was a serious crime because humanity lost the ' "future contributions" that would be "based upon [the destroyed group's] genuine culture, and ... well-developed national psychology" '.[336] It concluded that genocide was 'conceived of as the destruction of a ... group with a particular positive identity—not as the destruction of various people lacking a distinct identity'.[337] The tribunal conceded that debate over the prohibition of cultural genocide has continued among experts even after the Convention was adopted.[338]

As noted above, the original Secretariat draft of the Genocide Convention made reference to the targeting of the cultural heritage of a group including its cultural and religious sites, documents, practices, and language. This 'cultural' component of the definition was deleted because of post-war resistance to the resuscitation of minority protections. However, it was no coincidence that the revival of efforts to draft and finalize an instrument on the protection of minorities in the 1990s was accompanied by increased jurisprudence on the crime of genocide. This litigation before international courts has not only revisited the debate concerning 'cultural' genocide. It has again exposed the internal inconsistency within the Genocide Convention's definition of this international crime rendered by the deletion of those 'cultural' elements from Article II. That is, a group must have a distinct identity to attract the protection afforded by the Convention but acts which target their cultural heritage (and which render the group distinctive) are not prohibited per se. Confining such acts to establishing the *mens rea* of genocide alone, serves only to highlight this inconsistency rather than remedy it.

Nevertheless, the evolution of international criminal law from war crimes to include crimes against humanity (including persecution) and genocide has encapsulated the shifting rationale for the protection of cultural heritage at the international level.

5. Concluding Remarks

Whilst international humanitarian law was the first field in international law to bestow exceptional treatment upon cultural heritage, in the last 20 years there has been a recapitulation of the interplay between international humanitarian law, human rights law, and international criminal law in promoting its underlying rationale for protection: its importance to all humanity. As I have detailed in this chapter, with the rise of human rights from the mid-twentieth century, this

---

[335] ICJ *Genocide* case, at 194.　　[336] *Stakić*, Appeals Judgment, at 21.
[337] Ibid.　　[338] *Stakić*, Appeals Judgment, at 24.

rationale has undergone a significant recalibration. It was originally based on its importance for the advancement of the arts and sciences, and knowledge generally. This has now been eclipsed by an emphasis on the significance of cultural heritage in ensuring the contribution of all peoples to humankind. In conclusion, I wish to underscore three normative trends which consolidate this rationale and the internal shift that it has undergone.

First, the obligation to protection cultural heritage is not confined to states parties to the relevant human rights, humanitarian law, nor specialist cultural heritage instruments but extends to all states. This development intrinsically arises from the notion that if the protection of cultural heritage at the international level is grounded in its importance to all humanity, and this is a 'value especially protected by the international community',[339] then all states have 'a legal interest in [its] protection'.[340] Its nascent form is reflected in the 1972 World Heritage Convention and near universal uptake.[341] However, an early clear example of this type of obligation was contained in the 1943 London Declaration. It formally put persons on notice in neutral countries that the transfer of property from territories occupied by Axis forces would be declared invalid by the Allied Powers.[342] More recently, as noted above, the obligations contained in the 1954 Hague Protocol were extended beyond states parties when they were summarily incorporated into SC Resolution 1483 of 2003. This Resolution bound all UN member states to 'facilitate the safe return' and prohibit trade in cultural heritage illicitly removed from Iraq since August 1990.[343] In 2003 and 2007, the UNESCO General Conference and the Human Rights Council respectively confirmed that all states may bear responsibility in respect of intentional destruction of cultural heritage 'of great importance for humanity, to the extent provided for by international law'.[344]

Next, the progressive dissolution of the boundaries between protection of cultural heritage during armed conflict, belligerent occupation, and peacetime is

---

[339] *Jokić*, Trial Judgment, at 46. See also 1932 ICIC Resolution, *supra* note 145.

[340] *Legality of the Threat or Use of Nuclear Weapons,* Advisory Opinion, ICJ Reports (1996) 226, at 257; and *Legal Consequences of the Construction of the Wall in the Occupied Palestinian Territory,* Advisory Opinion, ICJ Reports (2004) 136, at 199 (in respect of obligations *erga omnes* generally).

[341] Convention concerning the Protection of the World Cultural and Natural Heritage, 16 November 1972, in force 17 December 1975, 1037 UNTS 151. As of September 2009, there were 186 states parties to the Convention and 192 UN member states. See Francioni, 'Introduction', in Francioni and Lenzerini (eds), *The 1972 World Heritage Convention: A Commentary,* (2008) 5. Cf O'Keefe, 'World Cultural Heritage: Obligations to the International Community as a Whole?' 53 *ICLQ* (2004) 189.

[342] See also Agreement between the United States, the United Kingdom and France in respect of the Control of Looted Works of Art, 8 July 1946, 25 *Department of State Bulletin* (1951) 340, Swiss Decree of 10 December 1945 concerning Actions for the Recovery of Goods taken in Occupied Territories during the War, and Swedish Looted Objects Law of 29 June 1945.

[343] SC Res 1468, at 7 (14-0-0), the United States and United Kingdom who are not states parties to the 1954 Hague Protocol voted in favour.

[344] Part VI of the Declaration concerning the International Destruction of Cultural Heritage, adopted by the 32nd session of the UNESCO General Conference on 17 October 2003, in UNESCO, *Records of the General Conference, 32nd session, Paris, 29 September to 17 October 2003,* (2004) v 1; and HRC Res 6/11, 28 September 2007, Protection of cultural heritage as an important component of the promotion and protection of cultural rights, para 5.

redefining the content of the obligation.[345] This was highlighted in the aftermath of the destruction of the monumental Buddhas in Bamiyan, Afghanistan, with the adoption of the 2003 UNESCO Declaration on the Intentional Destruction of Cultural Heritage.[346] Like the 1935 Washington Treaty and jurisprudence of the ICTY, the declaration marries references to war and peacetime protection. It provides that all states should act in accordance with customary international law and the 'principles and objectives' of international agreements and UNESCO recommendations during hostilities and peacetime.[347] It replicates the tradition of multilateral efforts covering cultural heritage dating back to the early twentieth century which meld preventative, protective, and punitive measures borne by states; foster international cooperation; and strictly circumscribe the military objective proviso.

The customary international law prohibition against the international destruction of cultural heritage during peacetime is less clearly defined than during armed conflict and belligerent occupation. However, support can be gleaned not only from pronouncements by United Nations bodies, like the Human Rights Council,[348] but the increased uptake of relevant treaties over the past decade.[349] Further, protection provided by international law during peacetime to cultural heritage of universal importance should necessarily be greater than that provided during armed conflict to which the military necessity proviso is attached.[350] Also, as explained above, international criminal law prohibits international destruction during peacetime when it targets cultural heritage because of its affiliation to certain groups.

Thirdly, and complementing this trend, is the growing convergence between human rights and humanitarian law in the field of cultural heritage (and cultural rights).[351] This has been enhanced by the embrace of a holistic understanding of cultural heritage through instruments for the protection of intangible heritage and endangered languages,[352] and the promotion of cultural diversity.[353]

---

[345] Art III, para 1, Declaration on Intentional Destruction.

[346] See Francioni and Lenzerini, 'The Destruction of the Buddhas of Bamiyan and International Law' 14 *EJIL* (2003) 619; and Vrdoljak, 'International Destruction of Cultural Heritage and International Law', XXXV *Thesaurus Acroasium* (2007) 377–396.

[347] Arts IV and V, Declaration on Intentional Destruction.

[348] HRC Res 6/11, 28 September 2007, seventh, eighth, and ninth preambular recitals and at 4 and 5.

[349] In addition to the 1972 World Heritage Convention, see Convention on the Means of Prohibiting and Preventing the Illicit Import, Export and Transfer of Ownership of Cultural Property, 14 November 1970, in force 24 April 1972, 823 UNTS 231. As of September 2009, the Convention had 118 states parties.

[350] See *Legality of the Threat or Use of Nuclear Weapons*, Advisory Opinion, ICJ Reports (1996) at 23–34 (the reasoning employed by the International Court to environmental protections can be applied similarly to those covering cultural heritage).

[351] Fifth preambular recital and Art IX, UNESCO Declaration on Intentional Destruction; and HRC Res 6/1, 27 September 2007 entitled Protection of cultural rights and property in situations of armed conflict.

[352] Intangible Heritage Convention, *supra* note 207, as of 1 October 2009, there were 116 states parties to this convention; European Charter for Regional or Minority Languages, 5 November 1992, in force 1 March 1998, ETS No 148; and Preliminary Study of the Technical and Legal Aspects of a Possible International Standard-Setting Instrument for the Protection of Indigenous and Endangered Languages, 17 August 2009, UNESCO Doc 35C/14.

[353] Universal Declaration on Cultural Diversity, *supra* note 207.

Complementing the evolution of international criminal law, these developments have arisen with the emergence of human rights and in particular, the re-emergence of minority protection.[354] Traditionally, the prosecution of crimes against humanity, in particular persecution and genocide, has almost exclusively relied on evidence of the damage or destruction of the physical manifestations of a targeted group's cultural heritage. However, as detailed above, the United Nations War Crimes Commission in 1945 when interpreting existing humanitarian law provisions for the protection of tangible heritage extrapolated them to include its intangible aspects. Also, the definition of genocide contained in the Secretariat's Draft Convention incorporated tangible and intangible cultural elements. Understanding and acceptance of the need for protection of intangible heritage, including language, augments efforts to prevent and punish the crimes of humanity and genocide and promote human rights.

While cultural heritage has attracted protection since the earliest codifications of the laws of war in the nineteenth century, it was not until the mid-twentieth century that the rationale for its protection which is promoted today was formally articulated. The crimes which were the subject of the Nuremberg Judgment precipitated the adoption of the UDHR, the Genocide Convention, and 1954 Hague Convention. Each of these instruments implicitly or explicitly reaffirms the special protection afforded cultural heritage because of its importance to all humanity. This protection is not afforded to cultural heritage per se. Instead, it is its role in ensuring enjoyment of human rights and the contribution of all peoples to 'the culture of the world'.[355] Half a century later, the crimes which were the subject of the ICTY's jurisprudence have served to alert the international community that such atrocities are not confined to the distant past and precipitated a recommitment to this underlying rationale through a further consolidation of the protection afforded cultural heritage by international humanitarian law, human rights, and international criminal law.

---

[354] Declaration on the Rights of Persons Belonging to National or Ethnic, Religious and Linguistic Minorities, *supra* note 208; and Framework Convention for the Protection of National Minorities, 1 February 1995, in force 1 February 1995, ETS No 157.
[355] Second preambular recital, 1954 Hague Convention.

IV

CODA

8

Are Victims of Serious Violations of International Humanitarian Law Entitled to Compensation?

Paola Gaeta

1. Introduction

Despite the expansion and development of international human rights law and, in more recent times, of international criminal law, victims of serious violations of rules of international humanitarian law (IHL) are still not considered to be entitled to reparation under international law. The common wisdom is that only the belligerent party as such has this legal entitlement, including for violations of IHL causing damage to specific individuals.

The underlying theoretical assumption of this legal construct is that the rules of IHL regulate inter-state or inter-belligerent conduct. Hence, they do not confer primary rights upon individuals, who therefore do not have the secondary right to obtain reparation for violations.[1] In practice, as a result, victims of violations of IHL are still considered through the lens of traditional international law, which renders them mere objects of rules addressing sovereign states. This is surprising, if one considers the extent to which human rights doctrine and the principle of personal criminal liability for international crimes have eroded this traditional paradigm, and contributed to the assertion that individuals, and not only states, possess rights and obligations under international law.

The purpose of this chapter is to examine to what extent the traditional approach to this issue is tenable today, when serious violations of IHL are at stake. I will confine the discussion only to *serious* violations of IHL, i.e. to actions that—once the other requirements are met—may amount to war crimes,[2] for the following three reasons.

---

[1] For the inter-state nature of the rules of International humanitarian law, see among others Ronzitti, 'Access to Justice and Compensation for Violations of the Law of War', in Francioni (ed), *Access to Justice as a Human Right* (2007) 95, in particular at 109.

[2] See the landmark decision of the Appeals Chamber of the International Criminal Tribunal for the former Yugoslavia (ICTY) of 2 October 1995, *Decision on the Defence Motion for Interlocutory Appeal on Jurisdiction, Prosecutor v Tadić*, para 94, where it specified that the conditions for the

First, serious violations of rules of IHL consist of breaches of rules 'protecting important values' and involving 'serious consequences for the victims'.[3] Therefore they involve the infringement of a particular kind of international obligation that the International Court of Justice (ICJ) has termed *'erga omnes'*.[4] It is therefore necessary to examine the extent to which the traditional approach to the issue of reparation for violations of rules of IHL can also apply to breaches of obligations that, because of the values they protect, escape the rigid bilateralism peculiar to many primary rules of international law.

Second, the issue of reparation for violations of IHL has been at the centre of the international debate in particular where *serious* violations are concerned. Significantly on this topic the United Nations' *Basic Principles and Guidelines on the Right to a Remedy and Reparation for the Victims of Gross Violations of International Human Rights Law and Serious Violations of International Humanitarian Law* were adopted by the General Assembly in 2005.[5] They refer, as the title suggests, to qualified violations of rules of IHL. This chapter intends therefore to contribute to

---

applicability of Art 3 of the ICTY Statute on war crimes, in the following terms: '(i) the violation must constitute an infringement of a rule of international humanitarian law; (ii) the rule must be customary in nature or, if it belongs to treaty law, the required conditions must be met...; (iii) the violation must be "serious", that is to say, it must constitute a breach of a rule protecting important values, and the breach must involve grave consequences for the victim. Thus, for instance, the fact of a combatant simply appropriating a loaf of bread in an occupied village would not amount to a "serious violation of international humanitarian law" although it may be regarded as falling foul of the basic principle laid down in Article 46, paragraph 1, of the Hague Regulations (and the corresponding rule of customary international law) whereby "private property must be respected" by any army occupying an enemy territory; (iv) the violation of the rule must entail, under customary or conventional law, the individual criminal responsibility of the person breaching the rule.'

[3] This is the explanation given to the expression 'serious violations' by the ICTY Appeals Chamber in *Tadić*, see *supra* note 2.

[4] In this regard, one cannot but quote the well-known *obiter dictum* of the judgment of the International Court of Justice in the *Barcelona Traction* case, where the Court underlined that 'an essential distinction should be drawn between the obligations of a State towards the international community as a whole, and those arising vis-à-vis another State in the field of diplomatic protection. By their very nature the former are the concern of all States. In view of the importance of the rights involved, all States can be held to have a legal interest in their protection; they are obligations *erga omnes*', Judgment, *Barcelona Traction, Light and Power ltd* (second phase), ICJ Reports (1970) at 32.

For the erga omnes character of some of the rules of international humanitarian law, see the ICJ Advisory Opinion, *Legality of the Threat or Use of Nuclear Weapons*, 8 July 1996, para 79, where the Court, although not yet defining them as rules establishing *erga omnes* obligations, stressed that 'many rules of international humanitarian law applicable in armed conflict'... 'constitute intransgressible principles of international customary law'. Instead, in the Advisory Opinion on *Legal Consequences of the Construction of a Wall in the Occupied Palestinian Territory*, 9 July 2004, the Court clarified that the rules of international humanitarian law 'incorporate obligations which are essentially of an *erga omnes* character' (ICJ Reports (2004), para 157).

[5] UN GA Res 60/147, 16 December 2005 (hereinafter, UN Basic Principles and Guidelines). For a comment on the Guidelines, see d'Argent, 'Le droit de la responsabilité internationale complété? Examen des principes fondamentaux et directives concernant le droit à un recours et à la réparation des victimes de violations flagrantes du droit international des droits de l'homme et de violations graves du droit international humanitaire', in 51 *Annuaire français de droit international* (2005) 27; van Boven, 'Victims' Rights to a Remedy and Reparation: the New United Nations Principles and Guidelines', in Ferstman, Goetz, and Stephens (eds), *Reparations for Victims of Genocide, War Crimes and Crimes against Humanity: Systems in Place and Systems in the Making* (2009) 19.

the existing debate on this crucial issue of the contemporary international law of armed conflict.

Finally, when perpetrated with the required *mens rea*, serious violations of IHL give rise to personal criminal accountability under international law for war crimes. In other words, it is now indisputable that there are rules of IHL which impose obligations not only on the belligerent parties as such, but also on individuals. If individuals do not comply with such obligations, and violate them with a culpable mind, they can be held criminally accountable under international law. It is therefore necessary to discuss whether, in a similar way to the development of criminal sanctions for individuals, rules of international law have evolved that entitle victims to compensation in the case of violations of some fundamental rules of IHL.

In addition, I will only discuss the issue of the individuals' right to reparation vis-à-vis the responsible state under international law.[6] I will mainly confine the discussion to monetary compensation, which is one of the forms of reparation for material damage that cannot be made good, in full or in part, through restitution in kind.[7] Financial compensation is indeed among the most frequent issues arising in the context of the right of individuals to reparation in cases of serious violations of IHL.

This chapter will begin by stressing the ambiguities of the relevant provisions on compensation enshrined in the Hague Convention IV (*Hague IV*) of 1907 and Additional Protocol I (*AP I*) to the Geneva Conventions (*GC*). Then the applicable rules under the general regime on state responsibility will be discussed, in particular the rules regarding violations of *erga omnes* obligations. This analysis will prove important to identify which states are entitled to ask for compensation within an inter-state framework or in the case of serious violations of the laws of warfare committed in non-international armed conflicts. Finally, some recent developments which indicate that under international law individuals have the right to obtain compensation from the state responsible for serious violations of IHL will be considered.

---

[6] Admittedly, in contemporary armed conflicts is not unlikely that non-state armed groups commit serious violations of the rules of the international law of armed conflicts. Assuming that these groups are internationally bound by such rules, it is clear that if individuals possess an international right to compensation towards the responsible state, it would be easier to reach the same conclusion—*mutatis mutandis*—whenever the belligerent party responsible for the violation is a non-state armed group. Also, and for the same reason, the paper will not address the issue of the individuals' right under international law to obtain compensation vis-à-vis the individual who has concretely committed the violation. The recent developments achieved in this regard with the adoption of Rome Statute establishing the International Criminal Court and, more generally, within the system of international criminal justice will be briefly discussed, to the extent they may help clarify the question of the existence of the right of individuals to compensation vis-à-vis the responsible state.

[7] See Art 36(1) of the Articles on State Responsibility for Internationally Wrongful Acts, adopted by the International Law Commission (ILC) at its fifty-third session (2001) and endorsed by the UN General Assembly Resolution 56/83 of 12 December 2001, (hereinafter ILC's Articles), which provides: 'The State responsible for an internationally wrongful act is under an obligation to compensate for the damage caused thereby, insofar as such damage is not made good by restitution.'

2. The Question of the Beneficiaries of the State's Obligation to Pay Compensation under Article 3 of Hague Convention IV (*Hague IV*) and Additional Protocol I (AP I)

It is well known that under international law a state that commits a wrongful act is liable to make reparation,[8] and that reparation consists of various forms which include monetary compensation.[9] As for violations of IHL, the obligation to provide for compensation is detailed in Article 3 of *Hague IV*, which provides that belligerent parties which violate the Annexed Regulation are liable to pay compensation.[10] This obligation is reaffirmed in Article 91 of *AP I*.[11] Neither Article, however, specifies who is entitled to compensation when the violation has caused damage to individuals: is the obligation to pay compensation due to the other belligerent party, or are the individual victims to be compensated?

The traditional understanding is that Article 3 of *Hague IV* and Article 91 of *AP I* simply codify the rule of international law according to which, when private individuals are injured by an internationally wrongful act, the responsible state is liable to provide reparation (and therefore compensation) only to their state of nationality, and not to the individuals who have concretely suffered damage.[12] It is therefore maintained that, when a violation of the Regulations annexed to *Hague IV* or a rule contained in *AP I* occurs, the obligation to pay compensation enshrined in these two provisions is towards the other belligerent party to which the individuals belong, and not to the individuals as such.[13]

Various arguments have been put forward in support of this proposition. The most important ones can be summarized as follows. On the one hand, it can be observed that, since Article 3 of *Hague IV* was adopted at a time when it was unthinkable that individuals might enjoy rights under international law, this provision cannot but reflect the inter-state structure of the international legal order.[14]

---

[8] See the dictum of the Permanent Court of International Justice (PCIJ) in the *Chorzów Factory* case, where the Court stated: 'It is a principle of international law that the breach of an engagement involves an obligation to make a reparation in an adequate form' (Permanent Court of International Justice, Ser A, No 9 (1927) at 21).   [9] See Arts 28 to 39 of the ILC's Articles, *supra* note 7.

[10] Article 3 of Hague Convention IV, Law and Customs of War on Land, provides: 'A belligerent party which violates the provisions of the [Regulations respecting the laws and customs of war on land] shall, if the case demands, be liable to pay compensation. It shall be responsible for all acts committed by persons forming part of its armed forces.'

[11] Article 91 of *AP I* provides: 'A Party to the conflict which violates the provisions of the Conventions or the Protocols shall, if the case demands, be liable to pay compensation. It shall be responsible for all acts committed by persons forming part of its armed forces.'

[12] See, for instance, Provost, *International Human Rights and Humanitarian Law* (2002) at 45, also for further reference. See also Ronzitti, *supra* note 1, at 100–111.

[13] See the authors quoted by Hofmann, *Compensation for Victims of War. Substantive Issues. Do Victims of Armed Conflict Have an Individual Right to Reparation?* Report to the Toronto Conference of the International Law Association (2006), available online at <http://www.ila-hq.org/en/committees/index.cfm/cid/1018>.

[14] See for instance d'Argent, *Les réparations de guerre en droit international public* (2002) at 444. See also Gillard, 'Reparation for Violations of International Humanitarian Law', in 85 *International Review of the Red Cross* (2003) 529, at 536–537.

Hence, since nothing in the text of Article 3 of *Hague IV* expressly provides that individuals must be compensated,[15] it cannot be maintained that Article 3 lays down the right of individual victims to obtain compensation from the responsible state. The same argument is made as regards Article 91 of *AP I*, which simply mirrors Article 3 of *Hague IV*. Subsequent state practice confirms this conclusion. Furthermore, national case law has refused to recognize that the aforementioned provision grants individuals the right to compensation.[16] In addition, the post-war settlements dealing with war-related claims have shown that states have considered the issues on compensation to be regulated within an inter-state framework, as a matter of purely inter-state concern.[17]

However, these arguments, while important, are not conclusive in regard to this matter. Some scholars have tried to demonstrate on the basis of the *travaux préparatoires*, that the scope of the two provisions implies that the individual victims are the beneficiaries of the obligation to make compensation.[18]

With respect to national case law, one cannot fail to note that the reasoning of domestic courts often amounts to a *petitio principii*. It is often simply maintained that Article 3 of *Hague IV* and Article 91 of *AP I* restate the rule on state responsibility, according to which only a state can present an international claim towards another state to enforce the latter's international responsibility. This is, however, exactly what should be demonstrated. As a matter of fact, the proper interpretation of these provisions cannot but take into account the developments that may have occurred in the field of international law on state responsibility.[19] As I will

---

[15] See d'Argent, *supra* note 14, at 784.

[16] Ibid, 785–788. See also Frulli, 'When Are States Liable Towards Individuals for Serious Violations of Humanitarian Law? The *Marković* Case', in 1 *JICJ* (2003) 406, at 418–421 and Ronzitti, *supra* note 1, 110–111.

[17] Dolzer and Stefan, 'The Settlement of War-Related Claims: Does International Law Recognize a Victim's Private Right of Action?', in 20 *Berkeley J. Int'l L.* (2002) 296. See also Tomuschat, 'State Responsibility and the Individual Right to Compensation before National Courts', typewritten text on file with the author, to be published in Clapham and Gaeta (eds), *Oxford Handbook of International Humanitarian Law* (Oxford University Press: forthcoming).

[18] Kalshoven, 'State Responsibility for Warlike Acts of the Armed Forces: From Article 3 of the Hague Convention IV of 1907 to Article 91 of Additional Protocol I and Beyond', in 40 *ICLQ* (1991) 827, who considers that the preparatory works of the Hague Convention IV 'provide convincing evidence that the delegates sought not so much to lay down a rule relating to the international responsibility of one State vis-à-vis another, as one relating to a State's liability to compensate the losses of individual persons incurred as a consequence of their direct (and harmful) contact with its armed forces'. In his view, Art 3 was adopted to address the 'liability of a State to indemnify enemy or neutral persons for damages incurred as result of acts committed by members of its armed land forces in contravention to the Regulations' annexed to the Convention. However, according to this distinguished author, it was the intention of the drafters only to include *enemy or neutral civilians* as the beneficiaries of the provision (at 832–833), and only in relation to small-case events (ie 'events involving direct, personal contact between offender and victim, rather then impersonal, large-scale, military operations such as a long distance bombardment, where the victim does not get to know the identity of the offender', at 834). In the same vein see also the expert opinions of Greenwood, 'Rights to Compensation of former Prisoners of War and Civilian Internees under Article 3 of the Hague Convention No. IV, 1907', reprinted in Fujita *et al* (eds), *War and the Rights of Individuals* (1999).

[19] In this regard, see the letter of the then President of the International Criminal Tribunal for the former Yugoslavia (ICTY), Claude Jorda, of 12 October 2000 to the United Nations Secretary-General, and reported in the *Report of the International Commission of Inquiry on Darfur to the United Nations Secretary General pursuant to Security Council Resolution 1564 of 18 September 2004*, available

endeavour to show below, the current regime of state responsibility for internationally wrongful acts does not exclude the liability of the responsible state for reparations vis-à-vis private individuals. It is therefore not conclusive to refer to the rules governing state responsibility for the purpose of excluding the right of individuals to reparation, without taking into account and discussing the developments that have occurred in this field since the adoption of *Hague IV* and *AP I*. In short, if one assumes that those provisions on compensation intended to codify the rules of customary international law on state responsibility, it is therefore necessary to examine what the content of these rules is at present. In addition, domestic courts have mainly dealt with Second World War claims: their findings, therefore, do not necessarily exclude that *at present* the aforementioned provisions may be interpreted differently, so as to recognize the right of individuals to compensation for violations of rules of IHL.[20]

With respect to the inter-state post-war settlements, it is important to note that they established schemes of 'war reparations'[21] which are patently at odds with the obligation to compensate violations of the rules of *jus in bello*. The post-war settlements were aimed at repairing injuries stemming from the war regardless of

---

at <http://www.un.org/News/dh/sudan/com_inq_darfur.pdf>, at para 597. In this letter, President Jorda emphasized that the general and universal recognition of the right of victims of human rights abuses to a remedy have a bearing on the proper interpretation of the rules on state responsibility for war crimes.

[20] See the decision of the High Court of Japan of 7 August 1996 in the *X et al v the State of Japan*. In its decision, the High Court stated that the applicants had no ground to claim compensation on the basis of international law, but noted that there is no evidence of any general practice or *opinio iuris* that the state that committed a violation of the rules of IHL had an obligation to compensate individual victims *at the time the incident occurred*. *X et al v The State of Japan*, Tokyo High Court, 7 August 1996, English translation in 39 *Japanese Annual of International Law* (1996) 116.

A similar stand has been taken by the German Federal Court and the German Constitutional Court in relation the so-called *Distomo* case. The case relates to the massacre which occurred in the village of Distomo, Greece, on 10 June 1944, when German occupying forces unlawfully killed hundreds civilians and wilfully destroyed private property. Relatives of the victims filed a claim for compensation against Germany before the Greek Court of Leivadia. The Court accepted the claim. However the plaintiffs did not manage to execute the judgment in Greece, due to the denial on the part of the Greek government, requested by domestic courts, to authorize its enforcement. For this reason, the plaintiff sought to obtain the recognition of the Greek judgment in Germany. Finally, the claim was dismissed by the German Federal Court of Justice on the basis of lack of jurisdiction of the Greek court, which failed to recognize the sovereign immunity of Germany before foreign courts. However, the Court noted that public international law could change gradually, but certainly in 1944 (at the time when the massacre was perpetrated) individuals were not directly protected by international law, and therefore only states or belligerent parties had a claim for compensation (see Pittrof, 'Compensation Claims for Human Rights Breaches Committed by German Armed Forces Abroad during the Second World War: Federal Court of Justice Hands Out Decision in the *Distomo* Case', in 5 *German Law Journal* (2004) 15, at 19–20, also for the reference to the Judgment). In the same vein the German Constitutional Court, in relation to the same case, when it stressed that changes in international law which may have occurred after 1944 were irrelevant for the case at issue (see Rau, 'State Liability for Violations of International Humanitarian Law—The *Distomo* Case Before the German Federal Constitutional Court', in 7 *German Law Journal* (2005) 701, at 710, also for reference to the Judgment).

[21] On the so-called reparations of war see the extensive study by Gattini, *Le riparazioni di guerra nel diritto internazionale* (2003), and the one by d'Argent, *Les réparations, supra* note 14. See also the ICRC Commentary to Art 91 of *AP I* and the reference provided in footnote 4.

whether the injuries resulted from the infringement of a rule of IHL.[22] The latter is however a condition for the applicability of the obligation set forth in Article 3 of *Hague IV* and Article 91 of *AP I*. In addition, war reparations were imposed on the vanquished country, and did not cover any injury or loss inflicted by the victorious states as a result of a violation of a rule of IHL. As the ICRC Commentary on *AP I* aptly observes, however, the purpose of both Article 3 of *Hague IV* and of Article 91 of *AP I* 'is specifically to prevent the vanquished from being compelled in an armistice agreement or peace treaty to renounce all compensation due for breaches committed by persons in the service of the victor'.[23] This implies that 'on the conclusion of a peace treaty, the Parties can in principle deal with the problems relating to war damage in general and those relating to the responsibility of starting the war... On the other hand, they are not free... to deny *compensation to which the victims of violations of the rules of the Convention and Protocol are entitled*.'[24] Therefore, post-conflict settlements concluded to deal with war-related claims have no bearing on the interpretation of the relevant provisions of *Hague IV* and *AP I*. This practice does not relate to the application of the obligation to provide for compensation enshrined in those provisions, being in clear contrast with their wording, scope, and purpose.[25]

3. Subjects Entitled to Reparation under the Rules of International State Responsibility for Wrongful Acts

Treaty provisions must be interpreted in the light of the context of the treaty, which includes evolution that has occurred in international law and, in the case at issue, in the law of state responsibility for internationally wrongful acts. Faced with the ambiguities of the text of Articles 3 and 91 of *Hague IV* and *AP I* respectively, it is therefore necessary to turn to the content of the rules on state responsibility, as they are in force today. This analysis proves all the more important if one considers that the issue of compensation for violations of IHL is not confined to the Regulations annexed to *Hague IV* and to *AP I*, and therefore to the proper interpretation to be

---

[22] As a distinguished commentator rightly observes, the post-Second World War reparation scheme for war-related damage regarding Germany was inspired by the principle that Germany was historically and morally responsible for the war aggressions and the atrocities committed during the war. For that commentator this is of the utmost importance for the issue of reparation for historical wrongs, which—by their very nature—go beyond the mere technicalities of the rules of international law on State responsibility. See Francioni, 'Reparation for Indigenous People: Is International Law Ready to Ensure Redress for Historical Injustice?', in Lenzerini (ed), *Reparations for Indigenous People* (2008) 27, at 38–39. [23] See ICRC Commentary to *AP I* (Article 91) para 3640.

[24] Ibid, para 3651 (emphasis added).

[25] On the other hand, in recent times some countries have established specific funds to make reparation to the victims of violations of humanitarian law and other human rights abuses. These funds clearly indicate that the relevant states considered that victims are entitled to obtain redress outside inter-state settlement or mechanisms (ibid). This practice too, however, is of no avail to the interpretation of the obligation to compensate under IHL. States which have established these funds considered they were not acting to fulfil a specific obligation arising from the laws of *jus in bello*, and therefore no inference may be drawn from this practice.

placed on the two provisions, but has a more general purpose. It also concerns violations of rules of IHL enshrined in other treaties and those established in customary international law. In addition, it is not limited to international armed conflicts (regulated, *inter alia*, by *Hague IV* and *AP I*) but extends to non-international armed conflicts as well.

The question that must be tackled is the following: under international law, are states liable towards private individuals to make reparations for (and therefore to compensate) the injuries caused to them?

A. The (ir)relevance of the Articles on State Responsibility for international wrongful acts

The Articles on State Responsibility of the International Law Commission (ILC Articles) do not directly deal with this issue.[26] They confine themselves to analysing the obligations of the state responsible for an internationally wrongful act vis-a-vis 'another State,... several States, or... the international community as a whole, depending in particular on the character and content of the international obligation and on the circumstances of the breach'.[27]

It would be incorrect to assume, however, that the ILC's Articles are irrelevant to the present discussion. Article 33 provides that the Articles do not prejudice 'any right, arising from international responsibility of a State, which may accrue to any person or entity other than a State'.[28] The rationale for this provision is provided for in the ILC's Commentary, which explains that the Articles do not exclude 'the possibility that an internationally wrongful act may involve legal consequences in the relations between the State responsible for that act and persons and entities other than States'. As the ILC aptly notes, 'State responsibility extends, for example, to human rights violations and other breaches of international law where the primary beneficiary of the obligation breached is not a State'. In short, while the ILC's Articles only address the issue of the (secondary) obligations of the responsible state towards other states or 'the international community as such', it is admitted that these obligations may also arise vis-à-vis non-state entities, including

---

[26] For some critical remarks on the approach taken by the ILC not to tackle the issue of State responsibility vis-à-vis individuals see Pisillo Mazzeschi, 'The Marginal Role of the Individual in the ILC's Articles on State Responsibility', in XIV *Italian Y.B. Int'l L.* (2004) 39, republished in Italian, with some minor changes, 'Il ruolo marginale dell'individuo nel progetto della Commissione del diritto internazionale sulla responsabilità degli Stati', in Spinedi, Gianelli, and Alaimo (eds), *La codificazione della responsabilità alla prova dei fatti* (2006) 415.

[27] Article 33, para 1, of the ILC's Articles, *supra* note 7. Note, however, that this provision refers to the obligations toward 'the international community as a whole'. This wording has been preferred to 'international community of States', in order to emphasize that the international community is not only made by states, but it also comprises individuals and non-state entities. In this respect see Crawford, 'The ILC's Articles on Responsibility of States for Internationally Wrongful Acts: A Retrospect', in 96 *AJIL* (2002) 874, at 888. According to Pisillo Mazzeschi, 'The Marginal Role' *supra* note 26, at 43, the ILC could have made it clearer that violations by a state of international obligations towards the international community give rise to the international responsibility vis-à-vis all states and also vis-à-vis individuals and non-state entities.

[28] Art 33, para 2, of the ILC's Articles, *supra* note 7.

private individuals. Therefore, as the ILC clarifies, there are cases where the individuals should be regarded as the holders of the right to reparation.[29]

It is true that the ILC has not specified in which cases individuals may be considered to be entitled to reparation. It has only given a general indication in this regard, and mentioned violations of the rules protecting human rights as an example. Therefore, and in line with this reasoning, to the extent that rules of IHL impose on states primary obligations that are owed to private individuals, the latter would be entitled to reparation for violations.

B. The obligation to repair in case of injuries stemming from violations of *erga omnes* obligations

The ILC Articles indicate, however, that breaches of international rules having an *erga omnes* character in some instances entitle the individuals who have suffered the ensuing damage, to reparation. This is the case of violations of obligations *erga omnes* that do not confine themselves to protecting a collective interest, but also confer rights on individuals. The elements in the ILC Articles and in the related Commentary that warrant such a proposition are explained in the following paragraphs.

1. Injured and non-injured states and the right to claim reparation under the ILC's articles

As is well known, in traditional international law reparation was considered to be the object of an inter-state legal relationship, even in the case of violations causing injuries to private individuals.[30] That the obligation to repair was due by the responsible state towards another state, and not to the individual victims of the

---

[29] Commentary on Art 33, at § 3, where the ILC explains: 'When an obligation of reparation exists towards a State, reparation does not necessarily accrue to that State's benefit. For instance, a State's responsibility for the breach of an obligation under a treaty concerning the protection of human rights may exists towards all the other parties to the treaty, but the individuals concerned should be regarded as the ultimate beneficiaries and in that sense the holders of the relevant rights. Individual rights under international law may also arise outside the framework of human rights. The range of possibilities is demonstrated from the ICJ judgment in the *La Grand* case, where the Court held that Art 36 of the Vienna Convention on Consular Relations "creates individual rights, which, by virtue of Article I of the Optional Protocol, may be invoked in this Court by the national State of the detained person".'

For some critical remarks on the saving clause contained in Article 33, para 2, of the ILC's Draft, see Gattini, 'Alcune osservazioni sulla tutela degli interessi individuali nei progetti di codificazione della Commissione del diritto internazionale sulla responsabilità internazionale e sulla protezione diplomatica', in Spinedi *et al* (eds), *supra* note 26, 431, in particular at 431–440.

[30] This legal construct implied that whenever the relevant rules of international law had been breached, and an injury was caused to individuals, the obligation of the responsible state to repair was due *only* to the home state of the victims. In other words, when material or moral damage was suffered by private persons, that damage was considered as material damage inflicted to the state of nationality and not to the individual as such. It was the state of nationality that was considered to have been injured, through the injury caused to its citizens; and it was the state of nationality that was entitled not only to claim, but also to obtain reparation for the injury suffered. The injured state could renounce reparation, or agree upon any form of reparation it considered the most suitable; it

violation (if any) was only natural at a time when the rules of international law simply regulated inter-state conduct and protected the reciprocal interests of states. In contemporary international law, however, it is recognized that certain rules do protect 'community values', ie values that the international community as a whole considers of fundamental importance. These rules impose obligations that, in a well-known *obiter dictum*, the ICJ has characterized as *erga omnes* obligations,[31] in that their violation is the concern of all states.

The recognition of the existence of international rules that provide for *erga omnes* obligations raises a few problematical issues in the field of state responsibility, some which have been tackled by the ILC in its work of codification. Among the issues which are relevant to the present discussion, the entitlement of states to claim reparations for violations of an *erga omnes* obligation must be addressed. In this regard the Commission has distinguished between the position of the 'injured' state, and that of 'non-injured' states.

The injured state is the one that is specially affected by the violation,[32] ie the state which suffers particular adverse effects because of the wrongful act and therefore distinguishes itself from the generality of other states to which the obligation is owed.[33] On the face of it, the relationship between the injured state and the responsible state would not be different from that stemming from the violation of an 'ordinary' rule of international law (ie one that establishes reciprocal or synallagmatic obligations). The injured state is entitled to claim the international responsibility of the responsible state, in particular to demand reparation for the injuries suffered, and to resort to counter-measures in case of lack of compliance by the responsible state with its obligations stemming from the commission of the wrongful act.

The relationship between the injured state and the responsible state, however, would coexist with a parallel relationship, namely that between all the other states (that the ILC's Draft indicates as 'non injured' states)[34] and the responsible state. The ILC Articles on State Responsibility do in fact provide that, in the case of a violation of an *erga omnes* obligation, all the other states (the 'non injured' states) are entitled to invoke the international responsibility of the wrongdoer state, including demanding reparation.[35] They are only prevented from applying the instrumental consequences of the wrongful act, ie resorting to counter-measures (something which continues to be a prerogative of the injured state).[36]

---

could even decide not to compensate the individuals who had concretely suffered damage, and use the monies for different purposes.

[31] See *supra* note 4.   [32] See Art 42(b)(i) of the ILC's Articles, *supra* note 7.

[33] See Commentary on Art 42, para 12.

[34] For the reasons why the ILC has finally adopted this wording, see Simma, 'I diritti umani nel progetto della Commissione del diritto internazionale sulla responsabilità internazionale', in Spinedi *et al* (eds), *supra* note 26, 399, at 405–406.

[35] See Art 48(1)(b) of the ILC's Articles, *supra* note 7. As has been aptly noted by Francioni, *supra* note 22, at 30, the recognition of a *locus standi* to any State for the invocation of state responsibility gives practical relevance to the wide concept of 'international community' enshrined in Art 33 (see *supra* note 27).

[36] They can resort, however, to 'lawful measures' (see Art 52 of the ILC's Articles, *supra* note 7).

Non-injured states, however, by definition must not have been 'specially affected' by the wrongful act, and therefore, by definition, they have not suffered any material or moral damage. Their entitlement to demand from the responsible state full reparation for the injury caused *cannot therefore be exercised to their own advantage.* The ILC was aware of this particular situation, and has provided that any non-injured state is entitled to invoke the performance of the obligation of reparation 'in the interest of the injured State or *of the beneficiaries of the obligation breached*'.[37] Although the term 'beneficiaries' is perhaps not the most appropriate,[38] it is clear that among the beneficiaries of the obligations breached, one may include the individual victims of the wrongful act, as the ILC itself has recognized in the Commentary on the relevant provision.[39]

2. *The holder of the right to reparation in case of violations of* erga omnes *obligations protecting individuals' interests*

The possibility for non-injured states to claim reparation in the interest of the beneficiaries of the obligation breached is of crucial interest to our discussion in at least two respects.

First, the right to claim reparation is detached from any material or moral injury suffered as a result of the wrongful act. This is peculiar to rules having an *erga omnes* character, since for the other rules (ie those having a bilateral or reciprocal nature) the state that has suffered damage is the only one entitled to claim and to obtain reparation. In the case of violations of *erga omnes* obligations, the entitlement *to invoke* reparation stems from the legal interest of every state to ensure compliance with rules protecting collective interests.[40] Non-injured states, however, would claim reparation to redress damage that others have suffered. In short, what the ILC has envisaged here is the *procedural right* of non-injured states to demand reparation as distinct from the *substantive legal entitlement* to obtain it.[41]

---

[37] According to the ILC, the possibility therefore offered to non-injured states to invoke reparation in the interest of the injured state (if any) or the beneficiaries of the obligation 'involves a measure of progressive development, which is justified since it provides a means of protecting the community or collective interest at stake'. According to Gattini, *supra* note 29, at 448, due to the lack of international practice outside treaty-based mechanisms, to speak of a 'measure of progressive development' is an understatement.

[38] According to Francioni the use of this term 'reveals the rather shy attitude of the ILC in addressing the role of non-state actors in the law of state responsibility' (Francioni, *supra* note 22, at 30). More critical in this regard Pisillo Mazzeschi, 'The Marginal Role', *supra* note 26, at 44, who points out how this term is 'an old and traditional one' and that 'it causes one to think of the individual as *de facto* beneficiary of norms addressed only to States and not as a true holder of rights'.

[39] See *supra* note 29.

[40] As Simma observes, Art 48 and the possibility for non-injured states to claim reparation in the interest of the beneficiaries of the obligation breached constitutes a clear demonstration of the willingness of the ILC to go beyond a rigid inter-state perspective (Simma, *supra* note 34, at 408).

[41] The ILC explains this situation in the Commentary on Art 48, by noting: 'certain provisions, for example in various human rights treaties, allow invocation of responsibility by any State party. In those cases where they have been resorted to, a clear distinction has been drawn between the capacity of the applicant State to raise the matter and the interests of the beneficiaries of the obligation' (para 12).

Secondly, it is only logical to maintain that the procedural right to claim reparation be exercised to the benefit of the subjects entitled to reparation. In this respect, the ILC's Articles provide, as noted above, that non-injured states can demand reparation in the interest of the injured state or of the beneficiaries of the obligation breached. For the ILC, therefore, not only the injured state but also the beneficiaries of the obligation breached, including private individuals, are entitled to reparation. Otherwise, one would fail to understand why non-injured states can demand reparation to their advantage!

There remain at least two important issues that are left unclear in the ILC's Articles and their Commentaries. First, when the violation of an *erga omnes* obligation protecting individuals' interests causes damage to a particular state (for instance, because the human rights of its nationals are seriously infringed), is the wrongdoer internationally liable to reparation towards both vis-à-vis the state of nationality and the individual victims? Or is it possible to contend that international responsibility only arises with respect to the individual victims, and that the right of the injured state is confined to claiming international responsibility on behalf of its nationals? Second, can the right of the non-injured state to claim reparations in the interest of the beneficiaries of the breach be exercised only when no state has been injured? Or does this possibility exist also when the wrongful act has injured a particular state?

With respect to the first question, it may be contended that violations of the human rights obligations of foreigners give rise to a dual international responsibility: towards the state of nationality and towards the individual victims themselves.[42] If one accepts this point of view however, the responsible state should not repair the damage inflicted on the individuals twice, ie to the state of nationality and to the individual victims, and some form of coordination must be envisaged. Another construct, however, is possible, and one could contend that, also in such cases, the international responsibility of the state only arises vis-à-vis the individual victims of the violation of human rights. The state of nationality will of course be entitled to present an international claim for reparation, but it will do so not to protect its own right, but rather the rights of its nationals.[43] In practice,

---

[42] See in this regard Bartolini, *Riparazione per violazione dei diritti umani e diritto internazionale* (2009).

[43] It must be observed that this legal construct is also in keeping with the development in the field of diplomatic protection observed by the ICJ in the *Diallo* case. In the 2007 Judgment (Preliminary Objections) the Court has recognized that individuals hold rights under international law and that diplomatic protection, which must be exercised on the basis of the principle of the nationality of the claims, is not limited to the violations of the rules on the treatment of aliens, but has widened to include internationally guaranteed human rights. 'Owing to the substantive development of international law over recent decades in respect of the rights it accords to individuals, the scope *ratione materiae* of diplomatic protection, originally limited to alleged violations of the minimum standard of treatment of aliens, has subsequently widened to include, *inter alia*, internationally guaranteed human rights.' ICJ, Judgment (Preliminary Objections), *Ahmadou Sadio Diallo (Republic of Guinea v. Democratic Republic of Congo)*, 24 May 2007 (still unreported, but available on the website of the ICJ, <http//www.icj-cij.org>), para 39. The tenor of the statement, in particular due to the reference to the rights conferred upon individuals under international law, cannot but imply that for the Court the diplomatic protection constitutes a means for the defence—by the state of nationality—of the rights of the individuals. The old conception, according to which the home state exercises diplomatic

when a violation of an *erga omnes* obligation protecting individual interests occurs, the ensuing relationship of responsibility would arise *only* between the responsible state and the individual victims. The state of nationality will be the *medium* through which individuals may obtain, at the international level, the enforcement of state responsibility.

The second question, namely whether the non-injured states must ask reparation primarily in the interest of the injured state (if any) and only subsidiarily in the interest of the beneficiaries of the obligation breached, is closely linked to the previous one. If one contends that, when an injured state exists, it is primarily in the latter's interest that non-injured states must ask reparation, the inference could be drawn that the injured state is the ultimate and unique holder of the right to reparation. This conclusion, however, seems not to conform with the opinion of the ILC. In the Commentary on the relevant provision, the ILC explains that the non-injured states have the right to claim reparation in the interest of the beneficiaries of the obligation breached because it is 'desirable' that, once there is 'no State which is individually injured by the breach', 'some State or States be in a position to claim reparation, in particular restitution'.[44] Why is this desirable? The ILC does not expressly clarify this point. One can speculate that, in case of violations of *erga omnes* obligations infringing individuals' rights, what really matters is that the individual victims obtain reparation thanks to the claim made internationally by some states. The same concern, however, would arise when an injured state exists. If the injured state is entitled to dispose of the reparation eventually obtained from the responsible state as it prefers, then individual victims would be better protected when the violation has not caused injury to any state. This result appears illogical. Once it is assumed that non-injured states can demand reparation in favour of the individual victims in order that the latter obtain some form of reparation thanks to the international claim, the same result should be guaranteed when—facing a serious violation of a human rights obligation—it is possible to identify an injured state.

It can therefore be maintained that when an international law obligation conferring primary rights upon individuals is breached, and causes damage to them, the law of state responsibility allows both the injured state and a non-injured state to trigger the international responsibility of the wrongdoer and to demand reparation

protection in its own right because an injury to a national is deemed to be an injury to the state itself, initially endorsed by the PCIJ in the *Mavrommatis Palestine Concessions* case (According to the PCIJ, 'by taking up the case of one of its subjects and by resorting to diplomatic action or international judicial proceedings on his behalf, a State is in reality asserting its own right, the right to ensure, in the person of its subjects, respect for the rules of international law' (at 12) and by the ICJ in the *Nottebohm* case ('Diplomatic protection and protection by means of international judicial proceedings constitute measures for the defence of the rights of the State' (at 24), seems now to have been abandoned by the ICJ.

[44] See Commentary on Art 48, where the Commission states: 'In cases of breaches under article 48, it may well be that there is no State which is individually injured by the breach, yet it is highly desirable that some State or States be in a position to claim reparation, in particular restitution.' The Commission, however, underlines: 'This aspect of article 48, paragraph 2, involves a measure of progressive development, which is justifies since it provides a means of protecting the community or collective interest at stake' (ibid).

(only the injured state, however, would be allowed to resort to counter-measures). This claim serves to *protect the rights of individuals,* ie to enforce the relationship of responsibility that arises between the responsible state and the injured individuals. In such cases, the claiming states will simply act on behalf of the injured individuals, so that the latter can obtain redress for the damage they have suffered.

4. Do Individuals Enjoy Rights under International Humanitarian Law (IHL)?

Can it be contended that IHL encompasses rules possessing an *erga omnes* character and attributing primary rights to individuals, whose violation would entail reparation for their holders? If one answers this question in the affirmative, then the analysis developed so far would lead us to maintain that any state could ask for reparation to the advantage of the victims of the violations; and that the injured state (which, in the context of an international armed conflict will usually be the state of nationality of the victims) too will be entitled to claim reparation on account of the injured individuals.

A. The individuals as holders of primary rights under IHL

That the most fundamental rules of IHL possess an *erga omnes* character seems to be indisputable, as has been recognized by the ICJ.[45] A different matter, however, is to establish whether such rules confer rights on individuals under international law, so that their violations entitle the holders of those (primary) rights to reparation for the injuries suffered. The question is a crucial one. In practice, what one should determine is whether the rules of IHL are simply inter-state dealings that, although protecting a collective or community interest to the benefit of individuals, do not differ from those rules by which states decide to regulate their conduct to protect, for instance, endangered species; or whether, like the rules for the protection of human rights, they possess an *erga omnes* nature but, at the same time, confer rights on private individuals.

In this regard, as has already been mentioned, the common wisdom is that the rules of IHL do not confer rights upon private individuals or private actors, but they simply regulate the conduct of belligerents and of neutral states. It is submitted that this legal construct is no longer tenable.

Admittedly, many of the treaty provisions of IHL relating to the conduct of hostilities are worded in the form of *prohibitions* incumbent upon belligerent parties, rather than in terms of *rights* accruing to specific persons or category of persons.[46] The provisions on the protection of persons who are or have fallen into the hands of the enemy are also worded in terms of obligations for the belligerents, by

---

[45] See *supra*, note 4.
[46] For instance, with regard to protection of civilians during combat operation, one of the relevant rules provides: 'The civilian population as such, as well as individual civilians, shall not be made the object of an attack': Art 51, para 2, of *AP I.*

imposing upon them the treatment that must be afforded to the relevant protected persons rather than spelling out the rights to which those persons may be entitled.[47] One could therefore contend that under these provisions the individuals concerned are mere *indirect beneficiaries* of obligations that are addressed to the belligerents, and which confer the corresponding rights only upon the belligerents as such.

However, this construct could have been propounded in the past, at a time when individuals had no status at all in international law. The development of the international law of human rights, and the parallel recognition that individuals are entitled to be protected in their own right against abusive state conduct, has had an enormous influence on the corpus of international rules and on their proper interpretation. Under contemporary international law, individuals are no longer considered the 'objects' of rights accruing only to states, but are also considered to enjoy rights themselves vis-à-vis states under international law. It would therefore be preposterous to affirm that the position of the individual as a holder of rights dissolves when their need to be protected against abuses reaches its peak, ie in situations of armed conflicts, when individuals are more vulnerable than ever. To state that the rules of IHL concerning the guarantees that belligerent parties must afford to civilians in combat operations and to persons in the hands of the enemy have a merely inter-state dimension amounts to asserting that, under this body of law, individuals are at the mercy of belligerents and entitled to protection only as mere objects of the belligerents' rights. This construction would mean that the relevant rules of IHL, when they apply, dispossess individuals of their entitlement to be protected against illegal conduct by belligerents; that they suppress individuals to a position no different from that of 'endangered species' in situations where, on the contrary, belligerents must not forget that they are dealing with human beings.

It should therefore not be surprising that, at least as regards the 1949 Geneva Conventions, one can find a common provision that contributes to clarifying who the holders of the rights corresponding to the obligation of protection incumbent on the belligerents are: they are the protected persons themselves, who can 'in no circumstances renounce in part or in entirety the rights secured to them in the Conventions'.[48] A similar conclusion can be suggested for the rules that intend *to protect civilians* from unlawful attacks by belligerents. Human rights law applies in situations of armed conflicts, and there is a set of human rights that continues to apply even when the state makes a declaration under the derogation clause contained in the human rights treaties. The right to life certainly belongs to this set of intransgressible rights and thus continues to protect civilians not taking direct part in the hostilities. The inescapable conclusion is that the relevant rules of IHL must be interpreted in the light of the development of international law in the field of human rights; hence as rules that, while obliging belligerents not to launch disproportionate and indiscriminate attacks against civilians, confer corresponding rights on the civilians themselves, and not on the enemy belligerent party.

---

[47] Article 12 of *GC I*, for instance, provides that members of the armed forces who are wounded or sick 'shall be respected and protected in all circumstances' and they 'shall be treated humanely and cared for by the Party to the conflict in whose power they may be'.
[48] See Art 7 of *GC I, II,* and *III*, and Art 8 of *GC IV.*

This construct, namely that rules of IHL confer primary rights on individuals, has also been echoed in some national case law. As a matter of fact, national courts have not found it difficult to state that individuals *possess primary rights under IHL*; what they have found difficult is to recognize that individuals enjoy, under international law, the *right to present a claim towards the state responsible for the violations of these rules.*[49]

B. The individuals as holders of 'secondary' rights under IHL

If individuals enjoy primary rights under IHL, the consequence is that their violation entitles them to the (secondary) right to reparation under international law.

That individual victims of serious violations of IHL have the right to reparation finds some support in international practice. First, one must refer to the *Report of the International Commission of Inquiry on Darfur to the United Nations Secretary-General*, where the Commission has maintained that

> whenever a gross breach of human rights is committed which also amounts to an international crime, customary international law not only provides for the criminal liability of the individuals who have committed that breach, but also imposes an obligation on States of which the perpetrators are nationals, or for which they acted as *de jure* or *de facto* organs, to make reparation (including compensation) for the damage made.[50]

Secondly, one must mention the ICJ's Advisory Opinion in the *Wall* case. In the operative part of the Advisory Opinion, the Court held that Israel was obliged 'to make reparation for all damage caused by the construction of the wall in the Occupied Palestinian Territory, including in and around East Jerusalem'[51]

---

[49] See, in this regard, the Federal Constitutional Court of Germany, in the *Italian Military Internee* case, Joint Constitutional Complaint, 28 June 2004, (English translation available at Oxford Reports on International Law, <http://oxfordlawreports.com>, para 38 a), which has however denied that individuals enjoy the right to bring a claim for compensation: 'In principle Art 3 of the Hague Convention of 1907 establishes no individual claims for damages but simply codifies the general principle under international law of responsibility for obligations between the contracting parties (cf. Art.1 of the Articles of the International Law Commission of the United Nations, International Law Commission—ILC, on the laws of State responsibility, Annex to Resolution 56/83 of the United Nations General Assembly of 21 December 2001). However, such *claims for damages under secondary law exist only in the international legal relationship between the states concerned. The claim for damages accordingly differs from the claim under primary law of the persons concerned to adherence to the obligations under humanitarian international law, as existing in the international legal relationship between the state occupying a territory and the population living in that area*' (emphasis added). In the same vein see the decision by the German Federal High Court of Justice in the so-called *Bridge of Varvarin* case (*35 Citizens of the Former Federal Republic of Yugoslavia v Germany*), 2 November 2006, para 10 a), ibid where the Court states: 'According to the jurisprudence of the Federal Constitutional Court, to this day only the State of nationality is liable for secondary claims for compensation based on unlawful acts of a foreign State against its citizens, *in spite of the development of the level of protection of human rights which resulted in the recognition that individuals could partly be subjects of international law and to the establishment of individual claim cases based on treaties*' (emphasis added).
[50] Report of the International Commission of Inquiry, *supra* note 21, para 598. The International Commission clearly wanted to refer also to serious violations of IHL. It grounded its proposition on the development of human rights law and the universal recognition of a right to a remedy to victims of serious violations of human rights and the effects that it has had on the law on state responsibility.
[51] ICJ Reports (2004) 202, para 163, 3, C.

as a result of the violations of international law established by the Court. In its reasoning, the Court also identified the beneficiaries of this obligation. It pointed out that since 'the construction of the wall in the Occupied Palestinian Territory has, *inter alia,* entailed the requisition and destruction of homes, businesses and agricultural holdings... Israel has the obligation to make reparation for the damage caused *to all the natural or legal persons concerned*'.[52] Admittedly, the Court has not specified that the obligation to repair the damage caused to all natural or legal persons concerned stems from the violations of the rules of IHL. For the Court, however, the construction of the Wall is unlawful under various rules of international law, in particular the law on self-determination of peoples, the rules on military occupation, and human rights. The failure by the Court to clarify which violations entailed the obligation to repair damage to private individuals can only mean that for the Court the matter was irrelevant,[53] namely that the obligation of Israel to repair the injury caused to individuals followed *naturally* from the illegality of the Israeli conduct under each of the aforementioned rules of international law, including those on military occupation.[54]

Finally, one ought to mention the developments which have occurred in the system of international criminal justice. In particular, the need to make reparations to victims of international crimes, including war crimes, is slowly becoming recognized before international and mixed criminal courts,[55] and has led to the inclusion of specific provisions to that effect in the Statute of the International Criminal Court (ICC).[56] Admittedly this development has occurred at the level of individual responsibility. The contention can be made, however, that if victims of international crimes have the right to reparation vis-à-vis the responsible individual, *a fortiori* they should possess the same right vis-à-vis the state on behalf of which the responsible individual has acted. International crimes are often the outcome of a system of state criminality, which is the reason why in international criminal law the obedience to orders and the official capacity of the individual who has engaged in the criminal conduct do not free that individual from criminal accountability. Once it is recognized that individuals who have acted *qua* state agents are liable to compensation under international law towards the victims of their crime, it is only logical to also recognize that the state on behalf of which they

---

[52] Para 152. See also para 153 where the Court underlined that the 'obligation to return the land, orchards, olive groves and other immovable property seized from any natural or legal person for the purposes of construction of the wall', as well as the 'obligation to compensate the persons in question' when the restitution 'should prove to be materially impossible'.

[53] In this regard, see d'Argent, 'Compliance, Ceassation, Reparation and Restitution in the Wall Advisory Opinion', in Dupuy, Fassbender, Shaw, and Sommermann (eds), *Völkerrecht als Wertordnung—Common Values in International Law, Festschrift für/Essays in Honour of Christian Tomuschat* (2006) 463–477. For a different view, see Tomuschat, *supra* note 17.

[54] In this sense, also d'Argent, *supra* note 53.

[55] See in for these developments Zegveld, 'Victims' Reparation Claims and International Criminal Courts. Incompatible Values?', in 8 *JICJ* (2010) 79, 86–92.

[56] Art 75 of the ICC Statute. On reparation claims before the ICC, see among others Jeangène Vilmer, *Réparer l'irréparable: les réparations aux victimes devant la Cour pénale internationale* (2009); Caesens, 'The ICC and the State as Partners in Prosecuting Crimes: Impact on the Victim's Right to a Remedy', in 3 *Human Rights and International Legal Discourse* (2009) 57.

have acted shares this form of liability to the extent that the wrongful conduct can be attributed to it.

C. How can the relationship of international responsibility of the state towards individuals be enforced?

The recognition that under international law individuals possess the right to reparation when they suffer from violations of rules of IHL, and therefore that there exists a private international cause of action for such violations, does not entail that they are automatically entitled to present a claim against the responsible state *at the international level*.[57] Admittedly, at first sight the recognition of a substantive right under international law which is not accompanied by the procedural right to enforce it before an international forum may appear meaningless. However, it is not really so if one considers the following.

First, individuals may obtain the enforcement of their right to reparation at the international level through the action of their nation state or through the actions of other states which—under the law of state responsibility—are entitled to claim reparation from the responsible state to the benefit of the individual. The position of individuals who are victims of serious violations of IHL is therefore not dissimilar from that of persons who, under domestic legal systems, are subjects of law but are temporarily or permanently deprived of the legal capacity to act (ie persons under the legal age). In other words, at the international level individuals could be equated with minors who can obtain the protection of their rights through the activity and the good will of their parents or tutors, ie the state of nationality or other states. It is in this vein, for instance, that the Agreement establishing the Eritrea–Ethiopia Claims Commission has enabled the Commission to pronounce on claims related to damage caused, *inter alia*, by violations of rules of *jus in bello*, claims submitted 'by each of the parties on its own behalf and *on behalf of its nationals*, including both natural and juridical persons' and '[i]n appropriate cases... claims [submitted by one of the parties] *on behalf of persons of Ethiopian or Eritrean origin who may not be its nationals*'.[58] With respect to the latter category of claims, the Commission has considered that a necessary requirement was the nationality (Eritrean or Ethiopian) possessed by the individual at the moment of the commission of the wrongful act.[59]

---

[57] At the domestic level, every legal substantive right can be made judicially enforceable before national courts: in other terms, at the national level, a cause of action always exists along with the right of action. By contrast, at the international level individuals may be granted legal (substantive) rights vis-à-vis the states (or other legal subjects of international law) without being provided with the right of action, ie the right to present a judicial or other kind of claim, before an international mechanism.

[58] See Art 5, para 1, and Art 5, para 9, of the Peace Agreement between the Government of the Federal Republic of Ethiopia and the Government of the State of Eritrea, available online at <http://www.pca-cpa.org/showpage.asp?pag_id=1151>. The emphasis in the text has been added.

[59] Partial Award, Loss of Property in Ethiopia Owned by Non-Residents, Eritrea's Claim 24, 19 December 2005, available at <http://www.pca-cpa.org/upload/files/FINAL%20ER%20 CLAIM%2024.pdf>, para 7.

In addition, again with respect to the latter category of claims, the Commission has considered that the claims based on injuries to non-nationals but made on behalf of the party concerned and not the individuals concerned were outside its jurisdiction.[60] This provision is notable, because the Commission has thus implicitly recognized that the relevant states, had they filed claims before the Commission on the basis of injuries against individuals having their nationality at the moment of the commission of the wrongful act, would have simply exercised a procedural right to protect the individuals' substantive right to compensation for violations of the rules of IHL.[61]

Secondly, individuals may enforce their *substantive* international right to reparation by turning to domestic systems and trying to assert their claim before national tribunals.[62] This situation is not unusual with respect to private international claims against states. One clear example of this in the field of the individual right to reparation vis-à-vis the state can be found in European Union law and relates to the liability of the member states of the European Union to make reparation for the prejudice caused to individuals by violations of European Union law. The individuals possess, vis-à-vis the member state, the right to be compensated for the violation of European Union law that has caused damage to them. As the European Court of Justice has affirmed, however, absent European legislation, the right to a substantive remedy can only be enforced within the competent national legal system, in accordance with its procedures and rules.[63] In practice, as has been correctly emphasized, one should distinguish between the existence of the right of an individual to reparation and *the law applicable to the ensuing relationship of responsibility between the state and the individual.*[64] As is often the case in the international legal order, the law applicable to this relationship is that of the competent national legal system. In other words, it is not unusual for rights conferred by international law on private individuals or other persons or entities to be only (or primarily) enforced by the domestic legal orders.

The extent to which national legal systems allow victims of serious breaches of IHL to sue the responsible state before their home courts may vary, and in some cases reparation claims might be (and have been) dismissed on national procedural

---

[60] See Partial Award in Eritrea's Civilians Claims, Eritrea's Claims 15, 16, 23, and 27–32, 17 December, available at <http://www.pca-cpa.org/upload/files/ER%20Partial%20Award%20Dec%2004.pdf>, para 19; see also Partial Award, Loss of Property in Ethiopia Owned by Non-Residents, Eritrea's Claim 24, *supra* note 52, para 7.

[61] No claim on behalf of individuals of Ethiopian or Eritrean origin has been filed before the Commission. The innovative purport of Art 5, para 9, of the Peace Agreement has therefore been significantly undermined.

[62] See Tomuschat, *Human Rights between Idealism and Realism* (2nd edn, 2008) at 373.

[63] In this regard, see D'Argent, *Le réparations, supra* note 14, at 792. See also Tomuschat, *supra* note 62, at 364–365. Another example is that of the European system for the Protection of Human Rights: as Art 41 of the European Convention on Human Rights provides, the Strasbourg Court may afford 'just satisfaction to the injured party' only to the extent that the internal law of the respondent party allows only partial reparation. Therefore, the applicant must first turn to the domestic system to obtain reparation for the injuries suffered (D'Argent. *Le réparations, supra* note 14, at 793).

[64] d'Argent, *Le réparations, supra* note 14; esp at 791–795.

grounds.[65] No doubt this situation is unsatisfactory because the outcome is often that the victims are left without a remedy.

One should note, however, that when claims have been brought before the national courts of the alleged responsible state, in most cases the dismissal of civil claims has been grounded on what I consider to be a misinterpretation of the relevant rules of IHL (for instance, on account of the alleged exclusive inter-state nature of the rules of IHL on the conduct of hostilities)[66] or on such doctrines as that of 'act of government', which cannot be reconciled with the rule of law as understood in our time.[67] In such cases, therefore, the dismissal of the claims cannot be held to be consonant with the correct interpretation of the law. In other instances, the dismissal was due to the applicability of a statute of limitations to civil claims. In this regard, it has been argued that, when claims relate to illegal acts that may also amount to war crimes, the principle of the inapplicability of statutes of limitations to international crimes ought logically to be extended to related civil claims.[68]

As for claims brought before national courts against foreign states, the question of the applicability of the doctrine of state foreign immunities usually arises. One international case regarding this thorny issue is currently pending before the ICJ.[69] Without entering into the wide debate of recent decades on the availability of sovereign immunities in the event of serious violations of rules of *jus cogens* (such as the rules on human rights and IHL),[70] I will simply underline an aspect that I believe deserves further analysis for the purpose of this chapter.

The doctrine of sovereign immunities was asserted and gained ground at a time when international law merely regulated inter-state conduct; its aim was to shelter

---

[65] For an overview and a discussion of these hurdles to national claims, see Gattini, 'To What Extent Are State Immunity and Non-Justiciability Major Hurdles to Individuals' Claims for War Damage?', in 2 *JICJ* (2003) 348, as well as Ronzitti, *supra* note 1, 104–114. Specifically on the doctrine of non-justiciability, see Ben-Naftali and Michaeli, 'Justice-Abililty: A Critique of the Alleged Non-Justiciability of Israel's Policy of Targeted Killings', ibid, 368.

[66] See in this regard the *Marković* case, where the Italian Court of Cassation dismissed an action brought by some Serb victims of the bombings by NATO-led airplanes of the Serb Radio-Television in Belgrade, by stating—*inter alia*—that the applicable rules (ie the rules of *AP I* to the Geneva Conventions) were inter-state rules: decision of 5 June 2002, English text in 128 ILR 652. The Italian Court consequently applied the doctrine of 'political act', thereby affirming that the judiciary had no possibility of pronouncing upon acts of war which fall within the remit of discretionary governmental powers. For a comment on this case see Frulli, *supra* note 16.

[67] See Tomuschat, *supra* note 17.

[68] D'Argent, *Le réparations, supra* note 14, at 794, footnote 2508 for the reference to some national cases on the applicability of statute of limitation to civil claims.

[69] ICJ, *Jurisdictional Immunities of the State (Germany v Italy)*, instituted by Germany on 23 December 2008, in relation to the decision of the Italian Court of Cassation not to consider applicable the rule of foreign state immunities in relation to claims concerning the practice of forced labour and deportation carried out by Germany during the Second World War.

[70] See, among others, Zimmermann, 'Sovereign Immunity and Violations of International Jus Cogens. Some Critical Remarks', in 16 *Mich. J. Int'l L.* (1995) 433; Clapan, 'State Immunity, Human Rights, and Jus Cogens: a Critique of the Normative Hierarchy Theory', in 97 *AJIL* (2003) 741; MacGregor, 'State Immunity and Jus Cogens', in 55 *ICLQ* (2006) 437; Giegerich, 'Do Damage Claims Arising from Jus Cogens Violations Override State Immunity from the Jurisdiction of Foreign Courts?', in Tomuschat and Thouvenin (eds), *The Fundamental Rules of the International Legal Order: Jus Cogens and Obligations Erga Omnes* (2006) 203.

foreign states from the national jurisdiction of their peers (*pares*) with respect to sovereign acts. As I have already underlined, the assumption was that, when the acts of a foreign state had caused injury to a private person, it was in fact another state that had been injured, usually the state of nationality. The latter state could therefore act at the international level, in diplomatic or judicial protection, to enforce what it considered to be *its own right*. The courts of that (national) state, therefore, were not authorized to exercise jurisdiction over the individual claim brought against the allegedly responsible foreign state, essentially for two reasons: (i) in order not to interfere with the decision of their own government to act internationally to assert the responsibility of the wrongdoer, and (ii) in order not to submit the foreign state to the domestic law of the country. The relationship of responsibility was an inter-state relationship, and it was only natural to consider that the matter had to be tackled at a purely international (ie inter-state) level.

The evolution which has occurred in international law, in particular the recognition that states have international obligations vis-à-vis individuals, naturally alters the scope and purpose of the doctrine of sovereign immunity.[71] A foreign state that violates a rule of IHL (or a rule of human rights) and causes damage to an individual is obliged to make reparation to the individual victim. The home state of the victim can act in diplomatic protection, but to protect the individual's right, ie to assert the international responsibility of the foreign state *towards the individual victim*. If it does not act in this manner, and the individual presents a claim before its own national courts against the foreign state, this of course might cause embarrassment to the home government at the political level. Nonetheless, in purely legal terms, the victims are simply trying to enforce the rights they directly enjoy under international law and that the government does not protect on their behalf. The *ratio* behind the recognition of foreign sovereign immunity in traditional international law no longer applies: the national judge will simply act as a stand-in for the government and make good its inaction. The judge might decide to reject the claim of the individual, as the case demands, as a matter of judicial self-restraint. This, however, will not be a *matter of foreign sovereign immunity,* but rather of deference of the judiciary to the political power.

Furthermore, the judicial examination of a claim before a national court based on the violation of a right granted to the individual by international law will not

---

[71] It is in this vein that the Italian Court of Cassation, in the *Civitella della Chiana* case, has stated that it would be highly contradictory to call for the application of the rules on state immunities for the sake of protecting state sovereignty when what is at stake is the application of international rules which protect individuals from abuses of state sovereignty ('... non avrebbe senso proclamare il primato dei diritti fondamentali della persona e poi, contraddittoriamente escludere la possibilità di accesso al giudice negando, in tal modo, agli individui la possibilità di usare i mezzi indispensabili ad assicurare l'effettività e la preminenza di quei diritti fondamentali conculcati dall'azione criminosa di uno Stato'). See Corte di Cassazione, Sezione I penale, judgment of 21 October 2008, n 1072, registered 13 January 2009, in 92 *Rivista di diritto internazionale* (2009) 618. For a comment, see Frulli, 'La "derogabilità" della norma sull'immunità degli Stati dalla giurisdizione in caso di crimini internazionali: la decisione della Corte di Cassazione sulla strage di Civitella della Chiana', in 3 *Diritti umani e diritto internazionale* (2009). See also Ciampi, 'The Italian Court of Cassation Asserts Civil Jurisdiction over Germany in a Criminal Case Relating to the Second World War. The Civitella Case', in 7 *JICJ* (2009) 597.

jeopardize the reciprocal independence and sovereignty of states, as required by the old maxim *par in parem non habet judicium* underpinning the doctrine of sovereign immunities. The national judge asserting his jurisdiction will not submit the foreign state to the *imperium* of the domestic law of another state; rather, he will act as a judge of the international community, putting in place the phenomenon of the *dédoublement fonctionnel* that is well known to international lawyers.[72] It is as though the international community, still a *communitas imperfecta*, avails itself of national courts to enforce the relationship of responsibility of the state towards individuals.

If one accepts this reasoning, the doctrine of sovereign immunity becomes unavailable whenever the claim is grounded on an alleged violation of international law. However, it will continue to apply in relation to a state's activities performed *iure imperii* in violation of the domestic law of another state.

5. Conclusion

International humanitarian law has undergone significant transformation. It can no longer be considered as a branch of international law merely regulating interstate conduct and only conferring rights and obligations upon states. This was true in the past, but it can no longer be considered true. Whenever illegal state behaviour has a direct and harmful effect upon individuals, it would be preposterous to contend that these individuals are not legally affected under international law, by stating that it is in fact their national state which has suffered the violation. This is an anachronistic view, which can no longer be maintained. IHL is no longer the '*jus in bello*'. It is a body of law which has gradually acquired a true humanitarian scope and purpose, as the international regulation of non-international armed conflicts clearly demonstrates. The aim of the bulk of these rules is to protect fundamental human rights, rights that cannot be trampled upon by states even in the event of armed conflicts. The international law of human rights has had a pervasive effect on many rules of international law, including IHL, changing the very scope and purpose of many of them. Individuals now hold primary rights towards states in the event of armed conflicts and therefore they also enjoy the right to reparation in cases of violations.

How can the responsibility of the state towards individuals be enforced? At the international level, the task is left not only to the state of nationality, which is often the injured state, but also to all other states. This possibility is expressly recognized by the ILC's Articles on State Responsibility, which provide that, as regards violations of obligations *erga omnes* conferring rights on individuals, both the injured and non-injured states can demand that the responsible state should fulfil the obligation to make reparation to the injured individuals.

---

[72] On the theory of the *dédoublement fonctionnel*, see the work of Scelle quoted by Cassese, 'Remarks on Scelle's Theory of "Role Splitting" (*dédoublement fonctionnel*) in International Law', 1 *EJIL* (1990) 210, note 1.

In addition, individuals can turn to the domestic legal order and bring their claims before the competent national courts. The fact that at the national level the exercise of the individual right to reparation has often been hampered by the application of doctrines such as that of sovereign immunity, of statutes of limitations or of non-justiciability, cannot be invoked to deny the existence of that right. It should instead prompt international lawyers to determine to what extent all these doctrines comply with the current evolution of international law and the progressive recognition of obligations of states towards individuals, including the obligation to make reparation for wrongs inflicted on individuals in times of armed conflict.

9

Post-conflict Accountability and the Reshaping of Human Rights and Humanitarian Law

Christine Bell

1. Introduction

The aftermath of conflict often sees two quite different demands for post-conflict accountability in terms of human rights and humanitarian law. The first demand is that those responsible for human rights or humanitarian law violations during the conflict are held accountable for those violations. The second demand is that third parties with post-settlement responsibility for 'implementing the peace' are held accountable where they themselves violate the rights of local populations. Both demands are variously made post-conflict by local populations and by international actors.

In this chapter I consider the ways in which human rights and humanitarian law have been argued to impose post-conflict accountability in both the above senses. While I do not seek to collapse the distinct legal, political, and moral issues which arise, I argue that the attempt to use human rights and humanitarian law standards to impose accountability has had similar dynamics across both cases. In both cases a lack of fit between regime and post-conflict political landscape has involved an interpretative revision of what the regimes require, that has moved them towards a loose common denominator implemented by *ad hoc* institutional innovation. Any account of the implications for the relationship of human rights and humanitarian law in post-conflict settings should take account of both sets of developments. To this end, this chapter sets out both processes of interpretive revision and *ad hoc* institutional innovation, discussing the consequences for each regime and the relationship between them.

The chapter proceeds as follows. In Part 2, I discuss, in general terms, the peculiarities of the post-conflict political environments with reference to human rights and humanitarian law. In Parts 3 and 4, I examine how the accountability standards of human rights and humanitarian law have been argued to apply post-conflict. Specifically, I examine the two quite different demands for post-conflict

* I would like to thank Gabriele Porretto, Ray Murphy, Fionnuala Ní Aoláin, and Orna Ben-Naftali for comments on earlier drafts. My thanks also go to Ita Connolly and Shauna Page for research assistance.

accountability set out above. Part 3 addresses the application of human rights and humanitarian law to those responsible for the worst atrocities of the conflict—often termed transitional justice. Part 4 addresses the application of human rights and humanitarian law to third party actors charged with peacebuilding, should these third parties violate the rights of the local population. In Part 5, I consider the implications of regime-merge and institutional innovation for the existing regimes of human rights and humanitarian law. I examine and evaluate what I suggest are three conceptualizations of the current legal landscape and its future direction. The first conceptualization ambitiously involves the attempt to articulate a new third-way combined regime—a *jus post bellum*—that is, a coherent attempt to develop a combined humanitarian law and human rights regime tailored to the political goals of internal constitutional revision. The second conceptualization is of a project of piece-meal reform aimed at producing new norms specifically targeted at filling in some of the 'gaps' between existing norms and post-conflict accountability demands. The third conceptualization of the way forward involves an attempt to narrate a form of transnational accountability which would build on, rather than attempt to rationalize, the legal pluralism and 'mess' of current developments. In conclusion (Part 6) I suggest the possibility of drawing on all three conceptualizations as reflecting different underlying meta-level understandings of the current 'situating' of international law itself.

2. Post-conflict Hybridity and Accountability

A. Post-conflict hybridity

The hybridity of the post-conflict landscape finds its roots in the hybridity of contemporary conflict itself. Intra-state conflict originating mainly within state borders, involving state forces and non-state armed opposition groups, for example in Sri Lanka, Northern Ireland, Sierra Leone, or Liberia, increasingly has inter-state repercussions. It spills across borders, draws in regional actors as conflict-underwriters or mediators, and attracts the attention and intervention of international organizations in particular the United Nations.[1] Most notably, contemporary practices of terminating intra-state conflict through negotiated settlement constitute a key international response. Even in the most domestic of conflicts, international actors—states, coalitions and international organizations—are involved in conflict resolution efforts, for example, as peacekeepers, international civilian missions, and international individuals on peace implementation bodies.

Conversely, just as contemporary intra-state conflict has international dimensions contemporary inter-state conflict typically has a connection to conflict within states. The main inter-state conflicts of the last two decades have arisen primarily between a coalition of state forces against an individual 'pariah' state and terminating with the capitulation of that state: namely the NATO intervention in

---

[1] Wippman (ed) *International Law and Ethnic Conflict* (2008).

Bosnia of the mid 1990s; the NATO intervention in Kosovo in 1999; and US-led interventions in Afghanistan in 2001 and Iraq in 2003.[2] All of these conflicts have had some type of articulated relationship to conflict within the target state, and have involved post-conflict attempts at post-conflict state reconstruction.

Both types of conflict have therefore left in their wake a post-conflict environment with some common features. Most centrally, the post-conflict environment is characterized by an international–domestic hybridity. Ending conflict requires both an internal political settlement that will be inclusive enough of military contenders within the state to convince them to stop fighting, and the external enforcement of that settlement.[3] The internal and external dimensions are linked. External actors are needed to reassure the state's opponents that the state will be held to its side of the bargain, in a domestic political and legal order that is every bit as 'anarchic' as the international legal system itself.[4] The typical post-conflict political and legal landscape is therefore characterized by 'international-domestic' hybridity where post-conflict governance is undertaken by international and domestic actors working together to implement the peace. Post-conflict entities are at once a national jurisdiction with technical continuity of statehood, and a space of transnational administration permeated by international actors and characterized by 'post-sovereign' elements such as binationalism and internationalization.[5]

Post-conflict societies are also characterized by a war-peace hybridity. Post-conflict seldom is *post*-conflict—even when a conflict has been terminated through a formally agreed ceasefire. War–peace hybridity can be seen in a 'no-war-no-peace' situation that tends to prevail in the short to medium term, in which the move from war to not-war is seldom linear, and where forms of violence often mutate in complex ways, rather than being eliminated. Parties to a settlement may renege on their commitments and return to violence covertly or overtly, or prompt their opponents to do so. Those parties not included in the settlement may act as 'spoilers' attempting to destabilize fragile accords through high profile dramatic acts, such as the assassination of Rabin post-Oslo accords in the Middle East (now clearly not 'post-conflict'), the Omagh Bomb by the 'real IRA' immediately post the Belfast Agreement in Northern Ireland, the post-Arusha Accord genocide in Rwanda, and ongoing violence in Iraq and Afghanistan. Ongoing conflict violence may continue and even increase (for example, Middle East, Rwanda); or reduce but also mutate into new forms (low-level inter-ethnic 'attacks', whose disorganization

---

[2] There have also been some 'pure' inter-state conflicts, involving two states and often revolving around border disputes, for example: Chad/Libya, Ethiopia/Eritrea, China/India, India/Pakistan, and Ecuador/Peru. However, even many of these conflicts also had closely related intra-state dimensions. The first war with Iraq of 1991 forms a clearer exception as an inter-state conflict with little (initial) relationship to events within the state.

[3] Bell, *On the Law of Peace* (2008), chs 5 and 10.

[4] Walter, 'The Critical Barrier to Civil War Settlement', 51 *Int'l Org.* (1997) at 335.

[5] Cf the concept of 'global administrative space': see Kingsbury, 'The Concept of 'Law' in Global Administrative Law', 20 *EJIL* (2009) 23, at 25 (defining it as 'a congerie of different actors and layers…that includes transnational institutions and transnational networks, as well as domestic administrative bodies that operate within international regimes or cause transboundary regulatory effects'.)

is difficult to combat, for example Northern Ireland); or forms of violence perceived as 'new' but nevertheless firmly connected to the conflict may arise, for example as violence against women in their home, exploitation and sexual trafficking fuelled by the presence of wealthy internationals, racist violence that targets those outside the main conflict groups, and organized crime (for example, Bosnia, South Africa). In short, a complex mix of war-acts, human rights violations, and 'ordinary' criminal law violations may be perpetrated by a range of domestic and international, state and non-state actors, in an environment in which clear categorization of the violence and perpetrator is impossible.

Finally, post-conflict environments contain a complex mix of state and non-state actors, in a state formation that itself is supposed to be in transition from an authoritarian illegitimate, violent, or exclusionary past towards a less authoritarian, more legitimate, or less violent and exclusionary future.[6] The post-conflict period is one of attempted transition to a new political and even constitutional framework, and the period of transition is often ambiguous as to the authorship and sources of legitimacy of this framework—and so typically all possible contenders are drawn into the peacemaking project—the government, its armed opponents, civil society, and international actors.

B. Post-conflict accountability

A working definition of accountability in this context is: having to answer for one's actions in terms of human rights and humanitarian standards, with some measure of sanction if violations are found.[7] Civil and political human rights standards found in the main international and regional human rights treaties, such as the International Covenant of Civil and Political Rights of 1966, but also in customary law require a state to answer for violations such as arbitrary execution and torture, not just in times of peace, but in times of conflict.[8] While some rights can be derogated from during conflict, key relevant rights, such as the right to life and the prohibition on torture, do not permit of such derogation.[9] These standards, where applicable, impose an ongoing liability post-conflict: no explicit provision can be found for a limited or partial post-conflict application.[10] Civil, political,

---

[6] See generally, Bell, 'Peace Agreements: Their Nature and Legal Status', 100 *AJIL* (2006) 373.

[7] Modified from Krisch, 'The Pluralism of Global Administrative Law', 17 *EJIL* (2006) 247, at 249 (quoting Oakerson, 'Governance Structures for Enhancing Accountability and Responsiveness', in J L Perry (ed), *Handbook of Public Administration* (1989) 114, at 114); cf de Wet, 'Holding International Organizations Accountable: The Complementary Role of Non-judicial Oversight Mechanisms and Judicial Review', 9 *German Law Journal* (2008) 1987.

[8] For a full review of both convention and customary law in this area see Orentlicher, 'Settling Accounts: The Duty to Prosecute Human Rights Violations of a Prior Regime', 100 *Yale L.J.* (1991) 2537. For discussion of the application of human rights law in times of conflict see Ben-Naftali and Shany, 'Living in Denial: The Co-application of Humanitarian Law and Human Rights Law to the Occupied Territories' 37 *Is. L.R.* (2004) 17–118; and more generally F Ní Aoláin and O Gross, *Law in Times of Crisis: Emergency Powers in Theory and Practice* (2006).

[9] See for example, Art 4, International Covenant on Civil and Political Rights of 1966; Art 15, European Convention on Human Rights and Fundamental Freedoms of 1950.

[10] See further *infra* notes 19–25.

social, economic, and cultural human rights treaty standards also restrain the power of those who govern with respect to the individual rights of those who are governed, and so seem relevant to third party exercising of public power. Similarly, humanitarian law found in the Geneva Conventions of 1949 (hereinafter Geneva Conventions), and Additional Protocols I and II of 1977 (*AP I* and *AP II*), contain standards which limit violence, for example, the prohibition on indiscriminate attack and the permeating need to distinguish between civilian and military targets. Again, the duty to enforce is not time limited but continues post-conflict. The Fourth Geneva Convention (hereinafter *GC IV*) further contains standards that both authorize and limit an occupier's power post-conflict, and again these standards seem relevant to the post-conflict exercise of public power by third party peacebuilders. While operating with different origins, both human rights and humanitarian law regimes have increasingly become viewed as an integrated set of standards, both capable of application during conflict.[11] However, where the standards materially differ, the *lex specialis,* or most relevant standard, should apply and where the conflict thresholds of humanitarian law are met, this would be humanitarian law.[12] The combined application of both regimes during conflict itself responds to the hybrid nature of contemporary conflict.[13]

The post-conflict political environment, however, makes any such orderly application of the regimes extremely difficult. The hybridity which characterizes the post-conflict landscape, as we will see, makes it difficult to decide what regime applies, when and to whom, and for what. This difficulty is in part a technical difficulty of how to apply the regimes to a situation that is in flux. However, I suggest that the difficulties are also of a quite different order with a clearly political dimension. Technical difficulties mask an underlying political struggle over the nature and direction of the transition. In the post-conflict context, demands for accountability of actors in the conflict or peace process, using human rights or humanitarian law, are rarely simply demands that 'one answers for one's actions'. The post-conflict political environment is one which attempts a transition from one state formation to another, and where the goals of transition are themselves contested among and between both local and international actors. Often the actual outcome of transition remains open: whether a coherent state will exist and what it will look like remain 'up for grabs'. Demands for accountability in this context are simultaneously challenges to the legitimacy of post-conflict political processes. Arguments for actors in the process to be held accountable in terms of international norms, often constitute surrogate ways of contesting the authorship and goals of the attempted political settlement: should those most responsible for violence be participants in setting its terms? Should international actors be setting

---

[11] See Ben Naftali and Shany, *supra* note 8; Orakhelashvili 'The Interaction between Human Rights and Humanitarian Law: Fragmentation, Conflict, Parallelism, or Convergence' 19 *EJIL* (2008) 161; and Roberts, 'Transformative Military Occupation: Applying the Law of War and Human Rights', 100 *AJIL* (2006) 580, at 595–590.

[12] On *lex specialis, see Legality of the Threat or Use of Nuclear Weapons,* Advisory Opinion, ICJ Reports (1996) 226, at 240; see further Orahelashvili, *supra* note 11.

[13] Cf Naftali and Shany, *supra* note 8.

the terms? Who should be accountable to whom? The assertion and denial of forms of accountability connect to the underlying meta-level negotiation over the nature of state that is to emerge, over who are the legitimate authors of its re-negotiated shape, and over where the power of the state will 'really' reside.

C. Joined up accountability?

The two forms of accountability, I argue, are linked in the ways in which both human rights and humanitarian law have been argued to be re-shaped by their post-conflict application. Interestingly, while both transitional justice and third party accountability can be termed 'post-conflict accountability' the literatures on the two forms of accountability barely intersect. The first issue has generated what is now accepted to be a distinct field of practice and legal inquiry—that of transitional justice. The second issue finds discussion in literature dealing with peacekeeping and peacebuilding. There are several apparently obvious reasons for this separation. First, each type of accountability seems to involve a different time-frame. Post-conflict transitional justice appears to be retrospective and look backward to the conflict, while questions of third party accountability appear to arise from what are clearly 'post-conflict' implementation tasks. Secondly, each type of accountability is often assumed to have a different moral starting point with differences in scale. Transitional justice is most strongly asserted with respect to war acts involving the systematic violations of human rights and humanitarian law, war crimes, and crimes against humanity, while third party accountability aims to address the 'errors' of third party enforcers whose primary motivation is to keep the peace. Thirdly, each type of accountability is often assumed to involve a different set of parties. Post-conflict transitional justice is often viewed as primarily relevant to the primary parties to the intra-state dimensions of conflict.[14] Conversely, post-conflict third party accountability seems relevant only to international actors. Finally, the difficulties of applying legal frameworks of accountability appear to fall apart around quite different dilemmas and questions of legitimacy. Post-conflict transitional justice is politically difficult because of an apparent 'justice–peace' dilemma that questions how normative standards which require some allocation of accountability can be squared with peace processes which work to an agenda of including all of those waging the war. Post-conflict third party accountability faces the political difficulty of when and how to persuade third parties to submit themselves to accountability for their own peacebuilding 'mistakes', and when and how to hold them accountable to a range of possible constituencies: host state, sending state, international organization, or 'international community'.

Despite these differences, it can be argued that both areas are connected in the ways in which they have resulted in a revised application of human rights and humanitarian law. Any account of the relationship between human rights and

---

[14] Although international standards also hold international actors involved in interstate conflict to account post-conflict, this is usually not discussed in terms of transitional justice and distinctive post-conflict accountability, perhaps because it is viewed so clearly as a matter of home state jurisdiction.

humanitarian law should have analytical power with respect to *both* sets of revisions. Seemingly obvious differences between the two types of accountability are less obvious when presented as questions of how norms connect with struggles over power and legitimacy. The idea that transitional justice and post-conflict justice focus on different timeframes, different parties, and quite different challenges to legitimacy, often overly invests in a 'conflict' and 'post-conflict' bright line and a view that local actors must earn legitimacy post-conflict, while third party international actors come with legitimacy which they must be careful not to lose. This view both obscures and neglects the ways in which local populations may experience a continuity of violence—albeit with changes in scale, in the permutations of actors involved, and in the political discourse around the meaning of the violence. Assumptions about the relative illegitimacy and legitimacy of local and international actors in peacebuilding can obscure the ways in which both sets of actors use questions of accountability in pursuit of broader political goals. For example, US implementation of 'de-Baathification' processes in Iraq under the banner of 'transitional justice' operated not as a simple attempt to promote the rule of law. Such processes also constituted an attempt to narrate the conflict in Iraq to which transitional justice applied, as being internal conflict in Iraq, rather than the US/coalition–Iraq international conflict, while simultaneously underlining both conflicts as being over. All this at a time when the term 'post-conflict' seemed inappropriate factually as an internal/international conflict continued to be waged with a cost in human life that has been argued to rival the abuses of the Hussein regime.[15]

Most crucially for this chapter, however, I suggest that a common dynamic colours the relationship between law and each post-conflict accountability demand. Both sets of demands involve similar questions over when and how international legal regimes can be moulded to what appear to be exceptional political difficulties. In overview, a lack of fit between the modalities of accountability offered by each regime to the multiple hybrid nature of the post-conflict political landscape, has created a dynamic reinterpretation of what the regimes should require post-conflict, and arguments that institutional innovation is required to enforce their application. I suggest that this dynamic of lack of fit and reinterpretation and invention, arguably present in all applications of norms to facts, have a particular impact in this context. Most notably, the lack of formalist clarity over when the regimes apply and what they demand has enabled arguments that any application must take into account the post-conflict political requirements of transition. The result, I argue, is a move towards a merged regime that does not merely view both as applicable with some *lex specialis* prioritization, but attempts to pull elements from each regime into a specialized post-conflict application that significantly revises each in the light of what are understood to be the political demands of transition.

---

[15] See further, Bell, Campbell, and Ní Aoláin 'The Battle for Transitional Justice: Hegemony, Iraq, and International Law', in Morison, McEvoy, and Anthony (eds), *Judges, Transition, and Human Rights* (2007) 147, at 156–157.

3. Transitional Justice

Turning first to post-conflict accountability for the violation of humanitarian law and human rights law during the conflict, in summary, the following story can be told. The post-conflict landscape with its assertion and denial of human rights and humanitarian law requirements of accountability can be argued to have significantly revised the standards towards a partial and somewhat messy regime-merge, enabled by institutional innovation. It can be argued that the process of 'fitting' the accountability requirements of human rights and humanitarian law to post-conflict political needs, occurring over the last two decades, has required a substantive modification. This modification has involved a move towards viewing the regimes as providing for a broad 'common denominator' shaped by the politics of transition. This common denominator establishes a normative imperative in the direction of a prohibition of broad amnesties, while leaving some (incompletely specified) scope for negotiating partial accountability as something less than full investigation, prosecution, and punishment for all violators and violations. This normative modification is not a formal one but, as we will see, nevertheless is one with legal effects at two levels. The first level is the articulation in soft law standards, state practice, international judgments, and academic commentaries, of a normative move towards prohibiting forms of amnesty for the most serious perpetrators and crimes, while leaving some (under specified) scope for amnesty as a conflict resolution tool. This normative move has been articulated to be required by the combined import of human rights and humanitarian law, as underwritten by international criminal law developments.[16] The second level is that of transitional justice mechanisms themselves.[17] These mechanisms have in effect provided for a 'contracted' set of standards drawn from both sets of regimes, which give effect to the 'no-blanket' amnesty/some-amnesty poles.

Each of the two levels is mutually re-enforcing. This norm-modification has taken place through a dialectical interaction between interpretations of what the regimes require post-conflict on one hand, and institutional innovation aimed at providing some form of norm-based accountability on the other. The normative poles prompt institutional innovation as the only way to give effect to both poles: new institutions articulate their rationale as lying in the need for a distinctively 'transitional' justice capable of mediating between accountability and amnesty. Conversely, the narrative of innovative institution as complying with the normative poles reinforces their normative effect. The broad contours, though not the detail, of the process of revision and institutional innovation can be traced through each regime.

---

[16] See below *infra* notes 34–40. For academic support see Gropengießer and Meißner, 'Amnesties and the Rome Statute of the International Criminal Court', 5 *Int. CLR* (2005) 267; O'Brien, 'Amnesty and International Law', 74 *Nordic J. Int'l L.* (2005) 261; Gavron, 'Amnesties in the Light of Developments in International Law and the Establishment of the International Criminal Court', 51 *ICLQ* (2002) 91; Slye, 'The Legitimacy of Amnesties Under International Law and General Principles of Anglo-American Law: Is a Legitimate Amnesty Possible?', 43 *Va. J. Int'l L.* (2002) 172.

[17] See *infra* notes 56–67.

A. Human rights law

As regards human rights law, an interaction of norm-promotion and institutional innovation has, over time, generated a new normative understanding. This understanding is that broad amnesties covering serious violations of human rights and humanitarian law are impermissible, but some level of amnesty capable of enabling is permissible. The development of this understanding has been gradual.

As the end of the Cold War saw a rise in negotiated settlements of protracted, social conflicts, it was not initially apparent that human rights had any regulatory claim. The initial difficulty of 'fit' was whether, post-conflict, human rights law imposed any ongoing requirements of accountability for conflict violence at all. Traditionally the ending of wars included broad amnesties for those waging the war, aimed at demobilization of troops and return of prisoners taken during the war.[18] This was assumed to be a political matter with the granting of domestic amnesty even a 'right' of states. Negotiated settlement of conflict up until the early 1990s often viewed amnesty as a key negotiation tool and the idea that there was a justice–peace dilemma did not figure.

It was with respect to the resolution of conflicts in Central and South America that the argument first came to be made that human rights law had a post-conflict reach. Writings from the early 1990s illustrate the argument, but also testify as to the need for the argument to be made. The articles of Roht-Arriaza and Orentlicher, for example, influentially argued that human rights law had post-conflict purchase as regards past atrocities.[19] Roht-Arriaza and Orentlicher both argued for an ongoing obligation to investigate and prosecute as grounded in human rights law, but also supported by the accountability requirements of humanitarian law and international criminal law. Their arguments shared some features. First, both responded primarily to Central and Southern America where impunity was one of the ways in which the conflict had traditionally been recycled. Secondly, both writers viewed the obligation to prosecute and punish as flowing more from the overall import and direction of human rights, humanitarian, and international criminal law when read as a unified body, than from any one convention or provision.[20]

In articulating a post-conflict reach for human rights law, both Orentlicher and Roht-Arriaza were forced to recognize the need for an interpretive application of human rights law, to fit the political requirements of transition. In particular, they sought to reconcile human rights law's apparent lack of capacity to allow for a balancing between accountability and political stability. How could human rights law, focusing on individual rights, and with a presumption of the general application of criminal justice, permit either some form of amnesty or some form of 'softer' accountability? Did it allow for partial accountability of some

---

[18] Du Bois-Pedain, *Transitional Amnesty in South Africa* (2007) at 302.

[19] Orentlicher, 'Settling Accounts: The Duty to Prosecute Human Rights Violations of a Prior Regime', 100 *Yale LJ* (1991) 2537; Roht-Arriaza, 'State Responsibility to Investigate and Prosecute Grave Human Rights Violations in International Law', 78 *Cal. L. Rev.* (1990) 449.

[20] See Orentlicher, '"Settling Accounts" Revisited: Reconciling Global Norms with Local Agency', 1 *IJTJ* (2007) 10, for an explanation of the context in which her 1991 article was written.

sort, sufficient perhaps to enable a rule of law basis for the society's future, but not so comprehensive as to destabilize the prospects for peace rooted in compromise between military-political actors?

Both Orentlicher and Roht-Arriaza suggested that an interpretive application of human rights law to permit such balancing was permissible. Both suggested that while wholesale amnesty could not be justified, neither was comprehensive prosecution required. Although they did not put it this way, they suggested that what was required by human rights law was sufficient good faith state action with regard to accountability to combat impunity. Orentlicher argued that

states operating under constraints commonly associated with political transition could satisfy their treaty obligations through exemplary prosecutions—focusing, for example, on those who appear to bear principle responsibility for systemic atrocities or on individuals believed to have committed notorious crimes that were emblematic of a regime's depredations.[21]

Roht-Arriaza suggested that the obligation most clearly applied to 'grave' human rights abuses rather than all human rights abuses by which she seems to mean torture, summary execution, and disappearances when in patterns tolerated by the state.[22] Moreover she also found that in each case 'a balance must be struck between the state's sovereignty interest' (which may be uniquely threatened by transitional prosecutions), and 'the international community's interest in protection of international human rights norms'.[23] Both Orentlicher and Roht-Arriaza therefore pushed for criminal accountability as a requirement of human rights law, but neither viewed human rights law as requiring full investigation with possible prosecution and punishment for all conflict deaths. Both writers, however, found it impossible to completely reconcile the human rights regime with the practical and political requirements for partial justice. They both acknowledged that neither human rights treaty texts nor jurisprudence made explicit allowances for the particular difficulties of transition, because human rights law had not been fashioned with a post-conflict application in mind.[24]

Ultimately, the very term 'transitional justice' came to signify the need for a differentiated application of justice standards, such as those of human rights law, suitable to post-conflict political needs. Within the emerging new field, the concept of 'transition to democracy' was understood to shape the type of accountability offered: pursuit of democratic transition both underwrote arguments that human rights law had purchase, but paradoxically also legitimated a partial approach in which it was viewed as formally requiring accountability only for the most serious violations.[25]

---

[21] Ibid at 14; see also Orentlicher, *supra* note 19, at 2548; and Roht-Arriaza, *supra* note 19, at 505–511.   [22] Roht-Arriaza, *supra* note 19, at 484 and 488.

[23] Ibid, at 495.

[24] Ibid, at 512 (Roht-Arriaza discusses and finds some room for the application of derogation regimes); Orentlicher, *supra* note 19, at 2606–2612.

[25] Teitel *Transitional Justice* (2000). Cf Arthur, 'How Transitions Re-shaped Human Rights: A Conceptual History', 31 *Hum. Rts. Q.* (2009) 321 (arguing that concept of 'transition to democracy' prioritized legal-institutional reform also over social justice and redistribution).

B. Humanitarian law

As the dilemmas of transitional justice were rehearsed across a range of other peace processes a further difficulty of 'fit' presented. Human rights standards apply only directly to state action, and indeed the state and its surrogates had been the central focus of Central American struggles against impunity. However, in most conflicts accountability of anti-state opposition groups was also an issue, and the thresholds of conflict triggering the application of humanitarian law have also been met. This prompted a turn to humanitarian law with its capacity to address non-state actor violence, to plug the gap. Similar problems of fit and reinterpretation, however, arose with regard to the application of humanitarian law. As with human rights law, towards the beginning of the 1990s humanitarian law's standards of accountability were not viewed as setting out a clear course of action with regard to the need for post-conflict accountability for conflict violence in intra-state conflicts. Although humanitarian law has provisions dealing with non-state as well as state action, and was specifically designed for situations of conflict, contentions that humanitarian law required post-conflict accountability again had to be argued for.

An interpretive development, similar to that of human rights law, was required to match humanitarian law to the post-conflict context. Although from 1949 onwards there has been a clear legal framework in the Geneva Conventions imposing legal requirements on states to prosecute for grave breaches of international law taking place during international conflict, a clear requirement of a duty to prosecute in internal armed conflict was at best unclear. Only a subsection of intra-state armed conflict is covered by humanitarian law—conflicts involving national liberation movements (Article 4(1) *AP I*), and conflicts meeting the threshold tests of *AP II* and Common Article 3 of the Geneva Conventions. Even where an intra-state conflict does fall within humanitarian law's parameters states are often reluctant to concede its application and (unlike with human rights treaties) there is no supervisory body to enforce and interpret the treaties.[26] Moreover, what these texts require as regards post-conflict accountability is not spelled out. There is no equivalent to the explicit grave breaches regime imposing a treaty obligation to prosecute for grave breaches of humanitarian law in international armed conflict. The argument that humanitarian law required post-conflict individual liability to be imposed through criminal law process required an interpretive revision.

Over time the application of individual criminal accountability to violations of humanitarian law in non-international armed conflict came to be firmly accepted in a range of state practice, and in the judgments of international courts and tribunals.[27] Moreover, a consequent duty to prosecute was understood to exist and to be ongoing, therefore having post-conflict application.[28] By 2005, international

---

[26] Ní Aoláin and Gross, *supra* note 8.
[27] See eg *Prosecutor v Dusko Tadić*, IT-94-AR72, Decision on the Defence Motion for Interlocutory Appeal on Jurisdiction of 2 October 1995, paras 96–136 available at <http://www.icty.org> (hereinafter *Tadić*). See also, *Prosecutor v Anto Furundija* IT-95-17/1-T, Judgment of 10 December 1998, at 151–157.   [28] Ibid.

acceptance that humanitarian law imposed an ongoing accountability requiring individual criminal responsibility was apparently so comprehensive that the International Committee of the Red Cross (ICRC) stated as customary law that

- individuals are responsible for war crimes committed in both international and non-international armed conflict;

- states are required to investigate such war crimes and if appropriate prosecute;

- states have the right to vest universal jurisdiction in their national courts for such crimes.[29]

However, a further difficulty of fitting humanitarian law to intra-state conflict was Article 6(5) of *AP II* to the Geneva Conventions which appears to require amnesty, providing that

[a]t the end of hostilities, the authorities in power shall endeavour to grant the broadest possible amnesty to persons who have participated in the armed conflict, or those deprived of their liberty for reasons related to the armed conflict, whether they are interned or detained.

As the pressure for post-conflict criminal justice as a requirement of human rights law increased, states that had rejected the application of humanitarian law during the conflict began to turn to it in peace negotiations.[30] This new-found attraction of states for humanitarian law lay in its perceived capacity to demand accountability not just of the state but of its non-state armed opponents, while also promoting mutual amnesty as a conflict resolution tool. While peace settlements incorporated provisions taken from humanitarian law to non-state actors in conflicts, domestic courts began relying on Article 6(5) to justify amnesties and truth commissions against human rights challenges.[31]

Combating this turning to humanitarian law as a justification for amnesty required an interpretive revision of humanitarian law as consistent with human rights law. Faced with questions as to the scope of Article 6(5) the ICRC in 1995 produced an explanatory interpretation of international law's one provision requiring amnesty—Article 6(5).[32] The ICRC argued that Article 6(5) had been designed to offer 'the equivalent of what in international armed conflicts is

---

[29] Henckaerts and Doswald-Beck, *International Committee of the Red Cross: Customary International Humanitarian Law* (2005) Volume I, at 551: Henckaerts and Doswald-Beck, *International Committee of the Red Cross: Customary International Humanitarian Law* (2005) Volume II at 3702–3704.

[30] See Campbell, 'Peace and the Laws of War: The Role of International Humanitarian Law in the Post-Conflict Environment', 82 *International Review of the Red Cross* (2000) 627; see also Roht-Arriaza, 'Combating Impunity: Some Thoughts on the Way Forward', 59 *LCP* (1996) 93.

[31] See, for example, *Azapo v President of the Republic of South Africa* 1996 (4) SA 562 (CC). See also, Roht-Arriaza, ibid at 96–98; Roht-Arriaza and Gibson, 'The Developing Jurisprudence on Amnesty', 20 *Hum. Rts. Q.* (1998) 843.

[32] Letter of Dr Toni Pfanner, Head of the Legal Division, ICRC Headquarters, to the Department of Law at the University of California of 15 April 1997 (referring to CDDH, Official Records, 1977, Vol IX, p.319) cited in Roht-Arriaza (1996), ibid, at 97.

known as "combatant immunity"' that was implicitly limited by commitments to accountability:

Article 6(5) attempts to encourage a release at the end of hostilities for those detained or punished for the mere fact of having participated in hostilities. It does not aim at an amnesty for those having violated international humanitarian law.[33]

While the ICRC's opinion clearly carries weight, the point remains that this opinion was driven by the need for internal regime coherence, and coherence with human rights law. The type of interpretation offered by the ICRC simply was not needed or given at the time of drafting (and does not appear in the contemporaneous commentary). The ICRC reading of Article 6(5) constituted an attempt to reconcile the Protocol's requirement of amnesty with the accountability requirements found in the other parts of humanitarian law, and indeed human rights law, so as to further underwrite the emerging prohibition on amnesty.

C. International criminal justice

These post-conflict revisions of international human rights and humanitarian law were also reinforced by moves towards the use of international criminal justice. International criminal law initiatives in essence codified a merged regime for post-conflict accountability. The *ad hoc* tribunals in Rwanda and former Yugoslavia created definitions of crimes that drew on the crimes of humanitarian law, concepts of 'crimes against humanity', and of gross human rights violations, but in ways that clearly addressed both international and internal conflict.[34] A similar list of crimes was used by the Special Criminal Court of Sierra Leone.[35] These provisions bolstered the move towards a developing requirement of universal jurisdiction for grave breaches of humanitarian law and towards a permitted and even required universal jurisdiction with respect to humanitarian law violations in internal conflict.[36]

The combined definition of crime approach was also followed by the Rome Statute of 1998 establishing the International Criminal Court (ICC).[37] While originally conceived as a response to inter-state conflict with antecedents that long preceded the peace agreement era,[38] the ICC's eventual establishment took place against a backdrop of intra-state conflict and associated transitional justice developments. The Rome Statute framework of criminal responsibility, like that

---

[33] Ibid.

[34] See Updated Statute of the International Tribunal for Former Yugoslavia, 2009; Statute for International Tribunal for Rwanda, 2004.

[35] Statute of the Special Court for Sierra Leone, 2002.

[36] Meron, *War Crimes Law Comes of Age: Essays* (1998) at 235–244; see also, *Tadić*; Henckaerts and Doswald-Beck Vol I *supra* note 29 at 608–609 (noting a requirement to prosecute with relation to serious violations of humanitarian law in non-international armed conflict).

[37] Rome Statute of the International Criminal Court, 1998 (hereinafter Rome Statute). The statute entered into force on 1 July 2002. See generally Schabas, *An Introduction to the International Criminal Court* (2006); and on drafting history, Bassiouni, 'Negotiating the Treaty of Rome on the Establishment of an International Criminal Court', 32 *Cornell Int'l LJ* (1999) 443.

[38] On these antecedents, see Schabas, ibid at 1–21.

of the *ad hoc* international tribunals and hybrid tribunals, offered a merged set of humanitarian and human rights legal standards capable of applying over a range of conflict scales, and, most importantly for current discussion, not limited to either 'internal' or 'international' conflict.[39] Importantly, the seismic normative development of a new international court and its lack of explicit transitional justice exception, also spoke symbolically to amnesty of serious crimes as lifted out of the discretion of domestic and international mediators. Post-conflict accountability for serious international crimes now appeared to be a straightforward legal requirement of a hierarchical criminal justice regime policed ultimately by the ICC.

And yet, the scope for compromise was not entirely eliminated. Prosecuting strategies targeted only those most responsible, and it soon became clear that very few perpetrators would ever see the inside of a court.[40] As we will see below, the application of international criminal law to intra-state conflict did not entirely eliminate scope for restorative justice mechanisms. Rather, international criminal law—particularly pre-ICC—can be viewed as creating a 'bifurcated approach', whereby international criminal justice was to hold 'those most responsible' to account, leaving more flexible quasi-law mechanisms to sweep up the rest.

D. Regime-merge?

Over time, therefore, a prohibition of blanket amnesty in intra-state conflict that nonetheless tolerates some unspecified forms of amnesty has emerged as a common denominator of human rights and humanitarian law, now supported by international criminal law. This common denominator does not find a positive law articulation in any regime, but must be 'read into' a unified narrative of what the differentiated regimes collectively require.[41] As one court has put it, the prohibition is a 'crystallising' norm of international law derived from diverse legal sources.[42] The corollary of a prohibition of blanket amnesty is that some level of amnesty is permitted and even required, and here too the permissibility of amnesty must again be garnered from a variety of legal doctrines.[43] The only direct treaty law provision for amnesty is Article 6(5) of *AP II* to the Geneva Conventions which only covers certain intra-state conflicts and which the ICRC contends does not apply to serious violations of humanitarian law. International legality of limited amnesty is also supported by the view that some domestic amnesties are outside international law's reach, and still constitute a political matter within the gift of the state.[44]

---

[39] Rome Statute, Art 5.   [40] See *infra* note 63.   [41] Slye *supra* note 16.

[42] *Prosecutor v Morris Kallon, Brima Bazzy Kamara*, Case No. SCSL-2004-15-AR72(E), Case No SCSL-2004-16-AR72(E) (13 March 2004), para 72. See also Orentlicher, Amicus Curiae *Brief Concerning the Amnesty Provided by the Lomé Accord in the case of the Prosecutor v Morris Kallon*, SCSL-2003-07.

[43] See Slye, *supra* note 16 (who has attempted to conduct an even broader 'regime merge' so as to produce specific criteria for 'legitimate amnesty' which are similar to the stated 'new law').

[44] Although there are arguments that quashing a conviction (because 'amnesty' is inappropriate) is required where fair trial standards have been violated, see Orentlicher, *Report of the Independent Expert to Update the Set of Principles to Combat Impunity, Addendum: Updated Set of Principles for*

The prohibition of broad amnesty has been normatively endorsed in soft law standards and UN policy statements and practice. Throughout the 1990s soft law standards were developed that articulated normative requirements of accountability for mass atrocity referencing both human rights and humanitarian law regimes. The 1989 Principles on the Effective Prevention and Investigation of Extra-legal, Arbitrary and Summary Executions, in Article 19, prohibit blanket immunity from prosecution for extra-legal, arbitrary, or summary executions.[45] Similarly, the 1993 UN Declaration on the Protection of All Persons from Enforced Disappearances prevents special amnesty for disappearances.[46] In 1997 the Joinet Principles provided a 'Set of Principles for the Protection and Promotion of Human Rights through Action to Combat Impunity'. Principle 25 set out limits to amnesty prohibiting its application to perpetrators of 'serious crimes under international law' while clearly contemplating that amnesty may be used nationally 'when intended to establish conditions conducive to a peace agreement or to foster national reconciliation'.[47]

This soft law move towards viewing forms of amnesty as unlawful was bolstered by UN practice and policy statements as the UN attempted to reconcile its peacemaking practices with its norm-promotion role.[48] In July 1999, the UN Secretary-General Representative in Sierra Leone, on the instruction of the UN Secretary-General, added a proviso to the UN signature on the Lomé Agreement between the Sierra Leonean government and the Revolutionary United Front (RUF), to make it clear that the 'United Nations holds the understanding that the amnesty and pardon in article IX of the agreement shall not apply to international crimes of genocide, crimes against humanity, war crimes and other serious violations of humanitarian law'.[49] This UN dissent served to 'normativize' and publicize its move towards a position as a 'normative negotiator'. It can be argued

---

the Protection and Promotion of Human Rights through Action to Combat Impunity. Geneva, United Nations, (2005), UN Doc E/CN.4/2005/102/Add.1, para 19 (hereinafter Updated Principles on Impunity) Principle 24(d)).

[45] *UN Principles on the Effective Prevention and Investigation of Extra-legal, Arbitrary and Summary Executions* (adopted 24 May 1984), ECOSOC Res 1989/65, UN Doc E/1989/89 (1989).

[46] GA Res 47/133, UN Doc A/47/687/Add.2 (1993).

[47] See, *Set of Principles for the protection and promotion of human rights through action to combat impunity,* E/CN.4/Sub.2/1997/20/Rev.1, annex II.

[48] One small part of this larger picture was a division between 'political' and 'normative' interventions in peace processes manifested institutionally in organizational tensions between its human rights actors in the Office of the High Commissioner for Human Rights, and its political actors in the Department of Political Affairs. See Hannum, 'Human Rights in Conflict Resolution: The Role of the Office of the High Commissioner for Human Rights in UN Peacemaking and Peace building', 28 *Hum.Rts. Q.* (2006) 1.

[49] *Seventh Report of the Secretary-General on the United Nations Observer Mission in Sierra Leone,* para 7, UN SCOR, UN Doc S/1999/836 (1999). Interestingly, the versions of the agreement available online (see Appendix 2) do not record this disclaimer. The UN does not seem to be able to produce a copy of the disclaimer (correspondence on file with the author). The Secretary-General's Report to the UN SC, while describing the rider, did not quote it, and subsequent citations of the rider seem to refer to this description, for example Schabas, 'Amnesty, the Sierra Leone Truth and Reconciliation Commission and the Special Court for Sierra Leone', 11 *U.C. Davis J. Int'l L. & Pol'y* (2004) 145, at 149; P Hayner, *Negotiating Peace in Liberia: Preserving the Possibility for Justice* (2007).

that the Lomé rider with its real-world impact, in terms of UN signature and controversy, gave the prohibition on blanket amnesty instant legal effect in a way that statements of commitment and soft law standards could not. As we will see, it also arguably paved the way to the United Nations Security Council (UN SC) later establishing a Special Criminal Court for Sierra Leone that operated contemporaneously with the Truth Commission.[50]

The new normative stance of the UN was reinforced on 10 December 1999 when the UN Secretary-General reported in a press release that he had issued guidelines to his envoys addressing human rights and peace negotiations.[51] These guidelines, at the time of writing, have not been made public.[52] The UN direction towards clear prohibition of amnesty was further consolidated by an intervention by the UN Secretary-General in his August 2004 Report on *The Rule of Law and Justice in Conflict and Post-Conflict Societies*, which reasserted a UN position of rejecting any endorsement of broad amnesty and capital punishment.[53] In 2005, Orentlicher updated the Joinet Principles and in Principle 24 reiterated Joinet's approach of restricting the use of amnesty while contemplating some ongoing use of amnesty.[54]

It can be argued that these standards operate to establish a broad and programmatic direction towards the prohibition of amnesty which still leaves some, possibly narrowing, room to manoeuvre. Interestingly, however, while there have been some attempts to provide a normative blueprint for a more explicitly 'transitional' justice, it has proved impossible to articulate a precise relationship between accountability and amnesty.[55] I suggest that it is impossible precisely because specification of the relationship would require an impossible shared understanding of how norms relate to the goals of transition, and some consensus as to what constitutes a relevant 'transition'. In the absence of such a shared understanding, any attempt to provide for an explicitly exceptional transitional justice runs the danger of undermining, rather than reinforcing, human rights and humanitarian law standards of accountability.

---

[50] SC Res 1315, 14 August 2000. Views are somewhat divided on how exactly the rider did this, and whether the rider created an impetus for accountability which was acted on once fighting was renewed, or whether the rider was in part responsible for the renewed fighting itself (see, for example, Schabas, ibid).

[51] UN Secretary-General, Press Release '*Secretary-General Comments on Guidelines given to Envoys*', 10 December 1999. These guidelines were updated in 2006.

[52] The rationale for privacy can be mooted to lie in the wish to keep the guidelines as an internal almost bureaucratic matter so as not to reveal mediator's hand. In the interests of disclosure, the author has viewed the Guidelines in the context of an expert meeting to advise on their updating.

[53] Report of the Secretary-General (S/2004/616) at the Security Council (New York), *Report on The Rule of Law and Justice in Conflict and Post-Conflict Societies* (2004) at 64(c).

[54] Updated Set of Principles on Impunity, *supra* note 44.

[55] A series of UN Commission and UN Council Resolutions on Transitional Justice have avoided attempting to articulate a relationship emphasizing the need to provide for transitional justice and the rule of law and setting out some process matters; see for example, Human Rights Council Resolution 9/10, Human Rights and Transitional Justice; Human Rights and Transitional Justice, UN Human Rights Commission Resolution 2005/70.

E. Institutional innovation

Normative development has taken place alongside a practice of transitional justice that has focused on innovative institutional responses aimed at providing forms of accountability that are attuned to post-conflict political difficulties. The difficulties in applying and reconciling human rights and humanitarian law regimes over the last two decades has often been resolved at the level of particular conflicts by creating new specialized quasi-legal and legal institutions. These new institutions in effect provided a particularistic 'contracting' of a merged regime, aimed at facilitating the political goals of transition.

There have been two main developments with regard to institutional innovation. The first development was the rise of quasi-legal mechanisms, such as Truth Commissions or Tribunals of Inquiry, which aimed to deliver forms of accountability other than that of individual accountability as prosecution and punishment. The second development—somewhat later in time—has been the bifurcated approach whereby international criminal processes were established to apply to the most serious offenders, with creatively designed local mechanisms, including forms of *de facto* or *de jure* amnesty, for those further down the chain of responsibility. It bears emphasis that this story of institutional innovation and patterning cannot be separated from the understanding of the development of international law's overarching normative imperatives—the two have been intricately linked in a dialectical relationship whereby each influences the other.[56]

1. *Quasi-legal accountability mechanisms*

At the domestic level, truth commissions and other 'restorative justice' mechanisms were increasingly turned to as a 'softer' alternative to criminal law trials, offering story-telling, truth, and reconciliation, aimed at underwriting the new constitutional order. The use of truth commissions as a key mechanism was significantly boosted by the diffusion of the high profile and attractive reconciliation, restorative justice rhetoric of the South African Truth and Reconciliation Commission. The attraction of truth commissions was that they offered an alternative to the arguably inappropriate dimensions of criminal law focused on an impossible and destabilizing, generally applied individual prosecution strategy of trials. Truth commissions could offer a specifically crafted list of violations drawing on human rights and humanitarian law (and therefore catching non-state actors as well as the state). They also claimed to be able to offer a balance between accountability and political reconciliation, and a measure of institutional as well as individual accountability—all difficult in the trial context. However, as the idea took hold that human rights and humanitarian law required ongoing accountability post-conflict, the question persisted, and even grew, as to whether these softer mechanisms satisfied the requirements of human rights law and humanitarian law post-conflict justice. Did these quasi-legal mechanisms give effect to human rights

---

[56] Cf Teitel, 'Transitional Justice Genealogy' 16 *Harv. Hum. Rt.s J.* (2003) 69.

law or did they merely constitute a 'necessary compromise' and a way-staging post en route to a more robust form of criminal justice?

The normative compliance of truth commissions persisted and grew at the level of the new normative developments which seemed to be marching ever towards prohibition of amnesty (even though practice lagged well behind). Thus, for example, Rome Statute debates considered whether there should be some sort of exception fashioned for truth commissions such as South Africa's, or other similar attempts at non-criminal justice accountability. The text eventually adopted, however, did not contain an explicit exception and left only limited room to take into account post-agreement transitional justice political pressures in how the statute was to apply. Article 16 provided that the UN SC could stay prosecution for 12 months by a Chapter VII Resolution,[57] and Article 53 provided the prosecutor with power to decide not to initiate an investigation or to stay a prosecution in 'the interests of justice'.[58]

Questions as to the legality of quasi-legal mechanism in terms of human rights and humanitarian law also persisted and grew at the local post-conflict level where political understanding as to what is possible and desirable tends to change over time. As the goal of sustaining a ceasefire gave way to longer term goals of peacebuilding, once-settled amnesties became vulnerable to arguments for accountability as necessary to establishing the rule of law. Deals as to amnesty, coupled, or not, with 'soft' accountability mechanisms such as truth commissions, began to be revisited. This turn towards increased individual accountability was bolstered in situations where military and political elites were perceived to have violated the spirit or even the letter of the peace settlement, and where domestic balance of powers had also changed. In Sierra Leone, for example, as the RUF failed to comply with both the Abidjan Accord, and later the Lomé Accord, with their generous amnesties, international actors supplemented the soft story-telling accountability of the Truth Commission provided for in the peace agreement,[59] with a hybrid Special International Court negotiated between the government of Sierra Leone

[57] Rome Statute, Art 16 provides 'No investigation or prosecution may be commenced or proceeded with under this Statute for a period of 12 months after the Security Council, in a resolution adopted under Chapter VII of the Charter of the United Nations, has requested the Court to that effect; that request may be renewed by the Council under the same conditions.'

[58] Rome Statute, Art 53(1)(c) provides that the decision on whether to initiate an investigation should not be made if '[t]aking into account the gravity of the crime and the interests of victims, there are nonetheless substantial reasons to believe that an investigation would not serve the interests of justice'. The prosecutor can also stay a prosecution according to Art 53(2)(c) where '[a] prosecution is not in the interests of justice, taking into account all the circumstances, including the gravity of the crime, the interests of victims and the age or infirmity of the alleged perpetrator, and his or her role in the alleged crime'. See further Schabas, *supra* note 37, at 185–186, (who notes that wording that might have more clearly protected South African-type mechanisms was not adopted, the statute ultimately preferring a vaguer and relatively ambiguous language of 'interests of justice').

[59] Peace Agreement between the Government of Sierra Leone and the Revolutionary United Front of Sierra Leone ('Lomé Agreement'), 7 July 1999 (hereinafter Lomé agreement) at <http:www.usip.org/library/pa.html> [last accessed 18 April 2010], Art XXXVI(2); the Truth and Reconciliation Commission was to 'provide a forum for both the victims and the perpetrators of human rights violations to tell their story, get a clear picture of the past in order to facilitation genuine healing and reconciliation' with power to 'recommend measures to be taken for the rehabilitation of victims of human rights violations'.

and the United Nations pursuant to UN SC Resolution.[60] The new mechanism did not replace the old, but was to operate simultaneously. Charles Taylor, amnestied by peace agreements in Liberia, was indicted by the Sierra Leonean Special Criminal Court, and post-Kosovo what had been an apparently unofficial impunity for Slobodan Milosević was replaced with a prosecution strategy before the International Criminal Tribunal on Former Yugoslavia (ICTFY). More recently, prosecutions were reopened in countries in which truth commissions and amnesty had been at the heart of political settlements, for example in Guatemala and Argentina.

The relationship between domestic truth processes and international law has been dynamic and interactive. While quasi-legal mechanisms often emerged and were presented as an innovative way of extending the reach of human rights and humanitarian law into a post-conflict environment without creating a disincentive to peace negotiations, they have increasingly come under pressure from international criminal accountability. Increasingly, they are viewed not as an alternative to international criminal law but as something which can sit alongside it.

2. *International criminal law*

The second post-conflict institutional innovation was the aforementioned establishment of *ad hoc* international criminal tribunals, of former Yugoslavia and Rwanda, and a series of hybrid international criminal tribunals such as those of Sierra Leone and Cambodia. Each arose in response to the particularities of the conflict in question, or processes completely unrelated to transitional justice, yet together they formed a pattern: the rise of international criminal law as a response to mass atrocity.[61] This rise was consolidated by the establishment of the International Criminal Court, an event which had origins independent of dilemmas of post-conflict accountability, but whose development increasingly became tied up with them.

These mechanisms appeared to mark a hardening of the transitional justice mechanism as focused on the delivery of individual criminal accountability. It can, however, be argued that what was institutionalized was not international criminal justice alone, but the need for a bifurcated approach to accountability.[62] This bifurcated approach is not bifurcated between international and domestic mechanisms alone, but in terms of hard (international) and soft (domestic) mechanisms. The limited capacity of international criminal trials to deal with the scale of mass atrocity, their expense, and the difficulty of attenuating them to broader conflict resolution goals such as reconciliation, has ensured that pressures for softer mechanisms have remained. International criminal law statutes cover only serious violations of international law, and therefore both the *actus reus* and the *mens rea*, which require matters such as widespread patterns and intent to destroy groups, tend to require

---

[60] Agreement between the United Nations and the Government of Sierra Leone on the Establishment of a Special Criminal Court for Sierra Leone, 16 January 2002; SC Res 1315 (2000) of 14 August 2000.   [61] Cf Teitel, *supra* note 25.

[62] See further Bell *supra* note 8, 251–253; Stahn, ' "Jus ad bellum", "jus in bello", "jus post bellum"?—Rethinking the Conception of the Law of Armed Force', 17 *EJIL* (2006) 921, at 940–941.

military seniority as a matter of fact (although not as a matter of law). Moreover, prosecuting strategies have not been generalized but have been targeted, focusing on those most responsible for such violations.[63] Thus, pressure for a truth commission and national approaches to the past persist in former Yugoslavia,[64] international law processes were supplemented by the Gacaca restorative justice process in Rwanda,[65] and the Truth and Reconciliation Commission in Sierra Leone continued notwithstanding the establishment of the Special Criminal Court.[66]

Moreover, the bifurcated approach has emerged as a possible response to the prosecutor of the International Criminal Court pursuing an increasingly uncompromising form of accountability for intra-state conflict in countries where peace negotiations have taken place or were underway. The Rome Statute provides in Article 17 that a case is inadmissible if the case is being investigated and prosecuted by the domestic state, unless 'the state is unable or unwilling genuinely to carry out the investigation and prosecution'. This 'complementarity' clause has come to the fore in debates over the relationship of the ICC to intra-state peace negotiations. Suggestions have emerged, in particular in draft peace agreements in Uganda, that domestic criminal law 'softened' by 'restorative justice' might be sufficient both to displace the international court's jurisdiction, and to effect a compromise between accountability as prosecution and punishment and some form of accountability falling short of that.[67] Such an approach, were it to be accepted by the prosecutor (although this is untested), would continue to build the bifurcated approach, with bifurcation not just between international and domestic criminal courts as a matter of complementarity, but also between criminal trials at the international level and more restorative justice criminal law approaches at the domestic level.

---

[63] Over time, the ICTFY prosecuting strategy has focused on 'the highest ranking political and military leaders', 'Office of the Prosecutor an Introduction' available at <http://www.icty.org/sid/287> [last accessed 18 April 2010]; in Rwanda as provided by the UN SC, the Prosecutor's strategy is to prosecute only those persons bearing the greatest responsibility for the crimes, and to seek the transfer of other accused to national jurisdictions, UN SC Res 1534, para 4 (the Tribunals' Prosecutors were requested to decide on trial or transfer) and para 5 (Tribunals only to confirm new indictments in respect of 'the most senior leaders suspected of being the most responsible'). The International Criminal Court prosecuting strategy focuses on 'those who bear the greatest responsibility for the crimes' (contemplating this to be supplemented by 'complementarity' with domestic process), 'Paper on Some Policy Issues before the Office of the Prosecutor', September 2003, p 3, available at <http://www.icc-cpi.int/NR/rdonlyres/1FA7C4C6-DE5F-42B7-8B25-60AA962ED8B6/143594/030905_Policy_Paper.pdf FN> [last accessed 18 April 2010].

[64] Truth Commissions were established in Serbia and Bosnia, but both failed in delivering final reports, see further 'Former Yugoslavia' at <http://www.ictj.org/en/where/region4/510.html> [last accessed 18 April 2010]

[65] See for example Clarke and Kaufman, *After Genocide: Transitional Justice, Post-Conflict Reconstruction and Reconciliation in Rwanda and Beyond* (2009)

[66] See Special Court Statute Annexed to the Agreement between the United Nations and the Government of Sierra Leone on the Establishment of the Special Court for Sierra Leone, signed 16 January 2002, 2178 UNTS 138 available at <http://sc-sl.org/DOCUMENTS/tabid/176/Default.aspx>; see also Schabas *supra* note 37 on the relationship between the two.

[67] See Agreement on Accountability and Reconciliation between the Government of the Republic of Uganda and the Lord's Resistance Army/Movement, 29 June 2007, UN Doc S/2007/453; Annexure to the Agreement on Accountability and Reconciliation, 19 February 2008 (<http://northernuganda.usvpp.gov/downloads.html> [last accessed 7 October 2010]). The latter agreement was not signed and neither were the agreements which would have implemented the entire framework and negotiations broke down.

F. Conclusion

In conclusion, as regards institutional innovation it is now possible to talk of a 'tool kit' of so-called transitional justice mechanisms to be used variously or together to address post-conflict accountability.[68] Domestic and internationalized truth commissions with varying mandates, hybrid criminal courts involving both international and domestic judges, trials before *ad hoc* and permanent international criminal courts, and security force vetting mechanisms—all have emerged as an attempt to provide some form of post-conflict accountability for conflict violations. These mechanisms typically draw on both human rights and humanitarian law to frame the violations for which accountability is owed. Moreover they respond to and reinforce what can be argued to be a *lex deferenda,* or 'normative expectation' with regard to what the regimes of human rights and humanitarian law require as a loose common denominator. It bears emphasis that the prohibition of blanket amnesty established as part of a 'regime-merge', and to which transitional justice mechanisms respond, is not clearly established by either human rights or humanitarian law on its own. The new normative understanding requires a synthesized narrative of what they compositely demand, as prohibiting some forms of amnesty, while leaving some unspecified room for amnesty.

4. Accountability of Third Party Actors

A broadly similar dynamic between lack of fit, normative revision, and *ad hoc* institutional innovation can be illustrated with reference to the post-conflict accountability of third party actors. Although the dynamic is similar the detail is quite different. The term 'third party actor' requires clarification. The contemporary post-conflict environment relies heavily on a diverse range of international actors involved in a diverse range of peace implementation functions. The scale and nature of international intervention is also varied, ranging from fully blown administration, to forms of peacekeeping, to involvement in domestic institutions such as hybrid courts.[69] Some forms of governance and peacekeeping are UN-undertaken, some are UN-authorized but conducted by groupings such as the North Atlantic Treaty Organization (NATO), and some, such as those in Iraq, are undertaken by other third party states on their own behalf.[70] Discrete parts of the United Nations also become involved in discrete issues, for example, the UN High Commissioner for Refugees (UNHCR) in return and repatriation of refugees and displaced persons.[71] Other international organizations can also find themselves with peace implementation roles; for example, the International Labour Organization has

[68] See UN Series, *Rule of Law Tools for Post-conflict States,* Office of the High Commissioner for Human Rights.
[69] For a full picture of third party involvement see Bell *supra* note 3, at 175–195.
[70] For a full review of international territorial administration see Wilde, *International Territorial Administration: How Trusteeship and the Civilizing Mission Never Went Away* (2008).
[71] See for example Arusha Peace and Reconciliation Agreement for Burundi, 28 August 2000, Protocol 4, Ch 3, Art 17, at <http://www.usip.org/library/pa.html> [last accessed 18 April 2010].

played a role in the implementation of the San Andreas Agreement between the Ejército Zapatista de Liberación Nacional (EZLN) and the Mexican government, undertaken under the rubric of its treaty monitoring with relation to the International Labour Organization's Indigenous and Tribal Peoples Convention 1989 (169).[72] International 'individuals' and civil society actors can also be given third party implementation roles.[73] These functions can be categorized in terms of four broad tasks: policing demobilization and demilitarization; guaranteeing and implementing an internal constitutional settlement; mediating its development; and administering in some form the transitional period.[74]

Two exercises of power in particular, however, give rise to demands for accountability to local populations: the use of force and the exercise of what are normally the powers of government. When international implementers use force and exercise governmental functions they in essence carry out the business of the state. The exercise of what is normally conceived of as domestic public power by international actors, like all use of public power, can give rise to human rights violations. Local populations have often asserted that the third parties are themselves violating legal rights found in international human rights and humanitarian law and indeed the domestic framework of peace settlements: in practice challenges to the actions of peacekeepers have included challenges to the use of force,[75] charges of sexual abuse,[76] use of administrative detention,[77] and in Bosnia, challenges to the constitutionality of the exercise of domestic legislative power by the Office of the High Representative.[78] Human rights challenges require to be addressed by third parties as they undermine peace settlement implementation efforts by undermining their legitimacy in the eyes of the local population. Given that peacebuilding typically involves a re-allocation of power from one side in the conflict to another, challenges to third party legitimacy tend to be seized on by 'spoilers'—that is recalcitrant parties who view settlement failure as their desired outcome—and can help build their political base locally.[79]

---

[72] See *Report of the Committee set up to examine the representation alleging non-observance by Mexico of the Indigenous and Tribal Peoples Convention, 1989 (No 169), made under Article 24 of the ILO Constitution by the Authentic Workers' Front (2004)* at <http://www.ilo.org/ilolex/english/newcountryframeE.htm> [last accessed 18 April 2010], in which the ILO examined the complaint as regards the Convention through the framework of the San Andrés Larraínzar Agreement between ELZN and Mexican Government, which were based on this Convention.

[73] For a full account of how peace agreements have provided for such roles see Bell and O'Rourke, 'The People's Peace? Peace Agreements, Civil Society, and Participatory Democracy' 28 *Int'l Pol Sci Rev* (2007) 293.

[74] See Bell *supra* note 3, at 176–195; and Kornhonen, 'International Governance in Post-conflict Situations', 14 *LJIL* (2000) 495.

[75] Allegations of torture and execution against Belgian, Italian and Canadian UN troops in Somalia (1992–5), see for example, *Report of the Somalia Commission of Inquiry* (2007) at <http://www.dnd.ca/somalia/somaliae.htm> [last accessed 18 April 2010].

[76] See *Special Measures for protection from sexual exploitation and sexual abuse*, Report of the Secretary-General, 15 June 2007 GA A/61/967 detailing sexual exploitation and related offences in the UN system in 2006, including sexual assault and sex with a minor.

[77] See eg *Al-Jedda v Secretary of State for Defence* [2007] UKHL 58.

[78] See *infra* notes 129–134.

[79] Stedman, 'Spoiler Problems in Peace Processes', 22 *Int'l Sec* (1997) 5; Bertram, 'Reinventing Governments: The Promise and Perils of United Nations Peace Building', 39 *Int'l Journal of Conf Res* (1995) 387.

While human rights and humanitarian law seem relevant, again both regimes have difficulties of fit. The post-conflict environment with its hybrid international/ domestic actors and ambiguous sovereignty does not sit easily with the assumptions of either human rights law or humanitarian law. The accountability offered by each regime is inadequate, both in reach and in enforcement mechanism, for dealing with the third party accountability issues that arise. The normal assumption that the state is capable of being the primary locus of human rights accountability does not prevail. The peculiarity of transitions from conflict gives rise to pressure for a form of regime-merge and institutional innovation that in its broad dynamic is similar to that described with reference to transitional justice. However, the detail and development of this dynamic is very different, and there is a less sustained, less coherent, institutional patterning. Once again, the broad dynamic of lack of fit and consequent regime revision and institutional invention can be briefly illustrated with reference to each regime.

A. Human rights law

Human rights law, as we have seen, is acknowledged to apply in situations of conflict and of peace, and the standards it offers appear to have capacity to hold international enforcers to account to the extent that they are using force or undertaking governmental-type roles. Human rights treaties impose a high standard of protection with regard to the right to life, capable of providing for accountability for killings by peacekeepers. Their strength, but also their weakness, is that they contemplate such killings as something other than potentially legitimate acts of war. As regards international governance, human rights standards are specifically designed to provide accountability for the exercise of government power vis-à-vis the individual, and so would seem to be relevant to international administrators when they exercise the powers of the state. Finally, unlike humanitarian law, in the event that states fail to provide mechanisms for adjudicating on human rights breaches, there is an international machinery in the form of treaty mechanisms capable of providing for some form of adjudication of a breach.

The difficulty is that human rights treaties regulate relationships between a state and the people within its jurisdiction, with the state obligated to deliver rights as minimum standards. As a technical matter, the rights contained in international conventions only apply to the state parties that sign the conventions and therefore do not apply directly to international organizations. The application of existing rights mechanisms to international organizations, including the United Nations, is not obvious and remains legally controversial.[80] While mission mandates and

---

[80] See generally, Devereux, 'Selective universality? Human-rights accountability of the UN in post-conflict operations', in Bowden, Charlesworth, and Farfall (eds), *The Role of International Law in Rebuilding Societies after Conflict: Great Expectations* (2009) 198; Cerone, 'Reasonable Measures in Unreasonable Circumstances: A Legal Responsibility Framework for Human Rights Violations in Post-conflict Territories under UN Administration' in White and Klaasen (eds), *The UN, Human Rights and Post-conflict Situations* (2005) 42; Mégret and Hoffman, 'The UN as a Human Rights Violator? Some Reflections on the United Nations Changing Human Rights Responsibilities',

regulations can provide for international organizations to undertake duties in ways that protect and promote human rights,[81] these seldom provide for a clear mechanism through which victims whose rights are violated can pursue accountability. There are similar difficulties with the application of customary international law to international organizations. Although the state technically retains its ongoing treaty and customary law human rights commitments, having abrogated its power to international organizations and often having given them immunity at point of entry through status of forces agreements, it cannot effectively hold international actors to account.

In response, commentators have posited a range of legal routes to finding the UN accountable.[82] Some commentators have contended that human rights apply directly to the UN by virtue of the constitutional standing of the UN Charter in combination with the International Covenants on Civil, Political and Economic, Social and Cultural Rights of 1966.[83] This argument views UN administrators as bound by human rights standards as part of its own constitution. Others have found *jus cogens* and customary law obligations to be directly applicable to UN administrators given the UN's status as a subject of international law.[84] A third route to application finds the UN to be subject to human rights norms through its usurpation of the state's functions—either as surrogate state, or as derivative or successor of the state. Each line of argument could, in theory, apply also to regional peacekeeping in terms of the respective constitutional foundations of the relevant regional organization (which also have roots in the UN Charter framework). The very existence of these arguments, however, testifies to an unhelpful lack of clarity as to UN human rights obligations. Moreover, these theories for UN accountability leave untouched the accountability of third parties other than states such as non-governmental organizations, private security contractors, companies, and individual actors.

Third party 'home' states would seem in principle to retain treaty responsibility to pursue the accountability of their own personnel. This form of accountability is unsatisfactory for local populations as it seems to deliver accountability to the wrong constituency. Nevertheless it is a form of accountability. However, asserting home state accountability in practice has exposed clear limitations on when treaty

---

25 *Hum. Rts. Q.* (2003) 314; Kondoch, 'Human Rights Law and UN Peace Operations in Post-conflict Situations', in White and Klaasen, (eds), *The UN, Human Rights and Post-conflict Situations* (2005) 19; 'Reasonable Measures in Unreasonable Circumstances: A Legal Responsibility Framework for Human Rights Violations in Post-conflict Territories under UN Administration', ibid, 42, at 68; Verdirame, 'UN Accountability for Human Rights Violations in Post-conflict Situations', ibid, 81.

[81] See eg UNMIK Regulation 1/1991, 25 July 1999, available at <http://www.unmikonline.org> discussed further below.   [82] For a full review see Devereux, *supra* note 80.

[83] Kondoch *supra* note 80, at 36. See also Dupuy, 'The Constitutional Dimension of the Charter of the UN Revisited', 1 *Max Planck Yrbk UN L* (1997) 1; White and Klaasen, *The UN, Human Rights and Post-conflict Situations* (2005) at 7; White, *The United Nations System: Towards International Justice* (2002) at 14–17. For arguments on the UN Charter as constitutional law see Fassbender, ' "We the Peoples of the United Nations": Constituent Power and Constitutional Form in International Law', in Loughlin and Walker (eds), *The Paradox of Constitutionalism* (2007) 269.

[84] Kondoch *supra* note 80, at 36–37, White and Klaasen *supra* note 80, at 7.

obligations apply.[85] Cases asserted under the European Convention on Human Rights, for example, have determined that:

- the Convention only applies when states occupy and exercise effective control over the area in which they operate, for example, excluding accountability for death from arterial bombing;[86]
- where the mission is formally authorized by the United Nations, UN SC authorization to carry out a specific operation or use 'use all necessary measures' may legitimize actions which would otherwise violate human rights standards;[87]
- where the operation is a UN one, responsibility lies with the UN rather than the third party state.[88]

Moreover, a review of the success of home-state trials and disciplinary hearings largely confirms local perceptions of impunity.[89]

B. Humanitarian law

Similar difficulties apply with reference to the application of humanitarian law. Once again it is unclear that this body of law applies to the peacekeeping forces of international organizations. While virtually all states are state parties to the Geneva Conventions, the UN itself is not, and direct accession has apparently been ruled out.[90] As Cerone notes, a further query over application lies in 'the notion that operations undertaken pursuant to the Chapter VII [of UN Charter of 1945] power of the SC are somehow exempt from the ordinary application of international law, such that even the IHL obligations of the member states participating in the operation are inapplicable'.[91] International legal accountability for private actors, to whom third party states contract out peace implementation duties, is even more unclear.[92] Moreover, the starting point of UN operations has been to provide for the immunity of peacekeeping and mission personnel from host jurisdiction. It has been standard practice for UN and regional terms of agreements between the international organization and the

[85] See further Hadden (ed), *A Responsibility to Assist: Human Rights Policy and Practice in European Union Crisis Management Operations* (2009).
[86] *Banković and others v Belgium and others* (App No 52207/88) Admissibility Decision of 12 December 2001 11 BHRC 435; *Al-Skeini v Secretary of State for Defence* [2007] UKHL 26.
[87] *Al-Jedda v Secretary of State* [2007] UKHL 58.
[88] *Behrami and Behrami v France* and *Saramati v France, Germany and Norway,* (App Nos 71412/01; 78166/01) European Court of Human Rights Grand Chamber Decision of 2 May 2007.
[89] Hadden *supra* note 85, at 121.
[90] See Palwankar, 'Applicability of International Humanitarian Law to United Nations Peacekeeping Forces', 294 *International Review of the Red Cross* (1993) 227. See Cerone, *supra* note 80, at 68–69.   [91] Cerone *supra* note 80, at 68.
[92] On issues of accountability raised by private contractors see 'Symposium: Private Military Contractors and International Law', 19 *EJIL* (2008); Faite, 'Accountability of Private Contractors in Armed Contract: Implications under Humanitarian Law', 4 *Defence Studies* (2002) 166.

host state to include immunity for its personnel, and now often also for private contractors.[93]

Humanitarian law's standards also seem inapposite to the type of accountability sought by local actors. As regards the use of force, humanitarian law authorizes the use of lethal force against enemy combatants, and permits some margin of error with regard to the collateral killing of civilians. Military action involving large numbers of civilian casualties is legitimate as long as the intention was to target enemy combatants, adequate planning and precautions were taken, and appropriate means used, even if large-scale civilian loss of life results. However, where peacekeepers are responsible for civilian deaths, as Hadden writes, the result 'will often be to cause a substantial reduction in the perceived legitimacy and acceptability of the international forces'.[94] Reliance on humanitarian law, which generally includes more scope for lawful killing than human rights law, undercuts the very concept of the political landscape as 'post-conflict'.

As regards the broader governance roles of international actors, and violations of rights other than the right to life, again there is a mismatch between humanitarian law's rationale, assumptions, and standards and the governance functions of third parties in contemporary transitions from conflict. For standards addressing the broader governance roles of third parties, one must look to humanitarian law's regulation of occupation. *GC IV* and the Hague Convention (IV) Respecting the Laws and Customs of War on Land of 1907 regulate a belligerent occupation, regardless of whether it is legal under *jus ad bellum* rules or not. Recourse to the law of occupation, however, is not automatic for international administrators. As Ratner notes, UN missions have tended to assume the priority of the human rights framework of accountability, while state-led international administrations have tended to view humanitarian law as the governing framework.[95] He argues that regime choice is more a 'default position' than a choice, determined by the nature of the third party: international administrations tend to be run by civilians who assume the primacy of human rights law, while state interventions run by military personnel tend to resort automatically to humanitarian law.[96]

Where humanitarian law is viewed as the appropriate framework there are further difficulties of fit. The underlying rationale driving the standards is an attempt to prevent the illegality of the acquisition of territory by force.[97] The law aims to protect the occupied state from being incorporated into the territory of the occupier. Therefore, 'the watchword is the legal maintenance of the status quo while protecting the basic welfare of the population, pending a final disposition of territory, typically a withdrawal from it'.[98] The difficulty for contemporary transitions is that rules designed to restrict an occupier's capacity to reshape the state's internal configuration restrict third parties whose imple-

---

[93] UN Model Agreement between the United Nations and Member State contributing personnel and equipment to the United Nations peace-keeping operations, A/46/185, Annex 23 May 1991; Hadden *supra* note 85, at 109.   [94] Hadden *supra* note 85, at 118.
[95] Ratner, 'Foreign Occupation and International Territorial Administration: The Challenges of Convergence', 16 *EJIL* (2005) 695, at 702–703.   [96] Ibid.
[97] Ibid.   [98] Ibid, at 700.

mentation function under a peace agreement is precisely that of 'transforming' state structures. *GC IV* limits on occupiers preclude actions that both military and civilian international presences undertake as a matter of practice, such as disapplying former laws, involvement in constitutional reform, and associated substantive reform of political and legal institutions.[99] The whole point of international implementation of contemporary transitions is to move away from the *status quo* associated with a war towards a situation in which the laws of war do not apply. International implementers aim to achieve this precisely by changing institutions and government by agreement. The assumptions and remit of the international humanitarian law of occupation and its modalities of accountability therefore seem inapposite to the third party enforcement tasks of international organizations. This has led to alternative forms of legal authorization being sought post-conflict. In Iraq, for example, the move towards ending occupation led to UN SC Resolutions being used to create extraordinary occupation powers, using the argument that *GC IV* did not provide for the needs of a gradual transition, such as the need for occupiers to engage in domestic constitutional reform, or management of oil resources.[100]

A third difficulty in fitting humanitarian law to post-conflict pressures for accountability is that it appears to offer accountability to the 'wrong' people. Accountability for third party actions is contemplated to be provided for by the domestic legal mechanisms of the third party state, with little formal international machinery to force states to comply, and no treaty monitoring mechanism.[101] Whether use of force or other violations of rights are at issue, for local parties the perception—and mostly the reality—is that international actors have *de facto* immunity from the international norms that they promote locally.[102] In short, there is a perceived 'accountability gap' between local populations and international implementer, which is not addressed by home state accountability in principle or in practice.

The difficulty of fitting and applying either humanitarian law or human rights regime to the post-conflict tasks which third parties undertake can again be argued to be producing forms of regime-merge and institutional innovation.

---

[99] A glance at the opening Art 47 of Section III of *GC IV* on occupation illustrates the mismatch between regime and contemporary transition: 'Protected persons who are in occupied territory shall not be deprived, in any case or in any manner whatsoever, of the benefits of the present Convention by any change introduced, as the result of the occupation of a territory, into the institutions or government of the said territory, nor by any agreement concluded between the authorities of the occupied territories and the Occupying Power, nor by any annexation by the latter of the whole or part of the occupied territory.'

[100] UN SC Res 1483, 22 May 2003; UN SC Res 1511, 16 October 2004; UN SC Res 1546, 8 June 2004. On the US justification for the need for these Resolutions see Bellinger, 'Summary of remarks available at State Department Legal Adviser Discusses U.S. Views on International Law, Security Council Powers under Chapter VII of the UN Charter', 99 *AJIL* (2005) 891, at 892–893.

[101] Ratner *supra* note 95, at 701. As Ratner notes, the international enforcement of state accountability is largely informal through lobbying, with only the Security Council or possibly the International Court of Justice being able to issue a binding directive to the state.

[102] Hadden *supra* note 85, at 112–113.

C. Regime-merge?

Post-conflict accountability pressures have forced attempts at new normative artic-
ulations. It can be argued that the hybrid international–domestic, war–no war,
post-conflict environment prompts recourse to the provisions of both regimes.
Again, this turning to both regimes is not a process of orderly harmonization with
prioritization of the most appropriate *lex specialis* where standards cannot be reconciled. Yet as Ratner, Roberts, and Stahn (from slightly different perspectives) have
all pointed out, the political context of post-conflict peacebuilding efforts points
towards the need to view the laws of occupation and human rights law as, in some
sense, a harmonized regime capable of servicing the needs of the contemporary
transition.[103] In practice, regime-merge has involved an attempt to draw on the
'spirit' or 'observance' of the regimes, rather than their letter, on the argument
that both offer relevant standards, which nonetheless require to be modified if
accountability is to be balanced with peacebuilding imperatives. Here the attempt
at formulating new norms is a complex effort to apply different standards to different third party functions, by applying different standards to different actors,
or different standards to the same actors when exercising different functions. As
with transitional justice, the concept of accountability that results is one in which
the letter of the law is attenuated to peacebuilding political goals. Normative and
institutional innovation illustrates the ways in which 'the spirit' or 'values' of the
regimes are invoked, rather than their strict application.[104] The search for accountability again reaches out to pluck from humanitarian law, human rights law, and
criminal law, eclectically and often simultaneously.

The point can be illustrated by a quick glance at some of the attempts at norm-
development, aimed at filling the accountability gap left by the lack of fit of human
rights and humanitarian law. In 1999, for example, the United Nations Secretary-
General issued a Bulletin, providing for the '[o]bservance by United Nations forces
of international humanitarian law'.[105] This Bulletin sets out a subset of humanitarian law provisions that are to apply to United Nations forces in situations of conflict
when 'they are actively engaged therein as combatants'.[106] It provides that in Status
of Forces Agreements concluded between the United Nations and a host state, the
United Nations will undertake to ensure that the force 'shall conduct its operations
with full respect for the principles and rules of the general conventions applicable

---

[103] Ratner does not aim to go so far as resolving the legal issues here, but states his purpose to be
'to show how any doctrinal approach, legal or political, must take account of the commonalities of
these missions', *supra* note 95, at 697. See also, Orakhelashvili *supra* note 11.

[104] See eg Art 28, UN Model Agreement between the United Nations and Member State contributing personnel and equipment to the United Nations peace-keeping operations, A/46/185, Annex
23 May 1991 (provides that UN peacekeeping operations 'shall observe and respect the principles
and spirit of the general international conventions applicable to the conduct of military personnel').

[105] United Nations, Secretary-General's Bulletin, ST/SGB/1999/13, 6 August 1999 (a Code of
'principles and rules of international humanitarian law applicable to United Nations forces conducting operations under United Nations' command and control', promulgated by then UN Secretary-
General Kofi Annan. The Code does not provide for the direct application of humanitarian law,
neither does it apply to peacekeeping forces under control other than that of the UN).

[106] Ibid, s 1.1.

to the conduct of military personnel'.[107] However, violations of humanitarian law are to be prosecuted in the national courts of the contributing state.[108]

In 2000, UN SC Resolution 1325 stated the UN's willingness to incorporate a gender perspective into peacekeeping operations and urged the Secretary-General 'to ensure that, where appropriate, field operations include a gender component'.[109] In 2006, a United Nations Group of Legal Experts, established in response to concerns about sexual violence committed by peacekeepers, submitted a Report to the General Assembly on the Accountability of United Nations staff and experts on mission with respect to criminal acts committed in peacekeeping operations.[110] The Report's emphasis was on placing criminal law accountability with the host state; however, it also raised the possibility that hybrid domestic–international tribunals might be an innovative way to enable local justice while responding to concerns of contributing states as to fair process and human rights protections for their staff.[111] The Report's attempt to plug accountability gaps remained limited—it only contemplated criminal accountability in cases such as sexual abuse which by their nature fell outside the definition of 'acts performed in the exercise of their official functions', and contemplated an ongoing backdrop of UN immunity.[112] The Expert Group appended a Draft Convention on the criminal accountability of United Nations officials and experts on mission, which included these limitations,[113] and also the limitation that the convention 'not apply to military personnel of national contingents assigned to the military component of a United Nations peacekeeping operation' and to other persons who status-of-forces agreements stated were under the exclusive jurisdiction of a State other than the host state.[114]

Regional organizations have also moved towards standard forms of codified application of international legal standards. For example, the European Union (EU) has developed a series of documents providing for general standards of conduct for all European Union Missions,[115] and guidelines for mainstreaming human rights and gender.[116] These documents set out principles aimed at 'behavioural'

---

[107] Ibid, s 3.
[108] Ibid, s 4. Moreover it does not apply to peacekeeping organizations under the command and control of regional organizations, even when deployed under UN auspices.
[109] UN SC Res 1325 of 31 October 2000, at 5.
[110] *Report of the Group of Legal Experts on ensuring accountability of United Nations Staff and experts on mission with respect to criminal acts committed in peacekeeping operations,* GA A/60/980 (hereinafter Report of the Group of Legal Experts).   [111] Ibid, at Section C.
[112] Ibid, at 9.
[113] Art 18, Draft Convention on the criminal accountability of the United Nations officials and experts on mission, ibid, provides that the Convention does not confer any right or impose any obligation which is 'inconsistent with any immunity of a UN official or expert unless the competent organ of the UN has waived such immunity…'.
[114] Art 2(2) Draft Convention on the criminal accountability of the United Nations officials and experts on mission.
[115] Generic Standards of Behaviour for ESDP Operations, Adopted by the Council on 18 May 2005, CEU 8373/3/05. See further Hadden *supra* note 85, at 106–107.
[116] Mainstreaming Human Rights in ESDP Missions, Adopted by the Council on 7 June 2006, CEU 10076/06; Conclusions on Promoting Gender Equality and Gender Mainstreaming in Crisis Management, Adopted by the Council on 13 November 2006.

standards of conduct and procedures for implementation, which include a requirement that provision be made for procedures of complaints and reporting misconduct. While extending clarified standards for accountability to EU Missions, discipline remains to be provided for by 'national authorities', or heads of missions in the case of 'contracted personnel'. Moreover, while these standards take a step towards accountability of the personnel of EU in terms of problematic behaviour, the EU Model Status of Forces and EU Model Status of Mission Agreements, promulgated initially in 2005, have been criticized for conferring a more extensive set of privileges and immunities on EU operations than current international practice warrants.[117] Neither do these Model Agreements include a provision similar to that of the UN Model Code, providing for 'full respect for the spirit and principles' of humanitarian law.

Some of the difficulties of applying norms to international organization are a specific version of the broader difficulties with the accountability of international organizations under contemporary international law.[118] However, while raising these general difficulties, in its specific form post-conflict third party accountability is particularly complex. Hampson's 2005 Report to the UN Sub-Commission of Human Rights, tellingly and perhaps ambiguously entitled 'Administration of Justice, Rule of Law and Democracy' provides a good example of the complexity. This Report addresses the accountability of 'international personnel' taking part in peace support operations, and thus covers a broad cross-section of the complexity of third party post-conflict roles: civilian and military personnel, international experts, international civil servants, and others such as the foreign staff of non-governmental organizations. It documents the complex, overlapping, and chaotic types of immunity which can pertain, and the equally complex, overlapping, and chaotic range of constituencies to whom accountability is owed, all of which point to different venues for determining accountability.[119] Even were the above matters more fully addressed normatively, they would not touch the full range of third parties such as private actors, judges, non-governmental organizations, and donors, many of whom stand beyond international law's easy reach, and whose functions would require specifically tailored standards.[120]

---

[117] Draft Model Agreement on the status of the European Union-led forces between the European Union and a Host State, 20 July 2007, CEU 11894/07; Draft Model Agreement on the status of the European Union Civilian Crisis Management Mission in a Host State (SOMA), 15 December 2008, CEU 17148/08. See further, Aurel Sari 'Status of Forces and Status of Mission Agreements under the ESDP: THE EU's Evolving Practice', 19 *EJIL* (2008) 67 (commenting on largely similar 2005 drafts of the Model Agreements).

[118] See generally, Klabbers, *An Introduction to International Institutional Law* (2nd edn, 2009) at 271–293; de Wet *supra* note 7; see also the Reports of the International Law Commission on the 'Responsibility of International Organizations' at <http://www.un.org/law/ilc/> [last accessed 18 April 2010].

[119] F Hampson, *Administration of Justice, Rules of Law and Democracy, Working paper on the accountability of international personnel taking part in peace support operations submitted by Françoise Hampson*, E/CN.4/Sub.2/2005/42.

[120] See eg Code of Judicial Ethics, ICC-BD/02-01-05, International Criminal Court.

D. Institutional innovation

With the jury still out on whether even a piece-meal normative revision is capable of garnering sufficient commitment from states to make it effective, institutional innovation has once again paved the way, providing a practice which reinforces the direction of norm-promotion attempts. This institutional innovation, like that of transitional justice, has involved effectively 'contracting' the application of elements of each regime through *ad hoc* devices. As in the area of transitional justice, a dialectical interaction exists with changing normative understandings of the accountability required by international law.

In particular, Status of Forces Agreements of the UN (SOFAs), while providing for immunity of troops from local state jurisdiction, since the 1990s have begun to also contract some application of human rights and humanitarian law. Although these agreements reaffirm the immunity of UN Troops from local jurisdiction, they now also contain provision of 'full respect for the principles and spirit of conventions concerning military personnel', including the Geneva Conventions.[121] Similarly, civilian missions can be contracted or regulated into some form of human rights commitment. In Kosovo, UNMIK Regulation 1 provides that 'all persons undertaking public duties or holding public office in Kosovo shall observe internationally recognized human rights standards and shall not discriminate against any person on any ground…'.[122] The limitation of these provisions is that it is somewhat unclear what respecting the 'principles and spirit' of the conventions, or 'observing' the standards, requires in practice, and the mechanism for enforcement remains through organizational disciplinary structures or home state criminal law jurisdiction, meaning that an accountability gap persists as regards local populations.[123]

In some cases, institutional innovation has attempted to create some form of direct accountability to local populations. The most innovative instances of institutional innovation with respect to governance have arisen in the context of post-conflict attempts to fashion constitutional settlements post-inter-state conflict. Precisely because they operate where there is little to no agreement, these examples demonstrate the type of innovation that is possible when international actors operate at the harshest end of international enforcement and most need to rationalize their own legitimacy.

An ombudsperson's office was set up in the UN Transitional Administration in East Timor (UNTAET) and the UN Interim Administration Mission in Kosovo (UNMIK), with the ombudsperson authorized to receive complaints against all the people employed by the United Nations, as well as against personnel working

---

[121] Agreement between the United Nations and the Government of the Republic of Rwanda on the Status of the United Nations Assistance Mission for Rwanda of 5 November 1993, UNTS 1748, Art 7.

[122] UNMIK Regulation 1/1991, 25 July 1999, available at <http://www.unmikonline.org> [last accessed 18 April 2010].

[123] See further Kolb, Vité, and Porretto, *L'Application du Droit International Humanitaire et des Droits de l'Homme aux Organisations Internationales: Forces de Paix et Administrations Civiles Transitoires* (2006) at 265 *et seq*, and 431 *et seq*.

for local authorities, but with no enforcement mechanism.[124] In Kosovo, for example, UNMIK has taken steps in effect to 'accede' to human rights conventions through technical agreements with the Council of Europe that bring them within the supervision mechanisms of the Convention on the Prevention of Torture and the Framework Convention on the Protection of National Minorities.[125] These agreements state that UNMIK is to provide the relevant information through a specifically designed reporting mechanism, and bypass the difficulties of a technical accession to the Conventions. A further step towards accountability took place in 2006, when an international Human Rights Advisory Panel was established to 'examine complaints from any person or group of individuals claiming to be the victim of a violation by UNMIK of the human rights of [eight human rights conventions]'.[126] The crafting of the Advisory Panel's jurisdiction operates practically to incorporate the conventions domestically as regards UNMIK by providing a domestic mechanism for their application.[127] Other *ad hoc* accountability mechanisms include a Personnel Conduct Committee in the United Nations Mission in Sierra Leone (UNAMSIL), and the Code of Conduct Committee in the United Nations Operation in Burundi. Both of these involved quasi-judicial mechanisms with no enforcement arm, in response to well-publicized abuses.[128]

To this example an exceptional instance of host state accountability over international actors can be added.[129] In Bosnia, the Dayton Peace Agreement (DPA)

[124] See Hampson *supra* note 119, at para 79 (A local ombudsperson's office was also set up in other PSO missions, including in the United Nations Mission of Support in East Timor (UNMISET).)

[125] See Agreement between the United Nations Interim Administration in Kosovo and the Council of Europe on technical arrangements related to the Framework Convention for the Protection of National Minorities, 23 August 2004, available online at <http://www.coe.int/t/e/human_rights/minorities/1._GENERAL_PRESENTATION/1._News/Agreement_UNMIK.asp#TopOfPage>. For full body of Reports and Committee of Ministers resolutions pursuant to this agreement see <http://www.coe.int/t/e/human_rights/minorities/2._framework_convention_(monitoring)/2._monitoring_mechanism/3._state_reports_and_unmik_kosovo_report/3._unmik_kosovo_report/UNMIK_Kosovo_gen.asp#TopOfPage>. Agreement between the United Nations Interim Administration Mission in Kosovo and the Council of Europe on technical arrangements related to the European Convention on the Prevention of Torture and Inhuman and Degrading Treatment or Punishment, 23 August 2004, available online at <http://www.cpt.coe.int/documents/scg/2004-08-23-eng.htm>. See further UNMIK press release at <http://www.unmikonline.org/press/2004/pressr/pr1216.pdf>. These agreements expressly note in their preambles that they do not make UNMIK a 'party' to the treaty in question [last accessed 18 April 2010].

[126] See, Ch 1, s 1.2, UNMIK Regulation No 2006/12 On the Establishment of a Human Rights Advisory Panel, UNMIK/REG/2006/12, 23 March 2006, available online at <http://www.unmikonline.org/regulations/unmikgazette/02english/E2006regs/RE2006_12.pdf> [last accessed 18 April 2010]

[127] The domestic incorporation had already happened through the 'Constitutional Framework for Provisional Self-government' of UNMIK/REG/2001/9 (Chapter 3) but appeared to apply only to the institutions of government listed in the constitution.

[128] UNAMSIL Press Release, 'Special Representative of the Secretary-General launches UNAMSIL Personnel Conduct Committee', 26 August 2002, <http://www.un.org/Depts/dpko/unamsil/DB/260802.pdf>; Peace Women website, 'Burundi: UN Mission Set up Units to Check Sexual Abuse', 15 November 2004, <http://www.peacewomen.org/un/pkwatch/News/04/ONUBConductUnit.html>. See further Hampson *supra* note 119, at 80–81 [last accessed 18 April 2010].

[129] There is a partial example also in Northern Ireland, where the international Bloody Sunday Tribunal was repeatedly judicially reviewed by the English Court of Appeal so as to overturn venue

provision established the Office of the High Representative (OHR) as the 'theatre of final authority' for the whole of the agreements, and these powers were subsequently extended to include the power to legislate when the domestic legislature was log-jammed.[130] The Bosnian Constitutional Court was subsequently repeatedly asked to consider the constitutionality of this OHR-promulgated legislation. In response the court asserted that 'the mandate of the High Representative derives from Annex 10 of the [DPA], the relevant Resolutions of the United Nations Security Council and the Bonn Declaration and that the mandate and the exercise of the mandate are not subject to the control of the Constitutional Court'.[131] Nevertheless, the Court simultaneously found that, 'in so far as the High Representative intervenes into the legal system of Bosnia and Herzegovina, the laws enacted by him are, by their nature, domestic laws of Bosnia and Herzegovina, whose conformity with the Constitution of Bosnia and Herzegovina can be examined by the Constitutional Court'.[132] This second part of its ruling operated as a *Marbury v Madison*[133] style judicial *coup d'état*,[134] which brought judicial review of the OHR back into play.

In this move, the constitutional court whose authority derives from one of the DPA's sub-Annexes, empowered itself to review the actions of the OHR which is the 'final theatre of authority' for the whole agreement—enforcement inversion. This innovation illustrates the capacity of peace agreement dilemmas of 'fit' to reshape and reconstruct both the international and indeed the domestic legal order established by the peace agreement. The Bosnian Constitutional Court's assumption of jurisdiction created a new relationship between international enforcer and domestic court (in this case itself an internationalized court), that reconfigured the third party role with respect to the peace agreement as treaty.

The above innovations are *ad hoc* attempts to respond to legitimacy crises which attempt to restore a connection between accountability mechanism and those whose rights are violated. The mechanisms both respond to the mix of international and domestic actors in the post-conflict state and further construct the post-conflict state as a space of hybrid governance characterized by transnational legal pluralism.[135]

---

and anonymity rulings of the Tribunal—raising the spectre of judicial review of the Tribunal's final findings. For judgments see <http://www.bloody-sunday-inquiry.org.uk/index2.asp?p=4> [last accessed 18 April 2010].

[130] These powers were provided in the Peace Implementation Conference, Bonn Conclusions, 10 December 1997, Art XI(2).

[131] *Twenty five Representatives of the People's Assembly of Republika Srpska,* U-26/01, (28 December 2001) at para 13. See *also, Eleven members of the House of Representatives of the Parliamentary Assembly of Bosnia and Herzegovina,* U-9/00 (3 November 2000), *Eleven members of the House of Representatives of the Parliamentary Assembly of Bosnia and Herzegovina* U-16/00 (2 February 2000), *Trideset i četiri poslanika Narodne skupštine Republike Srpske,* U-25/00 (23 March 2001), all available online at <http://www.ccbh.ba/eng> [last accessed 18 April 2010].   [132] Ibid.

[133] *Marbury v Madison* 5 US (1 Cranch) 137 (1803).

[134] The phrase is taken from Stone Sweet, 'The Politics of Judicial Review in France and Europe', 5 *ICON* (2007) 69, at 80.   [135] Cf Krisch *supra* note 7.

5. Re-conceiving the Connections

The hybrid nature of the post-conflict environment raises difficulties of which legal regime should impose what form of accountability, using what standards of accountability, in which forum. Two key post-conflict pressures for accountability have been addressed: accountability for conflict atrocities (transitional justice), and accountability for third party actors. The debates over accountability raise legal doctrinal issues of which body of law is applicable and what legal forum is available and suitable to enforcing the law. Some similar dynamics across both debates have been identified, namely, lack of clarity as to which regime applies; lack of fit between accountability need and either regime; narration of regime-merge as an attempt to draw on both regimes where they appear to offer appropriate standards; the shaping of the new 'unified' regime by the political demands of transition from conflict; and institutional innovation to effect compliance in practice. The terrain is interesting and fluid and its broader implications for international law remain difficult to assess. In an attempt to move towards that assessment I suggest there are three distinct conceptualizations of the project of developing a rights-based concept of post-conflict accountability. These conceptualizations can claim to be both descriptive and prescriptive, that is, to best describe how accountability and regime revision is being pursued, and to provide the best way of building that accountability in the future. Each conceptualization links to a particular view of the current 'situating' of international law vis-à-vis domestic legal systems more generally.

A. *Jus post bellum*

The first way to conceptualize the current state of affairs and way forward is as the development of a *jus post bellum*, that is, a specific post-conflict regime capable of drawing on both human rights and humanitarian law in pursuit of a peace-building project. Carsten Stahn, for example, tracing the connection between legal regimes and post-conflict peacebuilding requirements argues that existing practice points to the need to move beyond a dualist conception of *jus ad bello* and *jus in bellum*, towards a *jus post bellum*. This new post-conflict regime would draw on both human rights and humanitarian law and practice, so as to weave together standards capable of both restraining and enabling third party peace-building tasks.[136] Stahn roots this third regime in existing law and practice, such as that described above, as a set of rules which attempt to 'balance the interests of different stakeholders in transitions from conflict to peace' forged from the inter-action between 'the discretion and contractual liberty of warring factions' with 'certain norms of international law'.[137] Stahn's concept of a post-conflict regime finds some resonance in the work of Ratner and Roberts. Ratner points to the need to understand the commonality between both state-led 'occupations' and UN-led

---

[136] Stahn *supra* note 62.   [137] Ibid, at 937.

'administrations' with a view to addressing the accountability challenges that arise from what he asserts is a common set of problems. Roberts, discussing 'transformative occupation' and the difficulties of the law of occupation, also argues for the need to have recourse to human rights as well as humanitarian law standards and notes that 'it may be tempting to invoke an emerging or future *jus post bellum* as a better basis for handling these situations'.[138] While Roberts remains pessimistic about the possibilities of developing a more coherent *jus post bellum* regime either through *ad hoc* modification or formal revision of existing regimes, Stahn argues for such a revision. Stahn suggests both the need to depart from current understandings of the role of international law post-conflict. This 'adjustment' includes the need to distinguish between arguments over the justice and injustice of the conflict itself, and the post-conflict need to build a fair and inclusive settlement that respects objective rules, such as international legal norms, with the explicit aim of transforming the domestic order so as to remove the causes of violence. This last aim he suggests 'will ideally endeavour to achieve a higher level of human rights protection, accountability and good governance than in the period before the resort to armed force'.[139] More tentatively, Stahn proposes an initial substantive content to this *jus post bellum*, touching on both transitional justice and third party functions. He suggests the *jus post bellum* includes a move from collective to individual accountability and the harmonization of justice and reconciliation. He also suggests that it include provision for 'people centred government' that would 'create, *inter alia*, a duty for domestic or international holders of public authority in situations of transition to institute political structures that embody mechanisms of accountability *vis-à-vis* the governed population and timelines to gradually transfer power from political elites to elected representatives'.[140]

The argument for a *jus post bellum* merging of humanitarian and human rights law aimed at producing a set of standards has an appeal. It appears to offer a coherent and comprehensive framework of law that would differentiate between conflict and post-conflict imperatives. It is unclear, however, whether the suggestion of such a regime is intended as a practical suggestion, as a description of the inevitable track of current processes, or as an idealized outcome. The idea that a specific regime could or should be designed meets with some objections. First, international law-making processes do not seem up to such a revision as a matter of practice. The prosaic difficulties of drafting and agreeing a revision to such significant legal regimes as humanitarian and human rights law remain challenging. However, there is a deeper difficulty. Designing a new regime aimed at balancing standards of accountability with those of peacebuilding by attenuating current standards to enable domestic 'transformation' requires some agreement, first on what constitutes a 'transition', and secondly on the goals of transition. In fact any new regime would need a tight enough consensus as to what the imperatives of that transformation are, to enable any revision to human rights and humanitarian law to be tightly delimited by those imperatives. Yet, the goals of peacebuilding are

---

[138] Roberts, *supra* note 11, at 619–622; Stahn *supra* note 62, at 936–938.
[139] Stahn *supra* note 62, at 936.   [140] Ibid, at 941.

contested not just among local protagonists, but among international actors and between the two sets of actors. The existence of a transition and the prioritization of the political goals of the transition are often neither obvious nor uncontroversial. Moreover, articulation of political goals by both local and international actors is often viewed by the other as strategically manipulated and even dishonest. The question of what goals international actors should and do have post-conflict, cuts to the heart of debates over the appropriate goals of international intervention more generally. The very use of the term '*jus' post bellum* to describe the project of revising human rights law and humanitarian law has a legitimating function. The term suggests a post-conflict justice, when in fact the *post bellum* entity may be far from *post bellum,* the political goals of the transformers will be complex and, on occasion may have little to do with delivering local justice and democratic practice.

There is another—related—objection to a *jus post bellum*. As international law has lost its characterization as the law of states, it is already being criticized as the law of regimes, where the legality and legitimacy, for example of use of force, is determined not through moral and political debates over accountability, but through the technical arguments of experts as to which regimes apply with international law as 'the gentle civiliser of social systems'.[141] From this perspective the creation of a new regime might do little to provide for better accountability but rather open up new games and arguments as to when the regime was triggered, between different groups of experts. The hybrid nature of the post-conflict environment, and the ambiguity as to whether the war is actually over, and whether there is *in fact* a transition from conflict, points to the difficulty of applying a specialized 'post-conflict' regime.

Finally, it can be argued that there is a certain flexibility in the uncertainties and vagueness of the current loose normative understandings, which would be lost if they were codified. It can be suggested that establishing loose normative imperatives through practice and soft law, and *ad hoc* institutional innovation, stands a much more likely chance of delivering accountability than grand normative revision which also carries dangers of a 'backwards' revision by enabling a lower level of accountability to be applied even beyond the post-conflict setting.[142]

B. Piece-meal reform through norm-creation

The second conceptualization of current post-conflict accountability developments is as a project of piece-meal reform of human rights and humanitarian law regimes aimed at plugging the gaps with respect to whether and how they apply post-conflict. Again, this is potentially both a descriptive and a normative conceptualization. The project of piece-meal reform includes attempts to fashion greater home state accountability, and to argue for a new Draft Convention which might

---

[141] Koskenniemi, 'The Fate of International Law: Between Technique and Politics', 70 *MLR* (2007) 1, at 23, citing Fischer-Lescano and Teubner, *Regime-Kollisionen. Zur Fragmentierung des globalen Rechts* (2006) at 170.

[142] Cf Teitel, *supra* note 56, at 90–93; Roberts *supra* note 11, at 581.

include innovative mechanisms such as hybrid tribunals for providing for direct accountability to local actors.[143] Piece-meal reform also includes standard setting for international judges and actors,[144] and initiatives such as the UN Secretary-General's bulletin on international law.[145] It can be convincingly argued that the project of piece-meal reform is that which is most clearly underway. It can also be argued that this is the only project possible, given the difficulties with a more holistic normative revision discussed above.

The difficulty with piece-meal reform, however, is that while it appears to be a more modest project then a comprehensive regime revision, it suffers from some of the same barriers as holistic regime revision. As regards transitional justice, any attempt to fashion a clear transitional justice norm would need to specify what constitutes a 'transition' and which of the transition's political goals justify the attenuation of human rights standards, just as surely as a comprehensive regime revision. As regards the post-conflict accountability of third parties, it is often difficult to improve home state jurisdiction, and can be impossible to get them to accede to local or international jurisdiction over their troops in a discrete norm. Piecemeal reform may therefore in practice be as difficult as wholesale regime revision. Current practice bears this out: in place of a 'transitional justice' norm, stands increased normativization of the prohibition on blanket amnesty, with no real attempt to normatively delimit when and how partial amnesty or processes other than criminal justice might be permissibly used in pursuit of peace. In the shadow of the law, new games emerge in peace agreements, such as a commitment against impunity without a process of implementation,[146] or complete silence, which perhaps signify progress towards accountability,[147] but perhaps merely pay lip service to a new international demand while creating the *de facto* impunity seen as critical to a ceasefire. Similarly, the Draft Convention on the criminal accountability of the United Nations officials and experts on mission contemplates the ongoing use of troop immunity.[148] These constraints reflecting *real-politik* can be argued to be at once troubling and sensible. Impunity-enabling gaps are very important to the participation of the powerful in peacebuilding. The gap between transitional justice and human rights meet the demands of powerful military elites or war lords and are the price of their involvement in processes of negotiated settlement. The

[143] UN Draft Convention on the criminal accountability of the United Nations officials and experts on mission. [144] Code of Judicial Ethics, *supra* note 120.
[145] *Supra* note 105.
[146] See eg Art VII, section 5, Annex Programme of the Government of National Reconciliation, Linas-Marcousis Agreement, 2003, Côte D'Ivoire available at <http://peacemaker.unlb.org> [last accessed 18 April 2010] (providing that an amnesty law aimed at release of soldiers 'will under no circumstances mean that those having committed serious economic violations and serious violations of human rights and international humanitarian law will go unpunished', but not mentioning the mechanism for prosecution and punishment).
[147] Agreement on Permanent Ceasefire and Security Arrangements Implementation Modalities between the Government of the Sudan (GOS) and the Sudan Peoples Liberation Movement/Sudan Peoples Liberation Army (SPLM/SPLA) During the Pre-interim and Interim Periods, 31 December 2004, (providing for mechanisms for demobilization, demilitarization, and reintegration of combatants while not mentioning amnesty or a mechanism for the investigation of serious crimes under international law). Available at <www.usip.org/files/file/resources/collections/peace_agreements/ceasefire_agreement.pdf> [last accessed 7 October 2010]. [148] *Supra* note 112.

gaps in third party accountability meet the demands of the most powerful nations on earth and are the price of their committing personnel to peacekeeping and administrative functions.

C. Embracing legal pluralism and 'complex accountability'

A third conceptualization of the current terrain takes as its starting point the hybrid (international/domestic) and legally pluralist nature of the post-conflict political landscape, and acknowledges the mix of competing constituencies to whom accountability is owed, and the range of competing forums through which accountability claims can be pursued. This third conceptualization of the best characterization and way forward understands accountability to be taking place through ongoing negotiation of the respective spheres of legitimacy of international and national actors. This is a form of accountability that takes place through political debate involving narratives of legal legitimacy. Berman gives an example of how the challenge of neo-colonialism in Kosovo was used to hold international actors to account. He describes how in Kosovo local judges attempted a rejection of UNMIK regulatory power which in effect promulgated 'Serb' law by providing that '[t]he laws applicable in the territory of Kosovo prior to 24 March 1999 shall continue to apply in Kosovo insofar as they do not conflict with [internationally recognised human rights standards]'.[149] While not successful as a matter of technical legal enforcement, the legal challenge was politically effective, leading to the repeal of Regulation 1 and its replacement with regulation 24 which restored Kosovo's pre-1989 autonomy laws as a more neutral alternative.[150] Berman suggests that local allegations of a colonialist dimension to international administration required a response from international actors if the legitimacy necessary to effectiveness was to be preserved, and thus operated to hold them to account.[151] Berman sees a form of accountability being pressed through the domestic narratives of legitimacy that surround international intervention, particularly where links to problematic international pasts, such as colonization, can be invoked. Knoll echoes Berman's concept of accountability, pointing to the de-legitimizing dynamic that occurs when international administration governor functions are perceived to be in possible contradiction with its state-building functions; that is, when international actors pursue state-building in ways that produce forms of governance that local actors do not agree with.[152]

This idea that accountability derives from overlapping legal regimes with competing constituencies of legitimacy finds some theorization in the work of Krisch

---

[149] Regulation No 1999/1, UNMIK/REG/1999/1, 25 July 1999, s 3. The account of the case is found in Berman, 'Intervention in a Divided World: Access of Legitimacy', 17 *EJIL* (2006) 743, at 758 (citing *Le Monde* 17 August 1999 ('Vers une "loi du Kosovo", ni serbe ni yougoslave').

[150] Regulation No 1999/1, UNMIK/REG/1999/1, 25 July 1999; Regulation No 1999/24, UNMIK/REG/1999/24, 12 December 1999. See further Berman's account of the case's relationship to the broader political dynamics; *supra* note 149, at 758–764.

[151] Berman, *supra* note 149.

[152] Knoll, 'From Benchmarking to Final Status? Kosovo and the Problem of an International Administration's Open-Ended Mandate', 16 *EJIL* (2005) 637.

who sets out a similar approach to accountability in the context of global administrative law more generally. Krisch argues that the difficulty with accountability of
global governance is the question of to whom accountability is owed, and whether
it is a national, international, or cosmopolitan constituency. This difficulty is inherent in the transnational nature of global governance, and for Krisch it points to the
need to reconceive accountability in something other than single constituencies in
hierarchical legal orders. He argues, in the global administrative law context, for a
pluralist conception of accountability capable of responding to the new globalized
legal order through the idea that a range of mixed accountabilities—domestic,
international, and cosmopolitan—can operate to hold each other in balance
somewhat as the concept of separation of powers does within the domestic legal
system.[153] He proposes a heterarchical concept of accountability as 'mutual challenge' between constituencies. Krisch argues that this is not only a description of
the interaction of multi-level global governance and norms at present, but also that
it is normatively defendable rather than a way-stage post paving the route to a more
ordered and traditional form of accountability. Leaving aside the exact relationship of post-conflict environments to global administrative law projects as beyond
the scope of this chapter, it can be argued that the concept of accountability as
pluralist and heterarchical captures the present direction and best future prospects
for post-conflict accountability.

Again, there are a number of difficulties with 'complex accountability' as a useful
way of exploring the possibilities of non-hierarchical, multi-layered, and mutually
referencing processes of domestic and international accountability. There is something quite unsatisfying and intangible in this new conception of accountability,
that attempts to navigate between international, local, and third party state constituencies in a way that acknowledges the impossibility of any hierarchical ordering between spheres. This new accountability slithers between the descriptive 'is'
and the normative 'ought' and is curiously and intangibly situated as transnational
rather than within either the international or domestic legal context. It is a 'complex accountability' rooted in 'reciprocal monitoring and mutual constraint' of different accountability constituencies and sites, which must operate in the absence of
a 'fully effective coordinator'.[154] Yet, how one might access this accountability as
a local actor remains unclear. It is all very well to note that local political struggles
for accountability sometimes have an effect in producing greater accountability,
participation, and transparency, but this observation is of little use to a prisoner
languishing in 'administrative detention', or a rape victim seeking to hold an international peacekeeper to account. Moreover, the fact that the space occupied by
international actors is not just a transnational or international space, but also the
space of the domestic state—where international administration is completely con-
tiguous with the state's normal sphere of administration—heightens arguments
for accountability to the national constituency as paramount. The more international actors take over a range of state functions—acting as governors, holding

---

[153] See Krisch, *supra* note 7.
[154] Walker, *Policing in a Changing Constitutional Order* (2000) at 292–293.

the monopoly over the use of violence, making decisions over resource allocation, and dispensing criminal justice—the more there will be an attempt to hold them accountable to domestic constituencies through domestic institutions, even as they seek to reform those very institutions.

Unsatisfying as it may be, however, the conceptualization of current practices as sowing the seeds of a pluralist conception of accountability at least attempts to touch multiple and competing sites of governance which have competing theatres of legitimacy and competing constituencies of accountability. In so doing complex accountability seeks to enable both human rights law and humanitarian law to exert a moral and political force that carries beyond their strict application.

6. Conclusion

Each of the above conceptualizations stands as an account of the relationship between human rights and humanitarian law which would best capture and provide a basis for extending their post-conflict application. They have a relationship with wider debates as to the more general project of explaining and developing international law in its contemporary post-Westphalian dimensions.[155] The conceptualizations can be viewed as irreconcilable and rooted in quite different notions of how we are to conceive of the project of international law and therefore how we might best build projects of reform. The first conceptualization of *jus post bellum* conceives of the project of reform as one of 'integrity'—a project of applying universalizable norms from within a still hierarchical international legal order to new contexts. The second project of piece-meal reform attempts to re-order global, regional, and national law and mechanisms in a way that provides for accountability without the need for a broader account of the situating of international law. The third conceptualization embraces the de-situated new anarchy of legal forms and relations and attempts to construct a new concept of accountability to deal with it.[156] With regard to the meta-level 'dis order of legal orders' between international, transnational, and domestic law, Walker has argued that competing accounts of the current terrain can be reconciled if presented in moderate versions.[157] This observation can inform evaluation of the relative merits of the three conceptualizations of post-conflict applications of human rights and humanitarian law.

All three conceptualizations, if modestly understood, might be understood as contributing to our understanding of the post-conflict relationship of human rights and humanitarian law. This combined conceptualization sits with the above description of the common patterning across post-conflict accountability. I suggest it has explanatory power across the innovations with respect to both transitional justice and third party accountability. In both areas the complex dialectical relationship between the contracts that warring parties make with regard

---

[155] Walker, 'Beyond Boundary Disputes and Basic Grids: Mapping the Global Disorder of Normative Orders', 6 *ICON* (2008) 373.   [156] Ibid.
[157] Ibid.

to ending their conflicts and international human rights norms, propels paired processes of normative revision and institution innovation. These processes enable an ongoing negotiation of the normative foundation of both domestic and international constitutional orders. In this negotiation the tension between international law as universal principles and international law as imperialist project is inevitably present, as what Jouannet has called 'the ever present paradox of international law'.[158] This universal/particularist paradox can also be recognized as 'the ever present paradox of constitutional law'.[159] Recognition of a paradox indicates that rather than a choice between universalist and particularist versions of international law or constitutional law, the realm of law is that of ongoing negotiation between the paired universalist and particularist ambitions of international and constitutional law.[160]

From this perspective, each of the above conceptualizations of the post-conflict relationship of human rights and humanitarian law points to an important dimension of the negotiation. Talking about a *jus post bellum* can be a useful way of asserting the need for a clear but differentiated application of international norms aimed at accommodating attempts to create the conditions for peaceful co-existence which enable norms to be adhered to in practice. Embraced as a discursive project or a way of understanding the practical pressures which push for a distinctive normative revision the concept of *jus post bellum* has a value. The aspiration of *jus post bellum* as a search for a normative framework capable of responding to the constitutive politics of state reconstruction can be embraced, even as the project of fashioning it and precisely articulating its application is rejected as impossible and even undesirable.

Similarly, it is useful to understand better the ways in which discrete projects of piece-meal reform of human rights, and humanitarian law post-conflict 'gaps', identify important normative demands of peace processes and articulate broad normative aspirations. The attempt to 'plug the gaps' is also useful in identifying precisely what the gaps are—in the often ignored and unfashionable work of detailed mapping of which actors are doing what, through which institutions, in the post-conflict context. This project responds to the 'unknownness' of proliferating international and transnational institutional patterning and consequences generally: an unknownness that is accentuated in post-conflict societies where broad international patterning fragments further into country-specific *ad hoc* institutional manifestations—created virtually overnight by peace settlements.

Finally, the project of embracing the transnational dimensions of post-conflict accountability through the ongoing creation of pluralist and mutually constraining *ad hoc* mechanisms can usefully work to validate institutional innovation as

---

[158] Jouannet, 'Universalism and Imperialism: The True-False Paradox of International Law?', 18 *EJIL* (2007) 379.

[159] Or as Susan Marks has put it 'the riddle of all constitutions', by which she means the idea that democracy, conceived of as a process of ongoing ideals of self-rule and equality, constitute the ongoing riddle or challenge to all constitutions in which the possibilities for emancipation and oppression co-exist, Marks *The Riddle of All Constitutions: International Law, Democracy and the Critique of Ideology* (2007).   [160] Cf Jouannet *supra* note 158; and Marks, *supra* note 159.

equally as important a response as norm-generation. For example, a clearer clause and mechanism in a Status of Forces Agreement might be more effective than an international convention. Embracing the need for 'complex accountability' rather than new hierarchical institutionalization can also enable political imagination as to what might touch oppression in practice—for example, *ad hoc* hybrid tribunals first designed for transitional justice may have a useful 'read across' to attempts to find a modality for third party accountability that would satisfy the needs of local actors for local justice, while reassuring third parties of fair process.[161]

What synthesizes these three conceptualizations is an underlying commitment to accountability between those who abuse rights and those whose rights are abused, in terms of objective and even universal standards, as necessary to the broader attempt to articulate the proper use of public power wherever it lies.

---

[161] See arguments for 'hybrid' local state/international accountability mechanisms as a way of pursuing post-conflict accountability of third parties in Report of the Legal Group of Experts, *supra* note 110, at 29–33; Hadden *supra* note 85, at 116–117; and Durch, Andrews, and England with Weed, *Improving Criminal Accountability in Peace Operations* (2009), 19–20; Cf Zwanenberg, *Accountability of Peace Support Operations* (2005) at 177–179.

Index